9TH EDITION

Media Programming

STRATEGIES AND PRACTICES

Susan Tyler Eastman
Indiana University

Douglas A. Ferguson
College of Charleston

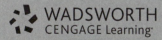

WADSWORTH
CENGAGE Learning·

Australia · Brazil · Japan · Korea · Mexico · Singapore · Spain · United Kingdom · United States

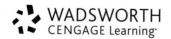

Media Programming: Strategies and Practices, 9th Edition
Susan Tyler Eastman & Douglas A. Ferguson

Editor in Chief: Lyn Uhl

Publisher: Michael Rosenberg

Assistant Editor: Erin Bosco

Editorial Assistant: Rebecca Donahue

Media Editor: Jessica Badiner

Marketing Program Manager: Gurpreet S. Saran

Art and Cover Direction, Production Management, and Composition: PreMediaGlobal

Manufacturing Planner: Doug Bertke

Rights Acquisition Specialist: Mandy Groszko

Cover Image: TV screen pixels close-up [©oriontrail/Shutterstock]

Graphics contained in this title are © 2013 Cengage Learning

For product information and technology assistance, contact us at
Cengage Learning Customer & Sales Support, 1-800-354-9706

For permission to use material from this text or product, submit all requests online at **www.cengage.com/permissions**
Further permissions questions can be e-mailed to
permissionrequest@cengage.com

Library of Congress Control Number: 2012930783

ISBN-13: 978-1-111-34447-4

ISBN-10: 1-111-34447-7

Wadsworth
20 Channel Center Street
Boston, MA 02210
USA

Cengage Learning is a leading provider of customized learning solutions with office locations around the globe, including Singapore, the United Kingdom, Australia, Mexico, Brazil and Japan. Locate your local office at **international.cengage.com/region**

Cengage Learning products are represented in Canada by Nelson Education, Ltd.

For your course and learning solutions, visit **www.cengage.com**

Purchase any of our products at your local college store or at our preferred online store **www.cengagebrain.com**

Instructors: Please visit **login.cengage.com** and log in to access instructor-specific resources.

Printed in the United States of America
1 2 3 4 5 6 7 16 15 14 13 12

Brief Contents

Detailed Contents

PART THREE

Understanding Key Processes 155

Preface

This book about media programming deals with both the structured and unstructured media. By **structured** we mean the traditional mass communication media of broadcast television and radio and the cable networks. These services have long sent prepackaged programs to viewers and listeners in linear series organized by time and day. We focus on ABC, CBS, Fox, NBC and PBS, and include CW, MyNetworkTV, Telemundo, TeleFutura and Univision and affiliated stations, the major cable networks, such as CNN, MTV, TNT, USA, HBO and so on, the satellite TV and telephone TV services, such as DirecTV and AT&T, and the radio and audio networks. Although these channels' programs can be recorded and replayed, on a structured service, each program was originally selected to fit in a single channel to create an image and set of expectations about that channel. Of considerable importance is the fact that many programs get replayed on co-owned channels or are later sold in syndication. Of even more importance is that this structured industry is moving toward on-demand programming, thus becoming more like the unstructured industry.

By **unstructured** we mean the parts of the huge online world that carry old and new television programs and radio shows, talk and music that come via the web to your laptop or tablet or cell phone— or perhaps your TV set. While we focus primarily on the unstructured services that provide television programs and movies, such as Netflix, Google and Hulu.com, we include the personal media of YouTube, Facebook and MySpace, as well as online gaming such as Farmville, Carville and Cityville, plus X-Box, Nintendo and their kin. We incorporate these in the unstructured group because they consist of giant masses of content from which users select however they prefer. Online media is inherently VOD (video on demand). Nonetheless, much of the online world is filled with non-programming and falls outside the purview of this book. But we do refer to blogs and podcasts, insofar as they are carriers of content that relates to the structured and unstructured programming media.

The primary reason for including both structured media content and rivaling unstructured content is that they share an economic and marketing universe. They compete for the attention of the same viewers, listeners and users, and they compete for the same dollars, although the revenue streams operate in different ways. And they are coming closer together. Indeed, over the next decades, broadcasting and cable will fade as broadband distribution rises, but for now, all must coexist and share the audience's attention.

Change continues to be the media's most enduring characteristic, and the contents of this book have most value when they not only describe and interpret the present but also predict the patterns of the future. The next media revolution is well begun, and the once-rigid barriers between methods of delivering programming are dissolving, as are barriers between domestic and foreign programming. The authors make educated assessments of likely changes in the near future, while science fiction imaginings edge closer and closer. 3D television without glasses is certainly coming but hasn't reached most living rooms yet.

The Changes

Six major shifts in the industry guided the revision for this edition. They can be summarized as conclusions or operating principles:

- **Multiplatform strategies inform media decisions today.** The conventional TV networks reacted to the newest media by trying limited multiplatform marketing, but changing economics and audience behaviors now make cable and the internet parallel to broadcasting, and if not yet equivalent, they are the future in programming and profits. Where once the broadcast networks viewed cable and the internet merely as vehicles for marketing their content, broadband and cable are now either full partners or full competitors to the broadcast media. Now every kind of receiver (computers, phones, tablets and TV sets) must be considered in every decision to buy, make or schedule programming.
- **Cross-media have become enmeshed media.** Diverse media outlets have been assimilated within giant media corporations. Broadcast network and stations, cable networks and systems and online video services now operate within single commercial conglomerates. This has led to conflicting goals within corporations in which programming decisions sometimes advantage some owned segments and disadvantage others to maximize overall profits. The full ramifications of Comcast's purchase of NBCUniversal, for example, will not emerge for a decade. While crossfertilization and reuse of broadcast programs on both cable and online is old news, the three kinds of media are now more deeply embedded—to the point where some distinctions have been erased. Television companies no longer act without full consideration of online impacts. And now radio is becoming audio and no longer separate from online, iPods or the telephone.

- **New media only partly subsume old media.** Television has gone from black-and-white to color to digital to HD and is going to 3D (although most screens lag behind and don't display HD signals, let alone 3D), while television is simultaneously going online. And only about three quarters of U.S. household have broadband access, not all of that high speed. LP records quite thoroughly replaced 78 RPM, but then CDs replaced records, and now online downloads to iPods and cell phones are replacing CDs. Radio has in part gone from analog to digital and from broadcast to satellite and to online, but HD radio has not yet been widely adopted in home, although it has become standard for new cars. In each big change, the strength and speed of the takeover has varied and in many cases, the old medium persists alongside the new.
- **Analog is dead, and digital is becoming HD.** The makers and distributors of media content now largely ignore the millions of analog receivers in homes (and cars) and presume they will inevitably join the digital age. Although cable, satellite and telephone distributors offer hundreds of channels as digital signals, the media companies expect to drop most plain digital in favor of high definition in the not-distant future. Households today may contain a mix of analog and digital media, but over-the-air television and radio consumers are getting left behind. While only about a third of digital subscribers now take high-definition service, the industry expects full conversion in a few years. While only half of households have high-speed internet access now, more than 90 percent will have it in a few years. Although the digital gap is shrinking, it persists between older and younger people and urban and rural households, despite sporadic regulatory efforts.
- **Reducing, reusing and recycling are now the driving strategies behind programming decisions.** While the traditional networks broadcast the classically defined the main program genres, new types of programs are emerging in spite of old terminology. Game shows and reality programs have merged and exploded across television.

Meanwhile, YouTube mushrooms with new program ideas, and Facebook illustrates the audience's need for interaction. While program types are expanding, schedules everywhere fill with reused tried-and-true favorites. Because the networks strive to reduce the total number of expensive programs they need to fill their schedules, an essential part of current strategy has become replaying of episodes more often and recycling shows on co-owned cable channels and online.

- **Wirelessness and pay are the directions of the future.** Although the traditional wired media of cable, satellite and telephone remain strong media businesses for now, wireless ways to receive television and audio are becoming commonplace. It is likely that virtually all entertainment media will become wireless (perhaps delivered via light rather than in the presently used parts of the spectrum!) and almost all media will require some sort of pay in your lifetime.

Chapter Organization

The organization of this edition of *Media Programming* has been altered to catch up with changes in ownership patterns and technology distribution, as well as to give greater prominence to the unstructured media because of their current interest to readers.

- Part One introduces the strategies and principles guiding the structured and unstructured media and tells what programmers need to know.
- Part Two looks at programming from the perspectives of prime-time broadcast—the gorilla on the block—as well as multichannel cable/satellite and online networks.
- Part Three builds understanding of the processes and problems of ratings and syndication, and if you don't understand them, you don't understand anything.
- Part Four focuses on the practices of specific kinds of programming situations.

- Part Five addresses the rapidly morphing audio media of music and information.

Although so much is changing right under our noses, this book largely preserves the classic media subdivisions as a convenience for chapters and because the process of amalgamation and reemergence remains ongoing ... ongoing. Someday, as in science fiction, all kinds of media will merge into mega-conglomerate media businesses serving all the different kinds of receivers. TV sets, laptops, tablets and smart phones—and who knows what—will be just different sizes and shapes of wireless computers. But we aren't there yet, not by a long shot.

Two indexes appear at the book's end, along with a brief bibliography and a long list of internet media sites. The authors also maintain a website at *www.media-programming.com* where updates and links are posted. The site can also be searched from *www.wadsworth.com*. Also at the book's close you'll find brief bios of the editors and authors.

The word television now encompasses much more than it did a handful of years ago. The impacts of digitalization, internet penetration and media consolidation continue to work their ways into viewers' homes and will remain the dominant forces operating to change programming strategies and practices in the coming decade. At the same time, the slow growth in the number of U.S. viewers and listeners is giving greater emphasis to serving the fast-growing Hispanic and Latino audiences and greater importance to providing programming for other countries. Concurrently, competition from foreign-made programs is attracting more U.S. viewers while rising local media industries in other countries are creating stiffer competition abroad for U.S. media companies. These will continue to be major pulls and pressures on overall programming strategy for the coming decade.

Our Thanks and Appreciation

We celebrate and appreciate our contributing authors and thank them warmly: William J. Adams of Kansas State University; Robert B. Affe of Indiana

University; Glenda Balas of the University of New Mexico; Robert V. Bellamy of Duquesne University; Matthew T. Kaiser of the University of North Carolina; Timothy P. Meyer of the University of Wisconsin-Green Bay; Gregory D. Newton of Ohio University; Matthew S. Pierce of Indiana University; Robert F. Potter of Indiana University; John von Soosten of SiriusXM; James R. Walker of Saint Xavier University; and Michael O. Wirth of the University of Tennessee. Working under someone else's deadlines and requirements isn't easy, but these contributors were gracious and responsive, and have our gratitude. We also give special thanks to those who contributed to past editions of this book. Much of what they had to say remains part of the present book.

We also thank those who wrote the boxed additions—the delightful blogs that spice up this book: James Angelini of the University of Delaware; Timothy B. Bedwell of Media Quarry, LLC; Andrew Billings of Clemson University; Mike Bloxham of Treadline Interactive; Dom Caristi of Ball State University; Frank J. Chorba of Washburn University; Edward Fink of California State University at Fullerton; Deborah Goh of Nanyang Technological University; Simon Licen of the University of Ljubjana; Patrick Parsons of Pennsylvania State University; Elizabeth Perse of the University of Delaware; Nancy C. Schwartz, The Academic Edge, Inc.; the late Daan van Vuuren of SABC; and David Weiss of Montana State University.

And most of all, we thank Rebecca Donahue of Cengage/Wadsworth, who has been the best editor we could have had, and whose gentle and thoughtful online presence much resembles the style of her predecessor at Wadsworth, Rebecca Hayden. The first of these two wonderful women made this book possible; the second helped us keep our sanity and sense of humor during this edition.

We dedicate this edition to the two Rebeccas, as well as to Lewis Klein and the memory of Sydney Head, who together had the original idea for this book so many decades ago.

Susan Tyler Eastman
Douglas A. Ferguson

Introduction to Programming

A Scaffold for Programmers

Susan Tyler Eastman and Douglas A. Ferguson

It's a wake-up call the first time someone says to you, "Wait. I'm watching a movie on my iPod." Or maybe it was an iPhone. Or an iPad. Americans use electronic screens of one sort or another for an average of at least eight hours a day. This book focuses on decisions affecting the content of those screens. The chapters look at the strategies of all kinds of television (broadcast, cable, online) and audio (radio, satellite, internet), as well as the daily practices of the electronic media industry. Although new technologies often capture our immediate attention, in the media world *content is king*, and we'll show you why. This chapter introduces the kind of *programming specific to the electronic media*—not what computer programmers normally do—and outlines the complex media industry.

What Is Programming?

Programming can refer to an outcome or a process. It can describe either *a group of programs* on a radio station, a television network, or cell phone, as in "I really enjoy the programming on that new cable channel"—or *the act of choosing and scheduling programs* on a broadcast TV station, subscription channel, or online service, as in "My job is programming; I pick most of the shows my channel carries." Like the programmer who handles many cable channels, the online programmer also has the job of choosing but for a video library rather than a single channel.

The processes of selecting, scheduling, promoting and evaluating programs define the work of a programmer, and they are the subject of this book, whether the programmer is a paid employee or you, the viewer! The word *programs* refers to units of **content**—some as short as tweets and YouTube videos, others as long as TV series and Hollywood movies. As you choose which online sources to watch, load up your iPod, or subscribe to Netflix or Spotify, you are programming for yourself, but someone else placed that content where you could get at it.

At a radio station or small cable channel, the person paid to handle the programming tasks might be called a program director or general manager (or "hey, you"); at a television station or network, the decisions are made the very highest corporate levels (the people called "sir") because so many tens of thousands of dollars, even millions, are involved in each decision. Regardless of the person's position title, the job will be to choose content that targets the desired audience, design a schedule, make sure the content is effectively marketed, and monitor the outcome—a job description that applies to both the established media and the newest media. Of course, it's highly likely that being talented at the job leads to more successes.

If a channel has weakly pulling shows, it needs new programming, in the most tangible sense, because owners usually seek large audiences for their advertisers. Always remember: *The main function of commercial media is to deliver an audience to advertisers.* Even Facebook and YouTube are supported by advertising. The new shows a programmer chooses must appeal to more viewers (or listeners in the case of radio, users in the case of the web) than did the old shows. Somebody organizes the hour to hour display of new videos on YouTube, just as somebody chooses the hourly sequence of television channels. But day to day, once the big decisions are instituted and the shows running, evaluation of some kind of audience ratings takes the front seat for programmers.

The Big Changes

The media world doesn't hold still, which keeps it interesting. In case you failed to notice, three changes in society and the industry have dramatically affected programming and continue to do so: *digitization, internet access* and *media competition*.

Digital Media

Digitization has displaced analog television broadcasting and changed the equipment that consumers use to receive television. Anything can be a "television" now, or so it seems. Box 1.1 asks whether you are really at the cutting edge. Digitizing television

1.1 Are You Really Watching HDTV?

A lot of people think they are watching HD when they're not. It takes three things to have an HD picture:

1. A digital HD screen for your TV or computer set, duh.

2. A program shot by an HD camera: Older cameras were not in HD format, and even today, many local events, including regional sports, are commonly produced using older non-HD cameras—even if the screen looks like the right spread-out aspect ratio. So if you watch a lot of old movies, you probably aren't getting them in real HD, even if they've been remastered.

3. A contract for HD service from your local cable, phone or satellite service. If you aren't paying for HD service, you're getting only a digital signal but not an HD signal. You have to pay extra for HD.

Look at detail in the close-ups: Can you see the whiskers grow?

Look for detail in the distant background: Can you see the faces and clothes of individual fans at a game?

Look for figure/ground separation: Do the foreground figures stand well apart from the background?

Get used to real HD because 3D is coming! And holography of some sort after that.

gave rise to DVRs (digital video recorders), which in turn enormously increased time-shifting of traditional television programs, as described in 1.2. Having people watch a show on different days at different times and via different media has had a powerful and often confusing impact on ratings and program scheduling. Consumers' desire for time-shifting led to such innovations as *on-demand television*, which in turn changed the meaning of a TV channel. Video-on-demand (VOD) is more like a library than a set of channels. Moreover, viewers now want HD (high definition) or even 3D reception on large screens in their homes as well as public places, leading to new production criteria for programs and much affecting what Hollywood does.

Nonetheless, nearly 8 percent in the United States, mostly in big cities where signals are strong, still get along without cable or satellite television (or the telcos' UVerse or FiOS) in their homes. (They have to go to bars to get the good stuff!) And only newer cars have HD radio. Smart phones and tablets now show some TV shows and other kinds of programming, another byproduct of digitization of television and the telephone. At the same time, smart TV sets let users switch between television and the internet. *The new media only partly replace the old media, but they have generated new ways for audiences to use media.*

Internet Access

That the internet has given rise to enormous changes almost goes without saying. Although everyday use of the internet has been widespread for more than two decades, it has become faster (although not fast enough for most people), wireless, and easier to use (except for the 25 percent of Americans still lacking high-speed internet access in their homes). For media programmers, the internet provides four things:

- replay of major movies and network television series and specials;
- original programs made for the web by amateurs or professionals (user-generated content and web series);
- websites that carry updates and background about television stars, program plots, and schedules (enhancements); and
- a gazillion places for program promotion and advertising.

Both program promotion and program replay matter: They influence the all-important ratings. Internet usage measures provide another kind of "rating."

As the whole world seems to know, the spread of the internet via wireless signals led to social media

1.2 The DVR Factor

Digital video recorders (DVRs) change viewing habits. Those who own them grow very fond of (and dependent upon) them. Those who have original or updated TiVos are often fiercely loyal to them—more so even than the owners of unbranded models from cable and satellite operators. Those who do not own them cannot understand all the fuss. They'll find out, eventually. Some forecasters predict that DVRs will be in 80 percent of television homes by about 2015.

To the uninitiated, DVRs appear to be glorified VCRs or recording DVDs, with video stored on a random-access hard drive. But DVRs can pause and instantly replay live TV, allowing more viewer control. DVRs play back while recording, allowing the viewer to time-shift more easily than ever before. The internal menu systems driven by daily downloaded program information make recording so very easy. DVRs beat VCRs hands down: no codes, no stop-start times, no clocks to set; just choose a program from the menu of upcoming options (or during a live promo or during the actual show) and hit record. Record a show once or every time it is shown, regardless of what time or day. There is no need to know what night a show is on because the DVR does all the thinking. It even can be told to ignore any show reruns during daily or weekly recordings. Viewers simply visit their DVR program menu and find what they want, when they want it. Dayparts are irrelevant. Channels are irrelevant. And commercials are meant to be skipped.

Even more important to conventional viewing patterns is that DVRs usually come bundled alongside enormous packages of digital services, including VOD. Because the TV services commonly have informational bands that appear for a few seconds across the bottom of screens, they do two things: Besides distracting the viewer from immediate involvement in the upcoming program, they certainly make using the up/down channel changing buttons (old-style surfing) quite unappealing. *Digital cable rapidly becomes menu-driven television, not channel-driven.*

Satellite services also come bundled with DVRs to make pay-per-view possible, and cable operators supply DVRs to digital, HD and 3D subscribers for a fee, with the goal of encouraging pay-per-view sales. Indeed, manufacturers of television receivers promise to build the DVR functions into the sets themselves. Many viewers don't want an additional box connected to their TV sets.

So what happens to programming strategies? Are the traditional practices of hammocking, tentpoling, bridging and leading-in (see Chapter 2) relevant in a DVR-enabled home? Some say not, but some say not so fast. Will the added expense keep most people away or will bundling of services make the price for adding a DVR insignificant? Guide listings are not universally popular. DVRs vastly improve them. How will widespread use of DVRs become? One for every TV in the house? A few viewers may remain content with the way things were before DVRs, but not many. Stay tuned in the coming years and find out.

communication. Once upon at time, AT&T and other phone companies were the social media. You called people on the telephone. Facebook, Twitter and the like have taken over as the vital parts of interpersonal communication, affecting daily personal life and even underpinning national uprisings in the Middle East and elsewhere. But *time spent on social media takes away from time for consuming traditional broadcast and cable programs.*

Competition with the internet for precious audience time has forced drastic changes in television programming. For example, competition drove the explosion of such cheap-to-produce quasi-reality shows as *Survivor* and *American Idol*; it upped the number of reruns during prime time; and it changed audience measurement practices. To compete, the internet found success with elaborate online games such as *Farmville*, a guzzler of user time. (Have you tried puppy watching? It's another time devourer.) Competition for audiences has motivated the adoption of "green" strategies (of a sort) for the big as well as small television corporations: *Programs must now be reduced, reused and recycled (and whatever other R-words you can think of) more than ever before.*

Media Competition

Finally, Comcast bought NBC Universal (creating NBCUniversal, for some odd reason). This giant step reflected consolidation not just within an industry segment but across competitive boundaries. And it was a "buy up" rather than lateral or down: A *cable operator* bought a major *broadcast network*, along with its ownership in a dozen cable networks. A newcomer bought an old-old-timer. Since the 1980s, broadcasting and cable have been primary rivals, battling head to head for viewers, but it normally takes a large group of cable networks to match the ratings of a single broadcast network in prime time. So for several reasons, this merger shocked many industry insiders. *Cross-media has now become enmeshed media.*

The number of cable networks exceeds 500, though many are co-owned by other networks or very small splinter services. The top 25 get by far the most viewing and have the most subscribers. No one can say how many program services there are online, but about a half-dozen are best known for providing web series, while YouTube, iTunes and their cohort supply virtually infinite and changing quantities of videos. In contrast, the number of broadcast networks seems to have stabilized at ten (or nine depending on who you count): The Big Four of ABC, CBS, FOX and NBC; plus CW, MyNetworkTV and PBS; plus Univision, Telemundo and TeleFutura, the three Spanish-language networks. (PBS often gets left out, leaving nine commercial networks.) But, around the edges, Google seeks to make YouTube into a broadcast network, and Netflix would like to join this exclusive group, so the number of networks could change.

One significant point is the growth in audiences for Spanish-language networks: Univision is the fifth largest network, far bigger than CW or MNTV or any single cable network. A major point is that Comcast's purchase of NBCUniversal from General Electric, as well as AT&T's, Google's and Netflix's aspirations, signal a major shift in the relationships among the controlling media entities, and these moves are the likely forerunners of more consolidation. And new relationships between the social media and the commercial media are in the wind.

Ownership powerfully affects programming. In addition to political slant, such as with Fox cable and MSNBC, the financial clout of an owner and the size of its total audience influence the purchase price of programs: *Money matters.* And the number of co-owned outlets directly affects a program's distribution: *Audience size matters.* The larger the financial risk, the more conservative big owners become. *Consolidation leads to more reduce, reuse and recycle rather than to innovation.*

The Themes

The pressures arising from these three big changes are *themes* throughout this book. All chapters in this book examine how programs (units of content) are selected (or not selected), how content is arranged in schedules or menus of various kinds (or all over some screen), how the content is promoted to audiences or users and advertisers, and how content and audiences are evaluated (at least by the industry, even if that's not how you see things). We are especially concerned with the limits arising from technology, financing, regulations, policies and marketing needs, and you should be too.

- One central premise is that how content is paid for determines much of its structure and availability, and the long-term trend is to pay for use (whether you like it or not).

- Another thrust is how the mass orientation and traditionally rigidly linear structuring of the broadcast media is adapting to emergence of personal and mobile media. (How much difference do you see?)

- We focus on the methods and processes of consumption of digital video and audio media, which are dissolving fixed ideas about "channels" and "dayparts."

- Still other recurring themes arise from the ways the once-clear distinctions between networks, syndicators and cable companies are fading, and while some former competitors are becoming enmeshed through partnerships and mergers, certain pressures keep other competitors well apart.

- Another recurring topic is how programmers struggle frantically on a daily basis for bigger shares of the overall American audience and specific sub-audiences.

- We are always concerned with how the big media conglomerates are co-opting and commercializing online, mobile, social and noncommercial program content.

- At the same time, the persistent patterns of daily work and living continue to influence the availability and arrangement of most media entertainment content (and you don't even notice).

- Finally, the realities of economics always overshadow all aspects of media programming.

Look for examples of how these themes emerge in the following chapters about specific media situations.

The Process of Programming

Programming is both a skill and an art. *The primary goal in programming advertiser-supported media is to maximize the size of an audience targeted by advertisers.* The only way to accomplish this goal is to satisfy the needs and wants of that audience, whatever they are today and tomorrow and tomorrow.

Present-day technology permits viewers themselves to choose programs from dozens of sources (such as broadcast stations, cable/satellite channels, SiriusXM, Netflix, YouTube), giving consumers more-or-less instant access to hundreds—even thousands—of programs. But oddly enough, most people prefer to let someone else do the programming chore. *Viewers tend to choose channels and websites, but expect someone else to have filled those channels/sites in an expert way.* Even YouTube viewers may choose a topic or known video to start with, but then they typically click on whatever follows (despite the commercials).

In the case of mass-appeal channels, such as the major television networks and larger cable networks and internet services, programmers go after as many viewers as possible. Most advertisers assume that the demographic groups they want to reach will be well represented in the total audience, if it's large.

To cover all bases, most big media companies have expanded their brands into groups of channels, such as the 5 channels of ESPN, the 11 channels of HBO/Cinemax HD, or the dozen or so channels owned all in or part by NBCUniversal and its owner Comcast. In the case of specialty cable and internet channels (called niche networks) such as the Military History Channel, Black Entertainment Television, Comedy Central and the Tennis Channel (or still smaller networks focusing on pets or cooking or cars or houses or shopping), the programmer may be more interested in pleasing a particular audience subgroup than in reaching an audience outside the targeted group. Of course, *the larger the size of that target audience, the easier it is to make money.*

Very narrowly targeted channels cannot survive long, even on the internet, unless they carry advertising (but if audiences are small, few advertisers will buy) and/or charge subscription fees—if enough people are willing to pay to get the service. But audiences tend to expect most programs to come for free, so other means of generating money are essential.

All programmers must deal with certain limitations, most of them economic. *Program resources are scarce. Good shows cost a lot of money. Unfortunately, bad shows are also expensive* (except on YouTube). Good or bad, the four largest broadcast networks combined (ABC, CBS, FOX, NBC) spend more than $10 billion annually on programs and rights to major events. Their collective share of the total audience shrank for several years but has currently flattened at about one-third of viewers at any given time. Audiences are available to consume media for only so many hours per day, and less of that viewing went to the Big Four networks as cable networks and then games and social media captured more of the audience. At the same time, Univision's TV audiences are swelling in size. In the case of television programming for which viewers pay a fee, there is a limit to how much they will spend before they start complaining to Congress about subscription fees.

One byproduct of smaller network audiences in the United States has been greater efforts to market U.S. program content in other countries. CNN is a worldwide service; Disney runs Spanish-language channels in South America and other parts of the world. Although ABC, CBS, FOX and NBC are quintessentially American channels, and their U.S. popularity depends on them staying so, their parent corporations can be increasingly involved with cable and broadcast channels in other countries. Just as U.S. car makers pushed for years to get into the gigantic Chinese car market, media program producers yearn to follow in their footsteps.

The following figure (see 1.3) illustrates the not-always-happy relationship between U.S. television viewers and television program services as a tug of war. The cartoon suggests that as audiences adopt new technologies, programmers must respond with new strategies for enticing and holding those audiences. Similarly, changing economic, regulatory, and social conditions usually result in acrimonious tensions between the sources of programs and their viewers, listeners and users.

How Programming Is Unique

If Irving Berlin was correct when he wrote that there's no business like show business, then what makes a programming product unique? How are programs different from other products that corporations make for the public?

Certainly, *ease of delivery* is key for broadcasting. What other product can be simultaneously delivered to nearly every consumer? Who else can attract the biggest audiences? The very biggest sports and entertainment events still go to the broadcast networks, for now.

In theory, anyone can conceive an idea and sell it to a cable channel or a broadcast network or put it online, but the big distributors (cable and broadcast networks through their systems and stations) continue to exert a large measure of control over which programs run. Barriers to entry still limit budding suppliers.

Nonetheless, it is possible for some programmers to start small and build national audiences. Oprah Winfrey started at a small station doing a local talk show before achieving national television prominence and creating her own production company and then more recently her own cable television channel (see 8.9 for more on *Oprah*). Facebook was only begun in 2004 and now reaches more than

three quarters of U.S. homes and represents maybe (at least at unsettled times) half of all internet use worldwide. Beginning with a website is the likely path for many future entrepreneurs.

Reaching a national audience is becoming less difficult. Internet cafes and Wi-Fi are proliferating, and a growing number of program suppliers are looking for nontraditional program providers. Netflix, Hulu and other online video rentals and sales services offer another potential avenue for program suppliers, and the internet's ability to stream audio and video programming—looking and sounding both the same and different from traditional programs—improves continuously. On the other hand, to remain competitive, the broadcasters have long been *first adopters of content production for new screen technologies*—first color, then HD, and now 3D programs.

Broadcast programming remains unique because there is *no apparent direct cost* to consumers for the most popular shows. Although cable and online programmers siphon away some desirable programs, the big broadcast networks are able to provide very popular drama, reality and comedy programs, along with top sporting events and live news coverage, seemingly absolutely free to the audience. Despite all the new media, *television remains the most used medium* (close to 6 hours daily), and advertisers know it. They pay for the programs in exchange for having their commercials presented to the audience.

Although the high cost of advertising is passed along to consumers, the advertiser's ability to market products to huge audiences actually decreases the per-item cost of many products because of *economies of scale*. It usually costs more for producers to market products to a small number of people.

Why should radio or television programmers care how "free" the programs are to the receivers? In the case of broadcast programming, the low cost to viewers generates audiences large enough to sell to advertisers. *Contrary to popular belief, broadcasters are not in the business of creating programs; they are in the business of creating audiences that advertisers want to reach.* Even in the case of cable/satellite channels and online sites, advertiser support is critical

1.3 Tug of War

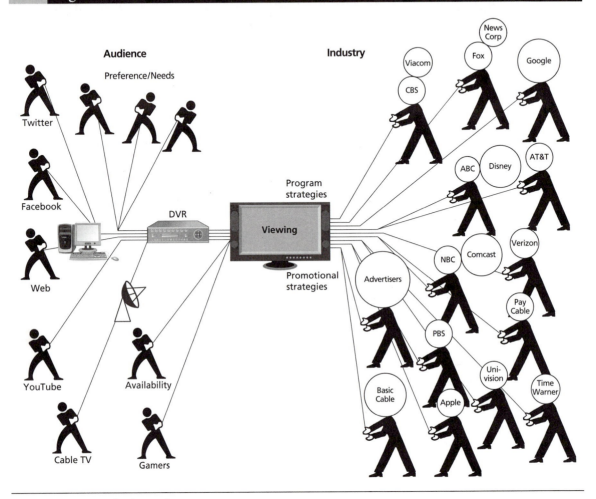

Reprinted by permission of Milton Hamburger.

to programmers because costs are seldom borne entirely by subscriber or user fees.

Programming is a unique product in that it is used to lure the attention of consumers so that advertisers can show those consumers commercial messages that help sell other products. Programmers work only indirectly for the audience; *the primary customer is the advertiser*, without whom there would be few programs to see or hear. Prime-time television might look like YouTube.

What Does the Audience Want?

The most important part of programming is understanding the audience. What appeals to viewers or listeners or online users? Quite simply, on the surface audiences want to be entertained, and they want to be informed. Speaking very generally, these two elements comprise the whole of programming content (see 1.4 and 1.5). But the devil is in the details, of course.

1.4 Recipe for Successful Production

A step-by-step procedure for the process of programming would go something like this. First, choose programs that seem to meet the needs and wants of an audience. Second, organize those programs into a coherent schedule that flows from one program into the next. Third, market the programs to the appropriate audience. Finally, evaluate the results and make necessary adjustments. This is the basic recipe for cooking the perfect program schedule.

1. Target a demographically desirable audience.
2. Choose appropriate programs for that audience.
3. Evaluate reasonable costs for program types and time slots.
4. Evaluate the competition to determine a scheduling strategy.
5. Make sure a program fits in with neighboring programs.
6. Employ talented performers whom the public likes.
7. Hire producers/directors/writers with a record of success.
8. Deal with currently popular subject matter.
9. Emulate comparable high-rated programs.

1.5 What Is Quality?

Whenever the word *quality* is attached to programming, viewers think they know what that means. Do they? Quality often connotes strong production values (lavish sets, famous performers, riveting scriptwriting, technical achievement) and critical acclaim. Those who fight to save quality programs often see some substantial social value in such shows.

So why is quality lacking in most television shows? Is it money, or could it be that the masses want circuses instead of high culture? Perhaps quality signifies only that a group of viewers finds some subjective value that is independent of objective criteria. If we cannot agree on what constitutes quality, does it really exist? Maybe those who use the phrase "quality television" really mean to say "programs that we really like."

Programmers are well advised to be careful with the word quality as long as so little consensus exists about what it is. It might be better to strive toward shows that are popular (or critically acclaimed) by external standards, rather than programs that have intrinsic quality.

The demand for entertainment encompasses a mixture of comedy and drama. Narrative stories represent the norm, and these stories have a beginning, a middle and an end occurring within each episode.[1] Characters have goals resulting from a desire. Along the way, they encounter some form of conflict. In a comedy program, the conflict is a humorous situation resolved in a way that causes the audience to laugh. Sitcoms usually appear in half-hour episodes. In a drama, the conflict results from a counterforce, often "the bad guys." Most dramas last an hour, occasionally longer. Nonnarrative reality programs are more like situation comedies with game show elements: they consist of a situation in which "people" compete to win. But the most successful of these shows also embody a narrative about participants carried over from week to week.

By the turn of this century, the former reality format (*Survivor* and *Fear Factor*) had resurfaced on a wave of game shows (*Who Wants to Be a Millionaire?*), which was soon overtaken by other types of blockbuster reality programs (*Dancing with the Stars* and *American Idol*) and two hit game shows (*Deal or No Deal* and *Jeopardy*). Many of these reality shows are competitions that generate a sense of urgency, like sporting events do, making them seem more important to watch than dramas or comedies.

Comedies, which had real staying power for decades, were consistently taking a beating in the ratings in the first decades of the 2000s, leading some critics to wonder whether viewers find serial dramas and series reality shows especially addicting. By mid-decade, the biggest draws were Fox's *American Idol* and such crime shows as *NCIS: Los Angeles*, *CSI* and *The Mentalist*. As has always been the case, however, such sporting events as the NFL games swamp all other shows in audience size.

Comedies and dramas are composed of various ingredients that appeal to most audiences: engaging dialogue, attractive characters, romantic themes, nostalgia, suspense and high emotion, to name a few. The audiences for all entertainment genres are also interested in seeing or hearing something novel, even if it is an old idea with a new twist (see 1.6). Reality shows, on the other hand, create a "human spectacle" that is every bit as scripted, primarily through postproduction editing, as programs with a preproduction script.

Information programming is also driven by novelty and entertainment value. Viewers want fresh stories that promise something new. Critics can complain about the trivialization of information, but network and syndicated news and information programming with an entertainment approach (infotainment) attracts big audiences. Consider, for example, the long-time success of *60 Minutes*, *20/20* and *The Today Show*. These programs mix popular topics with more serious information.

In their newscasts, local stations also necessarily pay close attention to the lighter side of community events, partly because there are fewer opportunities for hard news than on the national level and partly because "positive" stories appeal strongly to viewers. The trend has reached the point that younger audiences get much of their news from shows that actually mock the news, such as *The Daily Show with Jon Stewart*.

Looking at the types of programs demanded by audiences is one way to learn what people want, although it is not a perfect method. Some people say they want just comedy, for example, but some sitcoms have "serious" episodes that address social

---

1.6 **Uncovering the Mystery**

Merely asking television audiences what they want is difficult. Many times viewers do not know what they want until they see it, and a short while later they tire of it and crave something new. Programmers must become accustomed to dealing with fickle audiences. The only refuge is to uncover the mystery of how the audience makes choices about what to watch.

The process whereby audience members make choices is seldom clear, but researchers use three basic approaches to predict those choices. One way looks at the uses and gratifications of media consumption. This approach frequently substitutes the self-reported attitudes of viewers for more concrete information on their actual behaviors. A second way uses additional predictors of choice, such as market size, program length, awareness, cable/DVD/satellite penetration, and audience availability. Research findings in this area are equally unsatisfying or unusable

because really strong predictors, such as when the audience is available, are not usually controlled by the programmers (or the viewers).

The most promising way to predict choice seems to be to study the actual content of programs, but the industry has sponsored very little generalizable research. What element in a television or radio program is most important? Some say it is the likeability of the main characters. Others point to the compelling nature of the story or the format. Little research has been done in this area, perhaps because using structural predictors is easier than using content variables. In any case, studying programming as a serious topic is not easy. The networks and other program suppliers focus on the ratings and on testing ideas and pilots (see Chapter 2), but programming seems to remain one big gamble where instinct is more important than science.

issues, while some dramas venture into comedy. Adding to the general misinformation about programming is the fact that viewers and listeners believe they are programming experts merely because they watch or listen. Most people who tune to a broadcast program feel that they could do a better job of choosing the shows and selecting the time slots. If that were really true, of course, there would be no need for a book on how to be a programmer. Programming skills can be learned, but the art is a bit more difficult than it seems to many people.

The Lure of Lore

Everyone watches television, so nearly everyone professes to understand what programs ought to be like. Yet merely having preferences does not qualify a viewer—or a programmer—to make accurate decisions or judgments about program strategy. Because television viewing is so easy, the audience feels confident that putting shows on is really simple: Just make good programs and schedule them when they do not conflict with other good shows! Never make any bad shows. What could be easier?

Because it's too hard to explain, the professionals who work at the major broadcast and cable networks, along with their counterparts at the individual stations in each city, sometimes take a similarly simplistic stand. Always do this. Never do that. Give the people what they want (see 1.7). Or as Dick Block of the National Association of Television Program Executives (NATPE) preached, "Find out what works, what doesn't work."

Out of this no-brainer philosophy has grown a garden of "rules" that the wisdom of experience has nurtured. Call it folklore or just lore; many programmers believe that achieving success in television programming is a matter of avoiding common mistakes. Unfortunately, programming is much more complicated. But it is useful to examine some of the lore that has grown up around programming. Certainly some of it may be good advice. Like most lore, however, the student of programming should be suspicious of universal truths.

First, there is the matter of dead genres. A *genre* is a type of program, such as a western or a sitcom. At various times in the history of programming, common wisdom has declared each genre dead. Family sitcoms were dead in 1982, they said—until *Cosby* went on the air. Game shows were dead, they said—until *Who Wants to Be a Millionaire?* came along. Reality shows such as *America's Funniest Home Videos* were very popular in the early 1990s, and then they were dead—until they came back a decade later in the form of *Survivor*.

Second, program lore holds that there is a formula approach to building a successful show. For example, take a grizzled veteran in an action profession and pair that character with a young person to create dual appeal—something for both older and younger viewers. Or hire a big-name star from the world of movies, music or sports. The problem with such recipes is that they lead to bland television. Moreover, fans can name plenty of programs fitting these formulas that got quickly canceled—far more than shows that lasted on network television.

Third, program lore preaches that certain formats always fail. Anything with chimps. Science-

---

1.7 **A Programming Myth**

The late Sydney W. Head was a frequent contributor to earlier editions of this textbook, and he had this to say about programming:

A popular fallacy holds that innumerable workable new program ideas and countless usable new scripts by embryonic writers await discovery and that only the perversity or shortsightedness of program executives keeps this treasure trove of new material off the air. But television executives hesitate to risk huge production costs on untried talents and untested ideas. Even when willing, the results rarely differ much because mass entertainment remains the goal. A national talent pool, even in a country the size of the United States (and even for superficial, imitative programming), is not infinitely large. It takes a certain unusual gift to create programs capable of holding the attention of millions of people hour by hour, day by day, week after week.

Sydney W. Head

fiction drama has never spawned a major network hit, not even *Star Trek* (although *X-Files* came close). Never bank on satire. The list goes on… The internet has become the home for thousands of experiments in program content—most of these amateur, short-lived and attracting few repeat viewers in many cases, but attracting millions to the big successes. A few commercial websites, such as those produced by Comedy Central and some other professional producers, generate huge audiences for a time, but not for the many daily hours that characterize conventional television viewing. So far, only a handful of experimental online programs have given rise to new types of television programs for large audiences, but more may lie ahead. The same problems face radio broadcasters who want to compete with the big guys.

This chapter—indeed, the rest of this book—outlines what practitioners and scholars generally agree are the real fundamentals of programming. These are the building blocks that programmers construct with, whatever the medium, and they go well beyond the lore described above. It takes a gift to create programs capable of holding the attention of millions of people hour by hour, day by day, week after week. Competence in the field comes from understanding the sources of programs, the factors impacting audience size, and the influences of technology, economics, ownership and regulation on programming strategies and practices. Beyond them lies artistry—or magic.

Structural Considerations

Programming can be seen as largely a matter of choosing materials and building a schedule. These two processes—followed by promotion and evaluation—are the essence of what a programmer does on a day-to-day basis. Choosing programs depends on circumstances that are closely linked to the source of the programming, and depends even more on predicting what ratings each show will achieve. Similarly, scheduling is greatly influenced by whether the type of channel that will carry it is broadcast, cable, cell, tablet or online.

Sources of Programs

Four basic program sources exist for television and radio: **Network programs, syndicated programs, local programs** and **online programs**. These compartments, however, are by no means watertight. Produced shows sometimes develop into hybrid blends of local production and syndication, with an online counterpart. Network entertainment programs "go into syndication" to cable channels or broadcast stations after their initial plays on the national network; then they may be stockpiled online for On Demand replay and aired on tablets. Networks also produce special short segments of programs suited to tablets or smart phone reception.

Network Programs

The national, full-service, interconnected network is broadcasting's way of pooling resources to generate information programming. Newspapers shared news and features by means of news agencies and syndicates long before broadcasting began, but broadcasting introduced the elements of instantaneous national distribution and simultaneous programming. There are nine national commercial television networks: ABC, CBS, CW, FOX, MyNetworkTV (MNTV), NBC, and the three commercial Spanish-language networks (Telemundo—TEL, TeleFutura—TFA, and Univision—UNI), plus one public noncommercial television network (PBS). These ten supply broadcast programs by making or purchasing them.

Aside from news, talk and news-related public-affairs materials which they produce themselves, the six English-language broadcast networks buy most of their programs from the big Hollywood studios (all but one of which are owned by the parent corporation of one of the broadcast networks). Occasionally they buy from the very few remaining independent production firms. The tortuous route from program idea to finished, on-the-air network series is variously described in Chapters 2 and 7.

Network programmers for public broadcasting face still another situation. Originally designed as an alternative to the commercial system, much PBS programming comes ready-made from the larger member stations specializing in production for the network and from small independent producers, but it still buys programs, notably the British Broadcasting Corporation (BBC), which now has its own satellite channel carried on cable in the United States. While PBS selects, schedules and distributes its programming, no programs are produced by the network itself (although PBS now has its own satellite channels that compete with its affiliates, but it does not produce their content either). See Chapter 10 for more on public television's processes.

The Spanish-language networks draw much of their serial programming from Mexico's Televisa, a producer of movies and *telenovelas* (popular soap-opera-like serials with a definite ending after some months and usually with a moral or educational point). Some also comes from South America, particularly Brazil. Univision, the fifth-largest television network in the country, also produces several long-running programs, including the blockbuster of blockbusters: *Sabado Gigante*. TeleFutura, owned by Univision, attracts the second-largest prime-time audiences among the Spanish-language services. Unlike Galavision, a competing cable network, all three broadcasters produce newscasts and carry live and taped sports, especially soccer and tennis matches originating outside the United States.

About 200 cable program networks deliver the bulk of satellite and cable systems' content. Cable networks (called **subscription content networks** in Chapter 9) differ in major respects from broadcast television networks. In technical delivery, they are similar: in both cases a central headquarters (the network) assembles programs and distributes them nationwide, using orbiting satellites to reach thousands of cable systems and some affiliated stations (CNN Headline News, for example, goes straight to some stations).

But the financial and working relationships between broadcasting affiliates and their networks and between cable affiliates and their networks differ fundamentally. In addition to retransmitting broadcast stations, local cable systems supply hundreds of channels of satellite-distributed programming and must deal with hundreds of networks. The traditionally symbiotic relationship between each broadcast network and its 210 or so affiliated stations does not exist in the cable field. Most

programmers who work for cable networks also have far less input into the creative aspects of programming than do their broadcast counterparts.

The great bulk of cable network programming comes from the same sources as broadcast programming—distributors of feature films and syndicated programs—and, indeed, much of cable content has been old network programming, although this is rapidly changing as cable networks spend more for recent off-network hits and greatly increase their own production enterprises. Each cable network seeks for a single *signature* program that captures attention and gives definition to the whole network. At the same time, the multiplication of digital *splinter* channels (such as Encore Action, Encore Drama, Encore Love, etc., called virtual channels) has greatly increased the difficulty of the programmer's task of attracting a large audience for any one channel.

The internet has more varied program sources, drawing on both conventional television and radio content as well as on original commercial and amateur sources. The main sources for web series are *Hulu.com*, *blip.tv* and *revver.com*, although *YouTube.com* shows some web series, too. These series may have short or relatively long lives, but only a very few ever appear on over-the-air or cable television.

The traditional radio networks once offered by ABC, CBS and NBC no longer qualify as full-service networks. Those that have not been sold now resemble syndicators, supplying features and program inserts such as newscasts. Conversely, some radio program syndicators supply stations via satellite with complete schedules of ready-to-air music in various established formats, much like the TV networks supply schedules of programs, except that the stations now pay the radio networks for the content. Formerly, the radio networks paid the stations to air the commercials (called *compensation*), but that system is disintegrating.

Syndicated Programs

Local broadcast programmers come into their own when they select syndicated programs for their individual stations. They draw upon the following sources:

- **Off-network series.** Programs that have reverted to their copyright owners after the network that first aired them has used up its contractual number of plays (increasingly, the networks demand a share of ownership rights in many of their shows). These programs used to go directly to stations, but nowadays such cable networks as TNT, USA and A&E gobble up many of the best off-network dramas while TBS and the newer broadcast networks—CW and MNTV—take many of the popular sitcoms to rerun.

- **First-run syndicated series and specials.** Programs packaged independently by producers and marketed directly to individual stations rather than being first seen as network shows (for example, *Entertainment Tonight*, *Oprah* and *Wheel of Fortune*).

- **Feature films.** Movies made originally for theatrical exhibition, although this category has diminished because so many movies go to such premium cable networks as HBO, Showtime and pay HD channels. See 1.8.

| **1.8** | **Movies, Movies, Movies** |

Of all the program types, the feature film is the most in demand because of its popularity on so many different delivery systems. The term *window*—borrowed from the world of space flight where it refers to the limited time-space openings when conditions are just right for launching rockets—has been applied to the release sequence by which feature films reach their various markets. First, of course, comes the traditional window of theatrical release—films are either simultaneously released in several thousand theaters throughout the country or put out in stages of "limited release." Next in the usual order of priority come releases through the windows of DVD and pay-per-view cable, then regular pay cable, then broadcast networks, and finally general broadcast and cable syndication. Prices for licenses (and rentals) decrease at each stage of release as products age and lose their timeliness. However, studios sporadically experiment with different release cycles for specialized movies to see what makes more profit.

Local Production

Local programs are those shows produced "in-house," usually by professionals on broadcast stations (such as the local newscasts), but sometimes homemade by amateurs who find distribution on public access cable and online channels. Local newscasts play an important role in television and radio station strategies (but even newscasts, though locally produced, often contain a great deal of syndicated material as inserts). Aside from news, however, locally produced material plays only a minor role as a program source. It is true that all-news, all-talk, and all-sports radio stations depend almost entirely on local production, but those formats cost so much to run and have such a specialized appeal that they remain relatively few in number, exist only in the larger markets, and do not have television counterparts. Stations simply find syndicated material cheaper to obtain and easier to sell to advertisers. Localism is more worshipped than practiced.

The Uniqueness of Scheduling

Of all the programmer's basic skills, perhaps *scheduling* comes closest to qualifying as a unique radio and television specialty. Scheduling a station, cable system, or network is a singularly difficult process, and little that is comparable occurs online as yet. Even with hundreds of competing channels, the availability of the web, and the proliferation of remote controls and digital video recorders, the audience for one show normally influences adjacent programs. The influence can be to build up adjacent program audiences or to drag them down. Effective scheduling requires understanding one's own and one's competitors' coverage patterns, market and audience demographics. Most broadcast stations in a market compete directly for viewers and advertising dollars, but some viewers are more desirable than others, and programmers at stations without a network affiliation or with only a poor affiliation are disadvantaged compared with those programmers who deliver the most popular network programs.

Cable system programmers have different problems. They have to weigh the claims of competing services for specific channel locations. Being *repositioned* (moved to a higher channel number) used to be a very contentious issue between stations and cable until the FCC mandated that broadcasters get the same digital and analog cable channel numbers that they used for their over-the-air channels.

This FCC decision, combined with widespread adoption of digital cable, has pretty much made channel positions a nonissue. Nonetheless, if positions are vacant, cable operators prefer to give the choicest positions—the lowest in a group because they are easiest to remember—to the most popular (or most lucrative) services, whether they are broadcast or cable-only. *Cable operators especially favor the cable channels owned all or in part by their parent corporations.*

The Need for Promotion

The broadcast and cable networks forgo billions of dollars in advertising revenue in order to promote their programs on their own air, interrupting programs with clusters of promos and cluttering the bottom of the screen with animated program reminders. Such on-air marketing is essential for interesting viewers in new programs and new episodes of continuing series, and for retaining audiences by making them feel satisfied with the program array. In addition, millions are spent on paid program advertising appearing in other media, and on marketing endeavors in cooperation with such retailers as Kmart or McDonald's. Stations also cosponsor concerts and sporting events to attract audiences to local television and radio programs.

At the same time, having a presence in the online world has become a necessity for all ten broadcast networks. First PBS and then the five biggest commercial networks—ABC, CBS, FOX, NBC and UNI—developed huge multimedia sites on the web, and the major studios and most cable networks followed suit. Television and radio enthusiasts can now point-and-click their way through myriad home pages designed by the networks, their affiliates, the studios, the major cable channels, the programs, the fan clubs and even the program stars themselves. Unlike most blog and podcast sites, these are sophisticated promotional sites created to capture attention, generate buzz and feed the fans' yearning for closer contact with programs and their stars. Commercial interests sponsor most of these sites. Not to be outdone, this textbook itself has a section within *www.wadsworth.com*!

Fred Silverman, a giant in network programming history, understood that how programs were promoted was as important as how they were scheduled. The allocation of immensely valuable airtime to program promotion each year on every network and station is clear evidence that the industry is convinced of the truism that *the best program without promotion has no audience.* If the audience doesn't know what day, what time and what channel a program is on, the *old* viewers who miss the show will have a profound impact on the ratings; if *new* viewers don't see many exciting promos that convince them to watch a network's shows, their absence will certainly also have a profound impact on ratings.

It is crucial to understand that just a ratings point or two stands between the number one and number three broadcast network in most years (and maybe just a point more to number four). Promotion on and off the air is vital to maintaining and increasing standing in that elite group. The same situation occurs among cable networks and at the local level. Cable networks vie to be among the top 10 (or top 25), but most differ by only fractions of a ratings point. The slight advantage given by effective promotion can be the difference between making that top list and falling to some lower grouping, and *advertisers typically buy by grouping.* Local stations often vary only minutely in popularity, too, and a great deal of promotion of a newscast or radio format can boost one station above its competitors.

Promotion of online programs takes a different form nowadays. It largely consists of gaining favored placement in Google lists and other created listings of favorites or types of sites. Virtually all top placement is purchased on Google, at least under generic terms. This revenue contributes to a large part of a search engine's income. Placement is no longer luck of the draw or someone's idiosyncratic whim except perhaps on individuals' sites.

Networks, stations, systems and sites are also concerned with their overall images. Increasingly, fostering positive images around the world has value in building audiences for exported programs and associated products (this is called *branding*). Google and Apple have world recognition as brand names at least as widely known as those of Disney, CBS, Fox, NBC and the biggest movie studios, and they allot enormous budgets to increasing and maintaining those brand names. Promotion, then, is one path through the labyrinth leading to high visibility, high ratings and thus high revenue.

The Elements of Programming

The various strategies for selecting, scheduling, promoting and evaluating programs are derived from a set of assumptions about audience behavior. These broad assumptions, which are here organized into five groups, become the basis for strategies capitalizing on them, even in the changing media environment:

- Compatibility
- Habit formation
- Control of audience flow
- Conservation of program resources
- Breadth of appeal

Compatibility

Scheduling strategies take advantage of the fact that programs can be timed to coincide with what people do throughout the daily cycle of their lives. The continuously unfolding nature of radio and television allows programmers to schedule different kinds of program material, or similar program materials in different ways, into various dayparts. Programmers strive to make their programming compatible with the day's round of what most people do—getting up in the morning and preparing for the day; driving to work; doing the morning household chores;

breaking for lunch; enjoying an afternoon lull; engaging with children after they return from school; accelerating the tempo of home activities as the day draws to a close; relaxing during early prime time; and indulging in the more exclusively adult interests of later prime time, the late fringe hours and the small hours of the morning. And, of course, compatibility calls for adapting to the changed activity schedules of Saturdays, Sundays and holidays. Programmers speak of these strategies in terms of *dayparting*—scheduling different types of programs to match parts of the day known by such terms as early fringe, prime time and in the case of radio, drivetime.

Cable television's approach to compatibility has historically differed from broadcasting's approach. Each broadcast station or network has traditionally had only a single channel at its disposal (even if it shows up on two or three places in the electronic guide with different numbers). In consequence, broadcast programmers must plan compatibility strategies for what they judge to be the "typical" lifestyles of audiences. Most cable networks target more narrowly. Like the internet, an entire cable or satellite system accommodates so many channels that it can devote some to every type of audience at all hours, ignoring dayparts. They can cater to the night-shift worker with sports at 6 A.M., to the single-person household with movies at 6 P.M., to the teenager with round-the-clock videos—by using a different channel to serve each interest.

The daily share of viewing of the Big Four broadcast television networks (ABC, CBS, Fox, NBC) fell below the combined viewing of cable channels several years ago. Broadcasters' economics—and thus clout—have diminished dramatically because in such large metropolitan areas as New York City cable/satellite penetration has reached 91 percent.

Even so, many cable channels effectively shut down their program services during low-viewing dayparts (for example, 3 to 7 A.M.) and let *infomercials* reign. The owners find it hard to resist the guaranteed advertising income from program-length commercials at a time of day when the audience size is both too small to attract mainstream advertisers and not large enough to generate viewer complaints that the usual shows are missing. By contrast, *internet use climbs when television is weakest.*

Habit Formation

Compatibility strategies acquire even greater power because audience members form habits of listening and watching. Scheduling programs for strict predictability (along with promotional efforts to make people aware of both the service as a whole and of individual programs) establishes tuning habits that eventually become automatic. Indeed, in spite of having DVRs, some people will go to extraordinary lengths to avoid missing the next episode in a favorite series the moment it is aired. Programmers discovered the basic principle in the early days of radio when the *Amos 'n' Andy* habit became so strong that movie theaters in the 1930s shut down their pictures temporarily and hooked radios into their sound systems at 7:15 P.M. when *Amos 'n' Andy* came on. At about that time the fanatic loyalty of soap opera fans to their favorite series also became apparent, a loyalty still cultivated by today's televised serial dramas.

Ideally, habit formation calls for *stripping* programs—scheduling them Monday through Friday at the same time each day, just as evening news is stripped daily on network-affiliated stations. To strip original prime-time programs, however, would require building up a backlog of these expensive shows, which would tie up far too much capital. Moreover, networks want maximum latitude for strategic maneuvers in the all-important prime-time schedule. If a broadcast network stripped its three prime-time hours with the same six half-hour shows each night, it would be left with only six pawns to move around in the scheduling chess game instead of the two dozen or so pawns that the weekly scheduling of programs of varying lengths makes possible.

When weekly prime-time network shows go into syndication, however, stations and cable networks schedule them daily in strips (one episode daily at the same time), a strategy requiring a large number of episodes. *A prime-time series has to have been on a network for four years (with the prospect of one more year) to accumulate enough episodes for a year's stripping in syndication (including a substantial number of reruns).* Because few weekly shows survive five years of prime-time competition, the industry periodically faces a nagging shortage of quality off-network programs suitable for syndication. Syndicated game shows, such as the long-running *Jeopardy* and *Wheel of Fortune,* fill the gap. Necessarily, cable networks also pick up shows that had short runs, but for lower licensing prices.

Cable has adopted different patterns. Especially when just starting out, networks such as FX and Oxygen stripped sitcoms not only day to day but across most of each evening until their revenues permitted more variety in programs. Networks such as A&E, USA and TNT also strip expensive hit dramas that are freshly off-network in early evenings and prime time.

No one knows whether audiences find themselves more comfortable with the structured, compatible, predictable scheduling of traditional television than with a multitude of digital programming choices. Researchers investigating *channel repertoire* have often observed that, when scores of options are available to listeners and viewers, most tune in to only eight or so of the possible sources. For example, for many years, when Nielsen Media Research surveyed homes with access to 200 or more television channels, it used to find consistently that viewers watched only about 15 of them for more than one hour per week. Which 15 varies by household, of course. (Nielsen no longer tries to measure repertoire because the definition of "channel" has become so slippery.) The increased variety of program choices made possible by digital cable/satellite television and DVRs seems to have weakened viewing habits. Only about half of viewers (mostly women) choose in advance the programs they watch. The other half plays with the remote control.

Even so, some people may sometimes prefer to have only a limited number of choices. They find it confusing and wearying to sift through scores of options before settling on a program. We've all run across the complaint about having hundreds of channels and nothing to watch! *Broadcast scheduling, as a consequence of compatibility strategies and a tendency toward habit formation, preselects a varied sequence of listening and viewing experiences skillfully adapted to the desires and needs of a target audience.* People can then choose an entire service—an overall entertainment pattern (or "sound" in the case of radio)—rather than individual programs.

New technologies like DVRs have increased time shifting but are not likely to eliminate the average viewer's need to form patterns of behavior. Most people are creatures of habit, and television viewing is an activity that begs for routines. Indeed, DVRs may actually enhance habit formation because they make it easier to catch all the episodes of a favorite show, thus strengthening a habit. Grazing via remote controls diminishes for those who make use of their DVRs: Viewers can watch live TV and fill in the gaps when "nothing good is on" with saved favorites.

Control of Audience Flow

The assumption that audiences welcome, or at least tolerate, preselection of their programs most of the time accounts for strategies arising from the notion of *audience flow.* Even in a multichannel environment with dozens of choices, the next program in a sequence can capture the attention of the viewers of the previous program. At scheduling breaks, when one program comes to an end and another begins, programmers visualize the audience as flowing from one program to the next in any of three possible directions: They try to maximize the number of audience members that *flow through* to the next program on their own channel and the number that *flow in* from rival channels or home video, at the same time minimizing the number that *flow away* to competing channels or activities.

Many scheduling practices hinge on this concept. Audience flow considerations have traditionally dominated the strategies of the commercial broadcast and cable networks and affiliates (see 1.9). Blocking several similar comedies in adjacent time slots, for example, takes advantage of audience flow. By contrast, *counterprogramming* (scheduling programs with differing appeals against each other)

1.9

Television Versus Books, Newspapers, and Movies

Controlling audience flow becomes problematic because listeners and viewers have freedom of choice. Unlike a consumer faced with the limited decision of whether to buy a book, subscribe to a newspaper, or attend a movie, electronic media consumers can choose instantaneously and repeatedly by switching back and forth among programs at will. Hence, programmers cannot count on even the slight self-restraint that keeps a book buyer reading a book or a ticket buyer watching a movie so as not to waste the immediate investment. And, obviously, the polite social restraint that keeps a bored lecture audience seated does not inhibit radio and television audiences. Programmers have the job of holding the attention of a very tenuously committed audience. Its members take flight at the smallest provocation. Boredom or unintelligibility act like a sudden shot into a flock of birds.

is crucial to the strategies of small-audience channels that seek to direct the flow away from competing channels to themselves.

Fortunately for programmers, when watching television on large home screens, many audience members remain afflicted by *tuning inertia.* Although hundreds of options often exist in a cable, satellite, online, and tablet environment, *people tend to leave the channel selector alone unless stimulated into action by some forceful reason for change.* Many times, viewers are engaged in simultaneous activities that preclude a focused attention to what programs might be available on other channels. Moreover, programmers believe that children can be used as a kind of stalking horse: Adults will tend to leave the set tuned to whatever channel the children chose for an earlier program.

The greater number of program options provided by cable/satellite/telco and online services and the convenience of remote controls and DVRs have certainly lessened—but not eliminated—the effect of tuning inertia. Researchers recognize several ways the audience uses the remote control keypad to manipulate programming: *grazing*, hunting up and down the channels until one's attention is captured; *flipping*, changing back and forth between two channels; *zapping*, changing the channel to avoid a commercial interruption; and *zipping*, fast-forwarding a recording to avoid commercials or to reach a more interesting point. While grazing has fallen off, jumping between two programs (such as two games) and zipping through recorded commercials are commonplace. Moreover, the home playback unit has undermined Saturday evening ratings for both broadcast and cable programmers: Huge numbers of viewers regularly rent DVDs on Saturday nights from Netflix. Thus, tuning inertia continues as only a modest factor to consider in broadcast programming strategies.

Program flow is nearly irrelevant for some formats such as all-news radio, all-weather cable channels, and specialized subscription channels, which actually invite audience flow in and out. Some formats aim not at keeping audiences continuously tuned in but at getting them to constantly return. As a widely used all-news radio slogan goes, "Give us 22 minutes, and we'll give you the world." One cable news service used to promote itself in variations of "All the news in 30 minutes." The Weather Channel doesn't expect even weather buffs to watch for hours, just to return periodically.

In any case, the overall strategic lesson taught by the freedom-of-choice factor is that *programs must always please, entertain and be easily understood.* Much elitist criticism of program quality arises simply because of the democratic nature of the medium. Critics point out that programs must descend to the lowest common denominator of the audience they strive to attract. This fact need not mean the absence of program quality. After all, some programs aim at elite audiences among whom the lowest common denominator can be very high indeed.

Conservation of Program Resources

Radio and television notoriously burn up program materials at a high rate. This is an inevitable consequence of the continuousness attribute. That fact makes program conservation an essential strategy. See 1.10.

1.10 Reruns

Anyone who doubts the difficulty of appealing to mass audiences need only consider the experience of the older media. Of 25,000 to 28,000 new books printed in any one year, only less than 1 percent sell 100,000 or more copies; of 12,000 or so records copyrighted, fewer than 200 music recordings go gold; of 200 feature film releases, only 5 percent gross the amount of money reckoned as the minimum for breaking even. And yet audiences for these media are small compared with the nightly prime-time television audience.

Sometimes audience demands and conservation happily coincide, as when the appetite for a new hit song demands endless replays and innumerable arrangements. Eventually, however, obsolescence sets in, and the song becomes old hat. Radio and television are perhaps the most obvious examples of our throwaway society. Even the most massively popular and brilliantly successful program series eventually loses its freshness and goes into the limbo of the umpteenth rerun circuit.

A high percentage of the programming on cable networks and online consists of repeats of the same items. The broadcast networks also schedule plenty of reruns and now reuse their shows—*repurposing*—on their other owned broadcast and cable networks and online, as well as reformatting them for cells and tablets. Material related to the popular programs shows up in magazine articles, blogs and talk shows. The internet has stimulated production of new programs and program types, but on the whole, online and cable heighten program scarcity rather than alleviating it.

One further complicating factor, at least for hit series, is their easy availability on DVD. If someone really loves a show, they can buy a whole season or entire multiyear runs as a boxed set and need not search for it in reruns.

Frugality must be practiced at every level and in every aspect of programming. Consider how often audiences see or hear "the best of so-and-so," a compilation of bits and pieces from previous programs; flashback sequences within programs (especially in soap operas); news actualities broken into many segments and parceled out over a period of several hours or days; the annual return of past years' special-occasion programs; sports shows patched together out of stock footage; the weather report broken down into separate little packets labeled marine forecasts, shuttle-city weather, long-term forecast, weather update, aviation weather and so on.

The enormous increase in demand for program materials created by the growth of cable television and the internet would be impossible to satisfy were it not that the multichannel media lend themselves to repeating programs much more liberally than does single-channel broadcasting. A pay-cable channel operates full time by scheduling fewer than 50 or so programs a month—mostly movies—and runs each film four to six times. Furthermore, movies first scheduled one month turn up again in the following months in still more reruns, which pay-cable programmers euphemistically call **encores**. Even the basic cable channels rotate the showing of their movies and series, based on the idea that the audience at 8 P.M. will be different from the audience at 1 A.M. For example, A&E *double-runs* (plays the same episode of) many of its prime-time series, and the internet makes available archives of thousands (even millions) of old programs—all of which makes frugality in sharing and repeating programs even more crucial.

Beginning in the mid-2000s, several of the broadcast television networks began offering regularly scheduled repeats as part of their prime-time line-ups. Borrowing a strategy from cable, the broadcast networks recognized that viewers were accustomed to having multiple opportunities to see first-run shows within the same week. "This is inevitable," said Preston Beckman, the executive vice president of FOX Entertainment. "No network can program 22 hours any more, or in our case 15 hours."[2] Not surprisingly, the networks chose low-viewing nights for the repeats, conserving the cost of filler programming.

Programmers can also make creative use of low-quality shows. The SyFy Channel features packages of old monster and ghost movies, and SOAPnet replays old daytime soap operas for new generations of fans, just as Nickelodeon reruns old cartoons over and over. Another reuse strategy is evident in programs such as *Soap Opera Digest*.

A major aspect of the programmer's job consists of devising ingenious ways to get the maximum mileage out of each program item. One strategy is to develop formats that require as little new material as possible for the next episode or program in the series; another is to invent clever excuses for repeating old programs over and over; a third, the newest, is to adopt *multiplatform strategies* for each program as it is conceived. For the best programs, viewers seek more and more experience with each show, its characters, its plot twists, even merchandise. Programmers respond to the viewers' desire for more interactions by using *extensions* that may include websites and blogs, podcasts and other feedback. Nowadays, extensions spin off all hit programs. They show up in magazine articles and books while spreading across television in the form of program guests, guest hosts, and guest contestants. In the view of a programmer, there's no end to a good idea.

Before it ever airs, programmers plan versions of a show for broadcast television, for pay-per-view, for various internet locations, for tablets, for cell phones, for magazines, and so on, although such multiplatform approaches are usually only implemented when a show actually becomes a hit. The losers—without dedicated cult followings—just fade away. *The point is that any beginner can design a winning schedule for a single week on a single channel; a professional has to plan simultaneously for all media as well as for the attrition that inevitably sets in as weeks stretch into the indefinite future.* See 1.11.

Breadth of Appeal

Stations and cable systems recoup their high capital investment and operating costs only by appealing to a wide range of audience interests. This statement might seem self-evident, yet for many years, some public broadcasters made a virtue out of ignoring "the numbers game," leaving the race for ratings to commercial broadcasters. But this fundamentally unrealistic viewpoint has given way to the strategy of aiming for a high cumulative number of viewers rather than for high ratings for each individual program. This strategy coincides

1.11 Ripple Effect TV©

Truly successful TV programs are so compelling that they draw an audience that is not content to merely watch. The audience is hungry to go beyond the passive and to commune with others in chat rooms and virtual environments—to post videos, download additional content, buy the T-shirt, get updates on tablets and phones, and so on. If a program creates a deep enough sense of involvement (which is the currency of all interaction), then a creative extension backed up by a rewarding user experience will respond to that desire for further interaction with the program.

The programming for which program extensions work best can be thought of as Ripple Effect TV©. These are the programs that people talk about—the ones that show up most often in the blogosphere. With the ripple effect, the first broadcast is like a stone dropping in water. The biggest splash occurs at the point of impact, but thereafter the ring of concentric circles fans out to ripple across a range of platforms, bringing with it further opportunities to profitably harness the audience's sense of involvement—to allow that audience to develop itself into a community and to satisfy its desires—before coming back (i.e., to the original TV show's next episode) for more.

Michael Bloxham, Ph.D.,
Vice President, Trendline Interactive

with the goal of cable/satellite operators, whose many channels enable them to program to small audiences on some channels, counting on the cumulative reach of all channels to bring in sufficient subscriptions to make a profit. The internet inherently has this broad reach, although not the big profits—as yet.

The national television broadcasting networks continue to "cast" their programs across the land from coast to coast with the aim of filling the entire landscape. Of course, no network expects to capture all the available viewers. A top-rated prime-time program draws between 10 and 15 percent of the available audience, although extraordinary programs get nearly double that proportion of viewers.

Nevertheless, by any standard, audiences for prime-time broadcast television networks are *enormous*. Although the audience shares of the Big Four broadcast networks had dropped from 90 percent of viewers to less than 40 percent by 2012, a single program can still draw an audience so large it could fill a Broadway theater every night for a century. It is important to understand that a rating of 10 still means more than 10 million households are watching a program, and since households average 2.6 people, that means that 26 million people watched a show. Such size can be achieved only by cutting across demographic lines and appealing to many different social groups. Network television can surmount differences of age, sex, education and lifestyle that would ordinarily segregate people into many separate subaudiences.

A Model of Programming

As pointed out earlier, the process of actually doing the job of programming divides into four major parts. First, programmers must select programs to go into a program lineup—and separate lineups may be needed for large home screens, for tablets, or for online services. Then they must schedule the programs in an arrangement that maximizes the likelihood of their being viewed by the desired audience. Next, they must promote them to attract attention to new shows and new episodes of series and tell viewers where to find the shows. Finally, they must continually evaluate the outcome of their decisions. These complex decision-making processes of selection, scheduling, and promotion, modified by feedback from evaluation, ultimately determine the size and composition of the audience and suggest a series of pictorial models.

The model in 1.12 shows each of the major components exerting a proportional influence on the resulting audience. *The model shows that the*

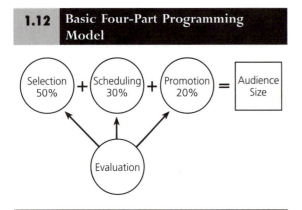

| **1.12** | **Basic Four-Part Programming Model** |

Reprinted by permission of Milton Hamburger.

selection component contributes roughly 50 percent to ratings; the scheduling component contributes about 30 percent; and the promotion component contributes about 20 percent. These proportions, however, vary widely for particular media, for particular programs, for different times of day, and even at different times in media history.

Selection, for instance, was probably much more important and promotion much less important in the 1950s when CBS and NBC dominated television viewing. Increasing competition in television came first from ABC and later from FOX, then from cable, then from even more broadcast networks (UPN and the WB which later merged into CW). Then PAX morphed into Ion, UNI grew up and added TeleFutura, Telemundo added viewers, and FOX invented MNTV. Now the internet, tablets and smart phones compete directly with broadcast television, altering the relative importance of each component in the television programming process. Moreover, scheduling has to be understood as operating now across the various media. *Overall, competition has boosted the importance of promotion and diminished the salience of scheduling, especially for new programs and new services.*

In contrast to television, for popular all-music radio stations promotion is sometimes the most significant component in the determination of radio audience size and composition. On-air contests and games have a great deal to do with music station

popularity. For all-news and talk radio and television, scheduling surfaces as the arena of competition and ongoing dynamism. For emerging web series channels, selection remains the key component.

If the model in 1.12 appears mechanistic, that is quite misleading. Even after more than a half century of concentrated attention, *programming remains as much an art as a science.* And nowhere is that more evident than in the enormous wealth of online programming. As the subsequent chapters will reveal, at all stages the processes and outcomes of programming are affected by the sparkle of insight, imagination and inspiration.

Selection

The figure shown in 1.13 illustrates some of the many components affecting the selection stage for electronic media that are spelled out in the following chapters. For the broadcast networks, these components include the scarcity of top-notch writers, the high financial risk of trying markedly different program ideas, and the escalating costs per episode for the onscreen and off-screen talent. For cable networks, the same factors are important for choosing programs, as is the need, usually, to target an underserved audience group. As significant as individual

| **1.13** | **Selection Factors** |

Reprinted by permission of Milton Hamburger.

programs are, even more important is the overall composite that creates a "format" for the cable or radio channel or internet site.

Additional factors that affect the selection of programs for cable and satellite networks include the need for differentiation from competing channels, costs relative to other program types, and the ability to capture space on local cable or satellite systems to reach an audience. On the internet, imaginative designs and antiauthority appeals to teen and young adults are key elements.

In radio and online music programming, enormous efforts go into choosing the songs that appeal to a particular demographic and psychographic group. Whether they are called music directors or programmers, the crucial task of the people making these efforts is to find and keep current the songs that the audience will tune in to hear.

Scheduling

It has been long understood that *the size of the prime-time television audience is affected by the amount and type of competing programs, the amount of viewing inherited from preceding programs, and the compatibility between adjacent programs* (see 1.14). The most studied of these

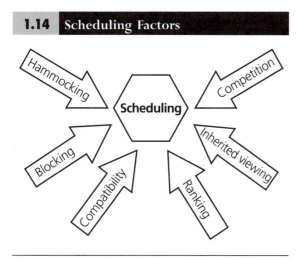

1.14   Scheduling Factors

Hammocking

Competition

Scheduling

Blocking

Compatibility

Ranking

Inherited viewing

Reprinted by permission of Milton Hamburger.

elements, the amount of inherited viewing between adjacent programs, has been consistently shown to hover around 50 percent in prime time. This means that half of the viewers watching Program B on a channel had already watched Program A on that channel.[3] Program B's other viewers come from other channels or are newly tuned in for the evening. Inheritance, however, is known to be much lower between incompatible programs and between nonadjacent programs. Few of the viewers of a romantic drama, for example, would choose to stay tuned for a violent action movie.

Moreover, inheritance is dramatically lower outside of prime time. One big exception is between two adjacent soap operas, when inherited viewing usually goes up. By contrast, only 10 percent of television viewers are likely to flow from program to program in the morning daypart because of the other activities and obligations of their daily lives— going to work, for example.

In radio, careful attention to each nuance of song rotation and news story rotation leads to ongoing scheduling adjustments. Similar attention to detail is required of online music and video, but as Chapter 4 explains, most of early focus was on the technology, and scheduling strategies have only recently gotten attention and continue to alter as they seem successful or unsuccessful. Most websites schedule by topic, genre or alphabetical name. YouTube and its many imitators let viewers know which clips and shows are "most recent" or "most popular" so that users can go directly to that programming.

Ordering by title or recency also applies to sites that replay actual television shows (*Netflix, Hulu* and *Hulu Plus, Crackle, TV-4-PC.com, your-free-satellite. com, free-internet-tv.com, the-free-tv.com,* and *various iPad apps*). Counts of hits reveal movements, and measures of time-spent-watching a show tell the presumed length of viewing (only presumed because computer users are often doing more than one thing simultaneously), but content on many sites that might be called "programs" doesn't divide into tidy half-hour-long and hour-long parcels. To date, systems haven't been refined for counting what's watched on smart phones, for example.

Promotion

The figure shown in 1.15 names some characteristics that impact the effectiveness of promotional spots on the air—such as the location of spots within a program, the position of those spots within breaks, the distance between the promotion and the promoted program (Next? Later tonight? Next week? Next month?), and the familiarity of the program to viewers or listeners. Such considerations as the physical environment of a message, the number of people reached, and the frequency of seeing or hearing the message also affect the efficacy of both on-air and print promotion. *Program promotion is constantly manipulated in the struggle to gain and hold ratings.*

Evaluation

Programmers must constantly appraise programs using ratings, hits or other measures, interpreted by the honed instincts and experience of the programmer. Here, evaluation refers to the ongoing interpretation of quantitative information and qualitative judgments that results in revisions of show selections, changes in the scheduling of already selected programs, and modifications in their promotion. One important result of increased competition from cable and new broadcast networks, as well as from the internet, has been to drive the process of programming into constant flux.

At local stations and at national and global networks, a static program lineup tends to lose ground, while ongoing refinements help to maintain and even increase audience size. This shifting of program times much irritates habitual viewers!

In 1.16, evaluation has a wide range of constituents, some directly related to program audiences and others of larger social scope. For example, the success of the competing programs affects a programmer's interpretation of ratings. A show with low ratings scheduled against a megahit on another channel might well be considered reasonably successful, whereas the same show in a less challenging location would be expected to perform much better in the ratings. Consider, for example, the inherent difficulty of trying to target men viewers (on networks other than the one with *Monday Night Football*) on Monday nights during football season.

In addition, the programmers' specific assumptions about an audience's behavior and viewing or listening motivations affect how programs are selected, scheduled and promoted. In one town, for example, workers start and end their jobs early, making afternoons a good time to program to them, whereas in another town, companies have var-

<table>
<tr><td>**1.15** **Promotion Factors**</td></tr>
</table>

Clutter · Familiarity · Location · Frequency · Construction · Distance · **Promotion**

<table>
<tr><td>**1.16** **Evaluation Factors**</td></tr>
</table>

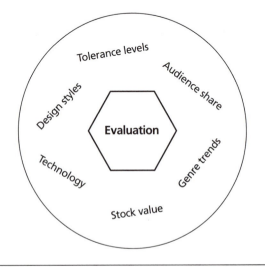

Tolerance levels · Design styles · Audience share · Technology · **Evaluation** · Genre trends · Stock value

ied schedules, lessening impact on the number of available afternoon viewers. Consider how complex programming would be in a country where the people speak not just one or two but 11 different languages (see 1.17 for a description of television in South Africa today).

Programmers' understanding of the impact and use of the newest technologies is also vital. Smart phones and tablets, as well as DVRs, have much affected the processes of program selection and scheduling, and the growth of online music listening has altered the strategies of traditional broadcast

---

1.17 Television in Many Languages

With a population of just 46 million people, South Africa has only five national television channels and no regional channels. Of these five, the South African Broadcasting Corporation (SABC), similar to the BBC in Britain and the CBC in Canada, programs and distributes three channels nationwide. These channels have to serve a population that speaks 11 different languages, and although much of the audience is bi- or multilingual, a large proportion does not understand English.

Most of SABC's programs are nonetheless in English, including such American daytime and prime-time shows as *Oprah*, *The District*, and *The Bold and the Beautiful*. South African–made "soapies" and mini-dramas are also very popular. Within these shows, programmers mix languages and also use English subtitling to overcome the language problem. To serve educational and political needs, national and international news is broadcast in 7 of the 11 languages at various times and on different channels. As you might imagine, scheduling becomes an enormous challenge!

The two competing (non-SABC) channels in South Africa broadcast only in English, although one of them, e-tv, presently attracts the second-largest audience in the country. The other is a subscription (pay) movie channel. All five of South Africa's television channels carry advertisements.

Daan van Vuuren
Former Director of Audience Research SABC, South Africa
Reprinted by kind permission of Linda van Vuuren.

---

radio stations. Other factors that programmers must constantly scope out are the trends in popularity of particular program genres, fads in star performers, styles in design and sound effects, and so on. *The programmer's nearly unconscious awareness of what is going to become popular and his or her ability to capture it in programming decisions comprise much of what is meant by the creative side of programming.*

Although some critics have decried the constant changes in television program lineups in the last decades, industry experience suggests that ongoing change is essential. Programmers tend to assume that audiences—especially the highly desirable young adults—are fickle, have short attention spans, become easily bored, follow fads, and find other forms of entertainment. It may be that many program ideas (and songs) wear out and become stale more rapidly than in the past, partly resulting from clones, reruns, repeat plays of music, or web chat about a series or song. It may be that performers peak for a shorter time than in the past as a result of constant media attention. It may also be that programmers perceive their careers to depend on identifying and eliminating tiny flaws in program lineups and formats. Whatever the reason, *ongoing feedback from the evaluation process is a critical component of the programming process.*

In sum, the basic model of selection, scheduling, promotion, and evaluation guides the approaches to specific programming situations that appear in subsequent chapters of this book. Collectively, the main model and its parts (1.12 to 1.16) illustrate some major components of the programming process that vary in the strategies for specific situations. These strategies, as well as the commonplace practices of programming—and the magical creative element—are the topics of this book.

External Influences on Programmers

Beyond learning the nuts-and-bolts programming framework, the novice programmer must deal with strong external pressures that powerfully—at times—affect decision making, for good or ill. Five sets of influences are outlined briefly in the following sections. Because the distribution system influences the kinds of programming chosen, technological issues are considered first. Without money (economic influences), of course, there can be no widespread development of new technologies. From economics flows some kind of structure, creating ownership influences. Whenever corporations and economies get in the way of individual rights, governments create regulatory influences. Finally, this chapter discusses what is morally right about the work of a programmer (ethical influences). For example, does the end (ratings success) justify the means (pandering to fickle viewers)?

Technological Influences

The long-term effect of media digitization has been to lessen station dependence on traditional national networks for television and radio programming, both as sources of original material and of off-network syndicated material; indeed, it tends also to reduce the number of local stations (see Chapter 8). The development of HD dramatically affected viewers' choice of channels, and 3D is next. Although 3D is attracting top-notch production talent, relatively little makes it all the way to home television receivers as yet. The newest portables can display entire television broadcasts, and some run on solar power. The broadcast networks may be the biggest guys on the block, but they find themselves less able to invest in high-cost series programming because of the audience's shift to watching cable networks, playing back rented and purchased DVDs and downloads, and playing games on the internet for long hours.

Contributing to this audience erosion is the increased difficulty of persuading affiliates to clear all requested time for network schedules. At one time the networks had considerable leverage over affiliates because the networks leased the coaxial-microwave relays that were the sole real-time program distribution system. Clearances of network programs were virtually automatic then. Now, however, satellites give affiliates many alternate sources of instantaneous delivery at reasonable cost. All this encourages the emergence of new program providers. Nonnetwork group owners play a prominent role among them.

Another huge technological influence is the inevitable creeping convergence of computers, telephones and television. There is little doubt that the various media have begun to come together in and out of the home. For example, the merging of personal communication assistants (Palm Pilots, Black-Berrys, Treos and their clones, best known by the older name of PDAs) with cell phones and tablets and Wi-Fi internet access signaled the arrival of portable web/television (see Chapter 4). Surprisingly, convergence came to handheld devices before it fully arrived in living rooms!

Economic Influences

There is a saying in business: "Good, fast, cheap—choose two." *The idea that quality, speed and price cannot all occur at the same time is also true for programming.* If most programming is like cheap fast food, then we should not be surprised that the quality is not high. The cost of extremely well-executed programming is high, and only two or three new TV series survive through a second season or longer (see Chapter 2). Each year, program development costs hundreds of millions of dollars. In other businesses it is known as Research and Development. In television it is called failure, or futility, or a wasteland.

The high failure rate of television programs attracts constant attention in newspapers and magazines and in TV news and talk shows like *Entertainment Tonight*, but when television shows are compared to other sources of entertainment, such as movies, books and Broadway plays, the TV failure rate does not seem so serious. The kinds of programs prevalent at any given time can be directly linked to economics. Some programs can be produced cheaply: soaps, game shows, talk shows, reality formats and tabloid news. In each case, there is little expense involved because there is no need for top-name stars or sophisticated writing. These shows may not win many awards, but they create audience demand without incurring huge costs.

Economic pressures also include the cost of waiting for a show to "grow" into its time slot. Considerable lore has evolved about several programs that had early low ratings and might never have become successful but that were, for various reasons, allowed to stay on the networks' schedules despite their ratings. Some shows seem to need incubation time to "find an audience." *Amazing Grace* was such a series, almost getting cancelled several times before rising in the ratings in the fifth year. Some program producers feel that the audience never gets a chance to discover some shows because cancellations come too quickly because so many millions of dollars are at stake.

In addition, a situation can arise where a show is canceled even when it finishes among the top shows for the week. Anyone who remembers *The Single Guy* or *Jesse* will realize that some successful shows owe most of their success to the preceding program. If the lead-in show has a huge audience, even a precipitous falloff can leave a strong audience share for the weaker following program, but programmers want shows that maintain or build the audience shares from the preceding shows. As Chapter 2 explains, *programs that "drop share" are canceled, regardless of seemingly high rankings.*

Ownership Influences

To function in media programming, it is necessary to know who the major players are. The six media giants in 1.18 are the companies that have enormous interests throughout broadcasting, cable and the internet. The major commercial television studios and producers appear in 1.19. As these charts show, these big companies own powerful media interests and combine production, distribution and exhibition of programs—the condition called vertical integration. The expansion of these mega-corporations into all aspects of media was an outcome of the repeal of the financial interest and network syndication rules (Fin-Syn).

Because much of media content is produced by network-run or network-owned studios, programmers must make difficult choices among competing company interests when acquiring shows. Enhancing the parent corporation's stock market value usually outweighs the importance of higher ratings on a particular channel, and executives at the highest levels are generally focused on maximizing revenue to the parent corporation. As Chapter 2 explains, to boost profits, when networks have a strong show, they give it their best time slot. When they have a strong show in a weak time slot, they often sell it to others (as Warner Brothers did with *Friends* to NBC). If a time slot is strong but the owned show is weak, the network normally tries to buy better programs from others. If both the show and the time slot are weak, then the network should recycle its own library (old movies) or buy cheap reality shows.

Ownership also directly affects programmers at the lower levels of the hierarchy. Nowadays, nearly all broadcast stations and cable systems belong to companies that own far more than one station or system. The profitability of broadcast and cable investments attracts corporate buyers, who gain important economies of scale from multiple ownership. Because they can buy centrally in large quantities, they can get reduced prices for many kinds of purchases, including programs. Current Federal Communications Commission (FCC) and Justice Department policies encourage the formation of multimedia companies and very large, diversified conglomerates, making group ownership the pattern of the industry. Although the failed merger between AOL and Time Warner was the first signal of the web's to major-player stakes, now Google and Facebook loom over the entire industry. And although AT&T owns only cable systems and phone lines, its executives ponder content ownership, for sure.

In broadcasting, the owner of two or more stations within a given type (AM, FM, TV) is called a *group owner*, while in cable television the owner of three or more cable systems is called a *multiple system operator* (MSO). To group MSOs with satellite and telephone companies that deliver television, the broader term *multichannel video programming distributor (MVPD)* applies. About three-quarters of the nearly 1,300 commercial American television stations are under group control (one-third are controlled by the top 25 groups), and big groups control about three-quarters of the 12,000 U.S. radio stations. In cable, the percentage of systems is even higher, with more than 90 percent owned by an MVPD.

1.18 The Players

Disney

ABC • ESPN • Radio Disney • ESPN Radio • ABC News Radio • Disney Channel • ABC Family • Lifetime* • A&E* • Disney XD • Disney Music Group • Walt Disney Pictures • Marvel Entertainment • Miramax Films • Pixar • Disney Theme Parks • Resorts • Disney Consumer Products (toys, books, software) • ABC Owned Television and Radio Stations

Time Warner

The CW** • TNT • TBS • CNN • CNN Headline News • HBO • MAX (Cinemax) • Boomerang • The Cartoon Network • Adult Swim • Kids' WB • TheWB.com • Warner Bros. Entertainment • DC Comics • Hanna-Barbera • New Line Cinema • Castle Rock Entertainment • Time Inc. (publisher of magazines and books) • Time Warner Cable Systems

NBCUniversal***

NBC • Telemundo • CNBC • MSNBC • USA Network • Bravo • E! Entertainment • SyFy • Lifetime* • A&E* • Style Network • Oxygen • Sleuth • G4 • VERSUS • The Golf Channel • AZN TV • FEARnet • NBC Universal Studios • Universal Pictures • Universal Theme Parks • Comcast sports (5) • NBC Owned Television Stations • Comcast Cable Systems

Viacom

MTV Networks (7) • VH1 (3) • Nickelodeon (6) • BET (4) • CMT (3) • Comedy Central • Spike • Palladia • TMF • Comedy Gold • VIVA • Xfire • Atom Entertainment Group • Neopets • GoCityKids • Quizilla • Paramount Pictures • Republic Pictures • Viacom International

CBS

CBS • The CW** • Showtime • The Movie Channel • Flix • CBS Television Studios (Paramount) • King World Productions • CBS Outdoor • CBS/?Paramount Television • CBS Consumer Products • Simon & Schuster • CBS Owned Television and Radio Stations

News Corporation

FOX • Fox News Channel • Fox Business Network • Fox Sports Channel • Fox College Sports • Big Ten Network • Fox Soccer Network • SPEED • Fuel TV • FX Network • National Geographic Channel • National Geographic Wild • MyNetworkTV (MNTV syndication) • Hulu.com • MySpace • AskMen.com • Foxsports.com • SKY • BSkyB (part) • STAR • Foxtel • GameSpy • Twentieth Century Fox Pictures • Twentieth Century Fox Television • Fox Searchlight Pictures • Fox Owned Television Stations • *The Wall Street Journal* and hundreds of newspapers and magazines worldwide

*Disney/ABC, Comast/NBC, and the Hearsl Corporation jointly own the A&E Television Networks, which owns A&E, Lifetime Networks (3), Biography, History channels (3), the Military History Channel, and Crime & Investigation Network.
** The CW Television Network, formerly WB and UPN, is jointly owned by CBS and Time Warner.
*** NBCUniversal is controlled by Comoast Corporation, which owns 51 percent along with GE, which retains 49 percent.

1.19 The Producers

The veteran movie and television producers were traditionally the Big Seven studios of the Hollywood entertainment motion picture industry until Sony bought MGM-UA in 2004 (reducing the seven to six). Currently, the Big Six studios are Sony (Columbia TriStar, MGM), Walt Disney Studios (Buena Vista, Miramax, Touchstone), Paramount (CBS), 20th Century Fox (News Corp.), NBCUniversal, and Warner Brothers (CW)—though many would focus on the main four: Columbia TriStar, NBCUniversal, 20th Century Fox, and Paramount.

In addition, the independent production houses make Hollywood their base of operations. Among independent producers, Wolf Films, Carsey-Werner-Mandabach, WorldWide Pants, David E. Kelley and Steven Bochco used to be regular and prolific producers for the networks and the syndication market. But independents are increasingly being acquired by large studios, as when New World bought Stephen Cannell Productions, Viacom purchased DreamWorks, King World Productions went to CBS after its split-up from Viacom, and Witt/Thomas Productions was taken over by Warner Brothers. Not much is left.

Consider the prime-time lineup in 2003–04. According to the Coalition for Program Diversity, that season CBS owned 98 percent of its programming. FOX owned 80 percent, ABC owned over 70 percent, and NBCUniversal owned nearly 60 percent of prime-time programming. The Coalition for Program Diversity unsuccessfully lobbied the Federal Communications Commission in 2003 to require that the broadcast networks buy 25 percent of their content from independent producers. Instead, now the networks have some kind of ownership in 100 percent of what they air, at least in prime time. Moreover, the five major networks now require company ownership in all that their O&Os buy in the syndication marketplace. This may be full or partial participation, but as you can imagine, the economics of independent production are no longer "independent."

This pie-splitting situation has driven buyouts and mergers and will soon kill off some production companies…if it hasn't already. As examples, consider the independent producers listed above. As of 2010, Wolf Films' television arm was officially "associated" with NBCUniversal, as was WorldWide Pants. David E. Kelley now does not do production on his own, instead working mainly for FOX or ABC. Steven Bochco, while still listed as an independent producer, no longer has any dealings with broadcasting. Witt/Thomas, a company that can trace its history back to the beginnings of television in the 1950s, has been taken over by Warner Brothers. Like Steven Bochco, Carsey-Werner-Mandabach refused to sell and found its television market dried up. It no longer exists.

William J. Adams, Ph.D.
Kansas State University

Group ownership of the right stations in the right markets can be remarkably profitable. ABC, CBS, FOX and NBC's owned-and-operated stations (O&Os) constitute the most prominent group-owned constellations. The O&Os of just ABC, CBS, FOX or NBC in the top three markets—WABC, WCBS, WNYW and WNBC in New York; KABC, KCBS, KTTV and KNBC in Los Angeles; WLS, WBBM, WFLD and WMAQ in Chicago—gross more revenue than any other groups. FOX, currently with the largest potential television reach, is owned by Rupert Murdoch, the international media magnate (see 1.20).

Each of the Big Four television networks and CW (jointly owned by CBS and Time Warner) now has about 200 affiliates and owned stations. MyNetworkTV (MNTV) has about 165 affiliates, and Telemundo (owned by NBC) has about 145, while ION (formerly Pax) had somewhat less reach at about 100 affiliates and soon became a syndicator rather than a network.

Perhaps surprisingly, although it is the fifth strongest network overall in ratings, Univision has just about 50 affiliates, as does its owned co-network, TeleFutura (see Chapters 2 and 7). In those 50 markets, Univision's ratings often exceed

News Corp. (which might easily be called the FOX Empire) is a giant among giants. Its annual revenue is nearly $35 billion, making News Corp. the third largest entertainment media conglomerate in America, barely behind only the Walt Disney Company (approximately $40 billion) and Comcast NBCUniversal (estimated $65 billion combined in January 2011, and yes, NBCUniversal is now one word).

News Corporation's holdings are vast. The annual report shows divisions in countries around the world for filmed entertainment, television, cable network programming, direct broadcast satellite television, newspapers and information services, integrated marketing services, book publishing and more. A sampling of media properties illustrates how vast the Fox Empire is.

- It owns all things 20th Century Fox, including film and television studios and distribution, music recording and publishing, product licensing and merchandising, Fox Searchlight Pictures and more.
- It operates all things FOX, including broadcast and cable networks, which cover the Fox Broadcasting Company—one of the "Big Four" networks along with ABC, CBS and NBC in America—plus MyNetworkTV, FoxSports, 27 owned-and-operated TV stations, many other Fox channels around the world, Fox News, FX, Fox Movie Channel, Speed, Fuel TV, FSN, a number of sports programs and networks globally, the STAR channels in Asia, Sky Italia in Europe, 39 percent of British Sky Broadcasting, various percentages of the National Geographic channels globally and more.

- Newspaper and information holdings include *The Wall Street Journal* (in America and Asia), the *Dow Jones Newswires*, *The Times* and *The Sun* in Europe, and almost 150 titles in Australia.
- The company owns HarperCollins Publishers in the western English-speaking world (U.S., Canada, Europe, New Zealand, Australia), and 40 percent of HarperCollins India.
- Digital media holdings include *MySpace.com* and the websites for all Fox shows (e.g., *AmericanIdol.com*, *TheSimpsons.com*).
- News Corp. even owns 32 percent of Hulu and 50 percent of the National Rugby League in Australia and New Zealand. (It once owned the Los Angeles Dodgers, too.)

The "fox" who controls this vast media empire is Rupert Murdoch (born Keith Rupert Murdoch on March 11, 1931), an Australian turned naturalized American (in 1985) who began his media career with one newspaper in Adelaide. Like all hugely successful moguls, Murdoch receives frequent criticism. A large scandal rocked his empire in the summer of 2011 when one of his British publications, *News of the World*, was implicated for illegally obtaining information and invading privacy, including bribing and phone hacking. The allegation that tipped the scale was hacking into the voice mail of murdered teenager Milly Dowler, possibly deleting messages and leading her parents to think she was still alive. The tabloid closed its doors, publishing its last issue on July 10, 2011. Soon after, News Corp. dropped

those of all other networks. Of course, how big each station's market is determines how many people can see the broadcasts, although cable channels spread reach even further. Some of the advantages and disadvantages of group ownership are spelled out in 1.21.

Because broadcast stations have a legal obligation to serve their specific communities of license, group owners must necessarily give their outlets a certain amount of latitude in programming decisions, especially decisions that affect obligations to serve local community interests. Beyond that,

broadcast group owners generally employ a headquarters executive to oversee and coordinate programming functions at owned stations with varying degrees of decentralization.

As for cable, the days of adding and swapping bunches of new systems has largely passed. The largest MSOs focus instead on competing with phone companies such as AT&T and Verison (its FiOS service supplies video; see Chapter 3). Systems tend to create geographically close groupings, thus generating savings in management. Some MSOs have given slightly more autonomy to their local its $12 billion bid to acquire the remaining shares of British Sky Broadcasting. Rupert and his son, James, were called to testify before a British Parliamentary Committee regarding the allegations. Murdoch denied responsibility for what happened, arguing that the decisions were made by those he trusted. However, he did say he was "shocked, appalled, and shamed" at what had happened, apologizing in an advertisement "for the serious wrongdoing that occurred." At the company's annual shareholders' meeting in Los Angeles on October 21, 2011, some called for his ouster, but Rupert and his sons James and Lachlan survived the vote, retaining control of the media empire.

The scandal caused many in America to question, once again, the rightness of behemoth media conglomerates. Can Fox news reporters and journalists from News Corp.'s many other print and electronic media be objective in reporting on the man who has the power to fire them? How can reporters be removed far enough from managers to operate independently, or can they? What do you think about media consolidation in light of the News Corp. scandal?

In addition to the phone hacking charges, other criticism is aimed at Murdoch, too. For example, while some of the programs on FOX television are applauded for their wit and innovation, such as *The Simpsons* and *House*, others are derided for their debauchery and meanness, such as *Family Guy* and *Hell's Kitchen*. No one can argue, though, that FOX network has spawned some megahits, such as *American Idol* and *Glee*. Murdoch has often claimed that he is

"a catalyst for change" in media. One implication is that, while a few people always condemn new ideas, the success of his enterprises demonstrates that hundreds of millions want to buy his programs, services and publications. Another implication is that his successes have forced others in the media business to change, too... and perhaps not always for the better.

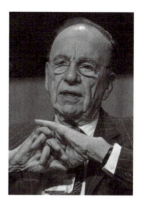

Photo of Rupert Murdoch at the World Economic Forum, January 26, 2007, used by permission under the Creative Commons Attribution-Share Alike 2.0 Generic license, courtesy of the World Economic Forum. *http://en.wikipedia.org/wiki/File:Rupert_Murdoch_-_WEF_Davos_2007.jpg*.

Edward J. Fink, Ph.D.
California State University, Fullerton

———

Columbia Journalism Review (www.cjr.org/resources/).

managers as they try to trim headquarters' budgets to reduce overhead. Nevertheless, cable group owners tend to centralize programming more than broadcasting groups do because cable has no special local responsibilities under federal law (as does broadcasting). Programming in the case of cable systems refers to what networks they carry, although many of the largest MSOs also own several cable program networks, so they also produce programs and have a vested interest in distributing them to all the markets they reach, irrespective of local preferences.

Executives concerned with programming, like those in every other aspect of broadcasting, cable, and new media, constantly need to update their knowledge of the rapidly evolving field and the rapidly increasing competition. The electronic trade press provides constant updates, but even more important are the many trade and professional associations that provide personal meetings, demonstrations, exhibits, seminars, and publications. Dozens of such associations bring practitioners together at conferences on every conceivable aspect of the media, all of which touch on programming in one way or another—

1.21 Group Ownership

The main programming advantages of group ownership are the cost savings in program purchases, equipment buys (such as computers, servers, and cameras), and service charges (such as by reps and consultants) that accrue from buying at wholesale, so to speak. Insofar as groups produce their own programs, they also save because production costs can be divided among the several stations in the group—a kind of built-in syndication factor. Moreover, group-produced programs increasingly are offered for sale to other stations in the general syndication market, constituting an added source of income for the group owners.

Group buys often give the member stations first crack at newly released syndicated programming as well as a lower cost-per-station. Distributors of syndicated programs can afford such discounts because it costs them less in overhead to make a sale to a single headquarters than to deal individually with many stations (see Chapter 6 on Syndication). A large group can deliver millions of households in a single sale. Large group owners can also afford a type of negative competition called *warehousing*. This refers to the practice of snapping up desirable syndicated program offerings for which the group has no immediate need but which it would like to keep out of the hands of the competition by holding them on the shelf until useful later. Also, group executives have bird's-eye views of the national market that sometimes give them advance information, enabling them to bid on new programs before the competition even knows of their availability. For their part, producers often minimize the risk of investing in new series by delaying the start of production until at least one major group owner has made an advance commitment to buy a series. Many promising program proposals for first-run access time languish on the drawing boards for lack of an advance commitment to purchase.

The stations in the top four markets that are owned and operated by the national television networks exercise extraordinary power by virtue of their group-owned status. Each such O&O group reaches about two-fifths of the entire U.S. population of television households, making their collective decisions to buy syndicated programs crucial to the success of such programs. Thus, these few group-owned stations influence national programming trends for the entire syndicated program market. So important to the success of programs is their exposure in the top markets that some

conferences on advertising, copyright, education, engineering, digital media, finance, law, management, marketing, music, news, production, programs, promotion, research, satellites and telephone, to name just some.

Licensing groups provide the legal and economic environment that ensures that artists get paid royalties for their works. The best-known of these associations, organizations and groups are listed in 1.22, with more about the most important of all associations to programmers—the National Association of Television Program Executives (NATPE)—in 1.23.

Regulatory Influences

The hottest topic in media regulation is *net neutrality*, the idea that FCC should develop rules preventing broadband companies from favoring their owned content and from charging fees for giving priority to certain signals on the internet. This disagreement pits giant broadband companies as Comcast, Google, Verison, AT&T and Time Warner against those who favor treating the internet like telephone lines, where all comers get free and equal treatment. The pivotal issue might be called "pay to play," meaning that distributors are likely to give favored treatment to companies that pay the most (see Chapter 4).

Broadcast radio and television, more than most other kinds of businesses, must live within constraints imposed by national, state and local statutes and administrative boards. Moreover, public opinion imposes its own limitations, even in the absence of government regulation. The trend to "let the marketplace decide" led to enormous media conglomerates and limited government involvement. Only a syndication companies offer special inducements to get their wares on the prestigious prime access slots on network O&O stations. These inducements can take the form of attractively structured barter syndication deals or cash payments to ensure carriage. The latter type of deal, known as a compensation incentive, occurs primarily in New York, the country's premier market.

Although O&O stations remain legally responsible for serving their individual local markets, they naturally also reflect the common goals and interests of their networks. As an example of a rather subtle network influence, consider the choice of the prime access program that serves as a lead-off to the network's evening schedule. An ordinary affiliate (that is, one bound to its network only by contract rather than by the ties of ownership; see Chapter 8) can feel free to choose a program that serves its own best interests as a station. An O&O station, however, must choose a lead-in advantageous to the network program that follows, irrespective of its advantage to the station. O&O stations also must take great care in choosing and producing programs to protect the group image, especially in New York, where they live next door to company headquarters.

The big cable and telephone system owners (MVPDs) have many of the same advantages as broadcast groups, however. Cable systems normally obtain licenses to carry entire channels of cable programming rather than individual programs or program series (see Chapters 3 and 9). Thus, major MVPDs, negotiating on behalf of hundreds of local cable or phone systems and tens of thousands of subscribers, gain enormous leverage over program suppliers. Indeed, a cable network's very survival depends upon signing up one or more of the largest MVPDs.

Group headquarters programmers and their sometimes extensive staffs impose an additional layer of bureaucracy that tends to slow local decision making. Local program executives know their local markets best and can adapt programming strategies to specific needs and conditions. A group-acquired TV program may be well suited to a large market but will not necessarily meet the needs of a small-market member of the group. When a huge MVPD such as Comcast makes a purchase for hundreds of different systems, not every system will find the choice adapted ideally to its needs. Group ownership imposes some inflexibility as the price of its economies of scale.

few rules remain that programmers must know to avoid possible violations within their jurisdictions.

Fairness and Equal Opportunity

Both broadcast stations and local cable-originated programming must observe the rules governing both the appearances of candidates for political office (*equal time*) and station editorials. The equal-time rule for political candidates demands that broadcasters and cable access channels (not cable or satellite operators) provide equal opportunities for federal candidates, effectively preventing entertainers and news personnel from running for office while still remaining on their programs.

Although the FCC has formally abandoned its specific Fairness Doctrine concerning discussion of controversial issues of local importance, many managers continue to adhere to the basic fairness concepts as a matter of station policy. Day-to-day enforcement of such rules and policies devolves largely on the production staff in the course of operations, but programmers often articulate station policies regarding balance and stipulate compliance routines. Fairness looms large in talk radio and talk television because the talk so often deals with controversial topics.

Monopoly

Traditionally, various rules have limited concentrations of media ownership, all of them aimed at ensuring diversity of information sources—in keeping with implicit First Amendment goals—although the recent trend has been to loosen the rules. Nonetheless, group owners of broadcast stations are

1.22   The Associations

Here is a list of important organizations, along with the home page listings (when available) for the World Wide Web.

Major Industry Trade Associations

National Association of Broadcasters (NAB): *www.nab.org*
National Cable & Telecommunications Association (NCTA): *www.ncta.com*
Radio-Television News Directors Association (RTNDA): *www.rtnda.org*
Writers Guild of America—West & East (WGAW & WGAE): *http://wga.org & www.wgaeast.org*
Independent Film Association (IFTA): *www.ifta-online.org*

Programming Organizations

National Association of Television Program Executives (NATPE): *www.natpe.org*
MIPTV: *www.miptv.com*
National Federation of Community Broadcasters (NFCB): *www.nfcb.org*
Alliance for Community Media (ACM): *www.alliancecm.org*
Media Communications Association International (MCAI), formerly the Independent Television Association: *www.mca-i.org*
Association of Independent Commercial Producers (AICP): *www.aicp.com*
Alliance of Motion Picture and Television Producers (AMPTP): *www.amptp.org*

Music Licensing Groups

American Society of Composers, Authors, and Publishers (ASCAP): *www.ascap.com*
Broadcast Music, Inc. (BMI): *www.bmi.com*
SESAC: *www.sesac.com*

Technical Societies

Society of Motion Picture and Television Engineers (SMPTE): *www.smpte.org*
Society of Broadcast Engineers: *www.sbe.org*
International Radio & Television Society (IRTS): *www.irts.org*
Visual Effects Society (represents special effects artists): *www.visualeffectssociety.com*
International Association for Radio, Telecommunications and Electromagnetics (NARTE): *www.narte.org*

Marketing and Sales Organizations

Television Bureau of Advertising (TVB): *www.tvb.org*
Radio Advertising Bureau (RAB): *www.rab.com*
Syndicated Network Television Association (SNTA): *www.snta.org*
Cabletelevision Advertising Bureau (CAB): *www.onetvworld.org*
Cable & Telecommunications Association for Marketing (CTAM): *www.ctam.com*
Promax: *www.promax.tv*

---

particularly sensitive to regulatory compliance in this area because they have a high financial stake in compliance and, of course, are conspicuous targets susceptible to monopoly charges.

For many years, cable franchises were regarded as "natural monopolies," because it seemed uneconomic to duplicate cable installations (*overbuilds*). Telephone companies, however, have stepped into this breach. Upgrading existing telephone lines to fiber permitted digital broadband delivery (called DSL), starting the trend for phone companies to compete for cable consumers by offering packages of telephone, internet connection and satellite television channels in some communities. Now Comcast's XFinity, AT&T's U-Verse and Verizon's FiOS battle head to head for subscribers in many large markets.

Localism

The FCC traditionally nudged broadcasters toward a modicum of localism in their program mixes, and expected licensees to find out about local problems

1.23 National Association of Television Program Executives (NATPE)

When television programmers formed their own professional organization in 1962, they called themselves the National Association of Television Program Executives (NATPE)—tacitly acknowledging that membership would be dominated by general managers and other executives who play more important programming roles than those specifically designated as programmers. Although programmers may track the performance of programs and come up with the ideas for new purchases, the executives are the ones who authorize the money—and make no mistake, programs are enormously expensive, running into the tens and hundreds of millions in large markets just to rerun off-network hits.

The broadcast station programming team usually consists of the general manager, sales manager and program manager. In cable organizations, the executive in charge of marketing plays a key management role and may have the most influence on programming decisions. In recent years, the role of program manager at many network affiliates has diminished as higher-level staff members frequently make programming decisions.

Syndicators put programs on display nationally and internationally at a number of annual meetings and trade shows. For showcases, they rely especially on the annual conventions of NATPE and the National Cable Television Association (NCTA) held each spring. Starting in 2003, NATPE faced some competition from the Syndicated Network Television Association (SNTA), which meets in New York in conjunction with the Association of National Advertisers (ANA) that every year holds its well-regarded Television Advertising Forum.

At the annual NATPE conventions, hundreds of syndicators fight for the attention of television programming executives, offering a huge array of feature films (singly and in packages), made-for-TV movies, off-network series, first-run series, specials, miniseries, documentaries, docudramas, news services, game shows, cartoons, variety shows, soap operas, sports shows, concerts, talk shows and so on. Trade publications carry lists of exhibitors and their offerings at the time of the conventions. (Chapter 6 gives a selection of syndicators along with examples of their offerings.) At the same time, the largest portion of sessions at recent NATPE conferences has been dedicated to the new media, but the attendees were largely new-media companies and content producers seeking ideas about how to gain distribution.

One industry source estimated that 90 percent of NATPE attendees continued to be focused on the traditional buying and selling of programs, while 10 percent were focused on the new media. Europe has a similar annual program trade fair, MIPTV. Formerly at that fair, the flow of commercial syndicated programming between the United States and other countries ran almost exclusively from the United States.

Public broadcasting first whetted American viewers' appetites for foreign programs. And with such specialized cable services as the Discovery Channel, featuring foreign documentaries, and Bravo, with foreign dramatic offerings, as well as AZN Television's Asian programs, and Univision's Mexican and Spanish programs, the international flow has become somewhat more reciprocal, although the United States is still much more often an exporter than an importer. Just as at the NATPE conventions, there is great interest at the MIPTV trade fair in innovation and new digital media.

in a station's service area and to offer programs dealing with those problems. In licensing and license renewals, the FCC gives preferential points for local ownership, owner participation in management and program plans tailored to local needs. However, localism seems to be getting less and less emphasis. Moreover, cable operators are not licensed by the FCC and so have no such federal public-interest mandate, and as a result, cable programmers differ fundamentally in their programming outlook from traditional broadcast programmers.

Nonetheless, increased competition for audiences now drives local broadcasters and cable operators toward increased localism. In many cases, localism has boosted the financial return for those stations with a long, honorable history of community orientation. It is good business to serve the community, not merely a requirement. On the other hand, economic forces lead to giant corporations for whom localism gets more lip service than action.

Copyright

With the exceptions of news, public-affairs and local productions, all owned programs entail the payment of royalties to copyright owners—whether broadcast, carried by cable, or distributed over the internet. (Of course, user-supplied content such as on YouTube only necessitates royalty payments when replayed on commercial services.) Programmers should understand how the copyright royalty system works, how users of copyrighted material negotiate licenses from distributors to use such material, and what limitations on program use the copyright law entails.

Broadcast stations and networks usually obtain blanket licenses for music from copyright licensing organizations, which give licensees the right to unlimited plays of all the music in their catalogs (in programs, promos or song play). For the rights to individual programs and films, users usually obtain licenses authorizing a limited number of performances (plays) over a stipulated time period. One of the programmer's arts is to schedule the repeat plays at strategic intervals to get the best mileage possible out of the product.

Stations and networks obtain licenses for the materials they broadcast, with fees calculated on the basis of their over-the-air coverage, but cable television systems have introduced a new and exceedingly controversial element into copyright licensing. Importation of distant signals have stretched the original single-market program license to include hundreds of unrelated markets all across the country—to the obvious detriment of copyright owners (the producers), the ones who stand to make money from the reuse of their programs. The Copyright Law of 1976 took at stab at solving this problem by introducing the compulsory licensing of cable companies that retransmit television station signals. It provided retransmission compensation to the copyright owners in the form of a percentage of cable companies' revenues that went directly to the Copyright Royalty Tribunal for distribution (mostly to sports rights holders).

The Cable Act of 1992 went further and insisted that cable systems receive *retransmission consent* from broadcast stations for their signals, which led some to believe that cable operators would finally pay broadcasters for retransmission. The issue seemed largely resolved when most affiliates of major television networks made deals with cable operators for a second local cable channel in lieu of cash payment.

In 2007, however, several small cable operators agreed to pay the CBS network a per-subscriber fee (*cable compensation*) for the right to carry its programming, a break-through for broadcasters. Although the initial amount was small (about $.50 per subscriber), the deal set a new precedent in cable/broadcast relations that gave broadcasters leverage in eventually gaining a second revenue stream (in addition to advertising), something long desired by broadcasters and, until then, adamantly refused by cable operators (more on this topic in Chapter 3). Nowadays, periodic battles erupt between broadcasters and cable MVPDs, threatening the loss of favorite programs or, horrors, a football game in one or another market until negotiated settlements are is reached. Chapter 2 deals more with this hot topic. The hungrier broadcasters get, the more they become anxious to share the subscriber dollars going to MVPDs.

A related copyright matter, the *syndicated exclusivity rule*, often called **syndex**, gives television stations local protection from the competition of signals from distant stations (notably superstations) imported by cable systems. The rule is based on the long-held principle that a station licensed to broadcast a given syndicated program has normally paid for exclusive rights to broadcast that program within its established market area. Satellite retransmission of certain stations (the half-dozen superstations) undermines this market-specific definition of licensing and divides audiences. The rule requires cable systems to black out imported programs that duplicate the same programs broadcast locally. Most syndicators avoid selling their shows to superstations in order to make the shows "syndex-proof."

Lotteries, Fraud, Obscenity, Indecency

Federal laws generally forbid lotteries, fraud and obscenity, and laws regarding them apply to locally originated cable as well as to broadcast programs. Conducting gaming and cheating audiences are definitely forbidden activities, and the fines are prohibitive. Shows that feature state-run lotteries, however, are an exception to the rule. If a state says stations can air the state lottery, the FCC doesn't care, but stations cannot run their own lotteries to make money. Programmers also need to be aware of special Communications Act provisions regarding fraudulent contests, plugola and payola (see Chapters 11 and 12).

Indecency, a specialized interpretation of obscenity laws, appears to apply only to broadcasting. The 1984 Cable Act sets specific penalties for transmitting "any matter which is obscene or otherwise not protected by the Constitution" (Section 639), but subsequent Supreme Court decisions affirmed that cable operators qualify for First Amendment protection of their speech freedom, as does the internet. This puts on those alleging obscenity the heavy burden of proving the unconstitutionality of material to which they object; in fact, several court decisions have overthrown too-inclusive obscenity provisions in municipal franchises. In practice, MVPDs have greater freedom to offend the sensibilities of their more straitlaced viewers than do broadcasters, whose wider reach and dependence on the "public airwaves" (electromagnetic spectrum) make them more vulnerable to public pressure. For some years, Congress has shown signs of tightening the restrictions on cable, including restrictions on nudity.

In a 1987 ruling, the FCC broadened the previous definition of prohibited words in broadcasting to cover indecency. That definition had been based on a 1973 case involving the notorious "seven dirty words" used by comedian George Carlin in a recorded comedy routine broadcast by WBAI-FM in New York. Responding to complaints about raunchy talk-radio hosts (shock jocks), the FCC has repeatedly advised broadcasters that censorable indecent language could include anything that "depicts or describes, in terms patently offensive as measured by contemporary community standards for the broadcast medium, sexual and excretory activities or organs." Raunchy radio content from Howard Stern led the FCC to levy a $1.7 million fine on his syndicator (see Chapter 12), eventually driving Stern to unregulated satellite radio. The increase in number and size of indecency fines that started in 2004 hastened the migration of most adult radio programming to Sirius XM. By the late 2000s, pressure on stations to excise certain indecent words from programming seemed ironic—given that the U.S. president and other elected officials had publicly used some of them.

Moreover, the FCC has designated late night as a safe harbor on television and radio for adult material. It is noteworthy that in this designation the commission used the words for the broadcast medium, implying that broadcasting should be treated differently from other media, a concept out of keeping with much FCC-sponsored deregulation. Thus, cable networks feel free to schedule dramas at 7 or 8 P.M. that most broadcasters would only air at 10 P.M.

Libel

News, public-affairs programs, and radio talk shows in particular run the risk of inviting libel suits. Because of their watchdog role and the protection afforded them by the First Amendment, the media enjoy immunity from punishment for libel resulting from honest errors in reporting and commentary on public figures. Unlike on the internet, broadcasters must take due care, however, to avoid giving rise to charges of malice or "reckless disregard for the truth."

Though the media traditionally had won most libel cases brought against them, by the early 1990s this trend had been reversed, and juries awarded huge fines. Moreover, win or lose, it costs megadollars to defend cases in court. Managers responsible for news departments and radio talk shows need to be aware of libel pitfalls and to institute defensive routines. These defenses include issuing clear-cut guidelines, ensuring suitable review of editing, and excising libelous matter from promotional and other incidental material. To assist local programmers, the National Association of Broadcasters (NAB) has issued a video that illustrates some of the common ways news programs inadvertently open themselves to libel suits.

Digital Must-Carry

Since the late 1990s, the FCC has pushed for conversion of all U.S. television households to digital reception both to foster efficiency and to release the traditional over-the-air (analog) channels for reassignment to Wi-Fi, mobile telephony, and other uses. A 2006 Geneva agreement set 2015 as the world switch-off date, after which no country need protect the analog signals in adjacent countries, and most countries have moved swiftly to convert. As of 2012 about 92 percent of U.S. households had converted, and the process went even more swiftly in Europe where the EU mandated switch-off at the end of 2012. The rise of 4G smartphones and tablets puts even more pressure on the system to free up spectrum.

The FCC's fundamental must-carry rules require cable companies to carry all locally-licensed television stations, and the HD regulations require carriage in the station's originating format (HD in most cases), while also providing a non-HD digital signal for subscribers without HD equipment. These rules explain the very long repetitive lists of channels each cable operator provides. What will happen, and how fast, with 3D is an open question, but when 3D becomes commonplace for stations, the must-carry rules are likely to apply.

However, splinter signals from a station do not have must-carry protection. Moreover, broadcast networks cannot charge cable companies license fees unless retransmission consent agreements have been reached instead of must-carry. As already mentioned, such negotiations have led big cable operators to hold specific signals hostage temporarily

(such as cutting football games or a network's entire signal) until fee agreements are reached.

Ethical Influences

Programmers continually wrestle with standards. They are not necessarily questions of media freedom but of taste. What is good taste? Like anything else, the definition depends on a consensus of the people who have to live with the definition.

Over a period of time, the erosion of public taste standards has mirrored the erosion of other aspects of public life (such as manners). Viewers might be more offended if television were the only culprit, but it is increasingly impractical to expect to be able to take a walk in the mall or go for a drive on the highway without being assaulted by someone's "free speech" in the form of a lewd T-shirt or scatological bumper sticker. In the process, the public consensus about "what is shocking" impinges on "what is good taste." Some viewers will defend a program with violent or sexual content by saying, "You think Show A is bad. It's not nearly as bad as Show B." Show A becomes the standard, and Show B is the exception, until Show C comes along. Then Show B becomes the new standard, and Show C the new exception.

The ever-widening spiral may not be rapid, but there seems to be a steady broadening of what is acceptable. Programmers are caught between the expectations of one audience that wants "in your face" entertainment and the complaints from another audience that struggles to hold onto civility. A minority of producers (and their networks) go for shock value and try to lower the standards one small notch at a time. Like the drops of limestone slowly accumulating on the floor of a cavern until a stalagmite forms, the amount of impolite language and situations has grown into high peaks in some programs on evening television, especially late-night shows. The exposed right breast of Janet Jackson in Super Bowl 2004's halftime show apparently was the final straw for the FCC, which immediately began to reassert its regulations against indecent programming, as it does periodically.

Not everyone agrees there is a problem with program standards. Here is a look at the arguments currently in vogue when the topic of ethical standards is discussed.

"It's just entertainment." The public derives its values from such institutions as family, schools, churches and the mass media, but as the authority of families, schools and churches declines, the content of radio and television programs takes on a larger role in the socialization of young people.

"If you don't like it, turn it off." True, but I can turn off only my own television set. My neighbors' kids will still be intoxicated by the violence in afternoon children's programs. They will also learn from prime-time television and soap operas that it's all right to be promiscuous. The cultural values of a nation are not wired to my individual ability to shut off my set. If someone poisoned all the drinking water in my area, you might say, "If you don't like it, don't drink it." I guess I could buy bottled water, but I have to live in the same society that my neighbors' children inhabit.

"Parents have the responsibility to monitor programming." This argument rarely comes from a parent, unless it's a parent who works as an executive at one of the broadcast networks. Anyone who thinks this will work is overly wishful. Children will see what they want to see if it is readily available at a friend's house, their daycare center, the mall or other group viewing locations. One person who has some control over the ready availability of seamy programming is the programmer.

"Censorship, even voluntary censorship, violates First Amendment rights." The Bill of Rights has 10 amendments, but somehow the first gets all the attention, perhaps because the media readily control what gets our attention. A lot of other freedoms are equally precious to the well-being of citizens, such as the right to a fair trial. The community standards of the present age would easily shock the framers of the Constitution.

A drinking water analogy is apt. If a very slow poison is released into the water supply and results in amoral, uninformed residents, then the culprits are those who work for the treatment plant. Likewise, those who choose and schedule programs for radio and television have the means to maintain some level of decency in the mass media.

How did things get so out of whack? When there were only three networks, the Standards and Practices departments held a pretty tight rein, but when pay movies and MTV came along, the competition for audiences heated up. Certainly, the most egregious examples of sex and violence come from movies and music videos, yet some viewers want still more adult content. The slow erosion of civil public behavior also affects media limits, but the amounts of sexual and violent content are merely surface issues. What matters are deeper concerns about how people in society learn to solve problems and get along in spite of differences.

The Pressures and Pulls

Well into this new millennium, the landscape of television continues to undergo a sea change, and you have to ride on it or with it. Currently, the industry pressures consumers to *switch from digital to high definition*. While broadcasting remains the largest and most powerful advertising medium, the new media check its growth.

The Federal Communications Commission has indicated that over the coming decades, *broadcasting will be replaced by broadband*. Eventually, *media entertainment may go entirely wireless*, replacing both broadcasting and cable (including most satellite transmissions). And some new technology will eventually replace the Wi-Fi of today, perhaps internet signals carried by light fixtures that fluctuate below our visibility. Magic, huh? Certainly more upheaval in the communications business world lies ahead.

Instead of a wealth of free programming, *all entertainment content may eventually require some form of pay*. We are evolving toward paying once for access to a movie or television program on any and all media devices. But there's a long way to go.

At this time, the strategy for the traditional media seems to be "if you can't beat them, buy them." In essence, a single company must program at least two versions of itself—one in broadcast (or cable) and one in broadband. In addition to online services, programs with ads now appear on cell phones and tablets, and Americans own nearly as many cell phones as television sets (and the Japanese seem to own more tablets than laptops). Indeed, worldwide, there are far more cell phones than television sets. Because the spread of advertising to multiple media threatens the traditional financial model of broadcasting, the big companies have bought, merged and developed their way into all aspects of media, becoming media giants with fingers in a wide range of media pies.

Influences work both ways: Although viewers quickly noticed that broadcast television adopted many features of computer screen displays, particularly in newscasts and sports, ironically, the current online world is growing to look more like the broadcast world. A cluttered screen doesn't work well on a cell phone.

Notes

1. Several narrative series have had another characteristic: Not only do individual episodes have ends, the entire serial concludes after some years, such as *Lost* and *24* and for telenovelas. This limited format has moved to cable channels such as Syfy, with series such as *Stargate Universe* and *Andromeda* that run to a conclusion.

2. Bill Carter, "MEDIA; TV's Loneliest Night of the Week Is Starting to Look Very Familiar." *New York Times*, June 21, 2004. *www.NYTimes.com/*

3. J. G. Webster, P. F. Phalen and L. W. Lichty. *Ratings analysis: The theory and practice of audience research*, 3rd ed. Mahwah, NJ: Erlbaum, 2006.

PART 2

Frameworks for Media Programming

Prime-Time Network Programming Strategies

William J. Adams and Susan Tyler Eastman

Chapter Outline

A chapter on prime-time network programming in this day and age! To many of you it must seem like a manual for the proverbial rearrangement of deck chairs aboard the Titanic—after it hit the iceberg and has sunk up to its deck. In the last half-decade, the broadcast networks (Six English-language now according to Nielsen) lost over half the audience they had and now have prime-time ratings that are the equivalent of those of the better cable networks. In 2009 both *Broadcasting & Cable* and *Variety* stopped publishing weekly ratings, probably because they were so embarrassing to the networks. Nonetheless, despite the shrinking size of network audiences, prime time still matters a great deal to a lot of people.

The ABC, CBS, FOX and NBC television networks are the most recognizable parts of their parent corporations although not the most profitable segments. They haven't been that for a long time. But even today they serve three key functions. First, the networks often act as *loss leaders* drawing attention to the programs and stars, despite being outdone in profits by owned stations (O&Os), cable networks, theme parks, publishing and other commercial interests. Second, they are systems for *cross-promoting* these other less visible corporate counterparts. Third, it can be argued that until recently the major networks' advertising and entertainment roles were most useful because they deflected criticism from other aspects of the company business. The TV networks act as magnets for people who want something to complain about—and noise about actors and TV shows limits potentially negative stories related to other corporate interests.

All roles have weakened, however, in the last few years. ABC, CBS and NBC's ability to generate and control news related to their corporate businesses diminished very fast once FOX's cable news, the internet and talk radio broke their collective voice monopoly (of course, a bad smell surrounds FOX's parent company for the goings-on in London). Nowadays, there is plenty of chatter about every success and every blunder made by any of the networks, sometimes with political and economic ramifications.

On the positive side, the networks represent brand names that are known around the world. The CW and MyTVNetwork, the newer English-language networks, strive to catch up with the established entities, just as the Spanish-language networks Telemundo and TeleFutura strive to catch up with front-runner Univision. Moreover, because network audience sizes have plunged in recent years, major changes in how the traditional networks select, schedule and evaluate programs have occurred, the focus of this chapter.

Blurring the Boundaries

During the last few years the separation between the five top media companies has begun to blur. This started when CBS and Time Warner partnered, turning the WB and UPN into the CW, thus also giving CBS access to Warner Brothers productions. Viacom owns Paramount and once owned CBS, and while officially Viacom and CBS are separate companies, they still share the same chairman and several other board members. Disney and ABC are wholly enmeshed, and Comcast, with its dozens of cable networks, now controls NBC.

At the same time, several networks have launched such joint online ventures as Hulu (see Chapter 4). It is owned by Disney, News Corp and Comcast/NBCUniversal. In 2011, Warner Brothers purchased Flixster and Rotten Tomatoes, thus giving it an outlet equal to Hulu. Warner Brothers plans to introduce a system that will allow videos downloaded on Flixster to be saved so that they, like DVDs, can be viewed at any time. How much they'll charge for this service and whether CBS will be a favored participant is unknown, but just the suggestion was enough to send Disney and Apple into fits. The takeover of Rotten Tomatoes seems odd as this site does not offer videos. It reviews films, and people were openly wondering just how valuable those reviews would now be when one of the producers of those films owned the site.

Regardless of what one may think about all this merging, it will continue. Even as you read this, the

Big Five are negotiating still other joint agreements in the areas of production and distribution. Broadcasting's survival in the face of Netflix and other internet innovations, while still facing the threat of rising cable audiences, necessitates new relationships among competitors.

Prime Hours

Of the more than 50,000 hours the nine broadcast networks program yearly, about one-quarter is singled out for special critical attention—the nearly 170 hours of commercial prime-time programming each week. That figure, multiplied by 52 weeks, equals more than 8,800 hours of prime-time network programs a year provided collectively by ABC, CBS, NBC, FOX, UNI, CW, MNTV, TEL (Telemundo) and TEF (TeleFutura).

Audience ratings throughout the day are important, of course, but prime-time ratings are the ones everyone takes note of, especially those of the Big Five (ABC, CBS, FOX, NBC and Univision). *The 22 prime-time hours—from 8 to 11 P.M. (EST) six days each week and from 7 to 11 P.M. on Sundays—constitute the center ring for the traditional networks, the arena in which their mettle is tested.* FOX programs 15 hours on seven nights of the week, competing head-to-head with the older networks. CW programs 13 hours (avoiding Saturdays), and MNTV programs 10 hours, dodging both Saturdays and Sundays. Univision fills 28 hours weekly, starting at 7 and running until 11 P.M.; some of this programming is duplicated on TeleFutura. Telemundo programs all of prime time but not necessarily with original content. (Filled with a mix of original production and syndicated Mexican and South American programs, Univision nonetheless beats all competition in some markets.)

Prime-time programs are the traditional source of virtually all off-network, online and much foreign syndication plus DVD, tablet and smart phone sales, and in consequence, remain the centers of long-term profit potential. Also, while the rating difference between prime-time and non-prime-time periods may not be as large as it once was, prime time is still the most heavily promoted and most talked

2.1 Original Programming's Role

The major difference between the broadcast networks and cable networks has long been the amount of *original programming* used. The top five broadcast networks (ABC, CBS, FOX, NBC, UNI) have it throughout their schedules. While the cable networks generally have original shows in only a portion of their schedules, there are so many cable networks that the amount of original programming available for off-network syndication coming from cable now almost equals that coming from the broadcast networks. Moreover, cable is moving toward more original syndicatable production (see Chapter 9) even as broadcasting moves away from it. As a result they are now challenging broadcasting for off-network syndication dollars. More importantly, as broadcasting has moved more and more into programs with no afterlife, and as they have continued to push half hour sitcoms for the syndication market, cable has begun to take over the international market.

about part of any schedule. It remains the focus of critical and regulatory concern. The prime hours make or break a network's reputation and continue to be the most visible part of an entertainment corporation's businesses (see 2.1).

The Scandals

When we talk about broadcast television, we are really talking about one small part of five giant entertainment monopolies that use their airwaves to endlessly cross-promotè the various parts of their businesses, to influence government and, when possible, to swallow or defeat competitive threats. The network morning shows have become thinly disguised vehicles for promoting the parent company's prime-time and cable interests. The magazine business is obsessed with promoting the latest stars, newest series, and happenings on the company's cable and broadcast networks. Even the venerable *60 Minutes* finds it an absolute necessity to interview the latest author from Simon & Schuster, owned by CBS. (To this day, few people realize the publisher and CBS are actually part of the same company, just as few of you students realize many of your expensive textbooks (but not this one) and *60 Minutes* come from the same company.)

They all do it. Fox News runs the latest results from *American Idol,* a FOX reality show, as if they were the news equivalents of another war, and virtually every FOX news personality just happens to have a book, which he or she mentions constantly, and which just happens to be published by HarperCollins, a News Corp-owned publishing house. NBC hypes government proposals as if they came from Heaven itself—as long as there's a contract in it for GE. ABC news shows end-lessly hype the goings-on at Disney, and CBS loves to work stars, who just happen to be in the latest Paramount picture, into their top programs.

In 2006, this cross-promotion resulted in a disaster for FOX when the public responded with outrage over O. J. Simpson's book on "here's how I would have committed the murder if I had done it." The reaction grew so loud it forced the cancellation of the book deal, a primetime "news" special interview, and resulted in the firing of a well-known editor at Harper-Collins (owned by News Corp). CBS executives breathed a sigh of relief as people forgot about their 2004 Super Bowl costume malfunction, about which the official line still remains "we knew nothing."[1]

In 2010 NBC got embroiled in the Leno/O'Brien late-night debacle (see Chapter 7), and in 2011 they were caught censoring the words under God from the Pledge of Allegiance at the start of the Davis Cup. In each case, there is little doubt that both the industry and Hollywood were truly shocked by the public's reactions. Why did uproar happen over these network programming disasters? The answer is they affected the few truly legendary shows still left on the networks. These bad decisions caught the population's interest and forced them to come face-to-face with what mainstream television had become. They didn't like it.

Vertical Integration

During the 1980s and 1990s, broadcast ratings fell. Stockholders panicked, and the networks were sold to other companies, which themselves were then taken over by giant international entertainment corporations. Although the giants became more and more powerful, they could not stop the ratings slide (see 2.2).

Faced with eroding audience shares, declining revenues and increased competition for viewers (often from other parts of their own companies), in the late-1990s the broadcast networks turned to the Federal Communications Commission. In response, in the 1996 Telecommunications Act the FCC relaxed many of the rules governing broadcasters. The most dramatic changes in regulations affected ownership, eventually permitting the networks to *own* stations reaching 35 percent of the population. Further FCC relaxation on ownership or the granting of exemptions has continued since that time allowing more cross ownership (owning radio stations, other TV stations, print interest and so on). With this enormously increased potential clearance for each network's programs (unlike affiliates, owned-stations can't decline any network programs, no matter how poorly some are doing), combined with the power of affiliation and very deep corporate pockets, the Big Four quickly took over the best stations in the top markets.

Moreover, the FCC also removed program ownership limits (the so-called *financial interest rules*), thus permitting the networks to actually *own* the programs they broadcast. The networks then used their clout to put an end to most independent production houses, eliminating competition and becoming, as never before in the history of electronic media, the true producers of their programs. *Thus, most of the programming process, from **production** of programs (by owned studios) to **distribution** via the broadcast or cable network through owned stations and cable systems or through the web-through owned web sites, to **publicity** from the TV and online units that promote everything, is largely controlled by a few enormous companies.*

Being vertically-owned limits what programmers can do. For example, each network increasingly feels pressure to program with series owned by its parent company even if those programs don't work. By 2004, no programs were aired that the networks did not at least partially own. Indeed,

2.2 Graph of Network Ratings

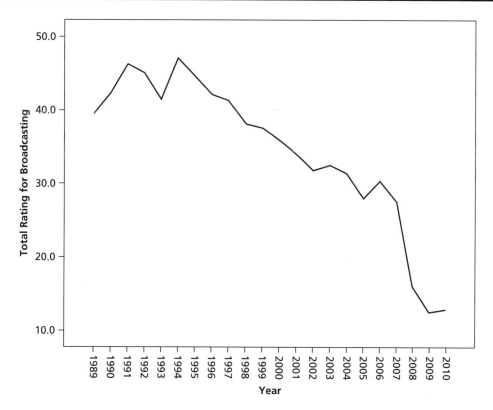

This graph shows the total ratings for all broadcast networks from 1989–90 to 2010–11. FOX was added in 1990–91. UPN and WB were added in 1994–95 and the Spanish language networks were added in 2006–07. For ratings by network see table 2.4.

in an ironic turn of events, the production arms of the Big Five companies (particularly that of Time Warner, which was strong in production but much weaker in distribution) were complaining that other members of the Big Five wouldn't even look at their proposals for new shows until they had been given a share of ownership. One outcome was that Time/ Warner partnered with CBS to create the CW to gain access to the CBS network.

Problems arise when business decisions made by the parent corporation fail to adequately consider their impact on the television network (see 2.3). In recent years, FOX and ABC have been in several

clearance fights with large cable or satellite systems over rights payments and over which other company-owned networks would have to be carried. These battles actually resulted in one or both of these two major broadcast networks being pulled off the air for a short time in some areas, with devastating results for short-term ratings and advertising revenues, as well as for long-term audience sizes. Then, over the New Year's holiday in 2010, News Corp went to the mat with Time/Warner cable over retransmission fees paid to run Fox O&O stations in nine major markets, even going off the air for a time. Time/Warner soon agreed to significantly higher fees. Suddenly there was a new standard and the other major companies wanted in. The allure of an extra one to two billion dollars in "found" money was just too great, even though it may mean even further erosions to their audience.[2]

Even worse, the entire industry seems bent on self destruction. In the face of massive declines in the audience, both unions and stars continue to demand ever-increasing salaries. A look at the network ratings in 2.3 indicates that the networks did not recover from the writers' strike that affected the 2008–2009 season. (*One axiom of programming is that loyal viewers who are forced to change their viewing habits rarely change back.*)

But the unions aren't the only problem. Back in 2003 it was huge news when NBC agreed to pay each cast member for *Friends* a million dollars an episode just to keep them for one more year. At the time, original episodes of *Friends* had rating of about 15. More recent problems with Charlie Sheen of *Two and a Half Men* revealed that he was being paid $2 million an episode, plus his share of syndication revenue and whatever other perks he contracted, but *Two and a Half Men* was only getting about a 4 rating, and that's less than half what the show was getting only a few years earlier. While it may have been the number one sitcom in the country just then, that is more a sad comment on situation comedies ratings than praise of the show.

As far as the major broadcast networks are concerned, production costs have just gone too high, which is one reason the cable networks are moving in fast on original production (see Chapter 9). They can do the same show for a fraction of the cost because salaries are lower (cable networks are exempt from many union rules) and they seldom produce their shows in Los Angeles.

Diminishing Audiences

As 2.3 shows, American broadcast network ratings have been falling over the last two decades. Indeed, the average primetime rating in 2011 was 2.9 for the broadcast networks (FOX highest at 3.8 and NBC lowest at 2). Indeed, by mid-decade, cable's collective ratings in prime time had passed those of the combined broadcast networks. By 2011, individual cable programs carried in prime time—like *Jersey Shore, Bill O'Reilly, True Blood, Deadliest Catch* and others—were beating competing network broadcast shows in the ratings, as were such Spanish language programs as *Sabado Gigante*, Univision's highly rated variety series, and *Soy Tu Duena* (Women of Steel) its top rated novella. Removing such megahit shows as *CSI* and *American Idol* from the analysis would drop the average ratings even further. It's easy to understand why problems with just one show, such as *Two and a Half Men* at CBS or the end of *Smallville* on CW, can throw an entire network into panic.

The Prime-Time Advertising Game

Traditionally, *prime time* has been the financial jewel in the media crown, pulling in billions of dollars each year for the networks. Until recently, the drop in audience size has been compensated for by higher advertising rates, by adding more spots within programs (many prime-time shows now air 20 minutes of ads per hour), and by producing fewer episodes. Increases in advertising rates, as high as 15 percent per year, have not been uncommon, and complaints from advertisers have been shrugged off. Where else can they go?

Most prime-time advertising spots are sold in late May and early June during the up-front sales period. Advertisers guarantee themselves access to top programs or desired time slots by locking them in at least three months in advance. Of course, because the programs have not aired, there are no ratings with which to set prices. Therefore, the prices for ads are based on *estimated* ratings provided by advertising agencies and *guarantees* provided by the networks. If a network does not make the guaranteed rating, it will have to run spots for free until the number of missed points is made up. If a program does much better than predicted, the advertisers get a bargain. The system appears to favor the advertisers, but that is seldom the case.

| 2.3 | Average Prime-Time Network Rating from September to May, 1980 to 2011 |

Year	ABC	CBS	NBC	FOX	WB/UPN/CW	UNI/TEL
1980–81	18.0	19.0	17.2			
1981–82	17.7	18.5	15.2			
1982–83	16.6	17.7	14.5			
1983–84	16.2	16.8	14.5			
1984–85	15.0	16.5	15.8			
1985–86	14.3	16.0	17.1			
1986–87	13.6	15.4	17.1			
1987–88	12.7	13.4	15.4			
1988–89	12.6	12.3	15.4			
1989–90	12.9	12.1	14.5			
1990–91	12.0	11.7	12.5	6.1		
1991–92	12.2	13.8	12.3	8.0		
1992–93	12.1	12.9	12.0	8.1		
1993–94	12.1	11.7	10.3	7.1		
1994–95	11.7	10.8	11.5	7.1	1.9/4.1	
1995–96	10.5	9.6	11.6	7.3	2.4/3.1	
1996–97	9.2	9.6	10.5	7.7	2.6/3.2	
1997–98	8.4	9.7	10.2	7.1	3.1/2.8	
1998–99	8.1	9.0	8.9	7.0	3.2/2.0	
1999–00	9.3	8.6	8.5	5.9	2.6/2.7	
2000–01	8.4	8.6	8.0	6.1	2.5/2.4	
2001–02	6.3	8.1	8.8	5.7	2.5/2.7	
2002–03	6.0	7.9	7.4	5.8	2.5/2.2	
2003–04	5.9	8.5	7.3	6.0	2.5/2.3	
2004–05	6.4	8.4	6.6	5.3	2.4/2.3	
2005–06	6.0	7.3	5.8	5.5	1.9/1.5	
2006–07*	6.2	7.8	5.7	6.2	2.0	2.0/0.5
2007–08	5.7	6.4	5.1	6.4	1.6	1.8/.6
2008–09†	2.9	3.1	2.8	3.6	.9	2.0/.7
2009–10	2.4	3.6	2.5	2.9	**	1.1/**
2010–11	2.3	3.6	2.0	3.8	**	1.2/**

Note: The chart combines ratings for ABC, CBS, NBC, FOX, CW, UNI and TEL in the September to May season years when they were operating with a rating above 1. The FOX network started broadcasting before 1990, but for the first few years its ratings were not reported in the trade press. Similarly, Univision and Telemundo were not included until 2007. At present, CW, Telemundo and MNTV get ratings of less than 1 (as small as .4 or .3) and shares of just 1, so they fall within Nielsen's margin of error and are not reported.

*WB and UPN were combined, for the most part, into CW in 2006.

†This season involved a writers' strike that affected the numbers

**Ratings dropped below 1 and were not reported.

24 Owners and Audits

A recent event illustrated how corporate profits can dominate the business decisions of subsidiaries. According to trade reports, Peter Jackson, internationally recognized for his *Lord of the Rings* movies, broke off relations with New Line Cinema, a Time Warner company, and would not participate in a New Line Hobbit prequel because Time Warner refused to permit an independent audit of the reported $4 billion income from the *Lord of the Rings* trilogy. This ended production until New Lines' options on the Hobbit ran out because, without the New Zealand production facilities, it was too expensive for New Line to do.

It is widely believed that New Line was only allowing companies that its parent owned to bid on such things as foreign distribution, broadcast and cable rights, DVDs, merchandising and so on. For the parent company, such arrangements provide a great advantage: All profits come to it, and money can be moved around so that taxes are lessened. The difficulty is that for independent producers such as Peter Jackson, this closed bidding practice costs tens of millions of dollars. In short, rather than allow the audit, New Line was willing to forgo a potential hit movie worth billions.

More recently, the producers of *Smallville* have been locked in legal battles with the CW. They claim the CW is giving Warner Brothers-owned stations and other Warner Brothers affiliated entities special deals for very low prices on *Smallville*, thus cheating the producers out of millions in profit sharing. However, insiders say this is just how things are done these days. In an ever-narrowing market, both in terms of product and competition, pressures come from all sides. No one part of the company is allowed to threaten the overall bottom line, even if that means massive losses in revenues for individual parts of the company or squeezing other people involved with the project even when the company must work with them in the future.

William J. Adams, Ph.D.,
Kansas State University

In actual numbers, although the ratings look small, each point represents a percentage of the 116 million television households in America (as estimated by Nielsen in 2012). Thus, a 2.4 rating stands for about 2 million households, each with an average of 2.6 people viewing. Even a rating as small as 2.4 means the program is attracting 6 to 7 million people at one time. Such ratings are sufficient for many advertisers and still better than average cable programs earn, but the biggest advertisers are getting nervous as they also have to pay a lot more for broadcast programs than for cable programs.

The ability to predict ratings is weak at best, and the networks tend to be very conservative in their guarantees. For the last few years, the networks have further protected themselves by refusing to sell the top-rated shows except as part of package deals. In other words, if sponsors want to buy time in a program like *The Mentalist* or *The Good Wife*, they also have to buy time in much weaker shows. In this way the networks assure the sale of time slots that might otherwise be left open. Of course, this means the sponsors have to take programs they don't really want and spend more than they would if they just bought the strongest shows. Although sponsors object, they continue to buy just as they always have. After all, where else are they going to go?

Until recently, that "where else?" question ended all discussion. It has always been easier for the advertising industry just to do what has always been done. For 20 years the compensation rates for the agencies placing advertisements declined steadily (from around 15 percent in the 1980s to the low single digits), giving them no incentive to make extra efforts.

As audience size continued to decline and network ad rates skyrocketed, however, the corporate sponsors themselves began to get back into the act. During the 2004–05 season, many of the biggest sponsors refused to go along with network attempts to make double-digit increases in advertising rates, forcing the broadcast networks to drop increases back to 6 to 8 percent. For the first time in that season, almost half of all prime-time slots had not been sold by the end of the up-front sales period, and cable and the internet reaped the benefits. The networks haven't forgotten this scare.[3]

In 2008 top advertisers refused to pay ABC, CBS and NBC a so-called integration fee of $125 million on top of whatever prices they had negotiated during the upfront sales period. Advertisers pointed out this fee made sense when someone had to physically insert ads into programs, a practice that no longer existed (and a fee that FOX, the CW and cable networks did not charge[4]). Advertisers also continue to object to the practice of calculating the ratings by totaling "live plus three days," a practice that drives up their costs (see Chapter 5). Both FOX and the CW are moving toward more integrated ads, in other words, product placement deals, and ABC and CBS are beginning to test the waters.[5]

Moreover, cable networks and the internet are no longer the only real competitors for advertising dollars or for content. Much of the challenge for advertising revenues seems to be coming from cash-plus-barter syndication deals (discussed in Chapter 6). Some syndicated programs outdraw most network shows, and the prices they can demand from the spot ad market reflect that power. By mid-decade, the syndicated *Friends, Seinfeld,* and *Two and a Half Men* pulled more than $200,000 per 30-second spot, and several others drew at least half that amount (see 2.4).

Advertisers must also deal with the new nontraditional ways of obtaining programming. For years broadcasters took comfort in the fact that they were free while all alternatives cost a lot. As the alternatives begin offering more choices and services than broadcasting, the industry quickly learned that many people were willing to pay for what they wanted (see 2.5).

In short, networks are no longer the economic powerhouses they once were, but the profits for their parent companies keep growing because they own most of the alternatives. Nonetheless, concern about program production is mounting. So far, the broadcast networks are still expected to produce the original programs that then feed the rest of the system. But as networks rely more and more on cheap reality programs, the pool of programs with an afterlife dries

---

2.5	**Cutting the Cord**

*W*ired Magazine compared the cost of the internet television with traditional TV (by which they meant signals delivered via cable or satellite). To equal the cost of cable or satellite, they calculated that the average person dropping cable or satellite would need a digital antenna to get broadcast stations ($50), Hulu ($119.88 per year), Joost, YouTube, TV.com, network Web sites (free), Netflix instant ($107.88 per year plus a Roku box at $79.99), and Apple TV or Amazon Video on demand ($229 for the Apple box, $1.99 per-show for average definition programs; for hi def, the authors figured $517.40 per year for one show per week night). The savings to move from cable/satellite TV to internet TV was $360 to $540 (depending on whether one was replacing satellite or a cable premium package) during the first year and $720 to $900 per year thereafter. Cutting the cord sounds like a good deal for savvy viewers, but what do advertisers and broadcast networks do then?*

William J. Adams, Ph.D.
Kansas State University

---

*Wired Magazine, Sept. 2010, "Wired's guide to picking your perfect tv setup." Wired.com/magazine/2010/08/ff_howto_watchtv/

---

up. Many reality shows can't be syndicated, can't be rerun on the air, can't be sold overseas or online, and have no value as DVDs. Once viewers know who won, they don't want to see the shows again.

FOX, however, figured out how to make extra money from the reality show *American Idol* and used the process to justify the cost of producing *Glee.* This new method is separate from traditional advertising or syndication revenues. *American Idol* gives massive promotion to singers (often several people going into the finals—not just the winner) who are then signed by Columbia Records, with whom FOX has a profit-sharing deal. These singers then go on tours using FOX-owned promoters with audience tickets sold through FOX-owned outlets. Much the same is true for *Glee,* which by all previous standards should be too expensive to be produced for television. But, not only does it produce top numbers (relatively speaking) with 18 to 33 year olds, it's also a hit in DVD sales, sales of recordings by the cast, tickets to cast tours, in internet sales of the production numbers (which can be downloaded after each show for a nominal price), and online sales of re-viewings of the episodes.

While these moneys don't go directly to the FOX network, they do go to News Corp thus making both shows worthwhile investments. As an added bonus, the other networks can't rush into production with *Glee* knock-offs as there are very few people in Hollywood who know how to do musicals anymore. After all, it was assumed to be a dead format. *This practice of creative aftermarket selling of a program and its participants suggests one profitable direction for broadcasting's future.*

In addition, too many spots in breaks and high ad rates have caused a rethinking among advertisers, and the result has been an enormous increase in *product placement* within programs on FOX and the CW. Product placement was standard practice in the early days of television, and it has been a big moneymaker in movies ever since ET followed that trail of Reese's Pieces. Cable networks have aggressively sought out companies to place their logos or products in prominent positions on original cable shows. But until recently, the broadcast networks were reluctant to follow the trend, calling it demeaning, and claiming it cheapened the value of the traditional spot advertisement and could possibly raise legal issues.

The smaller networks, however, with less to lose given their lower ratings, were willing to try. Soon, the cast of *Buffy the Vampire Slayer* was not only drinking but also mentioning Coke products, and a yellow VW was prominently featured in *Smallville*. As the money began to roll in, the traditional networks wanted a piece of that action, and soon brand-name products were appearing everywhere *except* in ABC, CBS and NBC's prime-time shows. Product placement became so common that Nielsen Media Research launched a new service in 2004 called Product Placement Measurement to allow subscribers to track their products and those of their competitors through various TV shows.

Also, product placement began to affect program content. Sears, while not the actual producer of *Extreme Makeover: Home Edition*, did make a huge investment, in return for which the reality show prominently featured Sears products in their makeovers. As a result, in the 2011 sweeps, *Extreme Makeover* ranked number 5 for product placement with 45 occurrences—still minimal compared with *American Idol's* 102 occurrences (it was number 1 in product placement according to Nielsen).

Perhaps the most interesting development, however, was illustrated by a deal TNT made to insert products into reruns of *Law & Order*. Generic products were digitally replaced with brand names that paid for the privilege. Sometimes described as *virtual advertising*, this is the next logical step in computer-generated content. Already widely used in sporting events, virtual ads do not require the actual placement of a physical product. The advertisement exists only in the computer.

With virtual ads, advertisers can aim their messages to specific markets. For example, Coca-Cola now pays to have the judges on *American Idol* drink their product. But through the use of virtual ads, in New York those judges could be drinking Vanilla Coke, while in California they sip Caffeine Free Diet Coke, and in the South it might be Classic Coke filling those glasses. The same process can be used to replace the generic products shown in older TV shows with high-paying brand names. Of more concern to advertisers is the fact that the same process can be used to replace an existing brand name with a higher-paying competitor. In the past, product placement was forever. No more. If Coke won't kick in more money, the stars may be drinking Pepsi in the reruns and Dr. Pepper on the DVD. The maker of M&M'S could finally correct its earlier marketing mistake and have ET follow their little chocolate product instead.

The *multiplatform strategy* was the next response to declining advertising revenues. The networks began distributing their most valuable properties across many media, packing the additional ad time—at high rates—with broadcast. Advertisers who wanted mass network exposure were then forced to develop plans for internet, cable, tablets and even iPod media. Beginning in 2008, CBS and NBC also began demanding that out-of-home viewing be counted and began placing dedicated screens in unusual places. By 2011, NBC had partnered with IdeaCast which has TV screens in over 900 health clubs and with the University Network which is on 181 college campuses. Similarly, CBS purchased SignStory outright, which operates screens in 1,400 grocery stores and partnered with Ripple which has 1,500 screens in specialty retail locations like Jack in the Box, and aligned with Automotive Broadcasting which provides screens in car dealerships.[6]

In 2010 ABC, CBS and NBC joined FOX and CW in moving production of their non-sitcom pilots out of California. Film L.A., which tracks production, noted a 42 percent drop in pilot production between 2005 and 2009. That didn't mean fewer pilots were being made; they just were not being made in California. By 2011, Los Angeles and the state had declared "runaway" productions a crisis, while Las Vegas was announcing plans to build a studio. This represents a loss of $100 million dollars to the Los Angeles region alone. The reason the production is moving out is simple: Costs drop dramatically. Not only do productions get out from under strict union rules, but they also get a 10 percent to 25 percent reduction in taxes.[7]

While ABC, CBS and NBC have only moved pilot production away, FOX, CW, Univision and Telemundo also moved actual series production out. While California is suffering a financial crisis, production in areas like Hawaii, Florida, Colorado and Chicago is booming. Canadian and Mexican studios are running at capacity. Univision and Telemundo have massive production in Miami and in Mexico; most of it is original programming, which they now syndicate to Spanish-speaking countries instead of just buying programs from them.

Audience Targeting

In 2003, James Poniewozik, writing for *Time* magazine (owned by Time Warner), noted the falling numbers for broadcast television and asked, "Does the mainstream still exist?"[8] He might better have

---

2.6 | **The Aging Audience**

Ironically, network audiences are aging, far beyond what most can imagine. As of 2010 (the latest published numbers), these were the median ages of network viewers:[9]

CW	34
FOX	44
ABC	51
NBC	49
CBS	55
Univision	34

Such aging scares network executives because the trend potentially affects advertising revenue and the viability of many kinds of programs. One response has been to focus on the ratings for certain desirable segments of the audience. The few youth-oriented programs being offered, such as *Glee*, get lots of hype. Even supposedly "young shows" often aren't: The median for *Two and One Half Men* is 50 and *Dancing with the Stars* is 60.

---

asked whether the networks would know the mainstream if they were drowning in it (see 2.6). For the last 30 years, the broadcast networks have relentlessly pursued one segment of the audience to the exclusion of other television viewers. Programs have been targeted toward the younger, more urban audience in the major population centers—matching the coverage area of the network owned-and-operated (O&O) stations—and away from the more thinly populated rural markets where the networks have no direct ownership interests.

Ideal Demographics and Flow

When NBC programming head Paul Klein first proposed the concept of ideal demographics back in the early 1970s, he believed the networks could go after his so-called ideal demographic group without losing the rest of the audience because at the time it was widely agreed that people watch television, not shows. In a three-network era, Klein reasonably assumed that viewers were forced to stay with one of the networks, so why not go after the most desirable audience? To Klein, that meant urban women 18 to 34 years of age. He believed they were the most susceptible to advertising and controlled the economy. They were also, it was claimed, the largest segment among the many demographic divisions.

When faced with critics who pointed out that the over-50 crowd had more money and that the potential television audience consisted of as many men as women, Klein simply dismissed the older audience as too set in its ways (to respond to advertising) and dismissed men as non-shoppers. Almost at once, there were signs he might be wrong. The year CBS and NBC introduced ideal demographics to the schedule, their ratings plunged, and ABC found itself in the unaccustomed position of being Number One. Klein thought that just proved his point. The audience hadn't left; they had just changed channels.[10]

By the mid-1970s there were clear signs of audience erosion. The networks denied it, claiming methodology errors in the ratings. By the mid-1980s there were no more denials. What had been a trickle was now a flood. Broadcasting was hemorrhaging viewers, largely to cable. As the audience got smaller, the ideal changed slightly and shifted to consist of urban women 25 to 49 years (all races). By 2004 "women" had been dropped from official statements, but many argued that it was still understood. When network ratings showed a massive loss of male viewers during the 2003–04 season (a combined broadcast network loss of almost two million men a night), advertisers weren't surprised. To paraphrase what they told the reporter, "What are the networks offering that men would want to watch?"[11] Indeed, targeting Klein's ideal audience had produced a programming "gender gap" between male and female viewers.

More recently the press has complained about a liberal versus conservative political gap in network programming.[12] Moreover, the assumption that younger women control shopping could now be challenged by a trip to any supermarket.

An obsession with 18- to 49-year-olds, called "the most desirable audience" or "the audience most demanded by advertisers," applies to cable and syndication as well as to broadcasting. A programmer for E!, for example, when commenting on its generally low numbers said, "I could create a stunt pretty easily that would pop a household rating, but I would bring in people my parents' age."[13]

Many syndicators seek the younger 18 to 34 audience, particularly for their daytime programming, even though this demographic group is practically nonexistent during daytime hours and not what many sponsors want. When ABC announced the cancellation of their soap operas in 2011 and replaced them with talk programs, sponsors pulled out en masse, pointing out if they wanted talk audiences, they'd have bought talk shows in the first place.

When asked about the popularity of reality shows, Betsy Frank, executive vice president of research and planning for MTV and one of the most quoted professionals in the business, pointed to the appeal to young audiences. She went on to argue that the ideal MTV viewer should be under 25. She pointed out that this group represents 70 million people, only 7 million fewer than the baby boomers.[14] It is ironic to note that MTV itself pulls ratings of only about 1 in this group, implying that only about 1 million of those 70 million potential viewers actually watch MTV.

At the broadcast network level, the programmers argue they know that targeting the ideal demographic group creates problems, but they have little choice because most advertisers demand this audience. ABC and NBC claim that two-thirds of all prime-time advertising money is spent on this group. Of course, this argument is a little like ESPN looking at its advertising and claiming advertisers only want sports. Realistically, what else could they buy on prime-time broadcast networks?

To be fair, CBS argues the ideal should be higher, 25 to 54 years to be exact (which happens to be closer to their audience demos), and FOX argues that 18 to 34 year old urban men should be included (a group they just happen to appeal to), but advertisers argue that the question itself is wrong. It may be that any demographic approach is outdated because so many companies now use *psychographics*, or lifestyle data, to target ads—not just age, sex and ethnicity.

Aside from a program's demographics, the networks look for *audience flow* from program to program. Each network hopes to capture and hold the largest possible adult audience, especially from 8 P.M. until 11 P.M. or midnight, with a recent emphasis on late-night offerings (a time period which draws a much larger percentage of young people). Network strategies are usually directed at achieving *flow-through* from program to program within prime time—that is, encouraging the audience to continue to watch from show to show, although this tendency grows weaker as the number of program options increase and as the hour gets later. *Networks continue to try to produce flow by careful scheduling, such as placing programs with similar story lines one right after another, although remote controls, digital guides, too many options and DVRs make flow-through difficult to achieve.* Nonetheless, virtually all traditional scheduling strategies have been designed to maintain this flow.

Classic Scheduling Strategies

Programmers believe that surrounding a newcomer with strong existing shows ensures the best possible opportunity for the newcomer to rate as high as the established hits. Several strategies have long been used to achieve protection for new and underperforming series. About a dozen strategies now dominate prime-time scheduling: anchoring, leading-in, hammocking, blocking, doubling, linchpinning, bridging, counterprogramming, blunting, stunting, supersizing, seamlessness, rotating and sampling.

Several of these protect new programs, others build flow or challenge competitors. While many years of practice have shown the usefulness of these strategies, they are becoming much less practical as they depend on a reservoir of strong, established series, and broadcasting now has very few of these available.

1. **Anchoring Strategy.** All schedulers use the strategy of beginning an evening with an especially strong program, the anchor show. Also known as the *lead-off*, this first prime-time show sets the tone for the network's entire evening. It is believed that this maneuver can win or lose a whole night and thus affect the ratings performance of a full week. *Programmers have traditionally believed that the network winning the ratings for the first hour of prime time also usually wins the entire night.*

A strong lead-off used to be considered so important that the major networks routinely moved a popular established series into the 8P.M. (EST) position on every weeknight, even if it meant raiding, and thus weakening, strong nights to get proven shows for lead-offs. A classic example occurred in 2003 when the WB moved *Smallville* to the first spot on Wednesday and on Sunday to shore up those nights, while FOX in 2010 put *Glee* as the lead-off to Tuesday, moved *House* back to the lead-off position on Monday and used *American Idol* as the lead-off on several days of the week.

As ratings continued to slide, fewer successes remain to move around, making this strategy fade in importance on most networks, even though their programmers continued to express faith in it. By 2007, NBC was scheduling cheaper scripted or reality shows to lead-off prime time; inherently, such shows are low-rated, at least to start, and thus would provide no lead-off power. At the same time, however, FOX led off Mondays with its hit *Prison Break,* and CW led off Thursdays with the strong *Smallville,* using these as evening anchors. CBS uses its many versions of the *CSI* franchise in a similar way.

2. **Lead-in Strategy.** Closely related to the lead-off or anchor show, the *lead-in* strategy places a strong series before a weaker (or any new) series to give it a jump start. Theoretically, the strong lead-in carries part of its audience over to the next program. A new series following a strong lead-in has a modestly better chance of survival as compared with a new series with no lead-in or a weak lead-in. To get a strong lead-in, the networks often shift strong series to new nights or times. No show

is safe in any schedule position, as *King of Queens* and *Becker* found out when they were moved from their strong Monday slot to act as lead-ins for the short-lived *The Brotherhood of Poland, N.H.,* and subsequently sagged in their ratings.

3. **Hammock Strategy.** Although scheduling strategies can help bolster weak programs, it is obviously easier to build a strong schedule from a strong foundation than from a weak one. Moving one of a pair of established series to the next later half hour and inserting a promising new program in the middle time slot can take advantage of audience flow from the lead-in program to the rescheduled familiar program, automatically providing viewers for the intervening series. This strategy is known as *hammocking* the new series—in other words, a possible audience sag in the middle will be offset by the solid support fore and aft (also called a *sandwich,* with the new show as the filling).

The 2003–04 season provided a classic hammock example with *The Apprentice* shoved between *Friends* and *ER.* Hammocking is one strategy that continues to be effective, but it can provide misleading information on the strength of the center show. For example, much was made at the time of the relatively high ratings for *The Apprentice,* but in truth, even in its protected spot, it lost almost 4 points compared with the *Friends* lead-in and 2 points compared with *ER.* Moreover, when moved to the unprotected Wednesday night slot, it dropped into the bottom third of the ratings. Hammocking guarantees a new series will get sampled, however, which automatically gives the new show a better chance. *The Apprentice,* slightly revised into *The Celebrity Apprentice,* and protected initially in a hammock, became one of NBC's few successful shows. This strategy, however, presumes a network has enough strong shows to create hammocks, an assumption that is increasingly rare.

4. **Blocking Strategy.** By 2011, this was the most used, albeit least effective, of all programming strategies. *Block programming* or placing a new

program within a set of similar dramas or sitcoms filling an entire evening (or at least 2 hours of one type) is a venerable and respected practice.

The *theory of blocking* is that an audience tuning in for one situation comedy will stay for a second, a third and a fourth—if the sitcoms are of the same general type. The first show in a group usually aims at young viewers or the general family audience. Each ensuing series then targets a slightly older audience, thus taking advantage of the fact that as children go to bed and teenagers go out or do homework, the average age of the audience goes up. Blocking works best during the first two hours of prime time but typically loses effectiveness later in the evening.

Traditionally, the only risk was believed to be that a new comedy might lack the staying power of its "protectors" and damage the program that follows. Today we know there are other risks such as *burn out*: So many programs of the same type that people get sick of the whole genre. We also now know that when broadcasters place too much reliance on just a few types of programs, the cost of those shows goes up dramatically. When Paul Klein declared no real need for variety back in the '70s, and that the networks could just concentrate on sitcoms and crime dramas, then the cheapest programs to produce that could still pull large audiences, he believed that the cost of production would go down. But costs went up. By the 1980s, half-hour sitcoms cost more than either westerns or science fiction hours. We now know that any time the networks rely heavily on any one genre, its cost skyrockets, making this a dangerous strategy in more ways than one.

Examples of blocking (also called *stacking*) are easy to find in prime-time schedules every year on all the networks. During the 2006–07 season, FOX formed a successful animated/family sitcom block on Sundays of *The Simpsons, American Dad, Family Guy* and *War at Home,* which is still mostly in place five years later. Recently, the networks have blocked hour-long dramas, games and reality for whole evenings—for example, CBS's *NCIS* to

NCIS: Los Angeles to *unforgettable* on Tuesdays or FOX's *Prison Break* to *House,* two cult hits one after another for a time.

5. **Doubling Strategy.** One hot trend, now that networks have fewer hit shows to work with, is creating blocks using the same show, running episodes of the same sitcom one right after the other. Called *doubling,* it started with FOX, which ran *Cops,* followed by *Cops*—and then finished the block with *America's Most Wanted.* In 2005–06, ABC doubled *Lost* on Wednesdays, while FOX doubled *That 70's Show* and NBC doubled *Scrubs.* By the next season, the CW was doubling *Reba* all across the schedule.

Since networks don't increase the number of episodes produced, the negative byproduct is that a much-doubled show must go into reruns even sooner—which can easily trigger burn out. ABC found this out when it overused *Who Wants To Be A Millionaire,* and it was also the case with *Deal Or No Deal, Are You Smarter Than A Fifth Grader* and the *Law and Order* franchise. Even at this writing, the powerhouse *CSI* variations are dropping in the ratings for the entire franchise.

One variation is to run an old episode followed by a new episode. By mid-decade, hit comedies, reality series and even a few hour-long dramas were being doubled and even tripled as with *Terra Nova.* Another variation involves stripping episodes on different nights like a miniseries. This has become a common practice with short-run series like *American Idol, Dancing With The Stars, Survivor* and *The Bachelor.* Shows such as *According to Jim, Extreme Makeover, Deal or No Deal* and *Arrested Development* have appeared night after night, but usually for just a few weeks at a time. Copying cable networks like USA, TNT and A&E, the broadcast networks occasionally turned an entire evening over to one show, as ABC did sporadically with *Desperate Housewives* and CBS did with the original *CSI.*

6. **Linchpin Strategy.** Most scheduling strategies rely on having enough strong programs around which to build a schedule for new series. However, with fewer and fewer real hits, the networks have had to find ways to use the few strong shows still left to them. This is one of those ways. Also known as *tentpoling,* the network focuses on a central, strong show on weak evenings, the *linchpin,* hoping to use that show to hold or brace the ones before and after it. This strategy was the basis for NBC's move of *Law & Order: SVU* to Saturday nights and CBS's move of *Cold Case Files* to 9:00 on Sundays. These moves also formed blocks, an added bonus, and demonstrate that scheduling strategies are often combined. NBC's shift of focus to its 9:00 shows—away from 8:00 anchors—exemplifies the use of linchpins.

7. **Bridging Strategy.** The bridging strategy is not as common in commercial broadcasting as the other strategies, but it has been useful to public broadcasting and such cable networks as TBS and HBO. *Bridging* has three variations. The best-known one is the regular use of long-form programs (one-and-a-half hours or more) that start during the access hour and continue into prime time, thus running past the broadcast networks' lead-offs and negating their strategies (for viewers who might have changed channels). HBO, for example, often schedules a hit movie starting at 7 or even 7:30 P.M. (EST) to bridge the start of network prime time.

The second variation of bridging involves starting and ending programs at odd times, thus causing them to run past the starting and stopping points for shows on other networks. This creates a bridge over the competing programs, which keeps viewers from switching to other channels because they have missed the beginnings of the other shows. For example, TBS regularly starts its programs at 5 minutes after the hour. As a result, TBS viewers are forced either to watch the next TBS show or tune into another program already in progress.

CBS has used the bridging strategy successfully in its Sunday night lineup. The network regularly runs Sunday football games (or other sports) beyond the hour point, thus throwing the rest of the night off by about 10 minutes. This means that the audience that watches *60 Minutes* is stuck with CBS for the night. NBC and FOX have copied this practice with their Sunday afternoon sports broadcasts. The alternatives for viewers are to leave a show before it is over or to tune in to the competition late.

A third variation on this strategy involves scheduling half-hour shows against hour-long shows on the competing networks. FOX, by placing a strong show like *King of the Hill* first, forced the audience to watch the weaker *Oliver Beene* or tune into the middle of hour-long programs on the other networks. The risk is that viewers may go to cable or turn to the DVR. Modern viewing habits, split screens and digital guides have further weakened this strategy as many people now watch more than one show at a time, just switching back and forth when something exciting seems to be happening.

8. **Countering Strategy.** The networks also schedule programs to pull viewers away from their competitors by offering something of completely different appeal than the other shows, a strategy called *counterprogramming.* For many years, for example, ABC successfully countered the strong, women-oriented series offered by CBS and NBC on Monday nights with *Monday Night Football*—until 2006 when the games went to ESPN. To counter *Desperate Housewives* and *Cold Case Files,* NBC introduced *Sunday Night Football.* ABC clearly counterprogrammed CBS's *Survivor* with *Ugly Betty.*

Traditionally, counterprogramming challenged the ideal demographics approach because it relied on finding a large, ignored group of viewers and scheduling a program for them. In the late-2000s, the CW was countering the older networks by programming for teenage women, while FOX programmed for young urban men. Univision counterprograms the English-language networks by stripping three shows, *Heridas de Amor, La Fea Mas Bella* and *Mundo de Fieras,* across the week from 7 to 10, Monday through Friday, then varying its 10 P.M. and weekend shows. Of course, the

mere fact they broadcast in Spanish is a counter to other broadcasters, and puts them in an entirely separate competition group in some markets, although Univision's own data shows many of its shows are watched by sizable non-Spanish-speaking audiences.

9. **Blunting Strategy.** Networks that choose to match the competition by scheduling a show with *identical* appeal are *blunting* the competition. For example, in the 2006–07 season, CBS and NBC ran *CSI: New York* and *Medium* against each other on Wednesdays, and ABC and NBC ran *Grey's Anatomy* and *ER* against each other on Thursdays, in each case effectively splitting the legal-show fans and medical-show fans. Such blunting attempts often don't last long as one show usually proves more popular than the other.

If two networks are already blunting each other, a third network that counterprograms often gets higher ratings than either of the other two networks. In other words, the two networks running similar programs split part of the audience, while the counterprogrammer, in theory, gets everyone who likes its program plus all those who dislike the genre being blunted on the other two channels. One recent example occurred when ABC ran the magazine show *Primetime* against *CSI* and *Medium;* another occurred when CBS ran *Shark* against *Grey's Anatomy* and *ER.*

10. **Stunting Strategy.** The art of scheduling also includes maneuvers called stunting, a term taken from the defensive plays used in professional football. *Stunting* includes scheduling specials, adding guest stars, having unusual series promotion and otherwise altering the regular program schedule at the last minute. Beginning in the late 1970s, the networks adopted the practice of deliberately making last-minute changes in their schedules to catch rival networks off guard. These moves—calculated and planned well ahead of time but kept secret until the last possible moment—were intended to blunt the effects of competitors' programs. Generally such maneuvers are one-time-only because their high cost cannot be sustained over a long period.

Scheduling hit films, using big-name stars for their publicity value, and altering a series' format for a single evening are common attention-getting stunts. *Glee* has provided a number of classic examples: Top musical personalities "drop in" on rehearsals. Such stunts have high promotional value and can attract much larger-than-usual audiences if well promoted. Of course, the following week, the schedule goes back to normal, so these efforts get people to sample shows but rarely create long-term improvements in series ratings.

CBS used another form of stunting when it paid more than $4 billion for rights to sporting events (including Major League Baseball) during the 1990s. This proved to be a financial disaster. Although the network expected to lose money most years, it hoped that the rewards from promoting CBS shows during the World Series and championship games would be worth the cost. Those hopes proved fruitless, and CBS lost tens of millions of dollars with no ratings improvements to show for it.

Investing in popular but unprofitable specials to promote other shows on a network remains a popular form of stunting, however. The Olympics are a perfect example. NBC acknowledged that the money paid for the 2004, 2008 and 2012 Summer Games would be more than it could get back, but it planned to use the games to promote and then lead directly into the new fall season, thus justifying the cost. It liked this arrangement so much it paid $4.38 billion for the next four Olympics (2014 to 2020).

Strangely enough, ABC, which first discovered the real value of sports, has pulled out of most megasports bidding, arguing that the big sporting events have become too expensive to be worth their price tags (although co-owned ESPN put in a losing bid on the 2014–2020 rights). ABC may well have been right because so far NBC's plans don't seem to be working when viewed from outside the network. On the other hand, perhaps NBC's image and ratings would be worse without the Olympics rights!

11. Supersizing Strategy. In recent years, the networks have developed a form of stunting used mainly for the sweeps months. This method, called *supersizing*, allows them to pull questionable series off the air without having to find another show to fill their time slots. To fill the time, the network adds length to their biggest hits and advertises them as *specials*. Supersizing is now common for hit sitcoms and reality series, although rare so far for hour-long dramas. Doubling can be considered a similar strategy with the same goal. Networks often schedule the supersized climax of their reality shows to coincide with sweeps weeks.

12. Seamless Strategy. In the 1990s the networks turned to still another strategy intended to accelerate the flow between programs. First NBC, followed by the other networks, eliminated the breaks between key programs (*Seinfeld* to *Frasier*, for example). Viewers normally make most use of their remote controls in the two minutes or so that has traditionally occurred between programs, thus running the end of one program right up against the start of the next avoids the opportunity for remote use. This is called a *seamless transition*, and its goal is to keep viewers watching whatever network they began with.

In another twist, ABC (soon copied by the other networks) instructed producers to cut out all long title and credit sequences and to begin every program with an up-tempo, attention-getting sequence. Titles then appear later in a program, some times as much as 10 minutes into the program after viewers have, presumably, been hooked. At the ends of programs, all networks have experimented with split screens and squeezed credits. Originally, some program action (or "bloopers") filled part of the screen to hold viewers' attention right into the next program (or very close to it). However, this space now usually contains ads or promos for the upcoming series. Another variation on this strategy involves running a "next" icon or a promotional crawl for the upcoming series over the last segment of the preceding show. Many viewers find this incredibly annoying, and the networks (and advertisers) know it, as witnessed by the fact that they never do it during the ads. But promotional crawls on programs have the added advantage of making home recordings off-the-air less desirable, and thus, the networks believe, a spur to DVD sales.

13. **Rotating Strategy.** This is a very old strategy being reintroduced because of a shortage of original episodes and the need to have original programming during sweeps periods. In the early days of network television, the very popular *Jack Benny Show* ran every other week, regularly alternating with another program. By 1960, this practice had disappeared, but then some cable networks reintroduced it in a slightly different variation. As they moved toward more original production, but usually ordered merely 10 to 13 episodes, cable programmers were faced with *the problem of what to do when original episodes ran out.*

They solved the problem by scheduling more than a single series for the same time slot. For example, Syfy Channel runs 10 to 13 weeks of *Warehouse 13*, followed by 6 to 8 episodes of *Eureka* followed by 7 episodes of *Merlin*. This allows Syfy's programmers to maximize the value of the original episodes while spreading out production costs, having a total of 26 episodes, which with reruns, fills a whole season. By 2011, the networks were beginning to do the same thing with reality series. For example, FOX and CBS each scheduled a hit, *American Idol* and *Survivor,* to run during sweeps and then filled the time between sweeps with other, far less popular programs. Until now, scheduling multiple series for a single time slot has been largely limited to reality shows on the broadcast networks, but the practice (and the need) is spreading.

14. **Strip Sampling Strategy.** In the last five years, a technique to get new programs sampled appeared: new series aired on several different nights across their premier weeks—*horizontal stripping.* The theory is that wide exposure will allow as many people as possible to see the show and thus will

follow it to its normal night. In a variation in 2010, *Cape* aired its premier episode on both network and cable channels during the first week—*cross-media scheduling.* To be effective, like many other strategies, such practices have to be combined with heavy promotion campaigns during the initial showing advertising the show's normal day and time.

Although these scheduling practices can readily be identified in prime-time network lineups, there is little reason to believe any has an overwhelming impact on viewing. Most were developed at a time when few people had remote controls or DVRs, and digital cable's wealth of channels and the internet didn't exist. On-demand options and recording via DVRs also encourage viewers to do their own scheduling. Today, the audience has little reluctance to change channels, and there is no shortage of places to go

The web carries rebroadcasts of highly rated or much-talked-about shows, further undermining network efforts to manipulate audience flow on television during prime time. Nonetheless, *most experts believe that well-defined and executed application of these programming strategies helps a broadcast network hold onto significant portions of the viewership.* They continue to believe this even in spite of falling numbers for network programs. On the other hand, the ratings might be worse ... or so networks like to think.

Appointment Viewing

For decades, scholars have argued about how people watch television. For most of the last 50 years, practitioners assumed people passively watched the set— not programs (the *least objectionable program theory*). In short, when they had time (availability), viewers tuned in and then looked for something to watch.

About a decade ago, some researchers began contending that people actively planned their viewing around specific programs that would continue their current mood or change a bad mood. This view proved to be a hard sell in an industry that had long dismissed the idea of program loyalty in all but a few cases. For example, everyone recognizes that many soap opera viewers plan their activities so they can watch their favorite afternoon programs—that is, *appointment viewing*. But, experts argued, this happened rarely in prime time, perhaps only with such megahits as *American Idol*, live sporting events, or occasionally with highly-touted miniseries (mostly the domain of public broadcasting and cable these days).

Some shows, like *Glee* and *NCIS*, generate loyalty and exhibit appointment viewing; their fans are willing to pay extra fees for on-demand viewing and DVD sets. When researchers looked closely at program preference, they found that viewers develop strong mental images about *when* their favorite programs are on and tune in with those programs in mind. This presented a very different view of habitual viewing, which had always been assumed to be a factor in channel or network loyalty. *This understanding of the power of viewers' mental images of network schedules led to intensification of the amount and type of on-air, print and online promotion in order to create and manipulate such mental images.* Simultaneously it led to renewed interest in creating programs that spur viewing by appointment—that is, shows that are so special or events so unique that viewers plan their time around them. On the other hand, the continual shuffling of the schedule is a practice that breaks down habitual viewing and thus increases viewer frustration.

It must be understood that despite program loyalty and appointment viewing, people do not tune in every week. Most viewers do not change other plans to watch even their favorite television programs. They find comfort in knowing the series will still be there next week and that they can watch missed episodes in rerun or on DVR.

DVRs have also profoundly changed people's views of when they have to watch. The *time-shifting* of favorite programs is now a common practice because DVRs make it easy; this has become so important that several days after a program first airs are now included in the ratings. Many programmers

were surprised to find that people were willing to buy DVD sets of complete seasons of their favorite television series. While ABC, CBS and NBC long resisted offering their shows in DVD sets, FOX and the CW made a sizable portion of their profits from these sets and even program for them.

Changing concepts of ordinary viewing behaviors makes the successful selection and scheduling of mass-audience programs increasingly difficult for programmers. The truth is, *as far as the major networks are concerned, programming is bait. It is a lure to get viewers to watch commercials and a commodity that can be resold to stations, mainly their own O&Os, as syndicated bait to get viewers for their ads.* The discovery that series could be resold as DVD packages forced programmers to begin to consider the actual value of the program itself (see 2.7). For programmers, however, appointment

---

2.7 **The Value Question**

To further complicate matters, the industry can't figure out which shows have resale value. FOX, for example, planned *The Simple Life*, its "Paris Hilton meets *Green Acres*" reality series, for fast DVD release. The network applauded as the series' ratings climbed, got the DVD set to the stores only one week after the series finished its run on the air, and then watched as sales went nowhere.

Meanwhile, *Firefly*, which FOX had dumped without even using all of the ordered episodes, went straight to the top of the DVD sales lists and stayed there. It was subsequently rushed into production again as a theatrical movie. At the same time, the success of *Family Guy* on DVD, another of FOX's cancelled series, was so great FOX un-cancelled it. Its performance on the network, however, was and still is only mediocre (ratings of about 2), revealing that loyalty and a willingness to buy a series on DVD are not necessarily related to broadcast audience size. The CW has known this for years as DVD sales make up a huge part of the profits for two of its series, *Smallville* and *Supernatural*.

viewing may not only refer to the planning of activities to allow the viewing of a series; it may also be a measure of how much a viewer enjoys a particular series and how much money and time he or she is willing to invest in it.

Prime-Time Ratings

Regardless of whether an advertiser wants sheer tonnage or a specific audience segment, currently, commercial spot costs depend mainly on the *absolute ratings plus 3 days* (= total estimated audience) of the programs in which the commercials occur. Nielsen is developing ratings for commercials from its minute-by-minute people-meter data, but those are not yet in common usage. A television advertiser, in contrast to an advertiser on a formatted radio station, must pay for all viewers, whether or not they fall within the desired target audience. *Estimated program ratings are the major determinant of the cost of a commercial spot.*

Ratings, however, lack precision. As pointed out in Chapter 5, network ratings *estimate* the viewing of 116 million television households using data collected from 12,000 cooperating families, and it is very unlikely that these estimates are exactly right. In fact, statisticians sometimes claim that no substantial difference exists between the 10th-rated and 50th-rated shows in prime time; the differences in their ratings could result from nothing more than inevitable sampling errors.

Because advertisers (and ad agencies) have agreed to base the price of a commercial spot on the absolute number, however, they ignore this inability to measure small differences. A top program such as *The Office* that has a rating of about 4 and an advertising price of $450,000 per 30-second spot will generate millions of dollars more in revenue than a program such as *Cougar Town* with a rating of about 3 and a spot price of $200,000, even though the difference in ratings between the two is statistically meaningless at the levels normally set by statisticians. The treatment of ratings as absolute numbers by both advertisers and networks has led to fights over unmeasurable fractions of a rating point and demands for more measurements,

produced more often. These demands have led to ratings being reported continuously and in a number of different ways, many of which are outlined in Chapters 5 and 6. As a quick heads up, for prime-time network programming, the most common of these are the sweeps, overnights, pocketpieces and multinetwork reports.

Sweeps and Overnights

Four times each year a highly controversial rating event occurs—the **sweeps**. In November, February, May and July, Nielsen Media Research uses people meters in the larger markets and diaries in the smaller markets to gather audience viewing behavior that is converted into ratings, shares and demographic information for local television stations and a growing number of cable networks. The sweep results, particularly the November and February periods when audience viewing levels are at their highest, directly affect the rates these cable networks and local stations (including network-affiliates and O&Os) charge for advertising time.

Traditionally, the summer sweeps were of less importance. One summer the ratings dropped so badly that affiliates began to balk at clearing network summer shows, but in recent years some of the biggest hits have actually started during the summer. This has led the networks to claim they have moved to a full 52-week season.

The stations demand that the networks display their highest-quality merchandise during the sweeps periods to attract the largest possible audiences and maximize ad revenues. This practice makes the four sweeps periods, especially November and February, highly competitive and, at the same time, not always the most valid indicators of a network's or station's real strength.

National ratings take several different forms. Aside from the sweeps, the *overnights* are the most avidly monitored ratings data. They are gathered through people meters which sample 25,000 people (5,000 for national ratings and 20,000 for local ratings) in 56 major markets. *The overnight ratings are used to monitor overall urban audience reaction to such "program doctoring" as changes in casts, character emphases and plot lines, and to compare the viewing of major sporting events on broadcast and big cable networks.* The overnights also indicate immediately whether a new program has "taken off" and captured a sizable audience in the urban markets. Advertising agencies also use the overnight numbers to make predictions about specific shows that then become the basis of ratings expectations (and sales rates).

For example, when *Smallville* first started, it was predicted to get a share of 3 but actually got a 7, thus making it a hit, even though its subsequent ratings were at the bottom for all series. Since that time, its DVD sales have made its rating almost irrelevant, as it has run for 10 years, never getting more than a 4. Indeed, CW was almost in a panic as it finally announced the series would end in 2011. Missing the predicted number (getting one much lower than expected) in the overnights during the first few weeks of a newly introduced program's run spells cancellation unless the ratings show a hint of growth—or unless the program is expected to have stronger appeal to a specific audience. *JAG* was canceled by NBC but picked up and run successfully by CBS, which argued that it had a strong rural and male appeal not represented in the city-based overnight ratings. CBS was subsequently proven right. Recently, when *Friday Night Lights* was dropped by broadcasting, it was picked up by cable and run successfully.

Sometimes international appeal is a factor in letting a show build an audience. For example, *Prison Break* was only a moderate rating success for FOX, but it showed strong international potential and offered a racially diversified cast during a year with little other racial diversity in prime time. Thus, *Prison Break* was renewed while higher-rated series were canceled. In 2010, *Hawaii 5-0* found itself in much the same situation. It was not high in the ratings, but its international syndication potential seems to be very high so it was proclaimed a hit.

Still other shows that are cheap to produce but have no aftermarket potential may be held because the shows' concepts are so valuable. For example, *Big Brother* has always had ratings of about 2 or 3 for CBS, hardly great numbers. But the show is

inexpensive to make, and the concept has been sold to producers in other countries, who use the same program idea and title but staff the house with people from their own countries. In Brazil, for instance, *Big Brother* is one of the highest-rated programs, and the contestants are considered major stars. While most game, reality and talent shows have no life after their first run, either as DVDs, off-network syndication or network reruns, the concept may have value and be syndicatable. Programs like *Who Wants to Be a Millionaire?*, *Deal Or No Deal*, *Dancing With The Stars*, *The Bachelor* or *Survivor* had no value to the international market as programs, but had great value as ideas. When syndicated, the other country actually produces it. While the money may not come directly to the network, it still comes to the parent company. Of course the money for traditional off-network syndication never came directly to the network either. And the process reverses: NBC bought the idea for *Voice* from non-U.S. sources. (Simply stealing the show, as Norman Lear did with *All In The Family*, is no longer an option.)

Other series, such as *The West Wing* and *Bones,* were only moderate rating performers but generated strong critical and special-interest appeal and thus remained on the schedule, giving them time to grow into true rating success stories, which led to big sales as DVD sets (and long runs on cable for *Bones*). Still other programs, such as *Heroes,* were designed to run on both a broadcast network and a cable network at the same time, requiring advertisers to predict combined ratings/shares. Some programs like *Monk* were not designed for running on both cable and broadcasting but have because parent companies try to double the value of an unexpected success.

Even though the ability to accurately predict the numbers, especially for new series, is very low, advertising agency predictions still have tremendous power. For example, during the 1999–00 season, advertisers predicted *Secret Agent Man* would get barely a 2 share. As a result, the series was canceled without airing even one episode. Who knows? Given a chance, the audience might have turned to it as they did to the summer surprise hits *Who Wants to Be a Millionaire?* and *Survivor* (the first one), both of which were predicted to generate ratings so low they didn't even get a regular season start. On the other hand, the same agency experts predicted that *Coupling* would be one of the highest-rated new series in 2003–04. It certainly did not live up to that prediction.

Pocketpieces and MNA Reports

The ratings report traditionally of greatest interest to the *creative* community, and the one most familiar to the public, is published every other week in a small booklet known as *The Nielsen Pocketpiece* (see 2.8).

It comes from the 12,000 national people-meter households selected to match census demographic guidelines for the entire country. Though this information is published only every other week, these data are available to Nielsen subscribers via computer the next day. A data bank provides, upon request, data not only for the nine major broadcast networks but also for selected cable networks.

As 2.8 shows, more than 11 million people watched CBS's *Cold Case* that Sunday from 8:15 to 9:15, and the program's average rating for the hour was 10.5 with a share of 15. At the same

---

2.8 Sample Pocketpiece Page

A-16 **NATIONAL *NielsenTV* AUDIENCE ESTIMATES** **EVE.SUN. OCT.17, 2004**

TIME	7:00	7:15	7:30	7:45	8:00	8:15	8:30	8:45	9:00	9:15	9:30	9:45	10:00	10:15	10:30	10:45	11:00	11:15
HUT	57.1	58.5	60.0	61.9	64.2	65.3	66.5	68.2	68.8	69.6	69.7	69.7	67.4	65.1	62.5	60.4	55.6	51.2

ABC TV

←AMER FUNN HOME VIDEOS→ ←EXTREME MAKEOVER:HM→ ED-8P ←DESPERATE HOUSEWIVES→ (9:00-10:01) ←BOSTON LEGAL→ (10:01-11:00)(PAE)

HHLD AUDIENCE% & (000)	4.6	5,020			8.8	9,670			13.1	14,340			7.3	8,010				
74% AVG. AUD. 1/2 HR %	7.5	4.0*		5.1*	12.6	7.9*		9.8*	17.3	12.4*		13.7*	10.2	7.5*		7.1*		
SHARE AUDIENCE %	8	7*		8*	13	12*		14*	19	18*		20*	12	11*		12*		
AVG. AUD. BY 1/4 HR %	3.7	4.4	4.8	5.4	7.3	8.4	9.1	10.5	12.1	12.7	13.5	14.0	8.0	7.1	7.1	7.1		

CBS TV

(1) ←60 MINUTES→ (7:23-8:23)(PAE) ←COLD CASE→ (8:23-9:23)(PAE) ←CBS SUNDAY MOVIE PERFECT STRANGERS→ (9:23-11:23)(PAE)

HHLD AUDIENCE% & (000)		11.1	12,120			10.5	11,460			5.3	5,840							
74% AVG. AUD. 1/2 HR %		18.8		10.6*		14.3		10.2*		10.7		5.3*		5.2*		5.0*		5.5*
SHARE AUDIENCE %		18		17*		15		15*		8		8*		8*		8*		10*
AVG. AUD. BY 1/4 HR %	14.8	9.7	10.5	10.8	12.5	10.3	10.1	10.4	10.9	6.6	5.6	5.1	5.2	5.2	5.0	5.0	5.6	5.4

NBC TV

←DATELINE SUN-7PM→ ←AMERICAN DREAMS→ ←LAW AND ORDER:CRIM INTENT→ ←CROSSING JORDAN→

HHLD AUDIENCE% & (000)	5.1	5,560			4.3	4,750			8.2	8,970			8.5	9,320				
74% AVG. AUD. 1/2 HR %	9.2	4.8*		5.4*	6.2	4.3*		4.3*	11.3	7.2*		9.1*	11.0	8.4*		8.6*		
SHARE AUDIENCE %	9	8*		9*	8	7*		6*	12	10*		13*	13	13*		14*		
AVG. AUD. BY 1/4 HR %	4.4	5.1	5.3	5.4	4.4	4.3	4.3	4.4	6.5	7.9	8.9	9.4	8.4	8.4	8.7	8.5		

FOX TV

(2) (3) FOX MLB ALCS GAME 4 NEW YORK YANKEES AT BOSTON (8:17-1:23)(PAE)

HHLD AUDIENCE% & (000)					9.5	10,440												
74% AVG. AUD. 1/2 HR %		7.4*			24.8		9.7*		9.2*		9.1*		10.8*		10.1*			9.1*
SHARE AUDIENCE %		13*			17		15*		14*		13*		16*		16*			16*
AVG. AUD. BY 1/4 HR %	6.9	7.8	9.2		8.5	9.6	9.8	9.4	9.0	8.9	9.4	11.4	10.2	10.5	9.6	9.5	8.8	

WB TV

←S HARVEY BIG TIME - WB→ ←CHARMED - WB→ ←JACK & BOBBY - WB→

HHLD AUDIENCE% & (000)	1.5	1,670			3.0	3,330			1.4	1,580								
74% AVG. AUD. 1/2 HR %	3.0	1.4*		1.7*	4.1	3.0*		3.1*	2.1	1.5*		1.4*						
SHARE AUDIENCE %	3	2*		3*	5	5*		5*	3	2*		2*						
AVG. AUD. BY 1/4 HR %	1.2	1.6	1.5	1.8	2.8	3.2	3.1	3.1	1.6	1.4	1.4	1.4						

PAX TV

←AMR MOST TAL KIDS-PAX→ ←DOC-SUN→ ←SUE THOMAS, F.B. EYE→ ←COLD TURKEY→ (PAE)

HHLD AUDIENCE% & (000)	0.5	560			1.0	1,050			0.9	1,010			0.3	350				
74% AVG. AUD. 1/2 HR %	1.0	0.4*		0.6*	1.3	0.9*		1.0*	1.3	0.9*		0.9*	0.6	0.4*		0.3*		
SHARE AUDIENCE %	1	*		1*	1	1*		1*	1	1*		1*	1	1*		1*		
AVG. AUD. BY 1/4 HR %	0.4	0.4	0.5	0.5	0.9	0.9	1.0	1.0	0.9	0.9	0.9	0.5	0.4	0.3	0.3	0.3		

U.S. TV Households: 109,600,000
(1) CBS NFL NATIONAL,VARIOUS TEAMS AND TIMES,CBS,(MULTI SEGMENT)(PAE)
(2) FOX MLB NLCS GAME 4,ST LOUIS AT HOUSTON,FOX,(S),(4:38-7:41)(PAE)
(3) FOX MLB ALCS GM4 PRE-SUS,NEW YORK YANKEES AT BOSTON,FOX,(7:47-8:17)(SUS)(PAE)

For explanation of symbols. See page B.

A-17   For SPANISH LANGUAGE TELEVISION audience estimates, see the Nielsen Hispanic Television Index (NHTI) TV Audience Report.

time, more than 10 million people watched FOX's Major League Baseball game, getting a rating of 9.5 and a share of 17 or so for that 8:15 to 9:15 P.M. hour of the game. ABC also did well with *Extreme Makeover: Households,* watched by nearly 9 million people; that show got a rating of 8.8 and a share of 13. NBC did less well in the competition, attracting just under 5 million people to *American Dreams* that week. The show got a rating of 4.3 and a share of 7. Just over 3 million people watched WB's *Charmed,* and it got a rating of 3.0 and a share of 5 (quite satisfactory for WB, now called the CW). The rating for the series *Doc* on PAX (now called ION) averaged about a 1.0, with about a 1 share.

At present, Nielsen is handling almost 1,300 computer requests for pocket-piece data monthly, suggesting that its people-meter data may eventually replace or diminish the importance of the over-nights. Unlike the urban nature of the overnights, the pocketpiece provides estimates for the entire nation, including ratings/shares and the all-important demographics for both prime time and daytime, plus general information such as average ratings by program type, number of sets in use by days and by dayparts, comparison of television usage between the current season and the one preceding, and other details.

Network programmers also find Nielsen's *Multi-Network Area Report* (MNA) very useful. The statistics in this report cover the 70 leading population centers in the country, represent about two-thirds of total television homes nationally, and break out the O&O markets. The networks use MNA reports to compare the performance of the major networks without the distortion caused by the one- and two-affiliate markets included in the national Nielsen reports (although few now exist). *MNA reports include the so-essential demographic breakouts and give the networks figures related to their owned stations without distortion from smaller markets where they have no ownership interests.*

As network ratings have fallen, the way the networks report them has also changed. Very few press releases or promotional materials actually refer to the ratings or shares anymore. Rather, they report the millions of people who viewed something (the rating times 2.6). They point to the percentage increase over last year, a show's first-place position in a time slot, the percentage of the ideal audience it captures, and so on—anything but the actual rating numbers, which are usually dismal. A decade ago programmers joked that the ratings books were designed to be complicated so that any programmer could find something that he or she was doing right. Now they keep the ratings a secret. Nielsen permits the ratings for only the top 25 programs to be reported in the press.

Prime-Time Scheduling Practices

The entire process of prime-time programming breaks down into three major phases: *deciding to keep or cancel already scheduled series, developing and choosing new programs* from the ideas proposed for the coming season, and *scheduling the entire group.* To understand program evaluation, selection and scheduling, the changing concept of a season needs to be spelled out.

Shifting Network Seasons

From the 1950s to the present, the main viewing year has periodically expanded or contracted until it settled on *40 weeks, usually running from late September to the end of May.* The remaining 12 weeks (*off-season*) occur in summer. Production cost increases combined with a high mortality rate decreased the size of episode orders for renewed series to 20 or 22 episodes by the 1990s, filling in the season with specials and reruns.

Nowadays, ABC, CBS and NBC tend to order just 6 to 10 episodes at a time, although occasional 22-episode guaranties are given to capture a high-profile producer or star. And network contracts now say "cancelable any time" (although Charlie Sheen sued claiming they had no right to cancel *Two and a Half Men,* or rather to cancel him, as CBS continued with the series). Even having 22 episodes fails to cover the May sweeps; but these sweeps are important to affiliated stations while being too expensive for the networks to fill with specials.

Because the network license fee gives the right to two showings of each episode for the one payment, and because the networks need to get their money's worth out of every episode, for the last decade reruns have begun early and often. They are usually scheduled at the end of the fall season in December (no ratings then) and between the February and May sweeps. Traditionally, weaker episodes used to be rerun in summers, but *the need to fill 40 weeks has resulted in reruns of nearly all episodes during the main viewing year*, with episodes of quickly canceled series, new pilots and original reality series saved for summers.

Specials, sports and limited-run tryouts fill the remaining weeks of the regular season. However, the definition of a "special" has become extremely loose. During a recent season, specials included rejected pilots, such fluff shows as ABC's *21 Hottest Stars Under 21*, and so-called news specials that were indistinguishable from the regular news magazines and reality shows.

It used to be that placing a program on *hiatus* (a rest or break) meant that it was awaiting cancellation. Over the decades, a few series came back from a hiatus with a new actor or plot line, and stayed on the schedule, but most just disappeared. Nowadays, if a series has 22 episodes to air, original episodes end before Christmas and then return in February or March to run without interruptions to the season finales in May sweeps.

Another option for filling gaps in the schedule is *stripping,* which refers to scheduling episodes of a program, usually a magazine series like *NBC Dateline,* on several different days across the week. This practice has not seemed to harm the numbers for news format shows, but it killed *Who Wants to Be a Millionaire?* as a network show. However, after a hiatus of a year *Millionaire* returned as a syndicated series, and later went back on ABC as a special. In more limited form, stripping has been employed with such situation comedies as *Till Death, Scrubs, Reba* and *That 70's Show,* and with such reality shows as *Next Top Model, Survivor* and *Nanny 911,* which often run two and sometimes three times a week. FOX dose this regularly with *American Idol* and *Dancing With The Stars.*

Limited Series

Starting back in the 1990s, the networks began interrupting the regular season with tryouts of new series in strong prime-time slots. March, April and the summer months became tryout months for *limited series* (generally four to six episodes). This off-and-on method of scheduling allows the networks to test a new program under the best possible conditions while preserving original episodes of the most popular series for the May sweeps.

Whether inserting a new series into the ongoing prime-time schedule is an effective strategy is debatable. *New shows usually get highly inflated ratings while in a popular show's time slot, but such ratings seldom hold up when new show moves into their much weaker permanent slots.* At the same time, constantly interrupting a popular show tends to cause its ratings to go down. Series tried out during the summer months suffer from the opposite effect. Because summer ratings are so low, even if a program significantly improves ratings for the slot, the absolute quantity of viewers seldom looks good, and the usual result is quick cancellation.

Many reality series, including *American Idol* and *Dancing with the Stars,* however, were planned as limited-run series scheduled during sweeps weeks. Having only a few episodes reduces production costs and allows the producers to stage much publicized tryouts around the country (that people pay to watch and participate in) between actual runs of the program. *Survivor* now follows the same year-round tryout scheme, but was originally a limited summer series.

In truth, *the majority of new series are aired first in limited-run experiments, not pilots.* The majority of new programs tried by ABC, CBS, NBC and FOX run for fewer than eight weeks. In contrast, UNI, TEL and the CW tend to leave new series on for a full season, but some programmers argue that this stems not from a different philosophy but from a lack of the money required to constantly develop replacements. (MNTV and TEF carry mostly rerun entertainment series.)

Programmers argue that limited-run series in all seasons are the wave of the future. They point to the success of such cable programs as *Monk* and *The Sopranos,* which ran 8 to 12 weeks, went off, and then came back later for another 8 to 12 weeks. This allowed cable programmers to stretch the run of the popular original series into the summer months, when they often wiped out the networks in the ratings.

However, as with most things concerning the networks, the situation is not quite that simple. In broadcasting, the combination game/reality formula used in *Celebrity Apprentice, Survivor, The Amazing Race* and *American Idol* forces programmers into a scattered scheduling approach. A new game has to start and run its course as one person is thrown off the show each week, and then end the game. It then takes several weeks to get the next episode of the game ready for broadcast. Something has to fill the weeks between the main reality series, so why not use another cheap reality game and then alternate them back and forth in the schedule? In cable, programmers used the broken-run strategy largely because they could not afford a full 22 episodes. They needed the money from the first run to produce the second run. This scattered approach to scheduling helped disguise the fact that there weren't very many original episodes being produced.

Network-planned limited runs of such high-cost series as *Lost* serve much the same purpose. Limiting the number of episodes produced each season keeps production costs down and produces revenue to support more production. Theoretically, this type of scheduling also builds anticipation in the audience, allowing a network to promote an upcoming series almost like a special event that hypes the ratings during sweeps weeks. ABC shocked many fans in 2007 by announcing *Lost's* end date of 2010, after a six-season run. The producers claimed that fans deserved the security of knowing that all the show's convoluted storylines would play out fully as intended.

Summer Schedules

In the late 1980s, the networks began using March and April, as well as summer, for testing new program ideas in short runs and airing rejected pilots that did not make the fall schedule. (Previously, these pilots would never have been seen by anyone outside the network programming department.) By the 1990s, not only were network ratings down but the costs for program development were so high that the networks could no longer absorb the expense of the development stages for new shows that never reached the air.

Summer became the arena for reruns of weak series episodes or episodes of quickly canceled series that were paid for but never used, and for episodes of never-scheduled shows or reruns of canceled series. *Running pilots as made-for-TV movies, summer specials, and short-run tests of series became three ways to recoup much of a network's investment.* By 2007, the networks had begun to repeat their top shows on Saturday nights, further exhausting their rerun potential for summers.

However, the practices of doubling, tripling and stripping episodes during the regular season, combined with airing many unscripted series, which cannot be successfully rerun, began leaving little that was fresh for the summer months. Indeed, the neglect of the summers by ABC, CBS and NBC made them a gold mine for the cable networks, which began killing the broadcast networks in the summer ratings. In addition, the affiliated stations worried about the extreme ratings drops during July sweeps.

FOX further complicated the picture when it discovered that summer was a good time to get people to sample series they did not normally watch. This network was able to build an audience for several of its regular series by continuing original episodes into summer, which were supported by active promotional campaigns. To take advantage of the potential for discovering its shows, FOX began heavily promoting its reruns as a "second chance to see what you have been missing." FOX's success was later copied by NBC in its "New to you" promotion that emphasized the fact that "if you haven't seen it, the program is new to you." By the early 2000s, this strategy was sufficiently successful to force the other networks to pay more attention to their summer schedules. Most networks now schedule at least one or two new series during the summer, although none seems intended to continue during the main season.

Even when a summer series generated a lot of talk or higher-than-expected ratings, as was the case with the short-run FOX series *Roar,* the show was dropped the minute September rolled around.

Until the breakthrough by extremely cheap unscripted (this doesn't mean no writers, it just means no union writers) series like *Survivor,* even when a summer series outperformed expectations, it was seldom picked up. Programmers generally wrote these offerings off before they ever went on the air. As a result, a show must break all records to get attention from programmers who have already moved on to next season's planning.

The original *Survivor* on CBS, which ran only during the summer of 2000, was such a surprise megahit. It spawned several **clones** (look-alike shows) for the subsequent season (*Temptation Island, The Mole* and *Big Brother*), and then *American Idol,* a summer copy of a British series, did the same thing for FOX. Suddenly summer was seen as the time to try reality series. *With the advent of original summer schedules and the promotion of reruns as original programming for people who normally watched the competition, the July ratings books took on more importance as a measure of network and pay-cable pull, as a limited vehicle for pre-fall testing, and incidentally, as a way to satisfy affiliates.*

Premieres

Traditionally, the networks premiered their new series during a much-publicized week in late September. However, in 2004, because of the late summer Olympics, the networks declared the end of fall premieres as such. The reality is that series have debuted in scattershot fashion for the last decade, usually throughout September and October (and occasionally as early as August or as late as November).

Theoretically, spreading out the premieres keeps new programs from getting lost in the rush, gives viewers maximum opportunity to sample each new network show, and accommodates interruptions caused by baseball playoffs, the World Series and other major events such as the Olympics. In fact, spreading out "premiere week" has diminished the excitement associated with a new season and

actually reduced the sampling of new shows. For example, viewers who find an appealing show at a certain hour in early September are unlikely to check out new shows when they debut some weeks later at the same hour. Viewers also won't stay around (or come back) when a new show they like vanishes for several weeks while the network stunts. *As a rule, fans of comedy will find another comedy at that hour and stick with it; fans of drama will become loyal to another drama.*

In addition, a large number of new network programs, particularly replacement shows, begin their runs in January or February, thus creating a **second season** on the networks. By late fall each year, the fate of most prime-time programs already on the air has become clear. Holiday specials usually preempt those destined for cancellation or restructuring, while more popular series go into reruns and special holiday episodes, which are often cut together pieces of earlier episodes with a loose plot—such as characters are trying to remember something—to tie them together.

By January or February the networks are ready to launch their second seasons—with almost the same amount of promotion and ballyhoo as are accorded the new season premieres in September or October. Nonetheless, they then promptly preempt the new schedule to promote and run special programming for the February sweeps, and then they introduce more new series in March. As a result, it is hard to argue that there are clear seasons any longer. Rather, network programming has become a round of constant changes. As a strategy, this is called the **continuous season** approach. Indeed, back in 2009, NBC said there were no more seasons, and the others have adopted the same practices. Schedule changes are occurring every week.

Program Renewal

Evaluation of on-air shows goes on all year. *The critical times for new programs starting are before the sweeps in November, February, May and July; those doing badly during sweeps are then quickly replaced before the next sweeps occur.* The final decision on whether to return an iffy program to the schedule the following fall is usually made between March and May because the networks showcase their fall lineups at their annual affiliates meetings during those months and up-front sales begin. Last-minute changes, however, occur right up to the opening guns in the fall.

Program Lifespan

The average *lifespan* of popular prime-time series has declined steadily over time. In the 1950s and 1960s, such shows as *The Ed Sullivan Show, Gunsmoke, What's My Line?* and *The Wonderful World of Disney* endured for more than 20 years. These records for longevity will probably never be matched again in prime time—with the exceptions of news magazines and cartoons like *The Simpsons*. By 1980, a program lifespan of 10 years was regarded as a phenomenon. By the 1990s, 5 years was an outstanding run for a successful series.

A decade later, because the networks became the producers, they gained a vested interest in the longevity of their programs. Series such as *Smallville, Supernatural, NCIS, 7th Heaven* and *Law and Order* are now moving back toward 10-year lifespans. The networks have become very reluctant to cancel anything that succeeds, even modestly, if they can make a profit from it.

Several factors accounted for this shortened lifespan:

1. Above all, the high cost of renewing writers, directors and actors after an initial contract expires

2. The increased sophistication or, some argue, the shortened attention span of the viewing audience

3. The constant media coverage of television shows and stars (as in *Entertainment Tonight, People* and *Us* magazines, the morning talk shows and so on), which wears out each series idea quickly

4. The practice of syndicating a series while it continues its network run, of releasing DVD sets, and of doubling and tripling (or other overusing while on the network), which leads to burnout

5. The scarcity of outstanding program forms and fresh, top-rated production and writing talent, as well as a network propensity for formulaic series, which leads to a great deal of copying and very low levels of originality

6. The loss of key actors because they become bored or move on to other projects

7. The move toward the cloning of prime-time hits, which results in a sameness that causes even the best ideas to wear out faster

The shortened lifespan of prime-time series reflects the complexity of program license contracts that generally ran for five to seven years. Each new episode of a program is assigned a *license fee*, whether the show is produced by the same company that owns the network intending to carry the program or another entity. The license fee size varies with cost factors such as costumes, special effects, sets, stunt work, the amount of location versus studio shooting, cast size, the producers' and stars' reputations, the program's track record, the demand for series in the same genre and so on. Traditionally, this cost represented about three-quarters of the actual cost of production and told the executive producers how much they were going to have to kick in to actually make the program.

When a series first makes it to the air, the network controls the contractual situation and usually requires several concessions from everyone involved. At this time, the producer commonly has to sign over such rights as creative control, spin-off rights, limitations on syndication and scheduling control. Everyone also agrees to a specific licensing fee for the run of the five-year contract, regardless of the program's success (after all, most shows fail). Typically, this licensing fee makes no concession for sharing the profits should the program become a hit. However, when the producer and the network now work for the same corporation, the leverage lies with the parent company (see 2.9).

Pivotal Numbers

Choosing which programs already on the air will continue and which will be pulled (renewals and

2.9   License Contracts

Traditionally, producers practice *deficit financing* (paying more to produce a series than the network pays in license fees) because the potential profit from off-network syndication can run into the hundreds of millions of dollars. If a show is a hit, the producers can make up any losses. Producers typically agree to licensing contracts lower than actual production costs in order to get their shows onto the networks so they have chances to be hits.

For those few shows that really succeeded, in the old days, at the end of the first contractual period (normally five years), the tables were turned: Now the producers and stars enjoyed the advantage because the series had a *track record*. In short, if the network wanted to keep making the series, concessions would have to be granted, usually in the form of much higher salaries or bigger shares in profits for the producers. *Friends* illustrated this dilemma when the stars each demanded $1 million an episode in 2003–04 even before any other salaries or production costs were figured.

Under such renewal conditions, a network could sometimes profit by dropping a popular show. But because finding hits has been so difficult, the networks generally decide it's better to give in rather than have another huge hole open up in their schedules. For example, NBC did bite the bullet with the moderate hit *ER*, paying $13 million per episode for one year just to keep this centerpiece for its Thursday night schedule.

The repeal of the financial interest rule, however, meant that the networks could (and do) now own the programs. Because the network is itself the producer, tables don't turn so completely (oh, actors can still get pushy, and the unions can cause trouble, as they did during the 2008 season), but all costs and profits belong to the same corporation, giving it enormous leverage over salaries and profit sharing. Although deficit financing is still practiced for tax purposes, it occurs between arms of the same company. One outcome of the new power relationship is that the networks seem to hold the few big hits longer even as cancellations for new series come quicker.

cancellations) is perhaps the easiest decision network programmers have. The decisions are based squarely on the network's *profit margin*—in essence, subtracting the cost per episode from advertising revenue. *Normally, revenue has been directly related to ratings.* Until the 1980s, a weeknight rating below 20 (or an audience share of less than 30) almost always resulted in a program's cancellation on any network. But because of steady network audience erosion, by the mid-2000s, the Big Four's numbers had plummeted to a *minimum weekday prime-time rating of 4 and a share of 9.*

If the profit margin is high enough, such as with CBS's series *Big Brother,* a show will be retained with even lower numbers. Thus, *profitability is the source of the power of reality programs.* A few, such as *American Idol,* have high ratings numbers, but most do far worse than hour-long dramas. But typically, unscripted shows are incredibly cheap to produce, making the profit margins enormous.

Entertainment series stalling in the bottom third of the Nielsens are usually canceled as soon as

possible, while programs in the top third are usually renewed. The most difficult decisions for network programmers involve programs in the middle third—*the borderline cases*—or programs that

1. are weakening but are nearing their fifth year.
2. are only just beginning to slide in the ratings.
3. are highly rated but draw the wrong demographics.
4. produce low ratings but draw a high percentage within a desirable demographic group.
5. have low ratings but high profit margins.
6. produce strong critical approval but marginal ratings.

Occasionally, the personal preferences of a top network executive, the reaction from critics, letter-writing campaigns or an advertiser's support may influence a decision, but the prevailing view is that *cancellations had far better come too soon and too often than too late.* Indeed, network programmers insist that advertisers and corporate headquarters will not tolerate a program that doesn't offer instant success.

Replacement series, however, rarely do significantly better than the original programs in the ratings (see 2.10), and they push development prices even higher. Therefore, large group owners occasionally pressure their networks to hold on to problematic shows. Group owners can affect cancellation decisions, as can direct participation from key sponsors, but this happens only rarely. For example, in 2003 Procter and Gamble pulled its advertisements (purchased during the up-front buying) from *Family Law,* saying the content was not what the company had been promised. As a result, CBS was forced to pull the offending episodes from the rerun schedule. In addition, the O&Os can affect a decision because they report to the same parent corporation. Such pressure can be positive (to hold) or negative (to kill).

More than the other networks, FOX and CW seem less traditional and readier to look for potential profits outside those generated by advertising. They are more likely to keep shows with strong off-network syndication or DVD sales potential, and seek shows with potential for non-direct sales from tours or music sales and on-demand or internet revenues.

Program Costs

In addition to ratings, profits left after subtracting licensing costs from advertising revenues influence program cancellations. Two prime-time programs of the same length, on the same network, with identical ratings will, ideally, produce identical amounts of revenue for that network. If, however, one of them has slightly higher per-episode licensing costs, say as little as $100,000 an episode, over the length of a season that difference would equal just over $2 million more in costs. It is clear that the program with the higher licensing cost will be canceled before the lower-cost series. In recent years, the networks have scheduled more program genres with low production costs—witness the proliferation of news magazines and reality shows in prime time.

Nonetheless, unexpected megahits like *Survivor* and *American Idol* have led programmers to promote

"the new reality revolution" because of the genre's low cost, in spite of disastrous rerun numbers and no syndication potential. Currently, a new reality show costs at least $1,500,000 per episode. Even such megahits as *Survivor* cost only about $3 million per episode, whereas the price tag for an episode of *Two and a Half Men* is close to $20 million. (Original cable series cost much less than the broadcast equivalent because they are done in non-union shops outside of California.)

Because the company controlling the network now usually owns the production, it has to cover all costs, so the fee itself is largely irrelevant except to the accountants at tax time. For accounting purposes, the license fee is still used to allocate the actual cost of production to various departments, and it tells the network how much it has to earn during first run and then during rerun to break even. How networks allocate these costs varies enormously and largely depends on what will generate the lowest tax bill at the end of the year. At present, one of the biggest cost factors is how a program is produced from a technical standpoint (see 2.11).

Because there are only a limited number of top producers and writers for any given genre, especially high demand for a particular type of show forces costs up. By 2012, the fee for a successful reality series had gone up almost 400 percent but was still far below the cost for any other type of programming (with the exception of news magazines like *20/20*).

A show's potential for profits in syndication also affects how high its license fee can go. Action hours have traditionally been expensive to produce but have been highly syndicatable in both the domestic and international markets. They are also highly desirable for the parent companies' own cable networks. However, following the takeover of most independent production houses, the number of original action series dried up. In 2004–05 there were only three action hours available in syndication, *Andromeda, Stargate SG1* and *Mutant X.* By 2007, no original action hours were on the market. In 2008, only one new series, *Legend of the Seeker,* was offered. It was produced in New Zealand, but distributed through Disney (ABC). For the broadcast

2.10 Time Slot Ratings

The history of ratings for the time slot a program fills may be the strongest measure of how that program will perform. After all, a "history" takes into account such factors as the competition, the leads in and out on all channels, the network's myths and policies, and the public's viewing habits and expectations. The reality is that more than 80 percent of the series scheduled in new time slots (new or moved shows) do not alter either the ratings or the ranking for their slots significantly. This means that a series placed in a top-rated time slot probably will be a top-rated series, and conversely, a series placed in a weak position will be weak.

The majority of the remaining shows get lower ratings than their time slot averaged in the previous season. This means that when a series does change the historical pattern, the change is usually for the worse. Chances are less than 5 percent that a program will significantly improve the ratings for the time slot even at the generally accepted 68 percent level (one standard deviation rather than the two normally used in research).

Low-rated shows are subject to a widely accepted condition called *double jeopardy*. According to this idea, low-rated shows have both low exposure and little chance of getting more exposure. This is because popular programs are chosen by more people, and those viewers are more committed to the shows. Thus, unpopular programs suffer from increasingly fewer and less-committed viewers.

Obviously the best scheduling ploy would be to place every series in an already strong position, an impossibility in programming. The slots open to programmers are usually ones where previous programs failed. In the last 20 or so years, more than half of all new shows have been scheduled in prime-time slots that already ranked in the bottom third of the ratings, and most were also in slots ranked third compared to the competition. Clearly, *the strength of a time slot should be considered when the decision is made to hold or cancel a series*.

This, however, has not usually been the case at the networks: *In practice, a program's rank and absolute rating overrule expectations for a time slot*. As a result, a series with a 9 rating would usually be held, while a series with a 4 would be cancelled, even if that 9 represented a loss of several points (by comparison with the lead-in program or the previous program in that slot) and the 4 represented a gain. Because there is only a small chance that a series will significantly improve the ratings for a time slot, considering ranking an absolute rating appears to be self-defeating in the long run.

Because the majority of available slots are going to be weak in any case, wisdom suggests holding onto series that improve the numbers and slowly rebuilding holes in the schedule would be sound practices. Because a short replacement series is very unlikely to do any better and is expensive to develop, common sense would also seem to advocate holding onto new programs longer to give them time to build audiences. After all, *Seinfeld* generated ratings of only 11 and 12 during its first year (which now seems incredibly high, but stunk back then), losing badly to *Home Improvement*. Nonetheless, the pattern of the three major networks has been "decide quickly" and "cancel fast."

2.11 Production Methods

According to data from NATPE, as of 2005, physically producing a program on film (not including the cost of talent) ran about $1,000 per minute. Tape was less expensive but still around half that cost. Producing the program digitally—using a digital camera and a computer for editing, special effects, and so on—ran about $7,000 for 45 minutes of high-definition product (less than $100 for minute). *This enormous cost differential—about one-fifth the cost of film—drove the high-definition revolution in Hollywood.*

networks, this meant a lucrative part of the syndication market had evaporated in less than five years. This part of the market has been taken over by cable which is now relied on for almost all hour-long syndicated product.

Crime dramas then surfaced as a means to fill network schedules at a somewhat lower cost than action hours, resulting in schedules full of *Law & Order* and *CSI* look-alikes. Although the network studios were cranking out afternoon talk shows and judges banging various gavels, they were generating few dramas outside of crime and lawyer shows. (The main exception was *The Mentalist*, the success of which gave rise to a handful of "psych" shows.) At the same time, the networks were having no luck producing new hit sitcoms, resulting in a certain amount of panic in the syndication market.

New Program Selection

Phase two in planning a new fall season—selection and development of new program ideas—poses more difficult problems than ongoing program evaluation. The four networks consider as many as 6,000 new submissions every year. These submissions vary from single-page outlines to completed scripts that come from writers or producers. *Decision makers favor ideas resembling previously or presently successful shows.* They even quietly agree that almost all so-called original successes are in fact patterned after long-forgotten programs. *American Idol,* for example is just the *Original Amateur Hour* with a snotty Ted Mack. *Glee* merges the musical with a dramatic series, a modestly innovative idea, copying a Disney cable movie and *7 Brides for 7 Brothers,* the last broadcast effort.

One year, NBC promoted its move toward new and daring ideas with *Titans,* described as a "quirky yarn about a big city lawyer returning to his hometown in Ohio," despite this being the same plot as *Providence, Judging Amy* and *Ed.* But then, none of the other networks have been any more original.

The newest way of generating additional network programs is *franchise programming*—cloning

an hour-long series into several more programs with only minor changes. Originality has never been a big selling point for broadcasters, but franchising programs creates extreme sameness because a franchised show merely has a different cast and perhaps location. By the mid-2000s, *CSI* had been cloned to three different cities (Las Vegas, Miami and New York) and blended with *JAG* to form *NCIS. Law & Order* had added a *Special Victims Unit* and *Criminal Intent,* and followed them with even more analysis in *Criminal Minds.* People were only half joking when they suggested that next we would have *Law & Order: SUV* where the characters would investigate crimes from large sponsor-placed vehicles.

Over at FOX, they were working on turning *American Idol* into a **franchise** by changing music styles or featuring contestants of different ages. For network programmers, franchising has three enormous advantages:

1. Generating hour-long programs for foreign syndication or whose premise can be syndicated internationally

2. Reducing decision making for new series ideas

3. Creating signature programs to be identified with a network, thus helping to set it apart from other program suppliers

Viewers have generally had to look to cable for fresh ideas in such programs as *Six Feet Under, Nip/Tuck, Burn Notice, Warehouse 13* and so on. But the most popular cable shows are sometimes reused on sister broadcast networks, as was the case with *Monk* and *Queer Eye for the Straight Guy.* This double scheduling of the same show is called repurposing and goes both ways. For example, NBC ran all three versions of *Law & Order* on its co-owned USA and later syndicated the original series to TNT. It also ran *Heroes* on the co-owned Syfy Channel. In fact, the entire SOAPnet channel seemed to be a way for ABC to rerun its afternoon soap operas at night for women who work during the day. One has to wonder what will happen to it now that ABC is down to one soap opera. But *Heroes* proved so popular with younger viewers that NBC broke the "avoid sci-fi" rule in 2008 and experimented with *Journeyman, Bionic Woman* and (unbelievably) the weird *Chuck*.

Program Concepts and Scripts

Many program concepts are dismissed out of hand; others are read and reread, only to be shelved temporarily—or even permanently when a network is worried that the idea might possibly be a hit but won't take the chance and doesn't want anyone else to chance it. A few, usually variations on present hits or linked to top stars or producers, get a favorable nod with dispatch. Such big-name directors as Barry Levinson, Oprah Winfrey or Rob Reiner are courted and given contracts to develop anything they want, but without promises to actually run the shows. *The networks fight desperately to find that immediate hit that will pull in a young audience.*

Of the thousands of submissions that land on the networks' desks, roughly 600 are chosen for further development. At this point, all parties sign a *step deal*, a contract providing development funds in stages to the producer. In the past, a step deal also set compensation rates if the show were successful and gave the network creative control, which are still important when a show is not wholly owned by one network.

As a rule, step deals authorize *scripts* or, in some cases, expanded *treatments*. The approved concepts often take first form as special programs, made-for-TV movies or, increasingly, test characters in established shows. For example, the characters Green Arrow and Aquaman were introduced in *Smallville,* both of which became strong contenders for their own series. In the end, the CW decided to keep them part of *Smallville,* but that may now change as that show has ended its run. If a concept was submitted initially in script form, a rewrite may be ordered with specific recommendations for changes in concept, plot or cast (and even new writers and in some cases, producers).

Until recently, ABC traditionally supported many more program ideas at this stage than CBS, NBC or FOX, but ratings shifts have led first CBS and then NBC to allot more money to develop new program ideas. *The network that has recently dropped the most in the prime-time ratings is always the hungriest for fresh ideas and the most willing to risk trying them.*

Before authorizing any production, the program executive will first order one or more *full scripts* and a *bible*. Nowadays, a network typically pays about $50,000 for a half-hour comedy script and $70,000 for a one-hour drama script. Exceptional (read *successful*) writers demand much higher prices. The bible outlines characters and their relationships, suggests sets that will be needed, and summarizes future script ideas or the way the program can develop during its proposed run. At this stage, the producer also looks for production locations—at least for the pilot—outside of California.

Advances and Pilots

A *pilot* is a sample or prototype production of a series under consideration. Pilots afford programmers an opportunity to preview audience reaction to a property. Each of the Big Four networks orders between 30 and 45 pilots to fill expected gaps in its new season lineup (fewer for CW and Spanish-language networks). Once a network decides to film or tape a pilot, it draws up a budget and advances start-up money to the producer. The budget and advance may be regarded as the third major step in the program development process.

Half-hour pilots cost from $1.5 million to $3 million, depending on things like sets, costumes, special effects, star power and so on, with one-hour drama pilots costing more than twice that amount. Traditionally, pilot production costs were generally higher than costs for regular season shows because new sets had to be built, crews assembled and start-up costs paid. (However, the ongoing costs for the few megahits have recently risen far higher than the costs of their pilots.)

FOX and many producers have denounced the pilot system because of its incredible expense and abysmal success rate. FOX demands 5- to 10-minute presentation films in place of full-blown pilots for many shows, but this radical idea has met strong

2.12 The Program Development Process

Process begins with the review of new ideas submitted in the form of pitch sessions, requested submissions, open submissions, or company-developed proposals.

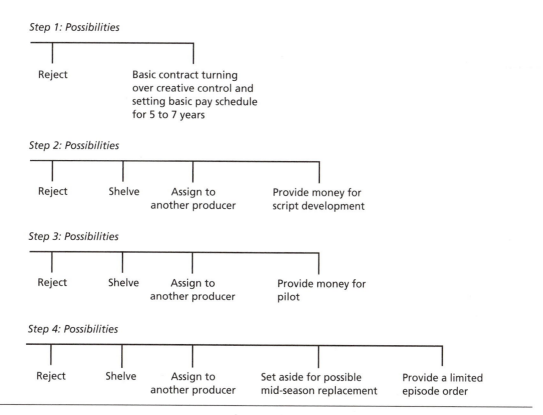

Step 1: Possibilities

Reject

Basic contract turning over creative control and setting basic pay schedule for 5 to 7 years

Step 2: Possibilities

Reject   Shelve   Assign to another producer   Provide money for script development

Step 3: Possibilities

Reject   Shelve   Assign to another producer   Provide money for pilot

Step 4: Possibilities

Reject   Shelve   Assign to another producer   Set aside for possible mid-season replacement   Provide a limited episode order

resistance from the other major broadcasters. Nowadays, of the approximately 130 pilots produced annually, many are formatted as made-for-TV movies. These can be played on regular movie nights and sold internationally as parts of movie packages, thus recouping the investment even if the series idea is not picked up. Series failing to make the final selection list for the fall season are held in reserve in anticipation of the inevitable cancellations. After seeing the pilots, the networks also "short order" some backup series, authorizing production of four to six episodes and additional scripts in case a backup show used as filler is unexpectedly successful. For a visualization of the development process, see 2.12.

The decisions to select series for airing based on their pilots usually take into consideration the following:

1. Current viewer preferences as indicated by ratings or profit margins

2. Costs

3. Resemblance between the proposed program and concepts that worked well in the past

4. Projected series' ability to deliver the targeted demographics for that network and its advertisers and its O&Os

5. Types of programs the competing networks air on nights when the new series might be scheduled

The following are of secondary weight but also relevant to a judgment:

6. The reputation of the producer and writers

7. The appeal of the series' performers (the talent)

8. The availability of an appropriate time period

9. The compatibility of the program with returning shows

10. The longevity of the concept (for example, in a program centered around children, the producer must remember children grow up)

Finally, increasingly relevant are these factors:

11. The number and type of countries that might buy the show or idea in syndication

12. The ability to reuse the show in another co-owned venture (another broadcast or cable network) or platform (internet or mobile media)

13. The size of the potential DVD sales market

14. The viability of inviting other companies to share the initial expenses

15. The possibility for advertiser tie-ins or cross promotion.

Of equal importance is whether the parent corporation can control the entire process from production to multiplatform distribution. The chief programmer juggles all of these considerations and perhaps others.

Schedule Churn

Stunting has resulted in a continual shifting of prime-time schedules, called *scheduling churn.* (Here the term *churn* refers to the continual shifting of programs within the network schedule and should not be confused with the term *subscriber churn* as it is used in the cable and pay-television industries.)

Moving programs in the schedule, using short runs and cancelling quickly are not the only causes of churn. These actions don't take into account network preemptions of their own shows, which have become distressingly commonplace. Indeed, over the last four years, each of the four major networks has averaged about a 40 percent preemption rate.

In most cases, these preemptions were caused by running extra episodes of an already existing series (for example, running hordes of back-to-back episodes of *Reba*)—or by reversing the existing shows (for example, so cleverly flipping *Grey's Anatomy* and *Desperate Housewives*) for just one week, or by blocking the network's franchise shows for a couple of weeks (such as running all the *CSI*s on the same night or all the *Law & Order*s, or just one version three times, or...or...). Such preemptions hurt the long-term ratings of the bumped shows: Lost audiences don't come back. Very few examples of churn were the result of airing specials.

In short, regularly-scheduled series were missing from their scheduled slots almost two out of every four weeks between September and May. The writers' strike can account for some of this during the 2008–2009 season, but nothing accounts for it during the other years. And the churn rate was even worse during the summer.

Changes now occur weekly and it's virtually impossible to tell when the network is trying a stunt, fixing a move that didn't work, or dumping a show quickly. It is hard not to agree with Brooks (see 2.13) that this constant motion represents panic.

A program that a network wants to get rid of can be canceled outright or *manipulated* (time-shifted or churned) until its ratings fall. Manipulation sometimes makes good public relations sense when a show is critically successful or widely popular—but not quite popular enough among the desired demographic groups. Some critics have suggested that this was the problem with *Touched by an Angel.* Analysis of program churn over the long haul leads to two conclusions:

1. *An individual program's ratings almost always fall when it is moved two out of three weeks (especially when moved in the second season).*

2. *A new series—one that had improved upon the time slot it was originally given—always fails when moved.*

Prime candidates for purposive schedule manipulation include programs with higher-than-average production costs that would cause managerial

2.13 Explaining Network Churn

Industry expert Tim Brooks, author of *The Complete Directory of Prime Time Network and Cable TV Shows*, blamed much of network churn on "panic." He pointed out that ratings had been declining since the mid-1970s but that the decline was not steady. Rather, ratings would first drop and then stabilize for a few years. When this happened, programmers would proclaim success, claiming they now had control of the problem (and then they would continue doing exactly what they had been doing).

These periods of stability were related to specific programs that, for a time, according to Brooks, brought in big audiences. During the 1980s, it was *Cosby*; then in the mid-1990s it was *Roseanne* and *Home Improvement*. Later the numbers again stabilized when *ER* and *Seinfeld* became hits, then *Survivor* further solidified them for a time.

When one of these shows eventually slid downward, though, the overall ratings for that network went into a free fall. When this happens, as it inevitably does, programmers panic.

Instead of changing the practices that seem to be driving the audiences away, they do more of them. For example, when ratings began another free fall in 1997, programmers went into another schedule-shuffling frenzy. By 2004, the heavy reliance on reality series had multiplied the problem because such series almost always decline significantly in audience size in their second seasons and have no afterlife in either syndication or as DVD sets. Those based on a gimmick, like *The Simple Life*, often fall apart completely. Franchise shows seem to hold up better in syndication, but never match the original in ratings.

problems if abruptly canceled (because they are supported by a highly-placed executive or advertiser). The 1995 shift of *Murder, She Wrote* on CBS from Sundays to Thursdays may have been an example of this type of move. Two notable shifts, *The West Wing* from Wednesday to Sunday in 2005–06 and *King of Queens* in 2006–07 from Monday to Wednesday, are probably examples of purposive schedule shifts. *Once low ratings or even a downward trend is achieved, network programmers can point to the numbers to justify cancellation (on the few occasions when some justification seems useful).* During panics, however, programs seem to be moved for no apparent reason: Merely showing the parent company that something is being done seems to be the real programming strategy at such times.

Promotion's Role

All broadcast networks use frequent *on-air promotion* and *online promotion*, as well as *paid advertising*, to introduce new and moved programs. Beginning as early as mid-July and continuing through November, networks intensify promotion of both their programs and their overall images on their broadcast and owned cable channels. For some big-budget or especially promising shows, paid advertising in program guides and magazines also helps draw audience attention, often through cross promotion deals with advertisers.

Concurrently, the networks open elaborate websites for each new program containing character bios and pictures, the *backstory* of the series and the current plot line, merchandise to buy, interactive chat groups, feedback options, recent episodes or previews of upcoming episodes and other elements. *On-air promotional announcements are believed to play a pivotal role in the ratings success of a program.* Particularly essential are the on-screen *tune-in messages*, now taking up a significant portion of airtime. *Websites have a different function: They are thought to build loyalty to the program and involvement with specific characters, both contributing to satisfaction with a series and to frequent viewing.*

In the fall, on-air *promos* plug every program scheduled to appear in a season lineup. Weak or doubtful offerings needing extra stimulus get extra exposure on all platforms, at least until the network surrenders. Not until a program is safely past the rocks and shoals of its first several airings (or until the network decides it can't risk more early trials) does promotion let up. At least minimal on-air promotion continues as long as a show is on the schedule, but websites fade away (from lack of updates) when a show seems destined for cancellation. At this point fan sites take over (see 2.14).

In addition, networks use *print promotion*, especially magazines and newspaper listings, to catalog offerings for particular evenings. For a long time, *TV Guide* magazine was so important to network television that programmers sometimes delayed schedule changes so that the alterations could make *TV Guide's* deadline for affiliate program listings. The promotional value of *TV Guide* was enormous until its format became unwieldy after the digital channel explosion. Cable systems now provide electronic guides, essential because of the huge numbers and types of channels (digital, HD, 3D), with several ways of sorting and classifying program titles.

Magazines like *People* and *Us* have become major outlets for printed promotional materials, often run as features and not identified as promotional material. Cross-promotion using morning shows and cable outlets carrying popular behind-

the-scenes specials is also critical for capturing attention. Some networks also join with major businesses, such as Kmart, Sears or McDonald's, to jointly promote the new season or a specific program.

Promotions in print, on the air and on the web are the primary ways networks invite viewers to try out programs. They are also the means by which the networks convince viewers to associate a program with a particular network (*franchising* or *branding*). At the same time, parent corporations are demanding heavy cross-promotion of a company's many subsidiaries—such as the CW using its TV shows to promote music from Atlantic, Elektra, Reprise, Rhino and Warner Bros. Records—which uses up air time that would previously have been used to promote episodes of individual programs. And it leaves less and less program time.

Changing Format Emphases

To minimize risk, networks continue to rely on the traditional winners in prime time—situation comedies, dramas and movies—and somewhat reluctantly added unscripted programs (in shorthand, *reality*) to this exclusive list. Another change has been the increased use of *specials,* a term encompassing one-time entertainment programs, major sporting events, and more infrequently, news documentaries or interviews. Nonetheless, the proportions as well as kinds of *formats* dominating evening schedules have altered over time (see 2.15).

Situation comedies and *crime dramas* have a long history in network television, stretching back to such shows as *The Life of Riley* and *Dragnet* in the early 1950s all the way through *The Big Band Theory* and *CSI* in the late 2000s. In one recent season, the broadcast networks offered over 75 sitcoms and 30 crime dramas; in a subsequent season, the distribution had flipped to 17 sitcoms and 38 dramas plus 26 unscripted shows (and another 22 dramas on Univision). The concentration of shows into sitcoms and dramas occurred because they:

- attracted sizable audiences in the young female demographics.

2.14   **Fan Sites**

Virtually every program has fan sites on the internet, and these remain long after the networks have forgotten a series. Indeed, one key function of fan sites is the more or less illegal sharing of taped episodes among fans. (According to *Variety,* studies have shown most people would use official downloads if they were available and at low prices; most people only pirate what the networks don't offer.) In addition, there are people who collect copies of virtually everything TV does, even if the networks don't think the offerings have any value. Somewhere out there are people who think *My Mother the Car* was a great show. Truth is, most people don't think of it as pirating when they find a show "in the trash" that the networks threw away. The networks, or at least their parent companies, might strongly disagree with that. At present, the networks are not keeping up with technology in their programming, their promotion, or their archiving.

- syndicate well off-network.

Unscripted shows supplanted some of this concentrated group because they:

- are comparatively inexpensive to produce.

Because of demand the cost of sitcoms and crime shows produced in the United States has escalated beyond that of most other formats. (Univision buys its soap-like dramas—*telenovelas*—less expensively from Mexico or produces them in Miami.) As a result, the crime drama has moved to the franchise route, and situation comedies have begun to all look alike. Although examples of top-rated shows in both of these types can be found, their overall success rate has declined steadily. Most years, the networks do not produce even one truly successful new sitcom (or drama).

Situation comedies fall into two main types: family-based comedies like *Two and a Half Men, George Lopez* and *How I Met Your Mother*—and occupational comedies like *Becker, The Office* and *Scrubs*. Together, these two types account for more than three-quarters of all situation comedies offered over the last 20 years. More unusual sitcom formats such as *10 Things I Hate About You* or *That '70s Show* occasionally turn up, but only in limited numbers. Crime dramas have slowly changed—from private citizen do-gooders like *Magnum P.I.* to gritty police dramas like *NYPD Blue* to investigations of somewhat revolting body parts like *CSI* and *Bones*.

The mid-1990s also saw the return of courtroom dramas, often in connection with a police show (as was the case with *Law & Order* and *Law & Order: SVU*), or on their own (as in *The Practice, Judging Amy* and *Without a Trace*). *Smallville*, an unusual comic book format, is most likely to become the franchise for the CW using the Justice League characters now part of *Smallville*.

Of the approximately 700 *specials* each year, more than 500 have been entertainment specials for young adults, such as the Justin Timberlake specials, the Charlie Brown Christmas specials and Univision's long-running *Sabado Gigante*, often considered a special even though it is part of the regular schedule. That's because of the type of program it is.

A fast-paced variety, talk, and game show, *Sabado Gigante* airs every Saturday evening and attracts huge Spanish-speaking audiences inside the United States and throughout South and Central America. About 100 specials each year on U.S. television are sports specials, including the annual Super Bowl and World Series games. The remaining 100 divide among dramatic specials and news specials, including interviews such as those by Barbara Walters, and occasional documentaries.

Entertainment specials often attract superstars (such as Robin Williams or Bob Newhart) whose regular motion picture work, performance schedules or health prevents them from participating in series programs. *Star-studded specials can invigorate a schedule, encourage major advertiser participation, provide unusual promotional opportunities, and generate high ratings and critical approval.* However, they cost a lot of money and are consequently rare. Programs such as *Glee* or *Saturday Night Live* now bring in these superstars as guests. In some cases, stars may actually beg, or rather have their agents beg, to get on the program. A flood of award shows, clones of the *Academy Awards* and *Grammy Awards,* are now promoted as "Star-Studded Specials," but few are as big a draw as the annual *Academy Awards.* Indeed, many so-called entertainment specials are merely long forms of regular series or regular episodes with big-name guest stars.

For example, the record-breaking final episode of *M*A*S*H* (amassing an extraordinary 77 share) was an extended episode of the existing series, as was the final episode of *Seinfeld. Friends* did several long-form shows leading up to their final episode, all of them called specials. Network programmers are awake to the possibility that too many specials differing sharply from the regular programming might interrupt carefully nurtured viewing habits beyond repair—hence, the trend toward long-form episodes of regularly scheduled series. Such shows also have the advantage of being relatively inexpensive to produce and promote, and they exploit existing audiences, thus reducing risk.

Nowadays, network *prime-time sports* consist of playoffs and championships in the major sports,

2.15 Is There a Doctor in The House?

Always a runner-up. That might be that way to describe medical dramas on the broadcast networks. Never the dominant format, but always there, usually in the top 10. However, over the years, they changed.

Back in 1948, medical programs were serious science. Starting on the old Dumont Network (and then moving to CBS), *The Johns Hopkins Science Review* was one of those shows critics loved and very few people watched. It offered the latest breakthroughs in medicine and other areas of science (a topic that has moved to evening newscasts). In the early 1950s, long before Googling, the program was where people went to get the latest word on the polio epidemics and the treatments. It was also where they went to see the latest information about rockets. When it went off the air in 1954, it was replaced with two shows: *Medical Horizons* on ABC—a series, like *Johns Hopkins*, which presented the latest breakthroughs, but only in medicine—and *Medic* on NBC, which dramatized case files from the Los Angeles Medical Association. *Medic* was more successful, but both typified the ways the medical profession was dealt with during the 1950s. Medicine was serious stuff, and even when stories were dramatized, they came "theoretically" just from the facts.

That all changed in 1961 when two groundbreaking shows hit in the same year. *Dr. Kildare* (taken from the movie of the same name) and *Ben Casey* both featured a brilliant, but nonconformist young doctor and his wise, older mentor. These doctors did more than cure sickness—with almost God-like success: They also solved an endless array of other people's personal problems. For the next 20 years, right up until *Trapper John,* they set the formula for successful medical dramas. But in 1972, a slight change began to creep in with the premiere of *Emergency.*

It's hard to think of *Emergency* as groundbreaking—but for the first time, a medical show had an ensemble cast, not just two major characters. What was meant to form a bridge between action-adventure and medical drama also formed a bridge between the existing formula and its next incarnation, which occurred in 1982 with *St. Elsewhere.* Set in a big-city teaching hospital, *St. Elsewhere* was a complete break from the programs with the God-like doctors that preceded it. Here doctors were all too human, with some driven by money, others by a yearning for fame. Instead of solving everyone else's problems, doctors started worrying about their own. The whole show was somehow less antiseptic, grittier, more inner-city, and the topics they dealt with ranged from breast and testicular cancer to AIDS to rape and gang violence and so on. This was the show that made it okay for men to appear nude, at least from behind. Doctors on television would never climb back up on the pedestals they had previously occupied. Even when the doctor is a certified genius, such as in FOX's *House,* he's still an arrogant jerk.

St. Elsewhere's most enduring legacy, however, was the ensemble cast. From that time, right through *Gray's Anatomy,* no one or two stars carried a medical drama. From the point of view of producers this has the huge benefit of allowing stars to leave and new ones be brought in without damaging the show. As a result, ensemble programs can run forever, so long as there's a sickness to tackle. Notably, not a single character who appeared in the early episodes of NBC's *ER* was still there when it finally finished its 15-year run in 2009, and yet the show continued to be a top-10 contender. By evolving over time, the medical drama has not only kept itself healthy but has been longer-lived than most formats.

William J. Adams, Ph.D.
Kansas State University

as well as special events such as the Olympics (see 2.16 about Roone Arledge's extraordinary influence). FOX and NBC, in particular, often use sports to fill the first two months of the new prime-time season, introducing regular series as late as November. Although the networks carry a great deal of football, basketball, baseball, tennis, and golf, and Univision has soccer, most of these shows are relegated to the weekends (see Chapter 7). Most soccer, wrestling, Nascar, and other sports command prime time only on cable, not on the broadcast networks.

Cable has become the true home of sports. Even ABC responded to pressure for the network to do something to attract more "ideal women," even at the expense of its traditional audience for the long-running

2.16 Roone Arledge: The Man Who Brought Sports into Prime Time

When Roone Arledge was first hired by ABC in 1960 as a lowly assistant producer, the television networks considered sports to be second-rate entertainment. Even professional team owners at the time believed that televised sports existed to sell tickets for the ballparks. Roone Arledge could not have disagreed more. He was convinced that sports programming could entertain the fans at home, and under his leadership, the sports broadcasting industry was completely recreated.

Arledge came up with a revolutionary approach to producing sports: He borrowed the production techniques of entertainment and used them to duplicate the experience of actually attending a game at the stadium. He used many more cameras, microphones and graphics in his sports telecasts than his competitors had ever used, and he experimented constantly with new technologies. Arledge and his team of talented engineers pioneered or refined the use of underwater cameras, handheld cameras, isolation cameras, field microphones, split screens, instant replay, slow motion and freeze frames. Their efforts resulted in new production techniques that heightened the drama of sporting events. Arledge also began the practice of focusing on the personalities and stories of the athletes. He invented what was called "up close and personal" coverage—airing pretaped biographical features of athletes right before their events—to involve viewers emotionally with the players and the outcomes.

During the 1960s, the television networks aired sports only on weekend afternoons. But ABC's successful prime-time broadcasts of the 1968 Olympic Games convinced Arledge, by then the president of ABC Sports, that sports programming could compete with sitcoms and dramas in prime time. *Monday Night Football,* an Arledge creation, premiered in 1970 and quickly became a phenomenal success in the ratings. (It is worth noting that CBS and NBC had both rejected the NFL's proposal for the show.)

During the 1970s, one sport after another moved into prime time, and fees for broadcast rights for sports skyrocketed because of soaring revenues from prime-time advertising.

In the following decades, sports programming expanded further into network schedules, and limited choices have given way to lineups containing dozens of channels devoted to exclusively to sports. In addition, many professional leagues, college conferences, and even some individual teams have started their own television networks (though they are more like syndicators than real networks). Also, some professional leagues have partnered with cable and satellite providers to offer premium access to all regular and postseason games. Sports has continued to dominate much of broadcast schedules, with league playoffs and championships consistently among the highest-rated programs year after year.

Despite starting with very limited resources, Arledge transformed ABC Sports into the preeminent sports network of the day and initiated a phenomenon that lasts to today. Although Arledge died in 2002, his immense influence will continue to be seen for decades to come. He forever changed ABC, and beyond that network, programming strategies and schedules for all television, the economics of professional and college sports, and the way that viewers watch sports on television.

Timothy B. Bedwell
Produce, Media Quarry, LLC.

Monday Night Football, and shifted the show to ESPN. (Also, ESPN makes more money for Disney than ABC does, which probably affected the move.) *Big sporting events do bring prestige to the network, are popular with affiliates, and fill out advertising packages by delivering male viewers of all ages, but the costs paid by broadcast networks for the biggest events no longer match returns.*

Unscripted programming is the overall term used by the industry to cover reality programs,

news magazines and game shows. It refers to the types of programs that do not require the expensive writing and controlled production used for other series. While such shows have writers providing ad-libs for hosts and outlining situations, the writing costs as well as talent costs are minimal compared with other genres. These three types of programs are certainly not new. The magazine format goes back decades, game shows ruled the airwaves during the 1950s, and artificial situation shows can be traced back at least as far as *Candid Camera*. What is new is the power they command.

Like the sitcom, there have been some immense hits in the *reality genre*. *American Idol, Survivor* and *Dancing with the Stars* have had staying power, but others, such as *Joe Millionaire*, did well once but fell apart once the gimmick was known. To date, nearly all reality series have dropped substantially in the ratings during their second outings. Even the most popular series in this format (with the two notable exceptions of *American Idol* and *Survivor: Vanuatu*) don't match on a regular basis the ratings of a *CSI, Gray's Anatomy, The Mentalist, The Office* or other top scripted series.

The power of reality is that it is incredibly cheap to produce: less than one-tenth the cost of scripted programs. The networks have also been able to standardize reality shows by fitting them into a rigid formula: A group of people you hope you never meet in real life backstab and cut each other's throats on the way to a big prize; during each show, one participant is thrown off after the group performs some outlandish stunt; the outcast then hits the morning talk shows and news circuit to hype the ongoing program. The only thing that changes is the situation. One variation that makes critics groan is the dumbed-down quiz show, epitomized by *Are you Smarter Than a Fifth-Grader?*. Because reality shows are so cheap to produce, they also provide a way to create original summer programming, thus helping the move toward a full 52-week schedule.

But the flurry of creativity that characterized some of the early entries has now settled into as formulaic a pattern as most sitcoms. One problem with reality series is that many of the concepts were borrowed from popular shows in Japan and Europe, and thus our versions are very hard to sell back. The other major problem is that each show needs a gimmick, and to maintain the shock value (and thus generate hype), the situations have been pushed closer and closer to outright pornography or life risking situations. We may yet get our first on-air tragedy.

Magazine series like *60 Minutes, 20/20, Primetime, Dateline* and so on are almost as numerous as reality series in prime time. The shows are produced directly by a network's news division and have earned consistent though middle-of-the-pack ratings for years. Like the other unscripted formats, magazine series are, comparatively, very cheap to produce, and unlike reality series, several have been able to run forever with little decline from their initial ratings. They also serve as prestige programs for the networks (see 2.17). *But like reality series, magazine shows have no afterlife. Neither type works well in rerun, and they have no life as a DVD set and no syndication potential, although in some rare cases their ideas may be franchised to other countries.*

Game shows enjoyed a brief resurgence in the late 1990s, were badly overused, and then appeared to vanish. Actually, they merged with reality series, most of which are now games, but in its purer form, the game show had been relegated to syndicated access time (for instance, *Jeopardy* and *Wheel of Fortune*).

Although increased costs have led to fewer movie nights over the last few years, three types of productions regarded as movies still fill some of prime time on the broadcast television networks: (1) *theatrical feature films,* those made originally for release in theaters; (2) *made-for-TV movies,* similar to feature films but made specifically for network television airing in a two-hour format containing commercial breaks; and (3) *miniseries,* multipart films made especially for broadcast airing in installments. All three types share these major advantages for the networks:

- They fill large amounts of time with material that usually generates respectable ratings.

- They make it possible to air topical or controversial material that may be deemed inappropriate for regularly scheduled network series or can be taken directly from the headlines.

- They permit showcasing actors and actresses who would otherwise never be seen on television.

- They allow the network to reward stars from their popular series by giving them a movie.

The three kinds of movies also share one major disadvantage—extraordinarily high cost for the

2.17

Tick tick tick tick. A ticking watch quickly became synonymous with CBS's groundbreaking, hour-long, investigative news magazine, *60 Minutes*, when it launched on September 24, 1968 (the stopwatch appeared after few episodes). Legendary news producer Don Hewitt (1922–2009), who directed venerable CBS newsman Edward R. Murrow for the first few years of *See It Now* (1951–1958), directed the first televised presidential debates in 1960 (Kennedy v. Nixon) and produced the *CBS Evening News with Walter Cronkite* for years, created this prime-time Sunday staple, serving as its executive producer until 2004. It is the longest-running, regularly-scheduled, prime-time broadcast program in American television. It has garnered 78 Emmys and five Peabody Awards. It was the top-ranked show for five years and among the top-10* Nielsen-rated programs for 23 seasons (1977–2000). It continues to be among the top-20 shows each week and the most-watched news magazine. *TV Guide* ranks it number six among its "50 Greatest TV Shows of All Time," and the only news program in its top 10.

Today's investigative techniques of hidden cameras, "gotcha" guerilla tactics, and re-edited interviews can be traced to *60 Minutes*. Originally hosted by Harry Reasoner and Mike Wallace, other journalists and commentators have come and gone in the 40-plus years of this storied program. Morley Safer, Lesley Stahl, Andy Rooney and others became household names and celebrity reporters thanks to this high-profile "magazine for television" (as Reasoner introduced it in the first episode). Part-time correspondents include a laundry list of legendary news personalities, including Ed Bradley, Connie Chung, Anderson Cooper, Walter Cronkite, Katie Couric, Bryant Gumbel, Lara Logan, Dan Rather, Diane Sawyer and Eric Sevareid.

Through the years, *60 Minutes* has been embroiled in controversy for some of its reporting. In 1982, a package asserted that General William Westmoreland withheld information about the Vietnam War from key people in Washington. Westmoreland denounced the story, and *60 Minutes* issued a statement that it did not believe the general was unpatriotic, while standing by the accuracy of the report. In 2000, the program landed an exclusive interview with Timothy McVeigh, the Oklahoma City

Bomber who had been found guilty and sentenced to death. McVeigh ranted against the U.S. government, and subsequently face-to-face interviews with death-row inmates were made illegal. In 1995, *60 Minutes* did *not* run a story, for which it was criticized. The producers had information that Brown & Williamson, a tobacco company, had disregarded information about the health risks of its cigarettes and had tampered with the tobacco to enhance the effect of nicotine. Don Hewitt hesitated to run such a scathing expose, and instead *The Wall Street Journal* broke the story. Eventually, *60 Minutes* aired an altered version, minus some of the most incriminating evidence. The Oscar-nominated film, *The Insider* (1999), dramatizes this incident. When all is said and done, though, it is expected that hard-hitting journalism, as championed by *60 Minutes*, will run into criticism sometimes; otherwise, it can be argued that the reporters are not doing their jobs.

Doing their jobs is a hallmark of the *60 Minutes* investigative team. Whether reporting on Vietnam and Watergate in the early years or the current presidential administration, this original and time-honored news magazine, which its creator, Don Hewitt, said married "show biz" and "news biz," is considered to be the preeminent investigative program on American television. It paved the way for many that followed, including ABC's *20/20* (1978), PBS's *Frontline* (1983), NBC's *Dateline* (1992), and others. It has been franchised in other countries, including Australia, New Zealand and Peru. Audio broadcasts of the show are distributed by CBS Radio, and commercial-free audio podcasts are available from iTunes. The TV broadcasts stream on CBSNews.com and CNETTV.com. The show has its own website at CBSNews.com and its own YouTube channel, *http://www.youtube.com/user/60minutes?ob=5*. It has spawned a few other series, such as the short-lived *60 Minutes II*, and it has a relatively new web series, *60 Minutes Overtime* (*http://www.cbsnews.com/60minutesovertime*), with internet-exclusive content beyond the TV program. A pretty good run for a show that just keeps on ticking....

Edward J. Fink
California State University, Fullerton

networks. Miniseries are typically the most expensive, and theatrical movies the second-most costly. Both are more risky in ratings than made-for-TV movies, but *all three remain popular because they fill big chunks of time and can be used to temporarily plug holes in the schedule until programmers can figure out something to schedule.*

Theatrical movies have declined in popularity because of exceptionally high costs and generally low ratings when run on the Big Three networks. The truth is that by the time a theatrical movie makes it to broadcast TV, it is already very late in its life cycle. It has played the theaters, run on pay-per-view, and is probably available on VOD. It may have been released for rental, run on cable movie channels and sold as a DVD. Consequently, ratings on the networks are almost always disappointing, even for the biggest blockbusters. Made-for-TV movies just perform better. Miniseries not only perform better but also have a strong afterlife in foreign syndication and as DVDs.

Many viewers and critics bewail the disappearance of the *dramatic anthology* format: a set of single-episode television plays presented in an unconnected series. What actually happened was that the anthology format went through a style change and returned as the made-for-TV movie. During the 1955–56 season, the very peak of the anthology era, dramatic anthologies made up about 526 hours of prime time. In the 1989–90 season, a peak year, 624 made-for-TV movies aired in prime time (not including those made for cable).

The best of these movies compare favorably with the best of the dramatic anthologies of the earlier era. Such movies also allow the networks to respond quickly to major news events. The Scott Peterson case was a movie even before it went to trial. The Elizabeth Smart and Jessica Lynch stories became competing films on more than one network, and the big guys fought about who was going to be first to do the Anna Nicole Smith story almost as much as the lawyers fought about who was going to get to bury her. Hot topics like drugs, sex and teenage problems can be dealt with in movies in ways a prime-time series just doesn't allow (see 2.18). TV movies shown on co-owned cable channels are another method of testing

new characters and plot ideas—especially for material that might be too risqué for broadcast networks!

The made-for-TV movie has replaced the pilot as the major method for testing new series ideas. Programs such as *Glee*, succeeded as television—or in this case cable movies (*High School Musical*)—before becoming series. Made-for-TV movies as pilots have four distinct advantages:

1. They can be profitable.
2. They can target a desired demographic group.
3. Audiences and affiliates like them.
4. They have international syndication potential as theatrical movies.

TV movie pilots now average $5 million to make (some as high as $10 million), but they pay their way whether or not the concept ever becomes a series. Even when they fail, the networks usually have made a healthy profit on the TV movie's initial run, its foreign syndication and the DVD sale. *Moreover, the made-for-TV movie has the advantage of being made-to-order to fit within a network's existing schedule. It can target a specific audience to maintain a night's flow and avoid the disruptions that specials often cause.*

The success of limited series on PBS's *Masterpiece Theatre* led the commercial networks into the production of multipart series presented in two to six episodes on successive nights or in successive weeks. Called *miniseries*, they could run for as long as 10 or more hours, typically beginning and ending on Sunday nights—the night of maximum viewing. Shorter miniseries tend to be scheduled on sequential nights, while longer series stretch over two weeks, skipping the evenings on which the network has its most popular programs. These extreme long forms, however, have become very rare because of their exceedingly high cost. Despite the advantages of blockbuster ratings, prestige, critical acclaim and series potential, the broadcast networks switched from long-form to *short-form miniseries* (four to six hours).

Such high-level fantasy concepts as *Merlin*, *Alice in Wonderland* and *Leprechauns*, the Romeo-and-Juliet takeoff, earned high ratings on the networks but also sold well internationally and as DVD sets

2.18   The Movie Mistakes

Occasionally, made-for-TV movies can show how badly out of touch with their audiences the networks can be. CBS was truly shocked by public reaction to its docudrama on President Reagan. It seems to have never occurred to CBS's higher-ups that much of the public would take offense at its portrayal of Mrs. Reagan as a shrew and the former President as a bumbling but affable storyteller. The public's reaction to the tendency to make things up for dramatic effect seems also to have stunned the Hollywood community. When the press picked up on the public outcry, Viacom quickly pulled the show from CBS and moved it to Showtime, which immediately declared it a hit and never showed it again. ABC reacted to the success of Mel Gibson's *The Passion of the Christ* (in spite of negative Hollywood and mainstream press) by rushing its alternative version of the *Passion* out for the 2004 Easter season, but the network seems genuinely surprised that *Judas* bombed. After all, the made-for-TV movie had a religious theme; why didn't it work? Recently a network announced plans for an animated series on Jesus Christ as a teenager having problems with his overbearing father. Will they ever learn?

William J. Adams, Ph.D.
Kansas State University

marketed on the air during the original network showing. NBC adopted the practice of putting delayed repeats on its cable networks about one week after initial broadcast airings, thus producing another round of advertising revenues. Widespread adoption of this multistep profit system, similar to the one used for Hollywood motion pictures, made the miniseries more popular than ever by the turn of the century. But a decade later, such event programming has become rare for broadcasting, budgets going instead to original production for cable.

Network Decision Making

Few program decisions precipitate as much controversy as the cancellation of programs. Because commercial television is first of all a business—with tens of thousands of stockholders and billions of dollars committed for advertising—the networks' overriding aim is to attract the largest possible audience in the ideal demographic range at all times, or at least to appear to be trying to do that. Networks always aim at the number-one position. Traditionally, ratings have been considered the most influential prime-time programming variable, and the networks make many controversial decisions each year based on these numbers. This often results in (1) canceling programs favored by millions of viewers, (2) countering strong shows by scheduling competing strong shows, (3) preempting popular series to insert special programs, and (4) falling back on reruns late in the season when the outdoors beckons and audience levels begin to drop off.

However, the type of program, the ranking as compared with the competition, the size of production fees, and the target demographic group may be as important as the ratings in cancellation decisions. New situation comedies, strongly desired by the networks' O&Os, and reality-based series are much more likely to be held than other kinds of series producing equivalent ratings. Also, series with low production fees are more likely to be held than more expensive programs, and finally, series that appeal to the network's concept of "proper demographics"—and some would now argue "political correctness"—may be held even when ratings are low. And occasionally, like once in a decade or so, audience outcry restores a favorite for a while, as in the case of cancelled and then revived *Jericho* on CBS or *Friday Night Lights*, which got new life on cable. Critical approval and the extraordinary promotional opportunity that public acclaim provides also figure in decisions to cancel or hold low-rated new programs (see 2.19 and 2.20).

2.19   The Critics

Acclaim usually has some effect only in the absence of other rating successes. The kudos for *Hill Street Blues,* for example, bolstered NBC's image at a time when it was sorely in need of prestige, persuading programmers to stick with the show even in the face of low ratings. The same connection between critical acclaim and patience even in the face of low ratings can be seen for the moderately rated *The West Wing* on NBC or *Bones* on FOX. Sometimes the networks decide to go along with the critics, at least until something with better numbers comes along.

On the other hand, critical shock also seems to be desirable as far as the networks are concerned. The WB openly admitted that it added a love affair between a high school student and a teacher to *Dawson's Creek* to generate negative press. ABC did the same thing with *NYPD Blue.* The nude scenes were there to stir up controversy. After the press furor generated by the Madonna/Britney Spears kiss, CBS was probably trying to trigger similar press attention with its 2004 halftime show at the Super Bowl. It just didn't count on how negative the public reaction would be. Many argue that the atomic bomb detonations on *24* and *Jericho,* the grittier aspects of *Prison Break* and the graphic details in *CSI* and *Bones* have also been designed to generate such shock. Instead of being bowled over, however, the critics have raved about the new realism.

The Risks and Rewards Ahead

Supposedly, the major networks prowl for the breakthrough idea—the program that will be different but not so different as to turn away audiences. *The Cosby Show* was one such show in 1984–85, as was *ALF* in 1986. *Married ... with Children* astonished viewers in 1987, *Roseanne* made a splash in 1988, *Friends* reintroduced the buddy sitcom in 1995, and *Malcolm in the Middle* suggested an entirely new idea for the family sitcom in 1999.

The biggest change was the rebirth of the prime-time game show with *Who Wants to Be a Millionaire?* in 2000—after an absence of nearly 40 years—and its combination with reality in the form of *Survivor.* Next came graphic special effects and mystery that produced the success of *CSI* beginning in 2002, and then the blatant sex in *Desperate Housewives.* Its success relaxed standards all through the broadcast networks. Then CBS came up with *The Mentalist,* which spawned a half-dozen medium and psychic shows. Most recently, FOX reinvented the musical with *Glee,* though few have attempted to copy it.

In recent years, all four major networks have had entire seasons without a single new hit. In truth, network programmers can only guess what the next hit will be and why it succeeds. A program failure is easier to analyze. It can result from the wrong time period, the wrong concept, the wrong writing, the wrong casting, poor execution of a good idea, poor execution of a bad idea, overwhelming competition, the wrong night of the week, and a dozen other factors. Conversely, success is very hard to analyze or copy, even though that has become the driving goal of the broadcast networks.

Although the actual cost of production has gone down dramatically through the use of digital technology and computer-produced effects, other factors have canceled out the savings and caused the full cost of production to continue to skyrocket. Some of those factors are directly related to programming decisions and seem to be the opposite of what many would naturally assume would happen. For example, the inability of programmers to produce successful shows has actually caused the price of production to go up. With so few true hits, programmers seem willing to pay almost anything to keep a successful program, as demonstrated by the incredible amounts paid to renew such series as *ER* and *Two and a Half Men.*

The networks are also locked in bidding wars for top specials and sporting events, again causing the prices to go through the ceiling. In a strange type of domino effect, however, as the top price levels have gone up, directors, writers, actors and people in all other branches of production have also demanded

2.20 The Censors

The broadcast *Standards and Practices Department*, a behind-the-scenes group, theoretically used to exercise total authority over all network programming. Cynically and often angrily called "censors," the department once acted as policeman and judge for all questions concerning acceptability of material for broadcast. It often found itself walking a thin line between offending viewers or advertisers and offending the creative community. It had to decide between the imaginative and the objectionable.

Members of the department typically read submitted scripts; attended rehearsals, filmings, or tapings; and often previewed the final products before they aired. They were everywhere. If, in the department's lordly judgment, a program failed to conform to network standards in matters of language or taste, it could insist on changes. Only a decree by the chairman or president of the company could overturn its decisions.

However, Standards and Practices was one of the first areas cut back when budgets grew tight in the 1990s, and as a result, this department has little day-to-day impact today (although its existence is loudly touted during election years when an increase in media criticism usually occurs). Moreover, even when it had considerable power, over the years the department's criteria for acceptability were forced to change. In the early 1920s, one of the hottest issues was whether such a personal and perhaps obscene product as toothpaste should be allowed to advertise over the radio airwaves. By 1983 the hottest question was whether NBC's censors would permit a new series, *Bay City Blues*,

to air a locker-room scene that included nude men photographed, as the producer put it, "tastefully from the back." By the mid-1980s, child abuse, abortion, and homosexuality were the problematic topics, while the 1990s brought the thorny questions of AIDS, condoms, obscene language, and, as always, how explicitly sex could be shown.

By the mid-2000s, concern focused on violence, nudity, drinking, and smoking, and one of the hottest issues was whether some reality shows were rigged. This question surfaced with the discovery that certain exciting scenes in *Survivor* were staged and that ABC network executives had overruled the judges in their *American Idol* clone, *Last Comic Standing*—a show in which the audience supposedly selected the next top comedian—apparently to produce a more demographically-friendly result. At the same time, gay groups and other liberal organizations were demanding more positive portrayals of gays in programming, and some producers wanted even more graphic and controversial depictions of sex in prime time.

The present situation has led to some very strange reactions, especially noticeable on cable. The Syfy Channel, for example, owned by NBC Universal, bleeps out bad words on some shows but ran *Tripping the Rift* for years, which is little more than animated porn. Now the network censors seem focused on political correctness and on gaining points with minorities, not on offending special interest groups like gays. As long as programs don't cross the lines set by the FCC, pretty much anything goes.

more. As a result, costs at all levels have gone up even as ratings have gone down. The network takeover of production not only didn't slow this process, however; it actually increased the rate of its rise.

At the same time, the incredible failure rates have resulted in an insatiable demand for replacement series. It is not at all uncommon for half of new prime-time series to fail by network standards within their first six weeks. These shows have to be replaced, and because development is the most expensive phase of production, the constant demand for new series has sent development costs out of sight. As these new programs rarely do better than the preceding series in those time slots on the same channels, one would presume, just considering the economics, that

programmers would leave most new series alone for at least a year to see if they could build audiences. The continual hope for that one elusive program that will break the trend, however, produces a type of feeding frenzy in which no programmers are willing to deviate from the present destructive cycle.

Predicting the future of any medium is a risky undertaking at best. As ratings and compensation continue to fall, eventually the largest non-network group owners may decide they can do better on their own. It would be natural for such group owners to either increase their participation in original syndication production for their own systems or join with disgruntled old executive producers as to form new production houses, thus in essence becoming networks themselves. For ten of its owned stations, FOX created MyNetworkTV to replace the prime-time shows that UPN formerly supplied.

Such scenarios suggest that the future American broadcasting system could more closely resemble the system that presently exists in such countries as Japan, rather than what is now familiar. In short, there would be more networks but fewer affiliates (and maybe way fewer stations, as Chapter 4 suggests). That is to say, the networks would be doing their own productions, which would then be distributed through whatever stations they own as part of a much larger entertainment wing of a corporation.

Companies like Hallmark have been doing production for years (nowadays Hallmark has its own cable network). Is it possible that they could join with other large companies to make their own shows? Many, like Sears and Procter and Gamble, seem to be threatening that now, arguing that they couldn't possibly do worse than the present broadcast system. Only time will tell how the present situation will work itself out. Only six things seem to be sure bets right now:

1. Television is not going to go away: Might change a bit, but it'll live.

2. The power of the big broadcast networks to control information and entertainment will continue to decline, forcing the networks to change into new entities.

3. The division between broadcasting and cable will continue to blur as the companies buy into one another and begin to mirror each other and make greater use of the internet.

4. Aftermarket selling of reality and other shows will become the centers of creative effort.

5. Virtual advertising and product placement will expand into regular programming as revenues from traditional advertising decline.

6. Multiplatform strategies will become part of every program proposal and central to all productions.

Indeed, the mixed broadcast/cable/online model now used by ION and Univision is the likely future of the business. In any case, one thing is clear: The next 50 years will bear little resemblance to the last 50 years.

Notes

1. Eggerton, J. (Feb. 9, 2004). Sexy halftime stunt has affiliates fuming. *Broadcasting & Cable*, pp. 6, 37.

2. Littleton, C. (Feb. 22–28, 2010). Free tv's found money. Nets and their affils revel in new coin from cable. *Variety*, pp. 1–37.

3. Becker, A. (March 3, 2008). Buyers give lowdown on upfronts. *Broadcasting & Cable*, pp. 3–26.

4. Eggerton, J. (Feb. 18, 2008). Advertisers rankled by network fees. *Broadcasting & Cable*, pp. 3–26.

5. Ives, N. (March 16, 2011). American idol returns to dominance in product placement. *Advertising Age*. adage.com/article/mediaworks/American-idol-returns-dominance-product-placement/1494191

6. Guthrie, M. (Jan. 21, 2008). Out-of-home tv: Now it's everywhere. *Broadcasting & Cable*, pp. 4–21.

7. Schneider, M. (April 12-18, 2010). Pilots depart from coasts: L.A., gotham deemed too expensive for nets. *Variety*, pp. 1–20.

8. Poniewozik, J. (December 29, 2003). Has the mainstream run dry? *Time.*

9. Bauer, D. (April 17, 2011). Broadcast tv audience aging faster than us population. Huffington Post. *www.huffingtonpost.com/2010/08/16/broadcast-tv-audience-agi_n_683009.html*

10. Klein, P. (1979). Programming. In S. Morgebstern (ed.), *Inside the TV Business*. New York: Sterling.

11. Amdur, M. (Nov.2, 2003). Case of the disappearing eyeballs: Big bucks at risk as nets suffer separation anxiety. *Variety.* variety.com/article/VR1117894931?refcatid=1275&printerfriendly=true

12. Gilbert, C. (April 21, 2011). How Democrats and Republicans use the media (very differently). *Journal Sentinel. www.jsonline.mobi/more/news/120368144.htm*

13. Romano, A. (July 22, 2002). At E!, Youth will be served. *Broadcasting & Cable*, p. 22.

14. Frank, B. (July 7, 2003), Check out why young viewers like reality programming. *Broadcasting & Cable.*

Multichannel Television Strategies

Susan Tyler Eastman and Michael O. Wirth

D o you get a lot of tweets and postcards from the company that supplies your television service? Or from the companies that don't? How many ads try to persuade you to add a zillion channels and upgrade to HD? Change to DirecTV? Switch to U-verse? Upgrade to Xfinity? Or add FiOS to your cell service? Competition among the wired and video service companies is fierce. The battle for subscribers and revenue has now moved to the mobile media, and soon will expand to potential adopters of 3D.

Multichannel Video Programming Distributors

New communications technologies and looser federal regulations created a whirlwind in the marketplace for multichannel service providers. Cable, satellite and telephone companies began blanketing homes and offices with combos of digital television, DVRs, on-demand video, voice telephony and fast (and superfast) internet connections. Cellular companies got into the game by offering 3G/4G and Wi-Fi internet connections and wireless video programming. Despite active competition, consumers' monthly bills grow steadily larger, easily to $100, $200 and, in some cases, even higher.

Cable, satellite and telephone companies are the major *broadband* carriers: They use telecommunications signals of far higher capacity than earlier in the twentieth century, thus "broader bands." Companies that provide broadband signals to deliver video programming are collectively called *Multichannel Video Programming Distributors*

(MVPDs)—or sometimes "multivideo program distributors" because the full definition is too big a mouthful. (In some jokes, they are the "most valuable program distributors.") Most MVPDs offer a mix of voice, internet and video services, so calling AT&T, for example, a "telephone company" or Comcast a "cable company" describes their history rather than their current broadband business. On the other hand, DirecTV is primarily a satellite video distribution company. For all types of MVPDs, it's *video* that accounts for the largest part of the revenue stream, but the distinction between video (or television) and internet has become largely one of hardware rather than content, and that hardware is slowly merging. *By 2015, it is expected that more than 90 percent of the country's households will subscribe to some kind of multichannel programming distributor,* some for a single service, such as internet or cable connection, but many for a large expensive "trifecta" of services. Only 1 percent of those subscribers will be dial-up households, the rest broadband. At the same time, online video distribution or "over the top video" will continue to grow with an increasing number of consumers choosing to "cut the cord" to get their TV over the internet. Current MVPD penetration is about 92 percent (see 3.1), and it should grow to over 95 percent within the next ten years thanks to a significant expansion in online video distribution. Most consumers will take a mix of services.

All three distributors, cable, satellite and telephone companies, provide wide ranges and changing lineups of digital video and audio programming. Cable and telephone companies also offer high speed internet and both wired and wireless voice services as they

3.1	MVPD Subscribership 2012		
	Subscribers	**% /116 m. USTV HH**	**%/107m. MVPD HH**
CABLE	70 million	60%	66%
SATELLITE	32 million	26%	30%
TELEPHONY	5 million	5%	5%
Non-MVPD	9 million	8%	8%

compete for customers, more or less. It's that "more or less" that makes the differences…and maybe the winners. As one Bell Atlantic (now Verizon) executive predicted, "The people who will win this game are the folks who provide depth and breadth in programming and knock-the-socks-off customer service."[1] Thus, *major players that offer the best service along with the most kinds of services—nearly all of which contain programming content of one kind or another—have the long haul advantage.* The broadband technologies that deliver multichannel media certainly give viewers more options and more flexibility, but at a high cost. And the huge expense of the complex technologies has forced many smaller companies to merge (or leave the game).

Irrespective of the kind of owner—cableop, satco, or telco (the short-hand terms for cable operator, satellite company, and telephone company)—the job of multichannel programmers is normally to *select, schedule, evaluate* and *promote* channels of television and audio programming out of the hundreds of content networks (described in Chapter 9) and to provide wired and wireless phone and internet services. However, the meaning of "select" is far different than in broadcasting as described in Chapter 2. Rather than select individual programs, MVPD programmers must choose whole channels for their lineups, depending as much or more on financial negotiations than type of content. Indeed, the biggest current battle is to determine how much money video distributors will pay the program producers and how various middlemen (banks, credit card companies, mobile phone carriers, software and hardware companies) will get their share of cell and video revenues. Moreover, the spread of HD followed by VOD and 3D has made the competitive marketplace even more complex and confusing for the programmer, the distributor and the consumer.

Video programming is predominantly a nationwide business. Nonetheless, a few *local* cable programmers remain that serve a city or limited region. These programmers' jobs focus on *producing* and then *scheduling* programs for one or more channels of local or regional cable or, more likely, web offerings, and they are discussed at the end of this chapter because they do matter to the communities they serve. But they aren't in the big game.

The Big Gamers

Three types of program retransmitters dominate the MVPD business: *terrestrial wired cable, direct satellite broadcasters,* and *terrestrial wired and wireless telephone phone systems,* although increasingly, the big cable companies offer both wired and wireless services. Collectively, the nine biggest MVPDs served more than 75 percent of the 116+ million U.S. television households in 2012, and since about 8 percent of households have no MVPD service, that leaves way less than 20 percent for all the smaller operators. In addition, foreign-managed companies of these types reach millions more subscribers around the world. (Is there any urbanite in the world under age 30 who doesn't have a cell phone?) Not surprisingly, the more than a thousand U.S. operators of these various distribution systems face common problems.

Cable Systems

The term *cable system* refers to geographically bounded and franchised wired companies using fiber optic and coaxial cable to deliver from dozens to hundreds of video and audio program channels to subscribers. Nearly all also offer broadband (high-speed) internet and wired telephone services, and the biggest cable systems also offer wireless (4G/3G/Wi-Fi) voice and video. Typically, local cable operators pick up signals from several orbiting satellites and terrestrial broadcast antennas and then redistribute them via cable wires to homes and other buildings. Subscribers pay from $40 to $150 or more per month for cable services; the total depends on the number of services taken by the consumer, how many *set-top boxes (STBs)* are being rented, whether they opt for digital video recorders (DVRs), and how many VOD movies were rented in a particular month. The most basic cable service—retransmission of local off-air local station signals and a few cable networks—may be available for as little as $30 or $40, but most households want (many would say "need") far more than

3.2	**Top Five Cable Operators, 2012**		
	Cable (millions)	**Internet (millions)**	**Phone (millions)**
Comcast	22.8	17,6	9.0
Time Warner Cable	12.4	10.0	4.5
Cox	4.9	3.9	2.5
Charter	4.5	3.3	1.8
Cablevision	3.1	2.7	2.2

3.3	**U.S. Satellite DBS Services, 2012**		
	N of sub (millions)	**% of TVHHs**	**Video Channels**
DirecTV	19.3	17	370
DISH Network	14.1	12	400

that, adding high-definition, premium, or 3D channels; DVR and STB fees; internet service; and/or both landline and cell phone service.

As the chart in 3.2 shows, Comcast (which also owns 51 percent of NBCUniversal) is the dominant force in cable television and home internet service and is third largest (after AT&T and Verizon) among providers of telephone service. Comcast, together with the other four largest multiple system operators (MSOs, the term for the companies that install the wires and manage local service in multiple franchise areas)—Time Warner Cable, Cox, Charter and Cablevision—serve about three-quarters of all cable subscribers. Comcast itself consists of hundreds of separate geographic franchises in 39 states welded into one huge operating company.

Satellite Systems

The term DBS is used only in the United States; in the rest of the world, *DTH* (direct-to-home) means all kinds of home satellite delivery services. As you probably know from frequent advertising messages, the two biggest companies providing domestic DBS service are DirecTV and DISH Network. Jointly, they have about 33 million subscribers (28 percent of multichannel households).

As 3.3 shows, by 2012 about 19 million households subscribed to DirecTV, and about 14 million subscribed to DISH, although such startups as VOOM and the Christian Sky Angel were trying

hard to bite off a tiny share of the business. The two main satcos provide service packages of between 60 and 400 channels and charge between $35 and $115 per month for their packages, while the newcomers offer only a few dozen channels, albeit at far lower monthly cost to subscribers.

If long-term success in the competition among MVPD services depends on their ability to provide consumers with all communications services—a "triple play" of video channels plus broadband internet access and telephone service—satcos are out of luck. Both big satcos supply plenty of HD (but not 3D so far), and DISH offers somewhat more channels while DirecTV offers exclusive sports packages. But neither has the ability to competitively supply high-speed internet connections or any kind of phone service unless they join forces with a terrestrial phone or cable company, which eats into profits (and is sometimes hard to explain to potential consumers). The third generation of just-launched communications satellites has far larger capacity than previous satellites Nonetheless, satcos are not likely to cost effectively compete with cableops and telcos (see 3.4), making satellite companies poor contenders for high speed internet customers except in rural places with no other options. The particular advantage of satcos is that they can bring service to the millions of households outside metropolitan areas.

Telephone Systems

The term *telephony* refers to service for both standard wired phones and wireless or cell phones. By 2012, analog voice telephone service had largely given way to a digital meld of voice and data in

3.4 Getting to Today's Satellite TV

atellite systems traditionally referred to three signal distribution methods:

(1) low-power C-band home satellite dishes (HSDs);

(2) medium-power Ku-band direct-to-home (DTH) satellite systems, such as Asia's STAR TV; and

(3) high-power Ku-band direct broadcast satellite (DBS) systems, such as DirecTV and DISH in the United States and SKY in Europe.

The oldest form of satellite program delivery, TVRO before the 1980s, required huge backyard dishes (often two or three yards in diameter) that were often banned by horrified neighborhood associations—but the business was really killed off by the scrambling of satellite signals and the FCC's requirement that home dishes be licensed (no more free out of market NFL games). Now consumers must pay for service through a cable or satellite company, and the large dishes have almost totally disappeared from urban and suburban backyards. (Only a few remain in the west and up in Alaska where signals are hard to get.)

The medium-power Ku-band DTH services lasted only a short while in America, selling off to DBS largely resulting from their smaller channel capacity and getting squeezed out of

the most desirable geosynchronous satellite slots because of aggressive bidding by DirecTV and EchoStar (DISH). The modern, high-power Ku-band satellites allow subscribers to use dish antennas of one to two feet in diameter. (The Japanese broadcast video and data using an even higher frequency band, Ka, to antennas the size of American half dollars.)

Between 2011 and 2012, a new generation of satellites was launched with ten times the capacity of earlier communications satellites. WildBlue and HughesNet, among others, offer satellite internet service with download speeds of 1.5 to 2.0 Mbps and upload speeds of 256 Kbps for a cost of around $80 per month for their fastest service offering. This is 30+ times faster than dial up, but considerably slower and more expensive than the high speed internet service offered by cableops and telcos (via FiOS and U-verse). In addition, it takes a measurable amount of time for signals to go up 22,000 miles and come back down again, which leads to noticeable delays and sluggish performance for internet users who participate in internet gaming or who watch streaming video feeds. As a result, such services are primarily aimed at rural markets that are not served by cableops and telcos.

the larger markets, and mobile service (meaning tablets or cell phones). Public and in-home Wi-Fi are other services that cableops and telcos can offer, and they have become an increasingly desired component of both television and computer access.

Counting who delivers how much of what is complicated by the two kinds of telephone service— wired and wireless. AT&T, Verizon, Qwest/Century-Tel, Comcast and thousands of small local phone companies provide wire line telephones, but the hot business is cellular service—where Verizon remains dominant because AT&T's threatened purchase of T-Mobile did not suceed.

Table 3.5 shows the percentage of subscribers with the two major kinds of service in the domestic market. AT&T and Verizon are clearly the national mega-giants, with Sprint much smaller and third in line with respect to cell phone service but Qwest/CenturyTel has 10% of landline subscribers. In

most urban areas, your local phone company has digital lines and is linked with a cellular company so that together they can provide any or all wire line phone, cell phone, and internet service (at least through DSL [digital subscriber line]). The largest phone companies also typically offer some type of multichannel video service. But the smaller companies lack the nationwide array of cell towers that AT&T and Verizon have; in spite of roaming contracts, calls just die in a lot of places outside the home area.

Verizon (FiOS) and AT&T (U-verse) have invested billions of dollars installing fiber and digital to upgrade a significant portion of their urban and business landline networks so they can offer broadband services capable of competing with those offered by cable companies. However, most rural areas continue to be served by twisted copper pairs that are inadequate for offering video or high-speed

3.5 Comparative Telephone Subscribership

	Landline Subs (% share)	Cell Subs (% share)
Sprint Nextel	0 (0%)	53 million (18%)
AT&T	39 million (45%)	101 million (34%)
Verizon	25 million (29%)	108 million (37%)
T-Mobile	0 (0%)	34 million (18%)
Qwest/CenturyTel	9 million (10%)	0.9 million (0.3%)

3.6 Wireless Cable

There is another small player in the MVPD game. Operating alongside cable companies are a few microwave distributors of video called *multichannel multipoint distribution service (MMDS)* operators, more commonly called (rather ironically) *wireless cable*. Wireless cable operators broadcast channels of local television and cable networks using microwave frequencies from an antenna located on a tower, tall building, or mountain. Homes, apartments, and hotels receive the signals by using a small microwave dish, typically about 16 to 20 inches in size. A set top converter, identical in function to a cable TV set top box (STB), has to be located near each TV receiver.

MMDS most successfully served portions of large cities where tall buildings are not too numerous to block the line-of-sight microwave signal, but their inability to simultaneously provide high speed internet connection and a large enough menu of video, coupled with signal security issues, killed them off except within apartment complexes where landlords want to provide a multichannel television service. The number of wireless cable subscribers has dropped below 100,000, which represents less than 0.1 percent of the multichannel video distribution marketplace.

Implementing another vision for using the MMDS spectrum in the late 1990s, MCI WorldCom and Sprint each purchased a significant number of MMDS operators (altogether, about 60 percent of the total MMDS licenses) with the intention of using this spectrum as the "last-mile" connection to homes for the provision of high-speed data and voice services. When sending video to cell phones and other wireless devices captured consumers' interest, the spectrum was re-deployed for wireless video and popularly named Wi-Fi.

Although still and moving video pictures are rapidly appearing on cell phones, pagers, and personal communication assistants (PCAs, formerly PDAs, such as Black-Berrys) using this MMDS spectrum, most of the material comes as short form video because of the small size of the screens. 4G smart phones (iPhones, Androids) with broadband capability have had a dramatic impact on mobile delivery of email, high speed internet, and data service.

internet connections. FiOS service is available to 16 million households in Verizon's wire line service area (i.e., it is available to about 60 percent of Verizon's potential wire line subscribers); U-verse is available to 27 million households in AT&T's wireline service area. FiOS and U-verse are only available to households actually passed by the upgraded networks. So cable companies continue to have the superior broadband network in most U.S. geographic areas.

FiOS is the only broadband network that takes fiber all the way to the home. Although this means that it can offer the fastest broadband internet service, it also means that it is the most expensive to build. U-verse is an IPTV (Internet Protocol TV) service that uses VDSL (very high bit rate digital subscriber line) to distribute signals via a significantly upgraded but less expensive network (compared to FiOS). FiOS and U-verse provide high quality, wire line competition for cable companies. However, they rarely compete with each other (because there is little overlap between the markets in which Verizon and AT&T offer wire line telephone service). FiOS has almost 4 million video/cable subscribers and about 4.5 million high speed internet subscribers. U-Verse has over 3.5 million subscribers to its video/cable and high speed internet services.

Selection Strategies

A strategy is a plan to achieve a goal, such as to win by defeating competitors. For MVPDs, the ultimate goal is to make money, of course, and generally, MVPDs make money two ways: by signing up subscribers for their various services and by selling advertising. They do best if they capture more subscribers—and hang onto them—than others in the same business. Each newer technology becomes a platform for potential profit, so corporations encompass many layers of strategies. Each small part of a system has its own goals and plans that normally have to be made to mesh with what the higher-ups want.

In the case of the highest corporate media levels, an overall strategy includes such segments as lobbying for regulatory advantages, minimizing tax ramifications, supporting research and development of new technologies, planning for growth, consolidation and mergers and so on. These strategic elements reach beyond the programming concerns of this book but may affect them. The meshing of various goals and strategies becomes more complex when many broadcast and cable networks operate under a single corporate owner, as is the situation with Comcast, Disney, Time Warner, Viacom and News Corp, who must strategize to effectively program for many of the fixed and mobile media. *Who owns a content producer and what else that corporation owns (and its overall financial condition) affects what its individual parts can do and not do.*

From the perspective of a single program network, *the goal is to make money for the parent corporation by selecting programs that attract audiences that advertisers want to reach* (usually the 18–49 age group). On the other hand, if

one channel is going after men 18–49, then other co-owned channels normally need to target other demographic groups—younger, older, women, or teens or kids, or people with a particular hobby or lifestyle interest (in cars, in cooking, in fashion or in specific sports). However, not all networks stick to a single audience all the time. The broadcast networks cast a very wide demographic net most of the time, but when the Olympics rolls around, all networks owned by whoever has the rights (for the last couple of decades, NBCUniversal) must share the huge mountain of programming and perhaps target somewhat different groups than their usual programs do.

And then there is Syfy Channel, owned by NBCUniversal. You'd think it would be full of science fiction movies and series, and it regularly carries *Star Gate Atlantis*, *Star Gate Universe*, or *Eureka* (mostly in summers) and disaster and monster films, but it also carries *WWE Smackdown*. And one night a week Syfy schedules people tiptoeing around old buildings with flashlights pretending that they see ghosts! The authors don't know who watches that.

The point is that selection of programs is as complex for cable networks as it is for broadcasters, but they are working across many channels instead of largely within a single channel (or one broadcast channel plus an online version, at any rate). At the same time, all program-related strategies have to take account of shifting seasons, program contracts and life spans, as well as the development and promotion of signature programs. Nonetheless, those content networks owned by an MVPD have even more considerations to weigh, some of which may narrow a network's choices to targeting audiences not served (at a particular day and time) by the rest of the media corporation. And they may narrow selection tactics to programs that work as well for smart phones and tablets as for larger screens. Because some MVPDs (satcos and telcos) do not own program content networks, and thus must concentrate on passing through programming owned by others, their selection strategies focus completely on negotiating pay for replay rights.

Some experts predict complete conversion to a totally on-demand video distribution system by mid-decade. Other experts predict a complete move to wireless distribution of television at some point in the future. However, several roadblocks will slow any transition. These include overlapping technical, legal, economic and marketing circumstances affecting cable, satellite and telephone delivery and reception and thus programming selection strategy. Not all factors inhibit innovation and change, however; some encourage them. *Successful programmers juggle all the variables of physical and legal limits, licensing and marketing costs, along with revenue potential, to select the best options for their coverage areas, and thus the mix of services necessarily varies somewhat from town to town and from one company's footprint to another.*

Many selection considerations relate to technology and law because the former is changing so rapidly, while legal applications and interpretations are trying to catch up. We look first at seven hot topics in media technology.

Technical Considerations

Just as one aspect of new tech becomes clear, some other development seems to undermine that understanding! But here are some tried and true elements of media technology.

1. Location and Income

Technology is not the same throughout an MVPD's territories, let alone throughout the country. Distribution and reception technology in urban areas is far advanced over rural areas, where great geographic distances and low household density make both wired and terrestrial wireless signals expensive, even impractical. The huge footprints of satellite signals better serve large rural areas.

Those who can afford to subscribe to the maximum of what's available have far more advanced and faster services. The less a household spends on tech, the slower it is likely to be. A related matter is tech dependency: Part B needs Part A in order to make Part B work. Households cannot access video on demand (VOD) without paying for an operator-supplied digital set-top box (STB). (TiVo won't work for Comcast's on-demand, for instance).

Technology is not the same from company to company. VOD comes under different names and with different characteristics. Comcast calls its service "On Demand," and if you have a Comcast digital STB, programs and movies (many free and some for a fee) are instantly available via an *On Demand* channel, and you can watch the same episodes and movies as often as you like. Some other cable companies, with less advanced tech, offer only *Pay Per View* (PPV) and charge per viewing of a rotating set of movies and specials. (Decoding and billing numbers can be supplied online or by telephone.) Satcos require subscription to their DVR service to get a much more limited form of VOD (compared to cable, FiOS and U-verse). Besides being slow (remember all those miles up and down the signals have to travel), while the files gets loaded onto your DVR's hard drive, the programs are only available for a limited time and then will be erased. If you want to watch a downloaded movie again, you need to pay again.

2. Capacity

Capacity is currently less of a problem for most MVPDs. Construction of optical fiber Hybrid Fiber/Coax (HFC) systems throughout the country in the 1990s combined with digital compression of video signals (so that more channels can be transmitted through the same amount of bandwidth) enormously increased cable's broadband carrying capacity. The end of over-the-air analog television in 2011, widespread consensus on distribution standards, and continued advances with respect to digital signal compression means wire line multichannel distributors have greatly expanded their technical capacity. Telcos can only bring competitive multichannel video services to communities where they have fiber wiring fully installed (see 3.7). However, rapid expansion of 4G/3G/Wi-Fi capacity for cell phones is occurring in high-usage urban areas, making video via smart cell phones (e.g., iPhones) and tablets (e.g., iPads) a reality.

It also takes time for companies to roll out the newest distribution technologies, and not all companies operate on the same schedule. One part of a city

3.7 The Role of Fiber Optics

Another element in the conversion to digital systems is fiber optics. Cable systems and telephone companies are evolving toward all-fiber communication networks because of their *much higher capacity* (as much as 1,000 times a comparable thickness of coaxial cable), *better picture quality* (because fewer and different types of amplifiers are required), and *greater reliability* (through redundancy because systems typically use only a portion of capacity and thus have plenty left over for backup channels).

In most systems, however, fiber installation ends at nodes that serve something between a neighborhood and a block or so of homes (fiber-to-the-node—FTTN)—because installing fiber all the way to individual homes (fiber-to-the-home—FTTH) will not be cost-effective for the foreseeable future. The cable industry believes that most services, including high-speed internet connection and VOD, can be adequately provided with FTTN, and that they can continue to increase system capacity as needed by moving the nodes closer to the "neighborhood" (i.e., having each node serve a smaller number of homes).

Users of up-to-date office campuses that are equipped with fiber all the way, however, commonly notice (and complain about) a significant lessening of speed and reliability at home—compared with their all-fiber offices,

dorms and classrooms—when part of the signal travels via ordinary telephone or cable lines. At present, FiOS offers the only complete fiber to the home (FTTH) service. If Verizon is able to identify a set of highly valued consumer services that require the additional speed achieved by taking fiber all the way to the home, it could gain it a significant advantage relative to its competitors. Failure to identify such a service will result in lower profitability relative to its competitors due to the higher costs associated with FTTH.

Although enough miles of optical fiber have been strung to reach to the sun (and probably back again), and fiber delivers data at the rate of one billion bits per second (a gigabit), fiber has been used primarily as a long-haul medium. Away from big cities, a shortage of high-speed, local-access connections between consumer residences and MVPD operators persists. As the quantity of high-speed internet connections increases, however, the number of special paid services via wire will dramatically increase, and the cost of these services may decline. Whether cable operators or telephone companies will ultimately dominate—or split—the delivery of high-speed internet service to U.S. homes has been a big question for the communications industry. At present, cable is winning with an almost 60 percent share of U.S. high speed internet subscribers compared to about 40 percent for telcos (see 3.1).

may have technologies available that other parts don't, causing negative consumer reaction (companies have to field lots of calls and say "sorry, not available in your area") and consequent political fallout.

The fundamental element in capacity is *operational bandwidth*, the width of the frequencies that signals can use. Years ago, plain-old-telephones used a mere 5 kHz of bandwidth, so high and low sounds were cut off. Cable began with MHz wires but today, the 1 GHz fiber platform is widely installed throughout urban areas. MVPDs view fiber and amplifier technology in terms of platforms, or levels of potential capability, and the 1-GHz platform has tremendous capacity. With appropriate design architecture, it can be utilized for mixes of digital signals

(video, audio, voice, data), and the number of functions it performs (and thus services it delivers) can be gradually increased over time...all the way to virtual projects and 3D. On the other hand, as new bandwidth intensive services are developed, such as holography if and when it ever becomes practical for television, the demand for spectrum will continue to expand.

3. Digitization

For cable, the high cost of upgrading systems to all-digital transmission and providing advanced set-top boxes has led the industry to utilize a *phased rollout* strategy. Cable operators seek to retain as many of their subscribers and advertisers as possible while moving step-by-step into digitization as the economic payback becomes visible. An overnight shift was impossible because it would have required all cable subscribers to have a digital set-top box for every television set in the home.

Although all broadcast stations supposedly ended analog transmission in 2011, most homes still have some analog TV receivers (with a digital conversion box). Additionally, the capital expenditure connected with the transition to digital was quite high, so MVPDs vie for high-end customers and look for services that will attract additional revenue. As the internet becomes a bigger part of the television system—and vice versa—subscriber choice will expand dramatically.

For satellite companies, digitization was never an issue. DirecTV and DISH Network launched their operations as fully digital systems, often touting the quality of their picture and sound in their marketing efforts to consumers. Although each of these DBS systems uses a different digital video compression system, both are able to deliver on their marketing promises. Satellite companies are, however, restricted by the number of transmission channels currently licensed to them by the FCC: 46+ for DirecTV and 107+ for DISH. Using present-day digital compression standards of 12 to 1, DirecTV can transmit more than 600 channels, and DISH can send around 1,300 to subscribers—far more than most cable systems offer. The extra bandwidth is used in a variety of ways including: distributing local TV signals back into local markets (i.e., local into local), for their slow internet and for delivering limited VOD services.

From the consumer's perspective, *digitization necessitates the eventual replacement of all existing television sets and usually devoting a higher proportion of discretionary income to subscriber fees*. HD and 3D are further add-ons. Because most people have several sets and won't throw out old ones that work, the industry has been forced to recognize that not all TV sets will be digital even in digital households and, moreover, that some of the remaining 8 percent of non-MVPD U.S. households will continue to depend on inexpensive down-conversion boxes for each TV set.

On the home recording front, the public's rapid adoption of digital music and DVD players killed off VCRs and videocassettes (except for the preschool children's market). About 86 percent of all households have DVD players. Although Blu-Ray won the DVD standards battle in home playback, victory came a bit late. Access to many of the same programs over the internet has slowed Blu-Ray's penetration, and creating libraries of DVDs is a practice that is likely to fade away. Consumers can load movies and TV shows at high speed on flash drives if they want portability, so the DVD becomes unnecessary. Meanwhile, Hollywood is rushing to play catch-up by digitizing its enormous libraries of old movies and television series to make them available online...once a bullet-proof digital rights management (DRM) system is fully in place.

4. High-Definition Television

Virtually all prime-time television programs and major sporting events on ABC, CBS, FOX, NBC and PBS appear in HD. Over 100 cable networks, including ESPN, CNN, TNT, A&E, USA, TLC, Comedy Central, several Discovery channels, the pay networks and most regional sports networks, as well as the largest television stations, offer much of their evening programming in HD.

Although more than 60 percent of homes have HD screens, nonetheless, three-quarters of viewing still occurs in standard definition for two main reasons. First, many consumers haven't hooked their sets up to HD signals—requiring a special HD set-top box from an MVPD for a monthly fee. Second, much TV viewing takes place on non-HD TV sets away from the main set, though such sets are slowly being replaced with HD-capable screens in homes. Moreover, older television reruns will continue to look like standard definition on any screen because of the way they were produced (the kind of cameras they were shot with).

DirecTV dishes and receivers can handle the standard compressed digital standard-definition signals (non-HD signals) and HDTV signals from satellites in both progressive format (scans like computers in 720p HD) and interlace format (scans like television

3.8   The Competing Scanning and Recording Systems

High-definition television (HDTV) contrasts with standard-definition television (SDTV) and lower-definition TV systems used in other countries. SDTV (480i) has 480 lines of resolution and uses interlace scanning. The HDTV system called 1080i has 1,080 lines of resolution and displays images using a form of interlaced scanning that first transmits all the odd lines on the TV screen and then the even lines. This system of HDTV is supported by CBS, NBC and the CW. The competing HDTV system, called 720p, offers 720 lines of resolution and displays images using progressive scanning, which means it transmits each line from top to bottom. This system provides image quality close to that of 1080i. Moreover, when transmitted at 24 frames per second instead of the usual 60 frames per second, cable operators can squeeze more

HDTV channels into their channel lineups. This system is, not surprisingly, supported by cable operators, as well as by ABC and FOX. One additional option is 480p, with 480 lines of resolution scanned one after another progressively on the screen. It allows for transmission of either multiple programs in the space of one channel or data services such as internet access. It is, quite logically, supported by Microsoft and various computer companies who use progressive scanning, and 480p is considered to be enhanced-definition television (EDTV) not HDTV. Finally, the SDTV standard in the United States is not the same as the standard in Europe and other places, just to keep things interesting. So don't buy a DVD somewhere else and expect to play it at home in the States.

in 1080i ATSC). The differences between systems are described in 3.8. Indeed, a single satellite receiver can function simultaneously as a digital television receiver for over-the-air signals and for high definition of both kinds and provide seamless switching among all channels, accompanied by Dolby Digital surround sound.

Of course, 3D is also beginning to penetrate the marketplace, with and without glasses. 3D will be a big draw for sports bars and other public places now, but 3D works best on the small hand-held or game screen at present. Without glasses, the viewer must look squarely at the screen to get the 3D effect (as on a smart phone or home game machine). In crowded informal settings such as bars, glasses are a considerable annoyance. (It is possible that the jump to holography will occur before any kind of 3D gets widely adopted.) However, as with HD, a large enough quantity of 3D games, programs and movies will have to be produced and distributed before consumers will become interested in investing in expensive 3D television sets. Creating such content will take a considerable amount of time and financial investment by the content creation and distribution industry. Additionally, the current lack of a de facto technical standard for 3D TV is also a

deterrent to marketplace penetration of 3D television sets.

5. On-Demand Television and Audio

In spite of the significant cost of doing so (cableops, satcos and telcos pay bigger rights fees for programs and movies stored in an on-demand library), cable operators have been rapidly rolling out various on-demand services because they have the potential for great profitability. Competing technologies exist, but Comcast's strong market power tends to set the standard for other cableops, as well as for telcos. In one system, content gets streamed in real-time though a set-top box or DVR; in another, content is downloaded to a computer, DVR or—for audio only—a portable media player. Internet television is a form of downloaded VOD, as is the format some airlines have adopted, called AVOD.

If the rights holders and distributors can agree on a mutually profitable fee structure, a complete shift to this form of interactive transmission by cable and telco operators is likely. In the decades ahead, many experts predict that very few *live* broadcasts will occur. Eventually, only a few networks will deliver real-time sports and breaking news; the rest of television will be on-demand programming, operating much the same whether the consumer seeks entertainment or information, and looking the same to the consumer whether the original source was once called a broadcast, cable, satellite, telephone, wireless or online network and whether the programs are watched on television, computer, smart phone or tablet screens—or no screens at all.

To imagine the near future of television, consider radio and its shift to MP3s and then internet downloads. *Ultimately, on-demand services will mean the realization of a greatly expanded channel universe by combining the vast resources of the internet with most preproduced and recorded video and audio programs and, less happily, with a large supply of commercial messages targeted to individual consumers.* The speed of this huge change, which is now in progress, depends on several things. These include the deployment of smart set-top boxes (with complex software) and the spread of greater standardization among technologies via open or flexible architectures (infrastructures that can transform any kind of signal into something the viewer can see and hear whenever they want to view it and on whatever screen on which they want to view; see 3.10 about MPEG-21). At the other end, the speed of transformation also depends on consumer willingness (that is, desire) to purchase video "by the program" in their homes.

6. Standardizing Standards

To take advantage of complex information flows and to seamlessly mix signals coming from many sources—from computer data, broadcast television, cable television, telephone, banking signals, shopping credit records, fax and so on—requires common standards—from sophisticated switching centers down to the basics of jacks and plugs—across the entire communications industry. Widespread adoption of the MPEG-2 transmission and storage formats for video and audio and MPEG-4 (the chip language for digital video compression) have been steps on the way to industry-wide standardization that apply to broadcasting, cable, satellites, telephone and the internet. Their utilization

allows program distributors—whether cable, satellite or broadcaster—to reconstitute programs and movies in viewable form on home equipment.

New and complex technical solutions are required to manage the delivery of these different content types in an integrated and harmonized way that has to be entirely transparent to the consumer of the multimedia services. Such solutions are coming but both technical and financial impediments slow the process.

Set-top converters, for example, have some downsides for subscribers. Most converters defeat the utility of the television's original remote control and interact poorly with purchased DVRs (such as TiVo), frustrating subscribers and generating complaints. Moreover, subscribers must pay monthly for *each* converter box, raising monthly bills in homes with many television sets. (The national average is three, and it is common to have as many as five or six TV sets and a mix of accompanying DVD players and DVR units.) Now that smart digital boxes have replaced analog boxes, cable programmers face difficult decisions about how to provide sophisticated capabilities without disrupting service to households with only elementary capability.

For a long time to come, there will be households (or secondary TV sets) that will need simple down-converters to take digital signals back to analog signals ($30 at the supermarket). DVRs incorporate hard drives and fancy computing functions, giving them replay, record, search and other capabilities, and they become increasingly sophisticated with each generation. *Cable operators are in a transition period, moving inexorably from limited addressability toward a totally addressable digital infrastructure* that should eventually eliminate one of DBS's current advantages over cable.

The newest intelligent boxes include a cable modem, advanced graphics, greater speed and a "triple-tuner" architecture that allow customers to simultaneously watch television, access blogs and vlogs on the internet, record several channels talk on the telephone and use their tablets to wirelessly interface with the set-top box. Rollout proceeds in fits and starts because of the increased capital investment required to deploy such smart boxes and because of the continuing development of new set-top box capabilities. Instead, set-top converters evolve and mutate, gaining abilities until they reach the full-service, intelligent two-way platform.

Once standardization of the technology is achieved—at some date in the future—such million-circuit converters (and DVRs) will probably move inside television sets, but adoption of such advanced technology will require replacement of all home electronic equipment, and thus widespread adoption will be slow in arriving. In the meantime, incorporation of high-definition signals and connections to other digital services must be worked out among industry competitors, further slowing implementation of new services. All the user interface hurdles will delay implementation of these and many additional technological advances.

7. Interactivity

It was once thought that program guides, home shopping and games would push the cable industry toward implementation of secure interactivity (two-way communication between users and cableops). Instead, *advertising has been the driving force in meshing the internet with television in home living rooms*. Advertisers want minute-by-minute access to usage patterns, and most want consumers to have the ability to click to access additional information about products that interest them, the kind of thing easy to do on a computer. Coming first to cell phones and tablets, as broadband gets to more homes, spillover into programming will occur. All kinds of programs—from education to cooking to comedies—may eventually avail themselves of the ability to ask viewers to respond in real time.

Interactivity via the internet has already revolutionized information gathering about audiences and methods of calculating audience size, and its spread to television is altering both the revenues available to cable, satellite and telephone companies and program content. For example, with some advanced interactive setups, viewers can tune in to a live sporting event, then choose their own camera angles, select the most recent statistics or purchase their favorite players' jerseys—all by clicking a remote.

Imagine watching a television show, then instantly ordering the soundtrack or a particular star's dress or sweatshirt, without even having to dig out a credit card. The charge for the item will simply appear on the monthly service bill. Viewers could also play along with a popular game show or do banking and pay bills without getting up from their living-room or office chairs—all by clicking a remote or, more likely, through use of their tablet. Although some of these functions can be done at present on a computer, all require more than merely clicking a button.

Some interactive options are already available from a number of cable and satellite operations: DISH in the United States; SKY Broadcasting in the United Kingdom; TPS and Cable Lyonnaise in France; PrimaCom in Germany; Via Digital in Spain; and Galaxy Latin America, the exclusive provider of DirecTV in Latin America. Such companies as Canoe Ventures, OpenTV, ICTV Inc. and Visible World have been working with MVPDs and programmers to expand viable business models for interactive television in the United States.

Legal Considerations

Selection strategies have a legal side, too, and we look at eight concerns here. Like all businesses, MVPDs must adhere to federal law, state law and municipal agreements, and several long-established policies promulgated by Congress, enforced by the FCC and upheld by the courts particularly affect programmers.

1. Universal Access

One congressional media policy is the goal of equality for rural and urban users. This goal has more than a century of tradition in government regulations encouraging and then demanding access to utility and telephone services for all citizens, and it drives many policy decisions regarding television and the internet. *Above all, communication technologies are viewed as essential to the proper operation of a democracy—for both their informational and their educational capacities.* Thus, *access* for all the public, irrespective of household income or geographic location, is a policy goal.

For several decades, the main method of implementing this goal was a federal mandate requiring the delivery of terrestrial radio and television broadcast signals to all homes. Historically, Congress viewed cable and satellite services as secondary to broadcast service, though the courts tended to equalize their value. Since 1996, access for all to the internet has been a goal, but implementation lags behind policy, largely because imposing regulations on the internet early in its development was widely seen as inhibiting innovation and speedy growth. Although dial-up access is now widespread in rural areas, regulators' attention has shifted to ways of encouraging affordable availability of broadband and wireless services.

An important part of that access is to AT&T's and Verizon's data networks. Although existing voice roaming rules allow local competitors to connect to other networks for out-of-area telephone calls (voice), it took a 2011 FCC decision to force the big guys to permit access for data—meaning sending pictures, doing email, searching Google and watching online video. Smart media require large amounts of bandwidth to accommodate all the things consumers want to do, and their expectations are the same whether they live in urban or rural areas. Providing consumers who live in rural areas with "adequate" access to broadband will require governmental subsidization through the generation of universal access fees along with the payment of higher monthly fees by these customers.

2. Must Carry

One of the most contentious regulatory issues of the 1990s—carrying well into the twenty-first century—is the required carriage of signals. The issue of **must carry** divides the program providers (networks) from the distributors (local cable systems, telcos and DBS companies) and even more vociferously divides local broadcasters from other multichannel video distributors.

Initially, the must-carry question was whether cable operators should be required to carry all

local broadcast television signals. Without a legal requirement forcing cable systems to carry all local broadcast stations, cable operators could have excluded some stations from easy access to cable viewers because the installation of cable connections usually means over-the-air antennas are disconnected. Cable operators could be expected to want to carry highly watched network affiliates of the major networks—but to have less desire to carry small-audience religious, foreign-language, educational, public and quasi-independent stations and shopping affiliates. Shopping channels, for example, compete for viewers with channels owned by the cable MSO or shopping channels with which the operator has a favorable financial arrangement. Any broadcaster excluded from cable systems would be greatly threatened financially because of decreased audience reach. Congress (eventually supported by the courts) decided cable "must carry all."

Next, the question shifted to whether *satellite* services, which wanted to carry the most highly valued local TV stations in each market, had to carry all *local broadcast* signals. Would DBS have to provide retransmission of all local stations (called **local-into-local service**), eating up considerable bandwidth and necessitating high scrambling costs because their footprints overlapped many markets? On the one hand, DBS providers had long sought the lifting of prohibitions *against* carrying *any* local terrestrial broadcast television stations; on the other hand, they said that being required to carry *all* local stations in order to carry *some* local stations, irrespective of content, would be difficult, very costly, and not in the public interest. Even with sufficient capacity, hypothetically satellite operators offering merely the affiliates of all nine broadcast networks plus a PBS station to all 210 markets would require the operators to catch more than 2,110 signals, scramble them, and then selectively unscramble 10 signals for each market.

It was decided that although DBS companies have the option of providing local-into-local service, they would not be required to do so. However, if they carry one local market TV station they are obligated to carry all the stations in that market. Today, DISH offers local into local service in all 210

Designated Market Areas (DMAs) and DirecTV's local-into-local service reaches more than 94 percent of U.S. television households. DBS subscribers typically pay a monthly fee to receive their local channels via DBS unless they purchase a program package that includes local channels as part of the cost of the package.

After the turn of the century, the contentious issue shifted to **digital must carry**. Although federal law required broadcast stations to shift from analog to digital signals, as long as a significant portion of the public could receive only analog signals, *broadcasters* had to (for economic as well as political reasons) distribute both kinds of signals. Most *cable* operators however, claimed that they lacked the channel capacity to provide two signals for every broadcast station (along with a wide range of both analog and digital cable networks) and that most households could only receive analog signals. At the same time, *broadcasters* argued that their enormous financial investment in digitization would be squandered unless local *cable* operators were required to carry both their analog and digital signals during the transition from analog to digital. The FCC declared that cable operators were required to carry *either* the analog *or* the digital signal, not both.

Once the conversion to all digital was accomplished, the battle shifted to **multicarriage**, or carriage of *multiple* digital (but non-HD) signals from one station as opposed to only carrying that station's high-definition signal. Congress's announced intention is to shift the country to high-definition television. Complicating the issue, the larger stations now argue that the most viable business model for many stations might be to divide a digital channel into a hybrid HD service (less than true hi-def) along with several other SDTV (standard-definition television) multicast program services, rather than fill it with only one channel of true HDTV. In essence, many broadcasters wanted to copy cable networks by becoming multichannel program suppliers and delivering multiple channels of programming (perhaps all news or local sports, all old movies or non-English programs—some hybrid HDTV and some not).

However, to date, *the FCC has ruled that a station is entitled to carriage of only one primary video programming stream under the current must-carry rules*. At the moment, carriage of secondary digital television programming depends on successful negotiations between local TV stations and MVPDs (cableops, telcos and satcos) through the retransmission consent process. At the same time, *Congress has made it very clear that it expects local TV stations to broadcast some form of HDTV, not just multiplexed SDTV*.

3. Net Neutrality

Then the whole topic of *must carry* rotated sideways to become a concern about the internet carrying (or not carrying) all content in the pipeline without favoritism or overage fees. Dubbed **net neutrality**, the fear is that internet service providers (cable companies especially) might install equipment that blocks competitors' programming, or even more likely, inhibit high-bandwidth usage by creating tiering systems or instituting overage charges. *The question to be decided is whether carriers should be prohibited from exercising data discrimination*. Some online games, for example, require huge amounts of bandwidth.

Another high-bandwidth usage group of services is **peer-to-peer communications (P2P)**. Although it originally referred to file sharing systems such as BitTorrent and Napster, the concept has been broadened to social communication among peers as in YouTube, Facebook, and social games. P2P ties up large amounts of bandwidth with services that typically don't make money for the carrier (or its parent corporation). In addition to concerns with usage based data discrimination, public interest advocates are concerned that broadband providers (cableops and telcos primarily) might favor their own content and applications (or of third parties who pay for priority) over other content and applications. Cable companies, for example, might rather consumers consumed its cable television networks than played elaborate games such as Farmville or chatted on Facebook.

The FCC established Net Neutrality Rules in late 2010. These rules: (1) require all broadband providers to publicly disclose their network management practices (transparency), (2) restrict broadband providers from blocking internet content and applications (no blocking), and (3) bar fixed (not mobile) broadband providers from engaging in unreasonable discrimination in transmitting lawful network traffic-including favoring their own content/applications or that of third parties who pay for priority over other content/applications (no unreasonable discrimination). No one is very happy.

4. Retransmission Consent

In 1992 Congress allowed local television stations to choose between being carried free of charge by cable systems or negotiating with the operators for some compensation for carrying their signals (*retransmission consent*). After some years in the courts, the law was upheld, and stations have the choice of opting for inclusion under the must-carry rules or giving permission for carriage, with the majority of stations picking the latter. In order to deliver local-into-local service, the Satellite Home Viewer Improvement Act of 1999 also required DBS companies to seek retransmission consent agreements with those television stations that chose this option over must carry, thus essentially treating all multichannel distributors alike, including telephone companies.

When the rules first went into effect, most cable MSOs refused to pay direct cash for any broadcast signal. Consequently, the broadcast networks (and other major group broadcasters) initially exchanged their owned-and-operated stations' retransmission rights for cable carriage of cable channels owned by their parent corporations, such as FX, MSNBC, Food Network and ESPN2. This worked for a while. By the turn of the century, however, Disney and FOX (along with others) were aggressively seeking leverage against such major cable operators as Cox and Time Warner. Their tactics included requesting more favorable channel placement (lower or "good" digital numbers—the easy-to-remember ones) on systems for all Disney or FOX-owned cable networks; asking MVPDs to pay relatively high monthly per-subscriber fees for carrying new cable networks owned by Disney or FOX; entering into an ad barter arrangements with cableops to get them to

"pay" indirectly for carriage of their local stations; and licensing some local news to cableops for local video-on-demand. *By contrast to the cableops, DISH, Verizon and AT&T decided in 2007 to pay direct cash for the rights to retransmit local TV stations, which rang loud warning bells of change in the industry.*

With the rise of strong competition in the MVPD marketplace among cableops, satcos and telcos, "must have" local television stations (ABC, CBS, NBC and FOX network affiliates) now have the leverage to negotiate direct cash payments from cableops (and other MVPDs) for carriage of their signals. In fact, **retransmission consent fees** are the fastest revenue growth area for big four network-affiliated television stations accounting for 12 percent or more of a many station's cash flow. Recently, some spectacular battles over retransmission consent between content owners and redistributors have flared. ABC, for example, cut its signal to Cablevision systems the day of the Academy Awards, which led to a settlement just as the Oscars aired; and Time Warner Cable and FOX settled a heated retransmission consent dispute the day before the Sugar Bowl.

Then **tablets** become the hot issue—and by extension other mobile media like smart phones. Viacom (owner of MTV and Comedy Central) and Scripps (owner of HGTV and the Food Network), supported by other content owners, demanded that *distributors* (Time Warner Cable and Cablevision) *pay a premium for streaming television channels to new media like iPads.* The cable operators in turn insisted that the right to distribute to other media was already covered by previous retransmission contracts for cable carriage.

There are *two* main concerns here: One is *who supplies the app for content channels*: Will consumers use apps arranged by their cableops, apps provided by content channels, or downloads through paid services like Netflix? Or all of the above? Having iTunes, for example, provide the app has advantages because it can log fees to an existing account, and its apps can be made to work only within the consumer's home, not as a mobile service (without extra fees). Every company in the middle of the

3.9   Mobile Wallets

Cell phones with embedded chips are set to replace credit cards and bank cards: A simple swipe, and a bill is charged or money falls from the ATM. But the same battle for pieces of fees charged for tablet apps is being fought over the cell phone among somewhat different players. The banks and big payment networks (Visa, MasterCard) want to continue to collect fees from merchants; Google and PayPal want a new system that gives them cuts as servicers like banks; and Apple and mobile carriers want to collect fees for every use of their phones. Consumer protection groups fear that any new system will cost consumers more, in part because fancy new equipment would have to be installed everywhere. Nonetheless, after a decade of debate, agreement is slowing inching forward. Isis, a joint venture by AT&T, Verizon and Discover, is experimenting with a system of mobile payment, as is Barclaycard in Britain and the United States.

3.10   MPEG-21 and the Future

One hopeful sign is the current tentative agreement on MPEG-21, a comprehensive new technical standard for multimedia on the near horizon. It speaks to the processes of exchanging, accessing and manipulating video and audio across all media—from the internet to broadcasting to wired and wireless transmissions of all kinds. It potentially divides the monetary pie for the participants in any exchange, and one of its great appeals is that it can readily exclude unpaid file sharing. Because different parties have intellectual property rights associated with multimedia content and understandably seek to acquire income from those who make use of their content, MPEG-21's appeal is that it integrates two critical technologies: one that allows consumers to search for and obtain content—either personally or through the use of intelligent agents—and another that presents content for consumption that preserves the usage rights (through payment of royalties) associated with the content. However, MPEG-21 is more a hope than a reality at present.

distribution process wants some revenue from the stream, and iTunes and Netflix naturally want healthy cuts (see 3.9).

The second main concern is *how to count audiences.* The more television viewed by consumers on iPads and other tablets, the greater the importance of counting every viewing of every program in order to sell advertising effectively. Chapter 5 outlines the measurement problems. How this will all work out and what it will cost consumers are unknowns (see 3.10).

5. Corporate Policies

In addition to legal carriage requirements enforced by the FCC, the policies of the parent corporation may impose restrictions on what a local system can and cannot carry. Some MVPDs, for example, have policies against carriage of adult programming. Moreover, parent cableops often sign agreements with program suppliers that have the net effect of compelling carriage of a particular cable network on all their systems irrespective of whether it might be the best choice for each market. A cable network naturally wants the largest possible audience and can offer discounts to a cableop to encourage wide carriage. Channels with a lot of violence and sexual material have been the biggest problems. With giant cable operators having thousands of local systems scattered across the country, standardized channel selection is unlikely to be an ideal fit for every location but it is economical for the MVPD.

6. Franchises

Historically, every cable system has had to win a *franchise* (a contract) from a local municipal government in order to operate in the local geographic area. Once cable operators receive a franchise, most are required to pay a percentage of their revenues into local government coffers. This is called the *franchise fee*, and cable subscribers see it listed on their monthly bills. Local government justifies charging operators a fee because they are making commercial use of local infrastructure (streets, trees, public rights of way) that belong to the whole community. Cable operators then list the franchise fee on the bill (typically about 5 percent of the subscriber's monthly statement) to inform cable subscribers about this so-called tax.

In addition, local franchise agreements often specify that cable operators must provide a specific number of *public, educational and government (PEG) access channels*. DBS companies also have public interest obligations amounting to 4 percent of their channel capacity. DirecTV, for example, carries C-SPAN, NASA TV, Link TV and others. The advent of Verizon's and AT&T's entrance into the multichannel television business led many states to replace local franchising with state franchising requirements for telcos in order to speed up their competitive entry into the multichannel video distribution business.

Periodic refranchising of local cable operators used to be a hurdle for each cable operator and local government every 10 years or so. Since 1992, local communities have been forbidden to grant exclusive or monopoly franchises, so telcos cannot be excluded. At the same time, local communities must legally prove that an incumbent franchisee has provided *inadequate service*—a difficult thing to demonstrate to a court's satisfaction—in order to refuse to renew an existing cable provider's franchise. When coupled with the ever-changing multichannel competitive landscape, cable operators appear to have a strong renewal expectancy with respect to refranchising, which, in theory, makes it more difficult for local authorities to negotiate for improvements. In sum, *federal regulations have generally freed MVPDs to program as they wish, with the exception of the must-carry and retransmission consent rules*. But a couple more sets of rules are relevant in some situations.

7. Syndicated Exclusivity

Another area of federal concern has to do with exclusive rights to show syndicated programs. Federal regulations now enforce the *syndicated exclusivity rule* (often called *syndex*), which requires cable operators (and now satellite and telephone program carriers too) to black out syndicated programs on *imported* signals (distant stations or satellite-delivered cable networks) in an area when any local station possesses exclusive rights to the syndicated program. For example, if both WGN, the Chicago superstation, and a local station in Indianapolis (or Kansas City, Fresno, Atlanta or wherever) happen to carry rerun episodes of *Frasier*, and IF the local station has stipulated exclusivity in its contract with the syndicator (usually for a stiff price), the superstation must be blacked out or covered up with another show in the franchise area when *Frasier* is on the local station.

Most importantly, the syndex rule also applies to sporting events carried by satellite. Because most local cable systems lack the insertion equipment to cover up one program with another, such superstations as KTLA, WPIX and WGN have tried to make themselves as "syndex proof" as possible by scheduling only original programming or paying for exclusive national rights to syndicated shows as WGN did with *American Idol Rewind* and *24*. Another example is TBS's having exclusive national rights to *The Andy Griffith Show* for many years but losing them to Viacom's TV Land when its term of license ended in the mid-1990s. DBS and telcos are also required to provide syndicated exclusivity to local TV stations. But the most valued syndicated programs are sporting events because they involve live original programming, huge audiences and big advertising revenue; in consequence, the cost for exclusive national cable or satellite rights for sports programs is usually very high.

8. Antennas

Another bone of contention has to do with regulations about antennas. The FCC's Over-the-Air Reception

Devices Rule removes the ability of local governments, property owners and covenant-controlled communities to restrict individual home-owners' ability to install outside antennas (dish or aerial) in order to receive video programming signals from television stations, wireless cable providers and satellite/telephone systems. The rule prohibits most restrictions that (a) unreasonably delay or prevent installation, (b) unreasonably increase the cost of installation, or (c) preclude reception of a signal of acceptable quality. The rule applies to subscribers who place video antennas on property they own, including condominiums and cooperatives that have an area for the subscriber's exclusive use (such as a balcony or patio) in which to install the antenna. The rule also applies to townhomes and manufactured homes, as well as to single-family homes, and in essence greatly increases the number of potential customers for wireless cable and DBS service.

Economic Considerations

By the second decade of the century, just over eleven hundred (1,162) separate cable companies operated in the United States, down slightly from a decade ago (1,191 in 2000). To reduce operating costs and increase operating efficiencies, cable companies bought, merged or swapped systems to create large *clusters* of geographically adjacent or nearby cable systems. Operating all (or most) of the systems in a local area under a single manager saves significantly in overhead and marketing costs. It has also allowed the cable industry to achieve the size required to generate the billions of dollars of cash flow required to upgrade the cable system plant in order to offer broadband, telephone service and video on demand services. *Clustering* is clearly more efficient than operating a patchwork of scattered systems in different counties and different states. Studies also show that above the 5-million-subscriber mark, significant economies of scale emerge. Because most U.S. homes can subscribe to cable if they want to, but only about half do, growth for cable companies can be achieved in only two ways: sell more varied domestic services (high speed internet service, telephone service, etc.) to existing subscribers and do a better job of acquisition marketing (taking subscribers

away from satcos and telcos and getting non-MVPD subscribers to subscribe). Nearly every aspect of the cable and satellite business involves cost expenditure as well as potential income. In deciding whether to carry a new channel, operators have to calculate whether the benefits (revenues) will outweigh the expenses. On the benefit side, revenues come mostly from monthly subscriber fees and advertising time purchases; on the outgo side, expenses include the cost of carrying and installing the program services, paying for copyrights, and paying for churn. *Understanding the basic economics of MVPD program delivery involves knowing who pays whom.*

In general, MVPDs pay to carry content. Most established cable networks require each local cable, satellite, or telephone operator to pay a monthly fee for each program service supplied, *calculated as a dollar amount per subscriber per month,* and ranging from a few cents per sub to more than $6 per sub for ESPN. A number of the more than 600 cable networks come without charge to redistributors (especially highly specialized services), and a very few actually pay the MVPDs for carriage (mostly retail or brand-new services offering short-term arrangements). In the past, Univision paid some cable operators a small amount per Spanish-surname subscriber (rates varied with the quarter of the year), but its great popularity ended the need for such payments. FOX paid cable operators for one year to add Fox Sports to their systems. Cableops now pay Univision and FOX a per-subscriber-per-month fee to distribute these networks to their subscribers.

Shopping services are a notable exception; they usually pay local cable operators a small percentage of sales as a carriage incentive and may operate as a barter network on an exchange-for-time basis, similar to the barter programs discussed in Chapter 6. A distributor such as Home Shopping Network presells most advertising spots, although a few local availabilities (*avails*) may be included as an enticement for the cable service to carry the channel. Nonetheless, most MVPDs pay out hundreds of thousands of dollars each month for the cable networks they carry.

Premium movie networks (HBO, Showtime, Starz, Cinemax and others) have a different licensing pattern: The local MVPD gets between 40 and 50 percent of the monthly fee paid by subscribers, and the remainder goes to the program network. This fee-splitting arrangement explains why MVPDs offer so many premium channels and are so anxious for their subscribers to upgrade.

One successful method of gaining shelf space for a new program service is to offer equity holdings (partnership) to MVPDs. Systems are more motivated to place an owned service advantageously on the system because they benefit from its success.

On-demand services threaten to change the game. If, eventually, all or most existing programs are constantly available, then what selection strategy can a corporation or a channel adopt? One part of current strategy is certainly for content producers to hang onto specific program rights as long as possible to force viewers to seek the most desirable shows via just one channel. Or alternatively, in the future, a corporation might create a large shared pool of VOD programs accessible from any co-owned channel—convenient for audiences but making measurement of individual program audiences very difficult. If all older programs are available constantly, then the strategy for selection clearly devolves on choosing new programs to produce, and airing them repeatedly to capture maximal viewership before releasing them into any VOD pool. At present, *program rights for streaming videos* (what VOD uses) are negotiated along with the right to air an entire channel of series or movies on an MVPD.

Still another expense comes from the rising cost of utility pole attachments. Utility pole attachment rates are regulated by the FCC for both cable and telecom services (including wired and wireless services), which pay a pole rental fee of $7 per foot per year. Cities and utilities that own the telephone poles that both cable and telecos attach to are hungry for revenue and thus are raising the rates for such attachments. This is one more pressure toward wirelessness.

1. Revenues

In general, MVPDs have two revenue streams: subscriptions and advertising. Cable ops and telcos make money by selling both subscriptions and national and local advertising, whereas satellite television companies have subscription revenues plus only national advertising.

Subscribing   The number of *new* subscribers in the United States to MVPDs has been slowly increasing for more than a decade. Consumers who want to sign up for cable or a competitor can do so as virtually all homes are "passed" by the wires or a satellite signal. Thus, the focus of the big MVPDs has been on upgrading current subs to higher levels of service. Fees for minimum service on cable have been kept low by federal mandate (that is, rates have been regulated), and basic service (the minimum level) usually includes only the local broadcast stations and local-access channels. But few people settle for just basic television service; they want broadband internet and more digital channels. So customer bills rise rapidly, keeping MVPDs profitable.

Typically, beyond the local stations' signals, additional channels are divided into tiers of programming, such as an expanded basic or "classic" tier, other digital service tiers including foreign language tiers, multiple premium movie and sports tiers, and several HD tiers and maybe 3D tiers. Acquiring HD in the home requires subscribers to rent one HD set-top box per television set, and it requires a subscriber to pay a monthly fee for HD service. Currently, major cable operators average $50 to $60 in monthly revenue from each subscribing household, and a customer's bill may easily exceed $150. MVPDs usually bundle television content with phone and internet services in "deals" with varying time limits so comparing across companies becomes tricky.

Altogether, cable holds flat at about two-thirds of multichannel households, and DBS serves almost one-third, and telco just less than a tenth. But MVPDs that provide superfast internet service are less concerned about cord-cutters than DBS because most cord cutters will be their internet subscribers anyway, and because content services on the internet are fast becoming pay services. As a result, cablecos and telcos will get their dollar share either way.

New enhanced services linked to the web are expected to be the "killer applications" of the next decade. Just as Google offers overlay of maps with other displays, so Autonomy and its competitors offer video insertion over real-life scenes. The first "wower" was a demonstration of moving images in a newspaper as one turns pages (as seen in Harry Potter movies!). Soon, a cell phone passed across store windows in a mall will overlay images of special sales or other information for prospective shoppers.

Advertising   On the positive side for cable operators, high programming costs can be offset in the case of the most popular cable networks because the local operator can sell up to two minutes of spot time per hour (*local avails*) on the most popular channels. (This advertising is in addition to the national advertising the cable content network sells.) Local advertising became a more viable source of revenue as an outcome of increased clustering of cable systems. In addition, cable systems owned by different companies can join to create large virtual geographic regions for the distribution of advertising messages. As with broadcasting, there is greater interest in purchasing ads on the most highly-rated (USA, TNT, Discovery) and tightly targeted (ESPN, MTV) cable networks. In contrast, satellite operators presently lack the ability to sell local advertising, but as spot beaming capabilities and other required technologies improve, the potential for DBS carriage of regional advertising increases.

Offering spots for local sale is a major bargaining point for cable content networks when renegotiating carriage contracts with local cable systems. For the most part, these spots are deducted from program time rather than network advertising time, so they cost the content network little. There is, of course, a practical limit to how much a program can be shortened to allow for advertising. Moreover, advertising spots that cannot be sold (such as spots in less popular programs or in lightly viewed time periods) offer little advantage to a local cable system.

2. Expenses

Carriage Fees   Cost is directly affected by whether the cable content network is advertiser-supported (most cable networks) or subscriber-supported (premium channels), whether the MVPD owns at least part of the network, and which additional incentives the network offers the operator. The cable industry has consolidated very rapidly, partly because getting larger gives definite advantages in negotiation for lower per-subscriber prices for program networks. If an MVPD controls a subscriber base of 10 million or

more homes—whether terrestrial or satellite—it has considerable leverage with program suppliers in negotiating monthly fees. As the largest operator of all, Comcast has enormous clout.

Estimates are that MVPDs collectively spend more than $35 billion on programming license fees each year, with approximately 75 percent of these payments going to advertising-supported cable networks. The fees per cable network vary from nothing to as little as a nickel per subscriber per month to about $6 per subscriber per month (see 8.11). ESPN, the most popular and most profitable of all channels, costs an average of nearly $6 per subscriber per month and requires operators to also carry ESPN2, ESPN Classic and ESPNEWS. For MVPDs, ESPN is an absolute must-have. In contrast, such smaller audience services as truTV (formerly called Court TV) charge in the neighborhood of $.35 per sub per month (which is still $35,000 a month in a midsized market with 100,000 subs). The fees paid to cable networks become a sizable monthly outlay for a system that carries 50 or more advertiser-supported networks to 10,000 or 20,000 subscribers, as the following equation shows:

$$\$.10 \times 50 \text{ services} \times 10,000 \text{ subs} = \$50,000$$

Thus $50,000 is the whopping monthly cost for just 50 networks in a tiny franchise area.

Just imagine what Comcast must pay each month for 300 content channels for 24 million subs! Even AT&T's U-verse has over 100 channels to pay for, times its subscriber list of almost 3.5 million. Moreover, network/distributor contracts sometimes specify even larger per-subscriber fees if the network is placed on an upper tier—under the assumption that fewer people will subscribe to an upper tier or package of channels. Inclusion on both regular digital and HD tiers is advantageous to content networks (and broadcast stations), so normally, MVPDs don't pay any extra fees for duplicating the same content. The fees are for *any* carriage at all (see 3.11). Such overhead costs underlie the battle over retransmission rights that is currently being fought between the owners of over-the-air television stations and MVPDs.

Compulsory Copyright   In addition to network fees, all cable and satellite systems pay *copyright royalty fees* to the Licensing Division of the U.S.

3.11 **Retrans Battles**

Programmers and cable system operators have always had a symbiotic but tense relationship. Each needs the other, but negotiations between the two over the price paid by (cable) distributors to program content suppliers has bred interesting and sometimes even headline-inducing clashes. In the 1980s, the flash-point involved popular basic channels. Cable operators beat back a proposed price hike for MTV in 1984 by launching a short-lived competitor, the Cable Music Channel. TCI, the nation's leading cable company in the 1980s, used a similar ploy to dampen a planned rate increase by ESPN. While fights over cable programming services, especially the expensive ESPN family of channels, continued into the 2000s, the focus has largely shifted to payment for local broadcast signals.

Broadcasters and the broadcasting networks historically have sought compensation for cable's use of their over-the-air programming. The Copyright Act of 1976 required cable distributors to pay a royalty for the use of distant broadcast signals (but not for local signals), and this provided some broadcasters and program producers, for the first time, with a modest income stream from cable. It wasn't until the Cable Act of 1992, however, that broadcasters were given the legal power to *withhold their local signals* if cable didn't pay. The traditionally pugnacious cable operators refused direct compensation in the first round of negotiations following the '92 Act. Cable executives

effectively declared that if people wanted local TV signals, they could buy antennas.

Ultimately, the two sides settled on a model that gave broadcasters extra channel capacity, in lieu of cash, to start new services, a reward that eventually turned out to be nearly valueless in the digital era. As those retransmission consent contracts came up for their regular three-year renewals in the late-1990s and into the 2000s, however, broadcasters became increasingly bold in their demands for payment. In what may have been a watershed showdown in late 2004, a smaller broadcasting chain, Nexstar Broadcasting Group, pulled its stations off of cable systems in four markets. Nexstar wanted direct cash payment for its channels. The cable operators said no. The blackout lasted 10 months and cost Nexstar millions. Two of the larger cable operators involved in the dispute, Cox and Cable One, eventually settled, not for cash but for guaranteed advertising purchases on the Nexstar stations. Some smaller cable operators, according to Nexstar, did finally agree to pay a modest retransmission fee.

Perhaps emboldened by Nexstar's move, in 2006 CBS president and CEO Leslie Moonves predicted his network would begin hammering out carriage fee agreements with cable operators over the coming years. Hearing this threat, in 2007 Time Warner Cable and the parent of ABC's stations (Disney Corp.) negotiated a high-profile distributor/supplier settlement. It provided a compensation

Copyright Office based on the number of distant signal over-the-air television stations they carry. DBS providers pay approximately 30 cents per subscriber per month per station to carry distant signals. (But remember that not all DBS subscribers necessarily choose to receive the distant signals being carried).

The formula for cableops and telcos is very involved. The basic approach to this requires cableops to pay 1.064 percent of each system's gross receipts for the first distant signal carried. For the second, third, and fourth distant signal they pay 0.701 percent of gross receipts and for the fifth and beyond, they pay 0.330 percent of gross receipts. On annual basis, the U.S. Copyright Office collects

compulsory copyright fees in excess of $100 million from DBS distributors and of more than $200 million from cable companies. Payment of these fees allows cable systems and DBS to carry such superstations as WGN, KTLA, WPIX, WWOR and others.

These funds are returned, proportionately in theory, to copyright holders such as the holders of rights for sporting events, music, movies, domestic and foreign television programs and so on, though there is some debate about whether sports rights holders get enough or too much from the royalty pool. From the operator's perspective, they are an additional expense. Copyright holders would like to eliminate the compulsory license for carriage of package that covered Disney's ABC-owned stations and its must-have cable channels (ESPN, ESPN 2 and the Disney Channel). The contract also guaranteed Time Warner's subsequent carriage of HD versions of the popular Disney properties. While details of such agreements are typically confidential, the package's terms were such that Time Warner could maintain it had not paid direct fees to carry the ABC stations.

That fiction eroded swiftly, however. Cable operators were, quietly, beginning to pay broadcasters for their local signals. In 2010, retransmission talks between Disney and Cablevision focused specifically on carriage fees for Disney's ABC stations. When discussions bogged down, Disney pulled WABC-TV off of Cablevision's New York area systems early on the day of ABC's scheduled coverage of the Academy Awards. It was a short-lived blackout, with carriage reinstated about 14 minutes into the awards show. Arbitration led to settlement, with trade press reports suggesting that Disney received between 25 and 50 cents per subscriber per month.

Later in 2010, Cablevision engaged News Corp. in a similar, but much more acrimonious, dispute. In October, the two companies came to loggerheads over carriage of a suite of channels that included the Fox Business channel, Nat Geo Wild, and the FOX broadcasting stations. Cablevision balked at the price asked by News Corp, and FOX pulled its signals from the Cablevision systems. The blackout

generated significant news media interest because it meant that Cablevision's New York area subscribers were deprived of FOX coverage of the start of the 2010 World Series. (Horrors!) The timing of the dispute was no coincidence, of course. The standoff lasted 14 days before millions of angry baseball fans forced a resolution just in time for Game 3 of the series. Terms, again, were not disclosed, but their nature could be divined from a Cablevision statement that declared, "Cablevision has agreed to pay Fox an unfair price for multiple channels of its programming including many in which our customers have little or no interest."

The price war between cable and the broadcast industry is likely to continue and perhaps escalate. In contrast to the 1980s, cable operators now feel like the underdogs in the battle and have asked the government to intervene. The FCC, in 2011–2012, was reviewing the rules. Meanwhile some cable operators took their cases directly to customers, informing them of the prices they now pay for off-air signals. Charter Communications and Suddenlink Communications reportedly include the new broadcast retransmission cost on subscribers' itemized bills. Charter lists the cost under "taxes and fees" as a "broadcast TV surcharge." (Of course, this is like the way cable operators tell subscribers how much of their bills get paid to their municipalities.)

Patrick Parsons, Ph.D.
The Pennsylvania State University

distant TV signals. However, so far, Congress has agreed with the MVPD industry that continuation of the compulsory licensing system is in the public interest.

Audience Churn: Another big problem is audience churn, or turnover. Subscribers who disconnect, even if they are replaced, cost the system in hookup time, administrative record changes, equipment loss and duplicated marketing effort. Annual churn rates are typically around 30 to 36 percent for basic cable and 50 to 80 percent for premium services and digital cable. For DBS providers, typical overall annual service churn is around 18 percent. The churn rate for

any local system or DBS service can be calculated for a year, or for any length of time, by dividing the number of annual disconnections by the average annual number of total subscribers; all systems keep careful track of their churn rates.

$$\frac{\text{Disconnects in a time period}}{\text{Average number of total subscribers in that period}} \times 100 = \% \text{ churn}$$

Not all cancellations can be prevented, of course, because people move, children grow up and leave home, and local economic recessions cause unemployment and cutbacks on services. College towns normally have lots of cable cancellations at the end of spring semester and lots of new connections in the fall, but *minimizing avoidable audience churn is one of the primary responsibilities that a service's programming and marketing executives share.*

Turnover on premium channels occurs more frequently than with the basic service. Instituting hefty charges for disconnecting single channels has reduced the practice of substitution, in which subscribers casually drop one premium channel to try another. Nonetheless, several premium channels such as American Movie Classics, Galavisión and Disney were forced to move from premium to basic services, and the challenges faced by other premium services have led to mergers and even occasional combined marketing efforts by such direct competitors as HBO and Showtime.

Given the easy availability of movies online and the increased ability of copyright holders to market movies directly to consumers, premium cable services will need to continuously reinvent themselves to remain economically viable in the future. HBO Go, which allows existing HBO subscribers to access and watch HBO content on mobile video devices (smart phones and tablets), represents one such attempt at reinvention. Nonetheless, unfavorable economics may eventually end stand-alone pay channels. But powerful companies survive by morphing into new entities.

Marketing Considerations

After technical, legal and economic considerations have been evaluated, the multichannel programmer still has to weigh several marketing factors in deciding whether to carry a particular network and how to position and promote it. *Cable and telco programmers seek to attract and hold both the local audience and the local advertiser; satellite programmers must seek both national advertisers and audiences.* To achieve these goals, both must *maximize new subscriptions* and *minimize disconnections.*

The nature of the local audience determines what has particular appeal. National research has established that nowadays the multichannel audience differs not at all from the over-the-air-only audience or even the online audience, but in particular markets, subscribers to a system may differ dramatically from national norms. One cable system, for example, may have more middle-aged, upscale, urban subscribers with higher-than-average incomes and deep broadband penetration, while another may have many more large families of mixed-age members, and fewer broadband subscribers. The upscale households might want documentaries, sporting events and HD, while the large families might want G- and PG-rated movies and kids programs. Foreign-language channels are highly desired in major cities, but less so in most small towns outside the Southwest.

Program services have to be chosen so that every subscriber has several channels that are especially appealing (see 3.12). In a big change from the past, the method today is to bring hundreds of tiered digital and HD channels to homes at 10 or 12 different price levels, accompanied by premium movies and pricey sports packages at the very high end (and 3D where available).

Scheduling Strategies

Up to this point, this chapter has been concerned with the technical, legal, economic and marketing factors that impact the *selection* strategies of cable and satellite programmers—in other words, how and why cable and satellite operators pick some services to carry rather than others. In addition, operators have scheduling, evaluation and promotional concerns.

Currently, cableops, satcos and telcos negotiate with a program supplier, such as a cable network or a television station, to carry its programs on a separate channel. For many years, much negotiation involved which channel number a station would get, but the 1992 Cable Act required that over-the-air stations have numbers corresponding to their over-the-air channel numbers (called *channel matching*) or be placed on a mutually-agreed-upon channel. The law never applied to DBS and never applied

3.12 The Phenomenon of Lift

Some services of particular appeal are considered to have lift in that they will attract subscriptions to higher tiers or premium services. *The major sports channels create lift on virtually all MVPD systems, and HD regional sports channels draw fans to an even higher tier.* Game channels have this impact for households with children aged 10 to 15 years. Lift generally diminishes as systems add more and more services, however, which has led to discounting and bundling of services that mix high and lesser appeal channels in upper-tier packages. Cultural channels are often marketed more for their balancing effect than for any lift they create, and similarly, public-affairs channels, classified advertising listings, and community access services are carried because they create a positive image for the MVPD even though they very rarely generate any increase in subscribers.

With the goal of gaining lift, one year HBO intensely promoted its hit series *The Sopranos* but found that its expensive marketing effort only temporarily doubled its subscribers, and that after a month, most new subs had canceled the service. A further strategy, adopted by the entire industry, has been to locate adult programming only on premium or pay-per-view tiers, which makes good economic and political sense because people who are willing to pay extra for adult fare can get it, while households that don't want adult programming to be visible need not be aware of it. Having adult fare, however, definitely provides lift.

to cable networks because they have no legally assigned numbers.

Moreover, the law never envisioned HD's rapid proliferation, so some strange temporary placements of stations occurred, but because it's sensible (and to avoid court cases or new Congressional action), over-the-air stations are getting channel matched as HD expands. For example, Comcast used 1000s as HD channel numbers, so the local broadcast Channel 6 (an ABC affiliate) on Channel 6 in basic service (which happened to be placed on 908 for a few years) now appears on 1006. Similarly, Channel 8 (a CBS affiliate) appears as 8 at the basic level (inexplicably at 912 in early HD) is now 1008 in HD. It seems likely that the 900 numbers will fade away as HD becomes widespread.

Cable systems continue to experiment with *content clustering schemes*—placing cable networks on virtual tiers according to their content or appeals (see 3.13). For example, channels can be grouped according to whether they are (1) all narrowly alike in content—such as sports channels, movie channels, or audio channels; (2) all alike in their appeal to a particular target demographic group—such as for children or Spanish-speaking viewers; or (3) typed broadly by content as in all entertainment or all news. For a time, most MVPDs tossed uniformity and moved to mixed entertainment and information tiers with something for most people and situations in each of several gradually expanding tiers (for higher and higher prices), until a subscriber got everything.

However, as part of the shift to higher and higher channel capacities (the great increase in the number of channels), Comcast has introduced a logical numbering structure in many of its systems, within its mixed tiers, that varies between content grouping and appeal groups. For example, broadcast stations hold the 1000s; news and weather channels appear in the 1100s; channels aimed at women are numbered in the 1300s; those for children in the 1500s; sports in the 1600s; movies in the 1800s; and the 1200s are "all others," meaning entertainment. This system means that adjacent channels will have similar content appeals, probably because children, news, and sports viewers tend to persist as users of the up/down arrows on remotes.

Interestingly, 3D channels are merely assigned content-related numbers like other HD, although premium HD movies (1900s), pay-per-view (1700s), non-HD sports packages (500s) continue to stand apart and can usually be added separately if a subscriber wants them. Clearly, Comcast shares the view that all subscribers will eventually become HD subs.

U-verse consists of about 100 channels, all HD, and they are grouped much like Comcast's, into all children's, all news and information, all premium (movies), all sports, and the catchall of "variety." Other cablecos, satcos and telcos utilize similar schemes to assign networks to their systems.

Wired and wireless systems have long employed three kinds of virtual lineups in their interactive electronic guides: Listings by day and time, the alphabetic listing of service names, and thematic clustering. Time listing is useful for finding what's on now or soon; alphabetic listing makes the search for a particular channel or program quick; clustering suits channel-by-channel selection within the grouping. None especially suits grazing. There are just too many channels.

One strategy that facilitates jumping is incorporation of social media into the program selection process. For example, a brief on-screen message might say "Others who selected this program also watched..." Alternatively, the names of the channels or programs that "friends" are watching might be highlighted (via interconnection with Facebook, Twitter, and the like).

At some point in the all-high-definition future, operators are expected to transition totally to menu- or topic-driven systems. Menu systems make channel numbers (and therefore lineup concepts) nearly irrelevant. Just as all channels coming through a VCR used to be converted to Channel 3 on the TV set, so in the future digital television sets might have only a single "channel" and receive all input from a converter (built into television sets), leading to the disappearance of the very idea of *channels*. Nonetheless, it is hard to conceive of a time when all set owners will want to subscribe to all services for all sets. For the purposes of pricing, some subdivisions will be needed.

Eventually, viewers are expected to have individual web search agents capable of "knowing" our individual likes and dislikes. The size and distribution of channel arrays then become irrelevant because search agents can jump around at lightning speed. Clustering would remain only as an aspect of

3.13 Uniform Lineups

Even within a single Nielsen DMA (see Chapter 5), having the most popular advertising-supported services on the same channel numbers on all cable systems makes selling advertising easier. Standardization within a market is called a **common channel lineup** to distinguish it from the ideal of consistent positions for services from market to market across the country (called a **universal channel lineup**). Nationwide standardization of channel positions has the particular advantage of making national on-air promotion more effective.

The goal of any kind of uniform channel lineup—local or national even for the dozen most popular services—is a long way from realization. The Los Angeles DMA was the first major market in which several cable operators agreed on a common channel array (in analog), and in the late 1980s newly constructed systems (new-builds) in Philadelphia and New York adopted uniform analog channel configurations. Those patterns seem to be surviving into the digital and then HD eras. The pattern adopted in Los Angeles, however, did not match the one adopted in New York.

Moreover, technical considerations limit the realization of such plans in many markets that have long-established systems. MVPDs are in varying stages of technical expansion into *virtual channels* (assigned numbers for users that have nothing to do with actual distribution frequencies). And users differ on their needs. Those who utilize "appointment viewing" and want to go straight to a particular show are unlikely to care about logical channel arrangements, and people who use onscreen guides find channel numbers irrelevant—although standardization among menus and search systems is another as yet unrealized goal. Annoyingly, how it all works differs from house to house and differs from hotel to hotel. But for those like children who use the remote's arrows, content adjacency is ideal. Uniformity makes sense for some viewers but is especially useful for effective promotion by networks and stations and, even more important, for lowering the cost of advertising.

guide listings, providing a way to scan options onscreen, should a viewer actually care to look with his or her own eyes.

Evaluation Strategies

Multichannel services have two evaluation concerns: evaluation of audience size and measurement of program popularity. These result in very different practices, and some are unique to cable because wireless and satellite systems do not carry local advertising.

Audience Size

Evaluation of MVPD audiences has been a long-time problem. *The overriding difficulty is that the audience shares for cable network channels cannot be exactly compared with over-the-air audience shares.* Although nowadays multichannel distributors collectively reach about 90 percent of the homes reached by broadcast television, each individual channel attracts only a portion of the people watching via cable, wireless, telephone or DBS (and not all cable networks appear on all or even most services).

Usually, cable network ratings range from 1 to 4 percent of total TV households in prime time rather than the 7 to 8 percent that the top local broadcast affiliate achieves. Looked at nationally, a top network TV show, such as *American Idol* or an *NCIS* season premiere might get a rating of 12 or 13, while a top hit on cable rates in the 4s and 5s (although NFL games often reach 8s and 9s on cable). During the height of interest in huge news events like the Egyptian and Libyan uprisings and Japan's earthquake and tsunami in 2011, CNN's and Fox News's ratings reached very high levels (such as 12s and 14s). Sporadic season-opening or ending episodes of cable dramas (such as *The Closer*) rise into the teens. The only cable networks to do consistently better is ESPN, and it fails to reach the level of top local affiliates most of the time.

However, without disasters or extraordinary events, these and other popular cable networks usually attract fewer than 2 percent of viewers individually. Nonetheless, the collective cable ratings in a market (for all the dozens of networks) often exceed those for the highest-rated station.

Advertisers had little interest in the small numbers of per-channel viewers (which are even smaller when the DBS and telco audiences are removed) until the cable industry came up with four strategies for increasing the number of people reached simultaneously and for making them more salable to national or regional advertisers.

The first strategy has to do with geographic coverage in portions of a state. Because the geographic area covered by an individual cable franchise is far smaller than the coverage areas of a single broadcast station, the cable industry now links franchises over a wide area (like the center of a state) by microwave or cable to create large interconnects. *Advertising interconnects* are arrangements for the simultaneous showing of commercials on selected channels. Of course, each operator must purchase expensive insertion equipment for each channel that will have local advertising added. (The ads usually cover up promotional spots sent by the networks, and how many and which ones can be covered by local spots are specified in cable network contracts with local cable operators.) Interconnects generally occur in or near large markets, however, leaving thousands of cable systems with unsalable (too small and undefined) audiences. Moreover, satellite services cannot be part of local interconnects. Their subscribers add to the national ratings but not to audiences for local or regional advertising.

A related strategy is *zoning*, which refers to subdividing an interconnect into tiny geographic areas to deliver geographically targeted advertising, which permits even small local businesses to purchase low-cost ads that reach only their neighborhoods. A dry cleaner, for example, hardly wants to pay to reach the other side of town where the competition operates—but might find two or three zones on its side of town ideal for reaching potential customers.

A third strategy is *roadblocking*—scheduling the same ad on all cable channels at the same time so that the advertiser's message blankets the time period. This can be done nationally by buying the same minutes of time on all major cable networks, or handled locally in one market by inserting the same ad simultaneously on all channels in an inter-connect. Then, no matter where a remote user looks on the lineup, the same commercial spot seems to be playing. (Some big advertisers buy all the broadcast networks also, thus airing a single ad virtually everywhere on television in the whole country at the same time.)

A fourth strategy has been to develop criteria other than ratings for wooing advertisers. Sales executives for the cable networks generally emphasize the *homogeneity of viewers* of a particular channel, meaning their demographic (age, gender) and psychographic (lifestyle, income) similarities. Viewers of MTV, for example, are alike in age and interests; weekday viewers of Lifetime are mostly women; viewers of the HGTV share a common interest in homes, furniture and gardens. The clustering of similar channels on digital services also makes it possible for an advertiser to roadblock a group of channels with homogeneous viewers.

Repetition and Ratings

On the programming side, *program repetition* is another strategy used to increase audience size. Sales executives for cable television report how many people saw a program *in all its airings,* rather than how many saw it on, say, Tuesday night at 9 P.M., the usual way that broadcast ratings used to be calculated (though they are wising up as their shows are viewed on laptops and tablets). *For cable, the size of the cumulative audience is often more salable than the audience for a single time period.* Reporting *cumulative audience size* makes programs seem more popular and more visible, thus better environments for advertising messages.

Promotion Strategies

Effective promotion of MVPD systems took a back-seat to technical problems for several decades. Once America was close to fully wired, cable systems began to pay more attention to marketing their services. Cableops used such traditional advertising tools as flyers on doorknobs and ads in local

newspapers to attract new subscribers. However, because money was tight as a result of huge capital expenditures and because cableops faced no multi-channel competition, most cable companies' marketing efforts were minimal at best for more than a decade. After the turn of the century, increased competition from satcos and telcos, coupled with the profits to be made from upgrades to internet and voice services, drove an explosion in competitive promotion.

Early on, competition from satellite services raised the bar for cable, and then telcos joined the battle for subscribers. To capture them from conventional cable, DBS and telco services designed clever marketing tools that carefully targeted specific groups of potential subscribers. No longer was one ad good enough to reach everybody. As thousands of its subscribers left cable for satellite service and later for telco service, the cable industry woke up and began spending the money to make more effective advertising tools. Mailers and TV and online ads touting the advantages of signing up for FiOS or U-verse or xfinity can't be avoided these days.

Another way to bolster (or retain) subscriptions is to promote exceptional program content and unusual program channels. When MVPD programmers are deciding which networks to carry, they consider how much promotional support a particular content network provides. On-air promotion as well as print advertising and merchandising has three advantages: It's valuable for boosting ratings for new programs, reducing subscriber churn, and creating positive images in the minds of subscribers and advertisers. National networks can supply professional-quality consumer marketing and sales materials, including on-air spots, information kits, direct mailers, bill stuffers, program guides and other materials that local systems lack the resources to create. In other words, some fees paid to national cable program suppliers are, in effect, returned in the form of advertising avails, co-op advertising funds and prepaid ads in publications such as *People* magazine that attract audiences to cable network programming (and thus to upgrade to more tiers of service).

Nowadays, cable, telco and DBS operators make use of both online promotion and on-air video insertions to get their messages across. Major content suppliers also maintain elaborate websites about key programs, another factor in subscriber retention. While use of print advertising in magazines and newspapers has declined, cable operators employ interconnects to run self-promotion on a variety of channels. They use spots that might otherwise have been sold, foregoing that revenue, to tout what the subscriber misses by not having HD service, what's available on VOD and premium HD channels, and how much more X service offers than Y or Z.

In the long run, having large numbers of subscribers who subscribe to high levels of service can be expected to bring in more revenue than the cost of the promotional spots and print ads to lure them to upgrade. Even more important is that such promotional spending has become critical to maintaining market share in the increasingly competitive multichannel video marketplace.

Local Origination on Cable

At the local level, cable programming means several very different things, with no equivalent on the part of satcos and telecos. On one hand, local cable refers to the programming activities of the 7,400 or so managers of cable systems or their MSOs. They may produce their own local/regional channels of information or entertainment, such as an all-day newscast or a high-school sports channel. On the other hand, broadcasters also make use of some cable-only channels to replay or multiplex additional channels of programming. Finally, local cable also refers to the programming activities of several thousand not-for-profit community access groups or centers. Theirs is the most local of all cable programming and has flourished in some cities for nearly four decades, although the internet is rapidly altering this kind of local cable programming.

Local cable channels consist primarily of entertainment mixed with infomercials, classified advertising channels, sports, and news and community affairs. When produced and controlled by the cable operator or a contractor, such channels are called local-origination (LO) channels, although the news channels tend to cover such wide areas that they are often referred to as regional cable. When produced and controlled by a local not-for-profit group, such channels are called community access. Local and regional cable-only channels have the long-term benefit of differentiating cable from competing wireless and DBS services and, in some cases, the short-term benefit of generating advertising revenue.

Entertainment Channels

Channels with original entertainment content produced (or purchased) by cable operators themselves are universally commercial and intended to supplement a system's profits. The programming is selected, scheduled and evaluated for its suitability for carrying advertising messages. Religious broadcasters (really, cablecasters) operate about one-third of local cable channels, and they typically mix syndicated programs with local and nationally distributed religious programming, including gospel music, discussions of gospels, sermons and religiously oriented talk, some of which are merely slightly disguised sales messages. In addition, a few foreign-language cable channels have a full spectrum of news, entertainment and talk in one non-English language. Many of these channels have dropped their over-the-air channels in favor of becoming digital-only splinter networks with national distribution.

The remaining local-origination channels around the country tend to operate as regional news channels or are programmed like independent television stations. When entertainment oriented, they can carry nationally syndicated series or movies—very old ones because the programs are licensed cheaply as a result of the relatively small cable audiences (compared with the audiences of broadcast stations or even cable networks). Such programs may be chosen and scheduled locally but, like syndicated programs on broadcast stations, are not very local. Toledo, Ohio, for example, has a popular LO channel called Toledo 5 or WTO5

3.14 Toledo's Local-Origination Channel

Because Toledo has only five local broadcast stations, TV5 was able to become the WB affiliate (now CW) for Toledo and to license a great deal of "good" unsold syndication. Now called Toledo 5 or WTO5, this local-origination channel carries off-network reruns, such as *Two and a Half Men*, *The New Adventures of Old Christine*, *Family Guy*, *The Cosby Show*, and *Friends* and first run syndicated programs such as *The Wendy Williams Show*, *The Tyra Show*, *Tyler Perry's Meet the Browns* and *George Lopez*.

Because the local newspaper (*The Toledo Blade*) owns the local cable company (Buckeye Cablevision) that owns Toledo 5/WTO5, the channel receives the enormous benefit of a listing at the top of the newspaper's grid, right under the local broadcast stations, instead of burial in the Ws where *TV Guide* places it (and similar channels).

The "station" has its own website (www.wt05toledo.com) and operates with a great deal more funding than the usual local-origination channel. The combination of having a national affiliation, only a few local broadcast stations in the market, supportive ownership by the local newspaper and carriage on Buckeye, Time Warner Cable and Comcast cable systems in Northwest Ohio and Southeast Michigan places Toledo 5/WTO5 in the forefront of successful local-origination channels that compete directly with broadcast stations.

that is remarkable for its off network and first run syndicated series (see 3.14).

On other LO channels, high school and minor league sports are especially effective for attracting audiences of considerable appeal to local advertisers. Local talk programs also provide an ideal environment for both local and national infomercials. Major national companies such as Sears, Verizon, Ford, General Motors and Procter & Gamble supply the bulk of direct-sell infomercials to cable systems, and these are supplemented by shorter infomercials from nearby car dealers restaurants, pharmacies, home builders and the like. Hyperlocal infomercials may be produced in the cable system's facilities (for a fee).

Classified advertising channels, often produced by local newspapers, have been another somewhat successful area for local cable, especially when operated in conjunction with a daily paper. Digital insertion equipment permits the quick updating of listings and the use of photographs (and some video), making local real estate, car, and other classified ads as well as Yellow Pages viable as auxiliary revenue streams for cable. Because the internet provides much the same opportunity for reaching out to viewers, however, religious broadcasters, retail companies and newspapers are generally operating websites with the same content they put on local

cable channels and are increasingly favoring the web over cable.

Local-Origination News Programming

News is a powerful environment for advertising messages and thus popular with many commercial entities that want to reach news consumers and make money. Having hyperlocal services helps systems attract and retain subscribers and keeps them in the good graces of local franchising authorities that grant them their licenses.

One strategy has been to replay broadcast newscasts on cable channels. Pittsburgh Cable News Channel (PCNC), for example, began in 1994 as a retransmission consent channel. (Federal law requires local television stations to give permission to cable systems for carriage of their signals and allows them to negotiate a fee or other compensation from cable operators in exchange for rebroadcasting their signal.) Many stations exacted cable channels of their own in lieu of monetary payment.

Most of these are solely rebroadcast channels, but a joint effort of WPXI-TV (Channel 11) and cable operator Tele-Communications, Inc. (now Comcast) created the Pittsburgh Cable News Channel that now carries live WPXI newscasts at 7 A.M. and 7 P.M. and multiple repeats of WPXI's latest newscast along with local talk and information shows (*www.wpxi.com/pcnc*). The pricing of ads on PCNC is comparable to that of local ad inserts on CNN and Headline News, and cable systems carrying the channel receive two minutes of ad time per hour. All other advertising revenue is split between WPXI and Comcast.

Modeled on CNN and its repeating counterpart, Headline News, a number of cable-only local and regional cable news channels (see 3.15) have been formed, some of which attract considerable industry attention. Although they require significant capital investments (in some cases, many millions of dollars) in equipment, crew, reporters and studios to get going and have high daily operating costs, their revenue potential is usually much greater than for entertainment channels because they attract more regular viewing. What the services share is their focus on smaller geographic areas from the "region" down to the neighborhood. Traffic reports are often street by street, weather reports describe in detail what is important in small geographic areas, and "news" moves down to the level of parades, store openings, and official city activities. This kind of information also transfers very effectively to online services integrally connected with these cable channels.

Local and regional cable-only news services differ from ratings-driven broadcast stations. The latter normally divide their newscasts into half-hour segments, devoting airtime to sensational crimes, fires and accidents, and also include nonlocal stories if they are likely to hold audience interest. On broadcast stations, local events get only a few minutes at most, and events likely to be of interest to only a few viewers are scrapped.

In contrast, hyperlocal cable-only news channels that operate live for several hours daily—increasingly 24 hours as they become established and profitable—can focus on neighborhood events on the scene and at length if they might be of interest to a few viewers. Most model themselves on CNN rather than the broadcast network newscasts and carry hours of live programming, although New York 1 News has been very successful using a half-hour news wheel (see 3.15). With the luxury of more time to dwell on events, regional and local networks

can spend hours on breaking events and enough time on stories about health, sports and entertainment events to avoid the taint of sensationalism.

Cable news producers' success with audiences and owners comes from an intense focus on local interests and, especially in times of stress, lots of ongoing weather and traffic reports. The details emphasizing the problems important to neighborhood residents and businesses appeal to viewers and advertisers, and the very low cost of such reportage appeals to cable operators.

In line with keeping expenses minimal, these regional/local channels take advantage of the newest robotic cameras and other automation, which may result in some odd pictures at times but reduces (compared with broadcast newsrooms) the technical staff necessary for them to function. The reporters tend to be young and inexperienced, are often interns or employees working for nonunion salaries, and carry their own handheld video cameras with portable video recorders, eliminating still other staff costs. By using portable tripods, reporters can even tape themselves at the scene of events and in interviews. As one reporter for New York 1 News put it, "I do a story every day. I dream it up. I set it up. I produce it. I report it, and I even edit it. I get to do everything."[2] The backpack video journalist who functions as correspondent, reporter, camera operator and producer has become the model for inexpensive news gathering.

Although financial support must initially come from a parent corporation with deep pockets and patience, major national advertisers have become increasingly interested in cable-only news and its online counterparts. Local and regional cable news channels can attract advertising from businesses too small to be able to pay broadcast station rates. Rates on New England Cable News are about $500 for a 30-second spot, compared with the $3,000 or so on a Boston network affiliate. Although such cable channels typically average less than a 1 rating for 24 hours, local disasters drive up ratings dramatically. For example, New York 1 News had ratings of about 6 for its live coverage of a winter snowstorm.

Local and regional cable news channels also have highly interactive internet sites to further enhance their viewers'/users' ability to selectively choose

The first and best known of the regional all-news ventures on cable continues to be **News 12 Networks**, which includes seven regional cable news channels in the New York area. Launched in 1986 by Cablevision as News 12 Long Island, News 12 Networks is a division of Rainbow Media, the programming arm of Cablevision Systems Corp. News 12 Networks offers 24-hour local news service in Long Island, Connecticut, New Jersey, Westchester, the Bronx, Hudson Valley, and Brooklyn (see *www.news12.com*). News 12 Networks reach 3.8 million cable households in the New York tristate area.

Each service supplies news about the local region to residents, beginning each morning with a radio-style mix of news, weather and hyperlocal traffic reports (for example, live from key points on the Long Island Expressway on News 12 Long Island). Then the service continues at a slower pace throughout the day with reports on local community events, live interviews, local news updates, and reprises of national and international news. Stories include everything from school parades to unsolved murders to reports on issues like garbage dumping and pollution. With a staff of 150, facilities rivaling those of nearby broadcast stations, and an annual budget of more than $10 million, News 12 Long Island, the flagship service, attracts enough advertising revenue to make a profit. Interestingly, its highest viewing comes in prime time.

Time Warner Cable established **New York 1 News** (NY1) in 1992 as a 24-hour news channel. NY1 and its 50 full-time news reporters and anchors serve New York City's five boroughs from an all-digital (and almost tapeless) facility. NY1 also provides NY1 Noticias, a 24-hour Spanish-language news channel launched in 2003, NY1 Rail and Road, a 24-hour cable news channel focused on the vehicular traffic and mass transit conditions in New York's five boroughs and a corresponding website, *www.ny1.com*, to complete its thorough approach to news coverage. NY1's

use of comprehensively trained journalists—who report, videotape, and edit their own stories—and broadcasts that are structured in half-hour programming wheels has become a global model for inexpensive news coverage. In addition to advertising, it attracts revenue by charging for consulting about low-budget news.

Northwest Cable News (NWCN), now owned by Belo Corporation, came on the scene in 1995 when KING Broadcasting (that is, KING-TV in Seattle, KREM-TV in Spokane, KGW-TV in Portland, and KTVB-TV in Boise) used its retransmission consent leverage to gain shelf space on cable systems in Washington, Oregon and Idaho to establish a 24-hour regional cable news channel. NWCN provides news programming, which is targeted to the geographic area it covers. As a result, NWCN achieves higher ratings than CNN Headline News, and it is available to a approximately 2.9 million viewers (see *www.nwcn.com*).

The **Texas Cable News** (TXCN) was established in 1999 as Belo's fourth regional cable news effort. Although some regional news channels choose to cover a metro area or even a limited part of a metro area, TXCN followed the design of NWCN by opting for coverage of vast regions (that is, the entire state of Texas) that include multiple metro markets. In 2000, Texas Cable News established *TXCN.com* as its online presence. TXCN has a staff of 30 (reduced from 75 in 2005) devoted to administration, operations and sales. It has no reporters of its own. Its newscasts depend entirely on contributions from its television and newspaper partners, *The Dallas Morning News* (owned by A.H. Belo Corp) and WFAA-TV8 in Dallas, KHOU-TV in Houston, KENS-TV in San Antonio, KVUE-TV in Austin, and the company's Washington, DC, news bureau (all owned by Belo Corp). TXCN is available to cable subscribers on 13 Texas cable systems, 10 of which are owned by Time Warner Cable (see *www.txcn.com*).

among news stories and to have news on demand. As a result, the same news information appears simultaneously on a cable channel and online. This serves to broaden the audience and is a key factor in establishing a successful media convergence strategy for local and regional cable news channels. In the long term, regional/local cable distribution may take over the role that local broadcast stations have

In Washington, DC, **NewsChannel 8** (NC8), owned by Allbritton Communications, was founded in 1991. NC8 is a 24-hour news channel available to approximately 1.1 million Washington, DC, metro-area cable subscribers. It uses a fiber-optic delivery system to deliver targeted local news (on a nightly basis with separate anchors and producers) and advertising (on a 24-hour basis) to suburban Maryland, Northern Virginia and the District of Columbia. NC8 operates three local news bureaus from which it originates live coverage (see *www.tbd.com/tv*).

The **Comcast Network** (formerly CN8) employs more than 400 people, and is a 24-hour regional cable news, talk, sports, and entertainment network owned and operated by Comcast. The Comcast Network was launched as CN8 launched in 1996 and is available to millions of cable homes in its Mid-Atlantic service area (Pennsylvania, New Jersey, Washington, DC, Maryland, Virginia and Delaware). Its programming is primarily locally produced regional news, entertainment and sports (high school, college and professional), with 90 hours per week of original programming including some live, interactive and on demand programming (see *www.csnphilly.com/pages/comcastnetwork* and *www.csnwashington.com/pages/comcastnetworkshow*).

NBCUniversal owns **New England Cable News** (NECN) is a 24-hour regional cable news network, which was launched in 1992 by Hearst and Comcast. NECN provides news, weather, entertainment, and sports to 3.7 million homes in a large number of New England communities. It has won many awards, including a George Foster Peabody Award, an Alfred I. duPont/Columbia University Broadcast Journalism Award, and a National Edward R. Murrow Award. In addition to its standard programming, NECN also regularly produces documentaries focused on issues of importance to New Englanders (see *www.necn.com*).

Begun in 1993, Tribune Company owned **Chicagoland Television** (CLTV) is a 24-hour regional cable news

channel that serves 1.8 million Chicago area cable households. CLTV shares content and staff with WGN-TV and the *Chicago Tribune*. Both the newspaper and CLTV are specifically oriented toward the suburban Chicago audience. One goal of the cable channel is to promote the value and expertise of the newspaper reporters, which should, in turn, improve newspaper circulation (see *www.cltv.com*).

Central Florida News 13 (CFN 13) is Orlando's only 24-hour local news channel serving the central Florida region. Started in 1997 and originally owned by Orlando Sentinel Communications (that is, the Tribune Company) and Time Warner Communications, Bright House Networks (formerly called Advance/Newhouse Communications) now owns CFN 13. CFN 13 is affiliated with CNN and provides local and regional news, weather, traffic, and sports programming (see *www.cfn13.com*).

The Dispatch Broadcast Group (which includes WBNS-TV, WBNS-AM/FM, and *The Columbus Dispatch* in Columbus, Ohio) launched **Ohio News Network** (ONN) in 1996, becoming the first state-wide 24-hour cable news channel in the country. ONN can be seen in more than 1.8 million Ohio cable households in such cities as Cleveland, Columbus, Cincinnati, Dayton and Toledo. ONN specializes in providing highly localized news, weather, and sports along with a regionalized approach to state-wide news coverage. It utilizes partnerships with a number of over-the-air television stations (including WBNS in Columbus, Youngstown, WEWS in Cleveland, WHIO in Dayton, WKRC in Cincinnaiti, WTOL in Toledo, etc. to rebroadcast local news programs and to share ONN stories with these stations (see *www.onntv.com*). For further information on local and regional cable news channels, visit *www.newschannels.org*, the website of the Association of Regional News Channels, and *http://en.wikipedia.org/wiki/Category:24-hour_television_news_channels_in_the_United_States*.

traditionally played because cable does not use scarce airwaves (although the broadcasters are likely to step in as owners and producers of content). Wired cable distribution, in turn, may soon be supplanted by wireless web services, which may be at least partially

responsible for the demise of some of the regional/local cable news channels that have shut down over the past decade. For example, Orange County Newschannel ended in 2002; the Florida News Channel failed in 2003; News 24 Houston died in 2004, as well as News 9 San Antonio in 2004; Southern Arizona News Network ended in 2010; and Local News on Cable or LNC5 died in 2010.

Community Access on Cable

In dramatic contrast to commercial cable, the access channels operated by community groups are noncommercial and driven by educational, artistic and public service goals. They tend to operate on the neighborhood and city level, rarely reaching outside county boundaries. Federal law permits local and state franchising authorities to require cable systems to provide channel space and sometimes financial support for community access services.

Although by law these services divide into three kinds—public, educational and government (PEG) channels—in practice, they usually operate out of *community access centers*. Such centers are noncommercial and local not just in practice but also in active philosophy, and they provide alternative programming that would never be viable on for-profit stations or local-origination cable channels. The mainstays of access content have been community-produced videos, video art, municipal meetings and hearings, and educational productions. Like commercial companies, they are finding the internet increasingly effective for reaching their audiences, and they face the same problem of having to fund the shift from analog to digital including HD.

Traditionally, *access* has meant two things to local-access centers: (1) access by community members to the means of television production through training classes, arrangements for loans of TV cameras, and the sharing of editing equipment; and (2) access by community members to an audience through the cablecasting of locally produced programs. The underlying principles guiding the staffs of access centers are the ideas of free speech for everyone, the egalitarian use of the media, the fostering and sharing of artistic expression, the accessibility of all people to affordable education and instruction, and open and participatory government decision making.

The internet is proving an even more effective vehicle for achieving these goals than cable, however,

and, with the drop in price and increased sophistication of video equipment, fewer members of the public are seeking the video training that access centers can provide, and their training equipment has largely become obsolete. Thus, the centers focus increasingly on digitizing their facilities to aid in the convergence of video and computer input and output.

A few access programs have moved up to wider distribution, and the flamboyant Bobby Flay, host of several shows on The Food Network, got his start on access television. The best of public access television get Philo Awards (the name comes from television inventor Philo T. Farnsworth), and the worst are played at the Found Footage Festival for comic effect. In the early 1990s, the hilarious "Wayne's World" spoofs about access television as part of *Saturday Night Live* helped raise awareness of public access television on the national level, for better or worse!

Changing Usage

The more than 1,000 access centers in America come in a bewildering variety of organizational setups, and many are finding common bonds with farseeing public libraries. As the repositories of printed books and periodicals move into DVDs, CDs and computer storage of ideas, their noncommercial, anticensorship, free-speech and open-access goals come to merge into those of community access television centers.

Many access centers, including one of the oldest in America—Bloomington's Community Access Television Service (CATS)—have located themselves within a community public library and receive financial support from the city, county, library (a taxing authority in Indiana) and cable operator. This particular center operates five PEG channels: a city government channel, a county government one (mostly meetings and some interviews); an educational channel called The Library Channel; a traditional public access channel where community members supply the content; and a SCOLA channel (news from other countries in their native languages).

In many other communities, once-separate local arts centers and local television centers have come together to become community media centers and are evolving into community communications centers. They can involve institutional networks, local libraries, health centers and schools, connecting them to each other, to community agencies, and to the internet, all of which have become central to their future survival. It is not the particular technology (television, books or computers) that ultimately matters but serving the mission in the community— the mission of public access to the means of communication.

Many of the community members who were once clamoring to gain local-access time to televise their home videos or local performances, however, can now exhibit continuously on personal websites, bypassing one of the motivators for public cable access. One striking aspect of the internet has been the rapid shift of art video and low-budget movies from cable access to the web. Video artists now fill multiple websites with original film shorts, and the internet provides places for the videos of birthday parties and church fairs as well as the more serious animation and dramatic films that once characterized local public access cable.

Educators, another group that formerly sought large numbers of cable access channels, have also turned increasingly to websites to provide interaction with students and parents. Homework instructions can go online; email allows personal messages from teachers to students or parents; and the cost of such sites is far less than for effective cable production. Religious groups that also clamored for more time on local-access channels now, on the internet, have more freedom to program as they wish. Nonetheless, church groups that wish to reach older, downscale constituents who tend to avoid computers still seek a significant portion of time on access television, creating problems for some managers as they see other kinds of traditional access fare fading in quantity.

In many well-wired communities, local governments are also finding websites effective for some of the kinds of information they produce. Long lists of community events, community service agencies and government office phone numbers suit menu-driven websites better than television channels. Users can access the websites at their convenience and select only the material of particular interest, unlike cable

channels that unfold programs over time. Live carriage of public meetings of municipal government, local school districts, environmental protection committees, councils, planning approval commissions, and live carriage of other ad hoc meetings on community issues continue to be carried on cable system local-access channels. However, the increased penetration and quality of high speed internet service has greatly increased the amount of online video streaming of public meetings of all types.

Nonlocal Programming

Although it was once thought that all access channels would carry only locally produced programs, some regional and national sources are now available to supplement what can be made locally. In addition to public broadcasting, noncommercial services such as SCOLA provide unedited segments of broadcast news from other countries in their original languages. Especially popular in university towns and cities with large foreign-born populations, SCOLA offers, over the course of a week, news, weather and cultural information from such varied sources as France, Spain, Germany, Poland, Hungary, Italy, Korea, Greece, China, Croatia, Slovenia, Lithuania, Latvia, Macedonia, the Netherlands, Moldova, the Ukraine, the Philippines and other countries.

The oldest distributor of access programming has been the Deep Dish TV Network, available to community access centers via satellite and now the internet. (The name *Deep Dish* refers to parabolic receivers as well as apple and pizza pie!) A not-for-profit program distributor, it is supported by donations and grants, as are Free Speech TV and Democracy Now! Independent and community producers create the highly diverse programs and largely political documentaries or analyses these satellite services circulate on such topics as housing, the environment, civil liberties, racism, sexism, AIDS, the Middle East and Central America.

Deep Dish identifies itself as "the first national grassroots satellite network" and quotes author Studs Terkel: "The idea of a democracy in this country is based on an informed citizenry, an intelligent citizenry—and you can't be intelligent without being informed."[3] These services appear unscrambled on commercial satellite transponders; the programs are carried by 200 or so cable systems, some public television, and radio stations (including NPR), and on the internet, and come directly to backyard dishes (HSD).

What's Sneaking Up

On-demand programming coupled with delivery of TV Everywhere represents the leading-edge of services for MVPDs. It has long been considered the cable industry's "holy grail." However, only recently has on-demand's cost fallen sufficiently to move it into commercial market rollout. Likewise, recent advances in wireless (4G/3G/Wi-Fi, tablets and smart phones) have made TV Everywhere both economically and technologically possible. More than half of MVPD subscribers have access to on-demand video programming and the rapid increase in wireless access devices and penetration of user interfaces between wireless and wire line networks is promising to make TV Everywhere a reality.

Existing challenges for VOD include: figuring out a way to get subscribers used to purchasing on a per-program rather than on a per-channel or per-package basis, negotiating low enough rights fees with Hollywood to make VOD profitable, and continuing to negotiate an earlier window for releasing movies to increase VOD value proposition for consumers (see Chapter 9). TV Everywhere challenges include investing the capital needed to provide consumers with the required technology so that subscribers can consume video content when (anytime), where (in the home or away from home), and how (on a TV, tablet, smart phone or laptop) they want to receive it. In addition to the technical challenges, MVPD distributors and programmers will also need to overcome the intellectual property rights associated with TV Everywhere.

The advertising industry's concern about DVRs has led to elaborate tracking of viewer patterns to learn how common commercial skipping continues to be and what factors minimize it. As DVRs proliferate (now approaching 50 percent penetration in

U.S. homes), advertisers will need to develop new strategies for getting their products out and messages heard. Product placement within television programs is one such strategy, and such marketing tricks as discounts, coupons and other kinds of fee reductions for watching commercial messages have also surfaced. In addition, some advertiser supported programmers have begun to require that fast-forward DVR functionality be disabled as a condition for providing programs on demand. How far this will go and how the public will adapt is unknown.

Cable, telco and satellite distributors moved rapidly into the HD service business and look ahead to 3D. In the short run, as HD set penetration continues to increase (over 60 percent of U.S. homes have at least one HD set), upper tier HD service offerings from MVPDs can be expected to generate significant revenue. However, once the transition to digital is complete, separate non-HD service tiers are likely to fade away, and all television will be HD (unless it's 3D or holography or something new we haven't yet heard of).

Although cable was long the clear market leader in the area of high-speed internet service, telcos are catching up where FiOS and U-verse are available to consumers. The question now is how much longer Verizon and AT&T will continue to supply the internet and wire line telephone service components of DBS's triple play packages. Cable telephony service has been growing rapidly thanks to the wide availability of VoIP (Voice of Internet Protocol) telephone service offerings by cableops. Today, cable has approximately 25 million VoIP telephone subscribers. Of course, telcos have responded with appealing packages of television, internet and voice telephone to counteract cable's move into telephony. Now that AT&T and Verizon have made the major capital investment required to build competitive broadband networks (FiOS and U-verse) to compete with cable in significant parts of their coverage areas, it will be very interesting to watch as things develop.

On the reception end, consumers await widespread distribution of truly intelligent converters incorporated into new television sets and computers, and user interfaces that provide seamless connectivity between wireless and wire line devices. Consumers also await improvements in interactive program guides and search approaches to allow them to personalize program viewing and searching. As the number of channels and programs proliferate, consumers need more efficient methods of identifying content (i.e., entertainment programs, news stories, etc.) they would like to consume. Great advances are on the immediate horizon in this area as MVPDs and other distributors develop much simpler and more intuitive ways for consumers to identify programs to watch. This includes incorporating such social media as Facebook and online connections like Amazon.com to get like-minded consumers to "share" what they like and don't like as part of the search process.

Sometime further in the future, it is envisioned that mass guides will evolve into personal search engines that utilize virtual agents that can be programmed by the user or that can learn on their own to make selections for individual users, from the huge sea of available entertainment, news and commercial content. An agent programmed for each individual will notify him or her about specific video content, blogs, vlogs and RSS postings based on previously expressed preferences or current wants and desires. The process of reprogramming an agent (by voice or perhaps merely by what is frequently chosen or requested) will eventually become transparent to users, and over time, increasingly sophisticated agent programs may become the equivalent of the semisentient computers in science fiction. Agents will eventually mutate into avatars (virtual selves) with virtual bodies that can interact with other avatars on the internet, far beyond the cartoon representations that exist today.

As broadband speeds become faster and faster and screens on handheld devices become bigger and brighter and keyboards become virtual, watching video content on tablets, smart phones and laptops will continue to improve as will user interfaces between wireless and wire line distribution devices. Nonetheless, history will repeat itself: Mobile media will supplement—not supplant—traditional media. Consumers will still want large TV screens in their homes (and public places) and desktop computers in their workplaces. However, 4G and Wi-Fi will have a dramatic impact on consumers, and the world will be a different place when most people can access the internet—for video, audio or text—whenever they want to and wherever they are.

Notes

1. Kenneth Van Meter, president of Bell Atlantic Video Services' interactive multimedia platform division, speaking before Kagan Services' Interactive Multimedia Forum, 18 August 1994, New York.

2. Seligmann, J, Covering the neighborhood. *Newsweek*, 13 December 1993, p. 6.

3. From the brochure cover for Deep Dish TV Network in New York, 2000.

Online Television Strategies

Douglas A. Ferguson

When you watch YouTube or Netflix, happily, you needn't follow a pre-structured schedule of programs, and you needn't watch on the largest available screen to see what's going on. Any handy screen will do. When you go online to watch a clip or show you missed on TV, you'll probably find links on the screen to other shows and clips that you might like. Just like in traditional television, the companies that supply online content have strategies to keep you coming back for more (and staying longer to watch the ads or pay a subscription). Online television strategies address the growing number of *unstructured* program options available on various screens viewed by the media audience. This chapter explores those online programming strategies, for web programs, social media and video games.

The New Programs

In a programming book, one expects to learn what online "programs" are, but their definition continues to be fuzzy and evolving. As in all media, entertainment and information are the major content types, but in the online world, they come in innumerable permutations, so it's more useful to distinguish among *web programs, enhancing information* and *interactive games* as the key kinds of online program content.

Just as in conventional television and radio, most online entertainment content is storytelling, and telling stories—real or fictional, in video or in games—is the primary task of what are collectively called **web programs**. Thus, on the internet, the term includes short and long video programs akin to television series, specials, documentaries, theatrical and made-for-TV movies, web-only newscasts and hosted entertainment/talk shows. Web programs fall into two distinct categories. First are the *repurposed* showings of traditional television programs, such as reruns of *The Daily Show* or *NCIS* via Netflix or Hulu and *NBC Nightly News* on MSNBC.com. The second type consists of *original* content produced specifically for online distribution, such as clips on YouTube or Revver. By 2012, Americans were streaming over 15 billion videos per month (see 4.1).

At the same time, promotional information associated with regular television programs (called **enhancement**) appears on websites supplied by any and all broadcast and cable networks, every Hollywood studio, most stations, most music producers and other key groups in the entertainment industry. Everyone wants you to watch what they provided. At the same time, those self-contained computer/phone options called *apps* (for applications, in case you've been trapped in a cave) provide program guides, live chat and other interactive functions that "enhance" the viewing experience. As you know from experience as well as the news, social media apps allow viewers in different locations watch television together as if they were in the same room, commenting on content and receiving enhanced information.

The third principal category of online media consists of **interactive games**. Certainly, its game function is one of the internet's unique aspects, and people can play solitaire or puzzles by themselves or interact with others at distant locations (sometimes with guns!) in elaborate video games. Notably, most video games involve entertainment and storytelling, just like traditional television, but with this added dimension of interactivity. You get to participate in the action, sometimes along with friends and strangers (until you get virtually killed, of course, or all your crops die).

Although the internet certainly contains mountains of "information," much of it is either related to retail sales and other businesses or consists of reference material (current and archived data) or personal/political content (such as individual websites and chat on a wealth of topics), and is thus outside the parameters of this book. *This chapter focuses on online content that is similar or at least related to what appears on television.*

Competition

Of the three types of online content, it is *web programs* that offer the most direct competition to traditional media (although electronic games pretty much wiped out the board game industry, at least for those old enough to read). But the online

4.1 Streaming and Capping

Streaming is the digital distribution of audio or video in near-real time, the closest thing to conventional over-the-air or cable/satellite television programs. *Streaming differs from broadcasting because the viewer receives a single transmission not intended to be seen at the same time that other viewers watch.* Just like with a television set, anyone with a computer and a connection to the internet can receive streamed pictures and sound, and the faster the connection, the better those pictures are. *The number of web users who are willing to watch streamed video grows as connection speeds increase.* Competition between cable modems and DSL to get you as a customer, like the competition between cable and satellite, has stabilized (but not yet driven down) the cost of broadband connections.

The introduction of unlimited data plans for internet and cell phone providers was a huge selling point when companies were first building a base of wired and wireless subscribers. But as more people began downloading more and more video programming, it became clear that a few people were hogging the bandwidth. So internet providers quietly introduced plans to cap, or limit, the amount of information that could be downloaded in a billing period, usually 250 gigabytes. The situation was analogous to banning really big eaters from the unlimited buffet line.

Because downloading was never a huge activity, except for a few, the introduction of data caps generated very little controversy. *But streaming is a different matter. Like downloading, streaming exhausts huge amounts of digital bandwidth. Unlike downloading a movie late at night, however, streaming takes place during peak hours.* While wireline providers like cable and telcos can expand their capacity to meet the demand, wireless was hitting the limits of peak-hour bandwidth as early as 2011. It makes sense (to some) to either throttle back activity or erect a monthly cap. Of course, if you have become accustomed to an unlimited data plan on your cell phone, you would see it differently. Suddenly the buffet line has become a menu of a la carte items, or you can only go through the line once, perhaps with a slightly smaller tray.

availability of streamed TV shows and movies certainly caused the greatest disruption to "the way things have been done." You can see this in the name that the television industry gave to streaming videos: *over-the-top (OTT) services.* Pricewaterhouse-Cooper (PwC) forecasts 9 million OTT viewers by 2015.[1] PwC also forecasts that the money consumers will pay for online video subscriptions (along with what distributors will pay to air the programs) will rise to $99 billion by mid-decade. Moreover, and perhaps even more disruptive to current economics, parts of the internet are now being distributed directly to portable devices (cell phones and tablets)—the so-called third screens (TV sets and computer monitors are the first and second screens). Viewers can go online at their offices or fire up their tablets at the beach to watch television, and sometimes they opt to watch conventional program channels unconventionally (see 4.2). Clearly, the typical settings for enjoying video entertainment have now moved well beyond the home.

Thus, online or on tablets, if they want to, viewers can watch repurposed content from regular television channels (via Netflix and Hulu Plus, for example). They can also watch made-for-web content from program producers who don't use traditional distribution channels (producers of YouTube clips, for example), creating industry competition between traditional and online television in these two categories. However, for viewers who "cut the cord" from cable and satellite providers, web programs are all in the same category (see 4.3).

Wi-Fi's Role

How many toys do you have? Are they separate or linked? In the last decade, an explosion of home networking has occurred in which household electronics devices, such as computers, TV sets, stereos, phones and video games, are interconnected around the entire house *without the need for wiring.* Operating on the Wi-Fi standard allows users to transmit

4.2 TV Anywhere and Everywhere

Thanks to online video, nowadays you can watch traditional TV almost anywhere. One way is to purchase a Slingbox. Hook your home cable or satellite to the Slingbox, and then tune in all of your channels with a broadband connection from any remote location. Copyright isn't a problem because you are already paying your multichannel provider for the right to watch. You are merely extending the reach of the cable coming into your home. With a Slingbox, you can extend that reach nearly around the world.

Cable operators' response to Slingbox was to come up with their own devices and "TV Everywhere" offerings. Thanks to tablets like the iPad and apps like that for Comcast's Xfinity, subscribers can watch television virtually anywhere. Over-the-top service is sometimes described by the "four anys": Viewers can watch *anything, anywhere, anytime, on any device*. A viewer connected to the web can watch on their second and third screens (desktop computers and mobile devices) what they pay to watch for on their first screen (television set).

Even without adding equipment, you can still watch regular channels (besides clips on websites) with services like FilmOn or ivi TV). Subscribers to these services get access to hundreds of worldwide TV and radio channels through their computers. Add a device such as Apple TV, and you can even transmit the video programs to your television set. (Does that feel like going around in a circle?) FilmOn is a subscription service, charging $10 per month to receive live programming, while subscribers to ivi TV only pay $4.99 for a comparable service (but FilmOn does offer a very brief trial service for free).

Handheld audio and video players also supplement media content received by cell phones. Apple's iPod Touch and iPad are the most common of the portable media players, and they are capable of storing (or streaming) hours of video, which can be displayed on a small (iPod Touch) or larger (iPad) screen. Unlike most cell phones, these devices can connect to Wi-Fi transmitters in the home or in some public spaces. Despite concerns that most people would not choose to watch a small screen, media analysts have observed that viewers seem willing to adapt to the largest or smallest screen that suits their situation at a particular moment. In other words, if 3.5-inch screens are all people have when riding on subways, then they'll use them until they get home to their beloved 42-inch HD display.

Of course, most viewers still prefer their video to appear on their home television receivers, and the bigger the better. Microsoft's Xbox 360 was the first device to offer PC-to-TV downloads, and other companies (Nintendo Wii and Sony Playstation) soon followed. Even without additional hardware, media companies have begun to anticipate the viewers' desire to watch online video on TV sets. Several manufacturers now offer HDTVs that have their own wireless connections, thus allowing viewers to bring internet video to their main TV sets (meaning that no computer needs to be in the same room as the TV set). A fifth of all new sets shipped in 2010 had such built-in connectivity.

streams of data (from computer keyboards, graphic cameras, photo printers and home video cameras) within a small geographic radius via radio waves. The central unit is typically a desktop computer with immense storage capacity that acts as a server for the rest of the home. The computer links to any number of cable boxes, alarm systems, stereo audio systems, video game consoles, video displays and who knows what that hasn't been invented yet.

Typically, Wi-Fi internet content comes to portable laptops anywhere in the house or yard. Also it can bring internet video to the main (biggest) television set, a device that has enjoyed a privileged location in the home for the past 60 years but where computers do not normally reside. The "smart" home imagined decades ago by futurists is finally beginning to emerge, and this includes new video and online abilities for those ubiquitous cell phones. But using Wi-Fi in homes has proved more technically problematic than envisioned because older equipment balks, and so it has rolled out slowly in homes.

Outside the home, connecting to the web is a simple matter of visiting a store or restaurant with

The term *cord cutters* applies to former cable/satellite subscribers who have "cut the cord" to save money by getting their movies and videos from Netflix, YouTube and Hulu Plus. Still, traditional television has a big advantage over video streaming: It can deliver HDTV-quality pictures, while video streaming via the internet remains comparatively limited in picture quality.

As you can imagine, the prospect of losing monthly cable subscribers to streaming video has worried some traditional suppliers and distributors of television shows. But other programmers are counting on the relative convenience of cable and satellite technology to save their businesses. Most homes are already wired to traditional sources, and current subscribers easily understand how to select programs from a cornucopia of options. Streaming video sometimes requires new devices and works best with home Wi-Fi networks. Meanwhile, major cable operators such as Comcast maximize their "TV everywhere and anywhere" options and promote a general shift to HD to stem the tide of competition from streaming competitors.

a free Wi-Fi zone. Travelers expect their hotel rooms to offer Wi-Fi networks; libraries and schools typically feature Wi-Fi capabilities. Some cities have public Wi-Fi, and many federal legislators consider free public access a right rather than a privilege, like public drinking fountains and restrooms. In addition, you can buy a monthly "Wi-Fi Anywhere" service so you aren't limited to public connections and can link in wherever signals reach.

Evolution, Not Revolution

A good guess is that consumer habits will evolve slowly as younger viewers grow older and older viewers learn new tricks. In many households, the price difference between full-cable service and web programs, however, may influence a cost-based switching decision, somewhat akin to the way cell phones convinced some households to cancel their landline phone service (while many younger people now never consider landlines at all). The broadcast networks and their allied production studios will also benefit from streaming video, because networks can spread their risk among additional distribution windows when they can repurpose programs to subscription services. The fly in the honey is who gets the money. A merging of interests will occur IF, and it's a big if, and when equitable splits of rights and royalties can be agreed to by dozens of parties. Economics will always be the driving force.

Web Program Providers

It won't come as a surprise that repurposed content on the web primarily takes the form of television shows and movies. As of 2012, the major providers of repurposed shows were Netflix, Hulu Plus, Apple iTunes and Amazon Instant Video. A second category of web content is original programming, for which YouTube and its close competitors are best known. Recent off-network and off-cable repurposed programs are sometimes free and thus supported by ads, as on Hulu, but the major online providers rely heavily on paid subscriptions. Original made-for-online content, on the other hand, is almost always free and supported by advertising. *Pretty much, you get what you pay for.*

Movies Plus

Netflix evolved from a distribution channel for rented DVDs through the mail to the largest supplier of program-length streaming videos. It streams professionally-produced content live over the internet rather than downloaded as a single file. Monthly subscribers with a broadband connection can watch Netflix through their computers, game consoles, smartphones, iPad-like tablets or web-enabled television receivers. The company still rents out movies, but in 2011 it began competing with the major television networks, producing original video content as well as continuing to stream older shows and movies.

Netflix was the first major supplier of professionally-produced content. For $7.99 (plus an additional $7.99 if you also want the option of DVD delivery to your mailbox), you can watch an online library of popular television shows and Hollywood movies. Its subscriber lists had grown to over 25 million by 2011, two-thirds of whom used the streaming-only option (before the price increase from $9.99 for both options to $15.98). Netflix online apparently made a sizable dent in the sale of DVDs, which declined a whopping 20 percent between 2010 and 2011.

Series Plus

Hulu was originally designed as a free website to stream content produced by regular television networks, plus a few original series. While CBS remains a holdout, NBC, ABC, FOX and many large producers like Viacom participate in streaming recently-shown programs on Hulu with few commercial interruptions. (CBS.com and CWTV.com provide network shows for online viewing of CBS and the CW networks, respectively.)

The catch is that each video is preceded by a *pre-roll*, which is a commercial that must be played (not on FF) before the selected clip begins to roll. Interestingly, 1 in 6 viewers abandon viewing a video clip during a pre-roll, but many viewers have begun showing greater acceptance of the tactic. After the pre-roll, viewers have the option of watching the remaining commercials sprinkled throughout the program, as is the practice on broadcast television, or see all the advertising at once in one very long commercial break. Initially, the number of commercials within programs was a fraction of those carried by over-the-air stations, which attracted many viewers to Hulu, but as advertisers got more comfortable with online video advertising, the commercial breaks became longer and longer.

As this chapter goes to press, Hulu is for sale. Netflix was not a bidder, but other interested companies include Google, Yahoo, Amazon.com, Microsoft and DirecTV. Hulu has no subscribers, per se, but it reaches over 30 million unique visitors each month.

Hulu Plus evolved as a subscription website that provided the same content as Hulu (with fewer commercials) but expanded its menu to include entire seasons of popular programs shown on regular television, sometimes offering multiple seasons of especially hot series. For example, Hulu Plus has all the *Saturday Night Live* programs dating back to 1975, hundreds of hours' worth. As with Netflix, Hulu Plus also streams theatrical movie releases from selected studios such as Miramax Films. The cost per month is $7.99, the same as Netflix. Hulu Plus focuses on well-known television series, but also features some original made-for-web content (especially during the summer months when regular network television is on hiatus). As of 2011, Hulu Plus had 875,000 subscribers.

Apple iTunes is another source of videos, typically downloaded rather than streamed. Although iTunes is best known for 99-cent music downloads, Apple sells individual video programs for $1.99, and because of its instantly recognized name, grabbed a steady group of customers. Customers using iCloud as virtual (online) storage for their music can also store videos, but the sheer size of video files may soon require a streaming solution instead of downloading, especially if portable devices are tied to offline storage ("the cloud"). The number of users is 50 million, although many download music instead of videos. The library of titles is estimated as 3,000 television shows and 2,500 movies.

Powerhouse **Amazon Instant Video** offers movies and TV shows for $1.99, similar to Netflix and iTunes. Its special deal is that members of Amazon Prime (a subscription service offering free two-day shipping for books and merchandise) receive unlimited, commercial-free, instant streaming of 5,000 movies and TV shows at no additional cost. Amazon Prime runs just $79 per year, which is less expensive than paying $7.99 to Netflix or Hulu Plus for 12 months. Despite its later start, experts predict that Amazon will eventually surpass giant Netflix, despite the latter service having become the largest single source of internet traffic in North America by May 2011.[2] And it might not take Amazon very long to do that, but no subscriber count is presently available.

Facebook, Google+ and other social media offer videos, too, but their presence on comScore's ratings lists is secondary to their primary mission of getting users to chat (and play games). Facebook is being used by Hulu to engage viewers by letting them post Facebook messages to friends while watching from the Hulu website. For example, a viewer on Hulu can make a comment during a video that appears on Facebook noting the exact running time within the show that the post was written. Facebook has 600 million unique monthly visitors worldwide, although Hulu is not available in every country.

Upstarts (Big and Small Ones)

Another mega-giant has joined the game: Wal-Mart started its own online video service called **Vudu** to compete with Netflix, but it uses the *pay-per-download* model. Vudu charges $1.99 per episode for network shows, also putting it into competition with iTunes. Some of the series presently offered by Vudu include *Glee, Modern Family, Weeds* and *Bones*. Vudu did 750,000 movie transactions in the last quarter of 2010, well behind Apple iTunes but even with Amazon.

On the smaller side, it's not clear what other services might try to capture viewers of specific genres, in effect, stealing them from Netflix and Hulu Plus. **Crackle** is an upstart provider of television shows (it has a handful of *Seinfeld* episodes) and somewhat-recent movies, and touts its free slate of programs, but it's too soon to know if Crackle will be able to gain sufficient advertising support to compete. Crackle has about 3 million unique monthly users.

Instead of a grab bag of programs, some web programmers choose a particular genre, such as humor, and focus on accumulating programs in that genre. For example, you might have tried **The CollegeHumor Network** or **Funnyordie**, which carry original videos made especially for online viewing. **AOL Media Network** (which delivers a variety of online videos to AOL subscribers, reaching 42 million users each month), **Vevo** (which specializes in online music videos, reaching 60 million unique monthly users), and **Megavideo** (which imitates YouTube) are other minor contenders offering

original videos, but the crop of competitors is so young that predictions are hard to make (see 4.5). Even YouTube (best known for free user-generated content) now offers an online rental service for a small number of Hollywood films.

A service that caters to cell phone users, **MobiTV**, offers its ten million subscribers more than 25 channels of streamed live television that show up as large as the phone screen. These include programs from the broadcast networks and such cable nets such MSNBC, CNBC, Discovery and the Learning Channel, along with originals from several web-only networks. For $9.99 per month (with no extra charge for cellular airtime), MobiTV offers its service via all major cell carriers. Not to be outdone, **Sprint TV** and Verizon Wireless' **VCAST** both offer their own mobile TV and music plans. Tablet-size portable devices like the iPad are making mobile viewing even more popular. What is clear is that lots of companies can see big dollar signs in the download and streaming video business.

Original Content Suppliers

Overshadowing most of the online world is the marvel of YouTube. Now a subsidiary of Google, it has been by far the most popular streaming site. Tens of millions of users upload and share videos among groups of people or openly for everyone online. Most of its content is user-generated content (UGC) along with some copyrighted materials uploaded by users (see 4.4). It is usually accessed via computers, but some material is available for television screens and some smart phones. About 500 million unique visitors worldwide watch YouTube each month.

YouTube soon proliferated into dozens of YouTube channels (similar to TV channels) and has become *web-based video-on-demand*: what people want and when they want it, in almost real time. People upload movie clips, TV clips and music videos, as well as amateur videos and video blogging and watch without needing to pay for any of it or even register (except for "mature" material so as to show they are old enough). As of 2011, YouTube reported that it was serving more than three billion videos a day, a staggering amount. Interestingly,

4.4 The YouTube Phenomenon

In 2007 Viacom started an uproar by demanding that more than 100,000 video clips, originally produced by MTV, Comedy Central or Nickelodeon, be removed from the YouTube site. The same month the BBC demanded that 100,000 clips from its own shows be removed. In both cases, YouTube leapt to comply. Meanwhile, the Japanese Society for Rights of Authors, Composers, and Publishers demanded that thousands of its producers' videos be removed, and NBC and CBS both filed complaints about their material appearing. Amusingly, Iran banned the site as "culturally undermining." The U.S. government also got in the act when it objected to rebuttals of the "public service" announcements they were uploading. After discovering fight and gang attack videos on YouTube, ITV in the UK claimed it was encouraging violence and bullying.

Of course, these attack videos have since become big hits on news services, which shake their collective heads in disgust even as they run the cuts for the hundredth time. Given such complaints, you might think that the existing media would keep its distance from this web upstart. You might also assume YouTube was on the verge of failure. You would be entirely wrong in both cases.

YouTube was founded in 2005 by three former PayPal employees using $3.5 million dollars in venture funding. In 2006, YouTube was named *Time* magazine's Invention of the Year and sold to Google for $1.65 billion. Worldwide, the public, to whom the service is free, consumes more than 2 billion videos a day. Members of the public can upload whatever they want so long as it meets the 15-minute time limit (although there are special categories without time constraints, but which require high-quality, original production).

By making it free, YouTube succeeded in avoiding the problems that had plagued Napster. While it hasn't ruled on the web as such, the Supreme Court has traditionally said members of the public can do whatever they want with materials sent into their homes or which they have purchased, so long as no money changes hands. YouTube gets its revenue from super-imposed ads and from an innovation: Commercial customers can also upload videos, but for a price. Even as Viacom was demanding removal, it was buying in. NBC negotiated its own

channel, and Time Warner touts YouTube as a great outlet for its music videos. The big entertainment companies don't hate YouTube; they just would like to control it. This is very lucrative action. Indeed, most of the material they demanded be removed is back on—just with official sanction.

YouTube is without doubt one of the great success stories of the web. It has exhibited immense flexibility by adding new channels, special groupings of videos, and even special categories (such as for comedians and amateur producers). The NHL even agreed to provide brief highlights of hockey games to the online service. In fact, many YouTube producers and entertainers have developed their own followings, becoming stars in their own right with their works featured on late-night broadcast television shows. Although critics once claimed that YouTube would find it impossibly expensive to maintain the required bandwidth and storage capacity, they have suddenly grown quiet. The public has welcomed the ability to participate in this one area of video freedom, and revenue from advertisers provides sufficient support.

While there are certainly many competitors who would like to see it fail, it was probably already too late after its first two years of operation. The public embraced this new outlet with amazing speed. Even as Brazilian model Daniela Cicarelli was demanding YouTube be shut down until all copies of an unauthorized video (of her having sex with her boyfriend on a Spanish beach) be removed, the video had already spread through hundreds of other websites. While YouTube makes no provision for downloading, the needed software can be found in a few minutes of surfing the web.

As Sean McManus, president of CBS News and Sports, noted: "Our inclination now is, the more exposure we get from clips ... the better it is for CBS News and the CBS television network; so in retrospect we probably should have embraced the exposure, and embraced the attention it was bringing CBS, instead of being parochial and saying 'let's pull it down'."[3]

William J. Adams, Ph.D.
Kansas State University

about three-quarters of the material comes from outside the United States, as does much of the viewing. But even more overwhelming is the fact that 150 million people view some of those videos every month.

Reaching into the once-sacrosanct sports world, to mixed horror and delight, YouTube has also begun to free streaming of live cricket matches and then NBA and NHL games. Currently, it is supported by advertising, but YouTube may develop a pay-per-month subscription service as Hulu did with Hulu Plus. Currently, YouTube lets members "subscribe for free" to one another's channels.

Dailymotion is a French-owned competitor to YouTube, with 93 million unique monthly visitors. It is the world's second largest video site. Dailymotion is more likely to include mature-themed videos, but otherwise is quite similar to YouTube.

Blip.tv is also similar to YouTube, but emphasizes web program series rather than standalone videos. Sometimes referred to as a "Hulu for original web series," Blip.tv provides more tools for creating and promoting content than YouTube, and offers a way for small-scale providers to make money from each viewing (sharing a portion of the revenue with Blip.tv, of course). Blip.tv has begun to shift its focus toward helping 32 million monthly visitors locate the most interesting and professional-produced content among its 50,000 video series. Some of its independent producers invest over $1 million in the series they produce, although that figure pales in comparison to the $1 million *per episode* of many broadcast series.

Vimeo is more artistic than YouTube and positions itself as a "respectful community of creative people who are passionate about sharing the videos they make." Like YouTube, it is free to use, but the 3 million people who upload their content are encouraged to buy a premium service (**Vimeo Plus**) for $59.95 per year, which entitles them to no intrusive "banner" advertising, ten times the storage, faster uploads and other privileges. About 20 million unique monthly visitors view its videos. By intent, Vimeo contrasts markedly with the sometimes tawdry or amateuristic tendencies of many YouTube videos.

YouTube has some other minor competitors: **Justin.tv** (popular with viewers age 13 to 18, **Veoh**

(known for long-form videos), **Flickr** (known for photos but stores videos, too), **Viddler** (for branding), **yfrog** (for Twitter), to mention a few. The resources of Google make it difficult for anyone to compete directly with YouTube for sheer size and dominance in the arena of original content, but the same was said of MySpace before its popularity was eclipsed by Facebook.

Regardless where it appears, *user-generated content is unique, and it competes for the attention of audiences who might otherwise watch other forms of television*. At its most basic, users sit at their keyboards and talk or perform for their web-enabled cameras. In an effort to entertain or inform viewers, they might also shoot digital video in other places and later upload it to sites like YouTube. A more elaborate effort is called a **mashup**, defined as a new video edited out of other videos from multiple (too often copyrighted) sources. To date, many video mashups have been parodies, sometimes accompanied by elaborate music mashups. Occasionally, as a gimmick, a network and an advertiser will encourage ordinary users to create content for distribution on mainstream channels, such as the homemade Doritos commercials that appear in each year's Super Bowl telecast.

Professional Web Videos

Beyond user-generated video and viral communication, an explosion of *professionally produced content* appears daily on an equally impressive number of broadband video channels. YouTube itself has begun to attract professional producers after its acquisition of Next New Networks, by launching YouTube *Next*. As mentioned, blip.tv and Vimeo also offer vast amounts of video from professional independent producers, who exist somewhere between the two extremes of commercial producers and silly amateurs.

The wide availability and frequent viewing of short online videos has led to the phrase *clip culture*, which refers to the presumption that viewers have acquired shorter attention spans. If a person is only interested in the highlights or the most important moment, then clips on the internet easily meet that demand. Internet technology has led to a rise in a kind of promotion that goes beyond word-of-mouth advertising. Viewers who forward to other users interesting videos or segments of information about programs or sites are indulging in a form of active publicity called *viral* communication. **Viral video** refers to images or programs that often get shared this way—for example, when the latest hit on YouTube is forwarded to thousands of "friends".

If a video becomes sufficiently popular, websites like *mashable.com* declare the clip a **meme** (referring to internet-spread ideas that attract intense notoriety). For example, fooling someone into watching a video that purports to be interesting but is really 1980s singer Rick Astley performing a music video became so popular at one time that it was labeled the "rickrolling" meme. Top-trending topics on Twitter are also candidates for becoming internet memes.

Local stations have also gotten into the act by streaming live content during their newscasts. **Livestream** is a tool for anyone wanting to launch a web television channel for free. Some broadcast stations (e.g., WSPA in Spartanburg, SC) use Livestream during live newscasts to show behind-the-scenes material during breaks. Other stations use Livestream to upload news clips.

Ubiquity

Regardless of how videos are generated by users (or what website distributes them), they have become ubiquitous. One reason is the ease with which they can be shared. Videos can be uploaded to a site such as YouTube, where an *embedded code* can be inserted into a Facebook wall, a news aggregator, a blog, a personal webpage, a Twitter tweet or even old-fashioned email. The ease with which computer users can click a button to play a show would have seemed a miracle just a few years ago. *For viewers battling boredom, it is easier to find something entertaining on the web than on regular television.*

Even watching regular television is an invitation to see YouTube videos, as the manufacturers of big-screen receivers integrate the web into their screens. A remote control with a YouTube jump-button is likely to attract an audience for popular videos on almost any topic, even clips from 50-year-old television shows. Viewers with older receivers can still watch YouTube through a TiVo DVR, Apple TV box or Roku box. Roku sells for as little as $59.99 and delivers Netflix, Hulu Plus and Amazon Instant Video to any TV set in a web-connected household with Wi-Fi internet.

The chart in 4.5 provides a snapshot of video online in May 2011. It lists ten online video suppliers

4.5 Reports on Online Video Use*

Source	Unique Viewers	Viewing Sessions	Minutes per Viewer
YouTube and other Google sites	147,158,000	2,173,422,000	311.2
VEVO	60,369,000	360,205,000	105.1
Yahoo! Sites	55,482,000	272,255,000	39.1
Facebook.com	48,189,000	176,076,000	19.3
Viacom Digital	46,535,000	241,026,000	74.2
Microsoft Sites	46,502,000	251,799,000	42.8
AOL, Inc.	42,271,000	246,592,000	45.7
Turner Digital	35,185,000	126,760,000	36.3
NBC Universal	30,622,000	67,251,000	21.1
Hulu	28,543,000	195,897,000	217.8
TOTAL FOR ALL SOURCES	**176,337,000**	**5,662,369,000**	**951.3**

*comScore Video Metrix

and the time viewers spend on each of them. The chart also shows how many viewers used video in that month, how many sessions were streamed to them, and the average time they watched at least for one month; this data changes fast.

Enhanced Viewing

Enhancements come in many types, and new ones are invented almost daily. Anything that expands or prolongs or enriches the regular television viewing experience is called an *enhancement*. First, there are references and links to websites. In addition to links in program webcasts, virtually all TV stations have streaming versions of their newscasts featured prominently on their web pages. Even the big guys (NBC, FOX) have created synchronized interactive links between their evening news broadcast and various websites. Moreover, nearly every sports event has an enhanced online viewing feature, with a logo in the screen's corner to remind viewers that they can access game statistics or enter contests online. Even syndicated game shows offer play-at-home online enhancements.

Another kind of enhancement consists of backstories and side stories and interviews that expand on what appears on regular television. This kind of enrichment both lengthens and deepens the fans' experience of a program and its stars, or so the makers hope. While some of this material appears in magazines, most of it now resides online on station and program websites. But viewers can also use social media to connect with other viewers without help from stations or channels. And the clear-winner among online enhancements formats is social networking via online communities in which participants engage in computer-mediated communication.

Social Networks

Social networks provide an extraordinary kind of program enhancement. Sometimes accompanied by *widgets* (downloadable software programs that feature media content), these sites provide the opportunity to interact, much like games. Not only can fans

read about and interact with their favorites, but as you know, they can discuss and compare and interact with "friends" and strangers.

Facebook is, of course, the largest such social network, with something like 600 million active users worldwide. It accounts for nearly 10 percent of all referred video streams, second only to Google, which accounts for more than half. Owned primarily by Mark Zuckerberg, along with other partners (but planning to go public soon), Facebook makes its revenue largely from banner ads provided by Microsoft and from Facebook credits (used to purchase items in games and other virtual applications). Like websites, Facebook groups have been created by stations, channels and viewers to enhance viewing experiences among friends, family and acquaintances, and in effect, solidify and expand fans' relationship to specific programs (thus making them excellent vehicles for advertising). To create or access Facebook pages, users must be 13 years old (supposedly) and register, although many younger children just lie. More than 40 percent of Americans have Facebook pages, and about 140 million Americans access the social network monthly.

Experimenting in 2011, Warner Brothers joined with Facebook to invite members to download the movie *The Dark Knight* (for 30 Facebook Credits, or $3). *Mature media companies are eager to protect their core business by following their users onto the internet in order to stay close to their current and potential customers.* Expect many more such joint efforts.

The second-largest such social site, **MySpace.com**, encourages its users to post videos (vlogs, which are video versions of blogs) that can be watched for information and entertainment value. But MySpace.com was sold in 2011 for $30 million, a fraction of the $580 million that Rupert Murdoch's News Corporation paid for MySpace.com in 2006, so the future of this social site has dimmed considerably. One exception may be musicians, who prefer MySpace over Facebook for posting videos and audio files.

Another widely-known enhancement is **Twitter**, a hip form of social media that allows users to *follow* people (most of whom they don't know personally, unlike Facebook friends). To "follow" is to agree to have someone's tweets (posted messages) included into your own personalized Twitter stream (analogous to a Facebook wall), so you only see comments you want to read, from those people you follow. People follow tweets in attempts to learn information, watch trends, monitor breaking news or engage in conversations with strangers who share an interest. Not everyone who loves Twitter bothers to tweet, although many users choose to share. If users of Twitter "overshare" details in their messages, their followers can choose to *unfollow* them. Following and unfollowing on Twitter is much more casual and tentative than friending and unfriending on Facebook.

Twitter has actually changed the way many people watch television in a big way—especially during special events like the Super Bowl or the Academy Awards. A person who is watching alone can *feel connected* by reading (and sometimes contributing to) a stream of *tweets* (Twitter messages of 140 characters or fewer, also known as *micro-blogs*) about the program. Watching "with" others alters the viewing experience by giving it more importance and making it more pleasant and interesting, and salience generally affects memory (an aspect that has not been lost on advertisers or programmers).

Using tweets, broadcast stations and national networks are able to entice followers with information about the normal televised content. Creating a buzz about a live event and creating a stream of human interest is no less riveting for some viewers than the links social media created among rioting Cairo citizens during the 2011 uprising against President Mubarak.

Many more people belong to Facebook than Twitter, but tweeting to strangers about television is easier when your friends don't happen to share your taste in programming. The focus of tweeting is thus on the program or channel rather than friendship. Bridging this divide is the introduction of social media tools to share *what you are watching* with *any* online community. It is too soon to know if viewers will really want to share what they are watching in the same way they seem to enjoy sharing what they are doing or thinking, but several websites and apps have begun to link viewers by letting them create social media profiles in which they can comment on television programs.

Other TV Apps

One of the simplest of these apps is called **tv Chatter**, which retrieves comments about programs directly from Twitter. A similar app is **yap.TV**, which uses a program schedule grid of programs currently showing that then leads to an unedited Twitter stream of comments based upon the selected program. The difference between the two apps is that the latter lets subscribers create their own "yaps" to compete with the "tweets" on Twitter. Yaps are public or can be contained in a "private party" group chat area.

NBC Live is the most elaborate app, offering three benefits for viewers. First, it provides a way to watch streaming versions of the most popular shows on NBC. Second, it encourages viewers to log in (either on the web or iPad) to interact with additional content (trivia, polls, cast commentary and fun facts about the show being viewed). Third, NBC Live offers a hosted social media forum, where viewers engage other fans of a particular program (and occasionally insiders from that show). NBC Live is clearly a promotional tactic to attract and maintain viewers to NBC programs.

Miso and **Tunerfish** are "check in" sites, where viewers tell what they are watching right now, similar to how they might share their present location on geo-location sites and apps like Foursquare, Gowalla, Facebook Places and Google Latitude. Miso provides badges as a reward for checking-in, an idea borrowed from Foursquare. Subscribers to Miso can also "follow" television shows, similar to the way Twitter users follow other people. Tunerfish is a phone app started by Comcast (who has very deep pockets) that is much like Twitter in the way it provides trending topics and a stream of users answering the question "What are you watching now?" Users can choose either "everyone" or "my friends" for finding out what others are watching. **Philo** and **Starling** are phone apps similar to Miso, but neither worked on the iPad we tested.

GetGlue is an app that focuses on media entertainment. Its creator calls it a window into the "taste graph" of entertainment. GetGlue organizes itself around a user's answer to "I am currently ..." with the choices *watching a show, listening to music, reading a book, watching a movie, playing a game, thinking about a topic, chatting about a celebrity,* and *drinking wine.* Users check-in to various media, receiving virtual stickers (which can be redeemed for actual stickers). Viewers can see a comment stream and assign ratings (of the thumb up or down variety), with or without comments. Does that appeal to you? Stickers, really?

IntoNow (owned by Yahoo, another elephant in the room) is a phone app for television viewers and provides a "popular" button for finding out what others are watching (and commenting upon or assigning a rating to the content). Like the Tunerfish app, IntoNow lets users see what friends or "everyone" is watching.

Television Without Pity (TWOP) is a website and cell phone app that encourages viewers to comment upon or create synopses of popular programs. **tvChaser** is an app that functions as an alphabetical search engine for television programs, providing much shorter synopses than those found on TWOP. Which of these will still be around by 2015 is anyone's guess. Place your bets!

Online Program Guides

In the 1990s the venerable *TV Guide* magazine created an online web service. Along with such companies as *www.zap2it.com,* such guides supply detailed tracking of half-hour by half-hour broadcast and multichannel offerings for all the larger U.S. markets. In addition to websites like theirs, there are dozens of apps for television that furnish program guides. Zap2It has released an app called *What's On* that takes the place of newspaper or the paper magazine form of *TV Guide* listings. It also includes times and locations for movies in local theaters. Not to be outdone, *TV Guide* came up with its own app for the iPhone and iPad, with local listings plus news about television.

Unlike printed program guides and their online counterparts, which are designed by the publishers in "one size fits all" fashion (per market), web-based television puts the user much more in control of the flow of information. Web-based television typically provides on screen access to very detailed websites like *www.imdb.com,* a searchable compendium of information on television and movies. Of course, there's always Wikipedia, but focused apps are usually more up-to-date on current programs and movies.

These enhancement apps are a tool for programmers (and fans) to make viewing more enjoyable. The future of such specialized social media is unclear, but the proliferation of cell phones and Wi-Fi tablets makes apps a tempting distraction for television viewers. Viewers are more likely to watch programs *live* than on a DVR when comments to friends or followers are concurrent with viewing. Live viewing (and commenting) also leads to less skipping of commercials. On the other hand, tablet and phone apps can serve as handy time-filler when advertising messages appear in live shows.

Video Games and Virtual Worlds

Video gaming is the third major type of online programming. How old would you guess most video game players are? What often comes first to mind are teenage boys wielding joy sticks in *Worlds of War* and the like or families jumping around playing Wii. But contrary to stereotypes about video game players, more than half the people playing online games are aged between 30 and 59, and they play everything from mahjong to Sudoku, word games and solitaire. Moreover, such games appeal to men and women almost equally, and they increasingly play them at home on their laptops while watching regular television.

Zynga has successfully launched such wildly-popular Facebook games as *CityVille, FarmVille* and *Mafia Wars* that rely on a player's friends, family and acquaintances to attain rewards in the games (see 4.6). Facebook also acquired another iconic computer game, *Civ World,* adding to its luster as the center for adult gaming. Facebook estimates nearly 300 million members play social games,

4.6 Zynga

Since 2007, Zynga has been enormously successful at creating lifestyle games to which a broad segment of users (typically people not ordinarily attracted to video games) often become addicted. Known as "the Google of games" to some observers, Zynga has built its fame on popular games like *FarmVille*, *CityVille* and *FrontierVille*. Although each game has stand-alone browser-based versions, most players participate with their friends via Facebook. By June 2011, Zynga had 270 million monthly active users. *CityVille* has 20 million daily players.

Most of the games rely on social media friends to assemble a community of game players who help each other achieve ordinary goals, like harvesting crops or feeding animals or constructing buildings. The objects in these games are virtual goods that convert to points or virtual money, with which players can purchase virtual items. Success in these games depends on effort, but players can also buy virtual goods from Zynga to advance further toward game rewards or sometimes avoid penalties. For example, virtual farmers can resurrect crops that died by paying roughly $2 in real cash to Zynga, which sells game "coins" (or Facebook Credits) in $10 or $20 bundles. Real-world poker tournament players recognized this tactic as a "re-buy" that allows a bankrupt player a second chance to play on. It is probably no coincidence that Zynga's very first social media game was *Zynga Poker*.

Thanks to enchanting graphics and time-based participation, Zynga captures players' attention with virtual activities that are fun to play with their friends at no cost—but then offers those same players additional benefits for a price. Zynga profits not from the free games but through the sale of virtual goods that players desire to advance in the game. Zynga's games follow the so-called freemium model, a combination of free and premium playing.

The more players play, the deeper they get into the games. Taking a day off, for example, hurts a player's points. It's not unusual for ordinary people who would never play video games to get drawn into the game, somewhat like an addiction. So a *FarmVille* player might get up early before going to work because their corn crop must be harvested before it withers. Manual harvesting takes longer than using a tractor, so the player feels the need to acquire farm machinery. Then, to operate the tractor, the players choose to either convert game points to buy gasoline or pay real money online (Zynga hopes) for game coins to purchase fuel. Playing the game is more mindful than passively watching television, although people often engage in both activities simultaneously.

CityVille is Zynga's most popular game, offering players the opportunity to build a virtual city, acquire energy points, and advance through experience levels. Zynga claims 61 million monthly users of *CityVille*. Players (often friends on Facebook) visit one another's cities and perform work in a reciprocal fashion. Friends can give gifts to other friends who play, just as they did in *FarmVille*. Thus, social media acquaintances who may have nothing to say to their friends each day can still share some kind of message to help the other in the game (e.g., "Mary has sent you a Zoning Permit" or "Can you send me an I-beam?"). Beyond the individual accomplishments rewarded in the game, players make friendly connections with people they know. If cities and credits can be virtual, why not build virtual friendships?

buying virtual goods like food and fuel to advance in the game. Slightly over half of all Facebook users log in specifically to play social games because of the real-time rules that foster addiction to playing.

Traditional media networks have tried to promote their offline programs during online gaming but have not met with much success thus far. What works better is to develop a television game show with an online game counterpart that is itself a promotional tool, fostering back-and-forth promotion of the two versions and advertising opportunities in both media. *Jeopardy*, for example, exists in daily syndicated television, online in several forms and in a box as a board game.

Then there are the heavy game players. They log in on ordinary web-connected computers to play **massively multiplayer online games (MMOG)** with hundreds or thousands of online friends and strangers. Youngsters (no less addicted than those parents who play *CityVille*) play online games like *Runescape* and the wildly popular *World of Warcraft* (in several versions). Monthly subscriptions are required for most of these games. Time spent playing typically *displaces* time spent viewing television, but teens sometimes do both, as do some adults.

Programmers and users classify the content of online and console games under the following five categories: role-playing (RP), first-person shooter (FPS), real-time strategy (RTS), turn-based strategy (TBS) and simulations (SIMs). Each game requires a downloaded program through which the player logs onto a network of users (or, in the base browser-based games, a "thin client" program operates the game). Some examples are described briefly in 4.7, and you can probably think of more!

Even standalone game consoles like Xbox 360 and Playstation 3 have moved from *solo* to *multiplayer games*. With built-in Wi-Fi devices, these consoles let players enjoy MMOGs like *Call of Duty (I, II, III, IV…)*, *Halo*, and that all-time parents' horror, *Grand Theft Auto* in all its permutations. The chief advantage of playing games on a game console is that such devices were designed specifically for

games. Thus, the game controllers are easier to use, the graphics are better, and connections have less "lag time" (because dedicated chips distribute the flow of information). Voice chat is also better implemented on game consoles than on computers. Game consoles also have advanced motion controls, such as Kinect for the Xbox 360.

Still another online game format consists of **virtual worlds**. These are computer-based simulated environments intended for users to inhabit and interact with via avatars. Defined as the web user's representations of his or her individual self, **avatars** occur in three forms: three-dimensional models, two-dimensional icons or text constructs. Very shortly after such sites first appeared, big commercial interests latched onto the branding and profit opportunities. For younger children, Viacom's *Neopets* has been especially successful. Nickelodeon's *Nicktropolis.com* targets children's desire to play games, watch videos, design personalized 3-D areas, and interact with other kids in real time—and also targets parents' desire for a "safe" online environment.

4.7 | **MMOGs**

The most popular MMORPGs (where RPG stands for role-playing game) are *Runescape*, *Final Fantasy* and *Tibia*. Players spend hours in a fantasy world where items are collected and exchanged for tools or power, and battles are fought. Websites such as *http://usfine.com* have also sprung up to help players move forward in the game, for a price.

MMOFPS games (first-person shooter) require the player to become a warrior, and the competitions are shown through a first-person field of view. Among the most popular games are *Combat Arms*, *AssaultCube* and *CrossFire*. MMOFPS players are usually awarded points for experience. Nexon is a major supplier of these games, and it makes money through monthly subscriptions and merchandise sales.

Beyond Protocol and *Battleswarm* are examples of MMORTS (real-time strategy) games, which fall into two respective categories: sci-fi and fantasy. Players typically get to be a king or a general in command of others. Large numbers of players can compete in these games set in a

persistent world hosted by the company that designs the content and charges fees.

MMOTBS (turn-based strategy) games are regulated by the tick on an online clock. Between the ticks, hundreds of players share the same field of conquest, where moves are made asynchronously and then locked in every 30 seconds or so, allowing players with slower (or intermittent) internet connections to simulate synchronous playing. *UltraCorps* and *Darkwind* are trendy examples.

SIMs (simulations) are a category of multiplayer games that includes poker, sports, auto racing and alternative worlds. Gamblers compete for play money (sometimes real, when the law allows) at such game sites as *Pokerstars* and *Full Tilt Poker*. Sports fans play a variety of games (one example is *Baseball Mogul Online*) which are similar to fantasy league competitions. *Kart Racer* is an example of an online racing game quite similar to MMORPGs, except that the role-playing is limited to driving very fast. Players of games like *The Sims Online* create their own alternate worlds.

Middle-school children are attracted to such semi-educational sites as *Gaiaonline.com* on which they use anime-type avatars (cartoons, manga) to interact in real time and earn rewards that "buy" virtual toys. Such sites earn their revenue from the purchases of clothing, hair clips, posters, stickers, games and so on. Such virtual-world models are moving into regular classrooms for more direct academic learning. For the adult population, the most popular virtual world site is *SecondLife.com*, a three-dimensional UGC where participants buy and trade virtual land and virtual dollars (using more spooky avatars). *Gaiaonline* and *SecondLife* peaked in popularity about 2009, but both still have large numbers of users.

A Conceptual Framework

When an innovation comes along that fundamentally changes the way people view the world, the term *discontinuous change* is used. At first glance, the use of online technology to distribute radio and television programming appears merely an extension of broadcasting—another way to receive the content—as with cable and satellite. The key difference, however, has been the degree of *interactivity* between the user and the programmer, a factor which created a sea change from the past. The seemingly infinite number of choices is another important difference: By 2012, there were more than 800 million *internet hosts* (which are comparable to channels).[4] Another change is that the formerly dominant media are now forced to compete with such unconventional forms of electronic entertainment as digital photo albums, visual encyclopedias, vlogs, virtual worlds and amateur podcasts.

Other chapters in this book have been structured around *strategies* for selecting, scheduling and promoting programs plus evaluating audience response. The "a la carte" nature of program offerings on the internet, however, has transformed many of the programmer's tasks. Instead of schedules of limited choices, the online audience has an abundant menu of near-limitless choices. Every listener and every viewer can construct his or her own media landscape. In this content-on-demand world, fewer people spend the same time enjoying the same program that other people are watching. Yet, *many viewers continue to expect that someone else will assemble offerings into a schedule, or at least a highly simplified menu.*

Although it is safe to define **online programming** as *media content available through a computer screen, tablet or speaker that displaces or substantially supplements the use of noncomputer media content*, it is only possible to sketch out some segments, not boundaries. Indeed, some handheld devices allow the screen to be wirelessly shared with a larger screen in a group setting (such as through Apple's AirPlay). While online content includes live and taped shows, described previously as streamed or video content, it can encompass virtual events, including chat rooms and group event simulations such as those just discussed (*Gaia, SecondLife*). *Online programming particularly includes but is not limited to web pages that promote programming delivered over conventional channels*, but does not include, for the purposes of this book, the archived sound bites and video clips found on journalism sites, which we set aside.

Conceptually, online programming compares with other programming as shown in Table 4.8. While the list of differences is not exhaustive, it is nevertheless helpful for framing the relative position of online distribution. Although these distinctions may seem peripheral to *how* programming is strategically scheduled, these conceptual differences are crucial for programmers' understanding of *why* new media are fundamentally unlike more traditional media.

The central uniqueness of the online world is its *interactivity*. Applications that are interactive account for an ever-growing slice of spending on the media. In the near term, we expect that cell phones, tablets, portable media players or some new multichannel television platform will better realize the full potential of new media systems.

Geography

Because they are distributed by middlemen—the broadcast stations and cable systems—ordinary over-the-air radio and television signals are limited

4.8	**Strengths and Weaknesses of Media Delivery Systems**			
System	**Reach Limited by**	**Revenue Streams**	**Bandwidth**	**Interactivity**
Broadcast	Geography	1. Advertising	High	One-way
Cable/Satellite	Channel capacity	2. Ads, plus subscriptions	High	Mostly one-way
Online	Bandwidth	3. Ads, subs, plus merchandise	Medium	Two-way

by geography. Back in the mid-twentieth century, networks were developed to link together stations and cable systems to create national services. In the 1980s and 1990s, multichannel media (cable and satellite) became collections of networks, limited by shelf space to about 600 digitally compressed channels (see Chapter 9).

Online, in contrast, is free of inherent geography and fixed channel capacity, but somewhat limited by the size of the pipe (*bandwidth*) through which programming must flow. Bundled fiber cables, however, are now replacing old-style coaxial cable and telephone lines, thereby increasing bandwidth. And internet cable modems and DSL have pushed delivery speeds to 5 megabits per second (mbps), with speeds up to 8 mbps for additional monthly fees. The theoretical limit of DSL remains 10 mbps, but cable is easily three times as much. Moreover, for larger cities, Comcast developed 50 mbps speeds and achieved 100 mbps over fiber connections, leaving DSL far behind. (Clearly, if you are a gamer 100 mbps is to die for!) When internet access comes through such connections, very high-quality video and audio are possible. Nonetheless, to match HD television quality, distributors must provide many megabits per second over shared access lines. *It is a rule of science that faster speeds produce better video and audio quality.*

Economics

The very essence of programming strategy is linked to how revenue flows from consumer to program producer, with the distributor (qua programmer) as middleman. All three forms of media programming

shown in Table 4.8 have offsetting benefits and drawbacks. The key distinction between broadcasting and multichannel distribution has been the number of revenue streams: Over-the-air radio and TV stations rely almost entirely on *advertising*, whereas cable/satellite services have dual income from *advertising and subscriptions*. Although the broadcast industry has only a single revenue stream to date (NBC has taken the first baby steps toward a second stream from cable operators), the "free" element of broadcasting allows nearly complete audience penetration: 98 percent of U.S. homes receive broadcast radio and TV stations, meaning nearly all 300 million Americans can see and hear them.

Thus, broadcast advertising is more efficient for reaching enormous numbers of people than cable or internet advertising, which means that broadcasters can charge more for the time in which commercials air. Online programming, however, has a third revenue stream from *merchandising* because its technology allows point-and-click purchasing of items related to media content. Once, such products and services could be sold only in the commercial breaks within TV shows. Now, companies like Zynga profit immensely by selling virtual goods (for which there is no manufacturing cost) to people playing online games. And Facebook and YouTube and dozens of others look to get into the virtual goods game.

The ability to attract subscribers to internet programming has been negatively affected by the "free" nature of the internet because, at the start, most content was reused broadcast material or a sorry sort of amateurism (UGC) lacking the production quality that viewers were used to. Nowadays, those who supply high-quality programs made-for-online must charge (like cable) and compete with those that seem free because they are advertiser-supported (in particular, broadcasters—and the pirate services that share their content with everyone for free). Web users have become willing to pay because they see the value and convenience of streaming video.

Convincing advertisers to evolve away from the long-established system of *cost-per-thousand* and *gross ratings points* has been a challenge for the online world. On the positive side, unlike conventional television's delivery of spot messages to an unknown audience, broadband video delivers a targeted message to actual users. By 2010, online video accounted for just 10 percent of all advertising dollars. Yet, the number of people who consume online video continues to grow (see 4.5), and that great size looks appealing to many with something to sell, so expect change there.

In traditional broadcasting, programs that under-deliver (have fewer than the predicted and thus paid-for number of viewers) necessitate the giving up of precious airtime in future programs for "make-good" commercials. In the online system, content providers cannot so readily hedge potential audience size. As a result, the traditional advertiser-supported model is slowly transforming into a *"pay-per-viewer" model for advertisers*. However, internet media analysts and executives correctly predicted that demand for *subscription video services* would eclipse the *pay-per-use* model *for consumers* because of greater convenience and predictability. By 2011, cord-cutters had generally traded the option of $10 per premium channel for lower cost channels hosted by Netflix or Hulu Plus. HBO and others have begun to shift their economic model, to avoid sharing the fate (demise) of established media giants like Blockbuster.

By now it is abundantly clear that *audiences prefer pre-roll advertising and commercial interruptions to paying for short clips of video*. On the other hand, the success of subscription services like Netflix and Hulu Plus suggests that viewers will pay for video subscriptions, especially in the case of movies and games.

Despite broadcast and cable's continuing importance, there are some highly positive features to being an online program supplier. No licenses and franchises are required, unlike for broadcast stations and cable

systems, and very little FCC regulation applies to online. Moreover, at present, the distinction between *distribution* and *content* is tenuous. Because there are very few distributors, content *really is* king. There are no bricks and mortar as with stations, cables and satellites. Very few barriers exist to consumption immediately after the creation step, and the size of staff required to maintain a website is much smaller than for broadcast stations or cable operations.

Most crucial to this book about media programmers, the job of the online programmer has uniquely become the job of librarian. Mostly, a programmer keeps track of things—the "things" being UGC videos submissions, updates to games, subscribers and members, players, special offers—and maybe advertisers (unless someone else handles them). Selection and evaluation remain valid functions, but the importance of scheduling is greatly diminished because everything is potentially available all the time. Daily promotion tends to be supplanted by research to find out who to promote to. The key job is helping users find what they want (before their patience runs out). Whether listeners and viewers prefer to create their own media landscapes or choose among packaged ones remains to be seen, but the online world is not a particularly friendly place to middlemen ... except for the very Big Guys.

In the online world, the focus is on *content aggregators* like YouTube and Netflix. The actual *content providers*—the people who produce short videos—either opt to place their "shows" on aggregator sites or to remain off-portal on *independent websites*. However, website programmers must rely on the *search engines*—such as Google and Bing—in order to be located by most users. *Programmers must decide whether to offer their content via major sites or to go it alone, hoping to be found by the search engines.* In the days of text-only search engines, this was a difficult decision, but video search has been integrated into all the major search engines, making it difficult *not* to be found. On the other hand, the numbers of entries turned up by Google and others sometimes run into the hundreds of thousands, and being buried on such long lists brings few hits. *The solution for players with deep pockets has been to purchase placement at the start of a related search as a form of advertising. Google.com and others charge advertisers for favorable placement during online searches.*

For those who have broadband, the choice between free and subscription internet content parallels that of broadcast and cable TV. Nowadays, the best content comes at a premium, but advertiser-supported free content is still pretty good. Those who decide to pay extra for content—that is, beyond the considerable monthly expense for high-speed access (which has other benefits such as fast email and instant messaging)—can save money by subscribing to a content provider aggregator that packages several services.

But an *authentication model* is popping up that provides protection for the existing MVPDs. What it means is that real (authentic) subscribers to a cable or satellite service will be favored online users of television programs. Authentication makes hot online content available to cable and satellite subscribers but not (or not now) to non-subscribers. Having a vested interest in forestalling cable disconnects because of all the cable networks its parent corporation owns, FOX was the first broadcast network to adopt the practice on Hulu, but others will soon follow suit. Only real (authentic) subscribers to a cable or satellite service will get to see FOX series immediately on Hulu, whereas non-authentic users will have to wait eight days to see repeats (or maybe forever, if this protective approach takes off—and it is expected to, although Google might keep an open system). If the authentication model becomes widespread, the chances of people dropping their MVPD subscriptions become considerably lessened. For the avid online user, getting to see episodes many days later isn't as appealing as seeing last night's episodes today. At a minimum, authentication practices are expected to slow down cord-cutting.

Strategic Considerations

If program strategists are middlemen, and the internet has no middle, then what is the role of program strategy? Considering the strategic themes outlined in Chapter 1 might lead to the conclusion that *selecting* online programs is different from selecting in the old media environment—but there are, however, enough similarities that programmers can make the transition from a time-bound broadcast world to an a la carte online world.

Daypart Compatibility

The utility of dayparting as a strategic theme was considerably weakened for broadcasters with the advent of themed cable channels in the 1980s and 1990s (for example, CNN, Game Show Channel, Cartoon Network). However, *the true goal of dayparting is to target sizeable groups of people,* and the use of a time segment is only one means to the goal. Online programmers who select programs for a given website certainly can match their content to a *compatible* audience. For example, ESPN Motion and other sports sites take advantage of knowing what fans like to see and delivering it to them.

In the earliest days of streaming video, the distribution of materials was a novelty, so targeting was minimal. Streaming was done because it was possible, not because there was any market demand. For example, downloading programs from mainstream television took so long they would rarely warrant most users' effort because it was easier just to watch TV.

But despite the fact that teens and college students account for a big chunk of the online video audience, the average age of U.S. viewers is an ancient 39 or so. Over and over, data compiled by such online research companies as Nielsen//NetRatings, comScore and Quantcast show that web surfers over 35 years old make up anywhere from half to two-thirds of YouTube's audience.[5] *Nowadays, the typical online user is no different from the typical television viewer.* Thus, the strategies used by the cable theme channels will find new homes online, with the key difference being the user's ability to select from a list of options (*online menu*), as in digital cable. *The programmer, as always, must construct an online menu that is compatible with the desired visitor to the website.*

Habit Formation

Freed from time constraints, the web can show anything, anytime. Programmers must count on first-time visitors being so impressed with their sites' contents they will find it rewarding and may even *bookmark* it (save the site's address). Social bookmarking sites like Diigo, Delicious and Google Bookmarks facilitate the sharing of bookmarks with one's friends. Present studies of *website repertoire* already note that users have a limited number of favorite sites (so much so that the idea of "web surfing" has become outdated except as a way to find specialized information). Entrance *portals* like YouTube and Hulu function like networks, connecting groups of content (in contrast to outlets like local broadcast stations). A main screen menu presents different categories of content (called *links*) that are sorted by interest area: news, sports, weather, travel, shopping, movies and so on. Portals do not hold the power they once did because people have become accustomed to searching via Google, Yahoo!, Bing and similar search engines.

The job of habit formation becomes making a favorable first impression and having the most user-friendly appearance and content—to the extent that that users think of certain sites as "the best weather radar site" or "the best online auction site," an evaluation that may also appeal to the "programmers" of search engines and get them top listing. Nonetheless, *paid search placement* is increasingly the deciding factor. With paid placement, the search engine grants preferential positioning to the client who pays them for the favor.

Another financial scheme is for the video aggregators to share revenue with the creators of short videos, especially when short *roll-in* advertisements precede the videos. In the case of YouTube (the aggregator), Google (the search engine) maintained the upper hand by acquiring it (YouTube) for $1.65 billion (which may sound like a lot of money until one recalls that Yahoo! paid $5.7 billion for Mark Cuban's *broadcast.com* website in the late 1990s during the dot-com heyday).

Habit formation is carefully considered by the producers of interactive games. It is not a coincidence that one website is called *www.addictinggames.com*; the best video games encourage long play and reward daily visits. Some games, such as *Farkle* on Facebook, punish players with fewer bonus awards if they miss a single day. Employers complain that employees play games too much on the job, but such is the addiction to daily play when virtual animals must be virtually fed and virtual crops wither without virtual water.

Audience Flow

When it comes to the notion of audience flow, most online sites follow the cable television model for specialized theme channels. As stressed in Chapters 1 and 2, *the main strategy is to invite audience flow in and discourage flow out.* On the other hand, much as multichannel programmers promote other channels, online programmers can *cross-promote content* by including new offerings (other programs) on the same screen page as those containing established programs (or other content). For such branded content providers as Cartoon Network and ESPN, cross-promoting among cable channels, online video games and pay-per-view videos is effective. The audience can be encouraged to watch the scheduled cable content as usual but is given the option to sample other forms of branded entertainment (or information) *without tuning away from the brand.* The internet and on-demand digital services strive to give loyal users alternate ways to remain with a program brand.

Because *surfing* (the online world's answer to *grazing*) is less common nowadays than in the beginning, new services need a developed programming strategy, beyond promotional support, to attract an audience. The *spinoff* approach and the *tie-in* approaches used by broadcasters can work well for online content providers. For example, *Angry Birds* was first developed as a game for mobile phones but later was spun off into television programs, both as an animated show and as a live-action version.

Conservation of Program Resources

Just as broadcast and cable programmers recycle material to optimize its value, online programmers put as much material onto their online menus as possible. *Unlike time-bound broadcast and cable programmers, the online content providers are not forced to rotate or rerun offerings because nearly everything is continuously available.* (Some MMOGs are exceptions because they have exact start and stop times for all participants, but others go on and on until all players lose interest.)

One consideration influences some providers to limit the availability of their material: Many programmers believe that *perceived scarcity* makes content appear more valuable to the public. For example, Disney carefully limits accessibility to its old classic films on videocassette and DVD to make them seem more special when they briefly become available in stores. If online content becomes too common or too readily available, the perceived worth of the contents (as compared with premium materials) may be diminished. One reason why cable viewers spend so much of their time watching HBO is because they pay extra for it, and the extra use justifies the cost. The lessons for website program services seeking subscription fees are to keep content original and promote the content as "special."

Just as with a hit TV program, a winning video gaming franchise can be developed into new versions. *Call of Duty* was an original first-person shooter game set in WWII that recycled popular concepts into *Call of Duty 2*, *Call of Duty 3* and *Call of Duty: World at War*. The program's distributor Activision chose the Vietnam Conflict as the setting for *Call of Duty: Black Ops* (selling $650 million in the first five days on the market) and then the brought the game series into present-day battles with the *Modern Warfare Series: Call of Duty 4: Modern Warfare*, *Modern Warfare 2* and *Modern Warfare 3*. Game players can buy new games or add-ons to existing games (such as *Call of Duty: United Offensive*). Activision also created games for consoles and hand-held games under the *Call of Duty* brand: *Finest Hour, Big Red One, Roads to Victory, World at War: Final Fronts, Modern Warfare: Mobilized, World at War: Zombies 1 and 2* and *The War Collection.*

Breadth of Appeal

A game like *CityVille* has a very wide appeal (over 60 million active monthly players by 2011), attracting all age groups. Other games by Zynga target the young, such as *Mafia Wars* and *Warstorm*, but older audiences are typically sought for wide appeal games like *FishVille* and *Café World*.

Online content is not immune to being categorized as broadcasting or narrowcasting, even though the term *webcasting* encompasses both. Like cable programmers, most online programmers have a choice between two tactics: to narrowcast *unique content* (such as sports highlights or games) or to broadcast *mainstream content* (weather, news, commerce). Eventually, it is likely that subscriptions models will proliferate on the web, and evolve into some kind of "basic" and "premium" content. Those who toil in the programming business should take heart that, regardless of the technology and distribution, *content remains the most important factor in influencing users.* Whether broad or narrow, broadcast, cable or online, programs have to have distinctive appeal that meets some consumers' needs and wants.

Specific Approaches

Experts know little about what strategies work and do not work in this new medium, just as "experts" were ignorant during television's inception or radio's early days. Many honestly thought radio would be used for education! In the present day, *repurposing* television and radio content has become an automatic process for news directors and station managers. Many television stations now offer access to their recent news broadcasts via web page. It has become a competitive necessity. Oddly enough, the most-watched local news videos are produced by newspapers, not broadcast stations. Whether the strategy of repurposing applies equally well to all content and all situations is an open question, but we'll certainly find out as new television seasons emerge.

Selecting Content

Shelly Palmer has described a media world of *linear* (scheduling in real time) and *nonlinear* (on demand with viewer control) television, where the value of content is best realized where that content is best viewed.[6] For linear viewing (plain old broadcast and cable television), he designates *emergent content*, meaning news, sports and live events. For nonlinear viewing (internet TV), he suggests *evergreen content*, meaning sitcoms, movies, dramatic hours and documentaries. The third type of content he calls *disposable content*, meaning talk shows, service shows (whose subjects have been rendered irrelevant because of technology) and infomercials. Disposable content is suited to either linear or nonlinear viewing.

Games have the best online growth potential. Games, contests, gambling and other kinds of online competition have become the "next big thing" in terms of interactive program content. Because they are free online and the brand names are known to parents, Disney and Toon games have gained enormous popularity with children as spinoffs, and many others are available for teens and adults. Some efforts have been made to distribute computer games for a fee over the internet, a successful strategy for capturing the person who has tried the free version and become hooked. *The most popular strategy to date, however, is selling virtual goods to game players, which has made Zynga a $10 billion company.* Can I sell you some virtual corn seed or a virtual parking place or maybe a virtual lottery ticket?

Running mini-lottery programs online has considerable (but unrealized) potential for the major media companies because the public is familiar with reports of lottery numbers and talk about winners as elements of television content, and the various kinds of media could be tied together. However, the FCC would almost certainly frown on close ties between any real gambling and media businesses. The commission has regulations in place that specify that any contesting that is lottery-like can only be incidental to the main programming service. Whether this subsidiary requirement applies to the internet is unknown. It is clear that the unregulated online world could run lotteries more readily than any other medium could. In the United States, online poker sites were shut down in early 2011, while the same poker sites operate freely in many other countries, making future uncertain.

Scheduling Content

So, how do the most popular online sites for TV shows list them so you can pick something to watch? What's interesting about the answer to this question is that the design, once created, is automatic. The programmer has to decide how to present the options, but no one has to manually update the suggestions. The computer is programmed to learn the subscriber's habits and make suggestions accordingly. Each content aggregator has a different set of strategies, so we will take a look at some examples:

Netflix: This service uses six highly-customized categories, different for each subscriber. Similar to the way Amazon makes book suggestions, Netflix offers its first category as "Top 10 [suggestions] for [name of specific user]." The text reads: "We create this *list based on your recent rental and watching history, ratings, queue adds, and taste preference settings.* We try to present a regularly updated selection of titles chosen specifically for you—older titles that you may have missed and new releases."

The second Netflix category is "TV Shows" and is *based on popular interest.* The third category is by genre, called "Custom category" [based on recent selections], then additional genres (e.g., "Children & Family Movies"). The fourth category is "New Movies to watch instantly" and followed by the fifth category, "Rate what you've seen to discover suggestions for you" (which is not really a category, but it appears as a fifth choice). The final category is "Local Favorites for [your city]" which targets subscribers by their location. Above these categories on the Netflix screen is a little menu bar with the following tabs: Genres (20 choices), New Arrivals, Starz Play, Instantly to your TV, and Suggestions For You.

Hulu: The free version of Hulu arranges its options in three categories—"Recent Episodes," "Popular Clips" and "Featured Content"—arranged in columns. Logging off or on does not affect the options displayed. Near the bottom of the screen, Hulu shows three additional categories—"Popular Shows," "Popular Movies" and "More to Explore." Hulu Plus (the monthly subscription version of Hulu) uses a different layout of category options, but with the same absence of custom suggestions: "Browse TV," "Most Popular Alphabetical"— with numerous screens of choices, with checkbox filters for "Currently on air," "Captions," "HD" and choice of TV only, Movies only or both—"Recently Added" and "Coming Soon." Does all this suggest to you that the assumption that people freely move around and choose whatever they like on the internet is kind of a fiction? There seems to be a lot of guidance here from the online services, just as there is in conventional broadcast and cable television.

Other Scheduling Strategies: *Cross-referencing* is the primary strategy for displaying content as a substitute for "scheduling" it. YouTube, for example, cross-references its clips so that the viewer sees suggestions related to the video just viewed. If the viewer watches a video featuring a particular politician, then all other videos featuring the same official will appear as choices. Sometimes general themes (humor or news) will trigger a menu of choices. Content providers have control over these suggestions and can choose to suggest videos for its paying video clients, which is somewhat akin to a *paid search placement*.

As discussed earlier, *dayparting i*s a minor consideration for online channels because the choices for users are so plentiful, more like cable and satellite services. Radio and television stations normally have *one* channel, so it makes sense to target the *one* demographic group most likely to be watching at a particular time of the day or day of the week—by age, gender or lifestyle. Online programs exist in nearly limitless cyberspace—where shelf space is endless and digital media can be ordered without regard to time or space. Similarly, *flow* is not very controllable for online programmers; users are as likely to travel horizontally as vertically, or even jump to distant sites, although sites try to keep themselves appealing and guide flow to other spots within the site.

At the same time, storytelling seems to be an inherently linear process, unfolding over time. Efforts to create innovative multiple paths for stories tend to evolve either into games or educational

activities—both of which are effort-full, not effortless entertainment. As converged media have arrived, web programming must consider users' personal goals, and target those users who want either relatively passive or active content.

Tiering is one scheduling strategy that successfully made the transition from the analog to digital TV and then to the online world. It is likely that consumers will purchase more higher-tiered programming more often than not, just as cable and satellite subscribers purchase premium multichannel programming (see Chapter 9). Indeed, much of premium programming from HBO, Showtime and Encore has moved to random-access schedules in homes with digital set-top boxes and DVRs, and such program services will move smoothly online as new home technologies spread. HBO2Go is a web app that delivers HBO content directly to portable media.

Promoting Content

The practice of online program promotion is still very young, but it is already clear that content providers need to promote their products and services using a mix of mass marketing and an abundance of online spot messages (the equivalent of "on- air" in broadcasting and cable) and on-screen invitations (comparable to print ads). The traditional media's interest in all things internet also provides many opportunities for *publicity* (unpaid promotion).

One avenue for the promotion of videos is the viral nature of the internet. Most online video sites encourage viewers to "share this video with a friend" or to "leave a comment" (which creates more involvement and increases the chance that an ordinary video will rise to the status of viral video). Social media sites like Facebook and Twitter are good tools for the web programmer.

Wikis are sometimes associated with hit televisions shows (FOX's *American Idol*, CBS's *Survivor*). A *wiki* is a website that allows internet visitors themselves to easily add, remove or otherwise edit and change available content, typically without the need for registration. In the case of FOX's *Glee*, fans can contribute their own explanations and interpretations of the storylines; meanwhile, the episode creators get feedback and generate excitement for future shows. Such collaborative processes allow mainstream content providers to be more closely connected to the eventual audience. A dedicated website further serves to promote the program, whether the show appears online or on the air.

Moreover, interactive media frequently generate email lists and sophisticated demographic databases of potential audiences for specific services. Nearly all websites that offer such content require the user to sign up for the service, even when it is free. That user's email address then becomes available (most sites ask permission) for updates. Instead of reaching merely *potential* users (as radio does with outdoor advertising), online services reach *actual* users, past and present, with their messages. Present users can also be encouraged to provide names of others who might be interested in the site, sometimes with a reward for the referral. In this way, online content providers can send messages directly to their subscriber base, without postage costs (although it may be *spam* to many people).

The standard online medium of *banner ads* reaches small targeted groups of online users, but getting promotional messages out to a wider audience will draw new users. After all, *many people can be persuaded to try out something new at least once, especially if it is free.* Such offers usually have a time limit, after which fees kick in. Because computers track when a given household has used up all free plays (of a program or a game), the service can flood the household with "time to subscribe" messages on multiple channels. In consequence, online promotion planners should budget money for paid advertising in other media. Although some adults still avoid online content, the traditional media of print, radio and television supply enormous potential audiences for online entertainment and information. *Despite the greater efficiency of online advertising, the reach of older media is important for building a base of users.* It needs to be combined with a targeted online approach.

Interactive media of several types can follow the promotional guidelines for the cable networks discussed in Chapter 9. For example, motion pictures will someday be released to video on demand immediately following their theatrical runs, assuming that video rentals become less effective in distributing movies and that studios are willing to take risks. Mass marketing ads that once said, "Now on VHS and DVD," now say, "Now available on demand." Other pay events carried online will require the same kind of promotion currently used by cable operators and DBS satellite companies. *Viewers won't care which way a movie comes to them.*

Online Measurement

As outlined in Chapter 5, Nielsen//NetRatings and Media Metrix measure the size of online audiences using two different methods: *online panels* and *server-side audits*. Both methods report mostly *cumes* (total unduplicated audience). Measuring total reach is a good tactic when a "channel" has not yet attracted a substantial audience. As convergence of the media takes place over the next dozen years, conventional percentages of the estimated total audience (ratings) and percentages of those actually using any service at a time (shares) will prove useful tools for measuring the kinds of online programming that garner a large core of regular users.

Like the national/local ratings for broadcast, cable and radio, internet audience measurement has proven to be dreadfully difficult and complex process. Companies constantly refine the process and constantly test to find new and more accurate ways to measure web audiences; the task is daunting. Nielsen's *Home Technology Report* describes some major complications that make accurate measurement annoyingly difficult. For example, because of the multiple interactions that can be happening on a single PC, information collected at the website level tells little about how content is actually being consumed. In some cases, PC users may access a website and then perform other totally unrelated operations while still keeping the original website online. Such uses may be widespread and varied but would be considerably different from the kind of use taking place when a visitor goes to a site, looks at it and, then closes it. Thus, measurements of "time-spent-viewing" on many web pages may be misleading.

Who are the users of website content? There were more than 150 million unique video streamers in the United States in 2011. Moreover, viewing is quite splintered; only one service (*NBC.com*) had as many as 5 million unique visitors. Although less than 15 percent of adults in the United States watch video online at once a week, men aged 18 to 34—that elusive group that advertisers so desire—account for nearly half of daily viewers of online video.

According to The Media Audit, the percentage of adults who spend at least an hour a day on the internet is significantly greater than the percentage of adults who spend an hour a day with the print edition of a daily newspaper (perhaps because most newpapers have gotten shorter!). Research has shown that about a quarter of adults spend seven or more hours per week on the internet—as much as withTV—and heavy use (however defined) has been growing faster among internet users than among users of other media. The percentage of affluent users is also higher for the internet than for other media. For evidence of the arrival of online media, one need only look at the success of Netflix, which barely registered in people's minds in 2009 and was a dominant force just two years later.

What's Coming Fast

The most likely strategy for the major film studios, big broadcasters and the other impacted "old" media, is adaption to the new environment, probably by buying in. An *adaptive strategy* has to be viewed from the standpoint of the established media and their "old" business models. The old way of packaging shows in arranged schedules is most unlikely to vanish completely. Many businesses adapt by changing their business model or product, after spreading into related areas and testing the waters (or in this case, testing the revenues). When the telephone industry saturated its growth potential by the 1980s, it looked to other information entities, like cell and cable. In contrast, when Kodak saw the impending doom of its film business in the 1990s, it dumped film rolls and got into the digital photography business.

In response to the question—Can streaming video sites with entertainment actually make money?—the answer is *yes*. Revenue is beginning to flow in many streams: advertising, sponsorships, transactions and commerce. The pay-per-view model works well, as long as others are no longer giving away content. As for advertising, it may work best when it is personalized—something called *one-to-one* marketing, where share of customer is more important than share of market. Privacy is also an issue, and the number of potential consumers for any given distribution platform must be large enough to justify the extra marketing effort beyond the usual mass media networks. Bandwidth limitations of the past are being eliminated. Faster connections and better video compression have made the online platform a practical way to distribute video content. The Blu-Ray DVD standard delivers HDTV movies on a single disc, but high-definition images are finding their way to the internet at a slower rate. On the other hand, a handheld tablet needs less resolution than a giant screen several feet away.

Faced with the announcement of big changes in store for old media in a new media world, some people wonder aloud whether people really want to interact with their TV sets. One should consider that the same question was asked about the personal computer, which was originally designed for doing such office work as spreadsheets, word processing and databases. The answer proved to be *yes*. Will people be just as enamored with interactivity from their TV as from their computer? The answer, again, seems to be *yes*.

Do people want to watch video over the web on their computers? *Yes,* if the added control and convenience are there. People want conveniences that make their lives easier. Way back in 2000, Gary Lieberman, analyst for Morgan Stanley Dean Witter, made the following pithy predictions about the future of online that have proven accurate.[7]

1. Once the tools and applications are in place, the revenue potential is huge.

2. Watching [home shopping channel] QVC, if you have a "buy" button on your remote, will be hard to resist.

3. Set-top boxes will not succeed unless they cost $300 or less.

4. Obsolescence will become the same problem for set-top boxes that it is now for computers.

5. Thin applications will be more successful than fat ones.

6. DVRs are like power windows on your car: Once you have them, you can never go back.

7. The first step will be video-on-demand.

8. The "killer application" will be a surprise, likely dreamed up in a dorm room.

9. Interactive TV will land in the middle of the PC and TV experience: You won't lean back as much as you once did, but you won't lean forward as much as you do with your computer.

10. Brand names will continue to be important.

11. Compatibility is a must.

When nearly all of America is finally online, and most have high-speed service, then the ubiquity of the broadcast world will no longer be so wonderful. TV Everywhere will have arrived, if you pay to get it. Unless you watch or read a lot of science fiction, it might be hard to imagine that consumers might download their favorite shows while channel-surfing through thousands of channels or letting a DVR robot download programs for them while they are away, but such changes seem likely in the coming years. Whoever designs the kind of remote control Americans will use will have a tough job. Will a trackball replace the mouse? Will voice-recognition do away with the lap keyboard? Will my iPhone or iPad replace the remote entirely? Can the public afford to pay individually for each show? Will product placement within sitcoms and dramas be enough to pay the stars' salaries? If the economics are wrong, the old mass audience ways will last much longer. If the new media demassify the audience, however, there will be no turning back. You will live in interesting times.

Notes

1. Tom, Lowry, "PwC Predicts Pay TV Boost" *Variety*, June 14, 2011. *www.variety.com/article/VR1118038523.*

2. Mermigas, Diane, "Send in the Cloud: Amazon Trumps Netflix, Others with Savvy Interactivity," 25 February 2011, *http://www.mediapost.com/publications/?fa=Articles.showArticle&art_aid=145717.*

3. Brian, Montopoli, "ACBS to YouTube: Who Loves You Baby?," July 17 2006. *www.cbsnews.com/blogs/2006/07/17/publiceye/entry1809404.shtml.*

4. Internet Systems Consortium, "ISC Domain Survey: Number of Internet Hosts," Redwood City, CA (n.d.). *www.isc.org/index.pl?/ops/ds/host-count-history.php.*

5. Louis, Hau, "Old People Like Web Video!," Forbes, November 14 2006. *www.forbes.com/2006/ 11/14/youtube-video-demographics-tech-media-cx_lh_1113webvideo.html.*

6. Shelly, Palmer. *Television Disrupted.* Boston: Focal Press, 2006, pp. 77–79.

7. Ken, Kerschbaumer, "For Lieberman, It's All About Perspective," *Broadcasting & Cable,* July 10 2000, pp. 52–56.

PART

3

Understanding Key Processes

Part Three Outline

Program and Audience Research and Ratings

Douglas A. Ferguson, Timothy P. Meyer, and Susan Tyler Eastman

Chapter Outline

"How could those idiots cancel that show? It was my favorite. Why do they always get rid of the good stuff and keep all the junk?" Sound familiar? It should. Most people have, at one time or another, heard the news that a favorite television show has been canceled. The reason? Usually the one given is "low ratings," a way of saying that not enough people watched the program. Why are the ratings so important? Why do so many shows fail? Can't a network executive tell whether a show will succeed in the ratings? In this chapter we look at ratings and other forms of audience research and explain what they are, how they are used and misused, and why.[1] We will examine the industry's current program research practices and qualitative audience measurement techniques and then, because of their special position in industry economics, explain and interpret audience ratings.

Decision-Making for Programmers

Media programmers (and all others in the advertising-supported media) are interested in one goal: *reaching the largest possible salable audience.* Programmers define audiences differently depending on particular circumstances, but regardless of definition, determining audience *size* is paramount. The separations between program creation and presentation and reception by the audience mean that programmers must always guess who will be there and how many there will be; then estimate how predictable and accurate those guesses are.

Because networks, stations and other content providers sell commercial time at dollar rates based on *predicted* audiences, it is no surprise that program and audience research is critical for the financial health of the broadcast television, radio, cable, mobile and online industries. Program and audience research, usually involving ratings, guides the process of selecting and scheduling programs to attract the desired audience and provide feedback on programming decisions.

The broadcast and cable industries use many research approaches to evaluate programs and audiences, most of which fall into one of three groupings (to date, internet companies have used only the third type):

1. Qualitative and quantitative measures of the programs themselves

2. Qualitative and quantitative measures of audience preferences and reactions

3. Quantitative measures of audience size

Qualitative research tries to explain why people make specific program choices and what they think about those programs. **Quantitative** research, in the form of ratings and surveys, reports what programs (and commercials, presumably) people are listening to or watching.[2]

Programmers use qualitative information on programs to select and improve programs and to understand audiences' reactions to program content; qualitative audience data help explain people's reactions to programs. Quantitative audience data generally provide measures of the size and demographic composition of sets of viewers, listeners or subscribers. Of all findings, however, *ratings are the major form of program evaluation, and they have the most influence on the other concerns of this book—program selection and scheduling—in the United States and, indeed, on the television industry worldwide* (see 5.1).

Newer on-demand delivery systems have taken most of the guesswork out of estimating audience size, although viewer reactions still require measurement. Cable systems can collect viewer information using the converter boxes that deliver the channels. Mobile devices can track what and how much is viewed by whom, assuming you are not watching a program on a borrowed iPad. Broadcasters are largely in need of audience estimates based on survey research with the aid of metered devices.

The Advent of People Meters

In the late 1980s, a sweeping change occurred in the national television ratings—the shift by ratings companies from measuring people's viewing using diaries and simple passive meters to measuring viewing using people meters, a much more elaborate, interactive measurement process. *People meters*

5.1 Ratings Research Is Everywhere

Dr. Wally Langschmidt was the founder of ratings research in South Africa. He was the colleague of such American and European luminaries of early media research as Arthur C. Nielsen, Alfred Politz and George Gallop. Dr. Langschmidt helped create the South African Advertising Research Foundation (SAARF). It promotes and monitors the use in South Africa of up-to-date standards in such audience measurement tools as people meters, diaries, and personal interviews. Dr. Langschmidt's most outstanding contribution, however, was to pioneer the concept of a single data source for all media—called the All Media and Products Survey (AMPS)—used today by both media and advertisers in South Africa. The AMPS survey gives the whole country a common trading currency that is used by both advertisers and broadcast program planners to evaluate the use of all media.

One big difference from the American system is that funding of market research in South Africa comes from a 1 percent levy on each advertisement carried on radio, TV, print, outdoor advertising, and cinema that is paid by the marketers. SAARF is run by a series of industry committees, and although the actual research is presently commissioned to Nielsen Media Research, SAARF's importance to the reliability of South Africa's media research is widely recognized, and its contract has been renewed every five years.

Daan van Vuuren, Ph.D.
Former Director of Audience Research
SABC, South Africa

Reprinted by kind permission of Linda van Vuuren.

consist of a computer and a handheld electronic device with which individuals signal when they are viewing. The "black box" computer is located near the television set, registering (from the handheld device) each viewer's presence and all channel selections. When first installed, background demographic information (age and sex) on every viewer in the household gets stored in the device's memory to be matched with the viewing information. As audiences develop more mobile habits, viewer information will be more user-specific with data stored such portable viewing devices as iPhones and iPads.

A/P Meters

In 2005 Nielsen introduced further refinements to its measurement devices, counting program viewing up to seven days after the original time of showing, to accommodate time-shifting with video recorders. These *active/passive (A/P) people meters* measure audiences with greater accuracy and less reliance on viewer participation by reading codes embedded into the programming—rather than by simply detecting the channel to which a set is tuned, as is done by the old metering system. At first, these meters measured only national audiences (a particular sample), but they soon moved into the larger markets for local measurement. In 2011 Nielsen

began measuring viewing on web-enabled television receivers.

Set-Top Box Measurement

A *set-top box* (STB) measures television viewing by connecting a counter to the (hated) digital cable box already installed in most homes. This method is expected to become more popular, if not liked, especially with small markets where diary-based ratings from Nielsen show wide differences from Rentrak's STB ratings. Even local people meters and passive meters have been shown to produce measurements that diverge from STB ratings, thus supporting a future shift to STB (but the good news for consumers is that set-top boxes will soon be buried in TV sets as they are in DVRs).

TiVo uses its own DVR box to offer STB measurement and sells the information on replaying commercials to advertisers. Programmers can glean useful information about how people pause and rewatch television shows and advertisers can assess the popularity of commercial messages by how often they are skipped (or played a second or third time). TiVo users probably don't, however, constitute a representative sample, but the service measures amount of time watching broadcast, watching cable, either in recorded mode or live and then on broadband, streaming versus downloads, podcasts and user generated content, so the service generates some useful data for the industry (even if it makes consumers wary).

Actually the term *set-top box* is becoming a misnomer, as fewer people have television receivers that even resemble a box. Such a device connected to flat-screen receiver is sometimes called a *digital converter box*, although the terms set-top box and STB are still widely used.

The Threat from DVRs

An ongoing consideration in the television and advertising industries centers on the adoption of DVRs, such as TiVo and various digital converters provided by cable and satellite operators. The DVR is a device that functions like a personal computer in that programs are digitally stored on the machine's hard drive. Like computer files, programs can be kept in storage or deleted once storage capacity is reached, and on some DVRs, programs can be burned to disks and saved as DVDs. Although home video recording of various kinds has been available for many decades, *widespread use of DVRs affects two relationships: that between producers and program*

distributors and that between advertisers and program distributors. Over 40 percent of homes had DVRs in 2012, but penetration was expected to increase to nearly all digital households by 2015. All satellite service subscribers get a DVR, and cable subscribers have the option of having either simple or high-end DVRs with high-definition service, and all of their benefits.

Traditionally, the A/P meters counted only the number of minutes spent viewing a program within a few seconds of transmission (now eight seconds to allow for DVR lag), the definition of "live" viewing. The valuable *overnight ratings*, for example, include only "live" viewing. But Nielsen produces other important data sets, such as "live plus same day," which measures viewing within 24 hours (to include DVR recording and playback), and "live plus seven," which measures programs recorded and watched within a week. In 2007 Nielsen introduced *C3 ratings* which measures average commercial minute ratings with three days of DVR playback. The system is a compromise between networks (who want credit for DVR playback) and advertisers (who only want to pay for viewers who are watching their commercials). Thus, producers, syndicators and advertisers negotiate with broadcast and cable networks about which set of numbers to accept as the standard.

5.2 **Tracking Bloggers**

Not all ratings services track television or radio and not all come from Nielsen or Arbitron. Technorati, a blog tracking service, tracks about 55 million blogs worldwide, in several languages (English, Korean, French, German, Italian, Chinese and others), to measure who is talking about which companies and what they are saying. Unlike ratings, this kind of surveying tracks both the buzz that aids new products and the negative write-ups that often doom new products. Such a service benefits marketers of products by monitoring online chatter that can supplement or contradict traditional advertising. In the same way, American media marketers play close attention to bloggers who discuss television programs, and many large companies have their own specialists (like commentators) who create daily blogs on a variety of topics, some of which are their own products and services. Brandimetrics and Nielsen

BuzzMetrics track blogs about specific client products and services in the U.S. NM Incite (a Nielsen McKinsey company) collects social media information that builds on BuzzMetrics. NM Incite helps clients take advantage of the power of social media.

Nowadays anyone can track topics because the Twitter stream of microblog messages (*tweets*) is indexed "live" by search engines like Google. A programmer can follow comments made during or after a program by searching the show title or a *hashtag* (e.g., #dwts for *Dancing with the Stars*). In addition, Twitter publishes the most-recent "top trending" topics on its home page. Even the walls of Facebook are revealed through the *youropenbook.org* website. Some observers believe the program ratings for a primetime show can be estimated by the amount of background chatter generated on social media sites (see also Chapter 4).

Another concern is that DVRs may upset the delicate balance that permits the television industry to pay for producing and distributing programs. All DVRs have the ability to skip over commercials while playing back a recording. If more and more viewers watch more and more television but skip the commercials, the financial infrastructure of the television industry becomes seriously threatened. Advertisers rely on television networks and stations to deliver audiences for the programs in which their commercials appear, and advertising revenue pays most of the bill. *If the viewing audience for commercials shrinks because of DVR use, then ad revenues will shrink correspondingly.* At some point, revenues might be insufficient to pay for program production and delivery. This would require a shift to an alternative way to pay for television programs—perhaps a pay-per-program system—that would make television a much less affordable commodity.

Even if DVRs eventually change the economics of television, audience measurement will still be needed. Recent research from Nielsen on TV commercial viewing by DVR users has softened many advertisers' concerns about skipping commercials, at least as long as fewer than half of all homes have DVRs.

One response to the threat of DVRs has been to expand *product placement* in programs. Now research firms measure the value of product placements (in daytime and reality shows) and sponsorships and look at the opinions of bloggers as a way to gauge improvements in products and marketing (see 5.2). As product placement invades television programming, a trend that began many years ago in motion pictures, the line between program measurement and advertising measurement begins to blur. This chapter, however, focuses on program and audience measurement because they are crucial to current programming processes and strategies.

Program Testing

The enormous expense of producing television programs necessitates testing them before and during the actual production of a show. In addition, promotional announcements that advertise programs are usually tested to gauge their effectiveness and ability to communicate a program's most attractive features.

Concept, Pilot, and Episode Testing

Concept testing involves asking audiences whether they like the *ideas* for proposed programs. Producers generally conduct this type of test before a program has been offered to a broadcast or cable network. *Pilot testing* occurs when a network is considering the purchase of a new series, and audiences are asked to react to the *pilot* episode. This process is described in detail in Chapter 4 (network prime-time programming). *Episode testing* occurs when a series is under way. Plot lines, the relative visibility of minor and major characters, the appeal of the settings and so on can be tested to gauge audience preferences.

ASI Entertainment, based in Los Angeles, is one of the best-known companies conducting program tests (and tests of commercials). Traditionally, ASI researchers invite people into a testing theater to watch a television program, a film or a commercial, asking them to rate it by pushing "positive" and "negative" buttons that are attached to their seats. Generally the participants are paid, often in products rather than cash, for taking part in the test. Computers monitor individual responses, producing a graph of the viewer's "votes" over time. These data are correlated with demographic and other information (*psychographics*) obtained via questionnaires from each participant (see 5.3).

Theater-style testing also takes place at the Television City research center at the MGM Grand in Las Vegas, an ideal location for assuming a nationally-diverse group of vacationers. Visitors are recruited to watch pilots and participate in surveys and focus groups. Five minutes before the screening begins, viewers are led into one of four studios to watch the most recent programs from CBS, MTV, Nickelodeon and other Viacom networks (this television-holdings giant manages the research center). A survey following the program lasts about 15 minutes; such incentives as T-shirts, caps, pins, key chains and computer software are used to get participants to fill it out.

5.3 ASI Theater Testing

ASI research has been criticized for its unrepresentative audience samples, yet it remains a major contributor to network and movie studio program testing in America. ASI provides valuable data because its audiences are consistent from one time to the next. It has established norms from all its previous testing of programs, films and commercials against which new findings are weighed. Given the many programs evaluated during past decades and the fact that few programs are really "new" in any significant way, comparing how well a new show tests to how others like it have tested in the past produces useful information. The results are especially noteworthy when a program produces a negative or low evaluation because the average ASI participant evaluates programs positively. Of course, not all programs that test positively turn out to be even modestly successful when put on a network schedule (factors independent of the show's content have more influence on ratings), but very few of those that test negatively at ASI later succeed.

Frequently, prime-time series that have slipped in the ratings are tested with live audiences to determine which aspects of the program, if any, can be manipulated to improve the popularity of the series. The testing instruments range from simple levers and buttons, such as those used in ASI theaters, to more controversial methods, such as skin conductance meters measuring respiration and perspiration. Programmers seek aids in understanding the weaknesses and strengths of a series that is performing below expectations. Sometimes the research suggests a change of characters or setting that revitalizes a program. (If research results are no help, the cynical programmer usually suggests adding a dog or a child.)

Concept and pilot testing stress general plot lines and main characters, seeking to discover if they are understood and appeal to a variety of people. Ongoing program testing focuses on more subtle evaluations of the voices, manners, style and interactions of all characters. In fact, different actors and plot lines are sometimes used for separate screenings to find out which cast and plot audiences prefer. Postproduction research can discover a poor program opening or an audience's difficulty in understanding the main theme of an episode.

Unfortunately, the theater environment can't reflect at-home viewing conditions and is thus a less than ideal research method. It does, however, supply detailed data that can be matched to screen actions, adding fodder for programming decisions. In many test markets where insertion equipment is available, researchers send alternate versions of pilot programs (and commercials) to different cable homes and interview the viewers on their reactions. This necessitates producing alternate versions of a program, however—a huge expense not lightly undertaken.

A popular method for program testing is using streaming video over the internet to reach test audiences. Online data collection simplifies the research process and reduces the chance for error in the data.

As more people watch video online, theater and cable testing may eventually be replaced, although both are still going strong.

Promotion Testing

Competition for audiences requires that most programmers continually produce effective promotional materials. Promotional spots advertise particular episodes of a series, special shows, movies, newscasts or unique aspects of a station's or service's programming (images and identities).[3] These *promos* can be tested before they are aired to find out whether they communicated what was intended.

Much of the promotional testing being done uses *online audience samples*. Strategic Media Research (SMR), a research and marketing company that has specialized in radio, began testing TV promos online at the turn of the century. Clients include MTV, VH1, Comedy Central, Country Music Television and Spike. Some testing firms used to conduct tests in shopping centers, intercepting people at random to invite them to view promos in return for cash or merchandise. Promo evaluation, especially for radio, sometimes includes group and theater testing that emphasizes such measures as *memorability*, *credibility* and *persuasibility*. After demographic data are gathered, other questions are asked and associated with participants' opinions. Promo-copy testing has become a standard practice in the industry.

As multichannel and mobile television entered the on-demand era, promotion testing increased in importance and became even more critical and more widely used. Menu-driven program selection (*video-on-demand*, or *VOD*) is more influenced by on-air promos and guide channels than by schedule-driven program selection, so media companies realize that promos need to be effective.

Qualitative Audience Research

In addition to program testing, which applies mostly to television programs and movies, stations use qualitative research to get audience reactions to program materials, personalities, and station or system image. Using focus groups is one such research method. Radio stations also use call-out research to test their programming, and network television and major-market stations make use of television quotient data (TvQs). *Qualitative audience research* is the most common phrase used in the industry to refer to all of these research techniques. (See 5.4 about the beginnings of qualitative research in the radio days.)

Focus Groups

One method of gathering information from a group of people is to conduct small group testing. A *focus group* is a set of 10 or 12 people involved in a controlled discussion. A moderator leads a conversation on a predetermined topic, such as a music format or television newscast, and structures the discussion with a set of questions. Predetermined criteria guide the recruitment of individuals for participation

---

5.4   Herta Herzog and Qualitative Radio Research*

Herta Herzog is perhaps best known for her pioneering "gratifications" research on 1940s radio serial listeners: "What do we really know about daytime serial listeners?" This study, as well as several of her earlier projects, marked Herzog as a key developer of personal interviews as an approach to learning about radio audiences. Her method was the forerunner of much of today's qualitative research into television and the internet.

As a graduate student in Austria, Herzog trained with Karl Bühler, an experimental psychologist who made several contributions to the psychology of thinking. Bühler argued that there were three sources of knowledge about human psychology: observation of human behavior, observation of the products of human culture and human introspection. By asking the proper questions, then, introspection could be obtained from ordinary people. Herzog's dissertation research was an early application of these ideas. She had six speakers, each different in sex, age, physical type and occupation, read the same passage over the radio on subsequent days of the same week. Then, Herzog distributed questionnaires in popular stores that shoppers mailed back

to her, analyzing them to learn what kinds of social and personal characteristics listeners derived simply from voice and diction. Later, Herzog developed the "depth interview," which involved open-ended questions and probes. She used this technique in her gratifications research about radio serials and quiz shows. The day after the 1938 War of the Worlds broadcast, she used this method to find out why so many listeners were frightened. These early interviews were summarized in a memo to Frank Stanton and became the basis for the interview schedule for the larger well-known study, "The Invasion from Mars."

Just as television was peeking over the horizon, Herzog left academia in 1943 to join the McCann-Erickson advertising agency, where she applied her techniques to motivation research. She stuck to the qualitative aspects of radio programs and commercials and developed ideas that others later applied to other media.

Women in Communication: A Biographical Sourcebook, edited by Nancy Signorielli. Copyright 1996. Reproduced with permission of ABC-CLIO INC. via Copyright Clearance Center.

in focus groups. For example, station management may want people who listen to country music or women aged 25 to 34. Finding people who fit the predetermined criteria (*screening*) can be costly, however, and specifying more qualifications results in a greater turndown rate, increasing the price for screening. Assembling a typical focus group generally costs between $4,500 and $5,000, including the fee paid to each participant ($50 is the standard fee, although it is sometimes as high as $150 for individuals difficult to recruit, such as physicians and other professionals).

Focus group research is especially useful for eliciting reactions to visual material and gaining insight into subtle responses to televised characters and individuals. These small group discussions can be used to develop precise questions for later field surveys of a large sample of people. For example, researchers commonly use focus groups to evaluate whether a station has enough news programming, whether music is too soft or loud, how people react to the newscasters, whether personalities are perceived as interesting or friendly and so on. The particular advantage of focus groups is that videotapes, newspaper ads and recordings can be evaluated in the same session, providing immediate feedback while avoiding confusion in recall after a lapse of time.

Approximately 200,000 media-related focus groups are conducted each year. The latest trend is to use internet-based videoconferencing for focus group observers to save travel costs and allow more people to observe the groups during the session. This technique is sometimes used to test new promos and programs. The biggest pitfall of high-tech focus groups is that many nonverbal behaviors are lost in the mediated setting. Videoconferencing technology, while continuing to improve, presents limited information from participating individuals. In a face-to-face focus group, cameras can record each participant and the moderator during the entire focus group, enabling researchers or clients to study group member reactions while another person is speaking. There are many important reasons why the data and results obtained from focus groups can't be generalized to a larger audience. An obvious limitation is the *small size* of the group. Even when a

number of different focus groups are conducted, the sample size will not allow for valid generalizations to thousands, let alone millions, of people.

Another major drawback is the *selection process*. Focus group participants are not selected using a statistically valid random sampling process, by any stretch of the imagination. *To generalize from a sample to the larger population from which the sample was drawn, random sampling procedures absolutely must be used.* In a random sampling process, every person in the population has an equal chance of being selected. A random sampling process greatly increases the chances of the sample's responses representing the population from which the sample is drawn. Even then, there is always a slim chance that the random sample may be nonrepresentative.

In addition to not being randomly selected, focus group participants differ from the general public by their *willingness* to spend the necessary time and to provide the types of information of interest. Researchers can never be sure if those who participate differ in really important ways from those contacted who declined participation. (Would you do it if stopped in a mall? Usually takes a couple of hours, and the "reward" is often store coupons.)

Other serious limitations that prevent generalizing to the larger population include participant responses that are elicited under *highly artificial conditions*. Normal viewing or listening behavior takes place in the household setting or at work (or in vehicles in the case of radio), not in the company of nine or ten complete strangers whom the participant has never seen before and will never see again. These conditions also increase the likelihood of *groupthink* or *contagion of ideas*. This means that one person's response shapes the subsequent responses of other group members and would not likely have occurred if each individual were interviewed separately. Sometimes a domineering and authoritative individual may intimidate other participants or pressure them to go along with a given expressed view, even if it is not what the others really think.

The specific *questions* asked, how they are worded, the order in which they are asked, and how they are presented verbally to participants also influence the quantity and quality of responses. Questions may elicit responses that would never have occurred spontaneously to participants outside the focus group setting. Finally, the *quality of the moderator* directly influences the focus group outcomes. Skilled moderators can make all group members feel comfortable and believe that their responses are equally valued, especially if participants disagree with what someone else has said.

Focus groups have enormous diagnostic value for programmers. "Why" questions are particularly well suited to focus groups, as well as any questions that require explanations that go beyond basic "yes or no" answers. And, just as group contagion can invalidate some responses, the group setting can successfully elicit responses that an individual may not have recalled when required to provide answers in traditional survey or individual interview settings; such responses may be elicited especially when members feel similar to other participants. Focus groups can also provide an effective means of developing appropriate questions to ask a larger random sample of audience members in future research that uses scientifically valid sampling procedures, so they're useful for learning what we need to learn.

Music Research

Radio programmers want to know their audiences' opinions of different songs and different types of music. They need to know which songs are well liked and which ones no longer have audience approval (which songs are "burned out"). *Call-out research* has been one popular, although controversial, method for discovering what listeners think about music selection.

Programmers conduct call-out research by selecting 5- to 15-second "hooks" from well-established songs and playing them for respondents over the telephone. A *hook* is a brief segment or musical phrase that captures the song's essence, frequently its theme or title. Using computers to place the calls, play the music and record responses automatically, programmers are able to ask randomly selected respondents to rate 15 or 20 song hooks on a predetermined scale. Often a scale of 1 to 10 is used, where 1 represents "don't like" and 10 represents "like a lot." Call-out

research indicates listeners' musical tastes at a given moment. If stations perform call-out research frequently (and some use it every day), a track record for each song develops, and based on it the music programmer can decide whether to leave the song in the station's rotation or drop it. When tied to the same songs for some time, it indicates song popularity but does not tell the programmer how often a particular song should be played. That remains the programmer's decision.

Another popular method of testing music is *auditorium research*. Programmers invite 75 to 150 people to a location where they jointly listen to and rate a variety of songs. Instead of rating just 15 or 20 hooks, as in telephone research, auditorium tests involve 200 to 400 hooks. Like call-out research, the method tells which songs are liked and disliked at the moment but not how often they should be aired (see Chapter 11 on Music Programming).

Music testing is expensive. Call-out research requires an investment in employees to make the selections and maybe the calls—as well as investment in computer time to analyze the results. Auditorium tests involve recruiting costs and "co-op" money for participants (usually $20 to $35). Those stations lacking facilities and personnel for music testing can hire commercial firms specializing in such work. See *www.musictec.com/method.html*.

Television Quotient Data (TvQs)

Many programmers use Marketing Evaluation, Inc.'s proprietary *television quotient data (TvQs)* to supplement Nielsen ratings. While Nielsen provides information on how many people watched a program, TvQs measure the popularity/appeal (likeability) and familiarity of TV programs and performers (from TV, movies, sports and other celebrity venues). TvQ data have been collected since 1963, relying on a panel of household members that since 1980 has included over 50,000 total households. Eight different services are provided: TvQ (programs), Performer Q, Product Q, Kids Product Q, Cartoon Q, Cable Q, Sports Q and Dead Q (performers from the past—don't you love it?!). Of these, TvQ and Performer Q are the best-known measurements.

Networks and programmers use the various TvQ services to identify actors who have "star" potential, given the assessment of both *recognition* and *likeability* that the scores provide. Some research companies use various Q scores to project the eventual success (or lack thereof) of a network series in syndication. Unlike ratings, these models factor in how people feel or felt about a program, not how many watched it. Like the Nielsen ratings, Q scores are numerical, but they are labeled "qualitative" because they assess how much performers and shows are liked. Nielsen ratings are objective measures of viewing, while Q scores are subjective measures of the appeal and familiarity of performers and programs.

Ratings Services

Ratings exert powerful influences on programming decisions by syndicators and station representatives (as illustrated in Chapter 6), by commercial network and station television programmers (as discussed in Chapters 2, 7 and 8) and by noncommercial television programmers (as covered in Chapter 10). Radio programmers also use ratings information to evaluate their market positions, choose formats and convince advertisers to buy time (see Chapters 11 and 12). And ratings are used in cable/satellite/telco distribution and online in specialized ways (see Chapters 3, 4 and 9). In fact, all programmers use ratings in program decision making, but how to use them isn't self-evident. Consequently, the rest of this chapter looks at the ways programmers interpret ratings data.

Using audience ratings is not restricted to programming applications. In fact, ratings were originally intended only to provide information for advertisers curious about audience size, and their value to advertisers continues to drive the ratings industry. Even today, unsponsored programs, including presidential addresses and political programs, are not rated by Nielsen exactly because they do not carry advertising.

Once the statistical reliability of ratings data became accepted, programmers began using audience measurement to gauge the success of their decisions. As competition among networks and stations increased, ratings became the most important decision-making data in commercial broadcasting. *Broadcast revenues, programs, stations and individual careers depend on audience ratings.* In the business of broadcasting, high ratings normally result in profits (and continuing careers). Broadcasting also has public service obligations and other aspirations and commitments, but on the purely economic side, a network or station will eliminate a program that receives low "numbers" if other, more viable options are available.

Cable/satellite rating cannot be compared directly to broadcast ratings because the potential audience viewing subscription channels is about 92 percent that of the commercial broadcast networks (61 percent are cable and 31 percent satellite/other). Moreover, scheduling is different: Many of cable's programs are scheduled in rotating and repeating patterns rather than one-time-only patterns—although this is changing because broadcasters now repeat their shows (you've noticed!), and cable has lots more original fare (you've noticed all those hours of cooking, racing, picking, digging, selling and on and on). Further, in addition to using standard ratings numbers, cable programmers analyze ratings to determine audience reach—how many people over a period of time viewed a repeated program or channel—much as public television programmers use ratings.

Articulating the power of audience ratings may sound crass to those who consider broadcasting an art form—or passé to those who are immersed in the internet—but in reality ratings continue to be the most important measure of commercial success. The efforts of most people involved in commercial broadcasting focus on achieving the *highest possible numbers*. Targeting more precisely defined audiences—such as women aged 25 to 54—is an alternate approach for television networks and stations that cannot immediately achieve a number-one position in the adults 18+ category.

In 2011, however, Nielsen finally began to rethink its decades-long interest in audience demographics, as broadcasters looked for a better way to measure the effectiveness of advertising. Nielsen Catalina, a partnership with a loyalty-marketing firm, offered a new model for measuring TV audiences based on *viewer-purchaser behavior*. Whether this new system will eventually replace demographics-based ratings remains to be seen. In the meantime, it is necessary to understand that many advertisers want demographic data so they can match their prospective customers to their commercial messages (whether those customers want to be matched is another question).

Alternatives to standard TV ratings emerge from time to time over the years, all proclaiming their inherent advantages over Nielsen data. The latest challenger is Optimedia US (owned by Publicis Groupe SA), whose "Content Power Ratings" (ironically abbreviated CPR) not only count TV viewers but also add in social media mentions on Facebook, Twitter and the like. Reporter Emily Steel provided some interesting comparisons of Nielsen program rankings and those from the CPR,[4] showing that *South Park* which is carried by Comedy Central, for example ranks #211 in the Nielsen rankings but is ranked #4 in the CPR. *Glee* (FOX) was #2 in the CPR but only #55 in Nielsen; *The Office* had a #6 CPR rank and was #105 on Nielsen. Other top programs were not nearly as far apart, such as *Grey's Anatomy* with an 11 CPR rank and a 28 from Nielsen.

Evaluating social media's role in stimulating viewing of particular shows is an emerging research phenomenon, and it obviously has some considerable significance for those TV programs that appeal to viewers who are regular social network users. Publicis Starcom Worldwide and Network Insights now measure the "positive buzz" on sites like Facebook and Twitter to assess its influence on new shows. For example, based on buzz, researchers predicted before the 2011–2012 season that FOX would have the most hits, followed by NBC, and were they right or wrong?

Which programs deliver the ideal reach and frequency of viewing by their target markets at the best possible price (aka, the biggest bang for the buck) is what advertisers want to know. Universal McCann continues to refine its statistical models that incorporate data that include TV viewership, company sales and other business data to estimate (guess) how much commercial time should be purchased and at what price not only on broadcast TV but on other media channels. Good luck with that.

Reaching the target market and staying within the allotted budget remain paramount in the minds of advertisers. What happens to those in the target market if they are in fact "reached" by the advertisers' messages remains an elusive area of audience research. *Regardless, no single model, no matter how complex, can be used for just any product or service category or brand within the category.* Different purchase cycles demand different objectives and tactics. New products or brands demand different ways of proceeding by comparison to well-established product/service categories or brands. No matter how great the advertiser's message is, it's obviously wasted if it doesn't find its way to target market consumers. The enormous difficulties of accurate audience/consumer measurement loom over many interrelated industries. (Lots of jobs here someday.)

Like broadcasters, advertising-supported cable networks also need ratings information to convince advertising agencies to purchase time. Premium cable services such as HBO use their national ratings to convince local cable systems that their programs are watched and important for promoting the local system. Video game producers and online and telephone services have their own versions of measuring audiences to show that their content is viewed. Understanding the basics of the all-powerful numbers is essential in all of these businesses.

High ratings, demonstrating television's widespread household penetration, also carry clout with Congress. Legislators generally use television to get elected and reelected, and politicians pay attention to their local broadcasters and the five largest national networks because they reach such enormous numbers of people. Increasingly, the major cable operators and most popular social media influence politicians because of their ability to reach certain types of audiences (especially upper socioeconomic levels).

The growth of social media comes at the older media's expense, but primarily for time spent looking at a screen. That time could just as easily be used for social networking, user-generated programs (such as YouTube) or traditional network shows delivered directly to mobile devices. Companies like Radian6 and others have already begun to measure some kinds of social media (see 5.2). Measuring the use of mobile devices in relation to social media and traditional media adds other layers of complexity to the following discussion of ratings.

Television Services

The most important distinction in television ratings is between *national* and *local* (also called *market*) ratings. Nielsen Media Research is presently the sole company in the United States producing nationally syndicated network audience measurements (although some of its clients are not too thrilled with the monopoly it has on data collection). Except for Arbitron's ARB-TV measurement of out-of-home television viewing, Nielsen is also the only company in the United States producing local station ratings for television (also leading to some criticism about methods and pricing).

Other research firms collect and analyze television audience measurements of specialized types for only a portion of the country. Nielsen covers the entire country continuously for network ratings, using a separate sample of 12,000 households with people meters.

The largest broadcast networks and the top 50 cable networks contract with Nielsen for this ratings service. Nielsen Media Research, hereafter called "Nielsen" for the sake of simplicity, is a subsidiary of The Nielsen Company. Nielsen Business Media publishes SRDS, the leading advertising database, and owns Scarborough Research and Billboard Publications. Only a third of the parent Nielsen Company's corporate efforts are directed at measuring what consumers *watch*, with the larger portion focused on what consumers *buy*. The division called Nielsen Online measures the use of social media and newer forms of mediated communication.

Sweeps

Nielsen conducts four nationwide measurements of audiences (*the sweeps*) for all local television stations—annually in *November, February, May and July*—producing the vital local television reports (see 5.5). These market-by-market reports allow stations to compare themselves with the other stations in their market. A separate ratings report (electronic as well as printed in a book) is published for each of the 210 markets in the country for each ratings period. These data are based on local people meters in the largest markets, a mix of diaries and local meters in the middle-sized markets, and diaries only in the smaller markets. The 25 metered markets operate on a sample of 400 to 600 homes that only partially duplicate the national people meter sample.

Today's ratings software can track hundreds of channels—broadcast or cable, terrestrial or satellite, PC or TV-delivered—and scan every channel every three seconds to report the tuning status of every TV set in the sample households. The data can be downloaded by conventional telephone or cell phone, reported the following morning as the overnights, and later compiled into the national people-meter database.[5]

A *ratings period* consists of four sequential weeks of data, reported week by week and averaged for the month. In addition to the four major nationwide television sweeps, large-market stations purchase ratings for as many as three more ratings periods (October, January and March). Midsized and smaller television markets perhaps purchase one ratings book beyond the four sweeps. The stations in a market contract individually with Nielsen for a ratings book, paying the cost of data collection, analysis, and reporting. In the very largest markets, stations pay as much as $1.5 million a year for ratings; in very small markets, however, the price may be as low as $10,000 annually. *It is important to understand that stations pay for ratings in their market, and the quality could be better if stations could afford to pay more* (advertisers, agencies and reps cover little of the cost). For example, samples could be larger and more representative, diaries could be more carefully double-checked, more call-backs could be made, and data analysis could be more reliable, but each of these steps would substantially increase the cost of ratings to the stations.

5.5 Nielsen Media Research

Nielsen gathers and interprets data on a wide range of consumer products and services as well as on television and the internet (but no radio). Nielsen's network audience estimates are reported in the *Nielsen National TV Ratings* (often abbreviated NTI for the division that collects the data), twice-a-year summary books, and in the abbreviated weekly booklets called *The Pocketpiece Report* (see Chapter 2 for a sample pocketpiece page). Besides the network-by-network ratings, pocketpieces (named for their size, designed to fit in a vest pocket in a suit coat) include the collective ratings for national public networks, basic cable networks and premium cable networks, giving network programmers a handy tool for comparing the performance of the networks and their competitors. DVD viewing is now fully incorporated into these reports. National viewing data are also reported in the other forms described in Chapter 6, often combined with product purchase and usage data.

Overnights: Nielsen also collects nightly ratings called *overnights* in the top metered markets, publishing this information every morning for the benefit of network executives and purchasing stations. Overnights, because of the smaller samples used and the big-city nature of the viewers, are only indicators of what the network ratings probably will be when the six-month NTIs are issued. But as more and more major markets are added to the overnight sample, the match between the overnight sample and the total sample comes much closer. About 70 percent of U.S. TV homes are in the overnight sample.

Local Books: Nielsen's other widely known task is the measurement of local market television viewing. These measurement reports are known as the Nielsen Station Index (NSI) and are published in *Viewers in Profile* for each market. Called the "ratings books," they are purchased by most television stations and advertising agencies. Nielsen household samples are drawn from the most recent national census, and the ratings are not weighted (adjusted to fit national or local population percentages). NSI prepares county-by-county reports on television viewing, various reports for commercial time buyers, several reports for cable

networks and system operators, and an online computer service for customized analysis of reach, frequency and audience flow.

Product Tracking: Nielsen also offers a tracking service called the Nielsen Scantrack. This national panel consists of about 30,000 households who use handheld bar-code scanners to record all purchases, including prices, and whether each item was on sale. This information is then correlated with television viewing data derived from people meters, as well as from magazine and newspaper data. Each household transmits all its media data (TV and print) weekly over phone lines to Nielsen's center for data analysis. This service has enormous benefits for corporate brand managers and advertising agency media buyers (though it may be a pain to the participants).

Computers: The measurement of television audiences now includes computer users as programs appear on the internet. Nielsen//NetRatings is a service designed to provide high-quality information about the internet in a special pocketpiece and other formats.

Spot Tracking: Nielsen has another service called Monitor-Plus, which uses computer recognition technology to identify all commercials airing in the top 50 major markets. The NSI data is combined with the commercial data to provide a minute-by-minute gross rating point measurement for each TV spot overall; the information is also broken out by brand category and by how it compares to competitors' spots. Monitor-Plus enables buyers and sellers to track advertising activity across 15 specific categories of media, including television, radio and print.

This Nielsen service rates television commercials, measuring the viewing of commercial spots—not programs—using its minute-by-minute ratings. The commercials are averaged across entire programs because per-spot data is too unreliable. This will be useful to advertisers because *industry experts have long estimated that commercial ratings are about 5 to 10 percent lower than program ratings.* That percentage can now be refined over time and eventually refined for different kinds of commercials in different program environments.

Diaries themselves continue to attract controversy in the 154 markets where they are still used as an economically feasible alternative to meters. In 2010, the Media Rating Council (MRC) withdrew its accreditation to the diary service known as Nielsen NSI. Officials at Nielsen expected the problem to be resolved, but the brouhaha served as a reminder that choosing a sample is complicated. In this case, it was determined by the MRC that Nielsen was using a flawed address-based system to replace an inferior random-dialing phone-based system (abandoned because 30 percent of homes use cell phones instead of landline phones).

Normally, station programmers purchase only the books for their own market, but programmers dealing with groups of stations may purchase all 210 local market reports for the entire country or a subset of books for markets where they have stations or cable systems. They can use these books to cross-compare the performance of programs in different markets, at different times of day, with different lead-in shows and so on. Other chapters in this book contain discussions about how ratings are used in specific sets of circumstances and point out specific weaknesses (see 5.6).

National Ratings

Network viewing estimates come from a nationwide people-meter sample of 20,000 households with and without cable. To be included in Nielsen reports, at least 3 percent of viewer meters (or diaries in local reports) must record viewing of a cable service. This means that only the top 30 or so cable networks figure in most ratings calculations. Multiple-set households are counted only *once* in total television households (TVHH), thus making the sum of the audiences to several programs telecast simultaneously often bigger than the number of households said to be viewing at one time (HUT) because one household may tune to more than one program. Indeed, *the average household has more sets than people.* As of 2012, *one ratings point represented the viewing of 116,000,000 television households (usually abbreviated 116.0 mill.), and each household represented 2.6 people.*[6]

5.6   The People-Meter Furor

Much questioning has long characterized attitudes toward rating services, but until 2004, most of this debate stayed well within the media industry. At the start of that year, Nielsen Media Research announced plans to introduce local people meters in New York City and Los Angeles, replacing set-top meters and paper diaries and providing previously unavailable demographic details about local viewers.

But when preliminary testing showed a huge drop-off in total viewing, especially among minority audiences, Nielsen faced loud charges of racial and ethnic bias in the press. Much of the criticism came from a campaign spearheaded by Rupert Murdoch's News Corporation and a coalition of black and Hispanic community leaders. In addition, producers of programs targeted to minority populations became worried that the new system would underrepresent minority viewing. On the other hand, many experts claimed that minorities had been oversampled for decades, which led to an apparent drop in viewing when they were more accurately measured. Attempts to quell suspicions were marked with numerous delays, and congressional investigations and audits were threatened, despite the issue being largely perceptual rather than substantive.

To improve its image and forestall legal action, The Nielsen Company had to lobby Congress, make big charity donations and undertake sponsorship of community events for minorities in several cities. (Insiders chuckled to think of Nielsen Media Research handing out pens, T-shirts and balloons in fair booths! This company doesn't sell anything to the public! Its high-priced products are sold only to other media companies.)

By the end of the year, the issue seemed resolved after outgoing NAACP President and CEO Kweisi Mfune announced support for Nielsen's use of people meters in local TV markets. But the issue could be resurrected at any time. Ratings are less than perfect to start with, and the services have a lousy history of accurately measuring minority viewing.

Radio Services

Only one company, Arbitron, provides *quantitative* local and national radio ratings. The consolidation of radio ownership in the late 1990s effectively drove out the need for competing services. Nielsen measures radio in 11 other countries, but not the United States, where it unsuccessfully experimented with a competing service between 2008 and 2010. Strategic Media Research converted its old Accuratings measurement (successor to Birch Ratings, if you've ever heard of that) into Accutrack, one of several similar services that *qualitatively* measure radio listening, but doesn't do quantitative measurements.

You may (or not) be surprised to learn that Arbitron measures radio audience sizes using *paper* diaries, supplemented by the internet for those who prefer responding online—but most of its ratings still come from paper scribbles. Arbitron's *Radio Market Report* tracks both in-home and out-of-home listening (in cars, offices and other places) for local radio stations in all of the 299 radio markets.[7] The data come from weekly diaries mailed to a sample of households in each market. Each person 12 years or older gets a separate diary to fill out for one week, usually running from Thursday to Wednesday when it is to be mailed back to Arbitron. New random samples participate each week, and each participant sending back a usable diary currently gets $3. The size of the sample depends on the history of response in the market and how much data collection the stations are willing to pay for (larger samples cost more money).

Data collection

Arbitron collects ratings for 48 weeks each year in the larger markets and for as few as 16 weeks in the smaller markets. This system is called *continuous radio measurement*, although it skips three weeks around Christmas/New Year's and one week in late spring. Arbitron also offers county-by-county reports of radio listening for about 42 customized survey areas and annual ratings for internet radio. It also provides *Arbitron Information on Demand (AID)*, an online computer service for radio diary research. Recent radio ratings from Arbitron are available at *www.radioandrecords.com.*

Arbitron's *Portable People Meter (PPM)* is used in the 48 largest radio markets, with daily samples ranging from 510 (Memphis) to 3,882 (New York City). *A PPM is the size of a cell phone or pager, and it records all daily electronic listening for several months.* (Have you ever seen one?) Monthly rating reports for the top ten U.S. markets are the goal, but so far the technology has had problems and more problems. Reports for the first 33 markets were released by 2009 and the remaining 17 by 2010.

Discouraged by the slow pace of the PPM releases, several of the biggest radio companies jointly funded a competing company, Media Audit, that uses smart phones as the measurement system. By 2012, Media Audit had measured over 80 radio markets.

Nationwide Radio

Radio's All Dimension Audience Research *(RADAR 108)*, owned by Arbitron, reports on the performance of the *national* radio services. RADAR reports cover the size and demographics composition of 50 radio networks operated by American Urban Radio Networks, Citadel Media Networks, Crystal Media Networks, Dial Global Media, Premiere Radio Networks, United Stations Radio Networks and Westwood One Radio Networks. RADAR reports are based on analyses of 48 weeks of continuous measurement using 395,000 members of Arbitron's diary and PPM databases. Arbitron also uses Mediaguide's broadcast monitoring technology to verify whether the radio commercials that were scheduled to be aired on affiliated stations of RADAR-rated networks were broadcast as indicated on the network commercial clearance reports. RADAR ratings are the only nationwide radio network ratings, and are reported for the top 10, 25 and 50 markets.

Online Radio

Since 2004, *comScore* has provided broadcast-type ratings for the online radio industry. It passively and continuously captures the online radio behavior across the country of nearly 250,000 U.S. listeners. ComScore reports weekly cumes, quarter-hour ratings and most demographics in the 15 standard broadcast dayparts for AOL Radio, Clear Channel

Online Music, ESPN Radio, Live 365 and Yahoo Music Launch-out. *Measurement is important to these big radio webcasters because it legitimizes a program service that reaches far beyond the usual geographic limits for a radio station* and supplies advertisers with the data they need to make informed decisions about media buys.

Online Video

In 2010, comScore updated its measurement of online video with the introduction of Video Metrix 2.0, which added the capability of distinguishing between program content and the advertising within the shows. *Video Metrix provides the television industry's only comprehensive measurement of the video marketplace*, with the ability to track video advertising, top television programs, viral videos and syndicated traffic. The comScore service also classifies video-viewing activity by TV dayparts. The largest primetime networks showed viewing to their respective video sites (as shown in 5.7).

Video Games

Until advertising began appearing in video games, user measurement was not a priority, even though video game playing was clearly replacing some traditional media behaviors (especially among the 18 to 34 male demographic). But by 2005, the video game industry was raking in more billions of dollars annually than the movie industry, a fact that made the advertising industry take note. Looking ahead in 2004, Nielsen expanded its definition of viewing to include "screen-based" advertising in order to include games, cell phones, wireless and other portable media, and began testing ways to measure viewing by game users.

Console-based video game systems account for 15 percent of teenage males' daily use of media during prime time. One recently altered factor was the move of "television prime time for young males" into the late-night time period, leaving 8 to 11 P.M. for games. Nielsen has developed *GamePlay Metrics* as a way of mining people-meter data collected on television and internet use, adding the passive collection of game titles, and matching all the data to

demographics and dayparts to inform the sale of advertising. GamePlay Metrics reports tell who is playing what game, the type of console used (applies to Sony, Microsoft and Nintendo, so far), the genre of the game, and what other media the players consume. The weekly data comes from the same 10,000 households used to provide television ratings.

The next generation of game consoles is likely to include special signals related to advertising in games that Nielsen can track, and such measurements will be extended to wireless (phone and PDA) receivers as fast as the technology can be developed. *Selling advertising within games and consoles is part of a national media trend to place ads everywhere and closely measure media usage.* Industry profits are needed to fund the enormous cost of developing subsequent generations of consoles, and later, wireless equipment and content.

Social Media

Social networking sites (*SNSs*) like Facebook and Twitter attract huge masses of viewers for their screen-based entertainment and information (in case you hadn't noticed!). At last count, Facebook had over 700 million members worldwide, and Twitter had 200 million users (but these numbers swell in the night). At this writing, the difficult problem of measuring their audiences is unsettled and evolving rapidly, but many companies are tackling solutions. Such companies as Attensity, Radian6, Statsit, Sysomos and Vocus retrieve text-based indicators of customer satisfaction (and dissatisfaction), but they barely skim the surface of the information that might be collected, and the data they collect is in no way the equivalent of ratings.

Specialized Audiences

Programmers and advertisers constantly pressure the rating services for more information about aspects of the increasingly fragmented media audience. On the television side, the larger audience shares captured by cable create demand for an even more precise understanding of audience viewing habits. Thus, in local market reports, the ratings companies break demographic information into smaller units (such as

5.7 **Sample Online Video Ratings**

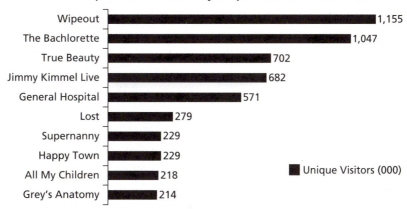

Top Shows on ABC.com by Unique Video Viewers June 2010

Show	Unique Visitors (000)
Wipeout	1,155
The Bachlorette	1,047
True Beauty	702
Jimmy Kimmel Live	682
General Hospital	571
Lost	279
Supernanny	229
Happy Town	229
All My Children	218
Grey's Anatomy	214

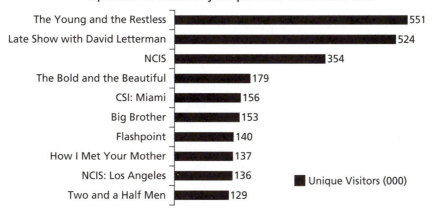

Top Shows on CBS.com by Unique Video Viewers June 2010

Show	Unique Visitors (000)
The Young and the Restless	551
Late Show with David Letterman	524
NCIS	354
The Bold and the Beautiful	179
CSI: Miami	156
Big Brother	153
Flashpoint	140
How I Met Your Mother	137
NCIS: Los Angeles	136
Two and a Half Men	129

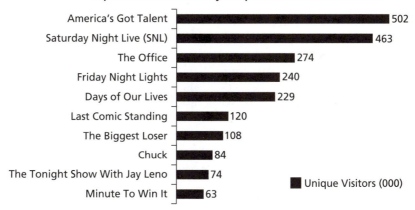

Top Shows on NBC.com by Unique Video Viewers June 2010

Show	Unique Visitors (000)
America's Got Talent	502
Saturday Night Live (SNL)	463
The Office	274
Friday Night Lights	240
Days of Our Lives	229
Last Comic Standing	120
The Biggest Loser	108
Chuck	84
The Tonight Show With Jay Leno	74
Minute To Win It	63

Reprinted by permission of ComScore.

10-year jumps for radio) and more useful categories for different groups of advertisers. In addition to the classic adults 18 to 49, 25 to 54 and the like, both women 18 to 34 and women 25 to 49 are now included, for example, as well as similar subgroups of men, children and teens.

In addition to local and national ratings reports, Nielsen and Arbitron offer various customized reports covering narrower views of the audience (for example, males aged 18 to 34, Hispanic women aged 25 to 54 or college students) and specialized programming, such as Nielsen's analyses of syndicated program ratings, which are particularly useful to stations making program purchases. Chapters 6 and 8 make a special point of the importance of syndicated program reports, which are illustrated later in this chapter.

Ratings Terminology and Measurement Computations

Nielsen collects television audience estimates by randomly selecting viewers from the 210 U.S. broadcast television markets. The number of markets varies slightly from year to year and has grown along with population increases. Nielsen calls the markets **Designated Market Areas (DMAs)**. These areas are roughly equivalent to **Areas of Dominant Influence (ADIs)** as determined by Arbitron for measuring radio markets. Many more radio markets exist, however, to account for listening in low-population-density areas. Nielsen collapses these very small markets with the nearest big city television audiences.

Survey Areas

For each market, Nielsen collects ratings data from more than just the DMA, as shown in 5.8. The smallest measurement unit is the **Metro Area**, the next largest is the local DMA, and the largest unit (part shown) is the **Nielsen Survey Index Area (NSI Area)**. *The NSI Area includes the DMA and the Metro Area but also encompasses counties outside the DMA where viewing can be attributed to a station in the DMA.* These three geographical areas are described more fully in the following sections.

NSI Area

The NSI Area includes all counties measured in a ratings survey, including counties outside the DMA when substantial viewing of stations inside the DMA occurs in them—viewership is usually the result of carriage by cable systems. *Rarely used by commercial television programmers (because DMAs are more useful), NSI Area figures show a station's total estimated reach or circulation.* As indicated earlier, reach tells how many people have viewed or listened to a station in the past, and it therefore suggests how many could view or listen in the future. In cable, reach tells how many households subscribe to basic cable service. Reach is an important measure for radio, public television, cable and online websites. Another name for reach is cumulative audience, or cume.

DMA

Each county in the United States is assigned to only one DMA. Generally, a DMA centers on a single city, such as Charleston, Denver or New York, but in some cases two or even three cities are linked in hyphenated markets, as in the Florence/Myrtle Beach and Springfield/Decatur/Champaign markets. All stations in these multiple markets reach most viewers, making the cities one television viewing market. Nielsen ranks each DMA according to the estimated number of television households within its counties. As of 2012, the top five DMAs in rank order were New York (with over 7 million TV households), Los Angeles, Chicago, Philadelphia and Dallas/Ft. Worth.

Metro Areas

The third geographical area, the **Metro Survey Area (MSA)** in radio and **Metro Rating Area (MRA)** or simply "Metro" in television, is the smallest of the three survey areas and is the one most frequently used for radio programming. The Metro includes only a small number of counties closest to the home city of the DMA, but often consists of only a single, gigantic county in some parts of the United States, especially in the West.

Because competing big-city radio signals generally blanket the Metro, urban radio programmers use it to determine the success or failure of

5.8   Diagram of a Television Market Survey Area

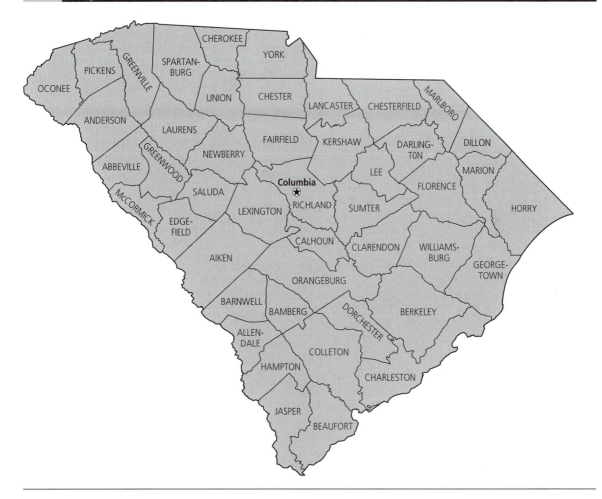

programming decisions. (Coverage patterns in out-lying areas may vary too widely to compare.) The Metro represents the majority of urban radio listeners, the bulk of office and store listening and a large part of in-car listening. Altogether, more than 280 Metro areas are measured by Arbitron for radio listening. Radio stations on the fringe of the Metro area are more likely to refer to Total Survey Area (TSA), which is comparable to NSI area measures. But television programmers rarely use Metro ratings because no demographic breakouts are available.

To use any of these ratings services for programming decisions, programmers must understand how the estimates are produced. Using ratings without this knowledge is like trying to play chess without learning the rules. Pieces can be moved, but winning the game is unlikely. Memorize the saying, "*Audiences count, but only in the way they are counted.*" Print it on your wall and make signs all over your home, and figure out what it means. We try to tell you in the following subsections which provide an overview of the basics of audience computations, but telling isn't understanding. That's up to you.

Ratings/Shares/HUTs

A **rating** is an estimate of the percentage of the total number of people or households in a population tuned to a specific station or network during a specific time period (daypart) such as morning drive-time or prime access (7 to 8 P.M. eastern/Pacific time). A **share** is an estimate of the percentage of people or households that are actually using radio or television and are tuned to a specific station or network during a specific daypart. *The sum of all program shares equals 100 percent, but the sum of all ratings equals the percentage of total viewers (one must include nonviewers to get 100 percent).* Ratings depend on a count of all *receivers*; shares on a count of all *users*. Shares are always bigger percentages than ratings for the same program or station because some people who could watch television (or listen to radio) are not watching (they are sleeping or playing games or actually working).

Ratings are always a percentage estimate of an entire population, whether the **population** refers to all households in the country or all people aged 25 to 54 or all adults 12+ or all women aged 18 to 49. Populations can be anything you say they are. A share is always a percentage of those households or people in that population using the particular medium at a specific time. To restate, *shares always appear larger than ratings because they are based on a smaller sample of people.* Fewer people use television (or radio or cable or the internet) than could use it if all were at home, awake and choosing television above other activities. Both estimates are percentages of an entire group, although the percent sign is often omitted.

Sales staffs use ratings to set advertising rates. Programmers generally use shares in decisions about programs because shares show how well a program does against its competition. *Shares eliminate all the people who are not watching TV and show how many of those watching TV are tuned to a program or station.* Programmers at broadcast networks and stations as well as cable services typically refer to their *shares of an actual audience,* not their percentage (ratings) *of potential households,* although newspaper articles often report ratings (or mix up the two kinds of data).

The combined ratings of all stations or networks during a particular daypart provide an estimate of the number of **households using television (HUTs), persons using television (PUTs),** or **persons using radio (PURs).** HUTs, PUTs and PURs are used to compute the shares for each station or network. Dayparts are more meaningful for radio audiences, which are less likely to time-shift their media consumption.

To illustrate these concepts, let's assume there are only four network television options in the United States (like in olden days) and that Nielsen's metered households (12,000 in reality, but rounded to 10,000 to keep this example easy) indicate the following hypothetical data for prime time:

Network	Household Viewing
ABC	1,904
CBS	1,928
NBC	1,976
FOX	1,222
None	2,970
Total	10,000

The HUT level is .703 or 70.3 percent (7,030/10,000), calculated by adding the households watching television and dividing by the total number of households with television (1,904 + 1,928 + 1,976 + 1,222 divided by 10,000 equals .703). The answer is changed from a decimal to a percentage by multiplying by 100. A HUT of 70.3 means an estimated 70 percent of all households had a television set on at the time of the measurement. The individual ratings and shares for the four networks can now be calculated.

$$\text{RATING} = \frac{\text{Households Watching a Network}}{\text{Households with Receivers}}$$

$$\text{SHARE} = \frac{\text{Households Watching a Network}}{\text{Households Watching TV}}$$

To calculate a rating, the number of households watching a network is divided by the total number of households that have receivers. To calculate shares, the number of households watching ABC, for example, is divided by the total number of households watching television.

Network Ratings	Share
ABC $\dfrac{1,904}{10,000} = .190$ or 19%	$\dfrac{1,904}{7,030} = .271$ or 27.1%
CBS $\dfrac{1,928}{10,000} = .193$ or 19.3%	$\dfrac{1,928}{7,030} = .274$ or 27.4%
NBC $\dfrac{1,976}{10,000} = .198$ or 19.8%	$\dfrac{1,976}{7,030} = .281$ or 28.1%
FOX $\dfrac{1,222}{10,000} = .122$ or 12.2%	$\dfrac{1,222}{7,030} = .174$ or 17.4%

The individual ratings for all the stations in a market during a given daypart should approximately equal the HUT. Network programmers primarily use rating and share estimates to compare program audiences, but often they also are interested in the specific number of persons in the audience. Ratings can be used to project to any particular population. For example, the data for the four networks listed produced these estimates for the entire United States (having a total population of about 116 million households):

Network	Rating × Population	Population = HH Estimate
ABC	.190 × 116 million	= 22,040,000
CBS	.193 × 116 million	= 22,388,000
NBC	.194 × 116 million	= 22,504,000
FOX	.122 × 116 million	= 14,152,000
	.699 (or 69.9%)	= 81,084,000

The number 22,040,000 represents the 211 million people estimated to be watching ABC (at this specific time). These calculations can be verified by multiplying the HUT, 69.9, by the total number of households: .699 × 112 million = 78,288,000, the total for the four networks.

Using part of a page from a Charleston (SC) Nielsen book (see 5.9), we can see how ratings and shares were computed for the local television stations WCBD, WCIV and WCSC. To calculate the rating and share for WCSC, in this morning/midday example, Nielsen first analyzed diaries from a sample of households (HH) in the Charleston DMA. It then projected the sample returns to the DMA household population. Approximately 8 percent of the total diaries were tuned to WCSC from 12 noon to 3 P.M.

If we assume that 8 percent of the diaries reflects 8 percent of the total households (always an iffy call but done constantly), the number of homes watching WCSC can then be calculated. An estimated 266,400 television households in the Charleston DMA (this information is supplied on another page) yields 21,312 homes for WCSC (.08 × 266,400 = 21,312). The share for WCSC was computed by using the HUT (see the H/P/T totals), which was 24 (percent). Twenty-four percent of 266,400 yields 63,936 HH, and when that figure is divided into WCSC's 21,312 HH, a share of 34 results. (Actually, the calculation is 33, but because the reported ratings are rounded to the nearest whole number, the math does not always work with whole numbers. Either the 8 rating is actually slightly larger than 8 and rounded down, or the HUT rating is slightly lower than 24 and rounded up.)

Further evidence of Nielsen's rounding can be seen in the 12 noon to 4:00 P.M. time period on the same page. In that time period of the Nielsen report, you will see that WCBD and WCIV both have "2" ratings, but each station's share is different. We can compute more accurate ratings by manipulating the basic formula, usually written as

$$\frac{\text{Rating}}{\text{HUT}} \times 100 = \text{SHARE}$$

The calculated value is multiplied by 100 to create whole numbers instead of decimals for shares and ratings. If we transpose to

$$\text{RATING} = \frac{\text{Share} \times \text{HUT}}{100}$$

we can rate more accurately:

$$\text{WCBD Rating} \quad \frac{7 \times 30}{100} = 2.1$$

$$\text{WCIV Rating} \quad \frac{8 \times 30}{100} = 2.4$$

Keep in mind that all ratings and shares are percentages and must include decimal points for all calculations, although to make their reports easy to read, ratings companies do not print the decimals (see 5.10).

5.9   Daypart Ratings Page

CHARLESTON, SC

DAYPART	DAYPART	DMA HOUSEHOLD			DMA RATINGS																																				PERCENT DISTRIBUTION			TV HH RATINGS IN ADJACENT DMA'S		
METRO HH		SHARE		IN MKT	SHARE TREND				PERSONS										WOMEN								MEN						TNS	CHILD					ADJACENT DMA					
R T G	S H R	DAYPART TIME(ETZ) STATION	R T G	S H R	S S H R	MAY '03	FEB '03	NOV '02	JUL '02	2+	12-24	12-34	18-34	18-49	21-49	25-54	35-+	50-64	18+	12-24	18-34	18-49	25-49	25-54	W K G	18+	18-34	18-49	21-49	25-49	25-54	12-17	2-11	6-11	MET	HOME DMA	#1	#2	#3	#1	#2	#3
1	2		7	8	9	10	11	12	13	15	17	18	19	20	21	22	23	24	25	26	27	28	29	31	32	34	35	36	37	38	39	40	41	42	43	44	45	46	47	48	49	50	51
<< 24		MON.-FRI. 6:00A-9:00A (CON'T) WTBS IT H/P/T.*	<< 24	16		25	25	26	22	12	4	6	7	11	11	13	17	16	20	15	4	9	12	14	15	14	13	1 6	9	10	11	11	3	7	6								
		MON.-FRI. 7:00A-9:00A																																									
9	34	WBLN W WCBD N	8	30	47	28	29	27	22	4	1	2	2	4	4	6	4	6	6	1	4	5	6	6	5	3	1	2	2	2	2	1				88	95	2		3			
5	19	WCIV A	4	16	26	15	16	17	18	2		1	2	2	2	4	3	5	3	1	2	3	3	3	4	2	1	1	1	1	1				87	94	1	4	1			
5	19	WCSC C	5	17	27	15	15	19	18	2		1	2	2	2	3	3	4	3		2	2	2	2	2	3	1	2	1	2	3				84	92		5	3			
1	2	WITV P	1	3			3	5	4	1																							3	3	60	100						
<<		WMMP UP WTAT F	<<																																							
1	2	DSNY	<<			NR	NR	NR	NR																								1									
<<		LIF	<<																																							
1	3	NIK	1	2		2	NR		4										1													1	1	1							
<<		TNT	<<				2																																		
<<		USA	<<			NR	NR																																		
<< 28		WTBS IT H/P/T.*	<< 27	17		26	26	26	26	14	1 5	7	8	11	12	14	19	17	23	18	6	11	14	16	16	15	13	1 5	9	10	11	4	10	9								
		MON.-FRI. 9:00A-NOON																																									
3	13	WBLN W WCBD N	3	12	27	13	14	11	10	1				1	1	2	1	3	2		1	1	2	1	1											78	93	2	2	3			
3	13	WCIV A	3	11	26	9	12	10	10	1		1	1	1	1	2	1	2	2		1	2	2	2	1	1										93	99	1					
3	14	WCSC C	3	13	31	24	19	21	21	2	1	1	1	1	1	3	1	4	2	2	1	1	1	1	1	2										75	91	6	3				
1	4	WITV P	1	5		3			4	1															1				1	1	1	1		3	2	63	100						
<<		WMMP UP WTAT F	<<																																							
2	7	WTAT F	1	6	15	5	6	6	8	1	1	1	1	1	1	1	1	1	1	1	1	1	1	1	1	1	1	1	1	1	1		3	2	79	93	5		2			
1	3	DSNY	1	2		NR	NR	NR	NR																								1	1								
<<		LIF	1	3		4			3				1									1	1	1	1	1																
2	7	NIK	1	6		4	NR	3	8	1			1								1	1	1	1	1							1	4	3							
1	3	TNT	1	3		4	7	4	2			1	1	1							1	1		1			1	1	1	1												
<<		USA	<<			NR	NR																																			
1	3	WTBS IT	1	2		3	4	3	2	1		1	1								2	1	1			1							1										
23		H/P/T.*	23		10	21	22	20	26	12	9	8	9	9	9	14	12	17	16	12	11	12	11	12	10	8	4	6	6	6	6	9	14	12								
		MON.-FRI. NOON-3:00P																																									
1	6	WBLN W WCBD N	1	6	11	13	10	9	6	1		1	1	1	1	1	1	1	1		1	2	1	1	1	1										72	95	1		4			
2	9	WCIV A	2	7	13	3	8	6	8	1			1	1	1	1	1	1	1		1	1	2	2	1											100	100						
8	36	WCSC C	8	34	67	38	34	35	30	4	2	2	2	3	3	6	3	8	7	3	5	5	4	4	3	2		1	1	1	1	2	1	1	72	89	5	4	1			
<<		WITV P	<<			4			2																								1	1	75	100						
1	4	WMMP UP	1	3	6			3	3											2	1	1											1		93	100			34			
<<		WTAT F	<<				4	3	5																								1	1	52	66						
<<		DSNY	<<			NR	NR	NR	NR																								1	1								
1	2	LIF	1	3			3		4	1		1	1	1						1	1	1	1	1	1																
1	4	NIK	1	3		3	NR	2	5	1	1										1	1		1								1	2	1							
1	3	TNT	1	3		5	2	2	2							1		1																								
<<		USA	<<			NR	NR		2																								1	1	2							
1	3	WTBS IT	1	4		2	2		3	1			1								1												1	1	2							
22		H/P/T.*	24		12	23	24	22	29	12	11	10	9	10	10	15	12	18	18	15	15	15	14	14	10	7	3	5	5	5	6	12	9	9								
		MON.-FRI. NOON-4:00P																																									
<<		WBLN W	<<																																74	90	5		5			
2	7	WCBD N	2	7	14	15	12	12	6	1		1	1	1	1	1	1	1	1	2	1	2	2	1	1								1			100	100						
2	10	WCIV A	2	8	16	4	9	8	9	1		1	1	1	1	1	1	2	2	1	1	2	2	1	1								1	1		71	89	5	5	1			
7	32	WCSC C	7	30	60	35	32	32	28	3	2	2	2	3	3	5	3	7	7	3	4	4	4	4	3	2		1	1	1	1	2	1	1	68	97	3					
<<		WITV P	<<			4			2																								1	1	83	100						
1	4	WMMP UP	1	3	7		3	2	4	1	1	1								1	2	1	1										1		68	78			22			
1	3	WTAT F	1	3	6		3	3	5													1																					
<<		DSNY	<<			NR	NR	NR	NR																								1	1	1							
1	4	NIK	1	3		3	NR	3	5	1	1										1	1		1	1								2	2	1							
<<		TNT	1	2		5		2									1																										
<<		USA	<<			NR	NR																																			
1	3	WTBS IT	1	3		2			2	1											1												1	1	2							
23		H/P/T.*	24		12	24	24	23	28	12	12	10	9	10	10	15	12	18	18	16	15	15	14	14	10	7	3	5	5	5	6	13	9	10								
		MON.-FRI. 3:00P-5:00P																																									
<<		WBLN W	<<																															1	100	100						
5	18	WCBD N	4	16	32	25	20	21	11	2	1	2	2	2	2	3	3	3	4	1	3	3	4	4	3	1	1	1		1	1				78	87	8	2	3			
3	10	WCIV A	2	8	16	4	9	9	10	1	1	1	1	1	1	1	1	2	2	2	1	1	2	2	1								2		93	93	3	3				
5	19	WCSC C	5	19	38	24	23	20	17	2	2	1	2	2	2	4	2	5	5	3	3	3	2	3	2	1			1	1	1	1	1		66	86	5	7	2			
1	2	WITV P	1	3			3	3	3													1														66	95	5					
1	2	WMMP UP	1	5	10	5		4	6			1	1	1				1				1	1			1		1					1		68	100						
2	6	WTAT F	1	5	10	5		2	4	1	1	1	1		1	1	1	1			1	1	1	1		1	1	1					1		71	85			14			
1	3	DSNY	<<			NR	NR	NR	NR		1	1																				2	2	2							
<<		LIF	<<				2		3	1	1							1															1									
1	3	NIK	1	3		4	NR	3	5	1	2	1									1	1	1										3	1	2							
1	2	TNT	1	2		2		3														1	1	1																		
<<		USA CON'T...	<<			NR	NR																																			
1	2		7	8	9	10	11	12	13	15	17	18	19	20	21	22	23	24	25	26	27	28	29	31	32	34	35	36	37	38	39	40	41	42	43	44	45	46	47	48	49	50	51

#1=COLUMBIA, SC   357,810
#2=SAVANNAH   284,160
#3=FLORENCE-MYRTLE BEACH 253,630

<table>
<tr><td>**5.10**</td><td>**A Visual Aid for Remembering the Formula**</td></tr>
</table>

The basic relationship among the three variables (rating, share, HUT) is easy to understand but sometimes difficult to remember. Here is a visual aid:

$$\frac{R}{S \qquad H}$$

(Putting the R "on top" is easy to remember because ratings are most important to the station or channel for advertising purposes.) Here's how to calculate: If you want R (ratings), cover the R with your finger. The result is S (share) multiplied by H (HUT). If you want share, cover the S with your finger. The result is R divided by H. Likewise, cover the H to calculate HUT: The result is R divided by S. (The number you get must be adjusted to provide a meaningful answer: If you multiplied, then divide the result by 100; if you divided, multiply the result by 100.) You may not get the exact result shown by Nielsen because the reported figures are rounded.

One final point concerning the 12 noon to 3 P.M. example is that the HUT/PUT/TOTAL line is 24, but if we add all the stations, the total rating is actually 16. The uncounted rating points mean that 8 percent of the households in the DMA were viewing cable channels for which no one channel received a 1 rating. Individual shares for all the stations should equal 100 percent when totaled, even if the tiny shares for cable viewing are unreportable.

PUTs/PURs

Ratings and shares for television generally represent households but occasionally refer to specific demographic groups such as women aged 18 to 49. Radio ratings always represent individuals or persons, and therefore, the term *persons using radio* (PUR) is used. *Persons using television* (PUT) is appropriate when calculations of individual viewers are made. Sales staffs and time buyers tend to be more interested in these calculations than programmers are, and one of the big advantages of people meters is

that they supply individual-person data as well as household data for the advertising industry.

AQH/Cume

Programmers use two very important computations in calculating ratings: **average quarter-hour (AQH) audiences** and **cumulative audience (cume)** estimates. Program audiences are typically measured in 15-minute intervals, hence "quarter-hour audience." Meters can, in fact, measure one-minute audiences (or even one-second audiences in comedy research, for example), but a person or household is counted in a quarter hour if the television was turned on for a minimum of five minutes during the measurement period.

Although radio and television diaries also measure audience size in 15-minute intervals, TV programmers use these data in much larger units—by whole program or daypart. Quarter hours are the particular concern of those who try to count fickle radio listeners. (Both time units may be too broad for accurately measuring channel jumpers and grazers and radio button pushers!)

Cumulative audience measures are appropriate for small audiences that would not show up in rating/share measures. Cume measurements indicate the number of different people tuned in during a 15-minute (or longer) time period. Cume figures are always larger than AQH figures, which are averaged.

The basic difference between AQH and cume is that in the average quarter-hour calculation, persons can be counted more than once in a total daypart. For instance, a person could tune to a station for five minutes, switch stations or tune out, and then tune back in to the original station during a later quarter hour. This viewer would be counted twice in an AQH calculation but not in an exclusive cume calculation because it counts only the number of different persons listening. Cume is considered to be the reach of a station because it tells you how many different persons were in the audience during a time period or daypart. It also reflects the growth or decay of an audience over time.

Public television and basic cable audiences are often too small for accurate measurement within one quarter hour, but cumulative ratings over a longer period of time may reflect more substantial audiences. Cumes can also be calculated for a single program over several airings, a common pattern in public television and cable measurements, permitting programmers to estimate the total number of people who watched a program. Commercial broadcasting with its special interest in the number of people watching one commercial spot generally uses AQH ratings.

Reach and Frequency Analysis

Salespeople most often use the concepts of *reach* and *frequency*. As we said earlier, **reach** refers to circulation or potential exposure—or the net size of the audience that actually gets the signal (gross would be all the people living in the country). **Frequency** refers to the number of times a person was exposed to a particular advertising message (or program). A high frequency means exposure to a message several times and indicates the "holding power" of a station, network, or program. *Programmers usually schedule several interesting programs in succession, trying to create audience flow and achieve a high frequency for advertisers among successive programs appealing to the same viewers.*

Television Market Reports and Other Programming Aids

Market reports (or "books") are divided into sections to allow programmers, salespeople and advertisers to examine an audience from many perspectives for a particular local DMA. In television, the major sections are: Daypart Audiences, Time Period Averages and Program Averages.

Daypart Audiences

The Daypart Audiences section divides viewing into 37 dayparts, a highly useful format for analyzing a station's overall performance in specific time blocks. For instance, Monday through Friday noon to 6 P.M.

provides a quick summary of the ratings and shares for all stations during that daypart. The page from a Nielsen book in 5.9, presented earlier, shows the crucial 3 P.M. to 5 P.M. period in the Charleston market toward the bottom.

Nielsen divides the viewers into 26 demographic (age and sex) classifications for both the DMA and the NSI station totals. *For just one station, 754 ratings cells are required in order to fill out all 26 Nielsen people categories and 37 daypart categories for station totals alone.* A single ratings book page contains an immense amount of data. Most programmers use computers to analyze the data.

A look at 5.9, presented in the previous section, shows that WCSC was the strongest television station in the market in the afternoon daypart, with a 7 rating/30 share in the DMA and 7/32 in the Metro. It was very strong with both W 18–49 and W 18–34 (the usual shorthand used in ratings analyses). No doubt this station was delighted because these demographics are very easy to sell to advertisers.

Programmers normally compare the current numbers to previous performances. **Tracking** a daypart shows how the station or program is doing over time. It is also important for selecting syndicated programs (see Chapters 6 and 8). Rarely will program decisions be based on only one book unless the numbers are very low and very credible, and no hope for improvement is in sight.

Time Period Averages

Television programmers are interested not only in broad dayparts but in quarter-hour or half-hour segments within them. This information, found in the Time Period Averages section of ratings books, is useful for determining a program's strength against the competition for a specific quarter hour or half hour. *Managers of affiliates look here, for example, to see how their local newscast stacks up against its competitors.* The Time Period Averages section also has an overview of access time and early fringe competition and shows lead-in and lead-out effects. Programmers use these data to analyze performance in time segments. (Salespeople use these data to determine spot ratings.)

Averages for the whole week, Monday through Friday, are included in the Time Period Averages section along with most prime-time network programming because it varies from night to night. These figures show performance during a daypart or time period when all days are averaged together, crucial data when a programmer is looking at stripped programming in early fringe and prime-time access.

Program Audiences

The last (but not least) major section of a television ratings book, the one television programmers most often use, is the **Program Audiences** section. Rather than lumping a program into a daypart, this section breaks each daypart and program into 30-minute segments (and some 15-minute ones) to isolate individual programs on different days of the sweep weeks. *The Program Audiences section is considered the "pure programming" section because each program is analyzed individually here.* It shows the titles of the shows and any scheduling variations from night to night. This allows programmers to examine ratings for their local news, say, night by night—and to eliminate the odd night when a sporting event, for example, cuts into the news time.

Look at the Program Audiences data for Charleston at 6 P.M. in 5.11. The numbers are the DMA rating/share and Metro rating/share for all weekdays (AV5—average for Monday through Friday). Notice that in DMA measurements, WCSC dominates the competition with a 25 share for its local newscast. The local news shows on WCBD and WCIV have a 15 share and an 11 share, respectively. The FOX affiliate WTAT came in fourth with a 7 share for *Judge Judy. This section permits analysis of individual programs without interference from ratings for adjacent programs.*

In summary, the sections of a television book provide programmers with at least four different ways to evaluate station performance. Daypart Audience data show broad time periods without regard to specific programs. Time Period Averages listings provide programming data by quarter hours and half hours on a daily basis and are useful

in analyzing competitive performance. Finally, Program Averages information isolates the "pure program" data. Each section answers different questions, and television programmers use every section as their questions shift.

Because mountains of plain ratings data are nearly too much to deal with, Nielsen also issues reports on specific demographic groups or types of programs or station market sizes in easy-to-use formats, on which stations, reps and ad agencies rely heavily. They also depend on other companies to reanalyze Nielsen's ratings data and to supplement the data with other research. Of all these additional services, *programmers find analyses of syndicated television programs the most valuable.*

Syndicated Program Reports

Affiliates and independents rely on off-network and first-run syndicated programming to fill parts of their broadcast days. *Because syndicated programs are expensive, however, station decision makers want to know about a program's past performance.* Will a program perform well in their market? Will its ratings justify its cost? Reps and program consultants especially want this information because they advise station programmers. *Projecting or estimating ratings success for a first-run product is an involved process that finally comes down to an educated guess. The potentials of off-network programs are somewhat easier to evaluate, but even here no hard-and-fast rules exist.* Lead-in programs, local competition and audience fads always influence ratings. Even the most successful network program may fail in syndication or perform below its network numbers at a given time or in a given market.

In making decisions about syndicated programs, Nielsen's *Report on Syndicated Programs* is helpful. (The major television rep firms also provide similar analyses in less bulky and unwieldy formats, such as the Comtrac report example featured in Chapter 6.) A page from the Nielsen analysis of *The Simpsons* is shown in 5.12. At the top-left corner of the page, you will find the number of markets telecasting the program, the distributor and other data such as the program type and the number of episodes available.

5.11 Program Audience Ratings Page

CHARLESTON, SC

WK1 7/10-7/16 WK2 7/17-7/23 WK3 7/24-7/30 WK4 7/31-8/06

PROGRAM AVERAGES

METRO HH RTG (1)	METRO HH SHR (2)	STATION DAY PROGRAM	DMA HOUSEHOLD RATINGS WEEKS 1 (3)	WEEKS 2 (4)	WEEKS 3 (5)	WEEKS 4 (6)	MULTI-WEEK AVG RTG (7)	MULTI-WEEK AVG SHR (8)	HUT (14)	DMA RATINGS PERSONS 2+ (15)	PERSONS 18+ (16)	PERSONS 12-24 (17)	PERSONS 12-34 (18)	PERSONS 18-34 (19)	PERSONS 18-49 (20)	PERSONS 21-49 (21)	PERSONS 25-54 (22)	PERSONS 35+ (23)	PERSONS 35-64 (24)	PERSONS 50+ (25)	WOMEN 18+ (26)	WOMEN 12-24 (27)	WOMEN 18-34 (28)	WOMEN 18-49 (29)	WOMEN 21-49 (30)	WOMEN 25-49 (31)	WOMEN 25-54 (32)	WOMEN 50+ (33)	WOMEN WKG (34)	MEN 18+ (35)	MEN 18-34 (36)	MEN 18-49 (37)	MEN 21-49 (38)	MEN 25-49 (39)	MEN 25-54 (40)	TNS 12-17 (41)	CHILD 2-11 (42)	CHILD 6-11 (43)
5		R.S.E. THRESHOLDS 25+%	13	13	13	13	4			3	3	14	9	10	6	6	4	4	5	4	4	19	17	8	8	8	7	7	7	5	18	8	8	8	7	24	15	20
1		(1 S.E.) 4 WK AVG 50+%	4	4	4	4	1			1	1	4	2	3	2	2	1	1	1	1	1	6	5	2	2	2	2	2	2	1	5	2	2	2	2	7	4	6
		5:30PM																																				
1	2	WMMP MON STEVE HARVEY	2	<<	<<	2	1	3	36			1	1	1						1		2	1	1												1		
1	1	TUE STEVE HARVEY	<<	<<	2	2	1	2	38			1	1									3														3		
1	2	WED STEVE HARVEY	1	1	<<	<<	1	2	38										1											1		1	1	1	1			
1	2	THU STEVE HARVEY	<<	<<	3	2	1	3	43	1	1	2	2	1	1	1	1					3	1	1	1	1	1		1	1	2	1	2	2	2	5	2	4
1	2	FRI STEVE HARVEY	2	1	<<	2	1	3	37			1						1	1	1	1	1						1								1		
1	2	AV5 STEVE HARVEY	1	<<	1	1	1	2	38	1		1	1									2														2		1
3	7	WTAT MON JUDGE-BROWN B	3	4	2	2	3	8	36	2	2	1	2	2	2	2	2	2	2	3	2	1	4	2	2	2	3	3	2	2		1	1	1	2	1		
3	7	TUE JUDGE-BROWN B	3	4	1	3	3	8	38	2	2	1	1	2	1	1	2	2	2	3	2		1	1	1	2	2	4	2	2	2	2			1			
3	7	WED JUDGE-BROWN B	3	4	2	2	3	7	38	2	2		1	2	1	1	3	2	2	4	2		3	2	2	2	3	4	1	2		1	1	1	2			
4	9	THU JUDGE-BROWN B	4	3	3	4	4	8	43	1	2		1	2	1	2	2	2	2	2	3		3	2	3	3	3	3	1	1								
3	9	FRI JUDGE-BROWN B	6	4	2	3	4	10	37	2	2	1	2	2	1	1	3	2	2	4	3	1	3	2	2	3	4	4	1	2					2	1		
3	8	AV5 JUDGE-BROWN B	4	4	2	3	3	8	38	2	2	1	1	2	1	1	2	2	2	3	2		3	2	2	2	3	3	1	2	1	1	1	1	2			
		6:00PM																																				
<<		WBLN MON ELIMIDATE	1	<<	<<	<<	<<		46													1																
<<		TUE ELIMIDATE	<<	<<	<<	<<	<<		49																													
<<		WED ELIMIDATE	<<	<<	<<	<<	<<		48																													
<<		THU ELIMIDATE	<<	<<	<<	<<	<<		56																													
<<		FRI ELIMIDATE	1	<<	<<	<<	<<		48																													
<<		AV5 ELIMIDATE	<<	<<	<<	<<	<<		49																													
<<		SAT E.R. B	<<	<<	<<	1	<<		34														1															
<<		SUN WHAT-LK-EV1-WB	<<	1	<<	<<	<<		34																													
7	16	WCBD MON NEWS 2 AT 6 PM	5	7	6	10	7	14	46	4	5	2	2	2	4	4	4	6	6	7	5	1	1	3	3	3	3	8	3	6	3	5	4	5	5			
10	20	TUE NEWS 2 AT 6 PM	6	10	7	9	8	16	49	4	6		1	2	4	4	5	7	6	8	6		2	4	5	5	6	8	5	5	1	4	4	5	5			
7	15	WED NEWS 2 AT 6 PM	1	11	6	5	6	12	48	3	4	1	1	1	3	3	4	5	4	6	4		1	3	3	4	4	6	3	4	1	2	3	3	3	2		
11	20	THU NEWS 2 AT 6 PM	10	11	6	12	10	18	56	6	8	4	3	4	6	6	7	9	8	10	8	5	3	6	6	5	7	11	6	7	5	6	6	7	7	1		
8	16	FRI NEWS 2 AT 6 PM	4	8	6	7	6	13	48	4	5		1	2	4	4	5	6	6	6	6		2	5	5	6	6	6	5	4	1	3	3	4	4			
8	17	AV5 NEWS 2 AT 6 PM	5	10	6	8	7	15	49	4	5	1	2	2	4	4	5	7	6	8	6	1	2	4	5	5	5	8	4	5	2	4	4	5	5	1		
5	16	SAT NWS 2-6 PM SAT	5	4	4	5	4	13	33	3	3				2	2	2	5	3	5	3			1	2	2	2	6	2	3		3	3	3	3	1		1
5	15	SUN NWS 2-6 PM SUN		5	3	7	5	14	35	4	4	2	3	3	3	3	3	5	3	7	4	3	3	2	2	3	3	7	3	5	4	4	3	4	4	3		
4	10	WCIV MON SIX OCLOCK NWS	4	5	6	3	4	10	46	2	3				1	1	2	4	4	7	4	1		1	1	1	2	8	1	2		1	1	1	2	1	1	
7	15	TUE SIX OCLOCK NWS	9	3	8	5	6	13	49	3	5	2	3	4	3	3	3	5	4	6	5	3	6	4	3	3	3	7	3	4	2	3	3	3	3			
6	14	WED SIX OCLOCK NWS	7	3	8	4	5	11	48	3	3		1	1	2	2	3	5	4	7	4		2	2	3	3	3	7	3	3		1	1	1	2			
6	11	THU SIX OCLOCK NWS	6	6	7	2	6	10	56	3	4		1	1	3	3	3	5	5	7	4		1	3	3	3	3	7	3	4	2	3	3	3	3			
6	13	FRI SIX OCLOCK NWS	3	4	7	6	5	10	48	3	4	1	1	1	3	2	3	5	5	6	4			2	3	3	3	7	3	4	2	3	2	3	3			
6	12	AV5 SIX OCLOCK NWS	6	4	7	4	5	11	49	3	4	1	1	2	2	2	3	5	4	6	4	1	2	2	2	3	3	7	3	3	1	2	2	2	3			
3	10	SAT SIX OCLOCK NWS	3	4	3	2	3	9	33	1	2				1	1	1	3	2	4	2			1	1	1	1	4	2	1		1	1	1	1			
3	10	NOR SIX OCLOCK NWS	3	4	3	2	3	9	33	1	2				1	1	1	3	2	4	2			1	1	1	1	5	2	1		1	1	1	1			
5	15	SUN SIX OCLOCK NWS	5	5	6	2	4	12	35	2	3	1	1	1	3	3	3	4	5	4	3		1	3	3	3	4	4	3	3	2	2	2	3	3			
6	16	NOR SIX OCLOCK NWS	5	5	6	1	5	13	34	3	3	1	1	1	3	3	4	4	5	4	3		1	3	3	4	4	4	4	3	2	3	2	3	3			
6	12	AV7 SIX OCLOCK NWS	5	4	7	3	5	11	45	3	3	1	1	1	2	2	3	4	4	6	4	1	1	2	2	3	3	6	3	3	1	2	2	2	3			
6	13	NOR SIX OCLOCK NWS	6	4	7	3	5	11	45	3	4	1	1	1	2	2	3	5	4	6	4	1	2	2	2	3	3	6	3	3	1	2	2	2	3			
12	27	WCSC MON LIVE 5 NEWS-6	11	11	15	10	12	25	46	6	8	2	2	3	5	5	6	11	9	14	9	1	2	4	5	6	6	16	6	8	3	6	5	5	5	1	1	1
12	24	TUE LIVE 5 NEWS-6	12	11	11	14	12	25	49	6	8	1	2	3	5	6	6	11	10	14	10	1	2	5	6	6	7	18	7	7	3	5	6	6	6			
12	26	WED LIVE 5 NEWS-6	11	10	9	16	12	24	48	7	9	5	4	4	6	6	6	11	8	13	10	5	5	7	7	8	8	16	8	7	4	5	4	4	4	2	1	1
14	25	THU LIVE 5 NEWS-6	17	11	11	16	14	24	56	8	10	6	4	4	5	5	6	13	10	18	12	6	4	6	6	5	7	21	8	8	3	5	4	4	5	4	1	1
11	23	FRI LIVE 5 NEWS-6	15	10	10	13	12	25	48	6	7	3	2	2	4	4	5	10	7	13	8	3	3	5	5	5	6	14	5	6	2	3	3	3	3	2		1
12	25	AV5 LIVE 5 NEWS-6	13	11	11	14	12	25	49	7	9	3	3	3	5	5	6	11	9	14	10	3	3	5	6	6	7	17	7	7	3	5	4	4	5	2		1
6	18	SAT LIVE 5 NEWS-6	8	5	6	5	6	18	33	3	4	1	1	2	2	2	3	6	4	8	6	2	2	3	2	2	3	10	3	3	1	2	2	2	2			
7	19	SUN LIVE 5 NEWS-6	5	10	5	6	6	19	34	4	5	2	2	2	2	2	3	6	4	9	6	1	2	3	3	4	4	10	4	4	3	2	1		2	1		
11	24	AV7 LIVE 5 NEWS-6	11	10	10	11	10	23	45	6	7	3	2	3	4	4	5	10	7	13	9	3	3	5	5	5	6	15	6	6	3	4	4	3	4	1		1
<<		WITV MON NEWSHOUR-LEHR	1	<<	<<	<<	<<		47																													
<<		TUE NEWSHOUR-LEHR	<<	1	<<	<<	<<		50											1																		1
1	1	WED NEWSHOUR-LEHR	<<	<<	1	1	<<		48																						1							
1	1	THU NEWSHOUR-LEHR	<<	<<	<<	1	<<		58																		1											
1	2	FRI NEWSHOUR-LEHR	2	<<	<<	1	1	1	49																		1	1										
<<		AV5 NEWSHOUR-LEHR	1	<<	<<	1	<<		50																													
<<		SAT S.C. OUTDOORS	<<	<<	<<	<<	<<		33																													
<<		SUN NOW W/B MOYERS	<<	<<		<<	<<		35																													
1	2	WMMP MON MOESHA	<<	1	2	1	1	2	46							1	1				1		1			1		1	1			1	1	1	1			1
1	2	TUE MOESHA	<<	1	3	1	1	3	49	1		1	1									3										1	1	1	1	3	1	2
1	3	WED MOESHA	<<	1	1	3	1	3	48	1		1	1	1	1	1	1					2	1	1	1	1	1		1			1	1	1	1	2	2	4
2	4	THU MOESHA	4	1	5	1	3	5	56	2	2	6	6	6	3	3	2				3	9	8	4	3	2	2		1	2	4	3	3	3	3	5	2	4
2	5	FRI MOESHA	2	2	1	3	2	4	48	1	1	4	2	1	1	1	1		1			3								2	3	3	1	1	1	5		
2	3	AV5 MOESHA	1	1	2	2	2	3	49	1	1	2	2	2	1	1	1				1	3	2	1	1	1	1		1	1	1	1	1	1	1	3	1	2
1	4	SAT MOVIE III	2	1	<<	2	1	3	33	1	1	1	1	1	1			1	1		1	2	1	1	1	1	1	1			1	1				1	1	1
<<		SUN RELIC HUNTER	<<	<<	<<	<<	<<		35																													
3	7	WTAT MON JUDGE JUDY	5	3	3	2	4	8	46	2	3	1	2	2	2	2	3	3	3	4	3	1	4	3	3	3	4	4	2	2		1	1	1	2	1		
3	6	TUE JUDGE JUDY	3	2	3	5	3	7	49	2	3	2	1	2	2	1	2	3	3	4	3	1	1	2	2	2	3	4	2	3	2	2	1	1	2			
3	6	WED JUDGE JUDY	6	2	2	4	3	7	48	2	2		1	1	1	1	3	3	3	5	3		2	2	2	2	3	5	1	2		1	1	1	2			
4	7	THU JUDGE JUDY	5	3	3	4	4	7	56	2	2		1	2	2	2	3	2	3	3	3		3	2	3	3	4	4	2	1		1	1	2	1			
3	6	FRI JUDGE JUDY	6	3	4	2	4	8	48	2	3	1	2	3	2	2	3	3	3	5	4	2	6	3	3	3	4	5	3	2					1			
3	7	AV5 JUDGE JUDY	5	3	3	4	4	7	49	2	3	1	1	2	2	2	3	3	3	4	3	1	3	2	2	3	3	4	2	2	1	1	1	1	2			

See Program Index for complete details of program start time, duration and weeks of telecast.

5.12 Syndicated Program Report Page on the Simpsons

MARKETS REPORTING	172
STATIONS REPORTING	184
TOTAL TV HH'S IN DMA'S	104,567,360
DMA % OF U.S.	96
EPISODES AVAILABLE	105
DIST: 20TH TELEVISION	
TYPE: SITUATION COMEDY	

REPORT ON SYNDICATED PROGRAMS
NSI AVERAGE WEEK ESTIMATES
NOV 2003

SIMPSONS M-F
30 MIN.

SUMMARY BY DAYPARTS

	DMA HOUSEHOLD SHARES BY MARKET RANK									DMA HOUSEHOLD SHARES BY MARKET RANK							
DAYPART	1-25		26-50		51-100		101+		DAYPART	1-25		26-50		51-100		101+	
	NO.OF DMA'S	% SHARE	NO.OF DMA'S	% SHARE	NO.OF DMA'S	% SHARE	NO.OF DMA'S	% SHARE		NO.OF DMA'S	% SHARE	NO.OF DMA'S	% SHARE	NO.OF DMA'S	% SHARE	NO.OF DMA'S	% SHARE
DAYTIME (M-F)†									POST PRIME (S-S)	11	7	8	7	5	6	16	3
EARLY FRINGE (M-F)	23	8	23	7	42	6	50	5	WEEKEND DAYTIME(S&S)	3	5	1	10	10	4	3	6
PRIME ACCESS (M-SAT)	9	8	5	6	13	4	12	5	WEEKEND PRE-PRIME(S&S)	11	6	2	9	8	6	11	6
PRIME (S-S)	4	4	5	5	4	3	7	3	AVG. ALL TELECASTS	25	7	25	7	49	5	73	5

	NO. OF MKT's	NO. OF DMA's	% U.S. TV	DMA HH AVG. QH RTG	DMA HH SHR	TOTAL HHLDS (000)	TOTAL HOUSEHOLDS AND PERSONS																
DAYPART							WOMEN						MEN				TEENS		CHILDREN			
							18+		18-49		25-54		18+		18-49		12-17		2-11				
							(000)	V/CVH	(000)	V/CVH	(000)	V/CVH	(000)	V/CVH	(000)	V/CVH	(000)	V/CVH	(000)	V/CVH			
DAYTIME (M-F)†																							
EARLY FRINGE (M-F)	138	138	86	4	7	3657	1622	44	1430	39	947	26	2222	61	1994	55	1328	36	1145	31			
PRIME ACCESS (M-SAT)	39	39	28	4	7	1277	598	47	532	42	389	30	824	65	748	59	473	37	377	29			
PRIME (S-S)	20	20	13	3	5	450	240	53	193	43	142	31	252	56	200	44	158	35	91	20			
POST PRIME (S-S)	40	40	40	3	6	1446	777	54	646	45	426	29	988	68	853	59	281	19	124	9			
WEEKEND DAYTIME(S&S)	17	17	10	3	5	309	140	45	121	39	118	38	162	52	140	45	122	40	89	29			
WEEKEND PRE-PRIME(S&S)	32	32	29	3	6	1093	506	46	421	39	329	30	688	63	584	53	336	31	308	28			
TOTAL DAY	172	172				3834	1799		1571		1071		2412		2144		1252		998				
AVG. ALL TELECASTS				4	7	33	15	47	13	40	9	28	21	63	18	56	11	33	8	26			

LINE 1	REPORTABLE STATIONS	FOUR WEEK AVERAGE TIME PERIOD AUDIENCES											PROGRAM AUDIENCE SECTION (SYNDICATED PROGRAM ONLY)										COMPETING FOUR WEEK AVERAGE TIME PERIOD AUDIENCES		
MARKET T.Z.	ON AIR	(THIS PROGRAM vs. PRECEDING HALF HOUR)																							
LINE 2	TOTAL DAY	DESIGNATED MARKET AREA										DMA %		STATION TOTALS								CORRESPONDING TIME PERIOD-3 HIGHEST COMPETING STATIONS		DMA %
STATION CH. NET. DMA SHARE			PERSONS SHARE %										(000) VS V/100VH		PERSONS (000) & V/100VH										
LINE 3 START NO. OF		DMA %	WOMEN			MEN			TNS	CHD	HH %		TOTAL HHLD	TOTAL ADULTS	WOMEN			MEN		TEENS	CHILD			HH %
DAY TIME T/CS.		HH RTG	SHR	18+	18-49	25-54	18+	18-49	25-54	12-17	2-11	HH RTG	SHR			18+	18-49	25-54	18+	18-49	12-17	2-11	STATION	PROGRAM	HH RTG	SHR
LINE 4		1	2	3	4	5	6	7	8	9	10	11	12	13	14	15	16	17	18	19	20	21			22	23
LEAD-IN-PROGRAM																										
ABILENE-SWTWATR CE 5																										
KXVA CH.15 F 5%																							KTAB	CBS EVE NWS	7	17
M-F 5.30P 16T/C		3	6	3	10	7	6	15	14	32	6	3	6	(000)	3	3	1	1	1	2	2	1	KTXS	ABC-WORLD NWS	7	17
THAT 70S SHOW		3	7	4	11	10	7	18	16	23	7			V/CVH		93	39	39	25	54	54	43	KRBC	NBC NITELY NWS	4	9
ALBANY-SCH-TROY EA 8																										
WXXA CH.23 F 5%																							WNYT #	NWSCH13 LIVE-6	12	24
M-F 6.00P 20T/C		2	3	2	5	2	3	6	5	6	10	2	3	(000)	9	8	4	4	2	5	4	1	WTEN+	NWS10-6 OCLOCK	9	18
#ACCESS HOLLYWD		1	2	3	5	3	1	1	1		1			V/CVH		94	42	41	23	51	47	12	WRGB	CH6 NEWS AT 6	9	17
M-F 7.30P 20T/C		3	5	3	7	5	6	10	8	4	10	3	5	(000)	14	16	7	6	5	9	8	1	WTEN+	JEOPARDY	12	24
#SEINFELD		3	6	3	4	4	8	10	9	4	4			V/CVH		118	50	43	34	68	55	8	WRGB	KING OF QUEENS	6	11
MARKET AVG.												2	4	(000)	11	12	5	5	3	7	6	1	WNYT	FRIENDS	6	11
														V/CVH		108	47	42	29	62	52	9				
ALBANY, GA EA 4																										
WFXL CH.31 F 5%																							WALB	NWSCNTR10-11PM	16	48
M-F 11.00P 16T/C		1	3	2	2	2	2	1	2	4		1	3	(000)	1	1	1	1		1				WVAG	NOT AVAILABLE	<<	
SEINFELD		2	4	4	4	4	4	5	3	21				V/CVH		98	58	38		40			WABW	VARIOUS	<<	
ALBUQ-SANTA FE MT 8																										
KASA CH. 2 F 5%																							KOAT-+#	ACTN 7 NWS 5	9	17
M-F 5.00P 20T/C		3	6	6	14	6	8	17	9	22	12	3	6	(000)	20	23	11	11	6	11	11	7	KRQE+	CBS EVE NWS	7	14
#SHARON OSBOURN		1	3	3	4	3	2	3	2	3	1			V/CVH		112	56	55	28	55	54	36	KOB -#	EYEWTNS NWS-5	6	10
M-F 10.00P 20T/C		3	5	4	8	5	7	13	10	17	9	3	5	(000)	18	21	8	8	5	13	12	4	KOAT-+#	ACTN 7 NWS-10	9	17
#KASA FOX2NWS-9		3	5	6	6	6	6	7	6	3	3			V/CVH		117	47	44	29	71	65	23	KOB -#	EYEWTNS NWS-10	9	17
MARKET AVG.												3	6	(000)	19	22	10	10	5	12	11	6	KROE-#	KRQE NEWS-10	8	15
														V/CVH		115	52	50	28	63	59	30				
AMARILLO CE 6																										
KCIT CH.14 F 6%																							KVII-+#	J KMML-/ACCSS	1	8
FRI 1.00A 1T/C		<<		8	12	15						<<		(000)	<<									KFDA	C KLBRN/HM MPR	1	7
HIGH SCH EXTRA		<<					2	3	4					V/CVH									KDBA	INFOMERCIAL	<<	
FRI 1.30A 1T/C		<<		8	12	15						<<		(000)	<<									KVII-+#	ACCSS H/JDG JD	1	11
#EXTREME DATING														V/CVH									KFDA	HM MPRV/CNN HD	<<	
MARKET AVG.												<<		(000)	<<									KDBA	INFOMERCIAL	<<	
ANCHORAGE YU 7																										
KTBY CH. 4 F 6%																							KTUU	NBC NITELY NWS	17	41
M-F 5.30P 20T/C		3	7	4	8	6	4	9	5	17	23	3	7	(000)	5	3	2	1	1	2	2	1	KTVA	CBS EVE NWS	7	16
DHARMA-GREG		2	6	5	9	6	2		2	4	12			V/CVH		70	34	31	29	35	34	26	KYES	DREW CAREY	2	4
M-F 6.30P 20T/C		3	7	5	8	6	4	6	4	15	21	3	7	(000)	5	5	2	2	2	3	3	1	KTUU	CH 2 NEWSHOUR	20	41
THAT 70S SHOW		5	9	9	15	10	8	13	7	16	27			V/CVH		103	47	43	38	56	51	24	KIMO #	WHEEL-FORTNE	6	12
																							KYES	FRIENDS	4	9
SUN 5.30P 4T/C		4	9	4	7	6	5	10	9	22	16	4	9	(000)	5	3	1	1	1	2	2	1	KTUU	NBC-NWS SUN	10	26
#DHARMA-GREG WK		1	3	1	2	2				6				V/CVH		64	23	23	23	41	41	23	KTVA	CBS NWS-SUN	2	6
																							KIMO	ABC NWS-SUN	1	2

For explanation of symbols, see lead page.

The second section provides overall ratings and share data by market rank and by daypart. It shows the number of stations carrying *The Simpsons* in both early fringe (138 DMA markets) and in prime access (39 DMA markets), presumably to appeal to young viewers in the late afternoon time period. *The Simpsons* averaged a 4 rating and 7 share in both dayparts, higher than for any other daypart. This section shows which dayparts and market sizes a program has played most effectively in, quite useful information for programmers. Demographic data by daypart fill out the rest of this section.

The third section of the page shows a market breakout of specific stations carrying *The Simpsons* in syndication. The first market, alphabetically, that carried the program was Abilene-Sweetwater, where *The Simpsons* ran at 5:30 P.M. central time on KXVA, a FOX affiliate on Channel 15, and it had a 3 DMA rating and a 6 DMA (Monday through Friday) share. In that market, *The Simpsons* got lower ratings than the three nightly network newscasts but was a close fourth place to the *NBC Nightly News* (4/9). *The Simpsons* held most of its lead-in, *That 70s Show,* which had a 3 rating and a 7 share. Programmers use this information to purchase or renew the show and to schedule it during a daypart with a lead-in that will make it maximally successful.

This third section of the page also provides data on the total number of persons viewing a program in key demographic groups. In Albuquerque-Santa Fe, for example, *The Simpsons* was viewed at 5:00 P.M. by 11,000 women aged 18 to 49 (representing 55 viewers per 100 homes using television), a substantial increase over the lead-in. Nielsen's report does not show the demographic breakdown for competing stations. The programmer can, however, turn to the page for *Jeopardy* (not shown here) and see fewer women aged 18 to 49. Because *Jeopardy* also has many more women 18+ than *The Simpsons,* the programmer can deduce that *Jeopardy* skews toward older women who may not fit the advertisers' target.

Before purchasing a syndicated program, station programmers typically choose markets that are similar to their own in size and regional

characteristics; they chart the performance of that program to determine its best daypart, its strengths and weaknesses against specific competing programs, and its demographic appeal. The *Report on Syndicated Programs* enables programmers to estimate the likely performance of a syndicated program and to schedule it effectively in their lineup. If a program proves unsuitable (demographically or in terms of ratings projections), the analysis is helpful in targeting another program to meet a station's programming needs.

The *Report on Syndicated Programs* is limited to program data about syndicated programs already on the air. Quite often stations must decide whether to purchase a program before it is released in syndication (or even produced). This is particularly the case with **first-run syndicated programs** (never on a network) and popular **off-network programs** (often purchased before any station has tried them out). (The subject of purchasing *futures* on programs is covered in Chapter 6.) In the case of off-network programming, national and local data from a program's network performance can be projected to the local market, though as you can imagine, many markets differ substantially from the national market. *Purchasing first-run syndicated programs is much riskier, though, because they lack both network and station track records.*

Computerized Services

All operations, including programming, are routinely computerized at broadcast stations and cable services of all sizes. Television ratings and syndicated program reports come on disks or online, and are more commonly accessed on computers than in paper "books," though the old name sticks. Local station programmers use computer software to schedule shows; print daily, weekly and annual program logs; and keep track of competitors' program purchases in the same way that reps track purchases for many markets.

A ratings book represents only a fraction of the data available from Nielsen. The books *exclude* county of residence, ZIP code, specific viewing and listening patterns and each individual diarist's reported age (in ratings books, age is presented only as group data, for example, women 18 to 34). But then there are the raw diaries. A diary also tells what the diarist was watching at 5:45 P.M. before he or she began watching the 6 P.M. news. *Nielsen stores this raw diary information on a secure website that stations can examine online.* The information allows programmers to analyze nonstandard dayparts, specific groups of ZIP codes, nonstandard demographics, county-by-county viewing and audience flow patterns. In addition, sales staffs use the terminals to compute audience reach and frequency. If a programmer wants still more information on selected programs on a market-by-market basis, Nielsen offers its *ProFile Ranking Report* (part of the Galaxy software), which provides detailed comparisons.

The management of any station, network or cable service that subscribes to Nielsen (or Arbitron for radio) can personally review the real viewer or listener diaries, an important service for popular music radio stations. The main reason for inspecting the raw diaries is to search for unexpected entries such as how listeners or viewers recorded the station's or service's name or call letters (or slogan or air personalities). Sometimes diarists name things differently than stations expect them to. A station can remedy incorrect attributions in subsequent ratings periods by submitting a limited number of different "nicknames" to Arbitron (or by changing a slogan if it is easily confused with a competitor's). Before computerized systems became available, first-hand diary reviews (usually performed by specialist companies located near the diary warehouses) were standard procedure after each ratings book was published (these guys and gals are now out of work). Computer tape now permits the information to be examined anywhere if the appropriate software is purchased.

On the national level, television programs are introduced, launched, bought and withdrawn constantly. *Keeping tabs on the daily changes in the program market involves constant record keeping based on information from the trade press and reports from reps and distributors.* One crucial set of jobs for local programmers is keeping track of local

program availabilities (syndicated programs not yet under contract in their markets) and their own station's program inventory, including contract details, plays and amortization schedules. Only the largest stations and rep programmers, however, have the resources to track all this crucial programming information and keep timely records. It can be a mess at small stations.

A great deal of information about program performance comes from *third-party processors* that sell research reports on national and syndicated television programs, using purchased Nielsen data. These services are based on the premise that raw information is less usable than processed information. For example, the Nielsen overnight ratings are analyzed by *WRAP*, a Windows ratings-analysis program from Audience Analysis, Inc. (AAI). Third-party processors like WRAP compete with Nielsen's two services (ProFile and Navigator) and with another major service, Galaxy, which offers additional analysis. Nielsen also offers a software package (N-Power) that provides access to household and individual-level viewing for television, and TAPSCAN is a third-party processor of Arbitron radio ratings. Station program directors can create rankings (called *rankers*) of all radio stations in a market based on daypart or demographic criteria. For example, stations could be ranked on *exclusive cume*, which is a measure of listeners who listened *only* to a certain radio station and no other. Some other third-party processors are described in 5.13.

Radio Reports

Audiences for the 14,000 radio stations in the United States are more fragmented than broadcast television audiences (although the spread of cable and satellite dishes is altering that condition for television). The largest radio markets such as Los Angeles have more than 80 stations, dividing the audience into tiny slivers per station. In general, *radio stations compare their share of the audience and their cumulative audience to that of other stations with similar formats in the same market.* The most popular stations use shares, and the least popular use cumulative audiences, although formats

---

Third-Party Analyses of Ratings

Scarborough Research provides a syndicated research service to newspapers, television stations, radio stations, cable systems, internet companies, advertisers and agencies. Scarborough is a joint venture of Arbitron and VNU Marketing Information. Scarborough provides syndicated studies to print and electronic media, new media companies, sports teams and leagues, agencies, advertisers and yellow pages. Categories include consumer shopping patterns, demographics, media usage and lifestyle activities for local markets. Scarborough surveys more than 180,000 adults 181 using a two-phase methodology. Phase I is the telephone interview, and Phase II is a self-administered questionnaire and television diary. A total of 75 leading U.S. markets are measured. Every market has two six-month field periods each product year, eliminating any seasonal bias in the data and allowing users to account for new store openings and media changes.

One of Scarborough's premier products is called PRIME NExT, composed of four separate reports: Profile, which compiles lifestyles and habits of a specific audience group; Crosstab, which classifies several audience groups at once for comparisons; Schedule Analysis, which combines various proposed schedules of media and cost for analysis;

and Media Analysis, which collates media reach information into Cumulative (more than one spot or insertion minus duplication) or Ranker (average) reports, or into graph mode (visually combining elements from either report).

Media Audit is a near competitor to the kinds of studies done by Scarborough, except that the former is accredited by the Media Ratings Council. Media Audit bills itself as a multimedia, qualitative audience survey covering about 450 target items for each rated media's audience. These qualitative data points cover things such as socioeconomic characteristics, lifestyles, business decision makers, product purchasing plans, retail shopping habits, travel history, supermarket shopping, stores shopped, products purchased, fast-food restaurants eaten in, soft drink consumption, brands purchased, health insurance coverage, leisure activities, banks used, credit cards used, and other selected consumer characteristics important to local media and advertisers.

Wimmer Research is also well known for its expertise in custom-designed telephone perceptual studies. These include music testing, interactive software, focus groups, micro/macro-market studies, the Persuasion Process seminar and optical scanning data collection services.

---

that lend themselves to tuning in and out (such as all-news stations) use cumulative audience ratings even when they are popular. The top 100 radio markets correspond closely to television DMAs, but some areas in the West and South have radio but no television, so we remind you that the total number of radio markets (299) is thus greater than the 210 television DMAs.

Ratings books for radio are organized differently from those for television. An Arbitron radio ratings book contains Share Trends, followed by Demographic Breakouts, Daypart Averages, Cume Estimates, Hour-by-Hour Estimates and a few smaller sections. The age and sex categories used in radio differ from those used for television because radio stations target their programming to more precisely defined demographic groups. Thus, age ranges for radio are smaller than those used in television:

typically just ten years (for example, 25–34). Most classification groups end in "4" for radio (24, 34, 44, 54 and so on); the groups used for television (18–49, 25–54 and so on) are broader, reflecting the more heterogeneous nature of television audiences and thus television advertising sales.

Metro Audience Trends

The Metro Audience Trends section reports a station's Metro shares for five ratings books—the current survey and the previous four surveys—covering a period of about one year. These data show a station's share pattern (its "trend") over time for four separate demographic groups: 12+, 18–34, 25–54 and 35–64. A hypothetical example for the demographic category of Total Persons 12+ is shown in 5.14. *A programmer can get a quick overview of all stations'*

5.14 Metro Audience Trends Page

	MONDAY - SUNDAY 6AM - MID					WEEKEND 6AM - MID				
	Spring 04	Summer 04	Fall 04	Winter 05	Spring 05	Spring 04	Summer 04	Fall 04	Winter 05	Spring 05
WAAA										
SHARE	3.3	3.7	**	3.2	2.6	3.0	3.7	**	2.9	2.1
AQH(00)	168	187	**	163	133	128	163	**	125	96
CUME RTG	10.7	11.6	**	10.8	10.0	5.9	5.9	**	6.2	5.1
WBBB										
SHARE	3.6	3.7	**	3.5	4.4	3.0	3.2	**	3.0	3.4
AQH(00)	183	187	**	179	228	128	143	**	129	150
CUME RTG	11.7	11.1	**	11.6	13.2	5.6	6.4	**	5.8	6.8
+ WCCC										
SHARE	8.0	7.6	**	7.8	9.4	7.5	7.0	**	7.8	9.5
AQH(00)	404	385	**	395	488	324	315	**	331	426
CUME RTG	16.7	14.9	**	15.7	17.1	10.4	9.5	**	10.0	11.1
WDDD										
SHARE	2.5	2.7	**	2.1	2.3	3.2	3.4	**	2.3	2.5
AQH(00)	124	140	**	108	120	136	150	**	97	112
CUME RTG	7.4	8.4	**	6.4	7.1	4.7	5.5	**	4.3	4.7

Metro Audience Trends

Footnote Symbols: ** Station(s) not reported this survey.
+ Station(s) reported with different call letters in prior surveys - see Page 5B.

Arbitron Ratings Co., used with permission.

performance in the market from the Metro Audience Trends section.

Consider as an example the Monday to Sunday 6 A.M. to midnight section in 5.14. It shows that from spring 2004 to spring 2005, WCCC clearly led the market and continued to have climbing shares and cume ratings (cumulative audience) in the last book. WBBB was the number-two station and had an upwardly trending cume. WDDD was at the bottom of the market with flat ratings. WAAA's 12+ share declined from 3.3 to 2.6, but the drop is less than a full ratings point, and the station's cumulative rating remained at 10 percent of the market (near the bottom of the hypothetical market). Up-and-down data tell a program director that the music probably needs some fine-tuning in the Monday to Sunday 6 A.M. to midnight slot. WAAA's programmer needs to examine additional pages in the book, however, before making any major decisions.

Demographic Breakouts

Pages from Arbitron's Specific Audience (see 5.15) and Listening Locations (see 5.16) sections illustrate different ways to display ratings and share data serving different purposes. Metro and TSA AQH ratings for several 10-year age groups broken out by gender (and Men 181 and Women 181), with Persons 12+ and Teens 12 to 17 listed separately, are presented in 5.14. In 5.15, Metro AQH population estimates are detailed for the three different places people hear radio (At Home, In-Car and Other) for drivetime and three other time periods. These data are reported separately for Persons 12+, Men 18+ and Women 18+ (5.13 shows only Men 18+). *These Specific Audience and Listening Locations data help programmers see which dayparts draw which audience subgroups and where listeners most use the station.* In combination with other information provided in an Arbitron book, they suggest how different programming (or additional promotion) can improve audience composition (and therefore salability).

Arbitron also reports an hour-by-hour analysis that includes ten demographic groups by AQH for the Metro area. A programmer can track a station's performance hour-by-hour from 5 A.M. to 1 A.M. to isolate particularly strong or weak hours during the broadcast day. Other sections of the Arbitron radio book include Exclusive Audience and Cume Duplication, both of which help radio programmers understand how listeners use radio.

5.15 Specific Audience Page

	AQH (00)													
	Persons 12+	Men 18+	Men 18-24	Men 25-34	Men 35-44	Men 45-54	Men 55-64	Women 18+	Women 18-24	Women 25-34	Women 35-44	Women 45-54	Women 55-64	Teens 12-17
WAAA														
METRO	174	55	8	15	21	8		112	28	35	30	6	12	7
TSA	186	55	8	15	21	8		124	39	35	31	6	12	7
WBBB														
METRO	322	142	18	68	43		6	177	39	69	41	13	9	3
TSA	370	167	18	78	56	1	6	200	42	87	42	13	9	3
+ WCCC														
METRO	636	269	12	23	36	47	59	366	22	19	51	44	88	1
TSA	667	281	12	23	36	53	60	385	22	27	51	46	95	1
WDDD														
METRO	135	55	9	8	18	4	8	69	5	11	19	7	13	11
TSA	135	55	9	8	18	4	8	69	5	11	19	7	13	11
WEEE														
METRO														
TSA														

Footnote Symbols: * Audience estimates adjusted for actual broadcast schedule.
+ Station(s) reported with different call letters in prior surveys - see Page 5B.

Specific Audience

5.16 Listening Locations Page

	METRO AQH (00)											
	MONDAY-FRIDAY COMBINED DRIVE			MONDAY-FRIDAY 10AM - 3PM			WEEKEND 10AM - 7PM			MONDAY - SUNDAY 6AM - MID		
	At Home	In - Car	Other	At Home	In - Car	Other	At Home	In - Car	Other	At Home	In - Car	Other
WAAA	18	26	13	9	27	21	12	8	6	14	18	11
%	31	46	23	16	47	37	46	31	23	33	42	25
WBBB	36	43	57	27	31	92	25	17	18	30	27	43
%	26	32	42	18	21	61	42	28	30	30	27	43
WCCC	129	49	77	122	33	140	118	29	14	114	34	56
%	51	19	30	41	11	48	73	18	9	56	17	27
+ WDDD	29	26	7	19	22	6	22	10	4	24	17	5
%	47	42	11	40	47	13	61	28	11	52	37	11

Footnote Symbols: * Audience estimates adjusted for actual broadcast schedule.
+ Station(s) reported with different call letters in prior surveys - see Page 5B.

Listening Locations

Arbitron radio data also come on diskette or online in a format called Arbitrend, which reflects the continuously measured markets and contains demographics. Programmers for music radio stations can also purchase (or write) software to accomplish most of the tedious work involved in developing a station's music playlist. (See Chapter 11 on creating music wheels.) One widely used software program on the market accounts for 50 different characteristics of a song when selecting its position and rotation!

Time-Spent-Listening

Programmers are rarely content with the bare facts reported by Arbitron (or Nielsen in the case of television), so they use all these various ratings to make many different computations. For example, radio programmers generally want to know how long their audience listens to their station. **Time-spent-listening (TSL)** is computed by multiplying the number of quarter hours in a daypart times the rating and dividing by the cumulative audience.

To illustrate, assume we have the Los Angeles *Radio Market Report* and want to compute the 18+ TSL for KABC-AM. We can pull the AQH and cume from the book to produce the TSL. The TSL for adults 18+ for this station, Monday to Sunday, 6 A.M. to midnight, is calculated using the following formula:

$$TSL = \frac{AQH \text{ in Time Period} \times AQH \text{ Audience}}{Cume \text{ Audience}}$$

$$AQH \text{ in Time Period} = 504*$$

$$AQH \text{ Audience} = 872 \ (00)**$$

$$Cume \text{ Audience} = 9{,}875 \ (00)$$

$$TSL = \frac{504 \times 872}{9{,}875} = 39.9$$

*There are 504 quarter hours from 6 A.M. to midnight, Mon.–Sun.

**Zeros indicate that these numbers are in thousands, for example, 872 means 87,200.

Therefore, the programmer concludes that the average length of listening to KABC for an adult 18+ is 39.9 quarter hours during a given week, 6 A.M. to midnight. A high TSL indicates that people (who listen) are listening for long periods of time, not that a lot of listening goes on. TSL refers only to the amount of listening by those who do listen. Television programmers also calculate time-spent-viewing using the same formula.

Turnover

Turnover indexes the rate at which an audience changes, or turns over, during a time period. Turnover is calculated by dividing the cumulative audience by a quarter-hour rating:

$$Turnover = \frac{Cume \text{ Households or Persons}}{AQH \text{ Households or Persons}}$$

A low turnover rate indicates a loyal audience, and high turnover means a station lacks "holding

power." *Television stations expect more turnover than radio stations and go after greater reach.* Turnover is calculated for public broadcasting and cable as well as for commercial radio and television. Tracking the amount of turnover on a graph over time provides a quick clue to changes in audience listening or viewing patterns for an individual station or service.

Cable Ratings

Nielsen reports cable network ratings data separate from broadcast network data for the larger basic and premium cable services (in addition to cumulative totals for all basic and pay networks within the *Pocketpiece* and *NSI Reports*). More than 90 percent of Nielsen's 10,000 people-meter sample are cable or satellite subscribers, and Nielsen issues its *Cable National Audience Demographics Report* covering the national audiences for the largest services drawn from people-meter data.

In general, the introduction of people meters has benefited cable services far more than most broadcast stations or their networks. In those 50 or so local markets measured with paper diaries, viewers tend to fill in diaries at the week's end, losing track of where VCR or DVD recordings came from and forgetting the names of the many cable networks, so the more familiar-sounding networks tend to get undeserved diary entries and consequently high ratings. Digital service adds a hundred or more to the usual list, only exacerbating this problem. People meters, however, record the exact channel viewed, the length of viewing (which is also recorded by traditional passive meters), and the composition of the audience. Many smaller local markets, however, continue to be measured with diaries or diaries plus passive meters.

On the local market level, individual cable networks are included in Nielsen's *Cable Activity Report* when they achieve a 3 percent share of audience (and pay the cost of data analysis and reporting). Nielsen measures cable service audiences along with broadcast station audiences in the all-market sweeps (using diaries or meters or both). Cable line-ups differ from franchise to franchise within one market, however, and accurate tracking of channel attributions ("I watched Channel 3") has been difficult. For example, the Washington, D.C., area has about 30 cable franchises plus ATT's FiOS and DISH and DirecTV, which place the dozens of cable networks (and some broadcast TV stations) on widely differing channel numbers.

Moreover, digital cable lineups can locate the same channel in two or three places (say, 24 and 316 and 1627, with no apparent numbering logic). *In consequence, ratings for the smaller services have not been stable even within a single market, let alone nationally* (see Chapter 9 on the dream of uniform channel lineups). Even though the Nielsen metered markets (covering more than 60 percent of all U.S. viewing) may eventually migrate to Active/Passive people meters (A/P) or portable people meters (PPM) that read codes embedded in the programs by the producers, *there will always be less reliable diary measurements in the smaller markets.*

To qualify for inclusion in the standard television sweep reports, a cable service must reach 20 percent of net weekly circulation. In other words, *20 percent of the market's television households must view it for at least five minutes during the survey week.* In the first year of reporting (in the dinosaur age of 1982), only HBO, WTBS-TV (the former Superstation, now the TBS cable network), Showtime and ESPN qualified. Two decades later, however, nearly all of the top 20 cable networks qualified in most markets, including (order varies somewhat from year to year) Discovery, ESPN, CNN, USA Network, TNT, Lifetime, the Weather Channel, ESPN2, Nickelodeon, Spike TV, A&E, TBS, the Learning Channel, CNN Headline News, MTV, Home & Garden Television (HGTV), C-SPAN, ABC Family Channel, the History Channel and Cartoon Network, each of which reaches over 90 million subscribers (see Chapter 9). Galavisión qualifies where Hispanic viewers make up much of the population, and other cable services such as WGN and WWOR easily qualify in some regions of the country. *Cable networks appearing on only some of a market's systems, however, have more*

difficulty meeting the minimum viewing level, even when they are regularly watched by the cable subscribers able to receive them.

Although each large cable system operator and network purchases cable ratings from Nielsen, they are also interested in research that identifies their most likely customers. Now a subsidiary of Nielsen, Claritas offers detailed demographic and behavioral information in annual reports. Nielsen's PRIZM (Potential Rating in Zipped Markets) report combines ZIP code information with Nielsen data, information from local governments, magazine subscription lists, automobile registrations, and other data sources. Such *geodemographic* information creates groups of population segments by lifestyle.

Arbitron competes with Nielsen on the cable front, using two techniques: Set-Top Solutions (STS) and the PPM mentioned earlier. STS collects viewer information directly from the cable converter box or DVR. The portable meters collect information from a pager-sized device carried by the viewer. Arbitron also offers three services to cable operators and networks: Scarborough, RetailDirect and Retail-Direct Lite. These services provide qualitative media and market consumer behavior information, but not ratings.

Premium Services

Pay-movie services have special measurement problems, of course (change any tech and "problems" rise up). *Movies, the largest element in their programming, appear in repeating and rotating patterns to attract large cumulative audiences for each feature.* This contrasts with the broadcast television pattern of scheduling a movie or series episode only once in prime time (typically) and seeking the largest possible audience for that one showing.

In digital households, subscribers may have six channels of HBO, six channels of Starz, eight channels of Encore, seven channels of various ESPNs, plus additional multichannel versions of the same networks in high definition. Even TNT appears in three places: analog, digital and HD; *thus, counting and matching viewing from system to system has nearly insurmountable difficulties.* In addition, six channels of ESPN Sports Pay-Per-View in digital and the same six again in HD appear on one cable system. And there are several on-demand channels on which older programs and events can be pulled up, for a fee. (These kinds of pay channels are measured by their buy rates, not household ratings.)

Indeed, *viewers shift the times they watch pay cable so much more than they do broadcast* television (by recording movies at home) that it becomes problematic to use the same measurement criteria. (See Chapters 3 and 9 on program evaluation and audience measurement.) Moreover, the total number of pay households is relatively small for all services except HBO, although nearly half of all television households take one or more pay services, in addition to digital service. And the large number of basic and pay-cable television networks subdivide the ratings into slivers much as radio stations do in major markets. Premium-channel cable programmers use the ratings information available to them to judge individual program popularity and channel popularity, but as yet pay networks rarely win specific time periods in competition with broadcasters. Frequently, *however, the cumulative audiences for all showings of a top-notch movie on HBO equal the size of a television network's audience.* Although pay-cable movies usually draw small audiences, original programming like *Game of Thrones* attracts critical acclaim, Emmy awards and stronger viewing levels.

Nielsen publishes a quarterly *Cross-Platform Video Report* and a comprehensive *Video Recorder Usage Study,* which can help pay-cable programmers make sense of reported viewing. The Nielsen Homevideo Index, as contrasted with the Nielsen Station Index, provides many additional specialized reports for cable programmers.

Rentrak specializes in measuring video-on-demand, which is becoming more important as portable video devices (such as iPads and tablets) reach greater acceptance with viewers. Mobile OnDemand is Rentrak's answer to measuring cellphone viewing and other portable use of media. Nielsen still struggles expanding its home-based measurement to portable devices, but competition from Rentrak and comScore will likely result in new products to keep Nielsen competitive in the future.

Cable Penetration Measures

Using figures supplied by Nielsen and the industry itself, the industry regularly updates cable statistics, reporting how many households have access to cable at the present time; such households are called **homes passed** (HP). As of 2012, more than 99 percent of U.S. households were passed by cable wires; that is, people in virtually all homes and apartments *could* subscribe to cable if they wanted to. **Cable penetration** is the percentage of television households actually subscribing to basic cable service (shown as household penetration in 5.17), which has held steady at about 61 percent. Actually, the total penetration by the cable *networks* had neared 91 percent by 2012, thanks to other multichannel distributors and the conversion to all-digital television.

Another important figure to the industry is *pay as a percentage of basic cable subscribers because those are the homes actually signing up.* NCTA no longer reports premium subscribers, but *a good estimate is three-quarters of basic cable subscribers take one or more pay channels.* It is estimated that, in addition to 70 million subscribers to cable systems, about 36 million households subscribe to DirecTV, DISH or other kinds of services, such as wireless cable, home satellite dishes in their yards or telephone companies. Giants like AT&T's FiOS provide the same cable networks to private homes and offices, but their penetration is, so far, a tiny percentage.

Like radio, cable, satellite and telephone services are also concerned with audience turnover. In cable, **churn** is the ratio of disconnecting subscribers to newly connecting cable subscribers (the number of **disconnects** divided by the number of **new**

5.17	2011 Cable Summary Report*
Total Subscribers (based on 60.6% of 116 million TV homes)	70,296,000
Homes Passed	128,500,000
Total Cable Systems	7,426
Household Penetration	60.6%

*www.ncta.com (Statistics), estimated, 2011.

connects). The problems associated with a high rate of churn are described in Chapter 9.

Because the audiences for many advertiser-supported networks are too small (at any one time) to show in Nielsen ratings books, a number of smaller basic cable networks estimate their audiences on the basis of customized research that adjusts the size of the universe of homes to match cable penetration in the markets the cable network already reaches. *Many cable networks reach only a portion of cable households, and of course, the audience for any one channel at any one time can be minute.* Direct comparisons of such customized cable ratings to ordinary ratings can lead to confusion because nonsubscribers are not counted. Especially for narrowly targeted cable services, advertisers want detailed demographic breakouts, which necessitate expensive customized cable research at the local level.

Online Research Services

Because of interrelationships among internet websites and the traditional media of cable, satellite, telephone and broadcasting, it is not surprising that Nielsen rapidly developed a system for measuring internet audiences. Nielsen//NetRatings is one of two major competitors in this field, the other being Media Metrix, the web's oldest rating service. Both use samples of home and at-work web surfers to monitor and estimate usage patterns.

Although cable, satellite and telephone delivery of television have certainly had a huge impact on audience behaviors, this impact pales in comparison to the profound and sweeping effects of the internet on television, as well as lots of other things, and it is still in the early stages of its development. How and why people use the web, what they use it for, and how these things affect other traditional or "old" media are yet evolving, but some trends can be gauged with fairly high accuracy (although others remain highly speculative). The situation for web audiences is extremely dynamic, almost volatile in many respects. Chapter 4 discusses in detail what online ratings show about audience behavior. One example is the measurement of *time-spent-online (TSO),* which by 2010 was 18 hours a week per adult, on average, and creeping up toward the 31.5 hours spent watching television weekly.[8] The methods and terminology used for measurement of online computer use are quite different from those used for broadcast and multichannel measurement.

Web Tracking Services

Nielsen//NetRatings publishes regular reports that include five sections: Audience Summary, Audience Profile, Daily/Hourly Traffic, Average Usage and AOL Audience Report. Audience Summary reports give a comprehensive profile of the entire web audience, including the *unique audience* (average number of different people who visit a site on each day during the course of the month), page views, audience demographics, frequency and time-spent information.

Audience Profile shows demographics for the total U.S. internet population. This report shows audience composition, number of sessions per period, average time spent per session and average pages viewed per session. Daily/Hourly Traffic breaks down the Audience Profile data by specific day and hour. Average Usage includes statistics on the number of sessions, pages viewed, pages visited per session, time spent per session and duration of the viewing of a page. AOL Audience Report shows average time spent and audience demographics for use within the AOL service.

The Nielsen//NetRatings audience-tracking software has several advantages over other approaches because of its accuracy. The software "sits in the datastream" and provides an unobstructed log of all web activity. This unique technique for tracking users automatically measures the viewing and clicking of ad banners (*bannertrack*), e-commerce activity (*commercetrack*), page views cached (that is, stored) by the browser program (*cachetrack*) and page loading times. The tracking is unobtrusive to users in order to limit bias and requires the absolute minimum in company intervention once installed. Software updates are also wholly automatic.

Nielsen has also begun to measure web-enabled television sets. Viewers who use such receivers to browse websites and stream web programs will be measured alongside their more traditional program choices. Nielsen also adapts its STB devices to collect viewing data for homes connected to FiOS, which is AT&T's answer to broadband distribution of web-based programs.

The other leading web tracking service, comScore's Media Metrix, produces a variety of reports from the continuous monitoring of internet audience behavior. The comScore company surveys 120,000 internet users recruited though random-digit dialing. Media Metrix also offers in-depth tracking of online transactions, at-work usage and activity on all web networks. The detailed description of the Metrix process illustrates the complexity of the problems and the seemingly arbitrary nature of some decisions that must be made to have a workable measurement system for online usage (see 5.18).

Rentrak also offers measurement of web program viewing through its Internet TV Essentials product. This service gauges how, what, where and why online television viewing takes place. Rentrak attempts to measure the shelf life of video content to help clients optimize their libraries of web programs. Two types of viewing are considered: live-streaming and per-transaction downloads, for either purchased content or rental showings.

5.18 The Media Metrix Method

Using its own patented metering methodology, Media Metrix *continuously* captures actual usage data from randomly recruited users, getting representative samples of tens of thousands of people in homes and businesses around the world (but excluding college labs, cyber cafes, airports, hotel business centers, public libraries and K–12 schools where there are certainly lots of computers …). The Metrix is a software application that works with one's PC operating system to passively track all user activity in real time—click by click, page by page and minute by minute, measuring only those users who visit the internet at least one day per month.

The unduplicated audience (*cume* or reach) is calculated by adding all at-home users to all at-work users and then subtracting all users who use *both* locations. Only the base-page *universal resource locator (URL)*, or page address, is counted, even if other files and items are associated with it.

By recording whatever keyboard or mouse activity is taking place, Media Metrix keeps track of each time the computer is turned on or off, when the machine is on, and whether a user is actively using the machine. Sixty seconds after keyboard or mouse activity ceases, the machine is declared to be "idle." Viewing time is not credited when the machine is in the idle state, but as soon as a user moves the mouse or presses a key, the meter resumes accumulating viewing credit to the page or application.

When the computer first boots up, the user must select his or her name from the list of registered users and press OK. After 30 minutes of "idle" time, the meter presents its user identification screen again to ensure that a change in user is captured. If at any time the user changes, it is a simple matter of clicking the meter's icon to recall the user identification screen. The meter applies viewing credit to only one application or program at a time. If, for example, the user is using a word-processing application while his or her browser is in the background downloading web pages, the word-processing application receives viewing credit—not the browser.

Whenever a page from the web is displayed in a browser, the meter records the full URL. The Media Metrix Meter records the name and details of each file coming into the PC over a network connection. The meter also records information about each graphic file, banner ad, sound file (wav, mid, mp3), streaming media and so on. The meter also can record additional detail on demand, such as specific activity within applications.

Once or twice per year, a certain percentage of respondents are asked to complete qualitative questionnaires to more fully describe their lifestyles beyond the key demographic data. Household-level demographics are updated annually by asking a representative from the household to visit a website and update the profile. Additionally, twice per year, a portion of the sample is provided with "scanning" software, which scans the PC to record the technical configuration and to log which software programs are installed. The weakness of the Media Metrix method is that it favors heavy web users and excludes light users (many of whom may be fearful of viruses and worms or wary of providing fodder for commercial advertising messages).

In addition to Nielsen//NetRatings, comScore Media Metrix and Rentrak, other services "audit" server-based information supplied by websites. I/Pro offers its I/Audit service, and Audit Bureau of Circulation (the same ABC that audits newspaper and magazine circulation) provides a service called the ABC Interactive Web Site Activity Audit Report. All these measurement systems have strengths and weaknesses that favor some sites and some kinds of usage over others. You'll be rolling in gold if you're the one who comes up with the technology that advertisers like, is fairest to all users and is most widely adopted.

Online Ratings Terminology

Page views (also known as *page impressions*) are usually defined as one or more online files presented to a viewer as a single document as a result of a single request received by the server. *Visits* are a series of interactions with a site by a visitor—without 30 consecutive minutes of inactivity.

Companies that focus on advertising measurement, such as ABC Interactive Audits, are concerned with such variables as ad display, ad download, ad impression, ad impressions ratio, ad request and click/ad interaction. To date, *banners* have been one of the most successful internet advertising methods, but for programmers, it is important to understand that advertising banners are not separate from the "program" content; they are somewhat like having a changing billboard in a live sporting event. Online, there is no flow, no break, and no need to zip or zap, although plenty of ad messages encourage the user to click away. The key measurement in e-commerce is the *click-through*, defined as the result of clicking on an advertisement that links to the advertiser's website or another page within the website (exclusive of nonqualifying activity and internal users).

As you would guess, different web tracking services use slightly different terminology. Media Metrix estimates a site's (1) *unique visitors* (the number of different people visiting the property in a 30-day period); (2) *reach* (percentage of projected individuals who visited a designated website or category among the total number of projected individuals using the World Wide Web during a given reporting period); (3) average usage days per user; (4) average unique pages per user per day and month; and (5) average minutes spent per person per page, per day and per month. As explained in 5.18, Media Metrix's measure of unique pages counts the number of different URLs visited by a person on a particular day. For example, a user viewing a stock-price page who hits the refresh button repeatedly throughout the day will be counted as visiting a single unique page for the day.

Nielsen//NetRatings has similar terminology, covering three critical areas: *site activity* (sites visited, URLs within a site visited, duration of visits and duration and frequency of sessions), *advertising activity* (actual ad banners viewed, advertisers, sites the ads ran on and ads clicked on), and *user profile* (age, gender, marital status, education, occupation, income and ethnicity). Of all these measures, programmers are most interested in *unique visitors* and *reach*, because they are most like broadcasting and cable audience measurements, and also perhaps *site activity* as an assessment of content popularity.

Matching

Attempts to combine the traditional media content of print or TV and related internet sites first occurred when NBC collaborated with Digital-Convergence.com to allow viewers to link their personal computers with television programming and advertising during NBC's 2000 Olympics, its national election coverage and its fall 2000 network television season. Advertisers could then track consumers interested in their products and tailor online information accordingly. The system enabled advertisers to communicate directly with these potential customers and not waste resources on those consumers for whom the brand is either irrelevant or not the preferred one. Whether the potential customers thought it was such a good idea is an open question.

All television networks continue to look for ways to "involve" the television and web audiences. TruTV argues that *cost per involvement (CPI)* is a key measure of return on investment for advertisers who fund programming. Originally, truTV (back when it was Court TV) introduced its "lean forward" campaign, noting that viewing TV while connected to the internet was different than the old "lean back" model of passive viewing. Now, the channel uses custom analysis of Nielsen data to assess the "stickiness" of its website for program viewers. It did, however, stop short of measuring the direct effects of product sales because, like most other advertiser-supported channels, truTV felt it could not be accountable for the creativity of the advertising message.

More recently, the issue has become *click fraud*, or concern for the accuracy of click counts. To the industry's dismay, two quite different kinds of fraud have been detected. In one case, a group of people flood a site with clicks in order to earn money (hosts of search ads make money according to how many people access the ad, and an extra-large number of clicks earns more money—enough to pay off conspirators). In the other case, companies with display ads normally pay to stay up on the site only until they attract a certain number of clicks, and then excess clicks can knock the ad off early (an advantage to a competitor).

Beyond this purposeful deception, measurement definition is an issue. For example, is a person two unique visitors or one if he/she accesses the same site from home and work on the same day? Eventually, the Media Rating Council is expected to establish uniform definitions for valid, invalid and fraudulent clicks, as well as standards for auditing tracking numbers (as soon as a million companies can agree on them).

Ratings Limitations

Although many broadcast, cable and web programmers are aware of the limitations of ratings and user counts, in practice these limitations are rarely considered. This does not result from ignorance or carelessness so much as from the pressure to do daily business using some yardstick. Programmers, program syndicators, sales staffs, station reps and advertising agencies all deal with the same numbers. In any one broadcast market, all

participants—those buying and selling programs, those selling and buying time—refer to the same sets of numbers (Nielsen reports in TV, Arbitron in radio), and they have done so for decades. The "numbers" for any single market usually show a consistent pattern that makes sense in general to those who know local history (such as changes in power, formats and ownership). Although broadcasters and the ratings companies know that the "numbers" are imperfect, they remain the industry standard. In practice the numbers are perceived as "facts," not estimates, like it or not.

Occasionally a gross error will require a ratings company to reissue a book, but for the most part, small statistical inequities are simply overlooked. To eliminate as much error as possible and refine methods suited to the newer media, the major ratings companies use advisory boards that suggest how to improve the ratings estimates. Because a change in ratings methodology always means additional costs passed on to broadcasters, the rate of improvement will continue to be conservative now that the shift to people meters has been accomplished.

The major limitations of broadcast and cable ratings are briefly summarized as follows. Until use of the internet as an advertising medium grows considerably, the problem of limited use overwhelms all other methodological considerations, and advertisers are the ones who pay for ratings research. But it won't be long. Advertising on Facebook, in particular, has had a monumental effect on advertisers' perspectives. All those hundreds of thousands and millions of eyeballs...Nonetheless, the following seven practical and theoretical problems limit the validity, reliability, significance and generalizability of broadcast and cable ratings data.

1. *Sample Size*
Although each ratings company attempts to reach a sample that represents the population distribution geographically (by age, sex, income and so on), a shortfall occasionally occurs in a market. Such shortfalls are in fact routine in radio market ratings and also occur, although less frequently, in television market ratings. In these instances, certain demographic groups have to be weighted to adjust for

the lack of people in the sample (such as too few men between 25 and 49).

Weighting by large amounts makes the estimates less reliable. The amount of unreliability is related to the (unknown) differences in responses between those who did respond in the sample and those who did not cooperate or bother to comply with all of the procedures. An expected return rate of 100 diaries from teenagers, for example, with an actual return rate of 20, should create strong skepticism about how representative the 20 responders are. The 80 who did not respond would undoubtedly represent this segment of the audience better and more accurately, but because their media usage is not known, the ratings services use the 20 responses and compound the error by assigning a weight of 5 to each of the 20 responses (to calculate the number of respondents in this age group as a proportional part of the total sample). Although weighting is a scientifically acceptable and perfectly valid procedure, it assumes that those responses being weighted closely represent those responses that are missing (see 5.19 for more on sampling errors). In our hypothetical example, the responses of too few individuals represent too many other people/households.

Sample size is the one limitation that comes to most people's minds when they hear about how ratings are compiled. The typical "person on the street"

5.19 Standard Error

The concept of standard error is not a ratings limitation but rather part of a mathematical model whose use reduces some of the problems associated with rating procedures. In practice, however, very few people using audience ratings ever take standard error into consideration. The "numbers" are seen as factual; sampling errors and other errors or weaknesses in research methodology are not considered in any way.

In essence, using the standard error model compensates for the fact that ratings are produced from a sample of people, not a complete count of an entire population. Whenever researchers project sample findings into the general population from which that sample was drawn, some error necessarily occurs. A standard error figure establishes the range around a given estimate within which the actual number probably falls. The range suggests how high or how low the actual number may be. The formula for standard error is

$$SE = \sqrt{\frac{p(100 - p)}{n}}$$

where SE = Standard error

p = audience estimate expressed as a ratio

n = sample size

For example, suppose that a random sample of 1,200 people produces a rating of 20. The standard error associated with this rating is computed as follows:

$$SE = \sqrt{\frac{20(100 - 20)}{1,200}}$$
$$= \sqrt{\frac{20(80)}{1,200}}$$
$$= \sqrt{1.33}$$
$$= 1.15$$

A rating of 20 therefore has a standard error of plus or minus 1.15 points—meaning that the actual rating could be anywhere from a low of 18.85 to a high of 21.15.

Another difficulty in calculating error is determining how confident we want to be of the results. It is possible to be very confident (with a 95 percent probability of being right) or somewhat confident (with only a 65 percent probability of being right). Nielsen ratings are generally calculated to the lesser standard. Most social science research uses the higher standard. Nielsen includes standard error formulas in all their ratings books for those wishing to calculate error in specific ratings and shares, but undeniably, printing the range for each rating/share would make ratings books unusable. Nonetheless, the range is the most accurate version of each rating or share, given its database, which may itself introduce a great deal more error.

response is "How can a few thousand people be used to measure what millions of people watch or listen to?" They are mistaken; the sample sizes used by the ratings companies are not the major problem. The *representativeness* of those selected for the sample is.

2. *Lack of Representation*

The major ratings companies long refused to sample from group living quarters such as college dormitories, bars, hotels, motels, hospitals, nursing homes, military barracks and so on. The problem with measuring such viewing is that the number of individuals who are viewing varies, sometimes greatly, making it nearly impossible to determine how many diaries or people-meter buttons need to be provided. The Nielsen people-meter ratings also fail to measure the number of people viewing in offices, workplaces, and country clubs—or who are watching battery-operated TV sets on beaches and at sporting events (there are more than 10 million portable TV sets in the United States, to say nothing of watching via computers, tablets or iPhones).

In the latest Total-TV Audience Monitor (T-TAM), a national survey, Nielsen Media Research estimated that about 44 million adults (and 32 percent of adults aged 18 to 49) watched television in out-of-home locations each week. As a result, Nielsen finally began including college students living away from home in its ratings because the survey showed that college apartments and residence halls were among the most common out-of-home locations for TV viewing. Nonetheless, only students whose families already participate in Nielsen's surveys can be included—so they do not represent new, independent families—but at least dorm, fraternity, sorority and off-campus apartment viewing now can influence ratings.

The *rest of out-of-home viewing,* however, only appears in special reports, not the weekly ratings. Nielsen argues that such viewing accounts for only a small percentage of total national television viewing and is therefore not worth pursuing (that is, is not cost-effective for broadcasters to pay to measure). Critics argue that, given that the number of TV households in America is 116.2 million, with 2.56 bodies per household, totally 297.2 million

people, the loss of 44 million more *out-of-house (OOH)* viewers is very much affecting program ratings, and that other OOH viewers need to be added.

TV programs and some radio formats that appeal to narrow demographic segments are widely known to go uncounted in calculating the ratings. Estimates for *Late Night with Jimmy Fallon* indicate that as much as one-fifth of the actual audience used to go uncounted by Nielsen's ratings largely because of the exclusion of the types of locations where many people watched the program (college dorms and bars). The same was true (and may still be to some extent) of Fallon's predecessor, *Late Night with Conan O'Brien*, and its competitor, *The Late Show with David Letterman*.

Also, cable sports services such as ESPN, watched in nearly every bar in the country, suffer from the omission of group audiences. At least 59 percent of ESPN's 5.4 million adult viewers watch outside the home each week. The wide popularity of sports bars in recent years (with multiple TV screens and patrons switching among different channels of ESPN) adds substantially to the inaccuracy of samples used to measure sports viewing. Group viewing of soap operas is another unmeasured phenomenon.

3. *Ethnic Representation*

Data for ethnic groups are among the most hotly debated aspects of broadcast and cable audience estimates. Ratings companies have long grappled with the difficulty of getting randomly selected minority households to cooperate with the ratings company by filling out a diary or having a meter installed. Companies have offered higher honoraria for participating in order to gain a representative sample of both Hispanics/Latinos and African-Americans. Nonetheless, many minorities understandably remain apathetic to the needs of ratings companies, despite financial incentives.

Critics argue that those minorities who agree to go along with prescribed procedures are much more like white sample participants and are atypical of the ethnic group they are intended to represent. Thus, a participating black family may not be like the vast majority of black families in a given viewing area. *Ethnic populations are undoubtedly undercounted, and those who are counted are often unrepresentative of their ethnic groups.* Because no standard of "truth" exists by which to compare samples to an entire ethnic group, ratings companies and advertising agencies inevitably use the numbers in front of them to make decisions.

Nielsen does identify African-American and Hispanic audiences in its local market rating reports, but the information in some markets is limited to penetration, counting their presence in the same table as multiset, cable and DVD homes. At the national level, however, Nielsen's monthly reports have an added 20 African-American demographic categories. In addition, primarily to serve Univision and Telemundo, Nielsen started its *Nielsen Hispanic Television Index (NHTI)* in 1992, but more recently, Hispanic viewers

of Spanish-language networks were folded into national people-meter ratings just like other television viewers. For markets with a significant Hispanic population, Nielsen has phased out it separate local ratings report for those homes (HSI) in favor of the NSI report.

In other countries, the enormous complexity of the racial and economic situation goes far beyond what U.S. ratings companies must deal with (see 5.20 on what is measured in South Africa). Everywhere, advertisers and media programmers need to know what languages their viewers or listeners prefer and what electronic capabilities their households have. In many developing countries, especially rural areas, viewing and even listening often takes place in large groups, which alters the relationship between a

---

5.20 Going Beyond Race

Once freed from apartheid, South Africa's volatile history of racial division and tension led its broadcasters and marketers to seek out ways to avoid categorizing people primarily by race in research. A Living Standards Measure (LSM) was developed that clustered people into ten distinctive segments on the basis of degree of urbanization, ownership of cars and major appliances, languages spoken, and access to basic services (water, electricity, telephones, media). Because LMS is a multivariate segmentation tool constructed from 29 variables, it is a far stronger differentiator than any single demographic variable. The full list includes such variables as the following:

Electricity	Flush toilet in house or plot
Electric stove or hot plate	Microwave oven
Water in home or on plot	Hot running water
Traditional hut	Built-in kitchen sink
Washing machine	Tumble dryer
Refrigerator/freezer	Deep freezer
Dishwasher	No domestic worker
Sewing machine	Vacuum cleaner or floor polisher
TV set	VCR in household
Home telephone	No cell phone in household
Pay/satellite channels	Stereo or music center
PC in home	Fewer than two radio sets in home
One or more sedan cars	Home security service
Home in Gauteng/Western Cape	Home in nonurban area outside Gauteng/Western Cape

The LSM is widely used in both programming and advertising to define target markets. It is also used in customized formats in other parts of Africa, and efforts have begun to use LSM as a global marketing tool.

Daan van Vuuren
former Director of Audience Research
SABC, South Africa

Reprinted by kind permission of Linda van Vuuren.

program and its audience from a programming perspective and certainly makes counting viewers or listeners even more problematic.

4. *Cooperation*

All ratings companies use accurate and statistically correct sampling procedures: People/households are selected at random to represent (within a small margin of error) the population from which they were drawn. For representativeness to occur in practice, however, the people/households originally selected must cooperate when the ratings company invites their participation. In the past, when Nielsen used the passive TV-set meters (before people meters were developed), cooperation was not an overwhelming problem. Since the late 1980s, cooperation rates for allowing the installation of the more complicated people-meter technology by Nielsen have steadily declined to alarmingly low levels. Studies have reported refusal rates of one-half to two-thirds for people-meter installations among those contacted in original random samples. Refusal rates were highest among ethnic minorities and younger adult males.

The same studies also reported sharp declines in the area of diary cooperation. Nielsen diary response rates for the November sweeps went from about 43 percent in the early 1990s to around 28 percent by 2000. Arbitron diary response rates went from 40 percent in 1995 to 35 percent by 1999. Again, participation differs among key demographic and lifestyle groups. Ratings for children and teens are hugely problematic. Moreover, long-term cooperation from all viewers continues to be a problem. Using a diary requires participants' willingness to train themselves to fill it out as they view or listen and to learn how to fill it out correctly. People meters require pushing buttons every 15 minutes as onscreen reminders interrupt viewing. They also require the householder to assign spare buttons to casual guests.

Nielsen's reliance on diaries continues in non-metered markets across the U.S. One of the authors of this chapter was selected to participate in the local market ratings one year ago and, again, this past year. Upon receipt of the diary and complete instructions, the author discovered that one of the first tasks was to list the TV channels regularly watched for each of the TV sets in the household. Since the author routinely "watches" more than 50 channels on a regular basis, sampling program offerings at various times of day or night, this was, at the very least an arduous task. The author felt like tearing pages out of the *Time-Warner Channel Guide* print publication and stapling them to the diary with the words "good luck" written on them. Moreover, the week selected for completing the diary was a totally atypical one in terms of outside commitments and events that would result in a completely unfair representation of a normal weekday/weekend viewing period. Suffice to say, the diary was not filled out and returned last year, despite follow-up reminders.

Not to be outdone, the Nielsen folks called again this past April, never leaving a message. Thinking that was the end of it, the author was then surprised to receive a diary and instructions for participation this year. Nothing had changed in terms of the process becoming more user friendly or more in line with how most people watch television. Again the diary was not returned, despite the usual follow-up reminders.

Based on the author's personal experience, it seems appropriate to ask how reliable the local market ratings were and will be, given poor cooperation rates to begin with and coupled with such a major piece of work to complete what was asked. The Nielsen folks would of course say that these were not usual circumstances, but coupled with other cooperation problems, the limitations of such procedures in a highly technological age seem obvious.

Another problem in gaining cooperation that has emerged in the last five years centers on having access to a representative sample to participate in the ratings (national or local market level). More and more households have no landline telephones ("cord cutters") and are not accessible through various household listing that could be used for the sample. Of those households with landline phones, many have caller ID and won't answer unfamiliar calls and/or have put their landline phones on do-not-call lists, which would make them unavailable to Nielsen.

Another way of collecting data, the *telephone coincidental method*—usually assumed to be the most reliable method—has its defects, too. A 2004 study conducted by Ball State University indicated that phone surveys are "largely useless" for determining media behavior. The three-part study combined phone surveys, diaries and observation with vastly different results: On average, people reported through phone surveys that they watched only 121 minutes of television per day. At the same time, diarists logged 278 minutes, and researchers observed individuals actually watching 319 minutes. Other results showed that phone survey responders said they spent only 29 minutes online per day, but diarists said they logged on for 57 minutes each day, while observations recorded people going online for 78 minutes a day.

Whenever cooperation rates are low, for whatever reason, the participating sample probably differs from those who declined. *Those who cooperate typically demonstrate a highly favorable view of the medium and generally use it more often than those who refuse to cooperate.* Refusals may indicate a lack of interest in the medium or, at the least, too light a use to warrant learning a fairly complicated but infrequently applied process. It is easy to visualize a single person or a young, childless couple who says to the ratings company, "No thanks, I'm (we're) almost never home. I (we) hardly ever watch TV at all." Thus, those who view more or use the medium more are probably overrepresented in the sample, resulting in correspondingly inflated viewing estimates and unrealistic measures of the total television audience's preferences. Of all the limitations on ratings, cooperation remains one of the two most significant and persistent problems.

5. *Definition of Viewing/Listening/Visiting*

And here's a head-scratcher: *No one seems to be even remotely certain of precisely what it means to "view" television or "listen" to radio.* It sounds so simple on the surface, but consider this: For those using people meters to be counted as "viewers," household members must activate the people-meter computer with the handheld device only while in the room where the television set is on. At regular intervals, viewers are reminded of the need to "log in" by pointing their handheld

device at the TV set. In all systems, the sole criterion for being a viewer is *being in the room.* Viewers can very easily be reading magazines, talking, thinking, playing a game—in short, paying little or no attention to the picture or sound—but are still counted as viewers.

Conversely, a viewer might be in a nearby room doing a menial task and listening intently to a program's sound. This person is normally not counted as a viewer. Being there may or may not constitute "viewing." More crucial, watching the same content via computer screen is not included as viewing. What the ratings services measure, therefore, are potential viewers—with the option of letting traditional television (or radio) receivers occupy their attention. To date, no commercial techniques measure viewing as a function of the attention paid to what is on or to the way that content is used. And viewing or listening via the new reception media appears only in special studies, not regular ratings.

Among radio audiences, the parallel problem is no uniform definition (or no definition at all) of what it means to "listen" to radio. When in someone else's car on the way to school or work while this person has the radio on, should the passenger be counted as a "listener" to station WXXX? How about offices where a radio station plays in the background while people work? Are they "listening"? Is the music or information what each person would have chosen had they been able to select the station? Moreover, what does "listening" mean? If a person is paying attention to other things and has the radio on for background noise or a kind of companionship, should that person "count" as a listener?

As for what it means to "visit" a website, the absence of universally agreed-upon definitions poses inherent interpretation problems when trying to understand what the numbers mean or represent. In this instance, the problem centers on defining what it means to "use" a website, a parallel to what it means to "view" television. To be counted as a site visitor, does one merely have to access the site to be counted or, perhaps more importantly, should that person count the same as someone who, while at the site, goes to other options or pages that are components of the site? Other questions that need to be answered include "What exactly does someone look at when at the site?" "For how long does the user look at a particular item or the site generally?" "Why were none of the options accessed?" "Why were one or more options accessed?" *As difficult as it is to come up with a valid definition of what constitutes "viewing" television, it seems easy by comparison to defining what goes on with a user while he or she is at a website.* The contemplate the strange things people do with smart phones ...

Both television and radio ratings are plagued by the industry's unwillingness to provide a standardized, widely agreed-upon definition of viewing and listening, and now the problem is extended to the online world. So long as the advertising industry remained satisfied with the ratings numbers generated for TV and radio, there was little reason for concern. As Nielsen moved to people meters, however, and as media choices proliferated rapidly through cable and satellite-delivered media services to the internet and mobile handheld media, the reported numbers for conventional media showed progressive shrinkage. Advertisers began to ask what was going on, and the broadcast and cable industries began to scramble for explanations. Broadcasting and cable have continued to point the finger of blame toward the ratings services, questioning their methods and the validity of the numbers they report. Lost in all the ongoing measurement arguments is the crux of the problem—no one knows what the ratings services are supposed to be measuring in the first place. This debate has no satisfactory means of resolution until basic definitions are standardized.

6. *Station Tampering*

A continuing problem for ratings is that sometimes stations attempt to influence the outcome of the ratings by running contests during the measurement period. Arbitron and Nielsen place warnings on the cover of their ratings books advising users of stations' questionable ethics. Of course, there is a gray area: Was the promotional activity (called *hyping* or *hypoing*) really a normal contest or one designed to boost (hypo) the ratings?

Warning labels are especially ineffective for the advertising industry when the agencies get their numbers from computer tapes or online services. There is no "book" on which a warning can appear. The problem of hyping has grown in recent years, with some local newscasts promoting huge cash giveaways during sweeps. Many industry experts predict year-round measurement for television that abolishes sweeps periods will eventually solve the hyping problem.

7. *Device Limitations*

Not everyone has faith in the reliability of people meters. After 30 years of depending on one ratings system, Nielsen's abrupt change in 1987 from passive meters and diary-based national television ratings to people meters created an uproar. The shift happened all in one year, and, with so much at stake, many in the industry felt unprepared. One objection to people meters centers on what happens when the handheld devices are not correctly operated. When mistakes are made, as is inevitable, viewing is invalidated and not counted in the ratings. Given the high likelihood that people will have occasional mechanical difficulties and that children and teens will "fool around" with the meter, much legitimate viewing may be lost. Nielsen argues the necessity of omitting figures where the device was misused, claiming that such inclusions would produce unrealistic figures. Nielsen further claims that in a national sample of 12,000 households, occasional omissions have only a negligible impact on ratings. Not everyone agrees, however.

Another people-meter problem occurs with *sample composition.* The difficulties previously discussed concerning who chooses to become part of the sample and who refuses are worsened, not resolved, by people meters. Nielsen's own studies show that *people-meter cooperators differ from noncooperators in that the former are younger, more urban and have smaller families* (they may also differ in other unreported ways). Older people and those living in rural areas are underrepresented in the people-meter sample, in part because of many people's reluctance to learn to use "another new technology." It is, however, recognized that Nielsen's previous national sample overrepresented older viewers and that the post-1987 sample composition more accurately represents the country's overall population.

A third limitation centers on a new form of resistance to allowing Nielsen to install the people-meter hardware. Installing the older passive meter involved little or no hassle for participants. People meters, however, require a substantial amount of wiring and hole drilling. For many people, allowing workers into their homes to do such work is an intolerable intrusion. And, of course, if households allowing the installation do so in part because they are eager to be part of the television sample, they do not represent the overall population and probably produce inflated viewing estimates and distortions in program preferences.

A fourth and final device-related limitation occurs because *people meters transform generally passive viewers into active viewers.* Every time a participant enters the television room or leaves, the handheld device must be activated. Such behavior involves more conscious decisions to view, and about what to view and when to stop viewing, than does usual television behavior. Research shows that most viewing gets done with little self-awareness on the viewer's part. Now, viewers with people meters must actively record their behavior, and the results are probably atypical viewing. Nielsen maintains that people-meter users rapidly become accustomed to them, and "normal" viewing habits soon return, similar to the way viewers become accustomed to using remote controls.

Nonetheless, the many problems with sample, hardware, and the unnatural state of "active" viewing resulting from using handheld controls have prompted Nielsen to forge ahead with *passive people meters.* These are electronic devices equipped with infrared sensors that identify people present in the room and record that information along with the tuned program. While these passive people meters may overcome the "activity" criticism, testing shows that many people feel that the camera needed to record a person's presence in the room has spied on them. Nielsen and Arbitron have also been testing

various kinds of portable people meters for many years, including a pager-sized PPM. (It has to be carried around or worn on the belt or wrist.) Until the technology of such ratings devices improves and is demonstrated as effective and appealing to audience participants in test samples, the problems inherent with the present system remain and pose major obstacles for interpreting what audiences are actually listening to or watching.

Whether a ratings system uses people meters, infrared sensors recording the presence of viewers in a room, diaries, household meters, portable devices or some yet-to-be-developed variation on these methods, ratings remain *estimates* of audience preferences, always subject to a certain undetermined margin of error (this margin may be quite small or very large; it is not known with any certainty). Previously, the media industry's temporary solution was to examine more than one set of numbers, but maturation of the industry has resulted in fewer independent sources of information about audiences (see 5.21, which discusses overreliance on Nielsen).

Moreover, considering numbers from multiple sources and multiple methods is a stopgap while awaiting a more valid measuring system. When all the numbers from different sources agree, certainly confidence in their accuracy rises. When there are variations, programmers and advertisers are left in the uncomfortable quandary of deciding which numbers to trust and which numbers to use. Some television programs and radio formats will not receive a completely fair rating regardless of which system is used—or even if a combination of measures is used. Children's and very light adult viewing will probably always remain uncertain.

Future Challenges

As the broadcast/cable and online/interactive worlds collide, we all expect big changes in the years to come. Traditional measurement services will certainly have to improve in order to measure smaller and smaller audiences with even greater accuracy. Google is set to challenge Nielsen with a

5.21 The Trap of Overreliance on Nielsen

One serious manifestation of the broadcast and cable companies' continued reliance on Nielsen data as their major if not sole source of audience viewing data occurred in the fall of 2003 and remains a matter of considerable controversy with huge consequences for advertisers and media distributors alike. As the ratings numbers came in for the first month of the fall network prime-time season, sharp, statistically significant declines in young adult males appeared. Among males aged 18 to 34, Nielsen reported declines as high as 12 percent; among males aged 18 to 24, the drop was 20 percent. For many advertisers who specifically buy programs that the network guarantees will have certain percentages of males in these age groups, this drastic reduction represented potential losses of millions of dollars in sales (and losses of millions in anticipated advertising revenue for the guaranteeing networks).

Network executives were quick to respond that Nielsen's sample was not representative of the total population of males aged 18 to 34 and that Nielsen's measurement methodology was responsible for the reported declines. Advertisers, by contrast, argued that such declines reflected a lack of interest on the part of young males in many network programs. Others pointed to the many activity choices that appeal more to young males than watching network television in prime time. Such choices include playing video games (for example, PlayStation II or Xbox) or computer games, surfing the web, writing blogs and downloading and listening to music, as well as passively viewing DVDs and other prerecorded materials. Nielsen fiercely defended its numbers and methodologies, providing detailed explanations that supported four conclusions.

1. Men aged 18 to 34 watched prime-time television with about the same frequency as in previous seasons, but they viewed for shorter periods of time; there are more days in which men in the key age group did not watch television at all.

2. Newly added sample members showed less decline in viewing than those continuing in the sample.

3. A combination of incentives and "coaching" of sample participants was successful in overcoming the fatigue of button-pushing.

4. Playing video games and watching DVDs did increase for men aged 18 to 24 years, but somewhat at the expense of DCR use.

It is clear that Nielsen numbers remain limited in their accuracy. While once the various parties were willing to overlook inaccuracies and agreed to accept ratings numbers as a common currency required for "doing business," the rise of competing media such as the internet and the threat of DVRs has generated a widespread challenge to traditional measurement practices.

media ratings system that links home computers wirelessly to television sets (and those ubiquitous boxes and DVRs). You can expect that electronic feedback on usage will be built into television sets, game players, smart phones, tablets and who knows what. This feedback will give advertisers near real-time and much more accurate measurement of media activity in general and commercial viewing in particular—whether you want it or not. The electronics that supply this information will be invisibly built into all your toys. So far, Nielsen is intent on acquiring smaller companies that use new devices that measure media activity and then folding the information into its existing, specialized reports.

At some time in not-so-far future, this type of real-time data collection could supplant Nielsen's people-meter ratings system, regardless of who owns and sells the data. Fortunately or not, technology to embed a "signature" into all forms of media content has been established, so the concept is out there. *Devices that track audience behavior are likely to solve the counting problem—if only the issue of what is to be counted can be decided (with sufficient agreement among the parties concerned).*

If DVRs make the practice of skipping commercials widespread, the future of advertising support for programming is also in question, leaving the likelihood of a pay-per-use system (on demand). *Audience measurement is largely for the benefit of advertisers.* If the audience pays for individual programs or channels, will the ratings really matter? Restaurants don't live or die by the little response cards people fill out at the end of the meal! The price of the meals, the number of patrons and the potential return visits measure success. In a similar way, networks may become retailers of their wares, just as book publishers and motion picture studios are. In the meantime, branded products with the name of major companies proliferate in television programs. Everyone is looking ahead.

Social media like Facebook and Twitter have been widely credited with energizing audiences for films, products/services and television programs/series. One objective is to *engage* viewers, turning them from indifferent, passive viewers into active, enthusiastic viewers who make specific programs a *must-see* on a weekly basis. Social media are also used to maintain interest in a series while it is on hiatus and especially as a new season approaches. Heightened anticipation is key to building interest and carrying it over to the start of a new season. Cable channels like TNT, USA and AMC are examples of cable nets that put a lot of effort into trying to fuel buzz for their series. Part of engagement is to get viewers talking (via the Internet social network sites) among themselves, sharing their thoughts on favorite characters, episodes, relationships, etc.

In an interview, CBS Marketing Group President George Schweitzer pointed out that "Technology is an enabler. It's enabling us to engage our viewers in the conversation—a two-way conversation where it used to be just one way."[9] He went on to provide examples where CBS series' stars are often active on Twitter with regular tweets, interacting with viewers where all Twitter followers can read the exchanges and participate themselves. He also added that social media enable CBS TV shows to fuel word-of-mouth that is presumed to help build and maintain the series' audience.

The rub comes when searching for a connection between those programs that are successful in exploiting social media and generating conversations among many thousands of followers and the corresponding rating. Do those series with lots of social buzz show ratings increases over those with less

buzz? What does it cost to continue active participation by the network in social networking? Will advertisers be willing to look beyond the cold numbers of ratings (overall and in key demographic areas) and be willing to pay more for the same numbers for a series that has ample evidence of an apparently energized and active audience? A survey in 2011 found that 40% of U.S. Internet users in the U.S. are fans or followers on Facebook and/or Twitter of at least one network TV show or network.[10] But, as CBS's Schweitzer concluded: "It's really hard to point to one specific thing, like Tweet Week, that affects ratings. From the amount of tweeting that there was, the responses we got and the thousands of new fans, we know that it [a show] was successful. But in terms of ratings, we'll never know."

Until there is a reliable means of measuring social network traffic's tie-in to the size of the audience (via ratings or other such measurement), networks will have to rely on persuasion to convince advertisers to pay more for those programs that are particularly effective in generating social network buzz. The biggest social media themselves could enhance their prominence among radio and TV stations and TV networks by producing some reliable indices of impact on audience size or higher levels of proactive consumer behavior for the advertised products and services. Calculating how many consumers use social network coupons or enhanced bar codes for specific products or services advertised on certain programs is one likely way of adding some more-or-less-solid numbers to the argument, but so far, privacy concerns seem to override such attempts.

Actual consumption, of course, speaks directly to advertisers' concerns. It is clear that social media are a growing source of online communication with incredible potential to alter the ways of doing business, but it is equally clear that much work—research, testing, public relations—needs to be accomplished by all parties with a vested interest in profiting from these new ways.

The latest challenge to the broadcast and cable industries comes from Nielsen's plan to introduce regular "commercial ratings" in addition to the usual program ratings. When specific commercials have numerical audience estimates attached to them, advertisers will be able to evaluate the program contexts in which their commercial appear, and this information may have major consequences for programmers. It may influence the selection as well as scheduling of shows if the evidence is clear that some types are better suited for gaining audience attention to commercials, as is already believed. And how the media operate and are to be paid for are clearly not the only important questions relating to evolving forms of television, radio and information consumption that the public and government need to address. Other chapters in this book raise plenty of concerns about the media future.

Notes

1. The word *ratings* had a clear meaning for much of the history of broadcasting until the introduction of content ratings in the late 1990s. Content ratings serve as labels to adults who supervise children's viewing. As the motion picture industry did in the late 1960s, the television industry bowed to government pressure and began putting program content ratings on shows in the late 1990s. This chapter deals with ratings in the traditional sense of audience measurement, not content labeling.

2. Quantitative data come from audience diaries, meters on television receivers, and occasionally from one-time telephone measurements (called telephone coincidentals) during or immediately following a specific program.

3. For more on this topic, see Eastman, Susan Tyler, Ferguson, Douglas A., and Klein, Robert A. (eds.), *Media Promotion and Marketing*, 5th ed., Boston, MA: Focal Press, 2006.

4. Emily Steel, "New Tools for Picking Hits," *The Wall St Journal*, May 23, 2011, p. B4.

5. The number of households varies annually, and the number of people varies according to census reports. These estimates are from Nielsen Media Research.

6. More information about Nielsen is available on YouTube by using "Nielsen Ratings 101" as a search term. The short videos are produced by Nielsen to reach potential panel members and clients. Each topic has its own video that breaks the research process into separate areas: introduction, designing the sample, recruitment, panel maintenance, and the future.

7. There are more radio markets (299) than television markets (210) because in big stretches of the southern and western United States there are places where no television reaches. In such places radio is useful and important. And stations and advertisers want those people counted.

8. Result comes from a meta-analysis (of multiple measurements) by eMarketer. *http://emarketer.com/blog/index.php/time-spent-watching-tv-tops-internet/*.

9. Interview published in the online source eMarketer (June 13, 2011 *www.emarketer.com*). *http://www.emarketer.tv/Article.aspx?R=1008429*.

10. Results released in the spring of 2011 from a survey by *The Wall St. Journal* and Harris Poll (press release, March 30, 2011). Wayne Friedman, "Social Media Increases Popularity For TV Viewer Comments," Media Daily News, *http://www.mediapost.com/publications/?fa=Articles.showArticle&art_aid=147734*.

Syndication for Stations, Cable, and Online

John von Soosten and Douglas A. Ferguson

Chapter Outline

W hat you see on your hometown television stations usually comes from somewhere else, even though the local station gets the big billing! The programs can be *network, advertiser supplied, local* or *syndicated*. This chapter deals with the fourth type, *syndicated programs*, which are mostly reruns of TV series, specials and movies generally sold to individual stations or station groups for exclusive showing in a single market.[1] These programs come from the distributor to the stations via satellite or Fire-Wire.[2] The local television station licenses a syndicated program from a *syndicator*, a national company that also licenses the same program to other stations in other markets but generally not to others in the same market, unless a second station is owned by the same group owner.

Have you run across listings for two different episodes of one show on different channels at different times in your guide channel? Under the FCC's cross-ownership rules, programs are frequently licensed to a group owner for airing on either of the co-owned stations in the same market. It is not uncommon for the same program to air on both stations, typically in different time slots, sometimes one right after another so you can watch double episodes. Just to keep you sharp, an alternative is that a given program may air for a period of months or even years on one station in a market and then be moved to the other co-owned station in that same market...and all run again.

Nationally, any "used television program" probably will not air simultaneously in the same time period in all markets and maybe not necessarily even on the same day or in the same daypart. The show probably will not air in every one of the 210 U.S. markets, and it probably will not air solely on affiliates of any single network. Hence, the program is said to be *syndicated*.

Although many programs may be licensed to national cable networks (which often precludes sale to local television stations) or online services like Netflix or Hulu, the term *syndication* typically applies to broadcasting. Although this chapter focuses on broadcast television, most of the principles and considerations discussed here apply equally to **cable syndication, online syndication**

and **international syndication**. The topic of **radio syndication** is discussed in Chapters 11 and 12 and **noncommercial syndication** in Chapter 10. The most common arrangements and methods of buying and evaluating syndicated programs are described in this chapter, but new permutations keep appearing. It is best to remember the old adage, "Just when you thought you'd seen it all..."

The Syndication Chain

The syndication chain reaches from the producer through various intermediaries to the station, and it begins with the program itself. By "program," we usually mean all the episodes of a series, anywhere from a handful to a hundred or more. Programs for syndication arise in one of four ways.

1. If the program was originally created exclusively for syndication and has not previously aired in any other venue (such as a network), it is said to be **first-run**; it is a program created for first-run syndication. *Ellen, Entertainment Tonight* and *Judge Judy* are easily-recognized examples of syndicated first-run programs. (Most new first run efforts are flops.) Foreign programs produced for airing in other countries and later placed into domestic U.S. syndication are usually considered first-run because they have not previously been seen in this country. (The rare program made for syndication that later gets sold to a cable or broadcast network—to the great joy of the producer—is called **off-syndication**.)

2. Programs that were originally created for one of the broadcast networks and are subsequently sold in syndication are called **off-network**. Previously aired episodes of *Family Guy, CSI: Miami, Everybody Loves Raymond* and *The Simpsons* are examples of off-network programs you've probably seen.

3. Shows that were created for the national cable networks were traditionally included in the off-network category. But as the number of such programs put into syndication increased, a separate **off-cable** designation developed. Generally, these are

shows that go from one cable network to another (not to co-owned broadcast networks).

4. The fourth category consists of **feature films,** including **theatricals** (made originally for exhibition in movie theaters) and **made-for-TV, made-for-cable** or **movie-of-the-week (MOW)** films. MOWs may be off-network, off-cable or first-run in syndication.

You've surely noticed that while most network shows air once a week, syndicated shows are stripped across the week. Remember that there are (usually) 52 weeks with 365 days in a year (you learned this in elementary school), and television never goes dark (you learned this in middle school). If you (being now a grown-up station programmer or syndicator) subtract 52 weekends, you have 261 daily slots each year to fill with various stripped programs. Maybe there are a handful of holidays with special programs (Christmas) and local sporting events (Indy 500) and local political debates (every other year), leaving you with about 250 days to fill. If you buy a syndicated sitcom and run each episode twice, you need exactly 125 episodes to fill a half hour daily for the whole year... and 125 of the next show, and 125 of many others... TV eats up programs. Keeps programmers busy.

Off-network shows are sold for several of years with a fixed number of runs per episode. It takes a long time—at one episode per week—on a network to build up enough episodes for syndication. For example, five years of *Two and a Half Men* generated about 110 episodes that then might be sold for three or five years for five to ten airings of each episode. Of course, because they are reruns of reruns, off-network shows don't get network-level ratings when syndicated to stations (and if streaming rights to the same show have been sold to NetFlix or Hulu, then its value to stations sinks a bit further).

In contrast, *first-run programs* are generally sold in syndication for one or two years at a time with a predetermined number of weeks of original programs (most of them) and repeat programs (fewer). For example, a 52-week deal might include 39 weeks of original programs (195 shows) and 13 weeks of repeats (65 of the original 195 shows), getting the station through every one of the 260 weekdays for an entire year. If the program is successful, the contract may be renewed for a year or two, usually at a higher price. And fresh episodes of first-run shows are produced for each subsequent season. Look in 6.1 for examples of the four types of syndicated programs, and in 6.2 for syndicated shows categorized by *program genre.*

The person who is responsible for delivering the program on time and on or under budget is called the *showrunner.* He or she is directly accountable for contacts with the production company and syndicator who financed the program. Moreover, if a program is not delivering satisfactory ratings, the showrunner is responsible for "fixing" or improving it.

The syndication chain involves both direct participants—one or more producers and financial backers, a distributor and the buyer (a broadcast television station, cable network, or foreign network)—and indirect participants, such as the programmers at the national station representative firms. All must

---

6.1 **Types of Syndicated Programs**

Off-Network: *Friends, Seinfeld, Everybody Loves Raymond, CSI: Crime Scene Investigation, The Parkers, King of Queens.* (Note that—just to confuse viewers—off-network shows may run simultaneously with new episodes on the broadcast network and with reruns or multiplexed episodes on cable networks and in off-network syndication.)

First-Run: *Dr. Oz, Ellen, Dr. Phil, Rachael Ray, Jerry Springer, Entertainment Tonight, Jeopardy!, Wheel of Fortune, Judge Judy.*

Off-Cable: *Nip/Tuck* (from FX to Logo), *Stargate SG1.*

Feature Films: Nearly any movie title once it leaves the movie theaters except recent movies still playing on pay-per-view, pay cable or a broadcast network before they go into syndication.

6.2 Eight Common Syndicated Genres

- Situation comedy. Most sitcoms are off-network (for example, *Friends, Family Guy, Seinfeld, Everybody Loves Raymond, The Simpsons*), although in the distant past some were created for first-run syndication—for example, some episodes of *Mama's Family* and all episodes of *Small Wonder*.

- Drama. These may be off-network (*Criminal Minds, Monk, Ugly Betty, CSI*), off-cable (*Sex and the City, Stargate SG1*), or first-run (*Star Trek: Voyager*) and may include action-adventure/sci-fi shows (*24, Alias*) and dramatic shows (*Dawson's Creek, The X-Files*). Although these shows were nearly all one hour long, a rare few are half-hour shows.

- Talk. Generally these are first-run, one-hour shows. They include *Dr. Oz, Dr. Phil, Maury, The Jerry Springer Show* and others.

- Magazine. Most commonly half-hour, first-run programs, these include *Entertainment Tonight (ET), Access Hollywood, TMZ on TV* and *Extra*. This category also includes the weekend editions of the same programs: *ET Weekend*, for example.

- Reality. This category is a catchall comprised mostly of first-run half hours (although the occasional first-run hour creeps in) and includes health shows (*The Doctors, Dr. Oz*), court shows (*The People's Court, Judge Judy, Judge Joe Brown, Divorce Court*), comedy shows (*Man Up Stand Up*), music shows (videos, dance music), and comedy-based shows (*America's Dumbest Criminals*).

- Games. These half-hour, first-run shows include "pure" game shows (*Jeopardy!, Wheel of Fortune*) and celebrity-driven, humor-based shows where the entertainment value is often more important than the game itself (*Family Feud*).

- Weekly. This category includes virtually all the aforementioned program types, but the shows are first-run and designed for broadcast once or twice a week, generally on Saturdays or Sundays (*Dog the Bounty Hunter, Man Up Stand Up*). Thanks to competition from cable networks, many stations run filler or infomercials.

6.3 Children's Genre

For years, children's programming was dominated by syndicated programs from a variety of companies; then production shifted to the networks. In recent years, syndication of children's programming has virtually ceased to exist. Kids' CW consists mainly of sitcoms and youth dramas that originally aired on CW/WB. Fox Kids has been rebranded as 4KidsTV and is children-oriented programming on Saturday mornings on FOX stations. The children's syndication business today is virtually nonexistent. The few syndicated kids programs that are available come from DIC Entertainment and independent producers (such as Litton) and are aired by stations seeking to fulfill FCC-mandated educational/instructional programming on weekends, often in early-morning time periods.

Along with public television, cable networks, especially Cartoon Network, Disney Channel and Nickelodeon, are the major forces for reaching kid viewers nowadays. Whether provided by the networks or acquired through syndication, children's programs fall into several basic categories: **animation** (*SpongeBob SquarePants, Fairly Odd Parents*), **live action** (*iCarly, Big Time Rush*), and theatrical **cartoons** (*Bugs Bunny, Tom and Jerry*).

talk in a mutually understood language. Although several systems for classifying programs exist, syndicators and programmers commonly use eight easily recognized genre categories (see 6.2). Children's programs used to be another major category of syndication, but no longer (see 6.3).

The Producer and Production Company

Many people think of producers as cigar-smoking, fast-talking, jewelry-bedecked guys "taking meetings" by the pool. A few may fit this description, but most would not stand out in a crowd. Actually, the producer—or showrunner—is the person who coordinates the diverse elements that constitute a television program. In some production companies, this person is called the executive producer; in others he or she is the line producer. Showrunners (or executive producers) oversee on-air talent, directors, writers, technical crew, line producers, production managers, production assistants and researchers. They "run the show" as the on-the-set boss and often come from a writer background. Showrunners often deal with talent agents, personal managers, union officials, the press and lawyers. They are answerable for everything: the program concept, the program content, the tone or mood of the program—in other words, the overall production.

A production company finances and produces television programs, hiring the showrunner and the staff and possibly proposing program ideas or financing the producers who bring in the ideas. Based on a pilot, maybe, or merely a written presentation, the production company sells programs directly to broadcast or cable networks or, alternatively, strikes a deal with a syndication company to distribute (syndicate) its programs to individual television stations. Often the production company is the syndicator itself and distributes the programs it has created.

The decision to begin production of a new program depends on (a) whether a broadcast or cable network is interested in the idea and advances development funds (see Chapters 4 and 9) or (b) whether the program is suitable for domestic and foreign syndication. U.S. cable and sales to foreign television networks are a crucial *aftermarket* for off-network programs and theatrical movies.[3]

For many years, hour-long dramatic shows had only modest syndication potential even after network airing, but such cable channels as TNT, USA, A&E and Spike have shifted to off-network dramas for early evening and prime-time weeknights (for example, *Law & Order, CSI, Without a Trace*), raising the prices for long runs of such hour-long series. Comedy has always been a gold mine, although most programmers insist that sitcoms must have young adult and youth appeal to succeed

in syndication. *Network carriage is important for giving a program high visibility, but syndication is where the profits lie.*

The Syndicator

Although some syndicators produce programs and others merely handle programs produced by other companies, all syndicators (also called *distributors*) supply programming to local stations on a market-by-market basis throughout the nation. Unlike ABC, CBS, FOX, NBC, CW, ION, MNTV, TeleFutura, Telemundo and Univision, syndicators do not have a single "affiliate" in any particular market. However, just to make things complicated, the parent companies of ABC, CBS, FOX, NBC and Univision also operate syndication companies as separate entities and generally forge strong relationships with affiliates of the parent corporation if possible. Nonetheless, syndicators can and often do sell their programming to any and all stations in a market.

Depending on the kind of programs offered by the syndicator, certain stations in a market may be more frequent customers than other stations. For example, some affiliates build programming blocks around game shows, others around talk shows. Although the syndicator may have more than one customer in a market, only one station is licensed to carry any particular program at a time. Thus, one station may license such first-run syndicated programs as *Dr. Oz* and *Dr. Phil* from King World (owned by Viacom/CBS); a second station in the same market may license *Inside Edition* and *Bob Vila's Home Again*, also from King World, and a third station in the same market may simultaneously license syndicated reruns of *Everybody Loves Raymond* and *CSI*, again from King World. And it's very likely that King World's *Wheel of Fortune* and *Jeopardy!* have been airing on one of these stations for decades.

Each station will have the exclusive right in its local market to all episodes of the series it bought during the term of the license. And because it means more money, the syndicator King World may try to upgrade the time period of one or more of these shows from a lesser-rated to a higher-rated time slot (even though the show may compete against another King World program on another station in the market). Syndicators also try to upgrade a show from a weaker station to a stronger station. For the syndicator, such upgrades usually result in more income from higher license fees, as well as higher rates for barter spots because of higher ratings. So station programmers must look to their own self-interest and be a bit wary of syndicators.

The United States used to have dozens of domestic syndication companies, but the number has declined in recent years after many mergers. There are also scores of other syndicators worldwide. All major domestic program syndicators and their hottest properties in the mid-2010s are listed in 6.4. Off-network hits such as *Seinfeld, Family Guy* and *Everybody Loves Raymond* average as high as $2 to $3 million per episode in combined syndicated revenue (from all stations). Of the firms in 6.4, six companies command more than three-quarters of the domestic syndication business: CBS Television Distribution, Disney-ABC Domestic Television, NBCUniversal Television, Sony Pictures Television, Twentieth Television and Warner Brothers Domestic Television

Distribution. All the other very large syndicators are divisions of the Hollywood studios.

Syndicators "sell" (license for a fee, hence *license fee*) the telecast rights to a program to a local station for a certain term and for a set number of plays. The syndicator or the producer of the program continues to own the rights to the show. Syndicators get a commission for distribution, and they can increase their revenues by selling national barter time (advertising spots) within the programs they handle. *At the end of the license term, the broadcast rights revert to the syndicator, who may now license the program all over again to any station in the market, including the station that ran the program in the first cycle or any of its competitors.* This occasionally results in some weird station-hopping by old shows.

The syndicator's client is both the group owner and the local television station or the cable network. After the FCC relaxed limitations on ownership of television stations in terms of both the percentage of the U.S. population covered and the number of stations permitted under common ownership in a single market, the dynamics of the sales process changed.

6.4 Program Syndicators

Syndicators	Programs
Carsey-Werner	*That '70s Show, 3rd Rock from the Sun, The Cosby Show, Roseanne*
CBS Television Distribution	*Dr. Oz, Dr. Phil, Wheel of Fortune, Jeopardy!, Judge Judy, ET, Rachael Ray*
Disney-ABC Domestic Television	*My Wife and Kids, According to Jim, Alias, Scrubs, Less Than Perfect, 8 Simple Rules, Who Wants to Be a Millionaire?,* Disney movies
DLT Entertainment Ltd.	*Benny Hill, Three's Company, The Ropers*
Hearst Entertainment & Syndication	*The Bravest, Popular Mechanics for Kids,* movies, cartoons
Litton Entertainment	*Storm Stories, Jack Hanna's Into the Wild*
MGM Domestic Television	*Cash Cab, Stargate Universe, Stargate Atlantis,* movies
NBCUniversal Television Distribution	*30 Rock, The Office, Access Hollywood, House, Law & Order, Maury, The Jerry Springer Show*
Sony Pictures Television	*Seinfeld, The Nanny, Married ... with Children, Who's the Boss?,* movies
Trifecta	*Punk'd, The Hills, Geek Meets Girl, Last Shot with Judge Gunn*
Twentieth Television	*Family Guy, How I Met Your Mother, That 70's Show, Are You Smarter than a 5th Grader?, Don't Forget the Lyrics, Divorce Court, Judge Alex,* movies
Warner Brothers Domestic Television Distribution	*Ellen, TMZ, The People's Court, Modern Family, Big Bang Theory, Without a Trace,* movies

Increasingly, *program purchasing and scheduling decisions moved toward corporate or group management and away from local television stations.* This is partly the result of the rapidly increasing costs of acquiring programming (as a percentage of a station's operating budget and expense versus revenue) and also because of the greater negotiating clout a group programming executive has when bargaining on behalf of several television stations—as opposed to the leverage a single station has.

At the group level, there are generally one or more programming executives. Frequently, upper management is involved in negotiating for programming on a group level, especially because of the consequences for multiple stations and the huge dollar amounts involved—often tens of millions for a single buy. These upper-level executives may include the CEO, president, CFO, executive and senior vice presidents and even owners. A lot of money is involved, and a single program buy usually affects several surrounding programs as well as advertising revenues.

At the station level, the people most commonly involved are the general manager, the business manager (financial person) and the program director (also called program manager, director of programming, or other similar titles). Many important program purchasing or scheduling decisions may be made by corporate management or station owners, bypassing the local general manager and program director altogether. These corporate executives, including the group programming executive, are generally not located in the same city as the station itself, a potential source of friction and poor judgment. In another twist, because of consolidation, the same program director may program two stations in the same market that are owned and/or operated by the same company. While in effect these stations compete against each other, the programmer will likely set up complementary program schedules on the two stations, hoping to maximize viewership on both of them.

The National Sales Rep

The outside party involved in the syndication chain is the *rep programmer*, who works for the national station sales representative firm that sells national advertising time for the station. The rep programmer acts as an ally for and consultant to the station about programming buys. In recent years, there has been much consolidation in the sales representative business, leaving just three major rep firms, each of which has separate sales organizations/divisions under its corporate ownership. This structure enables the firms to represent more than one television station in the same market, since the "separate" sales divisions within the same firm "compete" with one another.

- Clear Channel-owned **Katz Media Group** has Millenium (formerly Seltel and Katz Independent), Eagle and Continental divisions.
- Cox-owned **TeleRep** consists of MMT, TeleRep and HRP divisions.
- **Petry Media**, owned by Petry, has Petry and Blair divisions.

These companies (and several smaller ones) are station representatives, *national sales organizations selling commercial airtime on behalf of local television stations.* The media gorillas, ABC, CBS, FOX and NBC O&Os, are self-repped and have their own major rep divisions. Similarly, Univision stations and a few other large television stations are also self-repped. The names of station reps can be seen in trade publication articles, in advertisements, on research materials, in directories and even on television station letterheads.

Although the station representative is primarily a *sales* organization, reps do provide additional services to client stations including *marketing support, sales research, promotion advice* and *programming consultation.* Generally, the bigger the station, the more help that's offered, though the need is greater at smaller stations. Through these support services, the reps help client stations improve their performance in terms of audience delivery, which in turn leads to increases in advertising rates and, presumably, increased profitability for the station—and the rep, of course. (Although revenues may go up, profitability for the station sometimes does not because of increased programming and operating costs and other expenses.) Usually, no additional

6.5 The National Sales Rep

Reps sell commercial airtime on local client stations to *national spot* advertisers. As the advertising agency represents the advertiser in buying commercial time, the station rep represents its client station in selling the national time. Local stations sell commercial time to local merchants and other advertisers within their markets, and all commercial stations employ a *local* sales force for this purpose. In most cases, it is not economically feasible for a single station to employ a sales force to sell commercial time to *national* advertisers because there are far too many advertisers and advertising agencies in too many cities to be covered by a station's sales force. That's where the rep comes in. Rep firms employ sales people in major cities on behalf of local stations to sell to advertisers in those cities. (Several of the dozen or so reps have offices in more than 20 cities.) Because reps sell on behalf of many stations,

they can maintain sales forces of hundreds of people, selling on behalf of dozens of stations. The largest station representatives have client stations in as many as 200 markets.

The rep receives a negotiable commission from its client stations for the commercial time the rep sells. As a rule of thumb, a 10 percent commission rate is the industry norm, but because of the competitive nature of the rep business, such considerations as the overall state of the economy and market size may cause the commission rate to vary widely. Stations in larger markets and stations owned by large group broadcasters often pay only single-digit commission rates to their representative. Conversely, stations in smaller markets generally pay a higher commission rate because the dollar volume is considerably less than in large markets.

fee is charged for support services; they are included in the rep's sales commission (see 6.5). The major rep firms have programming staffs that work with programmers at client stations to shape and guide the stations' programming schedules.

Rep programmers provide ratings information that may support or call into question information that syndicators supply, and they advise client stations on the programs that will attract the most viewers in the demographic groups advertisers most desire to reach. At the same time, rep programmers must consider each station's programming philosophy, the mores of the community, and the quality of each program. (While all stations might like to carry *Jeopardy!* if they could, not all want to carry *The Jerry Springer Show*.)

One of the rep's most important functions is to regularly disseminate generic national research information and market-specific research to client stations. Most reps maintain close contact with all the big networks (ABC, CBS, FOX, NBC, CW and Univision), enabling them to supply an affiliate with competitive information regarding the other networks. Reps also publish ratings summaries and analyses of new programs, and they provide

exhaustive ratings information after each rating sweep period. Because of their national overview of programming and their own experience and that of their colleagues, rep programmers can often look at programming decisions from a broad perspective not available to a local station's general manager or program director.

Program Acquisition

Syndication is the arena in which most programmers expend much of their energies—and with good reason. *For most stations, the money spent annually to acquire syndicated television shows is their single largest expense.* The station that buys a syndicated program that turns out to be a dud or the station that overpays for a syndicated show may be in financial trouble for years to come. And the station that makes several such mistakes (not uncommon) has serious problems.

The general manager and the program director get recommendations from their rep on which shows should be acquired, along with a rationale for the acquisition and recommendations on the program's placement in the station's lineup. Although reps spend most of their time dealing with syndicated programming and therefore work closely with syndicators, agency reps do *not* work for the syndicators. *Reps work for the stations*; rep firms are paid commissions by client stations based on advertising sales.

Both the station program director and the rep programmer spend many hours meeting with syndicators, listening to sales pitches, and watching videocassettes or DVDs of sales pitches, research information, program excerpts or actual pilots. In the pitch, the syndicator's salesperson tries to convince the programmer of the program's merits and that the program, if scheduled on the station, will improve the station's ratings. Although the reps do not actually purchase the program, and although the syndicator must still pitch the station programmers directly, a rep's positive recommendation to the station paves the way for the salesperson when he or she contacts the station. Most syndicators' agents maintain close and frequent contact with the station program director and the reps. They inform reps of ratings successes, changes in sales strategy, purchases of the program by leading stations or station groups, and any other information they feel may win support from the rep. Syndicators often try to enlist the rep's support for a show in a specific time period on a specific station the rep represents.

Syndicators can be good sources of information about competing stations in a given market because they generally deal with all stations in a market and have a good idea of each station's programming needs and philosophy. Frequently, syndicators inform reps of programs during their developmental stages—like trial balloons that serve as a way to gauge the rep's reaction prior to beginning a sales campaign or shooting a pilot of a program.

Syndicator contacts with reps do not replace contact between syndicator and station. Rather, syndicators take a calculated risk with reps to gain support for a program. If a rep dislikes the show or does not feel it suits a station's needs, the rep's advice to the station can damage the salesperson's efforts.[4] Many stations have refused to buy syndicated shows because their reps did not endorse them.

Scheduling Strategies

When a television station acquires a program from a syndicator, its managers generally have a pretty good idea of how they will use the show. Normally, they look not only for a program that meets their needs but also for one that fits certain scheduling and business-deal criteria. As discussed in Chapter 2, several scheduling strategies are widely accepted.

- **Stripping.** Syndicated series can be scheduled daily or weekly, and programs that run daily in the same time period Monday through Friday are said to be stripped. In the case of off-network programs, 65 episodes (three network seasons) are generally considered the absolute minimum for stripping, allowing 13 weeks of Monday to Friday stripping in syndication before a station repeats an episode. As explained earlier, between 100 and 150 episodes are considered optimum for stripping, whereas 200 or more episodes can be a financial and scheduling burden to a station. Of course, first-run daily programs are created specifically for stripping. Typically, game show and comedy producers will generally shoot 195 original episodes (39 weeks) a year, with 65 episodes (13 weeks) repeated. However, some first-run strip shows will be produced fresh every day with no repeats (260 episodes over 52 weeks), as in the case of timely magazine shows like *Entertainment Tonight*.

- **Audience flow.** As a general strategy, programmers try to schedule successive shows in a sequence that maximizes the number of viewers staying tuned to the station from one program to the next. The shows flow from one to the next, with each building on its predecessor. The lead-in and lead-out shows are carefully selected to be compatible with a program in any given time period. Theoretically, the audience flows with the shows. Additional audience may flow into the program from other stations and from new viewers just turning on their television sets. Thus, audience flow is a combination of (1) *retention* of existing audience from lead-in, (2) *channel switching* from other stations and (3) attraction of *new tune-in* viewers.

- **Counterprogramming.** This tactic refers to scheduling programs that are different in type and audience appeal from those carried by the competition at the same time. For example, within one market from 4 to 5 P.M. Monday through Friday, station WAAA might schedule a talk show, WBBB might carry two court shows, WCCC might carry a magazine show and a reality show, WDDD might carry two situation comedies, and station WEEE might also schedule two sitcoms. And with WDDD and WEEE both carrying situation comedies opposite one another, one station might schedule sitcoms with ethnic appeal against the other station's general-appeal sitcoms, hoping to pick up a disproportionately large share of minority viewers. Thus, all stations are counterprogramming each other. In another example, within one market during prime time at 10 P.M., while the ABC, CBS and NBC affiliates carry network entertainment programs, the FOX, UNI and CW affiliates might schedule news. While the ABC, CBS and NBC affiliates air late-evening news at 11 P.M., the other stations might counterprogram with situation comedies, reality shows and other non-news programming. Again, one station might schedule programs with strong appeal to minority viewers in hopes of picking up additional viewers in what has become a highly competitive and increasingly fractionalized marketplace.

Deal Points

When the syndicator approaches the station or rep programmer, he or she outlines the terms and conditions of the offering. Most deals include the following deal points or terms:

- **Title.** In the case of programs entering syndication after a network run, the syndication title may be slightly different from the network version. Sometimes the title of a first-run program is changed from the time the program is marketed to the time it starts airing, often in an attempt to entice more people to watch the show.
- **Description of the program.** This includes whether it is first-run or off-network, the story line or premise and other pertinent information. While not an actual deal point, the syndicator may also

indicate potential strong points for audience appeal, including gender (for example, sitcoms having high female appeal or sports shows with strong male appeal), age (reality dating shows with young adult appeal or sitcoms that have kid/teen appeal), or ethnic (sitcoms with large minority casts).

- **Cast, host, or other participants.** Big-name or emerging talent is often a draw. In some cases, an ethnic host or cast may be a selling point. If additional episodes of a series are planned, notice of long-term contracts with the talent has value.
- **Duration.** The program may be 30, 60 or 90 minutes long, or another length entirely.
- **Number of episodes.** This point includes original episodes and repeats. Sometimes a minimum and maximum number of episodes are offered.
- **Number of runs.** The syndicator indicates the maximum number of times the station may air (*run*) each episode. In situations where a single company owns two stations in the same market, a provision might be negotiated in the contract to allow the program to run on either station, but the total number of runs in aggregate on the two stations will generally be the same as if only a single station were to run the show. In large part this has to do with the amount of money paid by the syndicator or production company in residuals to actors, talent, producers, directors and other creative personnel and the amount paid in music licensing and other rights payments. Generally, the greater the number of runs permitted, the higher these payments will be, regardless of the number of stations carrying the program. These additional payments go right out of the syndicators and/or the production company's bottom line, hence reducing profits. Another factor limiting the number of runs in syndication might include future sale to cable networks, which affects both the term (length) of the contract and the number of runs during that period.
- **Start and end dates.** Programs are sold for specific lengths of time, such as six months, one year, three-and-one-half years, five years or seven years. They may be sold months or years in advance of the start date (called *futures*).

- **Commercial format.** Each show is sold with a fixed number of commercial spots. For example, a typical half-hour program might be formatted for (1) *six-and-a-half internal commercial minutes* (in other words, thirteen 30-second units) in two breaks of two minutes each and one break of two-and-a-half minutes within the program plus (2) an *endbreak* (external) following the program, typically of 92 seconds. Some of the commercial time within the program may be retained by the syndication company for sale to its own national sponsors; this is considered *barter time* and is part or all of the license fee.

- **Price.** The cash price may be stated as either a *per-episode fee* (which is one inclusive amount for all runs of a single episode) or as a *weekly fee* (a fixed amount regardless of the number of times each episode is ultimately shown). The price charged for a program will generally vary by market size, with *stations in larger markets paying more for a program than stations in smaller markets would pay because at any given rating, there are more viewers per rating point in larger markets than in smaller ones.* Therefore, stations in larger markets can charge more for commercial airtime and with those higher revenues can pay more for programming than stations in smaller markets can. However, competition for a certain program in a highly competitive market can result in a higher license fee than in a somewhat larger market that is less competitive. Reasons for competitive levels can include the number of stations in a market (*more stations means more competition for a show and fewer shows to choose from—each show has a better chance of being sold because there are more potential customers*), more intense rivalries between competing stations or corporate owners, and the personalities and abilities of the programmers and the syndicators. Keep in mind that highly successful shows like *Jeopardy!* and *Dr. Phil* can command significantly higher license fees than less popular programs. Often the "buzz factor" has something to do with program pricing, like a car or movie that becomes hot because people are talking about it and not necessarily because it's the best car or movie for the price.

A syndication company's sales, research and publicity people can often create or enhance a program's perception in the marketplace. The price goes up for the show everybody is buzzing about, like Oscar winners.

- **Payment method.** Programs are sold for cash, for barter or for cash-plus-barter.

- **Down payment.** In cash or cash-plus-barter deals, the syndicator might request a down payment (typically 10 to 20 percent) when the contract is signed, which is sometimes several years before the station receives the rights to the show.

- **Payout.** Cash the station still owes to the syndicator (after the down payment) must be paid when the program begins to air. Typically, the balance is paid in installments over the life of the contract, similar to mortgage or auto loan payments.

Syndicator/Rep Rules

The relationship between syndicators and reps is generally friendly and mutually dependent. The syndicators need the reps' support in client markets; the reps need to get programming information from the syndicators. Yet the relationship must also be guarded. Because the reps are agents of their client stations, they must maintain their independence from the distributors with an impartiality befitting the trust placed in them by the stations.

Therefore, certain unwritten rules govern the relationship between syndicator and station rep. *Reps rarely make blanket program recommendations, and they do not endorse any particular syndicator.* Although reps often support or oppose a particular genre or programming trend, they are generally quick to point out that not every station in every market necessarily can be included in their assessment. Few programs will appeal equally in every market, and the stations' competitive needs differ greatly from market to market.

Another unwritten rule is that *rep programmers do not supply syndicators with privileged client-rep information.* As an extension of the station, the rep programmer does not want to supply information to syndicators that would help the syndicator negotiate

6.6 NATPE Pitching Contests

If or when you get a job in programming, you are likely to attend an annual NATPE conference. The sale of programs to stations is so integral to how programmers do their jobs that you might encounter a "pitch" competition, which is centered on the strategic considerations already presented. Syndicators attempt to sell (*pitch*) a program to stations or groups of stations. In a hypothetical syndication offering of an equally hypothetical off-network program, the prospective buyer must consider

- whether or not the station actually needs the program.

- the potential danger if the show ended up on a competitor (a virtual likelihood if her station passes on purchasing it).

- whether there is another program available that might be a better acquisition for her station.

- the time period when her station would schedule the show (and a backup time period if it didn't perform up to expectations).

- the actual network performance versus the show's projected performance in syndication.

- all the research (from the syndicator, the station rep, and her own).

- the cost of the program (raising the question of whether there is money allocated in the station's five-year future budget projections for a show at this price level).

The program buyer must put aside her personal feelings or biases for or against the show (it happens to be one of her favorites; in fact, she usually TiVos it to be sure she doesn't miss an episode) and make the decision on as much of a nonemotional business basis as possible. However, even the most conscientious programmers can rarely put aside all personal feelings and overlook either positive or negative buzz in both the television industry and their own personal worlds.

against the station. Privileged information includes prices the station would be prepared to pay for programs, prices it already paid for other programs, other programs the station is considering purchasing, its future plans and strategies, contract expiration dates and any other information that might harm the station's negotiating position; however, syndicators frequently provide such information to the reps.

Ratings Consultation

Station general managers and program managers talk regularly with their national reps. Rep programmers and station sales management are also in contact, albeit less frequently (and research directors, but most stations do not even have a research department). The rep programmer occasionally meets clients, either by visiting the station or when station personnel travel to New York, where all reps are based, to meet with rep sales management and with advertising agencies. Most general managers/program directors and reps endeavor to meet with

one another at the annual conventions of NATPE (National Association of Television Program Executives) and NAB (National Association of Broadcasters), as well as at network affiliate meetings.

A good working relationship between the station and the rep programmer is important. Consultation is not a one-way process; a rep does not presume to be an all-knowing authority dispensing wisdom from a skyscraper in New York. The consultation a rep programmer provides is a give-and-take exchange of ideas. *Just as the rep has a national perspective, enabling him or her to draw upon experiences in other markets, the station programmer generally knows his or her market, local viewers' attitudes and lifestyles, and the station's successes and failures over the years better than almost anybody else.*

Key Questions

Station management and rep programmers must consider some key questions as they work together.

- How well is the station's current schedule performing?

- Has there been audience growth, slippage or stagnation since the previous ratings report? Since the same period a year ago? Two years ago?

- What audience demographics are the advertisers and the station and rep's sales departments seeking? Is current programming adequately delivering those demos?

- Are older shows exhibiting signs of age?

- Has the competition made schedule changes that have hurt or helped the client station?

- Does the client own programs that can be used to replace weak programs, or must the client consider purchasing new programs for weak spots?

Generally, a station seeks audience growth over previous ratings books. Of course, for one or two stations to experience audience growth, other stations in the market must lose audience. And competition from cable and online also siphons viewers away from over-the-air broadcast television. The rep programmer seeks to help the station stem audience erosion and create growth instead.

Reps also help station programmers analyze the most recent ratings report. Both parties look for trouble spots. If a program is *downtrending* (showing a loss of audience from several previous ratings periods), the programmers may decide to move it to a different, perhaps less competitive time period. Or they may decide to take the show off the air entirely, replacing it with another program. Sometimes a once-successful but downtrending program can be *rested* or "put on hiatus," perhaps three months minimum to a year maximum, or for a part of the year, such as the summer. When the program returns to the air from hiatus, it often recaptures much of its previous strength and may run successfully for several more years. (*If the station does take the program off the air, it must still pay the cash portion of the license fee to the syndicator, and it must run the barter spots in the agreed-upon time period where the show had run, so this is not an easy decision.*)

The programmers may also note that a certain daypart is in trouble. A wholesale revision of that part of the schedule may be in order. They may need to rethink a station's programming strategy to decide whether current programming is still viable or whether the station should switch to another genre. For example, if a two-hour off-network action-drama block is not working, should the station switch to sitcoms or talk shows? A change of this magnitude is often quite difficult to accomplish, for the station usually has contractual commitments to run current programming into the future. Also, most viable programs of other genres are almost certainly already running on other stations in the market. It is usually easier to rearrange the order of the existing shows to see if a different sequence will attract a larger audience. It is also far easier to replace a single show than an entire schedule block.

Although household ratings are an important indicator of a program's relative performance, programmers are primarily concerned with *audience demographics*. Though there are dozens of demographic groupings, the most important demos are women 18 to 34 years old (W18–34), women 18 to 49 (W18–49), women 25 to 54 (W25–54), men 18 to 34 (M18–34), men 18 to 49 (M18–49), men 25 to 54 (M25–54), teenagers (T12–17) and children (K2–11). Generally, these are the demographic groups most desired by advertisers and therefore the target audiences of most programs, with W18–49 generally regarded as the single most important demo. Ethnic appeal can be an important consideration, especially in markets with relatively high minority populations.

Although most programs probably don't appeal equally to all of these groups, programmers try to schedule shows that reach at least several of these demos at times of the day when those people are available to watch television. Even if a program is not number one or two in household rating and share, a strong performance in a salable demographic may make the program acceptable despite the household rating. For example, the program may be number two or three in household rating and share but may have very strong appeal to young women, making it number one in the market in W18–34 and W18–49. And strong ethnic appeal to Hispanics or African-Americans may be an important factor in many markets. These groups have attractive demographics for many advertisers. Thus, the program might be acceptable for the station's needs despite its lower household ratings performance.

In another example, the program might be the third-rated show in its time period but may have exhibited significant ratings growth over previous ratings books. Therefore, the programmers may decide to leave the program in place because it is *uptrending* rather than downtrending. They may decide instead to change the lead-in show to try to deliver more audience to the target show. They may also decide to promote the show more to build audience.

A key issue in all these decisions is that *programming is usually purchased far in advance of its actual start date.* In the autumn of any year, stations are already planning for the following September, even though the current season has barely begun. Successful first-run shows are often renewed for several years into the future. Off-network programs are frequently sold two or three years before they become available to stations in syndication.

Once purchased, the station is committed to paying the agreed-upon license fee to the syndicator regardless of the program's subsequent network or syndication performance. Not uncommonly, a once-popular network program will fade in popularity in the two or three years between its syndication sale and its premiere in syndication. Although the station may be stuck with a program of lesser value than originally perceived, the syndicator does not waive or offer to drop the license fee. A deal is a deal. Conversely, some network shows increase in popularity as they continue to run; a station that bought early may pay a smaller license fee than it would if it had purchased the program a year or two later when its popularity was greater. Reps and their client stations thoroughly research, analyze and plan acquisitions carefully in order to purchase wisely—and then they place their bets and cross their fingers.

Research Data

As you can imagine, much station/rep consulting time is spent preparing information, researching program performance and formulating programming strategy using ratings information from Nielsen Media Research. Station, syndicator and rep programmers and salespeople regularly use the quarterly ViP ratings books to make programming decisions, sell

syndicated shows and sell advertising time. The syndicators and reps also have available to them additional Nielsen ratings information not generally purchased by stations because of its cost. These Nielsen studies include both national and local market reports. We repeat some reports already mentioned in Chapters 2 and 5 because here their relevance to *local* and *group* stations are what matters. Even reports focused on network programs tell local and group programmers how a possible future buy is doing now on the nets, and everyone in this business plans years ahead (or should).

National Reports

- **NTI.** *Nielsen Television Index,* based on people meters, provides daily ratings performance on a national basis for all network programs, including household and demographic audience estimates. The NTI ratings are also available as a weekly pocketpiece.

- **NTI Pocketpiece.** *The Nielsen Television Index Pocketpiece Report* weekly report provides national household and persons audience estimates for sponsored broadcast network programs. The *Pocketpiece* provides demos and household numbers for various dayparts. It is small enough to fit into a man's suit jacket pocket (hence the name) or a woman's purse, making it handy on sales calls. The *Pocketpiece* is also the oldest and best known Nielsen report.

- **Galaxy Explorer.** Nielsen's overnight NTI service provides national household ratings and shares and HUT levels. As a Windows-based system, users can analyze broadcast, cable and syndication audience estimates across user-selected demographics and user-defined dayparts for programs and time periods on both a daily and a weekly basis.

- **Galaxy Lightning.** Galaxy Lightning is a quick way to process standardized reports and to load data onto spreadsheets, which can then be manipulated and printed.

- **NPOWER.** Nielsen's NPower is a software package that allows individual users to analyze Nielsen data and create custom ratings reports on desktops or laptops. Subscribers can access a centralized Nielsen database, which is continually updated by Nielsen. The data includes audience estimates for broadcast, cable, syndication and Hispanic viewing.

- **NAD.** Nielsen's *National Audience Demographics Report* provides comprehensive estimates of viewership across a wide range of audience demographic categories. The *NTI NAD* is published monthly in two volumes and provides information on national network program viewership. The *NSS NAD* is a monthly book providing similar data for syndicated programming. *CNAD* is a quarterly report of cable network viewership. Unlike the other NAD reports, *CNAD* does not provide data on individual programs; it provides viewing estimates only for time periods and dayparts.

- **HTR.** Nielsen's monthly *Household Tracking Report* tracks program performance by individual network within half-hour time periods.

- **PTR.** Nielsen's monthly *Persons Tracking Report* tracks program performance in terms of household audiences and viewers per 1,000 viewing households (VPVH). The PTR includes both regularly scheduled programs and "specials."

- **CPT.** The *Household and Persons Cost Per 1000 Report* is an NTI report that gives advertising agency media planners and buyers estimates of the efficiency of network audience delivery.

- **HUT.** Nielsen's quarterly *Households Using Television Summary Report* provides HUT levels for individual half-hour time periods for individual days and weeks.

- **NTAR.** Nielsen's quarterly *Television Activity Report* compares the audience levels of all broadcast network affiliates, independent television stations, PBS stations and individual basic and pay cable networks.

Local Market Reports

- **NSI.** Since 1954, the *Nielsen Station Index* has been the system used to measure viewership in local Designated Market Areas (DMAs), including local commercial and public broadcast stations, and viewership of some national cable networks,

superstations and spill-in stations from adjacent markets. *NSI* provides metered market overnight ratings reports in more than 50 major markets and diary measurement in all Nielsen DMAs.

- **ViP.** Nielsen's *Viewers in Profile* report is the bible of local television stations, the infamous "book" by which stations (and sometimes careers) live and die. Most commercial TV stations subscribe to this report because they use it as the basis for the advertising rates the stations charge. All advertising agencies, syndication companies, and station reps get this report as well. Using NSI data, the *ViP* books show viewership over specific four-week periods (the "sweeps") in quarterly reports (November, February, May, July) in 210 markets and in October, January and March in selected large markets. The information is broken down for dayparts, programs and individual quarter hours. Ratings and shares are shown for households and key demographic groupings based on age and gender. There is also a very useful section that tabulates viewership as thousands of people rather than as rating or share. The data is shown as a four-week average and is also broken out for the four individual weeks and the 28 days of the ratings period. Both program averages (showing data for only a single program as a single number for the entire length of the show) and time period averages (which may include two or more programs in the same time period during the four weeks and are broken down by quarter hours or half hours) are provided.

- **NSS Pocketpiece.** Nielsen's *National Syndication Service* weekly report provides national audience estimates (in small size) for barter programs distributed by subscribing syndicators or occasional networks, including barter specials, syndicated sporting events and barter movie packages. (This is not the same as the network PT pocketpiece. Programmers are expected to have lots of pockets.)

- **ROSP.** Nielsen's *Report on Syndicated Programs* provides a complete record of all syndicated programs. The *ROSP* aids in the selection, evaluation and comparison of syndicated program performance.

- **Network Programs by DMA.** Nielsen's reports provide audience information for network programs by station within each DMA (market).

- **DMA TV Trends by Season.** This Nielsen report shows viewing trends throughout the year for all DMAs. It is produced once a year following the July ratings period.

- **TAR.** Nielsen's quarterly *DMA Television Activity Report* compares the audience levels of all broadcast network affiliates, superstations, independent television stations, PBS stations and individual basic and pay-cable networks. This report is similar to Nielsen's national NTAR report, except it is for individual local markets and includes spill-in stations from other markets.

- **NSI Report on PBS Program Audiences.** This report shows viewership of public television during each of the major ratings sweeps periods (November, February, May, July).

- **NSI Report on Devotional Program Audiences.** This report shows viewership of religious programs during each of the major ratings sweeps periods (November, February, May, July).

- **NHSI.** The *Nielsen Hispanic Station Index* report evaluates Spanish-language television viewing in 16 local markets that have significant Hispanic populations.

- **Galaxy Navigator.** Similar to Galaxy Explorer, Nielsen's Galaxy Navigator provides household ratings and shares and HUT levels for the individual local metered (overnight) markets. Using a Windows-based program, Galaxy Navigator enables the user to manipulate the reported data to customize reports.

- **Galaxy ProFile.** Galaxy ProFile is a PC-based analysis tool that the client can use to manipulate Nielsen data for all DMAs. Users can study the performance of individual programs across any and all markets, including comparisons in user-selected demos and with previous sweeps performances. Galaxy ProFile also provides time period analysis, genre analysis (that is, game shows, talk shows and so on), program block analysis, benchmark analysis and grid analysis.

In addition to this mountain of reports, which may also be purchased by syndicators, major station groups and large-market stations, Nielsen offers various internet (Media Metrix), sports, DVD, game-show, local-cable, pay-cable and other studies. If all this isn't enough, Nielsen can prepare special research reports exclusively for an individual station or tailored for a group of stations such as a rep firm's client list. (But your station better be in deep doo-doo to justify that expense!)

Specialized Program Analysis

Before the advent of personal computers, Nielsen provided printed reports to stations, syndicators and station reps, often at significant expense. Now the station reps themselves provide much customized research formerly available only from Nielsen. One example of such customized ratings research is the Katz Comtrac system, which has become an industry-standard research tool because it provides easy-to-use comprehensive overviews of station and program performances (see 6.7). Nielsen originally computed the Comtrac reports on its mainframe computers and then printed them as books, but since the late 1980s Katz has prepared the reports in-house for its clients on its own PCs more quickly and at significantly lower cost. Katz now distributes the reports to its client television stations on CD-ROMs. The stations can then analyze the data on their own computers, printing only the individual reports in which they are interested.

Katz's first page for *Friends* (one of several pages that cover all markets) tracks the show's shares in syndication in a condensed format. It shows which stations in which markets purchased *Friends* and when they scheduled it. As you can see, it then lists the shares for the time period performance in the three previous ratings books (May 2003, November 2003, and February 2004, as well as May 2004 in this example), also telling what kind of lead-in *Friends* had and the lead-in's shares.

In some cases *Friends* was not the program in the time period in previous ratings surveys, so the performance of whatever previous program was in the time period is shown. The previous program is indicated by a small letter next to the share number,

6.7 Comtrac Sheets for Friends

FRIENDS

Demos : HH = Homes, W1 = W18-49, W2 = W25-54, M3 = M25-54

Mkt	Market	Station	Affil	Ch		Time	Days	May '03 LI SH	May '03 HH SH	Nov '03 LI SH	Nov '03 HH SH	Feb '04 LI SH	Feb '04 HH SH	May '04 Hr Leadin	HH SH	May '04 Target HH RT	HH SH	%CHG May '03	W1 SH	W2 SH	M3 SH	May '04 Hr Leadout	HH SH	May '04 Top Competitor		LI SH	HH SH	W1 SH	May '04 2nd Competitor		LI SH	HH SH	W1 SH
32	CINCINNATI	WXIX	F	19	20T	7:30P	M-F	11	12	9	10	9	11	FRIENDS	7	4.3	8	-33	17	15	14	VARIOUS	12	WKRC	ENT TONIGHT 30	17	15	20	WCPO	JEOPARDY	18	14	16
33	MILWAUKEE	WVTV	W	18	20T	6:00P	M-F	4	7	4	7	4	6	KING OF QUEENS	4	2.4	5	-29	11	11	3	EVRYBDY-RAY MF	8	WTMJ	6P REPORT	20	19	11	WISN	WISN 12 NEWS	16	15	15
33	MILWAUKEE	WVTV	W	18	20T	10:30P	M-F	6	7	6	7	5	6	EVRYBDY-RAY MF	5	2.4	5	-29	8	8	3	KING-QUEENS B	7	WTMJ	TONITE SHW-NBC	22	19	19	WISN	ACCESS HOLLYWD	16	11	12
34	COLUMBUS, OH	WTTE	F	28	20T	6:00P	M-F	13	13	12	12	12	12	SIMPSONS B	10	4.9	10	-23	22	18	15	WILL & GRACE	9	WCMH	NEWSCH 4 AT 6	16	17	16	WBNS	10-EYWT NWS-6P	17	17	14
34	COLUMBUS, OH	WTTE	F	28	20T	11:00P	M-F	8	8	8	8	10	9	NEWSCENTER-10P	10	4.4	8	0	16	14	6	EVRBDY-RY MF B	9	WCMH	NEWSCH 4 AT 11	18	20	24	WBNS	10TV NIGHTBEAT	20	19	15
35	GREENVILLE-SPAR	WHNS	F	21	20T	6:30P	M-F	7	6	6	7	7	7	THAT 70S SHW B	8	3.8	7	17	14	12	14	FRIENDS B	7	WYFF	NBC NITELY NWS	16	15	15	WLOS	ABC-WORLD NWS	12	13	9
35	GREENVILLE-SPAR	WHNS	F	21	20T	7:00P	M-F	6	7	7	8	7	7	FRIENDS	7	3.8	7	0	14	13	12	SEINFELD	7	WLOS	WHEEL-FORTNE	13	15	10	WYFF	ENT TONIGHT 30	15	13	12
36	SALT LAKE CITY	KJZZ	I	14	20T	5:30P	M-F	7	8	7	7	5	4	HOME IMPROV MF	5	2.5	6	-25	21	9	8	FRIENDS	6	KSL	NBC NITELY NWS	11	16	13	KUTV+	2 NEWS AT 530P	16	14	16
36	SALT LAKE CITY	KJZZ	I	14	20T	6:00P	M-F	8	11	7	8	4	6	FRIENDS B	6	3.0	6	-45	19	10	6	WILL & GRACE	5	KSL	EYWT NWS-6	16	17	16	KSTU+	SIMPSONS	9	13	17
37	SAN ANTONIO	KENS	C	5	20T	10:30P	M-F	18	13	20	13	21	13	EYEWIT NWS-10	20	6.8	12	-8	12	15	10	D LETTRMAN-CBS	10	WOAI	TONITE SHW-NBC	18	16	14	KSAT	INSIDE EDITION	16	11	9
38	GRAND RAPIDS-KA	WOOD	N	8	20T	7:30P	M-F	5	7	9	9	11	9	INSIDE EDITION	10	3.4	8	14	9	10	8	VARIOUS	14	WWMT	JEOPARDY	25	23	15	WXMI	EVRYBDY-RAY MF	9	10	14
38	GRAND RAPIDS-KA	WXSP	U	15	18T	10:00P	M-F	2	1	2	2	2	1 a	VARIOUS	1	0.4	1	0	1	1	1	KING OF QUEENS	1	WOOD	VARIOUS	17	16	20	WWMT	VARIOUS	18	16	14
39	WEST PALM BEACH	WPEC	C	12	20T	7:00P	M-F	10	8	11	8	11	8	CBS EVE NWS	11	3.5	6	-25	10	8	8	ENT TONIGHT 30	7	WPTV	EXTRA	26	16	17	WPBF	WHEEL-FORTNE	8	16	9
39	WEST PALM BEACH	WTVX	U	34	20T	11:00P	M-F	4	3	3	3	3	3	VARIOUS	3	1.7	3	0	5	4	2	JUST SHOOT ME	3	WPTV	NWSCHNL5 AT 11	18	19	15	WPEC	NEWS12-11.00	18	16	17
40	BIRMINGHAM	WTTO+	W	21	20T	5:30P	M-F	5	5 b	4	5	5	7	SIMPSONS	6	3.8	7	40	12	9	14	FRIENDS B	8	WBRC	FOX6 NEWS-530P	17	15	14	WBMA+	ABC-WORLD NWS	18	14	12
40	BIRMINGHAM	WTTO+	W	21	20T	6:00P	M-F	5	8 c	5	8	7	8	FRIENDS	7	4.8	8	0	19	14	12	EVRYBDY-RAY MF	8	WBMA+	33/40 NEWS-6	14	16	12	WBRC	FOX 6 NWS AT 6	15	15	15
41	NORFOLK-PORTSMT	WTVZ	W	33	20T	7:00P	M-F	3	5	6	6	5	6	SIMPSONS B	5	3.0	5	0	12	10	9	FRIENDS B	5	WVEC	WHEEL-FORTNE	13	14	11	WAVY	ENT TONIGHT 30	14	12	15
41	NORFOLK-PORTSMT	WTVZ	W	33	20T	7:30P	M-F	5	6	6	6	6	6	FRIENDS	5	3.2	5	-17	10	9	8	VARIOUS	6	WVEC	JEOPARDY	14	14	13	WGNT	JUDGE-BROWN B	11	11	11
42	NEW ORLEANS	WNOL	W	38	20T	9:30P	M-F	6	5	5	5	5	5	EVRYBDY-RAY MF	5	3.6	5	0	6	5	3	SIMPSONS	6	WWL	VARIOUS	20	21	15	WDSU	VARIOUS	14	13	15
42	NEW ORLEANS	WGNO	A	26	20T	11:00P	M-F	4	5 d	8	8 a	5	5 d	ABC-NITELINE	5	2.2	4	-20	6	7	5	WILL & GRACE	3	WWL	D LETTRMAN-CBS	15	12	10	WDSU	TONITE SHW-NBC	10	9	7
43	MEMPHIS	WHBQ	F	13	20T	10:30P	M-F	8	11	7	10	8	10	KING OF HILL R	8	5.6	9	-18	13	13	9	THAT 70S SHOW	11	WMC	TONITE SHW-NBC	20	13	11	WREG	D LETTRMAN-CBS	18	13	10
44	BUFFALO	WIVB	C	4	20T	7:30P	M-F	14	10	15	9	15	9	INSIDE EDITION	14	4.6	8	-20	12	12	11	VARIOUS	15	WKBW	JEOPARDY	17	18	14	WGRZ	ENT TONIGHT 30	8	13	15
44	BUFFALO	WNLO	U	23	20T	11:00P	M-F	2	1	2	2	2	2	ACCESS HOLLYWD	2	1.0	2	100	2	2	1	COPS	2	WIVB	NW4 BUFFALO 11	20	21	18	WGRZ	CH2 NWS NTSIDE	19	19	18
45	OKLAHOMA CITY	KOCB	W	34	20T	6:00P	M-F	5	8	6	8	3	7	ON AIR-RYAN	3	3.9	7	-12	17	11	12	FRIENDS B	7	KFOR	NWSCHANNEL 4-6	18	19	18	KWTV	NWS 9-6	13	16	13
45	OKLAHOMA CITY	KOCB	W	34	20T	6:30P	M-F	8	8	8	9	7	8	FRIENDS	7	4.3	7	-12	15	11	9	VARIOUS	9	KOCO	WHEEL-FORTNE	15	19	13	KFOR	NWSCH4-630	19	16	14
46	GREENSBORO-H.PO	WTWB	W	20	20T	6:00P	M-F	3	4 e	4	4	5	5	THAT 70S SHOW	5	2.8	5	25	11	9	9	FRIENDS B	6	WFMY	WFMY NEWS 2-6	15	17	13	WGHP	FOX8 NWS-6.00P	14	16	14
46	GREENSBORO-H.PO	WTWB	W	20	20T	6:30P	M-F	4	5 f	4	5	5	6	FRIENDS	5	3.0	6	20	13	11	10	EVRBDY-RY MF B	6	WFMY	CBS EVE NWS	17	19	13	WXII	NBC NITELY NWS	15	14	15
47	HARRISBURG-LNCS	WHTM	A	27	19T	7:30P	M-F	8	6	7	5	6	4	HOLLYWD SQUARS	7	2.3	5	-17	4	4	4	VARIOUS	6	WHP	JEOPARDY	19	19	12	WPMT	EVRYBDY-RAY MF	8	11	18
48	PROVIDENCE-NEW	WLNE	A	6	20T	7:30P	M-F	4	4 g	4	3	4	3	ENT TONIGHT 30	3	1.8	3	-25	4	5	2	VARIOUS	4	WPRI	JEOPARDY	15	15	12	WJAR	ACCESS HOLLYWD	12	10	16
48	PROVIDENCE-NEW	WLWC	U	28	20T	11:30P	M-F	3	2 h	2	3 f	2	3	WILL & GRACE	2	0.7	2	0	6	5	3	DREW CAREY	2	WJAR	TONITE SHW-NBC	24	19	31	WPRI	D LETTRMAN-CBS	14	11	11
49	ALBUQUERQUE-SAN	KASA	F	2	20T	6:00P	M-F	5	7	3	4	3	4	DHARMA-GREG	4	2.4	4	-43	8	8	7	FRIENDS B	4	KOAT+	ACTN 7 NWS-6	14	13	12	KOB	EYEWTNS NW-600	10	12	15
49	ALBUQUERQUE-SAN	KASA	F	2	20T	6:30P	M-F	7	8	4	5	4	4	FRIENDS	4	2.5	4	-50	8	7	8	VARIOUS	8	KRQE+	WHEEL-FORTNE	12	12	9	KOAT+	ENT TONIGHT 30	13	11	15
50	LOUISVILLE	WDRB	F	41	20T	11:00P	M-F	11	10	8	8	9	8	FOX NEWS AT 10	10	4.5	8	-20	16	14	7	SEINFELD	10	WLKY	NEWS CH32 11PM	22	19	19	WAVE	WAVE NWS-11P	14	16	14
50	LOUISVILLE	WDRB	F	41	20T	12:00M	M-F	10	8 i	8	7 j	10	9 j	SEINFELD	10	3.7	9	13	18	13	12	FRASIER	9	WLKY	D LETTRMAN-CBS	14	13	14	WAVE	TONITE SHW-NBC	11	10	16
51	LAS VEGAS	KVVU	F	5	19T	6:30P	M-F	8	8	8	8	9	9	THAT 70S SHW R	7	4.4	8	0	15	10	8	FRIENDS B	9	KVBC	JEOPARDY	13	15	9	KLAS	EYEWT NWS-630	12	11	9
51	LAS VEGAS	KVVU	F	5	20T	7:00P	M-F	8	10	8	10	9	10	FRIENDS	7	5.4	9	-10	14	11	10	EVRYBDY-RAY MF	8	KVBC	WHEEL-FORTNE	15	13	8	KLAS	ENT TONIGHT 30	11	12	10
52	JACKSONVILLE, B	WJWB	W	17	20T	6:00P	M-F	5	5 c	7	5	5	5	HUGHLEYS B	3	2.2	4	-20	7	7	4	JUST SHOOT ME	3	WJXT	EYEWTNS NWS@6	16	17	15	WTLV	FIRST CST NW@6	13	14	12
52	JACKSONVILLE, B	WJWB	W	17	20T	7:00P	M-F	5	6	5	6	5	6	JUST SHOOT ME	3	3.0	5	-17	9	8	7	WILL & GRACE	4	WTLV	WHEEL-FORTNE	15	14	14	WJXT	ENT TONIGHT 30	12	11	16
53	WILKES BARRE-SC	WSWB+	W	38	20T	7:00P	M-F	1	2 k	1	2 f	2	2	WILL & GRACE B	2	0.9	2	0	4	3	3	SIMPSONS	2	WBRE	WHEEL-FORTNE	12	21	11	WNEP	INSIDE EDITION	36	16	15
53	WILKES BARRE-SC	WOLF	F	56	20T	10:30P	M-F	8	4 l	8	4	6	4	FOX56 NWS-10PM	10	2.6	5	25	8	6	6	BECKER	2	WYOU	VARIOUS	15	17	15	WBRE	VARIOUS	14	15	17
54	AUSTIN	KNVA	W	54	20T	6:00P	M-F	8	10	7	8	6	7	WILL & GRACE	4	2.9	6	-40	15	13	4	FRIENDS B	6	KXAN+	NEWS 36-6	13	14	8	KVUE	24 NEWS AT 6	16	13	11
54	AUSTIN	KNVA	W	54	20T	6:30P	M-F	10	9 f	8	7 f	7	5 f	FRIENDS	6	3.3	6	-33	13	12	6	VARIOUS	5	KXAN+	WHEEL-FORTNE	14	14	8	KVUE	ENT TONIGHT 30	13	11	15
55	ALBANY-SCHENECT	WNYT	N	13	19T	12:30P	M-F	12	10	17	12	15	12	NWSCH13-NOON	11	1.6	8	-20	15	16	7	DAYS-OUR LIVES	16	WRGB	YOUNG&RESTLESS	29	31	32	WTEN+	JEOPARDY	16	11	3
55	ALBANY-SCHENECT	WNYT	N	13	20T	7:30P	M-F	13	10	15	11	15	10	ENT TONIGHT 30	13	4.3	9	-10	16	16	2	VARIOUS	14	WTEN+	JEOPARDY	21	25	18	WRGB	KING OF QUEENS	11	10	11
56	LITTLE ROCK-PIN	KLRT	F	16	20T	6:00P	M-F	2	4	4	6	4	5	KING OF HILL	4	2.6	5	25	10	7	5	SEINFELD	6	KATV	CH 7 NWS-6	27	28	18	KTHV	KTHV NEWS 6P	14	15	14
56	LITTLE ROCK-PIN	KLRT	F	16	20T	10:00P	M-F	2	2	2	2	3	3	FOX16 NWS AT 9	3	1.9	4	100	5	3	2	THAT 70S SHOW	4	KATV	CH7 NWS-NGHTSD	12	24	19	KTHV	KTHV NEWS 10P	19	23	24
57	FRESNO-VISALIA	KMPH+	F	26	20T	7:00P	M-F	13	14	12	11	17	13	EVRBDY-RY MF B	14	5.5	11	-21	14	10	9	FRASIER	7	KFSN	JEOPARDY	15	15	5	KFRE	MASH	2	4	3
57	FRESNO-VISALIA	KMPH+	F	26	20T	11:00P	M-F	16	10 c	17	5 m	14	6	10 OCLK NWS	14	2.9	12	20	19	17	10	SEINFELD	10	KSEE	KSEE 24-NWS-11	17	17	12	KFSN	ACTION NWS 11	11	16	13
58	RICHMOND-PETERS	WWBT	N	12	20T	7:30P	M-F	18	14	18	13	19	13	ENT TONIGHT 30	18	7.4	12	-14	17	17	14	VARIOUS	14	WRIC	JEOPARDY	12	12	9	WTVR	MILLIONAIRE	9	9	7
59	DAYTON	WDTN	A	2	20T	7:00P	M-F	10	9	10	9	8	9	ABC-WORLD NWS	7	3.4	7	-22	9	10	8	JEOPARDY	11	WHIO	WHEEL-FORTNE	25	25	20	WRGT	SIMPSONS	6	7	13
60	TULSA	KWBT	W	19	20T	6:00P	M-F	5	5	6	7	5	5	THAT 70S SHW B	5	2.4	4	-20	14	10	4	FRIENDS B	5	KOTV	NEWS-6	23	19	21	KTUL	NWS CH 8 AT 6	15	19	19
60	TULSA	KWBT	W	19	20T	6:30P	M-F	5	6	7	6	5	4	FRIENDS	4	2.7	5	-17	13	10	6	VARIOUS	4	KTUL	WHEEL-FORTNE	19	21	18	KOTV	ENT TONIGHT 30	19	15	20
61	KNOXVILLE	WBXX	W	20	20T	7:30P	M-F	7	8	8	9	8	9	THAT 70S SHOW	5	3.6	6	-25	14	10	10	VARIOUS	7	WBIR	JEOPARDY	23	20	19	WATE	MILLIONAIRE	14	13	10

a: VARIOUS
b: HOME IMPROVMNT
c: FRIENDS
d: EVRYBDY-RAY MF
e: THAT 70S SHW B
f: WILL & GRACE
g: ENT TONIGHT 30
h: DREW CAREY
i: CHEERS
j: FRASIER
k: THAT 70S SHOW
l: FRIENDS B
m: SEINFELD
n: KING-QUEENS B
o: KING OF HILL

COMTRAC Syndicated Program Schedules, May 2004. Used by permission.

and the title is in the footnote at the bottom of the page. For example, in San Francisco the small letter *b* indicates *Cheers* ran in the three previous time periods; in Los Angeles, *Friends* was the February 2004 program because there is no small letter next to the number.

Next the Comtrac report shows *Friends'* current lead-in and shares in each market, and then *Friends'* own shares and ratings under the heading May '04 Target (including some abbreviated demographics), and its lead-out. Finally, the Katz Comtrac page shows *Friends'* two main competing programs in each market and their audience shares.

The Decision Process

When the syndicator visits the station, he or she makes a pitch to either the general manager or the program manager or both. This occurs, we hope, after the rep has consulted with the station and provided research support combined with experience and judgment—resulting in the rep's recommendation regarding the program the syndicator is selling. The station and the rep then analyze (via email) the terms of the deal and how they might use the program, if at all.

Each programming decision is different from any other. Each show is different; each deal is different. Markets and competitive situations differ; corporate philosophies and needs not only differ but may also change over time. The personalities and opinions of the syndicator, station general manager, program director and rep programmer all enter into the decision. *Although innumerable permutations and combinations exist, the basics of the decision-making process involve an assessment of need and an analysis of selection options.*

Determining Need

Perhaps the most important part of making any programming decision is establishing whether a program is needed and determining whether the program in question is the best choice to meet that need. Sometimes this task is easy. The need may be quite obvious. For example, a first-run program that many stations carry may fail to attract a large enough national audience and be canceled by its syndicator. It needs to be replaced on all the stations carrying it. In another example, despite increased promotion and a strong lead-in, a particular program on a given station continues to downtrend in several successive books and from its year-ago performance in the time period. It needs to be replaced.

At other times the need may be less obvious. A show may perform reasonably well but show no audience growth and finish second or third in the time period. Should it be replaced? Will a replacement show perform as well, better or not as well?

When a syndicator is pitching a station, he or she tries to identify or create a need for the station to buy the particular program being offered. Although the syndicator's assessment that an existing program should be replaced may be correct, he or she is looking at it strictly from the perspective of selling a program in the market. The syndicator's need to sell a particular show may not be the same as the station's degree of need (if any) to replace an existing program. And the syndicator doesn't have to find money in an operating budget to pay for the program, even if it fails to perform up to expectations. (When people buy new cars or televisions or hair dryers, they come with warranties. If they don't work properly, the consumers have recourse to the manufacturer.) *Television programs don't come with warranties; the station assumes all the risk, even if the show fails.*

The station and rep programmers approach the determination of need by first looking at the performance of the existing schedule and identifying trouble spots, including individual programs and entire dayparts. For example, three out of the four programs from 4 to 6 P.M. may be performing quite well, but one may be a weak link and therefore a candidate for replacement. In another situation, the entire 4 to 6 P.M. schedule might be performing poorly and need to be replaced, perhaps including a switch from one program type to another, such as from talk shows to reality and magazine shows.

Analyzing Selection Options

Once a need to replace a program has been established, a replacement must be selected. Programmers have six basic options at this point. Think baseball, for the alternatives are analogous in both television and baseball.

- **Do nothing at all.** If a station or a baseball team is trailing, it's sometimes best to leave the lineup unchanged, hoping for an improved performance or a mistake by the competition. Sometimes there's no alternative because the bench strength is either depleted or no better than the current players, so no stronger players or programs can be substituted.

- **Change the batting (or programming) lineup.** Swap the lead-off hitter with the cleanup batter, or swap a morning program with an afternoon show, or reverse the order of the two access shows. (There are many more examples.)

- **Go to the bench** for a pinch hitter or go to the inventory of programs "on the shelf" (already owned by the station but not currently on the schedule) for a replacement show.

- **Hire a new player** or buy a new show.

- **Send the player to the minors** or switch stations, but *only* if a company owns two stations *in the same market.*

- **Do not renew the player's contract** when it expires, and do not renew the program contract. This is no immediate remedy, but at least the station is no longer on the hook when the current contract expires.

Let's look at each option in greater detail.

1. Do Nothing

Although a time period may be in trouble, sometimes nothing can be done to improve the situation. The station may not own any suitable replacement shows. Other shows already on the air might be swapped, but the station and rep programmers might feel that such a swap would hurt another daypart (perhaps a more important daypart) or that the other program might not be competitive in the target time period. Then, too, potential replacement shows available from syndicators may be perceived as no improvement over existing programming, or they might be too expensive. Often, increasing promotion can help the show "grow." Finally, the programmers may decide to leave the schedule intact because it may take time for viewers to "find" the show and form a viewing habit. The rep may research the performance of the program in other markets to see whether the program is exhibiting growth. Sometimes the only choice is to do nothing at all.

2. Swap Shows

The second alternative is to change the batting order. Generally, the station and rep programmers look first at the station's entire program schedule to see whether the solution might be as simple as swapping time periods for two or more shows already on the air. Often a program originally purchased for one time period can improve an entirely different time period when moved.

In most cases, syndicators are delighted when a station moves a show from a time period with a lower HUT level to one with higher HUTs. *A higher HUT level means a higher rating, even if share stays the same or drops slightly.* For syndicators selling barter time in a program, higher ratings in individual markets contribute to a higher national rating, which translates into higher rates charged by the syndicator to the barter advertiser.

For a station, however, such a move may also mean paying higher license fees to the syndicator. In the case of *first-run* programs, syndicators often make *tier* or *step deals* with stations. At the time the deal is made, stations and syndicators agree on price levels for different dayparts, with higher prices for dayparts that have higher HUT/PUT levels and thus more potential viewers available. One price is agreed upon for morning time periods, a higher price for early fringe, and perhaps a still higher price for access. Four-tier agreements, which may also include late night, are not uncommon. Moving a program from one daypart to another triggers a change in license fee. It is to the station's advantage to negotiate a step deal to avoid a potentially expensive program playing in a low-revenue time period.

Step deals are relatively rare for off-network programs, which generally have a single license fee level priced by the syndicator that is based on the revenue potential of the daypart in which it is presumed the program will play. Thus, when a station buys an off-network sitcom or hour-long action-adventure show for access or early fringe, the price the station pays remains the same over the life of the contract. If the show is a ratings failure in access or early fringe and must be moved to a less lucrative morning or late-night time period, the station's financial obligation to the syndicator remains unchanged. Thus, a station can find itself with a very expensive "morning program," a daypart of significantly lower revenue potential than early fringe or access (meaning that the program may cost the station far more than the time period can generate in advertising income).

If the station buys an expensive off-network show that later is downgraded to a time period with lower HUT levels, the station may experience some discomfort in its bottom line (low profitability or a loss), but the consequences are generally not disastrous. If, however, the station buys several expensive shows that do not perform and must be moved to time periods with lower advertising rates, the economic impact can be quite serious. Because of the relatively long license terms of off-network shows (typically three to four years), a station may not recover for years when several such "mistakes" are made.

Depending on the program and how the contract is structured regarding stripping or weekend runs, it may be possible to move a Monday to Friday program from a weekday schedule to the weekend. Generally this is not possible with first-run strip programs (such as talk or court shows), which are designed for a five-day run, but the strategy may be possible with some off-network shows, particularly older sitcoms that are purchased on a per-episode basis.

3. Substitute Shows

The third alternative is to go to the bench for a pinch hitter. Programmers have a responsibility to manage existing products and at the same time remain competitive. It's not always necessary to spend more money to buy a new program. Sometimes the station already owns the solution to a problem. A simple swap of programs already on the air may not be the best answer. A station with strong bench strength may have enough programs "in the dugout" to replace a failing show in a competitive manner. Corporate accountants like this sort of solution because it does not add to a station's expenses, and it uses existing products that must be paid for whether or not they air.

The station and rep programmers look at the strengths and weaknesses of the shows on the shelf, which generally have aired before. They must ask some questions at this point. How well did these shows work? Have they rested long enough to return at their previous performance level, and if not, is their reduced level still superior to the current program's performance? Are the shows dated? Will they look "old"? Are the potential replacement shows suitable for the time period? Are they compatible with the other programs in the daypart? Are they competitive? Are they cost-effective? Do they appeal to the available demographic?

4. Buy New Shows

If the first three solutions have been examined and rejected, the programmers at the station and the rep generally consider purchasing a program. Because an added expense is involved whenever a purchase is made, the programmers must determine whether a new program will be superior to an existing show, and if so, whether it will be strong enough to offset the additional cost.

Although expense is a consideration in any programming decision, programmers as well as corporate and station management should always keep in mind one very important factor: *They must keep the station competitive.* Remember, their job is to deliver the largest mass audience with the strongest demographics. Although they must always keep an eye on the bottom line and therefore program in a cost-effective manner, a false economy will result from trying to avoid expense if the result would be to lose even more revenue. If ratings decline, eventually revenue will also decline.

Instead, programmers must balance expense against returns, determining the ratings potential and projected revenue when deciding whether a new purchase is practical and, if so, how much the station can afford. The rep's research can help project the future performance of a program, whether it is already on a station's schedule or will be a future acquisition. Anticipated performance plays a large role in determining the purchase price.

5. Switch Stations

When two stations in the same market are commonly owned, the contracts may have been negotiated to allow some programs to run on either station. Sometimes a program can take on a new life and appear fresher when switched from one station to another. Sometimes a program will become a better fit in the "other" station's lineup because of other program acquisitions or changes made to either or both stations. And sometimes it's just prudent to put a weakening program on the weaker of the two commonly owned stations to reduce the negative impact on the stronger station's performance. While in baseball the team might send a struggling player to its farm club, in television this works *only* in a situation where two stations in the same market are commonly owned, and the show can be put into the schedule of the other, presumably weaker station.

6. Don't Renew

Most companies own only one station in a market, and therefore, when a program is performing poorly, that station is stuck with it. Unlike baseball, where a player can be literally traded to another team run by a different owner, this is generally not possible in television during the term of the program contract. At contract renewal time, the current station may, in effect, turn a program into a "free agent" by not renewing it; the syndicator can then try to sell it to another station in the market. Moreover, unless the incumbent station has a contractual

right to meet or beat any offers from competing stations, the syndicator may elect to sell the show to a different station for its next cycle anyway, because the other station is stronger, can offer a better time period, is willing to pay more money, or offers to pick up additional programming from the syndicator if it takes the program in question. Sometimes, stations will *warehouse (*store unused) programs to prevent competitors from getting them.

Revenue Potentials

Based on a program's ratings and the sales department's estimate of *cost per point* (the number of dollars advertising agencies or advertisers are willing to pay for each rating point the station delivers), programmers can determine the amount of money the station can pay for a show. It works like this: *A rating point equals 1 percent of the television households in a market.* If there are 500,000 television households in market A, a rating point represents 5,000 households (HH). A show that receives a 15 rating in market A would deliver 75,000 households (5,000 HH per rating point × 15 rating points = 75,000 HH). Let's say that market B has 250,000 households. By a similar calculation, a 15 rating in market B would represent 37,500 households. Likewise, a 15 rating in market C with only 100,000 households would represent just 15,000 households viewing the program. This simple arithmetic illustrates the point made earlier in the "Deal Points" section that programs generally are sold at a higher price in larger markets than in smaller ones. *Thus, even at the same rating, the larger the market, the larger the number of viewers. Conversely, the smaller the market, the fewer the viewers. And the amount of revenue a station can expect varies accordingly by market size, as does the license fee for the program.*

Advertising agencies pay a certain amount for each thousand households, called *cost per thousand* (CPM). Let's say the agency assigns a $5 CPM. A 15 rating in market A would be valued at $375 for a 30-second commercial ($5 CPM × 5,000 HH per rating point ÷ 1,000 = $25 per point, then × a 15 rating = $375).

Let's say the station is considering a half-hour, off-network sitcom cut for six local commercial minutes and sold with six available runs over four years. (While the program may actually be cut for 6:30, including a 30-second barter spot, the general manager and program director at the station and the rep are concerned only with the six minutes that are available for sale to the station and rep.) The six commercial minutes in each episode translate to twelve 30-second spots per day. Revenue potential is calculated by multiplying the projected rate per spot at the anticipated rating by the number of commercials to give a gross revenue potential. The gross is now netted down (reduced) to allow for commissions paid by the station to salespeople, reps and advertising agencies. At a 15 percent commission rate, the station nets 85 percent of the gross. The net is now netted down again to a projected *sellout rate* (the number of spots actually sold over the course of a year is generally less than the number available). Most stations use a conservative 80 percent sellout rate for planning purposes; if they actually sell more than 80 percent of the available time, that's all to the good, and to the bottom line. This final revenue figure is called the *net net*. The calculation per episode would look like this:

$ 375	rate per 30-second commercial
×12	30-second commercials
$4,500	gross per day
×.85	net revenue level (after 15% commission)
$3,825	net per day
×.80	sellout rate
$3,060	net net per day

The $3,060 is the daily income the station can expect to generate during the current year for each run of the program.

To compute what the show would generate when it goes on the air, the station and rep sales managers inform programmers of the potential rate for all future years the show will be available. A typical increase in cost per point from year to year might run from as low as 3 percent to as high as 12

percent depending on inflation and local market economy. Using figures supplied by sales, programmers use this formula to project the net net revenue potential of the program over the life of the show. In this calculation, they also revise the rate based on the show's ratings delivery. A program that produces a 15 rating in its first run might be moved by its fifth and sixth runs (because it can be expected to weaken as it is repeated) to a time period with lower HUT levels, such as late night, and may generate only a 5 rating. Therefore, although CPMs are increasing, the lower rating will bring down the spot rate, lowering the revenue potential for the program in that run.

Let's look at a simplified example of the complete calculation. We'll assume the program is available two years from now. There will be 130 episodes of six runs each (780 total runs) over four years. The station plans to trigger the episodes as soon as the contract starts, running five episodes a week for three years, with no hiatus, until all 780 runs are exhausted. Coincidentally, this will take exactly three years (5 days/week × 52 weeks = 260 days per year ÷ 780 total runs = 3 years).

The various calculations of the revenue potential for each individual episode are shown in 6.8. The percentage rate increases are estimated by sales. This year and next year are the two years between the time the station buys the show and the time it goes on the air. Years 1, 2 and 3 are the years in which all runs will be taken. The years are not necessarily calendar years; generally they begin in September with the start of the new season or the program's availability date.

Now that we've figured the revenue potential per run of each episode as shown in 6.8, it's easy, based on projected usage, to compute the total revenue potential for each episode over the life of the contract.

But we're not quite done. Now let's figure how much the station can pay per episode. Stations assign percentage ranges in three areas: program purchase cost, operating expense and profit. Program purchase cost may run as low as 20 to 30 percent of total revenue for an affiliate, which gets most of its programming from the network, to as high as 50 percent for an independent, which must purchase

6.8

Run 1, Year 1	$3,439.44
Run 2, Year 1	3,439.44
Run 3, Year 2	1,945.34
Run 4, Year 2	1,945.34
Run 5, Year 3	1,313.76
Run 6, Year 3	1,313.76
Total net net revenue per episode	$13,397.08

or create all of its programming. Let's use a median figure of 40 percent for our example in 6.9.

With a total revenue projection of $13,397.08 per episode, the station using a 40 percent program cost figure would estimate the price per episode at $5,358.83. Because nobody figures so closely (that is, to the exact dollar), a range of $5,000 to $5,500 per episode would be a reasonable working figure. Multiplying these figures by 130 available episodes would establish a total investment of $650,000 to $715,000 for the program. The station would certainly try to negotiate a lower cost for the show but might be willing to go higher, even considerably higher, depending on how badly the station needed the program or if it perceived that the show was important to the station's image (to viewers and advertisers) and to its competitive position.

Unfortunately for the station, syndicators perform the same calculations. They generally quote a purchase price significantly higher than the station wishes to pay. In our example, knowing that the station could expect to make as much as $20,000

6.9 Calculation of Revenue per Episode

$5.00	current CPM
×1.05	(5% increase estimate)
$5.25	CPM next year
×1.07	(7% increase estimate)
$5.62	CPM Year 1 of show
×1.06	(6% increase estimate)
$5.96	CPM Year 2 of show
×1.08	(8% increase estimate)
$6.44	CPM Year 3 of show

Year 1: Runs 1 & 2 of each episode in access at 15 rating.

Year 2: Runs 3 & 4 of each episode in early fringe at 8 rating.

Year 3: Runs 5 & 6 of each episode late night at 5 rating.

Year 1		Year 2		Year 3	
$5.62	CPM	$8.96	CPM	$6.44	CPM
×5000	households	×5000	households	×5000	households
1000		1000		1000	
$28.10	Cost per point	$29.80	Cost per point	$32.20	Cost per point
×15	rating	×8	rating	×5	rating
$421.50	rate	$238.40	rate	$161.00	rate
×12	Commercials	×12	Commercials	×12	Commercials
$5,058.00	Gross	$2,860.80	Gross	$1,932.00	Gross
×.85	net revenue	×.85	net revenue	×.85	net revenue
$4,299.30	Net	$2,431.68	Net	$1,642.20	Net
×.80	sellout	×.80	sellout	×.80	sellout
$3,439.44	Net Net per run	$1,945.34	Net Net per run	$1,313.76	Net Net per run

in the access-time period if all six runs of each episode ran in access, but not knowing that the station might plan to take some runs in early fringe and late night, the syndicator might ask $10,000 to $15,000 per episode. The station might want to pay $3,000 to $4,000 but expect to pay $5,000 to $6,000 per episode and go as high as $7,500 if it really needed the show.

Obviously, the two parties have to reach a middle ground or the show will either be sold to another station in the market or go unsold to any station. And now the fun begins—negotiation.

Negotiation

Syndicators sell most programs to stations through good old-fashioned negotiation. Generally, the syndication company "opens a market" by pitching the program to all stations in the market. The pitch will be the same to every station in the terms and conditions of the deal (episodes, runs, years, availability date, price, barter split, payment terms) but may differ subjectively depending on the stations' perceived needs, strengths, weaknesses and programming philosophy. The syndicator will try to determine or create a need at each station with the hope that several will make an offer. In this ideal situation, the syndicator will be able to select which station receives the show based on the following considerations:

- Highest purchase price offered (if cash or cash-plus-barter)
- Size of down payment
- Length of payout
- Ability to make payments
- Best time period (particularly important to the syndicator for shows containing barter time)
- Strength of station
- Most compatible adjacent programming

Often the syndicator receives no offers initially but may have one or two stations as possible prospects. Negotiations may continue for weeks or even months, with syndicator and station each making concessions. The station may consider paying a higher price than originally planned or may agree to also purchase another program. The syndicator may lower the asking price or may increase the number of runs and years (if possible). The station may raise the down payment, and the syndicator may allow the station to pay out over more time. Negotiation is basic horse trading.

Bidding

Some syndicators of hit off-network programs have sold their programs by confidential bid to the highest bidder in the market rather than through negotiation. Here is how bids work. The syndicator opens half a dozen or so markets in a week. Each station receives a complete pitch, including research data, terms and conditions. Financial terms are *omitted* during the pitch. After several days, when all stations have been pitched, the syndicator faxes all stations simultaneously, revealing the syndicator's lowest acceptable price and certain other financial details. Stations are given a few days, perhaps 72 or 96 hours, to bid on the program. Bids from each station in the same market are due simultaneously so that no station has a time advantage over another. The syndicator analyzes the bid price, the amount of down payment offered, and other financial terms to determine the highest bidder. The highest bidder wins the program, pure and relatively simple.

The rep programmer usually becomes involved in advising client stations during the bidding process. Syndicators notify the reps of the markets coming up for bid, and the reps immediately notify their respective client stations. The reps provide their usual research analyses of the program's performance, coupled with their subjective views of how well the show will play in syndication and in the client's lineup. While the reps advise the stations whether or not to bid, it is ultimately the station's decision (with corporate approval) whether or not to bid and how much to offer. The reps frequently project the rating and help clients determine the amount of the bid if a bid is to be made.

Perhaps most important, the reps track *reserve prices* (asking prices) and reported or estimated selling prices in other markets. The rep programmer informs the client of these pricing trends to help the station determine a *bidding price* based on previously paid prices in similar markets. The rep also informs the client of down-payment percentages and payout terms in other markets, which serve as a guide to successful bidding.

Bidding is a fairly simple, clear-cut procedure for syndicator and station alike. There is no messy, drawn-out negotiation. The syndicator makes only one trip to the market, not repeat visits over many weeks or months. The sale can be accomplished quickly if there is a bidder at an acceptable price. Competition between stations is established, often turning into a frenzied escalation of prices by stations reaching ever deeper into their piggy banks to be sure they acquire the must-have program. And the syndicator generally achieves prices far in excess of the amounts that might be realized through negotiation. *But bidding works only for the must-have shows that are truly megahits.* An atmosphere of anticipation has to preexist, and stations must have a strong desire to own the program.

Stations generally dislike bidding. It often forces them to pay more than they normally would. In a negotiation, station management usually gets a feel for the degree of competing interest and the syndicator's minimum selling price. In a bidding war, stations get little sense of the competition for the show. A station may be the only bidder, in which case it bids against itself. It may also bid substantially more than any other bidder, a waste of money. In this situation, each station works in the dark, which can be unsettling. However, stations realize that if they want to be in the ball game for a bid show, the syndicator not only owns the bat and ball but also makes the rules.

Payment

Payment for programming takes one of three basic forms: *cash, barter* or *cash-plus-barter*. Payout arrangements vary and are usually negotiated.

Cash and Amortization

Cash license fees are paid as money (rather than in airtime, as with barter). In most cases, cash deals are like house mortgages or auto loans. An initial down payment is generally made at the time the contract is signed, followed by installment payments over a set period of time. The down payment is generally a comparatively small portion of the total contract amount, perhaps 10 or 15 percent. The remaining payments are triggered when the station begins using the program, or at a mutually agreed-upon date, either of which may be a month or two or several years after the contract is signed. If the contract is for a relatively short amount of time or a low purchase price, the payments will be made over a short period of time. A one-year deal may have 12 equal monthly payments, and a six-month deal may be paid in only two or three installments; however, a five-year contract may be paid out over three years in 36 equal monthly payments, beginning when the contract is triggered. No payments would be due in years four or five of the contract.

When stations buy programs for cash, whether negotiated or bid, they pay out the cash to the syndicator on an agreed-upon schedule, but they allocate the cost of the program against their operating budget via an amortization schedule. *Amortization* is an accounting principle wherein the total cost of the program is allocated as an operating budget expense on a regular (monthly) basis over all or a portion of the term of the license. Thus, stations control and apportion operating expenses to maintain a profit margin. Amortization does not affect the syndicator or the amount paid to the syndicator (payout).

Depending on the intended method of airing the program, amortization may be taken at regular weekly or monthly intervals or as the runs are actually used. In the case of programs intended to be played week in, week out without hiatus (such as most first-run and some off-network shows), amortization is taken every week or month without exception. This allows a station to predict its ongoing program costs, but it does not allow the station to avoid those costs should it remove the program from its schedule.

Alternatively, for most off-network shows and feature films, the show or movie is expensed (amortized) as runs are taken of the individual episodes or titles. The amount amortized each week or month will vary depending on the number of runs used. If a station must reduce operating expenses, it can do so by *resting* (placing on hiatus) a program or running less expensive movie titles. Conversely, in a period of strong revenues, a station can *play off* (run) more expensive shows or movies. In this manner, a station can control its operating costs to a degree. If, however, a station does not play off all the episodes before the end of the contract, it may find itself with unamortized dollars that have to be expensed. Thus, amortization can be a double-edged sword, and the programming executive has to be a bit of an accountant as well as a creative programmer.

Amortization Schedules

Amortization schedules differ from station to station, depending on corporate policy. Some stations use different schedules for different program types or planned usages. The two most widely used amortization schedules are *straight-line* and *declining-value.*

Straight-line amortization places an equal value on each run of each episode. If a program cost a station $10,000 per episode for five runs of each episode, straight-line amortization would be computed by dividing the five runs into the $10,000 cost per episode, yielding an amortized cost per run of $2,000 (20 percent of the purchase price, in this case). If the station had negotiated more runs at the same per-episode license fee, the cost per run would decline. For example, had the station purchased eight runs for $10,000, the straight-line amortized cost would be $1,250 per run. The lower amortized cost would reduce the station's operating budget by $750 each time the show is run. On a five-day-a-week strip over 52 weeks (260 runs in a year), the $750-per-run savings would total $195,000, a sizable amount. (Thus, it is important to negotiate well to get as many runs as possible.) The station would still pay the syndicator the full $10,000 per episode, multiplied by the total number of episodes.

With *declining-value amortization,* each run of an episode is assigned a different value on the premise that the value of each episode diminishes each time it airs. Thus, the first run may be expensed at

a higher percentage of total cost than is the second run, and the second run may be expensed higher than the third run, and so forth. A typical declining-value amortization schedule for five runs of a program might look like this:

First run	40 percent
Second run	30 percent
Third run	20 percent
Fourth run	10 percent
Fifth run	0 percent

If we compared the same program under straight-line and declining-value amortization systems, operating expenses would be as follows:

	Straight-line	Declining-value
First run	$2,000 (20%)	$4,000 (40%)
Second run	2,000 (20%)	3,000 (30%)
Third run	2,000 (20%)	2,000 (20%)
Fourth run	2,000 (20%)	1,000 (10%)
Fifth run	2,000 (20%)	(0%)
Total	$10,000 per episode	$10,000 per episode

In both schemes, the total amortized amount over the five runs is the full per-episode cost of the program. In the straight-line method, the station expenses each run (or "charges" itself) equally, even though the show's performance may decline as more runs are taken of each episode. An advantage of this method is that the initial run or runs are comparatively inexpensive, especially if the show performs well. A disadvantage is that the final run is just as expensive as the first run, even though the show's popularity may have faded and the ratings declined.

Under the declining-value method, the bulk of the amortization is taken on the initial runs, when the ratings would presumably be at their highest. Relatively few dollars would remain to be expensed in the final runs. In this example, 70 percent of the program's cost is taken in the first two runs under the declining-value system, but only 40 percent is taken for the same two runs straight-lined. If the show falls apart in the ratings after two or three runs, the station using the declining-value method has already put most of its financial obligation behind it, but the station using straight-line amortization has the bulk of the expense still to come.

In the example, using the declining-value method amortizes all the expense of each episode over the first four runs. Because stations sometimes fail to use all the available runs of a program, the fifth run at no charge can be quite helpful to a station. If the run is not taken, there is no charge against the show as there would be in the straight-line system. (Not all declining-value amortization schedules provide free runs; some companies place some value even on the final run, which serves to reduce the expense on the earlier runs, at least slightly.)

The straight-line system is frequently used to amortize first-run shows that are expensed on a weekly basis and generally run no more than twice per episode. *The declining-value system is often used for off-network programs and feature films* that are generally expensed on a per-run basis and are sold with 5 to 10 runs per episode or film.

Finally, amortization is only an internal allocation of dollars against usage. It does not change the payout of the license fee to the syndicator. The program may be fully run and amortized before payout is completed, or the station may continue taking runs of the show for years after the payout to the syndicator is complete, with the amortization of the episodes allowing the expense against the operating budget to be delayed until the programs are actually run. When all episodes are fully amortized and all payments made to the syndicator, the final dollars expensed in both amortization and payout will be identical.

Barter and Cash-Plus-Barter

The second payment method is *barter*. Barter is a fairly simple payment system. The station agrees to run national commercials sold by the syndicator in return for the right to air the program. No money changes hands. The syndicator makes all of its money from the sale of commercials to national advertisers, and the station gives up some of the commercial time it or its rep would have had to sell. A typical straight barter deal might give half of the advertising time within a program to the syndicator, with the other half available for station sale. For example, a half-hour program with six minutes of available commercial time might allocate three minutes to the syndicator and three minutes to the station.

Cash-plus-barter means exactly what the name suggests. Part of the license fee is paid in cash, albeit a lower cash license fee than if the show were sold for straight cash, and part of the license fee is given by the station to the syndicator as commercial time, which the syndicator sells to national advertisers. A typical cash-plus-barter deal for a half-hour show might be a cash license fee plus one minute of commercial time (1:00 national) for the syndicator, with the station retaining five-and-a-half minutes (5:30 local) for its own sale.

Barter can be both a blessing and a curse. On the plus side, barter can be a way of reducing cash expense at a station. In some cases, especially for untried and unproven first-run shows, stations may be more willing to give up commercial airtime than to spend money. If a syndicator takes three minutes of commercial time within a half-hour show and the station receives three minutes, the syndicator has received 50 percent of the available commercial time, and the station retains 50 percent. As you saw earlier, stations generally figure 30 to 50 percent of their revenue goes to programming expense, so barter may seem expensive. But because stations are rarely 100 percent sold out and may average only an 80 to 90 percent sellout over a year, the barter time the station gives up really represents only 30 to 40 percent of revenue potential.

Because most syndicated programs today contain some barter time, barter can be problematic. Some stations embrace barter so they don't have to spend real money. Others dislike it because commitments to many shows with heavy barter loads mean significantly less time for the station to sell, hence less revenue. A typical barter deal could result in as much as half of the commercial inventory not being available to the station to sell. Also, the station may not want to give its time to a third party to sell, often at lower rates than the station itself is charging, because the syndicator is selling many markets as a package.

Regardless of a station's feelings regarding barter, it has no choice about whether to pay cash or give up barter airtime for a show. The syndicator determines the payment terms, not the station. The station's only option is whether to run the program. If it doesn't like the terms, it doesn't have to clear the show.

Barter and cash-plus-barter are used primarily for the sale of first-run programs and the first syndication cycle of off-network programs because barter is an effective way for syndicators to maximize revenues to fully cover production and distribution costs. Producing first-run shows is generally expensive, and stations are often unwilling to pay sufficiently high license fees for untried first-run programs. The syndicator's other choice is to cover production and distribution costs by bartering a program. By combining cash payment and several barter commercials a day in the first syndication cycle of an off-network program, the syndicator can maximize revenue while allowing the station to spend less actual money than if the program were sold for cash only. Older off-network sitcoms, action hours and dramas are generally sold for straight cash with no barter because production costs have already been covered and demand for these programs is less.

Even though clearance in every market in the country is the goal, the syndicator must sell the show to stations in enough markets to represent at least 70 to 80 percent of all U.S. television households. Based on this minimum figure, the syndicator projects a national rating and, using a national cost per point, determines a rate for each 30-second commercial. The syndicator then attempts to sell all the national time in the show to national advertisers at, or as close as possible to, the determined rate. The syndicator tries to clear the show in the strongest time periods on the strongest stations to achieve the highest rating. The ratings from all markets clearing the show are averaged to produce a national rating that will, it is hoped, equal or exceed the projected rating. If the syndicator can get the 70 to 80 percent national clearance, sell all the spots at or

near the rate card price, and deliver the rating promised to advertisers, the syndicator will make money, and the show will stay on the air. If not, the syndicator will likely lose money, and the show might not be renewed.

In an effort to increase the rating and therefore the revenue potential, some syndicated programs are run twice during the same week. For example, a program that runs Monday through Friday during prime access and averages a 5 rating may be rerun the same night during the overnight hours (between 1:00 and 5:00 A.M.), where it might average a 1 rating. The prime-access 5 rating and the overnight 1 rating can be added together to *cume* a 6 rating. This cumed (or cumulative) rating is considered unduplicated viewing because most people would not watch the same program twice the same day. Thus, the program has a cumed rating of 6, which is 20 percent higher than the 5 it achieved in prime access. A 20 percent higher rating can translate into 20 percent more revenue, which could represent significant money during the course of a year to the syndicator.

Although no standardized ratio of national-to-local commercial time exists, half-hour straight barter shows typically range from two minutes national/four minutes local (generally expressed as 2:00N/4:00L) to as much as 3:30N/3:30L. Hour-long barter shows typically contain from 3:30N/10:30L to as much as 9:00N/5:00L. A one-hour cash-plus-barter program would typically be cut in the ranges from 2:00N/12:00L to 3:30N/10:30L, plus that would be the cash payment. The amount of national barter time the syndicator can withhold depends on the perceived demand for and strength of the program and the ability of the syndicator's station sales force.[5]

Cable and Syndication

Broadcast syndicators have found cable networks to be a ready and growing market for programs. Instead of sending a large sales force to call on three to eight stations in each of the 210 local markets to sell a program in syndication, that same program is frequently sold to a national cable network in a single deal. Often the cable price exceeds what might be made in broadcast syndication. Also, sales staff salaries and travel expenses are saved. With more potential customers needing to fill 168 hours a week of airtime, cable syndication has become an extremely lucrative marketplace.

More recent and vintage off-network programs, not to mention new and continuing first-run programs, are available than can be fit into traditional broadcast station schedules. The huge supply of programs and reduced broadcast demand have thus forced the creation of a cable aftermarket. Some cable networks program their schedules much as independent broadcast television stations once did, stripping off-network shows and movies (for example, USA's *Law & Order: Special Victims Unit* followed by a feature film) and vintage programs. Others buy failed network or syndicated programs at appealingly low prices because these shows either don't have enough episodes for syndication or have already failed in syndication.

A cable network can make an opportunistic purchase and program the shows effectively for its needs. Basic cable has become a hot competitive marketplace for feature films after their pay-cable and network exposure and before broadcast syndication. The same is true for off-network shows. Broadcasters' place in line is pushed further back, not nearly as central to program distribution when this chapter was first conceived. Even more disruptive has been the recent growth in online syndication, discussed previously in Chapter 4 and again later in this chapter.

To maximize revenue potential for network programs, the enduring trend has been to sell off-network rights simultaneously to both traditional broadcast stations and cable networks, with the latter bidding higher for the top shows. Although the types of deals may be limited only by the imagination and creativity of the sellers and buyers, perhaps the most common arrangement has become a weekly run on a television station (one showing of each episode) followed by a Monday through Friday strip run on a cable network. A popular and long-running program might also run simultaneously on different venues: (1)

on the original broadcast network with newly produced episodes for the network, (2) weekly repeats from previous seasons on local television stations once a week, and (3) the same weekly repeats on a cable network as a strip.

Yet another arrangement is a simultaneous run of brand-new episodes on both a broadcast network and a cable network. For example, from the beginning of its network run, *Law & Order: Special Victims Unit* ran on the NBC television network with a repeat play several days later on the co-owned USA cable network.

In still another arrangement, a program may be created for a basic cable network and simultaneous first-run syndication. For example, *The Invisible Man* was created with this idea in mind, taking its first run on the Syfy Channel followed by a first-run syndication appearance of the same episode two weeks later on broadcast television stations in syndication. Somewhat similarly, *Monk* was created for initial runs on USA and at a later date was played on the traditional NBC network.

Hollywood studios command steep prices when they sell off-network shows into syndication on cable networks. Table 6.10 shows some recent prices.

Inevitably, *the once-rigid relationships of syndication, broadcast television and cable will continue to evolve and interweave, leading to new and evermore innovative marketing schemes that involve online distribution.* Just when all participants think they understand how the business works, someone invents a better (or at least different) mousetrap.

Online Syndication

Online shows fall into the same categories discussed earlier in the chapter (off-net, off-cable, first-run, movies), but the sales process is still being formed. Wrote one observer: "online video syndication is still feeling its way … there are no rules for online syndication. And while everyone agrees that syndication is the future of online video, no one knows what the field will look like in 5 or 10 years."[6]

| 6.10 | Prices for Off-Network Program Sold to Cable Networks |

Hour-longs:

Show	Cable Net	$ per episode	Year
Hawaii Five-0	TNT	2,500,000	2011
Glee	Oxygen	500,000	2010
NCIS: Los Angeles	USA	2,200,000	2009
The Mentalist	TNT	2,000,000	2009
Ugly Betty	TV Guide	200,000	2009
Bones	TNT	450,000	2008
Criminal Minds	A&E	650,000	2008
Lost	Sci-Fi/G4	200,000	2008

Half-hours:

Show	Cable Net	$ per episode	Year
Modern Family	USA	1,400,000	2010
The Big Bang Theory	TBS	1,500,000	2010
The Cleveland Show	TBS/Adult Swim	500,000	2010
30 Rock	Comedy Central	800,000	2009
Curb Your Enthusiasm	TV Guide/TV Land	600,000	2009
Entourage	Spike	600,000	2009
It's Always Sunny in Philadelphia	Comedy Central	700,000	2009
Old Christine	Lifetime	350,000	2009
How I Met Your Mother	Lifetime	750,000	2008

YouTube, Vimeo and Blip.tv are planning to develop long-form, professionally-produced, first-run programs for online streaming, and others probably have similar plans. Blip.tv embeds sponsors' ads in contributors' videos and pays a share of the revenue to those who produce the videos (especially program-length series). While not everyone who has the talent to make compelling television shows can get a broadcast or cable deal, online distributors are now positioned to obtain revenue for any producer's content that can draw an audience. Funnyordie.com, for example, is a source of satiric programming, and it attracts audiences and thus advertisers.

A decade ago, websites like Atom tried to market informally-produced videos to advertisers but failed. However, now potential audiences are much better connected to wireless computers, phones and iPad-type tablets, with much faster streaming speeds.

Online viewership is projected to reach over 1.3 billion people worldwide by 2016.

Off-cable shows that went to broadcast stations, after some editing, are now sold directly to online distributors (in addition to the usual DVD sales). For example, after a six-season run of *Nip/Tuck* on the FX cable network, Warner Bros. Home Entertainment struck a syndication deal with Netflix to stream all 100 episodes of *Nip/Tuck*, as well as three other Warner Bros.-produced series, *Veronica Mars*, *Pushing Daisies* and *Terminator: The Sarah Connor Chronicles*.

DVD sales of off-cable series have been declining as more homes sign onto monthly subscriptions of streaming services like Netflix and Hulu Plus, which each charge $7.99 per month. By 2010, Netflix began offering producers $70,000 to $100,000 per off-network episode, just for streaming rights, which do not preclude syndication to other networks (except Hulu Plus, of course). It remains unclear whether Hollywood is entirely comfortable with this arrangement. Also, other companies that stream videos (Apple, Amazon, Google, YouTube) are very likely to start bidding wars for hit shows. Cable operators will likely compete with their own streaming services (TV Everywhere or Comcast's Xfinity—See Chapter 4).

At present, movies hold the strongest potential for online distribution. Netflix is the leader, streaming movies to 23 million subscribers in 2011. In contrast, YouTube streams an enormous 3 billion videos per day. And it has just begun to move to long-form content like movies. Hulu Plus also carries movies, and smaller competitors like Crackle show movies in addition to reruns of *Seinfeld. Where all this is going is pretty clear; the questions to guess at are how soon, how will it be paid for, and who owns everything.*

The International Marketplace

From the earliest days of television syndication through the late 1990s, the international syndication marketplace was fairly predictable and understandable. A program created in one country for domestic syndication, network or cable might also be sold in other countries, thus extending the revenue potential for the program. The basic syndication "rules" were pretty much the same in international syndication as in domestic. Then, as the twenty-first century approached, something entirely unforeseen happened: A totally new and exciting arena opened up, producing vast new creative and sales potential. Although the traditional international syndication market is still very active and important, new programming and marketing concepts are changing the face of the international marketplace. Let's look first at the traditional, tried-and-true international syndication realm.

The Traditional Pattern

Just as American syndicators have found multiple program sales opportunities in this country in network, syndication and cable, they have also extended the revenue potential of programs through syndication in international markets. Although most American television programs are produced in English, foreign broadcasters and cable networks find American programming very attractive. There is a worldwide appetite for things American (Mickey Mouse, Coca-Cola and McDonald's hamburgers, to name but a few); people in other nations also love American television shows and movies. Thus many, but certainly not all, American television programs find life in other countries. Often they are dubbed into another language. They may also be aired in English, either with or without subtitles, depending in part on the level of English spoken by citizens of a particular country and on the expense of dubbing or subtitling.

Even within the same country, some broadcasters may opt to dub, while others may choose to subtitle, and still others may air the program in its original language. Though policies among companies may differ for various reasons, often the expense of dubbing is the determining factor. As a matter of course, programs for young children are almost always dubbed: They can't read yet!

In many ways, the syndication process in the international marketplace is very similar to the domestic sales effort. Syndicators have websites, and salespeople send tempting emails and then visit stations and cable networks in cities throughout foreign countries. A domestic salesperson may go on the road for several days in the southwestern United States, traveling from Dallas to Albuquerque to Lubbock. Conversely, the international syndicator may go on a sales trip of several weeks, ranging throughout the Pacific Rim from Hong Kong to Tokyo to Fiji to Samoa. Although a domestic syndicator's biggest cultural problems may be regional accents and local food, the international salesperson encounters language barriers and quite different customs. Many certainly find this makes their jobs both more challenging and more interesting.

As in this country, programs are sold for various combinations of cash and barter time. The amounts of cash involved, however, are generally substantially less. The production costs of a program are usually recouped in the United States through sales to broadcast networks, local television stations and cable networks. International sales become the icing on the cake.

In some instances, especially for first-run syndicated shows, a program is created with American and international partners *cofinancing* the production and distribution costs and then splitting the revenue. For example, an American company may team with French and Australian partners. Generally, each coproduction partner retains the rights to the production in its own country or territory. The American partner may retain North American rights, the French company the rights to France and Europe, and the Australian producer the rights throughout the Pacific Rim. Rights in Asia, South America and Africa might be sold to an entirely separate company. The divvying up of rights often depends on the individual clout of the production partners and how much they are contributing to the production, including both money and facilities.

A program may even be shot in one of the partner countries such as Australia and may use talent and production crews from one or more of the countries represented. Sometimes this is done to meet national employment quotas or for nationalistic pride, but more frequently the purpose is to lower production costs. In the United States, we enjoy a high standard of living; we also have high labor and other production costs. Although shooting a series in a country such as Australia may sound exotic, it is usually done primarily with an eye on the bottom line.

Unlike program production in the United States, when shows are produced in other countries for airing in those countries or in the international marketplace, the producers must generally conform to various quotas. Often a country will require that certain percentages of the people employed for the production of a program be citizens of that country. This extends from the stars and other on-camera talent to the behind-the-scenes people, including producers, writers, technicians, wardrobe people, stagehands, secretaries and even drivers.

Quotas of a different sort must also be considered. Many countries regulate the percentage of a program schedule that must originate within that country, leaving the remaining portion of the schedule that may be made up of programs produced in other countries. For example, the European Union is very restrictive regarding the amount of programming that must contain European content. Furthermore, within a single European country, certain percentages must be created within that nation. In France, for example, not only must a certain percentage of the programs carried on the French network Canal+ be European, but some must also be produced in France. Within the EU, quotas are the same among all European countries, but quotas may be significantly different in other areas of the world.

In the United States, there are no restrictions or quotas whatever regarding either national program origination or employment. American producers are subject only to U.S. labor laws regarding noncitizens.

When a program is produced by or taped in several countries, quotas become even trickier. Selling foreign-produced programs to customers in another country requires consideration of that nation's employment requirements and content quotas, among other things. This is one of the reasons why fewer and fewer American prime-time series are finding their way onto other nations' television screens.

For years, most programming went in one direction: from the United States to other countries. Relatively little programming flowed from other nations into the United States. American dramatic and action shows generally sold best in other countries. Although car crashes, whodunits and prime-time soaps seem to have universal appeal, comedy shows often didn't fare as well. What's a knee slapper or rib tickler in one part of the globe may not seem so funny in other areas.

American movies have long been popular in most other countries. During the 1980s and 1990s, the Hollywood studios increasingly made *output deals* in which substantial amounts of programming from a studio were sold in advance in other countries. This helped to finance the production costs of the shows and to give relative assurance that a program actually would be produced. Some people have dubbed this period the Golden Age of Export.

The birth of new broadcast and cable networks in the United States and throughout the world in the 1980s and 1990s created a tremendous demand for fresh programming. The rise of the FOX network had enormous impact not only in the United States but also around the world. FOX programs such as *Beverly Hills 90210* and *The Simpsons* became so popular in other countries that they became *global brands*, much like Nike and Microsoft.

Many American cable networks have also become global brands. MTV has cable networks in many areas of the world programmed in the languages of the local countries. The Discovery Channel is also global, with localized programming in Africa, Asia, Europe, Latin America and the Middle East as well as in individual countries, including Australia, Brazil, Canada, Germany, Italy and India. Fox Kids Network, E! and TNT are also seen in many countries. And CNN is the original worldwide network, viewed around the globe since the 1980s.

Global branding has become commonplace in broadcast and cable circles. Often branding goes far beyond an individual program or character (see 6.11).

The Emerging Pattern

As the twenty-first century began, an extremely significant change occurred in the international marketplace. With deregulation and a single monetary standard sweeping Europe, there was a desire for strong locally-produced programming coupled with an ability to export such programming—to America among other places. As a result, *format programming* emerged as a dominant trend. (Formatting is essentially the same as franchising.) And unfortunately, we then saw the end of the Golden Age.

To understand format programming, think of *Wheel of Fortune* and *Who Wants to Be a Millionaire?*. Both programs were created in one country (*Wheel* by producer Merv Griffin and syndicator King World Productions in the United States, *Millionaire* by producer Michael Davies and the BBC in England). In each case, the format is licensed to broadcasters in other countries. Many of the

---

6.11   Global Branding by Nickelodeon

Nickelodeon has created branded blocks of programming both for its own international services and for sale to other companies in countries where Nick does not have its own operations. Nickelodeon provides not only several hours of the programs themselves but also interstitial materials such as promos and IDs and website content. As a further extension of branding and its image, Nickelodeon also licenses ancillary rights and services. Included are product licensing and merchandising (toys and games), video and audio products (CDs, videocassettes and DVDs), and publishing rights (books and magazines). Like many other companies, Nickelodeon believes its trademark is valuable, and it carefully guards the environment in which its programming and image are presented around the world.

As communications shrink the world, programs and program concepts are becoming both more global and more utilized. For example, Nickelodeon created *Rugrats* as a U.S. cable program. The show has since been aired around the world. In Great Britain alone, *Rugrats* can be seen on the BBC (the British Broadcasting Corporation's terrestrial broadcast network), Nick UK (basic cable and direct broadcast satellite) and Nick Replay (digital TV). With an eye to the future, when Nickelodeon develops programs or acquires program rights, their programmers attempt to do so for all Nickelodeon venues (Nick US, Nick UK, Nick Australia and so on). Such strategy is not unique to Nickelodeon; indeed, many multinational companies employ the same approach.

---

production elements (scripts, music, scenery design, sound effects, questions and so on) are provided by the program creators, but local hosts and contestants are used in each country. Scripts are tailored to local interests, habits and language (the American word *cookie* would be changed to *biscuit* in England, for example).

Even the name may be changed to reflect local culture and language. (For example, the most popular syndicated show in the United States is still called

Wheel of Fortune in Australia, but its name becomes *Roda a Roda* in Brazil, *La Ruleta de la Fortuna* in Ecuador, *Glücksrad* in Germany, *Roda Impian* in Malaysia, *Carkifelek* in Turkey, and *Chiêc nôn kŷ diêu* in Viet Nam. And *Jeopardy!* becomes *Your Own Game* [in Russian].)

In some cases, actual video portions of the program may be supplied. (For its preschool program *Blues Clues,* Nickelodeon provided all the animation; the various international broadcasters then chromakeyed their own local live actors over the animation.) Perhaps most important, the shows are produced in the local languages. Thus, *Wheel* has its own British Pat Sajak and successors to the classic Vanna White. Meanwhile, the British host of *Millionaire* was replaced by Regis Philbin in this country. Both shows air in Japan with Japanese hosts, in France with French hosts and so forth.

Format programming has tremendously affected international syndication. What had been pretty much a one-way flow of programs from the United States to other countries has been abruptly changed. *Product flow from Europe to the United States and other countries is now the largest ever.* This phenomenon has resulted in vast new creative and sales potential.

What Lies Ahead for Syndication

Syndication is a rapidly changing business. Headlines in trade publications frequently herald new and innovative syndication deals. Although it is speculative at best to imagine how the industry might look by the end of this decade, several scenarios are plausible.

1. **Innovative deal structuring.** As the financial stakes get higher and competition becomes fiercer, syndicators and stations alike will become more and more creative in their deal making. Broadcast syndicators will make offers more attractive to stations while simultaneously finding new ways to increase revenue to their own bottom line. This may involve barter, payout, additional daily or weekend runs, sharing use with cable, cofinancing

with station groups, hiatus periods and ancillary revenue sources. Deal structure will be limited only by the ingenuity of the participants and will be driven by the need to maximize profits for both syndicators and stations.

2. **Cost control.** Stations and syndicators are continually striving to manage costs. The days of heady economic growth and comfortable profits between the 1970s and early 1990s seem only a pleasant memory in the 2000s. In the wake of new competition from cable and the softening of the world economy, costs must be controlled. Therefore, whether in deal making, station operation or expansion of facilities or staffs, broadcasters and syndicators alike share a common goal: the need for efficiency, streamlining, mutually beneficial dealing and use of all assets. With FCC regulations allowing ownership of more stations by each individual broadcasting company, and with mergers of many syndicators, cost controls become ever more important, even as the programming deals are becoming bigger.

3. **Consortiums/coproduction/co-ventures.** All these terms mean much the same thing: Station groups and syndicators are increasingly finding new and exciting ways to work together as partners. Spurred by tough economic times and the need to control costs, station groups and syndicators can share costs and risks and, perhaps, profits. Station groups will continue to join forces with one another in noncompeting markets to develop and launch first-run programs to meet specific station needs. Increasingly, syndicators will join in these co-ventures. Because stations will hold an equity position in some shows, these shows will probably gain some extra promotion and perhaps be given a longer time on the air to prove themselves. In other words, coproduced shows will get a good shot at succeeding (if the audience likes them!).

4. **Cable, internet and mobile media.** Increasingly, programs created for original telecast via one delivery system are finding their way to another: over-the-air to cable and vice versa; network to either broadcast syndication or cable; cable to syndication; cable to foreign; foreign to domestic syndication.

And the internet and various mobile media will become increasing parts of these aftermarkets. Several crisscrossing paths already exist, and the line between network/syndication/cable is now blurring. In fact, the broadcast networks routinely promote their cable programs on network shows airing on local affiliates; talent is frequently utilized for both network and cable telecasts. As cable has grown and solidified its economic base, syndicators have played to that strength. Once traditional adversaries, now cable and broadcast have formed co-ventures that will benefit both. Just as politics make strange bedfellows, so too do the economic needs of the television industry.

The internet and mobile media have rapidly become the next challenges for broadcasters, syndicators and networks. Although the internet and smart phones offer great opportunities for extending program and product reach and for promoting a program or an entire brand, they also create huge challenges—even threats. Decisions must be made on how to sell a program on the internet and to mobile media, how to charge, and how to protect a copyright. Once a program or portion of a program is on the internet, it essentially becomes available to any person or company in the entire world. The owners of the program and the content copyright need to figure out how to protect their financial and other interests. Producers usually make programs because of their enormous revenue potential from domestic and international syndication, and the syndication process involves hundreds of millions of dollars annually across the United States. The rise of the internet and mobile media potentially challenges all these assumptions.

5. **Increasing role of reps.** Programmers at station representative firms will play an even greater role in the syndication process. As costs escalate and programming decisions become riskier, the rep programmer's expertise becomes more valuable. To control costs, many stations have eliminated the program director position and are using rep programmers instead. This trend is likely to continue.

6. **Increasing role of networks.** With the demise of the FCC's financial and syndication rules, the networks have become actively involved with the production of syndicated shows. Many expect the prime-access period (7 to 8 P.M. EST) to attract more off-network programs now that the Prime-Time Access Rule (PTAR) is long gone. First-run game shows and magazine formats have outlived their protected existence in the top 50 markets. Increased competition for hit off-network programs will affect the price for these shows.

Just as the children and teenagers of the 1950s and 1960s grew up watching *I Love Lucy, The Flintstones* and *The Brady Bunch,* so too the next generation found enduring favorites in *The Cosby Show, The Simpsons* and *Married … with Children.* Today's teens and adults expect police departments to conduct advanced crime-scene investigation because they watched so many episodes of *CSI, Without a Trace, Cold Case* and their clones. This generation has taken *Ugly Betty* and *Grey's Anatomy* into their lives. Television shows are valuable assets that can enjoy a long economic lifespan. Old favorites in broadcast syndication continue to play and play and play. And the needs of cable have extended the life of many seemingly lesser programs, while the internet offers worldwide opportunities to unknown producers.

While sitcoms are still important in syndication, hour-long network dramas generally are not as desirable for television stations because it is harder to find one-hour blocks of time on stations that will reach large audiences (outside of prime time—it's named that for the obvious reason). Also, because many hour-long shows tend to be serial in nature (*Grey's Anatomy, 24, Lost*), once the outcome is known from the original network run, the dramatic tension and viewer interest surrounding these programs tend to lessen. Their network rerun ratings are generally considerably lower than their original run rating, foretelling potential lower ratings in syndication. First-run series, on the other hand, draw viewers who are more likely to watch live, thus using DVRs less, which results in greater viewing of commercials.

Some of these hour programs may be sold in syndication as once-a-week hours for weekend runs, while others are sold directly to cable networks following their over-the-air network runs. Other hours (such as *Law & Order* and *CSI*) are sold directly to cable networks, bypassing syndication. For the rights holders, the lack of domestic syndication potential is often offset by sales to international buyers for broadcast in other countries.

The Peter Allen song "Everything Old Is New Again" at one time applied to the syndication potential of most programs going directly to television stations. Nowadays, especially with the rapid growth of cable and online networks plus tablets, program producers have many more potential buyers for programs when they finish their originals runs on network television. If only enough advertisers would catch up to pay for the game.

Notes

1. In the media business, a *station group* is made up of television stations in two or more different markets owned by one company, and relaxed FCC cross-ownership rules now sometimes permit a single company to own two stations within some larger markets.

2. FireWire, also called i.Link and Lynz, is Apple's standard for high-speed data transfer to computers (like USB). The system is copyrighted and fees are high, so FireWire is used by the television industry but not the general public.

Known technically as IEEE 1394, the descriptively-named FireWire system provides high-definition audio/video connections for speedy transfer of such programming as syndicated series episodes and movies. As you can imagine, "emailing" a whole movie or two dozen episodes necessitates high-quality and high-speed capacity.

3. A few shows move the other direction. The game show *Remote Control* went from cable to broadcast syndication, the first of a new stream of programs for the syndication market.

4. In cases where the rep is negative toward the program, avoiding an in-person pitch to reps generally has the advantage of minimizing the strength of the rep's recommendation to stations. Opinions tend to be stronger about shows that have been evaluated firsthand. Reps eventually see pilots or sample tapes of all shows their client stations are interested in, but delay sometimes works to the temporary advantage of the syndicator.

5. Barter splits may vary widely, even among essentially similar programs. For example, *Jerry Springer, Oprah* and *Jenny Jones* are all cash-plus-barter, one-hour talk-show strips, but the national/local barter splits are quite different, with *Jenny Jones's* syndicator having considerably more national time to sell than *Jerry Springer's* distribution company: *Jerry Springer,* 2:30N/12:00L; *Oprah,* 3:00N/11:00L; *Jenny Jones,* 3:30N/10:30L.

6. Troy Dreier, "Syndicate of Die," *http://www.streamingmedia.com/Articles/Editorial/Featured-Articles/Syndicate-or-Die-65694.aspx.*

PART

4

Television Programming Practices

Part Four Outline

CHAPTER

7

Non-Prime-Time Network Programming

Robert V. Bellamy and James R. Walker

Chapter Outline

The migration of television audiences away from the big broadcast networks to the ever-increasing number of alternative video outlets has greatly accelerated in the last five years—a phenomenon that won't be a surprise to you! As Chapter 2 pointed out, even a cursory glance at prime-time schedules shows that network TV has struggled in its attempts to reach and maintain audiences with value to advertisers. Similar pressures have come to major segments of non-prime-time. *In fact, network Monday–Friday daytime programming has experienced some of the most radical changes of all: The iconic soap opera format now is rapidly fading away, and more and more time slots are being returned to affiliates (who hardly know what to do with them). Talk programs have become indistinguishable from syndicated offerings and make up more and more of what is left of daytime network programming.*

For the popular media, *prime-time* television is *television.* Much of national and local coverage of television focuses on evening programs. Critical reviews, star interviews and Nielsen ratings for the top prime-time programs are readily available. Because prime time is the subject of such intense reporting, you might think the rest of the day is insignificant. Not true. Daytime talk and late-night comedy are frequently the most provocative and—significantly for the U.S. broadcast networks—*most profitable* shows on television. *The difference between what a program costs to produce and the advertising revenue it generates is its profit.* Because non-prime-time programs are generally inexpensive to produce and carry more ads than prime time, their ratings can be relatively modest and still supply huge profits for the networks. In addition, non-prime-time audiences are less demographically diverse, making it easier for advertisers to target their commercials to consumers most interested in their products. This means more compatibility between a program and its spots (less viewer annoyance) and less advertising waste (fewer commercials directed to wrong viewers) than in prime time with its larger but more diverse audiences.

Nonprime-time viewers are often more loyal to their programs than prime-time viewers. Many football fans plan their whole week around Saturday college and Sunday professional games, and the network programmer who preempts a weekday soap opera or *The View* for a special program will receive an avalanche of unpleasant tweets and emails. Despite steadily decreasing audiences, millions of Americans still use network evening news as a daily information ritual, and Letterman or Leno as a daily bedtime ritual.

Networks generating the largest advertising revenues have the most non-prime-time programming. Programmers cannot ignore the non-evening programs because there are many more hours to program than in prime time. More than any other type of programming, the non-prime period distinguishes the oldest broadcast networks (ABC, CBS, NBC) from their more recent competitors. The long-established presence of the Big Three in virtually all nonprime dayparts provides them with heaps of commercial availabilities to sell to advertisers. ABC, CBS, and NBC each sells more than three times as many commercial minutes as FOX, the most active of the other English-language networks.

The primary reason for this vast disparity in the networks' most basic product, *advertising availabilities*, is that the newer networks take a different approach to nonprime-time programming. With the important exceptions of sports on FOX, newer networks have not competed successfully in nonprime time. Instead of challenging long-running programs in early morning, daytime, and late night, the CW and MNTV try to capture viewers' attention in prime time, while ION strips older family-oriented reality shows. Univision, by contrast, successfully fills many of its nonprime hours with talk shows and *telenovelas* (television novels similar to soap operas, but with a definite ending after some months or years) and carries major international sports on weekends.

NonPrime-Time Dayparts

Nonprime time is a broad term encompassing all the programming dayparts other than prime time. The U.S. broadcast television networks program some or all of the following dayparts (reflected in eastern/ Pacific times) with several types of programming.

Weekday Programming

Overnight	2:05 A.M.–6 A.M.	News
Early morning	6 A.M.–9 A.M.	Magazine
Daytime	10 A.M.–4 P.M.	Soaps/Game shows/Talk
Early fringe	4 P.M.–6 P.M.	Children's*
Early evening	6:30 P.M.–7 P.M.	News
Late night	11:35 P.M.–2:05 A.M.	Talk/news

*Daytime children's programming has been abandoned by all the major English-language networks in recent years. This is another example of how niche-oriented cable networks (e.g., Disney Channel, Nickelodeon) have replaced one of the traditional functions of broadcast television.

Weekend Programming

Weekend mornings	8 A.M.–1 P.M.	Children's/ Magazine
Weekend afternoons	1 P.M.–7 P.M.	Sports
Weekend late night	11 P.M.–1 A.M.	Comedy/ Music

The size of the audiences in non-prime dayparts is considerably smaller than in prime time, but all nonprime-time dayparts contribute competitively and economically to a network's performance. Programming executives responsible for nonprime dayparts are as dedicated to competing for available viewers as are their evening counterparts. In prime-time programming, the "war" fought night after night is measured in daily ratings gains or losses. Although daily ratings are important to shows in nonprime time, the key to the battle is to get viewers into the habit of watching weekday nonprime programs every day or from week to week. With the exception of Univision's *Sabado Gigante*, all ten of the longest-running programs on the networks are non-prime series (see 7.1).

In *prime time*, ratings for the Big Four broadcast networks average between approximately 2.0 and 8.0 nowadays and range from about a 1.5 at the bottom end to about 8.0 or occasionally higher for top-rated shows in the key Adults 18 to 49 demographic. This huge variation means sharp differences in the prime-time advertising rates and profit ratios for the networks. For *daytime*, the average is between 2.5 and 3.0 with a range from 2.0 to 3.5, a quite different ball game. Although the revenues generated are more modest, the risks are also

7.1 Longest-Running Network Series

Top 10 Longest-Running Programs as of 2011*	Years on the Air
1. *Meet the Press*, NBC (premiered 1947)	64
2. *CBS Evening News* (premiered 1948)	63
3. *The Today Show*, NBC (premiered 1952)	59
4. *Face the Nation*, CBS (premiered 1954)	59
5. *The Tonight Show*, NBC (premiered 1954)	57
6. *General Hospital*, ABC (premiered 1963)	48
7. *The Price Is Right*, NBC, ABC, CBS (1956–65, returned 1972)**	48
8. *Days of Our Lives*, NBC (premiered 1965)	46
9. *NBC Nightly News* (premiered 1970)***	41
10. *The Young and the Restless*, CBS (premiered 1973)	38

* *Sabado Gigante* has been on the air 49 years (since 1962), but the first 24 were on a local South American channel; it has been a network show on Univision for 26 years.

**While in syndication, *The Price Is Right* had a concurrent prime-time run from 1956 to 1964 and two brief runs on prime time in 1986 and 1993.

***NBC, starting with *The Camel News Caravan* (1948–56) and then *The Huntley-Brinkley Report* (1956–70) to the present *NBC Nightly News* (1970–), has had an evening newscast on the air continuously for 63 years.

more modest. Nonprime programmers use a low-risk approach when building their schedules.

Using a low-risk programming strategy, programmers concede that blockbuster ratings and their accompanying high advertising rates are virtually impossible to attain. They take a more conservative approach, which limits production costs and uses tried-and-true formats. In addition, developing a schedule using a different series every hour of each weekday would be far too expensive—by a long shot. Thus, weekday programming is *stripped* (the same programs are scheduled on Monday through Friday at the same time). *Stripping allows viewers to build ongoing loyalty to a series while lowering the financial risks involved in program development.* To program effectively in nonprime time, the networks must assess the available audience in a particular part of the day. To do this, programmers examine HUT levels, clearances, potential advertisers and likely demographics of audience members.

Scheduling Strategies

Scheduling nonprime time presents a unique set of challenges for programmers. The programmer juggles two types of audience flow: *flow-through* from the first program to the second one in the daypart and *flow across* the weekdays from one day to the next. Flow-through is usually accomplished by using blocks of similar shows; flow across the weekdays is promoted by stripping a series in the same time slot each weekday. While we commonly see blocks of soaps or game shows on TV, late night is blocked too: a late-night talk show is usually followed by another late-late talk show. For news, talk and magazine programs, continuity comes from the regular presence of a familiar anchor or host that promotes flow from one day to the next. Also, such program genres as soap operas have a cliff-hanger narrative structure that connects each episode with the next day's episode, driving flow across days.

In contrast, weekend programming is scheduled *weekly*—like prime time—with one episode per week at the same time from week to week. Viewers return each Saturday or Sunday to get programming

that is less available on networks during the rest of the week, such as sports, comedy, music or extended news interviews. Viewers of Sunday morning political talk, for example, typically return week after week to keep up, and fans of a particular NFL team will religiously tune in every Sunday afternoon to see their favorite.

HUT Levels

HUT levels reach around 60 percent in prime time, while nonprime-time levels can be less than 10 percent. Because so few homes are using their television sets (or home computers), the potential ratings and advertising revenue are limited. But the opportunity to create a winning franchise for a time period remains: Even small audiences have value to advertisers. In fact, many clients cannot afford to advertise in prime time, so creative programming targeted to the "right" small audience is often very attractive to these sponsors. Weekends are a good example. Viewers who tune in on the weekend have a different mindset than prime-time viewers do. They often want more movies or sports than they have time to watch during prime time. *Longer chunks of leisure time can offset smaller HUT levels: Weekend viewers wind up spending more time watching television, despite their smaller numbers.*

The Struggle for Clearances

Nonprime time and prime time especially differ in the crucial matter of affiliate clearances. When a network schedules a program, an affiliated station has three options: It can clear the program (air it when scheduled by the network), it can decide not to clear it (preemption), or it can ask permission to air the program at a later time (delayed carriage). *Both preemption and delayed carriage, especially by major-market stations, hurt a network's national ratings because they reduce the potential audience for the program.* In order to increase clearances of network programming, especially in nonprime time, the networks succeeded in getting the FCC to raise the percentage of U.S. households they can reach with their owned-and-operated stations. Although most affiliates clear about 90 percent of their network's total schedule, the percentage in nonprime time, especially in the daytime, Sunday morning, overnight and late-night dayparts, is substantially lower. The O&Os naturally clear the entire network schedule.

In a surprising move after nearly 50 years of daytime programming, around the turn of the century, NBC (which ranked third in daytime programming throughout the 1980s and early 1990s) decided to scale back its daytime schedule because of low clearances. When NBC first offered *The Other Side*, a daytime talk show, it received only a 61 percent clearance rate; in other words, almost 40 percent of NBC's affiliates decided to schedule some syndicated series instead. *Besides eroding its potential audience, preemption and delayed carriage disrupt the scheduling strategies used to foster audience flow from one program to another.* For example, an ABC affiliate that carries *Nightline* following the local newscast provides a stream of viewers who are looking for information. When *Nightline* is delayed to allow the affiliate to carry a sitcom, much of the potential audience goes to bed or switches to an all-news cable channel. The delayed *Nightline* is less likely to attract a large audience when it follows comedy rather than news.

The corporate owners of the broadcast networks are also hedging their nonprime-time bets by offering programming to their own and other network affiliates through their syndication arms. Viacom, owner of CBS, also owns King World, the syndicators of former daytime powerhouse *Oprah* and its popular spinoffs, *Dr. Phil* and *Dr. Oz*. When affiliates of ABC or NBC purchase these talk programs, the shows compete with whatever CBS affiliates offer, a situation that more than irks CBS affiliates.

Advertisers and Demographics

A network has to determine which segment of the available audience it will go after (*target*), mindful of its competitors' programming and influenced to some degree by advertiser support for its programming. Then the network programmer's task is to put together a schedule of programs that will, at the lowest possible cost, do four big things:

- Attract the most desirable demographic groups
- Maximize audience flow-through
- Build viewer loyalty
- Capture the largest possible audience

One big difference between the major dayparts is that audiences during nonprime-time dayparts are more *homogenous* (similar in demographic composition) than prime-time audiences. Typically in nonprime time, the three networks schedule the same program type head-to-head (all soaps, all talk, all games, all soft news and so on), which creates fierce competition for single audience group. When selecting the shows for a particular daypart, the networks necessarily give primary consideration to these elements:

- Demographics of available audiences
- Competitive counterprogramming opportunities
- Economic viability

The questions are whether an audience group is large enough to split profitably, whether there is a chance to capture another big group, and what the cheapest option is that will still please enough advertisers.

Indirect influences on programming practices also come into play. Daytime programs rely on drug and food companies for advertising revenue. Hence, programmers are wary of scripts or interview programs that tackle subjects such as tampering with painkillers or rat hairs in cereal. For three reasons, *daytime programming is in much closer touch with its advertising messages than prime time.* First, daytime programs contain more commercial minutes per hour. Second, because many programs were once both sponsored and produced by advertisers, there is a tradition of sensitivity to advertiser needs. Finally, two major companies, General Foods and Procter & Gamble, dominate the advertising time in daytime, and until very recently, the networks could not afford to offend them. (Now most networks are owned by even bigger guys.)

Genres of NonPrime-Time Programming

There are seven key genres of nonprime programming: (1) sports, (2) daytime soap operas (including telenovelas that also air in prime time), (3) game shows, (4) news/magazines, (5) talk shows, (6) children's programs and (7) comedy/music programs. Most of these program types are identified with particular dayparts: sports with weekend afternoons; soaps and game shows with daytime; children's programming with Saturday mornings; talk/comedy shows with weekday late night; and comedy/music with late nights on Saturdays. Different strategies and practices necessarily associate with each genre of programming, as well as different levels of cost, and the development processes for new shows vary considerably. Not all of these categories are mutually exclusive. For example, the third and fourth hours of *Today* are as much a talk program as they are a news/magazine. *The View* and *The Talk* are talk programs (duh) but include interviews with newsmakers like the news/magazines. In addition, ABC schedules the cheap-to-produce reality genre in daytime (and prime time)-most recently, *The Chew* and *The Revolution*.

Sports

In case you haven't noticed, on the broadcast networks, weekend afternoons (1 to 7 P.M.) are dominated by live sports coverage, and they are allowed to run on into the once-sacred prime time if the events are popular. *Sports are indubitably one of the most important forms of programming in television.* One of the chief reasons for sports' popularity with the network higher-ups is their consistent ability to attract an audience of young men who are extremely difficult to attract with other types of regularly scheduled programming (duh). In addition, sports provide a much-valued location for zap-proof advertising and promotion. Sports telecasts are brimming with opportunities for the insertion of ads, promotional spots and announcements that cannot be avoided by the viewer unless she or he

also risks missing part of the action. Sports also are one of the programming forms that provide excellent branding opportunities for networks, such as "NBC—The Home of the Olympics," *FOX NFL Sunday* and so forth.

A network's sports division is responsible for acquiring the rights to games and events and for producing the telecasts. It must work closely with the programming division because of the complexities associated with live sporting events, including overtime pay and weather-related cancellations. The networks' sports divisions negotiate with the sports leagues to guarantee that start times occur when the majority of viewers can watch. Those sporting events that do not attract a prime-time-sized audience are carefully scheduled elsewhere so as not to interfere with the all-important prime-time entertainment programs.

Noninterference with prime time diminished as a concern in recent years, however, because of the rising popularity and enormous cost of major team sports, particularly football. The late afternoon NFL games and even post-game programs regularly run into Sunday prime time and often contribute to high prime-time ratings, bumping *60 Minutes* and other Sunday shows. NBA (National Basketball Association), MLB (Major League Baseball), and NCAA (National Collegiate Athletic Association) playoff games now regularly appear in prime hours. When Disney shifted ABC's *Monday Night Football* to its ESPN cable network because of declining ratings, NBC promptly filled the prime-time broadcast NFL void with *Sunday Night Football* while re-branding Sunday night prime time as *Football Night in America*. Most regular season team sports coverage remains in weekend afternoons and early evenings (and on cable), while most major postseason contests are featured in prime time.

Sports Programming in a Multichannel Environment

Although major sports are not the low-cost programming option they were in the early days of television, *programming costs are always relative in television.* Although CBS claimed to have lost millions of dollars on sports rights in the early and mid-1990s, within a few years the network once again spent enormous sums to regain a piece of the NFL Sunday afternoon package and to renew its NCAA Men's Basketball Tournament coverage. This occurred after the network's prestige was seriously damaged by its loss of the NFL to the less-established network in 1994.

FOX used the NFL and later MLB, NASCAR (National Association for Stock Car Auto Racing), and, to a limited degree, the NHL (National Hockey League) to establish itself as a legitimate member of the Big Four to both viewers and the financial community. One result of FOX's new leverage was its ability to upgrade its affiliates in several markets, mainly at the expense of CBS. The question of cost, then, involves more than simply the profit or loss made from the ratio of program costs to advertising revenues: *Losing major sports can undermine the legitimacy and degrade the financial value of a broadcast network.*

Cable has clearly had a huge impact on televised sports programming. Networks such as ESPN, ESPN2, ESPNU, Versus (VS) and the regional Comcast Sports, Fox Sports and Root Sports Nets exist only because of their sports coverage. *Cable's saturation coverage has raised the profile and value of sports on television, even as it drains ratings from broadcast networks for all sports but the NFL.* Only the NFL has consistent increases in regular-season ratings—at a time when most other broadcast network ratings are declining. ESPN, for example, now pays the NFL more per year ($ 1.1 billion) for *Monday Night Football* than any of the Big Four broadcast networks pay for their Sunday afternoon (CBS, FOX) or Sunday night (NBC) packages. Although network sports ratings, like the ratings for all other network programming, have had some attrition in the wake of cable and internet competition, the falloff is much less than that of other program genres. In fact, ratings for the NFL, NBA and even the NHL have recently increased while the ratings for MLB, NASCAR and other events have remained stable in the last few years. *An important point is that even the limited*

ratings attrition for sports is offset by sports' increased value as one of the few programming types that attract the male audience so valued by advertisers, in spite of ever-proliferating entertainment options. In addition, such high-profile events as the Super Bowl, the Olympics and the World Series continue to draw enormous audiences and provide substantial promotional opportunities for the host networks at critical times of the year (the February sweeps and early in the new broadcast season).

The solution to the tug-of-war over sports has been for broadcast networks to partner with cable networks to share rights to sports programming. The most prominent examples are Disney's ownership of both ABC and the ESPN networks, which have shared NFL, NBA and NHL packages; the FOX/Fox Sports Net combination, which shares MLB; and the more recent Comcast/NBC merger, which shares the NHL and is likely to become a more aggressive bidder for sports to feed both the network and Comcast's numerous Regional Sports Networks (RSNs). Cable networks are able to offer most of the near-daily regular season games, leaving broadcast networks to focus on the postseason and key regular season contests.

There are also shared rights arrangements among separate companies where early rounds of team playoffs and golf and tennis matches appear on cable networks, with later rounds shifting to networks. The split of NBA between ESPN and ABC is another example of leveraging the value of sports television. In fact, the sports divisions of ABC and ESPN have been merged and now operate in tandem more often than they operate as competitors.

The sports anthology program, exemplified by ABC's long-running *Wide World of Sports*, was a casualty of the changes in sports television.[1] The minor sports that were typically covered by anthologies have, for the most part, benefited from the explosion in televised sports by gaining individual contracts on broadcast or cable (NASCAR, WNBA and Major League Soccer). There has been a redefinition of what constitutes a successful program: now there is more emphasis on the "quality" than the quantity of ratings. This situation has enabled NASCAR to gain lucrative network television

7.2 Nascar on Television

Almost $4.5 billion. That's the price FOX, ABC/ESPN and TNT paid to carry NASCAR races for the eight years that started in 2007. The deal's hefty tag recognized NASCAR's high television ratings as the second most-watched sports programming after the National Football League. Among its most valuable assets are the Nextel Cup races.

Starting in the 1960s, ABC aired NASCAR races as part of its *Wide World of Sports* program, and after two decades, shifted NASCAR off broadcasting and onto cable (ESPN), a relationship that lasted another 20 years. ESPN is widely credited for popularizing NASCAR—so much so, indeed, that at the turn of the century, NBC and FOX snapped it up—but unexpectedly, the ratings slid in mid-decade. The slide led to the creation of the "Chase for the Nextel Cup," an end-of-season playoff series in which only the top ten drivers were eligible for the final ten races. These races energized the entire season and attracted much larger audiences, taking NASCAR to the No. 2 spot. When NBC decided not to renew NASCAR's contract in 2005, ABC/ESPN jumped at the opportunity to air the races again, agreeing to pay an estimated $270 million to air 17 Nextel Cup races (the remaining races were split among broadcasting and cable outlets).

NASCAR is widely popular, but whether ABC/ESPN's investment will pay off over that long a haul remains to be seen. Competition from the NFL is hard to beat. NASCAR ratings have also been sagging, including double-digit dives in the 2009 and 2010 seasons. NASCAR officials and network executives "study the reasons" for the drop, but many journalists blame a clash between race times and NFL games, colorless story lines about the drivers, and the spacing and timing of the many, many commercial breaks.

Debbie Goh, Ph.D.
Nanyang Technological University

contracts (see 7.2). *The "a little something for everybody" approach of sports anthologies is less viable as a means of keeping program audiences in the multichannel environment because it virtually encourages channel changing.*

The idea of multiple sports in one program lives on in the biannual Olympic Games and the various X Games (the "extreme" sports that have a particular appeal to young audiences). Although the Olympics cannot be regularly scheduled in a conventional sense, the 1992 decision of the International Olympic Committee (IOC) to have the Summer and Winter Games alternate every two years enormously increased the value of the games to television. NBC, in fact, gave up competing for rights to the NFL, MLB and NBA in the mid-1990s in favor of the lower-cost NASCAR and, even more important, in favor of branding itself as the "Network of the Olympics." ABC Sports had used this same branding strategy with great success to build its ratings and credibility in the 1960s and 1970s, and NBC has succeeded in tying itself to all Olympics in the public's mind. (Some people are surprised to hear that any other network ever carried the Olympics.)

With the Winter Games scheduled in the February sweeps and the Summer Games coming right before the fall season rollout two years apart, the various Olympic events provide hundreds of hours of prime-time and nonprime programming and also supply a key promotional platform for touting NBC's other programming. The Olympics were also the first major experiment with *multiplatform programming*, a practice that has now become standard for the Olympics and other long-season sports while stimulating the new media by providing highly visible and valued content.

Non-Live-Event Sports Programming

Non-live-event sports programming on the networks today generally consists of (1) pregame and postgame programs and (2) sports-league-produced programming for children and young adults. Since the success of CBS's *The NFL Today* in the 1970s, broadcast and cable networks have developed similar shows for other sports. *These wraparound shows help networks to more fully brand programming blocks and expand the programming hours devoted*

7.3 Mister Olympic Broadcasting

Duncan "Dick" Ebersol is best known for producing large-scale events, most notably the Olympic Games. Long an American television executive, his career began at ABC Sports where, mentored by Roone Arledge, he became the first-ever television Olympic researcher. In the mid-70s, he moved to NBC and created such enduring successes as *Saturday Night Live* and *Friday Night Videos*, as well as *Later with Bob Costas*, under his own independent production company.

In 1989, Ebersol returned to NBC to become the president of NBC Sports. He immediately negotiated the acquisition of the rights to broadcast the NBA, and in the following years brought the NFL, MLB and Nascar under the NBC umbrella. His most influential decision, however, was to turn NBC into "The Home of the Olympics" in the USA. In 1993, he secured the rights to the 1996 Atlanta Summer Olympics (the 1988 Seoul and 1992 Barcelona Games had been acquired before his arrival at the network). This was the first of several record-breaking contracts that would bring the broadcaster every summer and winter Olympics between 2000 and 2012.

Under Dick Ebersol's guidance, NBC effectively became the biggest single sponsor of the Olympic Movement (the International Olympic Committee and the organizations it coordinates). Broadcast rights add up to half of the entire revenue generated by the movement, and NBC alone contributed $820 million to the $1.28 billion collected from broadcasters of the 2010 Vancouver Olympics. This massive role gives the network some influence on the scheduling of Olympic events. For example, in the 2008 Beijing Games, in contrast to past practice, swimming finals were scheduled in the morning sessions to allow NBC to broadcast them live in prime-time, rather than in tape delay due to the time zone offset. In addition, the network expanded its coverage from Beijing to an unprecedented 3,600 hours, most of them through such outlets as online channels, digital platforms and on-demand footage. Such a flood of significant (and popular) content contributed in a major way to the rapid development of these new media platforms.

Ebersol unexpectedly resigned from NBC in May 2011, just weeks ahead of the negotiations for the U.S. rights for the 2014 and 2016 Olympic Games. Despite his departure, the network secured exclusive U.S. Olympic TV rights through 2020 with a $4.38 billion contract that includes four summer and winter games.

Simon Licen, Ph.D.
University of Ljubljana

to sports *without paying additional rights fees.* In addition, powerful sports entities can demand airing of league-produced shows. This began when the NBA forced former broadcast partner NBC to schedule *NBA Inside Stuff*, a youth-oriented feature magazine about the league, as a condition of its contract with the league. Similar programming and a variety of promotional spots are now standard in major sports television rights deals.

Soap Operas and Game Shows

Daytime programming (9 A.M. to 4 P.M.) has traditionally been one of the most lucrative dayparts for television networks. Its profit margin often challenges that of prime time because the cost per program in daytime is substantially less. *The money needed to pay for one hour of prime-time drama will cover the costs of a week's worth of daytime soap operas.* Moreover, *daytime profits help networks offset extraordinary program investments in other dayparts.* Because viewer loyalties are intense and developing successful new programs is difficult, the newer networks were reluctant to try to develop daytime programming—which turned out to be smart. Cost advantages have greatly declined in the last few years because the audience for network daytime programming has succumbed to the lure of popular syndicated offerings on stations, cable and online.

Currently, of the major English-language networks, only ABC, CBS and NBC have a substantial stake in daytime programs Monday through Friday (see 7.4), although each of the Big Three have much

7.4	Network Weekday Daytime Programming	
Network	**Hours**	**Programs**
ABC	4	*The View, General Hospital, The Chew, The Revolution*
CBS	5	*The Price Is Right, The Young and the Restless, The Bold and the Beautiful, The Talk, Let's Make a Deal*
NBC*	3	*Today* (3rd and 4th hours), *Days of Our Lives*

*NBC's *Today* has expanded into this daypart in the last decade, first from 9–10 A.M. ET in 2000 and from 10–11 A.M. ET in 2007. The fourth hour of *Today* is an example of how the concept of *brand extension* has come to television. This last hour is related to the parent program only by title as it has completely different hosts (Kathy Lee Gifford and Hoda Kotb), little if any interest in news, and much more emphasis on entertainment, comedy, fashion and food. Because of these differences, this particular brand extension of the iconic *Today* brand is aired out of pattern (usually in early afternoon) in some major markets.

reduced the amount of programming they schedule in this daypart in the last decade. Telemundo and Univision, however, maintain a major presence in daytime with telenovelas that air during several hours of their Monday through Friday schedules.

In addition to having lower programming costs in the daytime, the networks schedule about 21 minutes of non-program material (commercials, promos, public service announcements and so on) per hour compared with about 17 minutes in prime time. Although daytime audiences are much smaller than prime time, daytime programming fills more hours per day, and each hour provides more commercial slots. In prime time, top dramas, situation comedies and ambitious miniseries have enormous talent costs; sports programming has huge rights fees, and breaking news coverage is expensive. Those kinds of programs become loss leaders, often costing far more than the advertising revenue they generate.

But daytime programmers face enormous competition from cable television and syndicated programming. The collective number of viewers for syndicated programming, for example, now regularly surpasses that for daytime television on the major networks.

Daytime television seems to have the most potential for audience erosion. Compared with the 1950s and 1960s, the number of viewers who are at home in the daytime has decreased. Because many more women work, children stay at childcare centers rather than at home. The networks have

additional worries as the numbers of younger viewers (aged 18 to 34 and 18 to 49) continue to decline for each of the networks. Cable/satellite networks, the internet, video games and home video also contribute to this decline.

Soap Operas

For about 50 years, soap operas were the cash cows for their networks. Production and talent costs are considerably less than for prime-time programming. Soaps are shot primarily in digital studios with multiple cameras and receive far less costly postproduction editing and sound "sweetening." Typically, the producers, directors, writers and actors hired for soaps produce five hours of programming a week, compared producing the 30 minutes of a prime-time sitcom. Despite the seemingly lower quality, CBS's highly rated *The Young and the Restless* does better at making a profit and delivering its target audience—women 18 to 49—than many of the network's prime-time offerings (see 7.5).

In addition, the soaps built loyal constituencies that lasted for decades because viewers followed a set of compelling characters nearly every weekday. Networks developed this habitual viewing by stripping daytime soaps in the same time slot five days a week. Viewers become so determined to see their favorite soaps that daily activities are planned around making time to watch, and episodes are regularly *time-shifted* when necessary. *Soap operas continue to be one of the most time-shifted programming genres.*

7.5	Network Soap Opera Ratings		
		HH Rating	**W 18–49 Rating**
CBS	*The Young and the Restless*	3.6	1.7
CBS	*The Bold and the Beautiful*	2.2	1.0
ABC	*General Hospital*	2.1	1.4
NBC	*Days of Our Lives*	2.0	1.2
ABC	*One Life to Live**	1.9	1.0
NBC	*All My Children**	1.9	0.9

*Cancelled in 2011.
"Ratings: Another New Low for GH in Women 18–49," (2011, May 12), *Soap Opera Network*, http://www.soapoperanetwork.com/ratings/item/4567-ratings-another-new-low-for-gh-in-women-18-49-viewers.

Despite this long and enormously successful history, *the most important recent change in network daytime programming is the decline of the soap opera as a major genre.* Since 2010, four long-running soaps—*All My Children*, *As the World Turns*, *The Guiding Light* and *One Life to Live*—have been cancelled. This surprised many observers because soaps survived and even thrived after millions of women began to work outside the home in the 1970s and 1980s; they even found new popularity among college students and others who time-shifted them for viewing at more convenient times. Soaps fell from their perch as the prototypical daytime program genre for four reasons:

1. The total daytime audience has eroded greatly since the 1990s when even the lower-rated soaps were able to draw about five million viewers. Today, only the highest rated of the remaining soaps (*The Young and the Restless*) regularly attracts this many viewers.

2. The audience for soaps is ageing faster than that of other programs. The loyalty that made soaps such a successful genre has not transferred to younger viewers who can watch most anything they want on television at any time of the day via cable, time shifting and on demand programming.

3. Despite efforts to trim costs and with a price structure much less costly than prime-time dramas, soap operas still cost more to produce than talk and other "reality" programs.

4. Today's seemingly never-slowing pace of life makes it more and more difficult for viewers to devote the time and effort required to follow a program for five hours a week. Daytime viewing has become "grazing" in which viewers drop in and out of programs. This works to the advantage of relatively simple non-scripted programs such as magazines, reality and talk.

None of the problematic dimensions for soap operas are likely to change; this makes the remaining four network soaps likely to be the last of the English-language U.S.-produced soaps. This is a sea change from traditional television practice and another indicator of the big challenges that local, regional and national television programmers face.

Game Shows

From the 1950s until the 1990s, game shows were the other profitable mainstay of network daytime programming. Typically, several episodes of a game show were taped in a single day, and these shows used the same sets and props for years. In exchange for on-air announcements, advertisers provided the prizes awarded to contestants. Usually only the host got a big salary, and production costs were very low.

Four kinds of competition have nearly driven games daytime network lineups:

1. The popularity of familiar first-run syndicated game shows (including *Jeopardy!* and *Wheel of Fortune*)

2. The growth of cable/satellite networks dedicating some or all of their schedules to games (GSN, formerly the Game Show Network)

3. The draw of network big-money games (*Deal or No Deal* and *Who Wants to Be a Millionaire?*) in prime time

4. The rise of syndicated talk programming

This last, syndicated talk, is much more lucrative for most stations than network game shows. Remember that stations get only network compensation and limited advertising slots for a network show, whereas they can sell all the advertising time in syndicated shows. They have particularly hurt the clearance rate for game shows—which has led to their virtual demise as a network daytime staple.

Two network daytime game shows remain, however, both on CBS: *The Price Is Right* and *Let's Make a Deal*. One of television's all-time longest-running programs, *Price* was the first hour-long game show (it was even 90 minutes for a short time), and developed a near-cult following among homemakers, shift workers and college students. Its network run still seems secure as the program has also developed a devoted following among young people, and host Drew Carey is popular with younger viewers, as well as with more traditional daytime audiences. The continuing success of *Price* led CBS to revive *Let's Make a Deal*, a game that has been on and off network and syndication daytime and prime-time schedules since the 1960s. The newest version, hosted by Wayne Brady, places much more emphasis on the show business talents of its host than the older versions and shows signs of becoming a daytime staple (until the next major upheaval).

Weekday News, Information, and Talk

In addition to their own intense competition, the broadcast networks face increasing challenges from strong local stations in major markets in the early morning daypart. Local stations in large markets, including New York, Miami, Chicago and Washington, are producing their own early newscasts and magazine programs (see Chapter 8). Because of their strong local emphases, these competing shows have garnered strong ratings against network offerings.

If network programs are to remain strong competitors in the major markets in the morning dayparts, they must adjust to the changing environment by doing what local competitors cannot. Because network morning shows cannot compete for *local* appeal, the key to successfully attracting mega-audiences lies in continuing to interview the most important national and international news and entertainment figures, and in shipping their popular morning personalities off to exotic locales or the sites of hot national news events.

Early-Morning Newscasts

Each of the Big Three provide early-morning newscasts on weekdays, running from 4 or 5 A.M. to 7 A.M. The networks hope to bolster their 7 A.M. programming by getting flow-through from these earlier programs, but they also realize that many affiliates produce their own morning news shows during part of this time period. Therefore, they try to accommodate affiliates with multiple feeds of these early newscasts. All have beginning and end points at the top and bottom of every half hour, so an affiliate can "dump out" or join a network morning newscast after 30 or 60 minutes.

Morning Magazines

In the period between 7 and 9 A.M., the Big Three networks compete head-to-head with magazine format programs. The long-running *Today*, *Good Morning America* and a CBS challenger appearing under numerous titles (*The Early Show* since 1999), have contested this time period for several decades. These morning magazines provide news headlines, weather forecasts, and interviews ranging from soft entertainment to hard news. Because they resemble print publications, they are called *magazines*. Like print magazines, they contain a series of feature articles, have a table of contents (*billboard*) at the beginning to tell viewers about what will be on that day, and are bound together with a common cover and title.

The magazine format is especially suited to the early-morning daypart when most viewers do not watch for extended periods of time. As people ready themselves for the day ahead, they catch short glimpses of television (see Chapter 8 on *dayparting*). The segmented magazine format allows viewers to watch for short periods of time and still see complete stories. News and weather updates allow viewers to start their day with useful information. All national magazines include local breaks in which affiliates air brief local news, local weather or traffic updates. FOX affiliates usually compete with other affiliates by having their own long-form local newscasts (but nothing from the network).

Morning magazines are a valuable tool for promoting the network's prime-time offerings. For instance, when a network has scheduled a prime-time miniseries, the hosts of the morning magazine interview the stars or appear on the set of the miniseries. Correspondents from prime-time news magazines (*20/20, Dateline*) frequently make guest appearances on their network's morning shows to promote features on that night's program. Conversely, prime-time programs can help boost the ratings of morning magazines. For example, CBS's *The Early Show*'s ratings increased for a time when it began to capitalize on the success of the network's prime-time *Survivor* series. Each of the morning magazines has weekend editions that further extend their brands.

By early 2011, NBC News's *Today* was still dominating the ratings over its rivals—as it had done for over a decade. ABC News's *Good Morning America* was second, and CBS's *The Early Show* was a weak third and likely facing yet another revision (see 7.6 for more on the battle for morning magazine leadership). To some extent, the relative popularity of the leading morning shows is connected to the night-before ratings (*tuning inertia*). If NBC is the number-one network, the television set is often switched off at night with the channel position on NBC, and a disproportionate number of viewers turn on their sets and see morning programming from NBC. Similarly, ABC has an advantage when its shows win the ratings the night before. Despite presently out-rating its two traditional network rivals overall, CBS has never had much success in the morning and probably does not benefit from tuning inertia. Of course, NBC's strong late-night lineup helps *Today* much more than its presently low-rated prime-time lineup.

Despite relatively low ratings, the competition between the networks for early-morning viewers is always intense because the advertising revenue is so great. The stakes get even higher during ratings sweeps. To make the shows more attractive, the cast and crew often travel to exotic locations during a sweep. Although the cost of remote productions is higher, they often return higher ratings and create a promotional hook to tempt audiences. During one sweeps period, CBS scheduled an entire week of its morning magazine inside the studios of *Late Night with David Letterman* while *Late Night* was in London. This provided cross-promotion for both shows.

Daytime Talk

Traditionally, the talk show was used to fill hour-long gaps in a network's daytime schedule and target the desirable 25 to 54 female audience. Further, if a talk-show host connected with the audience, a series attracted very loyal followers who watched daily. With studios and equipment almost always available, talk shows are one of the most easily instituted and adaptable of genres. Indeed, with outstanding success, syndicators have stolen the genre away from the broadcast networks with such syndicated talk as *Oprah, Dr. Phil, The Jerry Springer Show* and *The Ellen DeGeneres Show*. Back in the 1980s when *Donahue, Oprah* and *Geraldo* were redefining the daytime talk show, the networks stuck with their successful soap operas and game shows in daytime, losing the programming initiative to their syndicated competitors. In the era of corporate consolidation, some of these programs began being syndicated by the same media conglomerates that owned the networks.

The Big Three have recently re-entered the daytime talk business. This is a reaction to the decline of soap operas as a viable format and the inexpensive cost of mounting a talk show. ABC started the new wave of network daytime talk with *The View* in the late 1990s. The late-morning show (11 A.M. currently) has a unique four-host format that includes television icon Barbara Walters, its creator and producer. *The View*'s continuing success in both ratings and in its format expansion to international markets, led NBC to expand *Today* to both the 9–10 A.M. and 10–11 A.M. time periods. As mentioned above, the third and, especially, the fourth

7.6 The Morning Magazine Shows

NBC's *Today*

NBC pioneered the magazine format with the 1952 premiere of *The Today Show*. Over the years viewers have become very attached to the show's hosts and regular guests. Popular *Today Show* personalities have included Dave Garroway (its original host), John Chancellor, Hugh Downs, Barbara Walters, Tom Brokaw, Jane Pauley, Willard Scott, Bryant Gumbel, Katie Couric, Matt Lauer and Meredith Vieira.

Each of these hosts and regulars had a long run, bringing stability and familiarity to the program. These are essential ingredients for ratings success in a daypart where viewers' behavior becomes routine, as most people start each of their weekdays in much the same manner. *The Today Show's* sole big ratings dip, which took place in the early 1990s, has been attributed mostly to revolving hosts following the departure of Jane Pauley. *The Today Show* successfully rebounded in the mid-1990s with a new generation of morning stars and, renamed *Today*, has been the clear leader in morning network ratings. Lauer and Ann Curry are the present hosts/anchors for the first two hours, supported by a roster of familiar specialists such as weatherman Al Roker and big-name contributors from the NBC News.

ABC's *Good Morning America*

Like the newer networks of today, in its first decade or so (prior to 1975) ABC did not offer any network service until 11 A.M. Then it challenged the well-established *Today Show* by introducing *AM America* and aiming for a younger early-morning audience. ABC believed that its target audience, women 18 to 49, were less-habituated viewers than the over-50 age group that had been drawn in large numbers to *The Today Show*, and that these younger women would sample the new program. By 1980 the retitled *Good Morning America (GMA)* had moved into first place overall in the ratings.

Although *Today* had re-established its first-place position by the mid-1990s, *GMA* remains securely in second place. After unsuccessfully experimenting with younger, supposedly "hipper" anchors in the late 1990s and early 2000s following the departure of long-time anchors/hosts Charles Gibson and Joan Lunden, ABC returned Gibson and added popular prime-time news personality Diane Sawyer. When Gibson became the *World News* anchor in 2006, newscaster Robin Roberts was promoted to co-host, making Sawyer and Roberts the first all-female

morning magazine program hosting team. The network also invested millions in a new studio, complete with *Today*-like windows showing adoring fans outside.

Increasing stability has closed some of the ratings gap between number-two-rated *GMA* and number-one-rated *Today*. Sawyer replaced Gibson on the nightly *ABC World News* evening broadcast in 2010 at which point George Stephanopoulos joined Roberts as co-anchor.

CBS's *The Early Show*

CBS has languished in third place in the morning news ratings since the beginning of three-network competition in early mornings in the 1970s. Even when ABC was out of the picture, CBS always ran a dismal second to *The Today Show* regardless of whether they were trying straight news or "infotainment." The failure of CBS to establish a morning franchise is one of the enduring mysteries of network television. The network has always trailed the competition regardless of format, personalities or ratings for the rest of its morning performance. A recent CBS attempt at a star-driven *Today/GMA*-style program (complete with a window for fans to gather!) was *The Early Show* hosted by former *Today* host Bryant Gumbel. Debuting in late 1999, Gumbel (and co-host Jane Clayson) lasted barely three years before being replaced by four co-anchors—including Harry Smith, a veteran of a previously unsuccessful CBS attempt at developing a morning program. As of early 2011, Erica Hill and Chris Wrigge were the two main anchors, but they had a very brief tryout. By late in 2011, CBS had acquired former PBS talk host Charlie Rose and OWN host Gayle King for its morning show. These two will probably last longer than most CBS morning predecessors if only because it would take a good offer (and strong contract) to get them away from their own long-lasting shows. But if history is any guide, their time in these jobs will also be limited.

The money that successful morning programs generate makes it unlikely that CBS will give up on its nearly 40-year effort to create a successful morning news and infotainment magazine. Nonetheless, the huge number of options for viewers even at this time of the day on broadcast, cable and the internet make for increasingly long odds that CBS can capture enough of the audience and buzz to compete strongly with NBC and ABC in the early-morning ratings race.

hour of *Today* have minimal connection with the parent program.

More recently, CBS has rolled out *The Talk*, a program that follows the same basic pattern as *The View*. In addition to the traditional Big Three, both Telemundo and Univision rely on popular talk shows to fill substantial parts of their daytime schedules.

Evening News

Although ratings have and continue to decline, particularly among the young, the evening newscasts remain the centerpieces of the ABC, CBS and NBC television news organizations, and the same is true of Univision. Along with daytime and late-night programming, evening newscasts help distinguish these full-service networks from their more recent competitors (FOX, the CW, MNTV, ION), thus enhancing their brand identification.

The advertising revenue generated by these news programs remains substantial. Evening newscasts also give the broadcast networks prestige as major players in national and international politics. In the early days, evening newscasts provided a service to affiliates, most of which then had very limited, if any, news operations. CBS and NBC introduced the nightly 15-minute newscast to network television in 1948, and by the 1960s, the newscasts had expanded to 30 minutes. Although modest by today's standards, the expenses incurred by a network news operation during those early years were often far more than the income derived from advertising on the newscasts.

Today, evening newscasts face difficult competition from cable news networks and internet news services. Busy viewers don't need to wait until 6:30 or 7 P.M. for a network newscast because 24-hour news channels (CNN, CNBC, CNN Headline News, MSNBC and Fox News Channel) and hundreds, maybe thousands, of news websites sponsored by newspapers, television and radio stations, wire services and the networks themselves, can be reached anytime. In addition, the newscasts on the larger local affiliates compete with the network newscasts for national and sometimes international

stories using satellites to bring in high-quality coverage with on-the-spot video.

Thus, *network news may not remain a staple of non-prime-time programming if current trends persist* (see 7.7). Less than a third of the adult public now watch any of these telecasts with any degree of regularity, down from more than half in 1990 and almost three-quarters in 1980. Also, network, local and cable news audiences slipped precipitously in viewers younger than 30, perhaps because younger adults are more likely to seek news from other alternatives, such as the internet and mobile media. This demographic trend suggests that audiences for evening newscasts may continue to decline.

Nonetheless, network newscasts continue to bring in sizable advertising revenue for the networks. Despite increased competition and lower ratings, these newscasts also remain important as promotional tools. Affiliates benefit because the networks promote the evening's prime-time schedule during commercial breaks. Just as with early-morning magazine programs, the network's news division can promote other news programming within the newscast. For example, ABC promotes *Nightline* as well as its website (*abc.com*) within its nightly newscast, while each of the networks generally incorporates promotion for their own news magazines (CBS's *60 Minutes* and *48 Hours Mystery;* NBC's *Dateline NBC;* and ABC's *20/20* and *Prime Time Live*) within their evening newscasts. Indeed, all the networks push their websites in every newscast and many promotional spots.

Time zone differences present a challenge to both programming departments and the news departments. The solution has been a multiple-feed schedule. The first feed of a network newscast is generally 6:30 to 7 P.M. eastern time. Because some affiliates delay this newscast and the time would be inappropriate for the mountain and Pacific time zones, a second feed is scheduled for 7 to 7:30 P.M. eastern time and a third from 6 to 6:30 P.M. Pacific time. Breaking or updated news stories can be inserted into the later feeds.

Because most network newscast elements (news gathering, scheduling and technology) are about the same across competitors, *news personalities become*

7.7   The Evening Newscasts

NBC *Nightly News*

NBC first offered a regular nightly newscast in 1948, the *Camel News Caravan* with John Cameron Swayze. Swayze was not an experienced journalist and eventually was replaced in 1956 by Chet Huntley and David Brinkley. The renamed newscast, *The Huntley-Brinkley Report*, was a ratings hit, becoming the top-rated news program in the late 1950s and for most of the 1960s. When Huntley retired in 1970, NBC retitled the show the *NBC Nightly News* with Brinkley and John Chancellor as the main anchors. Following NBC's declining news ratings in the late 1970s and early 1980s, Tom Brokaw was moved from *The Today Show* to the *Nightly News* anchor position in 1982. As NBC added cable networks (CNBC, MSNBC), the *Nightly News* became a source of programming material for these newer news/talk outlets. *Nightly News*'s stories are frequently the major focus of evening programming on these cable networks, and archived *Nightly News* reports have been repackaged to provide new programming for its cable partners.

Brokaw stepped down as *Nightly News* anchor after the 2004 presidential election and was successfully replaced by Brian Williams, a frequent guest anchor on the *Nightly News* and former anchor of a long-running CNBC evening newscast. Heir to ABC's Peter Jennings because of his similar wry manner, NBC's Williams is currently the most popular of the network evening newscasters.

CBS *Evening News*

Walter Cronkite replaced Douglas Edwards as anchor of the *CBS Evening News* in 1962 and remained until his retirement in 1981. In times of crisis, more people tuned in to Cronkite than to any other newscaster. During the 1970s, polls repeatedly showed Cronkite as the most trusted source of news. Dan Rather took over the helm of the *CBS Evening News* upon Cronkite's retirement, but Rather's credentials as a highly experienced journalist would have meant little had his chemistry not matched that of his predecessor.

Even though the ratings of the *CBS Evening News* declined after Cronkite's retirement, Rather continued to dominate the evening news ratings until the late 1980s when the reign of ABC's Peter Jennings began. In June 1993 CBS decided to pair Rather with veteran reporter and weekend anchor Connie Chung. The combination did not work out, and ratings did not improve. Two years later, Chung was demoted from the

anchor desk, and the president of CBS News was fired. In 2005, Dan Rather stepped down following criticism of his role in a news story that used faked documents.

Long-time CBS correspondent Bob Schieffer was interim anchor until September 2006 when Katie Couric (former co-host of NBC's *Today*) became the sole weeknight anchor. Although Couric and her producers attempted to shake up the conventional formula of an evening newscast with more interviews and guest commentators, such moves were met with large amounts of criticism and no improvement in the ratings. The newscast soon reverted to the standard anchor-centered newscast that has been a television mainstay for over 50 years. After five years of not being able to lift the newscast out of third place, Couric left in 2011 to be replaced by veteran CBS correspondent Scott Pelley.

ABC *World News*

ABC has been airing nightly newscasts since 1953, but for three decades it failed to pose a serious news threat to CBS and NBC. In 1977, in a bold move, ABC appointed the head of ABC Sports, Roone Arledge, to supervise its news division as well as its sports division. Arledge had made ABC the number-one network sports organization with his unconventional strategies—introducing offbeat sporting events and building up the dramatic aspects of sports competition. During his tenure as head of news, ABC assembled a team of highly respected journalists, including Peter Jennings, Sam Donaldson, Diane Sawyer, Ted Koppel and David Brinkley, catapulting ABC into the lead in the evening news ratings for some years.

Most observers credit anchorperson Peter Jennings with the success of *World News Tonight*, as he actively served as executive editor and wrote (or rewrote) many of the stories, adding his own wry style. After the departures of Brokaw and Rather, Jennings' 2005 death was a shock to many viewers and industry insiders, closing an era of network news stability, now called the classic era. After an interim period, Elizabeth Vargas and Bob Woodruff were named as Jennings' successors in 2006. However, Woodruff's grievous injuries suffered while he was covering the Iraq war put an end to the new anchor team after less than one month. Charles Gibson became the anchor of the renamed *ABC World News* later that year. Diane Sawyer became the second woman to solo anchor a network evening newscast when she replaced the retiring Gibson in 2010.

critical for winning the ratings competition. News anchors that can connect with other members of the news team and the audience are essential as the centerpieces for building loyalty. All three networks produce high-quality newscasts for which the ratings have been nearly equal for a very long time, but they risk losing the next generation of news viewers to cable and the internet if younger personalities are not developed to anchor these programs. Prime-time newsbreaks, vacation replacements and weekend newscasts often are the training grounds for new anchors and reporters.

As of the end of 2010, the *NBC Nightly News* was solidly in first place in the evening news ratings with an Adults 25 to 54 rating of 2.0. *ABC World News* was second with 1.7, followed by the *CBS Evening News* with 1.4. The networks have tried to distinguish the three newscasts from each other and from cable by creating segments within the newscasts. CBS's "Eye on America," NBC's "It's Your Money," and ABC's ongoing "Person of the Week" provide hooks for promotional announcements. The networks believe that viewers will link such segments to a particular network and get into the habit of watching a particular network for a favorite segment. Alternately, they may follow up on that network's news website. The news websites also offer viewers a chance to view features or even full newscasts on demand, although with reduced picture and sound quality.

Late-Night News

In November 1979, ABC News seized on the American viewing audience's fascination with the Iran hostage crisis and began a late-night newscast to summarize the major events of the day. The show evolved into *Nightline*, an in-depth news program hosted by Ted Koppel until 2005. Then a three-anchor multi-topic format was developed, currently hosted by Cynthia McFadden, Terry Moran and Bill Weir. Critics, however, pointed to less depth than in the single-story format and frowned on the rise in popular culture stories.

Because it counterprograms the network and syndicated talk shows, *Nightline* continues to draw a loyal, upscale audience. Traditionally, the series' ratings fell or rose sharply depending on national crises, wars and other disasters. Although the program is typically a half-hour in length, it sometimes expands for extremely important stories. On those evenings, *Nightline* can obliterate all the competing programs.

Such major news events as the disputed 2000 presidential election, the events of 9/11, the invasion of Iraq and later the Arab Spring triggered big upward spikes in the size of its audience. Even when major events are not taking place, *Nightline* has become a solid ratings performer (often finishing first in its time slot). *The key to its success has been ABC's vigorous campaign to have the show cleared live in most TV markets.*

Overnight News

The overnight time period (2:05 to 6 A.M.) has the lowest viewership of any daypart. Be it second-shift workers, nursing mothers, bottle-feeding fathers or insomniacs, however, there is *some* television viewing in the overnight period, but the network competition is not as spirited as in other dayparts. Unlike in prime time, where HUT levels are around 60 percent, overnight HUT levels are just 10 percent. Given the relatively low number of viewers, the potential ratings for individual overnight programs are thus quite low. Some affiliated stations sign off in the overnight hours, leading to lower clearance rates that further reduce ratings. Therefore, in the overnight time period, a 1.0 rating (meaning over 3 million people) is considered very strong (even in a nation of over 300 million people).

Given the low ratings and the low HUT levels, one might wonder why a network would bother to schedule any programming overnight. Even with 16 minutes of commercial time per hour, the entire daypart is worth only a few million dollars to each broadcast network. If the network can keep costs below the advertising revenue in the daypart and promote forthcoming shows, however, the effort is worthwhile because the risk is low. In addition, overnight news gives network affiliates programming at no cost to sustain their broadcast signal for 24 hours a day.

ABC's *World News Now* and CBS's *Up to the Minute* are the traditional overnight news series, although their names have changed over the years. Scheduled about 2 A.M., these shows compete against syndicated news programming offered to local stations by CNN Headline News. NBC's cable partners, MSNBC and CNBC, also offer information alternatives on cable/satellite networks. Each network does what it can to keep the costs of production low. *Up to the Minute* was one of the first network news services to provide video stories *on demand* over the internet, now common practice for television news organizations.

Following their overnight programming, networks offer early newscasts that lead into and provide updates for their local affiliates' news programming. At 4:30 A.M., NBC enters the competition with *Early Today*, a joint venture with its cable/satellite partner CNBC. At the same time, ABC airs *America This Morning* and CBS carries *CBS Morning News*. These early-morning news efforts lead into the networks' morning news magazines: *Today*, *Good Morning America* and *The Early Show*.

Weekend News and Information

Although weekday news and information programs receive the most attention, weekend programs include some of the longest-running series in television. In addition, weekend news and information slots allow networks to extend successful program brands such as *Today* and *Good Morning America* into new hours.

Weekend Magazines

ABC, CBS and NBC each program weekend morning magazines. On both Saturdays and Sundays, NBC airs a one-hour *Today* and ABC carries a one-hour *GMA*. CBS offers a two-hour Saturday version of its weekday magazine, *Saturday Early Show*, and also *Sunday Morning*, a 90-minute program that reviews news of the past week and surveys the world of fine art, music, science and Americana.

Sunday Morning, first with host Charles Kuralt and then with Charles Osgood, has been a fixture on CBS for over 30 years and delivers a surprisingly solid rating for the time period. These weekend shows allow network news divisions to utilize veteran news staff members while also developing and experimenting with new talent on the air.

Sunday News Interviews

ABC, CBS and NBC have traditionally aired public-affairs interview programs on Sunday mornings, and FOX has joined them. The format usually consists of a panel of journalists interviewing recent newsmakers about current issues and events. These shows have longevity rare in modern television: NBC's *Meet the Press*, network television's longest-running program, began in 1947, and CBS's *Face the Nation* began in 1954. ABC inaugurated its own public-affairs show, *Issues and Answers*, in 1960, which was replaced by *This Week with David Brinkley* in 1981. After Brinkley's retirement, the title was shortened to *This Week*, and Christiane Amanpour now hosts it. *FOX News Sunday*, which is allied with the Fox News cable channel, joined the competition in the 1990s. *Meet the Press*, hosted by David Gregory, presently draws the largest audience followed closely by *Face the Nation*, hosted by Bob Scheiffer. *This Week* is third and *News Sunday*, hosted by Chris Wallace, typically brings up the rear.

Although these news interviews do not attract large audiences, they remain on the air for two key reasons. First, all four of *these programs have become important news events in and of themselves.* Elected officials and top reporters appear on them to be seen and quoted; they have a chance to express themselves at length on important issues; and they themselves watch these programs avidly. Their words on Sunday morning television often become Sunday night's and Monday morning's news. This is especially important because Sunday is usually a slow news day. Second, *the programs attract desirable upscale audiences, and as a result, prestigious advertisers are drawn to the shows.*

Despite attractive attributes, many stations are hesitant to clear these relatively low-rated programs on weekends. Affiliates can make more money carrying infomercials or paid religious programming. To provide affiliates with more flexibility, multiple feeds of the programs are scheduled, giving affiliates plenty of scheduling options. However, many affiliates still refuse to clear the time.

Children's Programming

Children's television programming best illustrates the massive industry changes caused by the proliferation of program outlets. Because a child's brand loyalty is to the program and not to the network, an upstart network such as the former WB could leverage its *Pokémon* program in several time spots, making the WB, at least for a time, the number-one network in both the weekday kids' and the traditional Saturday morning children's block.

The dominant position of basic cable network Nickelodeon is further evidence that children are major users of cable television services (see 7.8). Consistently ahead of any of the Big Four broadcast networks in children's ratings, Nickelodeon has used such popular series as *SpongeBob SquarePants*, *iCarly* and *Zoey 101*, among others, to become *the* major force in children's television (both on cable and at cousin company CBS) and an increasingly powerful force in motion pictures and product licensing.

After decades of dominating Saturday morning children's programming, the rise of Nickelodeon, the Disney Channel, Cartoon Network and the once powerful Fox Kids network drove all three of the older broadcast networks into downplaying the time period. Post-2000, a pattern of leasing kids' shows from cable became the norm. The three-hour ABC Kids, for example, is provided by parent company Disney, which recycles its Disney Channel and Toon Disney cable programming on the network. ABC calls this "New-to-ABC Kids' episodes. Not surprisingly, popular Disney animated theatrical films, such as *Toy Story* and *The Lion King*, provide the self-serving inspiration for many of the programs in the block.

NBC, which abandoned most cartoon programming in favor of *tweens* live-action programming (*Saved by the Bell*) in the 1990s, formed (with ION) the more economical Qubo Kids lineup, airing shows on Saturday afternoons that target 4- to 8-year-olds. The CW is programmed by 4 Kids Entertainment, an offshoot of the major children's television syndicator Saban, presently under the *Toonzai on* CW4Kids label, demonstrating the continuing popularity of Japanese anime for young viewers. FOX, which at one time was a dominant player in children's programming, had abandoned the genre by 2011.

For some years, CBS "rented out" its Saturday morning block to Nickelodeon; then it tried education-blended-with-entertainment for older children, for example, *Wheel of Fortune 2000* and *Sports Illustrated for Kids*. Still slipping in the ratings, in 2007 CBS rediscovered animation, installing a lineup of six new animated half-hour series from Canadian producer Nelvana, under the KOL brand name. Today, the two-hour CBS kids' block is called *Cookie Jar* TV. Despite major efforts, all the broadcast networks must continually struggle against the attractions of cable and websites directed toward children.

In addition to ratings and economics, programmers must also consider factors specific to children's programming. One factor is that federal rules mandate minimum amounts of prosocial and educational programming (see 7.9). Although such rules are often perceived as vague and easily satisfied, programmers in other dayparts do not face such content-specific rules. Even Univision has had trouble figuring out what would be acceptable (see 7.10)

The Children's Television Act also required broadcasters to *air educational and informational children's programming* (knows as E/I). At license renewal time for stations, the FCC is required to consider whether a television station has served the educational and informational needs of children. Broadcasters are now obligated to air programs serving a child's cognitive/intellectual or social/emotional needs. These rules, of course, apply to stations, not networks, but many affiliates and all the O&Os want help from their networks in fulfilling

7.8 "Watching" in New Ways

While kids and tweens still watch a great deal of television, not all viewing habits are equal, and traditional television shows are finding it harder to appeal to older children. Because entertainment programming is now accessible through a myriad of platforms, from home computers to cell phones and iPads, television programmers are increasingly employing cross-platform initiatives to reach school-age kids. Instead of delayed rollout, Cartoon Network's animated series *Class of 3000* launched with a website featuring online sneak previews, streaming episodes, downloadable songs, podcasts, ringtones, wallpapers and messenger icons, plus a funkbox game that lets kids create their own music. Nickelodeon has renamed its 5–7 P.M. programming block *ME:TV* to reflect the proliferation of web-based activities for kids.

Interstitials between episodes of *SpongeBob SquarePants* feature short videos of kids participating in polls and games, and the program showcases videos submitted to *Nick.com* by kids. Viewers can go online to submit questions to Nick's hosts and celebrity guests or visit *www.Nicktropolis.com*, a virtual world where kids create their own avatars and personal rooms in order to play games, interact with network characters and connect with friends. Such activities may seem secondary enhancements to adults, but for children, they are becoming the new definitions of *watching television*.

Nancy C. Schwartz, Ph.D.
The Academic Edge, Inc.

7.9 Children's Programming Requirements

The FCC has long studied children's television programming. Members of the public, including special-interest groups and parents, have repeatedly stated their concerns about "kidvid." The main concerns regarding children's television programming have long been the overcommercialization of children's programming, the blurring of distinctions between program content and advertising messages, and the absence of educational content.

In 1990, Congress passed the Children's Television Act, requiring the FCC to impose advertising limits on children's programming of up to 10.5 minutes on weekends and 12 minutes during the week. The act also restricted the use of host-based commercials, ones that feature characters from the program in the advertiser's message. At the time, for example, a number of commercials featured the Mighty Morphin Power Rangers; the act eliminated those ads

featuring the Power Rangers or products with the Power Rangers pictured on them during the airing of *Mighty Morphin Power Rangers* or within 90 seconds before or after the program. Had the commercials aired, then the entire program would have been considered a program-length commercial and, therefore, in excess of the maximum allowable advertising time for one hour of children's programming.

This was a clever stratagem to force stations to exhibit some sensitivity to children's vulnerabilities. The prohibition on host-based commercials was aimed at decreasing the confusion a young child likely has in distinguishing commercials from a show's content. Even before the Children's Television Act, networks (as well as syndicators and broadcasters) usually placed interrupters or bumpers between programs and commercials. Nonetheless, research shows that young children remain confused.

the children's requirements. All of the programs presently offered by ABC, CBS, NBC and the CW on Saturday morning meet the E/I standard. However, the FCC does not specify the number of hours or the actual series that would satisfy the act, so there is always some unease.

After the act was in place, the FCC cited statistics showing that educational programming on the networks had actually fallen from 11 hours a week in 1980 to just 5 hours by the early 1990s. The Commission reacted to these findings by adopting new rules in 1996 designed to strengthen the existing

7.10 Univision's Expensive Mistake

In its most aggressive action regarding children's programming to date, the FCC fined Univision $24 million in 2007. This was the biggest fine ever for an individual company and a shock to an industry that has a history of being rather casual about what is and is not "educational." In the early 1990s, for example, several stations were using *The Flintstones* and *The Jetsons* to fulfill their educational requirements. Univision's fine arose from two years of labeling one of its soap operas as "children's" programming. *Complices al Rescate* ("Friends to the Rescue") follows the lives of two identical 11-year-old girls who swap identities, lose family members and friends, and suffer injustice. Because of the plots' complexity and the many adult themes, the FCC determined that the episodes had little value for children. The telling point was that about 80 percent of the advertising in the episodes was directed toward adults.

act. Chief among these were rules that did the following:

- Established a guideline of a minimum of three hours per week of core programming per television station

- Defined **core** programs as those that are regularly scheduled on a weekly basis, broadcast between 7 A.M. and 10 P.M., at least 30 minutes long, and that have as their significant purpose "serving the educational and information needs of children"

- Adopted new public information initiatives to benefit parents, such as requiring on-air identification of core children's programs and providing this information in parents' guides

Another factor is that children's programming is very much fad driven: Children's interests are fickle and change quickly. Chances are very good that the current *SpongeBob* phenomenon will fade in a few years and be replaced by the next big thing. *Scooby Doo, Power Rangers, Pokémon* and *Teenage Mutant Ninja Turtles* have all had their days in the ratings' sunshine.

Still another factor is that children's television is often an excellent example of the *synergy* so heralded when corporations merge. The most popular programs are used to market a dizzying array of toys, games, clothing, fast food, snacks, videos and motion pictures. One has only to walk through the various children's sections of a major store to see how popular children's programs become strong franchises for marketing a vast array of products, a phenomenon that dismays many parents.

Production and Development Processes

The development process for *animation* is different from that of prime-time or other daytime programs. Development of an animated children's series begins about 12 months before telecast, with pickups of new series exercised in February or March to allow producers six to seven months to complete an order for a September airing. The first stage is a **concept** pitched to the network programmers. The next steps are the **outline**, which describes the characters and the setting, and the **artwork**, which provides the sketches of the characters in several poses and costumes. If a project passes these stages, the next step is to order one or more scripts, which usually go through many drafts before final acceptance.

Pilot programs are rarely commissioned for cartoons because of the long production time and high costs. The usual contract for a season of animated programs to be aired weekly specifies production of only 13 episodes. If it airs any cartoons, the network generally schedules each episode four times during the first season.

The development process for *live action* is similar to that of animation, but it substitutes a **casting tape** for the artwork. In hopes of lowering per-episode production costs or of targeting a slightly older target audience, the broadcast networks have focused on live-action programs for several years.

The large number of repeats that networks can employ offsets the high cost of children's programming to a large degree. Popular children's programs can have each episode broadcast dozens of times over a period of years (besides spending time on cable and being syndicated to stations). Unlike most programs, which lose substantial audience share with reuse, both live-action and animated children's programs are less affected by repeats because the audience changes frequently with a new generation of youngsters to discover every old program. In addition, children generally enjoy the familiarity of program reruns more than adults do.

Despite network cuts, the children's television market remains strong, vital and profitable to networks that have carved out a substantial niche inside the genre. Even with their recent ratings problems, most of the broadcast networks are likely to maintain at least some Saturday morning presence through coventures that allow the broadcast networks to maintain a reduced Saturday morning schedule, but that target young viewers carefully and use the programs with proven popularity on cable and/or in syndication. The advantages for the Big Four are that they no longer have developmental responsibilities for children's programming and no longer need take on the entire financial responsibility.

In addition, even in an era of continuing deregulation of television and equation of the public interest with the corporate interest, the FCC and Congress would likely object to a network's complete abandonment of children's programming. Although always affected by economic cycles and the fickleness of the audience, children's programming is likely to remain popular and profitable because it can be linked to other profit centers in entertainment, motion pictures, video games and the internet.

Late-Night Talk/Variety

The studio-based talk/variety show is a prime example of low-risk programming. Its minimal start-up and ongoing production costs make it a perfect format for the low-budget realms of both daytime and late-night television. On the other hand, it's had its problems (see 7.11) with changing hosts.

Although other genres have been tried, the talk show remains the network genre with the greatest longevity in the late-night time period. Currently, NBC airs three consecutive talk shows (*The Tonight Show with Jay Leno, Late Night with Jimmy Fallon* and *Last Call with Carson Daly*) in the late-night period; CBS airs two talk shows (*Late Show with David Letterman* and *The Late Late Show with Craig Ferguson*); while ABC competes with *Jimmy Kimmel Live* following *Nightline*. FOX has failed several times to develop competing talk/comedy programs (*The Late Show Starring Joan Rivers, The Wilton North Report, The Chevy Chase Show*) and presently does not program the daypart.

As in prime-time series development (see Chapter 2), pilots are often produced for nighttime talk shows. Producers test a variety of elements prior to a talk show's release in attempts to gauge a show's potential: Commonly examined are the sets, the band, the sidekick, and the pacing of the show, but of course the key is the appeal of the host. When a network signs a major star to a talk-show contract, the network may decide to economize by producing **rehearsal shows** rather than a full-scale pilot. The late-night talk show has some of the same benefits of the morning talk show. The talk show can promote network offerings by booking same-network guests. A well-known celebrity appearing in a forthcoming made-for-TV movie can make a timely appearance on Leno or Letterman to promote the show's exact airdate and airtime.

After the merry-go-around (Version 2.0), late night gradually settled down. On NBC, Leno's *Tonight* (Version 2.0) is currently followed by *Late Night with Jimmy Fallon* and then *Last Call with Carson Daly* (a popular former MTV personality).

CBS's decision to gamble on David Letterman after he left NBC was a win. CBS had been struggling in third place in late night, and its new *Late Show with David Letterman* gave CBS an instant ratings success in this time period. Following *Late Show's* success, the network lured Tom Snyder away from his cable talk show on CNBC and gave him his own program, *The Late Late Show*, following Letterman. After Snyder retired, CBS hired Craig Kilborn, former host of Comedy Central's news spoof *The Daily Show*. After Kilborn's departure, comedian/actor Craig Ferguson took over the hosting duties.

7.11 The Late-Night Merry-Go-Round

Although not the first network late-night program (NBC's *Broadway Open House* has that distinction), NBC's *The Tonight Show*, with an over 55-year run, is the model for all television talk/comedy/variety programs and a model of stability with only five regular hosts in five decades: Steve Allen, Jack Paar, Johnny Carson, Jay Leno, Conan O'Brien, and Leno again. Carson, the host of *The Tonight Show* for the three decades from 1962 to 1992, was such a mammoth ratings success that the network added a one-hour show following *Tonight: The Tomorrow Show* with host Tom Snyder, which ran from 1973 to 1982.

After guest-hosting frequently for Carson, David Letterman was given his own daytime show on NBC in the 1980s. Because of low clearances and low ratings, his program lasted only four months. Guessing that Letterman's offbeat style might better suit late-night audiences, NBC replaced Snyder's program with the now-legendary *Late Night with David Letterman*. Letterman developed a cult following among young viewers, particularly college students, who made up a large portion of the show's audience.

Letterman's show attracted an especially desirable target audience with little falloff toward the end of the program, and to capitalize on the potential flow of viewership, NBC added another half-hour to its late-night lineup in 1988. The show, *Later*, was originally hosted by NBC sportscaster Bob Costas.

When Carson retired from *Tonight* in 1992, NBC had to decide who would replace him. Of its two final candidates, the network chose stand-up comic and frequent guest host Jay Leno over Letterman (driving Letterman to CBS after he lost this too-long too-public decision). Because *Tonight*'s audience had aged dramatically toward the end of Carson's reign, Leno retained the opening monologue that Carson had made famous but changed the show's style, band and routine to draw a younger audience. Leno's musical guests were selected with careful attention to the younger target audience. *The Tonight Show with Jay Leno* has been consistently the highest-rated of the network late-night programs.

With big ballyhoo, Conan O'Brien moved from *Late Night* to *Tonight* in 2009, and former SNL star/actor Jimmy Fallon took over *Late Night*. O'Brien had been promised the *Tonight* show back in 2004 at which time Leno was initially supposed to retire. Instead, in 2009 Leno was awarded a nightly prime-time program (10:00 P.M. M–F) which turned out to be a major failure so serious that it harmed all of NBC's prime-time schedule—a harm that still hadn't been rectified years later. So O'Brien finally got the tonight slot, but his ratings on *Tonight* were less than had been expected and considerably less than what Leno had been generating at 11:30. So Leno's prime-time program was cancelled early in 2010, and after O'Brien vocally refused to give up the 11:30 time spot, he was dumped and replaced by the return of Leno. (With renewed publicity, O'Brien moved to TBS and started a new talk/variety program, *Conan*.) This game of musical chairs was a major embarrassment to NBC and the most controversial and publicized event in prime time since the Leno/Letterman struggle to replace Carson in the early 1990s.

Prior to acquiring the services of Letterman, CBS had run original dramas (most of which were relatively inexpensive international coproductions) and repeats of prime-time programs. However, CBS had long sought its own "signature" talk-show personality to compete with Carson. First with Merv Griffin in the 1960s and 1970s and then Pat Sajak in the late 1980s, the Eye network failed to make a dent. Carson's departure and NBC's choice of Leno over Letterman to host *The Tonight Show* allowed CBS to obtain Letterman.

Although rarely winning the time slot, *Late Show* has been a highly lucrative program for CBS.

The success of Letterman led ABC to try unsuccessfully to woo him away from CBS. ABC, even more than CBS, has consistently failed to establish late-night stars. From Les Crane in the early 1960s through Joey Bishop, Dick Cavett, Jack Paar and Rick Dees over the years, ABC has found limited late-night success with repeats of prime-time dramas and, since 1981, with ABC News's *Nightline*. Before 2003, ABC tried *Politically Incorrect*, a

7.12	Late-Night Network Ratings Season Cumulative as of May 2011		
Program	**Network**	**Number of Viewers**	**A 18–49 Rating**
Nightline	ABC	4.0 million	1.0
Tonight (Leno)	NBC	3.9 million	1.0
Late Show (Letterman)	CBS	3.6 million	0.9
Late Night (Fallon)	NBC	1.8 million	0.6
Late, Late Show (Ferguson)	CBS	1.8 million	0.5
Jimmy Kimmel Live	ABC	1.7 million	0.5
Last Call (Daly)	NBC	1.0 million	0.4

"Gorman, Bill. (2011, May 12). Jay Leno and Jimmy Fallon Deliver #1 Finishers vs. ABC and CBS Competition for Late Night Week of May 2-6." *TB By The Numbers.* http://tvbythenumbers.zap2it.com/2011/05/12/jay-leno-and-jimmy-fallon-deliver-1-finishes-vs-abc-and-cbs-competition-for-the-late-night-week-of-may-2-6/92379/.

comedy/political discussion program, in the post-*Nightline* slot, but declining ratings and, according to many observers, the controversial post-9/11 comments of host Bill Maher led to cancellation. Its replacement, *Jimmy Kimmel Live*, is a Hollywood-based talk program hosted by a cable personality best known for his appeal to young men via Comedy Central's *The Man Show*.

FOX had three notable late-night talk-show failures prior to withdrawing from the daypart. None of the three—*The Late Show Starring Joan Rivers* (1986 to 1987), *The Wilton North Report* (1987 to 1988), and *The Chevy Chase Show* (1993)—attracted significant audiences away from competing talk shows. As of 2011, only the Big Three competed against cable and syndication for late night viewers on weeknights (see 7.12). With cable increasingly competitive in late night with its own talk/variety or comedy programs (*Daily Show, Colbert Report, Conan, George Lopez*) there is little opening for FOX to re-enter the fray.

Late-Night Weekend Entertainment

Programmers of late-night (11 P.M. to 1 A.M.) weekends generally attempt to reach viewers aged 18 to 34, but they face competition from a variety of sources in this daypart. First of all, on any given Saturday night, many in the desired target audience have other things to do than watch television. Second, cable and syndicated movies capture substantial audiences among this age group. As a result, to reach young adults, networks have tried to grab attention with truly unique programs on Friday and Saturday nights, including outlandish comedy, news and music formats. With only a handful of exceptions, however, they have been unsuccessful, so affiliates fill late-night weekend time with syndicated fare and infomercials.

One of the rare successes in network late-night weekend programming history is NBC's *Saturday Night Live* (*SNL*). Debuting on NBC in 1975, *SNL* remains an often innovative 90-minute comedy/variety program airing on Saturdays at 11:30 P.M. *SNL* features regular cast members and a different guest-star host each week. Ratings sometimes reach 6.0 total and close to 3.0 in Adults 18 to 49—huge ratings for a time period when HUT levels are so low. In some weeks, *SNL* out rates all other Saturday night network programs including prime time. Many former cast members have become famous film and prime-time television stars, including Chevy Chase, Mike Myers, Bill Murray, John Belushi, Eddie Murphy, Dana Carvey, Chris Rock, Adam Sandler, Will Ferrell, Amy Poehler and Tina Fey.

Because producing a fresh 90-minute sketch-driven comedy is so demanding, NBC occasionally gives the cast and writers a rest and has offered some specials and a variety of packaged, thematic best-of-*SNL* shows in its time slot. During the crucial November, February and May ratings sweeps, however, first-run shows air for at least three consecutive weeks.

As is the case with most successful series, *SNL* has had its imitators over the years, the most obvious being ABC's *Fridays* that lived and died in the early 1980s. So far, *SNL* has had only one long-running network competitor, FOX's *MADtv*, which ran from 1995–2009. Similar to *SNL*, it uses a repertory company of young comedians performing comedy sketches, including popular culture satires and recurring character bits. The one-hour program started at 11 P.M., a half-hour earlier than *SNL*, allowing it to counterprogram the local news on NBC affiliates and bridge the start of *SNL*, thus capturing viewers interested in comedy before *SNL* takes the stage. In late 2006, FOX began to program the 12 to 12:30 A.M. post-*MADtv* spot with *Talkshow with Spike Feresten*, and alternate this with repeats of prime-time series. Both *MADtv* and *Talkshow* left the air in 2009 to be replaced by *The Wanda Sykes Show* that lasted only one season. Reruns of *Fringe* and a reality competition program entitled *30 Seconds to Fame* were being scheduled by FOX by 2011.

The Effects of Consolidation and Cable

Network non-prime-time programming is in transition. There is no question that daytime, weekend and late-night programming can be lucrative dayparts. The combination of relatively low costs for program production (with the exception of sports) and loyal audiences has produced substantial profits. Why then are many of the remaining network programs losing audiences? Why have the networks scaled back or abandoned their programming in some of these dayparts (for example, NBC on weekday afternoons, FOX in late night)? The answers to these questions lie in the changing nature of the broadcast network television industry in the early years of the twenty-first century.

The huge profits from daytime and some other nonprime dayparts are no longer a secret. *Local stations now realize that they can generate much more revenue from syndicated programs or even infomercials than they can from the compensation (cash and/or advertising availabilities) offered by networks for clearing their programs* (see Chapter 8). This has reduced clearance levels for non-prime dayparts and led to the scaling back of network offerings. Because of low clearances, the newer broadcast networks have not even attempted to program many of the non-prime dayparts.

However, there is no need to worry about the networks. Their corporate owners are increasingly the owners not just of cable networks, but of both the local stations and the syndicated programming that has replaced network programming on those stations in many nonprime dayparts, and they are buying up online services (witness Hulu). The Big Four networks constitute the largest owners of major television stations, and their O&Os are typically much more profitable than their networks. In addition, co-ventures, such as seen on Saturday mornings between cable networks, broadcast networks and syndicators, are likely to become the norm in other time periods and spill over into the internet and as offerings for mobile media. *The old lines of demarcation are rapidly dissolving in the television industry—as they did a generation earlier in the radio industry.*

Several non-prime network programs continue to have fiercely loyal audiences. The problem for the networks is that these audiences are aging and not being replaced by younger viewers who are divided among many more viewing options (and other entertainment media) than were their parents. In particular, programs that have traditionally drawn a loyal but older audience (soap operas, news) must adapt or run the risk of becoming unprofitable—at which point they will likely be so altered as to be unrecognizable or simply disappear.

The most important factor to consider with regard to both the present and future of nonprime network programming is this blurring of the traditional distinctions between network, syndicated and cable programs. Relaxation of the financial interest and syndication rules (see Chapter 1) allowed networks to establish themselves as program suppliers to affiliates and nonaffiliates. Increasingly, broadcast networks are both programmers and syndicators both domestically and internationally. The continuing relaxation of the television station ownership cap has made the corporate owners of the broadcast networks more active program buyers.

While integrated station and network ownership can be used to guarantee clearance for a network program, it can also be used as clout for "sibling" syndicated programming. For example, the revenue goals of a Viacom/CBS-owned television station might be fulfilled by a CBS network program. On the other hand, it might be more lucrative for the station to acquire a syndicated program such as *Dr. Phil* from King World (a syndicator owned by Viacom) or a film from Paramount (another Viacom Company). The parent company (in this case, Viacom) cannot lose in any of these scenarios. Moreover, Viacom can use its clout to gain the necessary clearance for a new syndicated offering in exchange for the rights to a successful show. In addition, Viacom is not tied to the needs of CBS or its local affiliates and can auction off its syndicated offerings to whatever local stations are willing to pay the most. Viacom (or Disney, FOX, NBC Universal, Time Warner) cannot lose.

This is the new television. The low HUT levels in nonprime time have allowed the big media conglomerates to experiment in the "new world" of television programming. There is much more change to come in all dayparts, as the decades-old distinctions between broadcast networks, cable networks, syndicators and program producers fade into the fog of corporate consolidation and the rise of online and tablet television.

Note

1. Despite the demise of regularly scheduled sports anthologies on the networks, the *Wide World of Sports* brand continues as the name of a sports entertainment attraction at Disney World. The Walt Disney Co. is, of course, the parent company of both ABC and ESPN.

Television Station Programming Strategies

Robert B. Affe

Chapter Outline

The dinosaur could not adapt to a radically changed environment ... and died out; Somewhat more recently, vacuum tube manufacturers lost their market to transistors; film cameras were replaced by digital cameras. In business, as in biology, the key to survival is adaptation. Media companies of the past that have ridden the peak of the wave of technological, economic and demographic change have prospered; those companies able to merely cope with change have hung on to survive, if only temporarily; companies that failed to meet the demands of change have been extinguished. The dynamics of programming a television station have radically changed over the last 15 years or so, buffeted by overdue regulatory reform and technological revolution in the form of digital communications. Consider the impact of the internet, digitized signals and personalized mobile communications devices. Whereas most individual stations were programmed autonomously ("inside the building") for most of the twentieth century, today the television station is at the end of a pipeline of business imperatives imposed from above. (The sole exception is news programming, discussed later in this chapter.)

On many levels—technological, financial, demographic, marketing and regulatory—broadcast programming is hurtling through creative and economic developments that are breathtaking to its viewers and gut-wrenching to its participants. Now that the predictability and easy profitability of past decades have declined markedly, station owners, programmers and industry observers warily look to the horizon to see what lies ahead.

The Regulatory Wave

The two waves that broke over the programming business formed far offshore during the 1990s; one flooded the business immediately, with a long term impact; the second wave took a longer, slower time to crest, but had an equally formidable consequence. The first was regulatory reform, which had several parts. For starters, after decades of patchwork revisions, in 1996 the U.S. Congress finally revamped the enabling legislation of the electronic media business,

the (antique) 1934 Communications Act. The effect on the programming business was profound. Numerical restrictions on station ownership were lifted. Media companies could own, theoretically, as many stations as they wanted (and the giants wanted a lot!), up to a cumulative population reach of 39%. Almost immediately, television station companies were no longer small, informal collections of media properties. The economies of scale created by the 1996 act imposed a discipline of managerial realities from above, affecting production, purchase, scheduling and promotion at television stations.

Some of the most enthusiastic station-buyers were the networks themselves. Always at the vanguard of the economies of scale that drive commercial television, three of the four major networks leapt to add to their portfolio of stations. By 2011, FOX owned 17 stations, CBS owned 14 stations, and NBC 10. Only ABC held back with a smaller portfolio of 8 stations.

For station programmers, the most visceral change was the fact that the relationship between the local station affiliate and the network was uprooted. Always precarious and wobbly at best, the balance between the powerful national programmer and the local outlet was tipped unequivocally toward the network. The days of the locally owned and operated commercial television station were over. The first and second generations of station owners sold out ... and moved on.

Another regulatory change with convulsive impact was the FCC's decision to let the networks return to the lavishly profitable business of program syndication. This abrogated the established financial-syndication rules (fin-syn) and ripped program-making away from the independent producers and put it into the hands of big studios with which the networks had close "marital" relationships (Disney owns ABC, Paramount once owned CBS, Fox owns FOX). Once free to do so, it was an easy play for networks to produce their own programs and then reap the profits of selling them in the programming aftermarket. Soon the independent producers were finished off (as described in Chapter 2), and the Hollywood studios made theatrical movies and television largely for the favored network.

Finally, the FCC has backed away from its traditional insistence on a local orientation for broadcasting. The result has been an increase in the quantity of affiliates of some network and an overall decrease in the number of unrelated (independent) station owners. Another by-product has been more substitution of remote owners for local ones and a concomitant decrease in locally produced programs.

The Digital Wave

No business operates in a vacuum, immune to outside forces, and television programming is no exception. Many factors affect the environment in which a station makes decisions about program selection, scheduling, evaluation and promotion. In technology, the major change has been the adoption of digital signal transmission. As of 2009, all licensed stations (which excludes cable) were required to broadcast a *digital signal* (although some stations sought exemptions from the FCC). This has resulted in superior-quality signals, although they are not necessarily in high-definition formats and do not necessarily result in better reception for all receivers.

At the same time, stations acquired the ability to *multiplex*—to send several channels of programming on their assigned frequency—while previously they could send only one channel. *From an economic perspective, going digital required an enormous financial outlay, and the station owners thought multiplexing would provide compensating income.* Moreover, as an advertiser-supported medium, broadcast television is hyper-responsive to the overall national economy. When the economy expands, advertising budgets likewise expand; in a period of economic contraction, advertising budgets are usually among the first budgets cut by companies.

Another pressure comes from new and intensified competition—first from cable, then from the internet and mobile media. Networks and their affiliates no longer capture the majority of television viewing. Combined ratings for the top 20 cable networks now often equal or pass broadcast ratings. Yet the broadcasters were slow to convert to digital signals and continue to be slow to convert to HD.

And the demography of the audience is altering. More affluent viewers are abandoning the networks in droves; younger viewers are, too, finding that the flexibility of the internet and mobile media better suits their lives. The median age of television viewers is rapidly growing older (past 50 years of age), accelerated by the fact that younger consumers spend increasing amounts of time in online and gaming pursuits. In a business that relies on young, brand-conscious consumers, the graying of America signals a demographic derailment for national advertising via broadcasting.

Sources of Television Programs

In nearly all circumstances, station decisions about programs are evaluated for both their creative (content) and financial (business) considerations. When home viewers enjoy—or disparage—a program on the screen, what they see is the result of professional programmers' evaluations of that show's relative creative and financial merits.

Nearly all programs are *produced* by one of four entities: the networks, the television production divisions of the movie studios, the very few remaining independent producers (more common in radio broadcasting than television now), or the local stations themselves. A producer needs a customer for any program, and television programming is relayed to homes via one of three outlets—from a network to its affiliates, from a syndicator when purchased by the station or its group, or from original production at the station (called *local*). The chart in 8.1 illustrates how several popular programs have come to the screen via different producers and modes of distribution.

Not all networks are program producers because two are co-owned and operated as a unit with the dominant network. ABC, CBS, FOX and NBC are active producers, but CBS/TW-owned CW and FOX-owned MNTV are not; they carry mostly syndicated or "repurposed" product from their parent companies. Both Univision (UNI) and Telemundo (TEL, owned by NBC) produce a wide range of Hispanic programming—and import from Mexico as well—but TeleFutura (TEF), owned by UNI, produces primarily sports.

8.1   Program Distribution

	Produced by:		
	Network/Station	**Movie Studio**	**Independent Producer**
Distributed via:			
Network	*NBC Nightly News* (NBCUniversal)	*CSI* (CBS)	*America's Got Talent* (Freemantle North America)
Syndication	*Rachael Ray Show* (CBS TV)	*Ellen* (Warner Bros)	*Wendy Williams Show* (Debmar)
Local station	Local newscasts (self-produced or repeated from another local station)	—	—

For purposes of discussing programming, here are three classifications of stations. Most visible are the network owned-and-operated stations (the *O&Os*, pronounced "oh and ohs"), which are generally the top stations in the biggest markets. For example, ABC-TV, Inc., (owned by Disney) in turn owns the ABC Television Network, which in turn owns and operates eight television stations, among them WABC-TV (New York), KABC-TV (Los Angeles), WLS-TV (Chicago), WPVI-TV (Philadelphia) and KGO-TV (San Francisco). In the shorthand of the television trade press, it is often reported that a network has "made" or "lost" money. That is a largely inaccurate way to report the fortunes of a broadcasting company. It is important to remember that network television is a *program service*; in other words, it is an *expense*. The network's programming service is not designed to maximize profit. The *real* money is made by selling commercials in high-rated programs at the network-owned stations. This is why the networks continue to beef up their portfolios of owned stations and aggressively lobby Washington to raise the limits on station ownership still further.

As you undoubtedly know, *affiliates* are stations that have agreed to run all the programs distributed by one of the nine major commercial networks and have signed an affiliation contract. The Washington Post Company, for example, owns six television stations, and its Houston station (KPRC) is affiliated with the NBC network and has the exclusive right to run NBC's programs in the Houston television market. It is called a *network-affiliated station*. Other stations owned by the Washington Post Company, however, are affiliates of other networks.

A true *independent station* has no formal relationship with a network and instead obtains its programs from a variety of sources, mostly syndicators or rerun programs. During a brief 15-year period (roughly from 1980 to 1995), independents sprang up across America, corresponding to a spurt in the economy and consequent demand for advertising time. The economy was *so* good, in fact, that four new networks—FOX, PAX, UPN and the WB—were formed, and most of the then-independent stations chose affiliation.

Today, most of the former UPN and WB stations are affiliated with the CW or MNTV (PAX died and eventually reemerged as ION—which morphed quickly into a syndication service). In addition, more than 200 stations are O&Os or affiliates of one of the Spanish-language networks (Univision, Telemundo, TeleFutura or one of the smaller networks). However, the number of owned stations and affiliates varies widely for the nine biggies (see 8.2).

Altogether, 95 percent of all commercial broadcast stations today are either O&Os or affiliates of one of the nine commercial broadcast networks. In addition to ION, a few very small broadcast television networks exist alongside the well-known ones, for example, America One (formerly Channel America), MTV2 (formerly The Box), and Trinity Broadcasting Network (TBN) and other religious networks. They

8.2 | Network Affiliates and Owned Stations

	Owned Stations	Affiliates*	U.S. Penetration
ABC	8	218	96.8%
CBS	14	204	96.9%
CW (CBS/TW)	—	195**	95%
FOX	17	180	96.1%
ION	58	95	83%
MNTV (FOX)	—	167	96%
NBC	10	207	97%
TeleFutura (Univision)	18	34	75%[†]
Telemundo (NBC)	13	50	93%[†]
Univision	19	66	97%[†]

*America One, for example, has 152 affiliates, but they are low-power, cable and satellite affiliates only; moreover, the network is not promoted on the air, so its affiliates appear to be independents.

**CW also has 15 cable-only digital affiliates.

[†]These percentages are of Spanish-speaking households, not total TV households.

tend to have secondary rather than primary affiliations, largely with digital-cable or low-power or very small market stations. If they have primary affiliations, these tend to consist of less than a handful of stations.

Network Programming for Affiliates

In television, the station–network relationship is modeled on the pattern established in the days of radio. The operators of the first radio stations quickly realized that broadcasting's programming demands were an all-consuming flame. As difficult as it was to create programming for large-city stations in the early days, it was nearly impossible for smaller-market stations to fill their program days. The owners of WEAF, including General Electric, fed that station's programming to their co-owned station in Washington, D.C., WCAP. In effect, the cost of that program to the local station was zero. That experiment was so successful that when stations outside the company clamored for programs, General Electric created a relationship in which the

company would send programs through long-distance telephone lines to the local station. In return, GE inserted their commercials inside the program, and at the program's conclusion, the local station could air its own commercials. Thus the first network was created.

Subsequent networks, including television and cable, continue to be patterned after this model. *The classic network model maximizes the economies of scale in the broadcasting business because the cost of producing one program can be spread over hundreds of affiliates.* In return, with one commercial, an advertiser can have its message sent nationwide in the same program at the same time. In network-distributed programs, the network keeps approximately three-quarters of the commercial time, and the affiliate retains a quarter of the time for sale, traditionally the source of immense profitability.

Another advantage is that the local affiliate has *exclusivity*, the sole right to the network's programs (or at least, the right of first refusal). The full-service networks (ABC, CBS and NBC) supply about 12 to 16 hours of programming daily to their 200+ affiliates—nearly 100 hours per week across all time periods—which is about one-half to two-thirds the amount a station needs. UNI supplies even more hours to its affiliates. Getting the rest is the primary occupation of programmers at the stations (and the other networks supply even fewer hours, making the programmer's job much larger).

But downsides to the network–affiliate relationship exist. Some affiliates are weak stations with poor signals, low-rated newscasts or overall inadequate performances, all of which disadvantage a network and cause it to look for stronger affiliates. From the affiliates' perspectives, some networks' programming is rated lower (the CW, MNTV, Tele-Futura) than that of other networks—or a network's specific programs might not be as popular in a particular market as in the country overall. For example, ABC has traditionally targeted the urban audience, but some of its affiliates are in rural locations where urban material doesn't always suit the viewers. Nonetheless, both networks and affiliates need each other to provide what they themselves lack: The networks lack local presence, and the affiliates lack the financial resources to program all their broadcast days.

The Big Four

At the apex of their dominance and profitability in the late 1970s, the Big Three—CBS, NBC, ABC—attracted more than 90 percent of all prime-time viewing and advertising dollars. By the early 2000s, their collective share of prime-time viewing had slipped beneath 35 percent. Although alternative forms of video entertainment, in the aggregate, have chipped away at the networks' near-monopoly of television, commercial network television continues to remain the best vehicle for mass advertising in America and thus continues to be economically viable. The newer broadcast networks, the cable networks and internet websites attract higher concentrations of narrowly targeted audiences, but they cannot come close to contesting the networks for delivery of mass audiences.

In 1994, FOX upended the cozy three-way balance that had operated for four decades. Initially, FOX's affiliates were former independent stations, usually the highest-rated independents in their respective markets, but still inferior in audience

share and revenue to their competitors, the affiliates of the long-established networks. In addition, most of the FOX affiliates lacked newscasts. Chairman Rupert Murdoch soon put them on notice that his affiliates would produce local news—or lose the FOX affiliation. FOX successfully raided many traditional affiliate rosters, especially those of CBS, and the Big Three reluctantly became the *Big Four*. FOX captured the crown jewels of the industry by acquiring the broadcast rights to NFL football starting with the 1994 season. By securing the NFL rights, other affiliates suddenly saw the immediate threat of losing loyal viewers, irreplaceable revenue and an unmatched platform for promoting network programming. The impact of the NFL deal shook the underpinnings of the relationship between the Big Three networks and their affiliates, particularly for CBS, whose affiliates opened their eyes to the advantages of switching their allegiance to FOX.

Before 1994, affiliation switches were rare. Viewers, broadcasters and networks basked in the security of loyal, long-term relationships. When FOX announced a series of affiliation switches in major markets, it unleashed a flurry of activity, breaking a logjam and causing a downstream realignment of affiliates in nearly every large market in which the Big Three networks did not already own stations. In Philadelphia, Boston, Detroit, Dallas, Atlanta, Cleveland, Seattle, Tampa, Miami, Phoenix and many other markets—covering nearly one-quarter of the U.S. population—one or more long-term affiliation relationships were broken up, and FOX substantially upgraded its affiliate lineup. By doing so, it achieved station *parity* in network television (reaching equal numbers of households via roughly the same number of owned-stations and affiliates).

CBS was severely wounded by the raid on its affiliates. The network lost decades-long relationships in large markets and had to spend scores of millions of dollars in advertising, promotion and publicity, introducing viewers in many markets to the local channel that was the new home of CBS. The costs were more than monetary; in many cases they were a slap to the prestige of the "Tiffany Network." In Detroit, for example, CBS lost its Channel 2 affiliate to FOX and had to decamp way up the dial to Channel 62. (It was not exactly in the same spectrum with police and fire calls, but it was close, from CBS's perspective.) In Miami, CBS lost its traditional position on Channel 4 and moved to Channel 6, which had a serious signal-reception problem in the northern half of the market. In Atlanta, CBS lost Channel 5 and moved to Channel 46. CBS was staggered by the FOX raid, and it took years for the network—and thus its affiliates—to recover.[1] Today, CBS, NBC, ABC and FOX have between 197 and 226 affiliated stations each (including O&Os) on their rosters.

The Small Ones

In January 1995 two new networks debuted in the same week: "The WB", owned principally by Time Warner, and "UPN", originally owned by Paramount and Chris-Craft Broadcasting, then by Viacom/CBS. These so-called netlets did not provide the full programming slate to their affiliates. Instead, the WB and UPN focused on the heart of a station's schedule, the prime-time hours, adding young-adult-skewing programming and children's animation on weekdays and weekend mornings. The new networks patterned their rollout on the model devised by FOX in its early years, introducing one or two nights of prime-time programming per year.

After a decade of low ratings, CBS and Time Warner shut down the networks, and in about the blink of an eye, came up with the CW, cherry-picking the old schedules for the best programs. Since the new network could have only one affiliate per market, it captured the best ones (sometimes stealing from the Big Three because NBC's programming was ailing at the time). That left dozens of former UPN stations (many owned by FOX) and others without a network, so FOX invented MyNetworkTV (MNTV, named like FOX's MySpace.com).

The new networks' game plans avoid competing for ratings with the Big Four across all dayparts. Instead, the CW and MNTV program only when they can be competitive, which means primarily prime time, and primarily weeknights. Even FOX does not program three hours of prime time every night, unlike the Big Three. FOX programs two

hours, then expects its affiliates to air late news at 10 P.M. (9 P.M. central) to get the jump on the late newscasts aired by affiliates of the other networks. Affiliated broadcasters are left with large portions of weekdays and weekends to fill.

The other English-language network, Paxson, launched its PAX service in 1998, concentrating on family-friendly programming, both first-run and syndicated, and morphed into ION in 2007 (after a couple of other tries at a new name), but it lagged in ratings and familiarity to audiences. In order to foster programming without sex and violence (suitable for family viewing), it attempted to tightly control the programming of its affiliates using a contract that limited the carriage of syndicated series. Many affiliates soon abandoned the contract, ignoring it and eventually jumping ship for more popular programming from MNTV or the CW. Consequently, ION stopped trying to be a network and shifted to a rerun service, purchasing long sets of older off-network series, currently offering *Without a Trace* (over and over), *Ghost Whisperer* (over and over), and lots of *Criminal Minds*. Dropping its "holier than everyone else" attitude, it carries *Look Sexy Now*. It does not produce newscasts or live talk, instead filling time with paid programs (mostly religion) and informercials.

One of the major benefits of the FOX, CW and MNTV affiliations is that they give a network-quality look to their affiliated stations, which were predominantly weak independent stations before the mid-1990s. As much as any other factor, by their guerrilla style of picking off younger network audiences, the newer networks have contributed to the blurring of identities between affiliates and the former independents. Independents used to be characterized by a "local" look ("local" used pejoratively in this case), providing prime-time programming consisting of old movies and even older syndicated products. Today, it is virtually impossible to distinguish between the two former classes of stations in network prime time.

The Spanish-Language Three

One of the huge success stories in broadcasting in the last generation has been Spanish-language programming. The Hispanic population of the United

States is now the largest minority population, as well as the fastest-growing minority. Furthermore, this population is densely settled along the states bordering Mexico (Arizona, New Mexico, Texas), and the Mountain states, with significant population clusters in Florida, North Carolina and metropolitan New York, Chicago and Atlanta. The three major Spanish-language services—Univision (and its sister network, TeleFutura), and Telemundo, owned by NBCUniversal—overwhelm markets that have a strong Spanish-speaking presence. Indeed, UNI typically outdraws English-language competitors in many time periods and has altered the national advertising market.

Spanish-language broadcasting is concentrated in markets with large *absolute* numbers of Hispanics (New York, Los Angeles, Chicago, San Francisco, Dallas, Miami) and also with large *percentage* numbers (Austin, San Antonio, Albuquerque, Bakersfield). The Hispanic population of the United States was officially (at least) 16 percent as of 2011, projected by the U.S. Census Bureau to increase to 20% in 2030, and to 30% in 2050.

Univision, a publicly traded independent company (formerly Spanish International Network or SIN), was founded in 1962 and was the first non-English-language network in the United States. It owns 18 full-power and 8 low-power outlets, has 66 broadcast affiliates and is carried on about 18,000 cable systems, FiOS and both satellite services, giving it reach into nearly all of the 210 broadcast markets. It has been the fifth-largest U.S. television network for many years. Its best-known programming consists of Mexican telenovelas produced by Grupo Televisa, major international sporting events—especially soccer—and *Noticiero Univision*, its nightly newscast.

Its co-owned sister service, TeleFutura, schedules to compliment Univision's programming on another 18 full-power and 15 low-power owned stations and 34 broadcast affiliates, along with about 270 cable affiliates. In addition to such blockbuster programming as *Sabado Gigante*, soccer and hot telenovelas, both networks carry newscasts and some noncommercial programs. In 15 markets, their duopoly status puts UNI/TEF stations near the top of all stations.

Univision also owns the cable network Galavisión, some music services, Univision Radio and *www.univision.com*, a very popular website. In addition to its efforts to capture a younger demographic, Univision claims to have the largest unduplicated prime-time audience, with two-thirds of its viewers unavailable to any other network.[2] During hot soccer matches, Univision sometimes leads ALL U.S. networks in prime time in adults 18–49. One year, the highest recorded rating for Univision (a 35.9) was a tribute to the murdered Tejano singer, Selena. As a further measure of its influence, the concept for the Univision serial, *La Fea Mas Bella*, was licensed and re-introduced on ABC as "Ugly Betty."

Telemundo (TEL) is the second-largest producer of Spanish-language television programming in the world, and the second-largest Spanish-language television network in the United States. Founded in 1954, Telemundo has about 160 broadcast and cable affiliates. As a symbol of the growing importance of the Hispanic advertising market, Telemundo was purchased by NBC in 2002 and gained substantial financial support for program production, both for its own affiliates and for shows for international distribution. Because of its majority stake (51%) in NBCUniversal, Comcast now owns Telemundo, solidifying the network's domestic presence on about 600 cable systems, in addition to ownership of six full-power and five low-power stations with 50 broadcast affiliates. This combination gives TEL video presence in about a quarter of U.S. television markets. Its popular movies, reality programs, talk shows and telenovelas make it the No. 2 network TEL offers the largest amount of bilingual programming, with English subtitles, because it distributes internationally as well as targeting U.S. Spanglish speakers.

Another Spanish-language network, Azteca America began operations in 2001. Headquartered in Los Angeles, this network has approximately 60 affiliates, receives some of its programming from its sister network in Mexico, and reaches nearly all the Hispanic market in the States. The Hispanic population is younger than the population as a whole, a particular advantage for broadcasters who can attract them. Its median age is 27.4, versus the overall median population age of 36.8, and the Hispanic audience has a higher percentage of young adults and children, making it ideal for national consumer advertisers. Traditional package-brand advertisers now allocate larger budgets to reaching this audience, and the profit potential of Spanish-language networks and their stations has become self-evident. For example, at times, in Los Angeles, Miami and Fresno ratings, Univision stations have led their markets in adults aged 18 to 49 and adults aged 18 to 34 across the entire broadcast day. Combined with the increasing household income of Hispanic families, Spanish-language broadcasting is a growth segment in an otherwise-mature (and threatened) broadcasting business.

The Network–Affiliate Agreement

Each party to an affiliation makes specific promises to the other party; the legal document binding both parties is called an *affiliation agreement* (and sometimes programmers go around moaning that they can't do something because of "the agreement"). To summarize, the network agrees to provide its program service to the affiliate on an exclusive basis. *Exclusive* means that only one station in each market may broadcast the network's programs (except that refused programs can be licensed to another station). Further, the network will pay the affiliates a negotiated fee for broadcasting its programs. This fee is called *network compensation*, or just plain *comp*. Network compensation can easily exceed $1 million per station in the larger markets. Ironically, comp is more important to stations in the smaller markets, where it can represent up to 10 percent of total revenues and spell the difference between profit or loss for the affiliate.

In return for comp, the affiliate promises to broadcast the programs as delivered by the network and to allow the network to retain about three-quarters of the commercial time within each network program (to sell the time in the national market). *The exchange of local commercial airtime for network*

programming is the justification and foundation for the entire network–affiliate relationship. This is the central idea of the network–affiliate relationship (see 8.3). For example, one variable in a commercial station's profit formula is the number of advertisements it can air. Although the number of commercials allotted to an affiliate is only about one-quarter of the total number of ads in a given program, small variations in that "about" can mean the gain or loss of a lot of money for the station.

As you probably know, the commercial breaks for the local station are called *station breaks* or *adjacencies*. In a half-hour program, the affiliate's commercials come at the end of the program; the network's commercials fall within the more desirable real estate—within the program itself. In an hour-long program, half the affiliate's commercials fall at the end of the program, half within, while (again) all the network's commercials occur within the program. Thus, hour-long programs have more value to stations—ratings being equal—because some of the "within spots" can sell at higher rates.

8.3 ▐ **The Soi-Disant "Networks"**

The scramble for programming and the oversupply of local stations has resulted in the creation of self-described television networks, such as occur in radio broadcasting. These are not networks in the true sense of the word; they are national programming or syndication services that can be used to fill low-rated time periods. Low-rated stations that cannot afford competitive prices for syndicated programs and lack the ratings to attract barter advertisers make considerable use of them. ION is one exemplar (and MNTV comes close). Another such program supplier is Bounce TV, appealing to black American audiences. Bounce debuted in 2011, with affiliated stations reaching about half the domestic U.S. viewing population either via cable, satellite or broadcasting. Such quasi-networks don't pay compensation, don't have newscasts, and usually don't sell time in the national spot market. Their programming is either very local or purchased from syndicators. If there is national advertising in the shows, the syndicators put it there.

Tension between a network and its affiliate governs the entire relationship. In the network-affiliate detente, each party thinks that the other is getting the upper hand in the deal. The networks believe that the affiliates are reaping windfalls from obtaining high-quality and commercially attractive network programs *plus* receiving compensation. In contrast, the affiliates grouse that the networks are hogging most of the commercial *inventory* during network programming as well as piggybacking on the affiliates' success and reputation in the market for news and local programming. These arguments raged back and forth for decades, indicating that the relationships were roughly equal in strength. Of course, in markets where the affiliate is competitively superior (because of strong news performance or such outside factors as signal strength or lack of strong competitors in the market), its resentment of the network is correspondingly higher than in a market in which the affiliate is weak.

In truth, networks and affiliates have long had need of each other. *Under the traditional network model, each party trades what it has for what it needs: The network needs local affiliates to gain access to the market, and affiliates need the economies of scale that enable the network to provide the big-budget entertainment/sports/news programming that affiliates would otherwise be unable to produce on their own.* What lies on the horizon may not fit this model. As the internet captures more of television viewers for programming other than TV shows, and as both production and comp costs rise, the industry may be forced to adopt something close to the syndication model ... where the highest bidder gets each program. But for most stations, at least the bigger, more profitable ones, that day lies in the fuzzy future, not nearby.

Preemptions

Occasionally, an affiliate might decide not to air (i.e., might *preempt*) a network program for any of a number of reasons. Most commonly, a station might preempt when it

- has a local news emergency that requires live, on-the scene coverage.

- decides to air a program it produced on its own, such as a local parade, local news special, sporting event and the like.

- deems the content of the network program inappropriate for local viewers.

- wants to keep all the advertising time and revenue for itself (which occurs most frequently on weekends during the Christmas shopping season, when local stations try to maximize commercial revenue during the busiest advertising time of the year).

Usually, when an affiliate preempts a network show, the station will reschedule the program in another time period (called *delayed carriage*) but will lose whatever compensation accompanied the regular airing (not all programs qualify for comp). If the affiliate refuses to *clear* (air) the program at all, a Big-Four network will then offer it to another station in the market in order to have some audience in the market for the program and its ads. As you can imagine, the networks keep careful track of exactly how many preemptions each affiliate makes, and that number can be a powerful bargaining chip at the time of affiliation agreement renewal or when affiliates request higher compensation. To protect themselves, affiliates negotiate in advance for the right to preempt a limited number of programs during the year.

It is important to recall that networks are not licensed by the FCC—only stations are—and affiliates must keep their eyes on their next license renewal dates by offering some programming in the public interest. Sometimes an affiliate contests its network's complaints about preemptions on the grounds that the substitute programs better served the community's interests and made the affiliate a stronger station in the market. This is a compelling argument when a network repeat episode is preempted in favor of a local news special about education in the region; it is a plausible argument when a network is preempted in favor of a championship game in which a local college team is playing; and it is a weak argument if the network is preempted in favor of a syndicated entertainment program, broadcast solely for the purpose of selling more commercials to improve the station's quarterly revenues.

News and Local Programming

"News is what someone, somewhere wants to suppress; everything else is just advertising,"

> — Alfred Lord Northcliffe, British press magnate from the early part of the last century

Television, like its parent radio, was originally developed as a community-oriented medium, serving both local viewers and advertisers. Limited by unreliable equipment and the financial/organizational constraints of an infant industry, early television was predominantly a *live, local* medium. The early days of television were experimental, thrilling, agonizing and just plain chaotic.[3]

When the U.S. Congress passed the Communications Act of 1934, it established the FCC as broadcasting's licensing and regulatory authority, authorizing the Commission to regulate broadcasting "in the public interest, convenience, and necessity." As a matter of philosophical and practical forbearance, the FCC has historically given broad latitude to stations in the programming area to meet their statutory obligations, even though the epicenter of a station's mandate remains *serving the public interest.* The surest path to public service has been through news and local programming. Television news is omnipresent and its prospects for the future are relatively undiminished (why is explained in this next section), but there is always some criticism of its quality and presentation (see 8.4).

The Role of Local Newscasts

Newspapers devote only a minority of their pages to news reporting. Did you know that this so-called *newshole* amounts to no more than 20 percent of newspaper space? The rest of papers consist of advertising and features (syndicated columns, Sudoku, Dear Ann or Abby, comics, Miss Manners, crossword puzzles and so on), and a big chunk of what is euphemistically called "news" is sports. Though television is justifiably criticized for its

8.4 The Not Real News

One of the most enduring criticisms of television news is that it is not "real news": that television news is somehow counterfeit when compared with print journalism. Many complaints about contemporary television journalism begin with the cliché, "Edward R. Murrow would be spinning in his grave if he saw television's coverage today of [insert issue of choice]." Then the critic offers what Murrow's opinion *would* have been, were he still alive to have one. Interestingly, Murrow himself clearly anticipated the distinctiveness and limitations of the new medium and said, in effect, "Television news is a combination of show business, advertising and news."[4]

Television journalism, being so invasive in our lives, is often compared on an apples-to-apples basis with print journalism, a comparison which is unfair to both. Newspapers have been regularly published in America for nearly 300 years, protected by the First Amendment from punishment or licensing restrictions, while television has been plugged in for nearly 70 years as a captive of its technological, economic, competitive and especially regulatory environments. Of course, just as some newspapers are trashy and some world-class, with all degrees between, so television stations vary in quality, commitment and competence.

excessive interruption by commercials, in its defense, we should note that it allots about 75 percent of its newscasts to programming content and only about 25 percent to commercial time. You may think that is far too much, but it pays the bills.

The real competition for both newspapers and television is really the internet, of course. It supplies news (and not so news) reports on demand, and there stories can be contracted or expanded in a live-like format for as long as the user is interested. Such flexibility and user control has driven many people away from both print and television news—except in times of disaster when television (usually) shines.

In addition to the obvious community benefits of having news content on the air, local news programming serves the broadcaster's commercial objectives quite well in the following six ways:

1. **Risk mitigation.** When a station buys a syndicated program, the result of that purchase can be a hit, a dud or something in between. Admittedly, no station sets out to deliberately buy a failure in the syndication marketplace. No matter; *regardless of the ratings of the program, the station must honor its contract and continue to pay the broadcast license fee and continue to air the barter commercials, even if the program is taken off the air.* News programs, in comparison, are rarely abject failures and can nearly always be resuscitated by a "news doctor."

2. **Exclusivity of product.** No competitor can steal a station's newscast or copy the name of the newscast. The names, faces and personalities of the on-air talent are exclusive to the station, too.

3. **Brand-building.** The newscast's content and production values can be styled so as to match the station's desired market identity, which results from its entire mosaic of network programming, syndicated programming, news/local programming and other community exposure. Affiliates that are number one in news generally are number one in their markets in prime time as well. How much their news ratings are attributable to their network's appeal in prime time and how much the prime ratings can be linked to the affiliate's news success is debatable; what is *not* debatable is that *local news and prime-time success are linked.*

4. **Customization of product.** In response to market forces beyond their immediate control—such as time of day, competing programs, changing popular tastes—the station can alter its newscast's content and format. For example, the news can be modified to offer more or less of hard news or softer coverage (such features as health or personal finance stories), or the weather report can be expanded or given more prominence in the newscast. If those alterations do not work, the original format can be restored and other changes put into place. No network or syndicated program can offer such a luxury.

5. **Cost containment.** Any locally produced telecast is a budgeting challenge to a business as sensitive to cash flow as a broadcast station. News is particularly expensive because of the need for sophisticated news-gathering electronic equipment, on-air talent, newscast sets, and behind-the-scenes producers, editors and so on. The start-up price tag is high, but such costs can be accurately estimated and budgeted—unlike the syndicated market, where the law of supply and demand causes fluctuations from year to year in the price of syndicated shows. In addition to reliable budgeting, the cost of adding an *additional* newscast is incrementally small; most of the expenses (equipment, sets, talent) are fixed and therefore already covered. Adding another half-hour of news in some cases might require only an additional news crew consisting of a single reporter and a photographer. (This is a lesson well learned from all all-news cable channels and continuous online reporting!)

6. **Revenue enhancement.** News programs can be enormously profitable for stations. First, unlike the limited amount of commercial inventory allowed to stations in network and some syndicated programs, the station owns all of its newscast inventory and, if budgetary needs require, can easily expand that supply by shortening the newscast and adding commercial time. Second, advertisers usually object to their products' commercials being placed during controversial network or syndicated programs. An airline, understandably, won't want to sponsor the movie *Airplane*, just as a travel agency will probably avoid *Titanic*. Such programs are said to be on an advertiser's *hit list*.

Newscasts, fortunately, are usually not hit-listed, and a large universe of potential advertisers is available for the sales department to approach. A third benefit is that the advertising community regards news as the most prestigious category of television programming. An image-conscious company that would reject the notion of advertising in an entertainment program might well consider advertising in a news program as an acceptable alternative. Stations use their newscasts as bait, as a means of enticing new or reluctant potential clients to expanding their advertising to more parts of the television schedule.

As of 2011, there were 968 stations offering local news, with approximately 26,500 staff employed in news departments. Generally speaking, the larger the market, the more competitive the product: Nearly 60% of station news departments turned a profit, and almost half of all station revenue was generated during news programs (though revenues don't look that good every year). Industry polls showed that the average network affiliate was up to 5½ hours of news each day by mid-decade. This spotlights the changing nature of the station business: As audiences drift away to cable/satellite networks and internet activities, stations use news to strengthen their brands and turn a profit. The old days of "noblesse oblige" in news are long gone: It's all about the money. In 2011, the FCC released an alarming report about the state of local television news.[5] The report was scathing, indicating that while the amount of news and the number of news outlets in a community might be increasing, the amount of local investigative news had not. The report equally criticized the FCC itself for a lack of proper oversight in its responsibilities as overseer of licenses of the public's airwaves. Only four times in its history has the FCC denied a license renewal to a station on the grounds of failure to fulfill public interest obligations.

One of the unintended after-effects of the pay-tv age has been that some consumers are left with *over-the-air* (*OTA*) viewing as their only choice, and these viewers tend to be poorer and less-well-educated, the downscale market. The OTA component has been variously estimated at between 8% and 14% of the total viewing audience, although current levels of MVPD subscribers suggest that the true amount is nearer 8%. But the point is that minorities make up much of this group: Specifically, 24% of the Asian market, 17% of the black market, and 23% of the Hispanic market watch OTA only. Overall, twice as many homes with less than $30,000 annual income watch over-the-air television exclusively. This group is more likely to watch local news than national cable news, although local television news is largely a combination of sensationalistic criminal reports and fluff.

Local TV news has taken on the visage of radio, deploying teasing strategies to keep the viewer watching, while spooning out as diluted a mixture of information as possible to keep them watching. Given that down-scale viewers watch disproportionately more television, this is an example of entertainment masquerading as news. Across the country, news consultants spout templates of cookie-cutter wisdom while driving out local interests and accents. No longer are reporters true journalists; most are hit-and-run news readers or attractive people looking to move up to a larger market. Many local news readers open their program by saying, "thank you for joining us." Rather an insult to the viewers. Some misguided stations have even offered contests for newswatchers. The desperation of some stations to hold on to their viewers is sometimes painful to watch...but we do.

Other Local Programming

There are two basic categories of local programs: *regularly scheduled shows* (mostly produced out of the news department, such as public-affairs discussion programs and weekend sports wrap-ups) and *special events* (such as ball games and parades). Some nationally important programs that are produced locally still exist—mostly in the biggest markets for such special events as Philadelphia's Mummers' Parade on New Year's Day, the Boston Marathon and so forth—but local programs no longer drive the financial or programming goals of a station, and the news department produces the few that remain, even in the largest markets. The venerable *Chronicle*, at 7:30 P.M. weekdays on Boston's WCVB, for example, has been on the air since 1984 and is the only large-market, locally produced newsmagazine program in America. The exception illuminates the void (see 8.5).

8.5 Why So Little Local?

Local programming has four main liabilities. They are primarily related to its labor and cost structures.

1. Labor-intensive. In contrast to the physical simplicity of airing a network or syndicated program (which can require—at most—one or two technicians to supervise master control, videotape machines and digital servers), a local program can require some dozens of personnel working over weeks or months to plan, produce and edit just one program. Even the most modest of programs requires personnel to host, write, edit, produce, direct and crew the production.

2. Cost-intensive. Budgeting is complex for a local production: There must be an accounting for talent fees, production crew, equipment, insurance, storage, construction, rentals and all other related expenses of the production, all of which are borne by the station. To keep the production's on-air "look" comparable with network and syndicated programming, the show's budget must not skimp. Although television is said to be a "forgiving" medium for production quality standards, the local program would defeat its own purposes if it looked amateurish. Occasionally, some production costs can be recouped if the station is able to syndicate the program to other stations. The most frequent example of this is when a sporting event gets syndicated to a regional cluster of stations.

3. Advertising considerations. If the local program is a one-time-only telecast, it might be difficult to find advertisers willing to buy time in it. Advertising agencies desire predictability; they want to have some pre-telecast notion of the kind of program they are buying and some realistic estimation of what the program's ratings will be (to justify the advertising buy to their clients, who are usually much more careful with spending their own money than the advertising agencies are). Unless the production is a regularly scheduled program or a local traditional event, the advertiser might shy away from a novel program. This is particularly true of national advertisers, who generally will not sponsor an unknown local program. Local advertisers, however, are more likely to support a local program because their advertising is less ratings-sensitive than that of national businesses. Local businesses can measure advertising success by other factors, which are sometimes as basic as an increase in the number of telephone calls or customer traffic at their stores.

4. Promotion intensive. Unlike the help they get for purchased programming from networks or syndicators, stations are solely responsible for promoting their own products. Heavy promotion of a local production, especially if it meets with resistance from the sales department (because promos use up time), is dangerous; it could result in a disproportionate creative effort for a minimal revenue return.

For group-owned stations, local production can be a laboratory, a means of field-testing programming before a launch in syndication (because that's where the really big bucks are). For instance, Oprah Winfrey hosted a local talk show on WLS-TV in Chicago before her program went to national syndication in 1986. Maury Povich and Regis Philbin reached syndicated fame after their respective programs' successes at local stations. At the other end of the personality spectrum, Howard Stern had a test run on local television in New York (WWOR-TV), years before his program went to national broadcast syndication in the late 1990s, and ultimately found its level on late-night cable and then satellite radio.

Syndicated Programming

To fill the time periods when its network does not supply programs, a station usually must enter the syndication marketplace for substitutes (spend lots of money). See Chapter 6 for a detailed discussion of the syndication processes for off-network and first-run programs.

The Prime-Time Access Rule

In an attempt to encourage stations to live up to their public service mandate and, not incidentally, make the network–affiliate relationship more balanced, in 1970 the FCC issued a regulation that chopped off one hour of prime-time television per night. (Until then, network prime had started at 7 P.M. Eastern/Pacific/6 P.M. Central/Mountain and aired for four hours.) The 7 to 8 P.M. hour was dubbed *prime-access time*, and the regulation was called the *Prime-Time Access Rule (PTAR)*.

Under PTAR, the commission limited affiliates to three hours nightly of network programming and prohibited stations in the largest 50 markets from airing any off-network syndication in prime access. (An exception was made for network news programs so that they would not count toward the three hours. A second exception was made for Sundays because, at the time, the networks aired family-oriented programming on the most heavily viewed night of the week, reasoning that seems silly today.) The FCC naively imagined that the 7 to 8 P.M. time period would be occupied by local productions, public-affairs shows and more local news.

Of course the "rule of unintended consequences" applied. Rather than produce more (low-rated) public-affairs programs, local stations realized that they had just been handed a great gift. They could now run syndicated programs (so long as they were not of the off-network variety) in what was formerly prime-time territory, and they got to keep *all* the extra commercial inventory and the revenue that went with it!

Although PTAR was repealed in 1995, it is highly unlikely that the Big Three networks will get their lost hour back. *Access* is the highest-viewed non-network time period during the day, and stations generate too much commercial revenue to acquiesce in returning the time to the networks. Now that off-network reruns can air in access in any market, the increase in potential programs has driven prices down for both off-network and first-run programming, and local stations make even more money.

Off-Network Syndication

Unlike other tangible properties for which a price can be established (such as land, automobiles, textbooks

and even personal services), there is no *inherent value* to any given television program. Ultimately, the market value of a program is set by the price at which the buyer's offer price and the seller's acceptance price overlap. As explained in Chapter 6, a program entering the syndication marketplace can sell at wildly varying prices, depending on such factors as a station's programming needs, the demographic "fit" of the program, the financial resources of the station, and the competitive landscape in the market. There is no set formula for calculating a price based on market size or location. Programs are not a fungible commodity where comparison shopping can be undertaken; each program is different, and its syndication performance is unpredictable.

The syndication contract is an exercise in simple mathematics. The syndicator sells the exclusive right to air the program in one of two ways—on a weekly license basis or on a per-episode basis.

1. **Weekly license.** This is the most commonly structured form of syndication. The station pays a weekly rate for the program (paid monthly), which is satellite-fed to the station. There is *barter* advertising in the program, where the syndicator has sold advertising time within the program, and the station has no say in the scheduling of individual episodes. The station must play the program once every day. (The station may choose to contract to play the program twice a day if the license fee is increased, usually by about 50 percent.)

2. **Per episode.** This is the original method, in which the station enjoys more control over the scheduling of the program. As long as the syndicator gets paid (monthly), it does not care whether the station airs the program every day, twice a day, or not at all (called *resting* or *shelving*). There is generally no barter in this method. The station contracts for a specific number of telecasts over a stated period of time. In general, the station may play each episode up to six times before additional residual rights kick in.

In either case, when a program is sold into off-network syndication, it enters the marketplace upward of two years before its actual syndication date on the air. For example, when *Everybody Loves Raymond* launched on the CBS network in 1996, it was immediately evident that it would have a future in syndication. Eyemark, the program's syndicator, began the sales process in 1998, anticipating a syndication start date of 2000. From that date and until the eventual network run ends, episodes of *Raymond* will air on both the network and in syndication.

Once enough network episodes have accumulated (usually after four seasons of 22 new episodes each), approximately 90 episodes are released into syndication. So, in the fifth year of network production, typically, a program begins its syndication life. In network seasons five through cancellation, the program is simultaneously in syndication. As each network year ends, and the network's broadcast rights expire and return to the syndicator, those 22 episodes pour over into the syndication contract, adding to the number that the local station is able to air.

While a program is still on the network, the station benefits in three ways from having the syndicated version:

- **National exposure.** A network previously spent heavily to promote the show as a hit, not only on its own network but also through advertising in the rest of the media. The national name recognition rubs off on the syndicated version of the program.

- **New episodes.** Every year the station gets the rights to the previous season's network episodes, which were broadcast only twice each. These "new" episodes (new to syndication, anyway) are underexposed because even fans of a program cannot be expected to catch every episode during its network run.

- **Advertiser access.** Advertisers are businesspeople. They crave predictable results. They know and respect the drawing power of network programs, but if a network asks too much money for commercials, advertisers know that they can buy spots for less money in the same program at the syndication level, and the commercials will still be seen nationally.

From an economic standpoint, syndicated programs pose both opportunities and perils. On the opportunity side, the big benefit is the commercial inventory. In off-network syndication (*off-net*, for short), the station keeps most (if not all) of the commercial time, creating the possibility of generating more revenue from airing a syndicated program than a network one.

Another benefit lies in brand-building for the station. During non-network dayparts for affiliates (and ALL the time on stations without a network), stations have the entrepreneurial challenges of selecting and scheduling programs of strong appeal to their viewers. Each station works with blocks of sitcoms, movies, talk shows or court shows, perhaps with a mix of sports and news, to develop a particular identity in the minds of the local audience.[6]

For the afternoon lead-in to local evening news, affiliated stations can often acquire syndicated programs that are more complimentary to their high-profile afternoon and evening news programs than those their network provides. Finally, stations can use syndicated programs to cater to local tastes. *Networks have to program for a national audience or audiences reached by their owned stations, which tend to be in the largest markets necessarily having different demographic and socioeconomic characteristics than small-city and rural America.* The syndication marketplace makes available programs that might be a better fit for regional or market tastes.

At the same time, there are perils. When an individual station commits to licensing a syndicated program, it bears the entire financial risk of that decision. If a network program fails, the network will eventually replace it, at no cost to the affiliate. If a syndicated program fails, the station is still obligated for all the costs of the program throughout the contract period (and has to run any prepaid ads).

The station also has to cover the cost of promotion for its syndicated commitments, usually "spending" some of its immensely valuable commercial inventory. In contrast, network programs generate national exposure and national publicity—to the eventual downstream benefit of local stations. On a network schedule, a given program is aired on the same day, at the same time, everywhere: *60 Minutes* is on every CBS station on Sundays at 7 P.M./6 central, for example. In contrast, syndicated programs are on the air at different times everywhere. Although syndicators do support their programs with advertising and promotion (to add value to their barter spots), there is no comparing that effort with a network advertising campaign, and a station must bear the lion's share of promoting the program locally. If an off-network program has no barter spots in it, the syndicator will have no financial incentive to spend any money on advertising.

Another risk lies in the absence of exclusivity. Once a program is on a network, it seldom moves to another network. A local affiliate can be confident its network hit will continue to be aired on its station for the length of the program's run. In contrast, a syndicated program is under the control of the syndicator. A first-run syndication contract can be as short as one year and often is as short as two or three years. Once the contract period is over, the syndicator can move the program to another station that offers to pay more, and there is little loyalty to stations in the syndication business.

Movies

By the time a local broadcast station can air a syndicated movie, the film's appeal is often exhausted from overexposure. As a result, a once-valuable program franchise has been co-opted by bigger and deeper-pocketed cable competitors. Today it is highly unusual to discover a movie on local television that one has not had many opportunities to see elsewhere. Movies in syndication have *devolved*; once a marquee attraction carrying a premium purchase price, movies are now an economy-of-scale program choice, a low-cost product for a moderate return on the investment. The situation differs for affiliates of the Spanish-language networks, where movies imported from South and Central America may still be fresh for American audiences.

Infomercials

The infamous program-length commercials, euphemistically called *infomercials*, sell everything under the sun—kitchen appliances, weight-loss "systems,"

real-estate seminars, exercise equipment and self-improvement courses. Infomercials are the "elephant in the parlor" of television that station executives prefer not to discuss. These misfits of the programming world are pilloried in the industry, ridiculed by the public, and parodied on programs ranging from *Saturday Night Live* to *The Simpsons* ("Hi, I'm Troy McClure, and you might remember me from other infomercials such as *Smoke Yourself Thin* and *Get Confident, Stupid!*").

So why would a station air such easy-to-scorn programs? The answer is that infomercials are usually paid for in advance, and thus they provide quick cash to stations. No station brags about airing these programs, but at the end of a budget period, a station can preempt a program in a low-rated time period and sell the time period to an infomercial provider for a rate far in excess of what the station could otherwise generate in revenue. Most infomercials run in such out-of-the-way time periods as overnight and early mornings on weekends, although occasionally one will pop up in plain sight—for example, opposite a Super Bowl or other mega-telecast. And the lowest-ranked stations in a market are the most likely to fill part of their days with infomercials.

How can the infomercial provider afford to pay such a premium rate? The success of an infomercial depends not on its rating but on the so-called *response rate*, the number of persons who call the toll-free number and sign up for a service or order the merchandise. No matter how seemingly odd the product being pitched appears, rest assured that somewhere there is a person on the phone right now ordering it. *Infomercials are proof, indeed, that television continues to be the world's most influential advertising medium.*

Station Dayparts

There are 24 hours in a day, 168 hours in a week, 8,760 hours in a year. It is literally impossible for programmers and advertisers to work with every one of all these hours on an individual basis, and not every hour in the day is equally important. For example, on any station, 9 P.M. is a far more significant time period than 2 A.M. In the name of efficiency and expediency, for the benefit of all parties in the business—programmers and advertisers alike—the hours of the day have been grouped into *dayparts*. The dayparts represent the approximate behavior of the imaginary typical American television household. The best-known daypart, of course, is prime time. Although it might at first seem to be an arbitrary division, the grouping of hours of the 24-hour day into dayparts generally reflects the presumed lifestyles and viewing patterns of the average American viewing household. The generally accepted dayparts and their time periods appear in 8.6.

Although necessarily arbitrary, the division of the day into dayparts does indeed reflect large portions of most people's lives. For example, most people awaken in the morning between 6 and 9 A.M. (corresponding to the *early-morning* daypart), get off to work or school by 9 A.M. (start of *daytime*), and

return home in the afternoon between 4 and 6 P.M. (*early fringe*). About two-thirds of American households watch television during the evening, peaking around 9 P.M. (*prime time*), although peak viewing by teens and young adults occurs later. Between 10 and 11 P.M., viewing levels begin tapering off as families and older people prepare for bed, then drop precipitously after 11 P.M. (late fringe).

Broadcasters and advertisers must agree on these dayparts, which are established by Nielsen Media Research, in order to conduct the multibillion-dollar business of setting advertising rates and selling commercial time at America's more than one thousand commercial television stations. *In addition to configuring advertising expenditures and revenue, the dayparts also set the boundaries for the programming strategies that capture the time, money and effort of broadcasting producers and executives.*

Early Morning (6 to 9 A.M.)

As a lead-in to network morning news programs (*Today, Good Morning America, The Early Show*) that commence at 7 A.M. local time, many network affiliates air local news (or the early early network show). In response to the evolution of American lifestyles toward more working couples, single working parents and longer commuting times, America's workday is starting earlier and ending later. Although HUT levels are modest at dawn, most people who are awake before 7 A.M. are awake for a reason: They are preparing to go to work. These people are likely candidates for news because they are employed (and are disproportionately commuters), and they therefore meld the desirable advertising markers of income and education to the accompanying lifestyle and purchasing patterns of working people. In response to the availability of these viewers, advertisers are attracted to early-morning news programs.

These viewers usually cannot commit to watching an entire program, however, so the information is frequently repeated, with headline, traffic and weather updates occurring throughout the hour or half-hour newscast. This kind of format is called a "news wheel." In fact, viewers *listen* to the morning news as much as watch it while they get dressed, prepare

---

8.6 Time Periods and Dayparts

6 to 9 A.M.	Early morning
9 A.M. to 12 noon	Morning
12 noon to 4 P.M.	Afternoon
4 to 7 P.M.	Early fringe
7 to 8 P.M.	Prime access
8 to 11 P.M.	Prime time
11 to 11:35 P.M.	Late fringe
11:35 P.M. to 2 A.M.	Late night
2 to 6 A.M.	Overnight

These dayparts are standard for the eastern and Pacific time zones. In the central and mountain time zones, the dayparts change slightly: Essentially, prime time starts an hour earlier and ends an hour earlier, and early fringe, access, and late fringe move correspondingly an hour to accommodate the earlier hours of prime time.

Central Time Differences:

4 to 6 P.M.	Early fringe
6 to 7 P.M.	Prime access
7 to 10 P.M.	Prime time
10 to 10:35 P.M.	Late fringe
10:55 P.M. to 2 A.M.	Late night

breakfast, shoo schoolchildren out the door and prepare to leave the house themselves. The video product is treated as background chatter, much like radio. In larger markets that have the longest commute times, the early-morning news starts as early as 5 A.M.

The 7 to 9 A.M. time period has traditionally been a network preserve. *Today* has been on NBC for 60 years and *Good Morning America* on ABC for nearly 40 years, deeply embedding viewing patterns. Most daytime viewing is habitual viewing, and the networks try to establish that habit as early in the day as possible. CBS affiliates have suffered the most anguish in this daypart because their network has had only indifferent success over the years with its many morning efforts (see Chapter 7). Its affiliates obviously want their network to succeed, but they cannot wait indefinitely for it to do so; thus, lack of clearance exacerbates the network's problems.

During the first decades of television, when most television markets had only three stations, a network program could not finish worse than third in the ratings. Today, with nearly every available channel allocation licensed to an operating station, a network program can—embarrassingly—place beneath a syndicated program, falling to fourth, fifth or worse in the ratings. Despite CBS's expenditure of tens of millions of dollars to build a successful morning news franchise, many CBS affiliates are preempting their network's *Early Show*. They are producing their own local news programs or scheduling syndicated programming more attractive to their *lead-out* audience at 9 A.M.

In deliberate contrast to their network competitors, FOX affiliates blaze their own trail. In an attempt to capture a share of news-related advertising dollars, FOX affiliates in most markets avoid a head-on competition with network affiliates, instead producing a news product heavily weighted toward local news, local entertainment and personalities. In many markets the distinct FOX formula works to great success, beating the traditional network newscasts. The FOX strategy is that to copy the approach of CBS, NBC and ABC is futile; the international/Washington/New York orientation of the networks is both redundant and unimportant to viewers more interested in events in their own towns.

At 7 A.M., UNI carries *Despierta America* ("Wake Up, America"), which is the Hispanic equivalent of *Today* or *Good Morning America*, and contains talk, entertainment and half-hourly news updates. Over on Telemundo, the morning offering is *Levantate* ("Arise!"). The newsholes of these programs, however, tend to be even smaller than that of the English-language morning "news" programs.

Affiliates of the smaller networks counterprogram this daypart with syndicated entertainment, predominantly sitcoms or reality programming (or the dreaded infomercials). Using entertainment is an effective strategy: it avoids competing with the news business and concentrates on the smaller audiences of children and adults who don't watch news. The business strategy of these stations is not so much to maximize profit as to minimize programming costs in a low-priority daypart.

Morning (9 A.M. to 12 Noon)

The Big Three networks do not program the entire three-hour morning block; the supply varies from one to two hours, depending on the network. As a cost-sensitive measure as well as a nod to the reality that generating a morning audience is difficult, NBC in 2007 extended *Today* for a fourth hour, to 11 A.M., CBS has continued with *The Price Is Right* in late morning, and ABC airs *The View* at 11 A.M. Affiliates then complete their lineups with a mixture of first-run programs, talk and local news. The scheduling strategy is to complement the demographic appeal of programs supplied by the network.

With a relatively low HUT level providing a shaky foundation for success, the attrition rate for syndicated morning programs is high. Programmers do not have the luxury of allowing a program sufficient time to attract its audience. There are no "out of town" tryouts, unlike in the motion picture or theatrical industries. If a program fails to attract a stable audience within a reasonable period of time, then, like their network counterparts, station programmers move it to another time period or, more often, cancel it.

An intriguing characteristic of both morning and afternoon daytime is that if a new program can weather the first couple of years of attracting a loyal audience, a kind of "TV inertia" takes over, and the program enters "Video Valhalla," remaining on the schedule seemingly permanently. (*The Price Is Right*, for example, has been on the CBS daytime schedule since 1972.) Viewers during daytime tend to be homemakers, senior citizens, students and shift workers. Although they have large blocks of time to watch programs, they are not fully attentive to the programs. So producers structure their programs to enable viewers to join, depart and rejoin a daytime program easily; that is why game shows have lots of noise and require minimal levels of sustained concentration and why soap opera plots proceed so slowly.

For the rest of the morning, UNI carries *Quien Tiene la Razon?* (Who is Right?), in which guests relate their respective sides of a personal conflict/dispute, to be resolved by the moderator. Following is *Casos de Familia*, a program about familial stresses. The rest of the daytime schedule on both Univision and Telemundo mirror the staple of daytime programming: relationship programs, soap operas ("novelas"), game and talk shows.

Afternoon (12 Noon to 4 P.M.)

The only local newscasts before evenings are generally around the noon hour, a vestige of an era when more adults were home midday, and they have shifted to focus on office workers. In addition to reporting on that morning's news stories and aggregating more news-targeted ad dollars, the midday news promotes the station's other programming, particularly the late afternoon news.

The four main choices for the afternoon time period are soap operas, court shows, talk and game shows (see 8.7). For affiliates of the Big

---

8.7 **The Beloved Soaps and Games**

Soap operas are the most venerable program format, but nonetheless, few are left. ABC's *General Hospital* debuted in 1963. On NBC, *Days of Our Lives* premiered in 1965. Of all the networks, CBS soaps have had the greatest longevity until recently; now only *The Young and the Restless* is left (see Chapter 7). Networks and advertisers love soaps for the same reasons:
Because they are seriously habit forming (Fans of soap operas watch not for years but for decades … and, in some cases, for generations), and because that viewing loyalty can be translated into consumer loyalty when the same products sponsor the same soap for many years. Advertising relies on repeated messages to be effective. A viewer watching the same program every weekday for years, with the same products advertised over and over, is a rare commodity in an increasingly fragmented advertising environment.

Lest one conclude that all first-run television in daytime is devoted to exploiting the dark or voyeuristic side of human nature, there are more lighthearted categories of programs. The popularity of program formats is cyclical: Just as soaps were fading, games rose again. Game shows might be out of favor for some years, then return to popularity seemingly overnight. Game shows are traditional and quintessential daytime television fare. They are suitable for all viewers; the content is mostly questions and answers; viewers can play along at home—and feel superior when the contestants muff an easy question.

To keep the pace of the game interesting, game shows are usually a half-hour in length. Research has shown that the best companion program for rounding out the hour is another game show. That is why so many game shows are found together in a one-hour block. Even though technology has ramped up the production values of game shows, the basic elements remain unchanged: question/answer format, relatively low skill level, vicarious viewer participation and a clear payoff or disappointment. None of life's ambiguities for game shows; every game produces a winner or a loser.

Speaking of winners, even though one might think that a cash prize would be a more desirable or useful prize, an under-realized appeal of prizes is the "fantasy" aspect: the opportunity to win a dream vacation, a world cruise or an expensive car. The vicarious enjoyment of watching a contestant win a fabulous prize is always greater than watching someone win cash money.

Three, after the midday break for local news, the afternoon daypart is the mother lode for soap operas. (Network executives get irritated when "the soaps" are referred to as such, preferring to have them called "daytime continuing dramas.") Affiliates of ABC will certainly carry *General Hospital*. Affiliates of CBS will doubtless air *The Young and the Restless*. Affiliates of NBC will carry *Days of Our Lives*. The Hispanic stations follow the same pattern, using first-run or rerun *telenovelas* in the afternoons. These Spanish-language serials resemble soaps in their close focus on individual emotional ups and downs, but they have a much shorter lifespan (maybe a year or so) and contain a more obvious moral or educational point about families or society.

The remaining stations in a market counterprogram with various judges (*Judge Judy, Judge Alex, Judge David Young, Judge Joe Brown*) and justices. If the best court shows are not available, stations usually go for talk such as *Martha* or *The Ellen Degeneres Show*, or in urban markets for off-network sitcoms such as *Everybody Hates Chris* or *Tyler Perry's House of Payne*. Otherwise, hundreds

and hundreds of episodes of old game and reality shows are available as reruns, but talk dominates.

Needless to say, the afternoon is the most programmatically stable and consistent daypart for viewers, networks, and advertisers. Talk programs have become a mainstay of daytime program schedules, but the mortality rate for such syndicated talk is high. Approximately 80 percent of all syndicated shows that make it to broadcast do not make it to year two. But once a program has established itself as an audience favorite, it can stay on the air for almost as long as the distributor wants. Even if a popular host departs, the program can remain if the format is popular (see 8.8). The daily syndicated talk show *Live with Regis and Kathie Lee* enjoyed a successful 12-year run and even survived the departure of Kathie Lee Gifford in 2000. Kelly Ripa joined the program (retitled *Live with Regis and Kelly*) in 2001, and the ratings *increased*. Then, Regis finally retired in 2011, ending more than a half-century on television.

Another popular daytime program category is court shows, in which a real or ersatz judge hears disputes and rules on them. The appeal of programs

8.8 Filling the Air with Talk

Talk-show formats run the emotional spectrum. At one extreme is the soufflé of nearly lighter-than-air content: interviews with celebrities publicizing their latest movie, television program or successful drug rehab (for example, *Live with Regis and Kelly*). In the middle are decorating and homemaking hints (*Martha*) or light humor with chat (*The Ellen Degeneres Show*). At the other extreme is the exploitative treatment of guests' troubled psyches or relationships, where personal and interrogatory confrontations delight or repel viewers (for example, *Montel Williams, Tyra Banks, Jerry Springer*). Industry research indicates that there is a vicarious appeal to these exploitative programs: Viewers at home, no matter how troubled their own personal circumstances, feel relieved that their own lives are not as pitiful as those of the victimized guests who are telling their tales of woe to Jerry Springer on national television.

Why are talk shows so common (in both senses of the word) in television syndication? The major reason is cost or, more accurately, *lack* of cost. Syndicated talk programs are relatively inexpensive to produce; in contrast to scripted shows, talk programs are seemingly improvised. There are no screenwriters, only low-paid "researchers"; there is no expensive location shooting because all programs are shot in studios; there is no cast of expensive stars, usually just one or two hosts; and many hosts are paid less than "stars" (but not Oprah—see 8.9) because the more relaxed schedule allows them to take on other work after that day's program is taped. In contrast, the shooting schedule for a scripted Hollywood program requires 12-hour days, script rewrites, memorization of lines, laborious camera setups and so on. The low cost threshold makes it easier for a talk-show producer to adjust the content to appeal to viewers' changing tastes and interests.

8.9 Oprah Winfrey

Born in Kosciusko, Mississippi, in 1954 to unmarried teenagers, Oprah Winfrey lived the first six years of her life in rural poverty with her grandmother. At the age of 6, she moved to Milwaukee's inner city to live with her mother who worked as a maid and was on welfare. She was molested by her cousin, uncle and a family friend at the age of 9 and became pregnant at the age of 14 but lost the baby. She was then sent to live with her father in Nashville, Tennessee.

This is not a very likely resume for one of the most influential women in America and, according to *Forbes*, the richest African-American of the twentieth century. As the story goes, while attending a party at a ranch in Montecito, California, she fell in love with the location and wrote a check for $50 million to buy the 42-acre estate. At the same time, according to *urbanmecca.com*, she is the most philanthropic African-American of all time. She has helped raise hundreds of millions to fight AIDS in Africa and to fund a girls' school in South Africa. Her Angel Network alone has raised more than $50 million dollars, and since she covers all administrative costs, 100 percent of donations go to charity. But that is the widely publicized background of Orpah Gail Winfrey. (Named after a person in the Bible's Book of Ruth, she found her name hard to pronounce and spell, so she shifted the *p* and the *r* and became Oprah.)

On the other hand, her bios say, her grandmother taught her to read by the age of 3, she skipped two of her earliest grades, and she won a scholarship to attend Nicolet High School at age 13. In Tennessee, she was an honor student, voted Most Popular Girl, placed second in the nation in dramatic interpretation, secured a full scholarship to Tennessee State University, and won the Miss Black Tennessee beauty pageant. Her broadcast career began at Tennessee State on a local radio station. When she started to anchor the news at Nashville's WLAC-TV, she was not only the youngest anchor, but also the first black woman anchor in the station's history. In 1976 she moved to Baltimore to coanchor WJZ's six o'clock news, and then cohosted a local talk show and a local version of *Dialing for Dollars*. In 1983 she moved to Chicago to take over WLS's low-rated morning talk show *AM Chicago*. Within months the show had passed *Donahue* and was Chicago's highest-rated talk show. Renamed *The Oprah Winfrey Show* in 1986, Oprah decided to go national at a time when the experts "knew" the country was not ready for a black woman host of a talk show.

In the preceding year, the country had been introduced to Oprah. Her role as Sofia in *The Color Purple* won her a nomination for best supporting actress—but a nationwide TV talk show host? Many of the stations that picked up her syndicated program were last in their markets with nothing to lose. Astoundingly, Oprah quickly passed Phil Donahue, the reigning talk show king, and soon had double his audience. Critics and experts were perplexed, and most reacted with left-handed compliments at best. *Time* magazine wrote, "Few people would have bet on Oprah Winfrey's swift rise to host of the most popular talk show on TV. In a field dominated by white males, she is a black female of ample bulk." A TV columnist referred to her as "a roundhouse, a full-course meal, big, brassy, loud." *The Wall Street Journal* was marginally kinder when it reported: "It's a relief to see a gab-monger with a fond but realistic assessment of her own cultural and religious roots." But it was *Newsday* who hit the nail on the head when a columnist wrote, "Oprah Winfrey is sharper than Donahue, wittier, more genuine, and far better attuned to her audience if not the world."[7]

Since that time Oprah has founded a successful production company, cofounded the cable television networks Oxygen and own, published two successful magazines, produced a musical version of *The Color Purple*, founded a website visited by 3 million people monthly, cowritten five books, developed a channel for satellite radio, and agreed to produce two new reality shows for ABC. To quote Bill O'Reilly, "I mean this is a woman that came from nothing to rise up to be the most powerful woman, I think, in the world … and she's done it on her own."[8]

William J. Adams, Ph.D.
Kansas State University

like *Judge Judy* is twofold: First, the personality or character of the magistrate is entertaining; second, the actions and reactions of the litigants are heart-rending, comical or just plain irritating. In any case, for societal good or ill, such programming makes for compelling television. A good court program is one part confrontational talk show ("Your Honor, he stole my pen." "*I did not.*" "He did, too, Your Honor." "*Did not.*"), one part game show (who wins the ruling?) and one part (a small one) introduction to the U.S. legal system. The overwhelming litigiousness of our society is mirrored in the court shows appearing on television as of the date of this writing: *The People's Court, Divorce Court, Judge Judy, Judge Jeanine Pirro, Swift Justice with Nancy Grace, Judge Karen's Court, Judge Alex, Judge Browne, Judge Mathis* and *Cristina's Court.*

The "reality" program craze, kicked off by *Survivor* in 2000, spawned daytime progeny in the form of "relationship" shows. Television has a proud legacy of relationship shows: *The Dating Game* (1965), its direct spinoff, *The Newlywed Game* (1966) and *Love Connection* (1984) all drew on our natural curiosity about the personal lives of others. In the twenty-first century, that has all changed. The relatively sweet, innocent relationship programs of the past that masqueraded as game shows have yielded to voyeuristic hook-up segments, focusing less on locating Mr. Right and more on finding Mr. Right Now.

Afternoons fill with talk because it is absolutely the cheapest programming, and the easiest format to change if ratings are low. Occasionally, a station will run a sitcom that failed in a higher-revenue time period or a sitcom that has outlived its usefulness and is being programmed purely for amortization purposes.

Early Fringe (4 to 7 P.M.)

This daypart's unusual name harkens back to the first 25 years of commercial television, when this time period immediately preceded prime time (which started an hour earlier than it does today). Therefore, the hours before prime time were said to be on the "fringe" of prime time and, thus, *early fringe.*

From the networks' perspectives, early fringe is a low-priority time period, so program time is returned to the local stations.[9] From 4 to 7 P.M. (4 to 6 P.M. central/mountain time), the networks rely on their affiliates to schedule local news or syndicated talk. Industry research has consistently demonstrated that the best lead-in program for a newscast is ... more news! This is makes sense: Viewers who are predisposed toward watching any one newscast are interested in news and therefore more likely to watch an additional newscast than would a viewer who doesn't usually watch the news. The results of this research happily match the budgetary facts of life for news production: It's expensive to *start* a news operation but relatively economical to *expand* it. Over the last 15 to 20 years, newscasts have replaced expensive and unpredictable syndicated programs at 5 P.M. In the largest markets—New York, Los Angeles, Chicago and Philadelphia among them—some newscasts start as early as 4 P.M.

A station can generate more advertising revenue in early fringe than in prime time with a judicious combination of programs. HUT levels during early fringe, while not as high as those in prime time, nevertheless average two-thirds of prime viewing. Especially during winter months, viewing spikes upward once darkness falls. In this early fringe period, station programming strategies generally have either a news or an entertainment orientation. As the afternoon progresses and older children return home from school, followed by employed adults, the average age of the audience increases, and so does the appeal of the programs. This technique of matching program content to gradually aging demographics is called *aging an audience*, and most stations, whether news- or entertainment-oriented, follow this pattern in the daypart (as the networks do in prime time).

The most content-malleable of programs, newscasts vary their topics over the course of this daypart to go along with the audience. The earlier afternoon newscasts tend to be lighter on news, emphasizing feature stories and afternoon rush-hour reports that reflect the interests of the available audience. As the afternoon wears on into early evening and more paycheck-earners return home, the news becomes harder-edged, with more news content and less fluff.

News stations surround their newscasts with news-compatible programs. These programs might be female-oriented programs such as *Dr. Oz* or *Dr. Phil* or court shows like *Judge Judy* or *People's Court*. For years, Oprah Winfrey was a programming juggernaut. Oprah was the center of the syndicated talk world until her decampment from broadcast to her own "OWN" (Oprah Winfrey Network) in 2011 (see 8.9). Her program was scheduled to devastating effect in most markets at 4 P.M. to funnel viewers into the local newscast. *Oprah's* ratings frustrated competing stations' attempts to get ratings traction in the late afternoon. Only when a program with an equally strong personality came to the television screen was *Oprah* challenged.

Stations that decide not to compete head-to-head against the Big Three affiliates' newscasts usually opt to counterprogram—with comedy. While news attracts an audience that trends older, with higher-than-average incomes and education—by contrast, comedy audiences in early fringe are younger, but they are also less affluent and less well educated. One might find young-skewing sitcoms or talk shows appearing at 4 or 5 P.M. (*Tyra, Wendy Williams*), followed by slightly older or family sitcoms opposite the news programs (*Frasier, Everybody Loves Raymond, Friends, The Simpsons, King of Queens*), which in turn are followed by the

strongest sitcoms on the station's schedule in access (*Seinfeld*).

Whether a station is programming from a network, syndicated or news/local source, it wants to retain as many of its viewers as possible through the sequencing of programs in its schedule. As explained in Chapter 1, this is called audience *flow*: The strategy of scheduling programs similar enough in appeal that current viewers will stay with the next program while new viewers tune in. As the audience composition changes during the day, the program lineup changes along with it. But as 8.10 discusses, the strategy of seeking flow has been eviscerated by the growth of multiple programming providers and mobile devices.

Prime Access (7 to 8 P.M.)

In television's infancy, prime time started at 7 P.M. (6 P.M. central/mountain time). As the industry reached adolescence, most of television's participants—stations, advertisers, producers—believed that the networks exercised a stranglehold on both the access to the airwaves and the pricing of advertising and production. After years of lobbying pressure, in 1970 the FCC imposed the *Prime-Time Access Rule (PTAR)*. In essence, PTAR prohibited stations from running more than three hours of

---

8.10 Flowing Away

Surveys show that about three-quarters of computer users report watching at least one entire television program online, and about half watch shows that they never saw previously on television. Although men are usually thought to be more technology- and adaptation-friendly, research has shown that women equally report having watched "television" programs online or on a mobile device.[10]

Flow is not as critical a concept as it once was. Before cable brought multiple channels to the home screen and before ubiquitous remote control handsets made channel changing a push-button procedure, the viewer had to physically rise from the sofa to change the channel. The incentive to change the channel had to be greater than the inertia to remain on the sofa. Once a channel was selected, the viewer tended to stay with that station for the rest of the evening, and programming executives obsessed over the idea of program flow. Today, with hundreds of viewing options available and the ability to change channels as easily as pushing a button, viewers can surf channels at whim. In addition, DVRs make saving programs or stopping momentarily (without missing anything) easily possible, and mobile media make industry-created "schedules" a thing of the past. Flow is a fading programming strategy even for stations, and the objective of consumer retention now takes place in an infinitely more challenging universe.

network-originated entertainment programming per night during prime time. (Recall that the FCC cannot regulate networks; the FCC's writ extends only to the stations it licenses. Networks are not licensed and therefore cannot be regulated by the FCC. There is a backdoor, however; the FCC can regulate the *stations*—that is, the O&Os—that a network owns.)

The impulses behind PTAR were twofold, and while the first was idealistic, the second was as subtle as a blow to the head. The first impulse was to create opportunities for stations to produce their own local programs, given that their mandate from the FCC was to operate in the public interest. This opening gave stations access to prime time; hence the name of the new daypart: *prime access* or just *access*.

The second impulse behind the rule was to create a more level playing field between the following:

- The networks and their affiliates
- The networks and the advertising community
- The networks and the program production community

After initially celebrating their victory over their network partners, suddenly affiliates realized that they had to come up with one hour of programming each night. Not only was making programs a costly time- and labor-intensive proposition, but it turned out that the public as a whole wasn't interested in watching the second-rate programming that was produced.

Into the breach came the program producers, creating new programs for what formerly was prime time. The viewers were there, the advertisers were there, and the games and magazines appeared. A handful of first-run syndicated shows (*Wheel of Fortune, Jeopardy!, Entertainment Tonight, Extra, Access Hollywood, Inside Edition!*) have dominated the ratings in this time period for many years. The magazine shows are hybrid programs consisting of entertainment, show business and celebrity news wrapped in a newscast format. The upside is that, unlike sitcoms in syndication, which can be expensive and risky, magazine programs are plentiful, and the rough equivalence of supply to demand results in stable purchase prices. Plus, entertainment talk and celebrity news never seem to go out of style, which means steady ratings and predictable advertising purchases, an ideal scenario for a business characterized by novelty, fads and the fickleness of public tastes. As a result, new shows have a tough time breaking through. Demographics play a key role in selecting programs, especially for stations that cannot buy the top show but can counterprogram to a different advertising target (for example, men aged 18 to 49).

Prime Time (8 to 11 P.M.)

This marquee time period for the networks is discussed in detail in Chapter 2. Viewing levels are highest, industry prestige is highest and potential advertising revenue is highest during this daypart, and for Big Four affiliates, profit margins are higher than in other dayparts. Affiliates preempt these most visible of network-supplied dayparts carefully—only with cause.

There *is* local programming in prime time; it is news. FOX, CW and MNTV supply their affiliates with only two hours of programming nightly, not three as the older networks and Hispanic networks do. FOX, in particular, compels its affiliates to program local news immediately after two hours of prime time—at 10 P.M. eastern/Pacific, 9 P.M. central/mountain. This is not just a bold counterprogramming move (news against three entertainment choices): It allows FOX affiliates get a one-hour jump on the affiliates' late newscasts as well; many early risers cannot stay awake past 11 P.M. to watch news.

Many affiliates of the smaller networks, with only a two-hour supply of network prime-time programming, follow the path of FOX. News departments are a profit center for major broadcast stations, and the facilities and output of a big news department can be leased to a smaller station in the market that lacks the budget to produce its own newscast. Many MNTV and CW stations thus outsource their newscasts, airing news produced for them by larger stations (usually the local FOX, CBS or NBC affiliates). These newscasts are not time competitive for the Big Three affiliates but run at the earlier hour while these affiliates still carry network shows. All of the advantages of newscasts come together with an *early* late newscast.

- It counterprograms the broadcast and many cable networks.
- It gives the station a one-hour jump on the affiliates' local news.
- It gives access to broadcast-wary advertisers.
- It fulfills a station's public service requirements.
- It gives a high-ratings track record in the time period.
- It displays the station's identity in a high-visibility time period.

Another advantage, albeit more minor, that comes from the news franchise is the occasional practice of repeating the late-fringe newscast during the overnight hours. While it might at first seem that a news rerun is stale programming, there are viewers who did not watch the original telecast, and the "news-lite" content of much local news does not detract from its timeliness. Also, there is no programming cost for a repeat, unlike the cost (in dollars or advertising time) of an outsourced program from a syndicator.

Late Fringe (11 to 11:35 P.M.)

As dayparts are delineated to reflect the typical behavior of the "average" viewer, a new daypart comes into play at 11 P.M., as older viewers begin getting ready for bed and younger viewers eventually turn from the internet to television. Late fringe is another example of the interconnectedness of the network–affiliate relationship. The local affiliates of ABC, CBS and NBC rely on their networks to provide popular programs during prime time, thus generating a strong lead-in audience for local late news. Even though news viewing for any given station is acknowledged to be a form of habit, viewers do not always act like they are "supposed to." Local affiliate late-news ratings can spike up or head downward, depending on the network lead-in. HUT levels, however, start dropping precipitously around 11 P.M.

(10 P.M. central). The Big Three networks, after three hours of prime programming, take a rest and throw the time period back to their affiliates, which invariably program their own local news.

With three hours of prime-time programming momentum as a lead-in, late fringe is a key ratings and revenue daypart for a Big Three affiliate. In the early days of television, late news was regarded as little more than an update of the early-fringe newscast, but in recent years, with the advent of the 24-hour news cycle and cost efficiencies in news production technology, late-news programs are regarded as separate programs and are important profit centers.

As a revenue-enhancement technique, affiliates of the Big Three networks stretch their newscasts to 35 minutes in late fringe, creating another commercial break. Going to all that trouble to add just one more commercial break might not seem like a dramatic addition, but over the course of one year, the arithmetic compounds into large multiples. If four commercials are placed in that extra pod five days a the week, 52 weeks a year, that translates into 1,040 extra commercials in a year. If a large-market station charges only $2,000 for a commercial, adding just one more break means $2,080,000 gross dollars in a year—with virtually no additional costs to generate that revenue! An intelligent media executive can turn a minor scheduling change into a financial "force multiplier."

Not everyone wants to watch the coverage of human debasement that much of local news consists of immediately before going to sleep, and some viewers already watched an earlier newscast. These viewers are likely customers for the many kinds of entertainment programs. Stations not airing news have a wide choice of syndicated programs to offer viewers uninterested in news and information just before going to sleep. Late fringe is a strong time period for stations without a network feed; strange as it seems, the strongest ones often outperform local affiliate news. FOX-owned stations during the last few years have adopted the strategy of acquiring top-performing (and expensive) off-network sitcoms as a counterpunch to what they see as the uniformity of local news product. *The Office* and *Seinfeld* work well here. Even stations with smaller program budgets can select from a wide range of first-run barter programs with appeal to some part of the demographic spectrum.

With the rise in the popularity of talk shows, another effective programming move has been to schedule a second, repeat telecast in late night for viewers unable to watch the original telecast during the day. *Oprah*, for example, used to be rerun late at night in several large markets, including New York, Los Angeles, Chicago and Philadelphia. Smaller stations also rerun daytime content, soaps, games and sitcoms—or turn to older movies.

For the programming executive, one advantage of late fringe over early fringe is that late fringe reaches an elusive quarry—men (particularly young men) aged 18 to 49 or 25 to 54. Men watch less television overall than women or children—calculated either by hours spent watching or variety of programs viewed. Young men, in particular, are more likely to watch narrow categories of broadcast programs: sports, some action-oriented movies and action-oriented reality programs. In late fringe, however, men are available, and in addition to sports they do watch comedies and risqué, first-run late-night programs, making these shows ideal for stations that choose to go after young men in that time period.

Late Night (11:35 P.M. to 2 A.M.)

Affiliates of CBS and NBC virtually always clear their network's programming during this daypart— *The Tonight Show with Jay Leno*, followed by *Late Night with Jimmy Fallon;* and *The Late Show with David Letterman*, followed by *The Late Late Show with Craig Ferguson*. Counterprogramming with more serious fare, ABC covers the newsbeat with *Nightline*, followed by the entertainment of *Jimmy Kimmel Live*. The overwhelming majority of Big Three affiliates are content because these programs attract larger audiences than they could lure with first-run or off-network syndicated programs. Moreover, the program content is not as restricted as it is in prime time because there is no measureable children's audience at such a late hour.

For the competing stations, late night is an ideal time period to experiment with offbeat syndication ideas. HUT levels are relatively low, so a failed idea will not hurt much financially, and an unexpected hit can generate a long-term occupant of a late-night time period. Expectations are not very high; there are disproportionately more men available, and if a program is a hit, it can make money in the daypart and perhaps even be moved to a daypart that generates higher revenues.

Overnight (2 to 6 A.M.)

Networks do not program first-run entertainment overnight because HUT levels are way too low to justify the costs of daily production and distribution. Thus, overnight becomes an arena for repeated telecasts of syndicated programs and repeated newscasts as well as a sanctuary for failed programs or old movies to fill the long predawn hours.

Although HUT levels are at their nadir (about 10 percent) and the time period is a low priority, stations wisely do not completely ignore these hours for three reasons. First, in the 24-hour world, *some* viewers are always available at all times, and advertisers can still be found to buy commercial time, even if at very low rates. (Commercial spots run in very cheap time periods are rather affectionately called "a-dollar-a-holler.") Even if an overnight commercial costs as little as 20 dollars, a small news station may air two dozen of them per hour or 100 per overnight period. Multiply $20 by 100 commercials a night, seven nights a week, 52 weeks a year, and the result is a not inconsiderable $728,000 per year. *Every time period counts, and every dollar counts.*

A second important reason for not ignoring overnight is more tactical. If the station signs off the air, the local cable company might use the now-empty channel space to carry a service with content that might alienate the broadcaster's regular viewers when they turn the television on the next day. The content could be as mild as a home-shopping channel or as spicy as an adult movie service. Suffice to say that the station wants to keep control over all programming coming from "its" cable position.

Third, if a station signs off, the few viewers who were still watching at that hour will turn away to another channel. When they turn the set on again, it will be on a different channel. Why invite customers to sample a competitor? There is enough free or cheap programming, combined with old movies, to fill up the overnight schedule. All else failing, another format ideally suited for late night is that of the infamous program category known as infomercials.

Between midnight and daybreak, little locally produced news exists. The syndicated *Poker After Dark* is as popular in the middle of the night as anything could be. If stations want news overnight, they either clear the overnight services offered by ABC (*World News Now*) or CBS (*Up to the Minute*) or go into the syndication marketplace to broadcast, for example, CNN's broadcast service or specialized newscasts offered by other program vendors. Financial newscasts are becoming increasingly popular, given the universal viewer interest in the subject of money and the advertiser attraction that upscale viewers represent.

Weekend Programming

On Saturdays and Sundays, networks readjust their programming away from their heavy viewers (women) to attract the demographic that watches most of its television during the weekend: men. Predictably, sports programming dominates the screen on weekends, especially on affiliates of ABC, CBS, FOX, NBC, TeleFutura, Telemundo and Univision. Advertisers are willing to pay a premium rate to attract men, who watch little in prime time but account disproportionately for expenditures on big-ticket items (automobiles, financial services, sporting equipment) and specialty purchases (alcohol, men's personal care). Even with relatively low HUT levels, affiliates find their adjacencies in top network sports events enormously valuable. If a station's network is not providing sports programming, odds are that the affiliate is counterprogramming with female-oriented movies or similar syndicated fare, although a few stations go after teens with weekly syndicated dating programs.

Station Promotion

A station's two constituencies, viewers and advertisers, need to be continually reminded of the existence of specific station programs. While the promotion manager is ultimately responsible for *promoting, advertising* and *publicizing* the schedule, the programmer's intimate knowledge of program audiences and viewing behavior may be invaluable for designing on-air promotional announcements.

On-Air Promotion of Programs

Among all the mass media available for publicizing a lineup, the station's own air time is the most effective for reach- and cost-efficiency. The station's loyal viewers can easily be located in the market—they are already watching the channel! The station can then redeploy its unsold advertising time by scheduling on-air promos. To ward off the sales manager's pressure to preempt important promos to place last-minute commercial buys, stations will often reserve a position for a promo, called a *fixed spot*. Very generally speaking, these fixed spots are the equivalent of a 30-second spot in each network hour or a 30-second spot in each half hour of syndicated programs. A promo might be dedicated to one program or to two or more programs. The latter is called a *combination spot*, or combo spot. With sales pressure always on, stations favor combo spots for two reasons: It is more efficient to promote as many programs as possible in one space (or amount of time), and using combo spots increases the chances of program flow.

The trend in the last several years has been toward fewer on-air promos. Since many former independents have aligned with the newer networks, much of their promotion comes from their networks in prepackaged spots. Also, consolidation has compelled corporate owners to eschew the long-term strategy of brand-building in favor of running more commercials (and thus fewer promos) to meet short-term financial targets. Having said that, the fundamental principles apply. The most practical way to design an on-air promotion strategy is to remember that "like goes to like." *In other words, similar programs or programs with similar audiences should be promoted toward each other*. The trade name for this technique is cross-promotion. *The station sets its priorities for on-air promotion according to two criteria: the potential profitability of the program and the importance of the program to the station's overall branding strategy.*

One category of programs generally fits both criteria: local news. Local news is one of the station's most significant profit centers, and because it is produced at the station, this program genre totally customizable in content, audience appeal and commercial format. Moreover, news programs remind viewers of other news programs; therefore it makes sense for the 7 A.M. network news to contain a promo for the 12 noon news. The noon news likely will promote the next news program at 5 P.M. The early-fringe newscast will promote the next newscast, and during prime time, there will likely be several reminders to "stay tuned for the late news."

There are two general kinds of promos: topical and image. For newscasts, a *topical spot* is a promo about a specific story: the update on the day's biggest trial, or a live shot of a traffic accident accompanied by a promise of coverage of the wreckers hauling away the vehicles during the next newscast. A topical promo is timely and story-specific. By contrast, an *image spot* for news should create a general impression of the news product's overall identity in viewers' minds. Typical image spots might be fast-paced scenes of anchors in motion who are interviewing people out in the field, prodding unseen faces over the telephone to make dramatic revelations, then racing to the news set with their hot stories just in time for the beginning of the program. (Irrespective of whether this is what they actually do, such promos are designed to create positive images of experienced, professional journalists.)

Topicals and image spots are also the norm for non-news program promotion. After the news promos are scheduled, the remaining promo time is allocated according to station needs. Most often, the lion's share of promos belongs to the programs that produce the highest revenues, for example, those programs during early fringe and access.

Lastly, those programs "on next" usually get a promo—a vestige of the time when the forces of program flow were stronger than they are today.

Promotion in Other Media

Outside media—radio, newspapers, billboards—traditionally occupied a large proportion of the television station's advertising efforts. Over the last several years, however, the downstream effects of deregulation have created many unintended (and unforeseen!) consequences, largely as a by-product of concentrated media ownership. Today, when companies can own up to eight radio stations in a market, radio ad rates are too aggressive (meaning very high) for television stations to afford the same kind of saturation radio campaigns seen just a few short years ago.

Cable, too, is starting to price itself out of the broadcast advertising market, particularly in those markets with a heavy concentration of ownership or an aggressive *interconnect* (electronic connection among a consortium of separately owned but geographically contiguous cable companies). Although the price per commercial seems beguilingly low on many channels, the number of viewers per cable program is so small that it drives the cost-per-viewer price inefficiently upward. *In short, television is a victim of its own attractiveness as an advertising vehicle. Compared with other media, television remains the most cost-efficient buy for both reach and frequency, but that efficiency is declining.*

One solution for most stations has been to develop enticing internet sites that both supply extended content for viewers who want more news and program information, and promote the station's news, programming and overall image. *The downside of internet promotion is that only viewers who make the effort to go to the site are exposed to the promotion, and network sites tend to be bigger lures than local station sites—except in the area of local weather and local events.* Thus most web programmers place sidebars that promote entertainment alongside key news items—to draw the user's attention to additional content that is above and beyond what drove the person to the site.

What Lies Ahead for Stations

Predicting the future of the local television station business has been difficult for the last decade. On one hand, the technology is moving away from program-source scarcity to program-source abundance. On the other, parent media corporations continue to derive predictable—if not outright superior—returns from their affiliates.

Digital Technology

The number-one threat to over-the-air broadcasters (as well as advertising-supported subscription television) comes from technology that frees the viewer from the addiction of passive viewing: DVRs, tablets, smart phones and video-on-demand. Although these technologies have done little harm to broadcast revenues so far, their household penetration is climbing swiftly. Losing control of viewers spells the eventual end of commercial breaks as they presently exist because DVRs allow viewers to "skip over" breaks entirely.

The remarkable thing is that digital television and DVR use is not diffusing slowly the way new media technologies have in the past—instead, in a period of less than three years, digital totally supplanted analog television. The newest generation of converters allows for storing lots of recorded programs in memory and represents a marriage between the computer and the television set, a plus for cable and satellite viewers *but* not *for broadcast stations.*

On the other hand, the predominant motivation to watch television is to relax. Given their history with new technologies, it is clear that much of the American audience is unwilling to read any instructions, learn any sequences or steps, or wait for their TV set's operating system to boot up. The safe money says that new media innovations should bend over backward to accommodate loyal viewers in such a way that they won't need to know about bandwidths or protocols—so they can swim in the digital stream without understanding it. All of this is predicated on the effective design of very smart converters and their remote controls, of course, and because there are so many ifs, broadcasters must watch and worry.

Competing Newscasts

It is an axiom of the business that news will continue to be a mainstay of television programming into the indefinite future. Television's eternal appeal is that it is a "live" medium. No other medium has the immediacy of television. Increasingly sophisticated and miniaturized technologies give stations a level of production quality and time-responsiveness that were unimaginable only a few short years ago.

The main challenge will be competition, not just at the local level—where competitors are expanding and upgrading their news product—but also from competing industries jumping into the news business. One of the viewer benefits arising (albeit indirectly) out of the massive consolidations in cable ownership in the 1990s is that many cable franchises in large markets now offer around-the-clock *local* news channels of their own (such as News 12 Long Island and many others; see Chapter 9). To varying degrees, these local news channels are like mini-CNNs. They represent a serious threat to the dominance of broadcasting as a local medium. Their lack of network commitments means they can cover ongoing local stories as they unfold during the day, whereas broadcasters usually are forced to wait until their regularly scheduled newscasts.

Moreover and maybe worse, local cable news shows can undercut the relatively high advertising rates of broadcast newscasts by offering more commercial availabilities, lower spot rates and more flexible packaging opportunities to local advertisers. What is particularly grating to affiliates is that some of these national and local news outlets are owned by their own network partners! (For example, News Corp. owns Fox News Channel as well as the FOX Broadcasting Network; Time Warner owns CNN as well as New York 1 News.)

Other emerging competitors are the internet and mobile media. Use of the internet for news programming offers the ultimate of both extremes: global instantaneous distribution and individualized news products for the consumer. At present, the web's news capability rests largely in distributing news that was originally generated for television or print and then was adapted for the internet, accompanied by mountains of professional and amateur blogging. It was thought that true news competition would wait until computers were as easy to use and as plentiful as television sets, but then Wi-Fi proliferated, making computers mobile. People began accessing news from practically anywhere they could open a portable computer. Next, cellphones, personal assistants (Blackberrys) and music players added video to their equipment, meaning internet access could be truly anywhere, anytime, if a bit reduced in size.

At this writing, the major media companies are extending themselves into all these new media, using their branding power to stake claims to content areas in an attempt to follow the audience wherever it goes. Although internet-generated news products are not yet profit centers for their participants, the ultimate profits and marketing advantages of these new media are too potentially enormous to be ignored, and that leaves broadcasters nervous.

Channel Migration

As of February 19, 2009, all analog television transmission stopped, and television stations began sending digital signals. The largest stations (and networks) broadcast now in high definition—which uses the entire allotted bandwidth—but many stations have chosen standard definition with the option of multiplexing additional signals. So far, the options for paid use of that extra bandwidth are scarce, but it was expected to be the savior: to become a revenue stream that would cover the enormous cost of digitalizing station facilities. But the FCC will eventually require some number of hours of HDTV (rather sooner than later) and is likely to limit reselling or reusing channel bandwidth. Because of pressure from other users of the airwaves, the FCC may also reclaim bandwidth resources from stations long before many are ready to give them up.

The Mutation of Broadcasting

Although broadcasting has traditionally been a free service, the American consumer is increasingly becoming accustomed to paying for media. Smaller companies owning stations in markets with network-owned stations but not producing programs themselves face heavy leverage and consequent pressure to sell to the larger companies. The traditional local orientation of broadcasting has begun to flicker, to be rekindled by industries that have economies of scale on their sides: cable and the internet. These competitors now provide not only local service but also increasingly customized entertainment and news content to individual consumers.

Broadcasting of some sort will stay around because it is universal and free, which is in the nation's best interest, but the number of stations per market is likely to fall drastically in another decade or so. For the immediate future, however, local broadcasting will remain a highly profitable business, although its owners are likely to squeeze every dollar of profit they can from it now.

Nonetheless, the maturation of the television industry means that the original business model of distant networks and local affiliates is disintegrating. Competition from newer media means that free television has to resign itself to no longer being the biggest and gaudiest float in the television parade. Video entertainment has become global, instantaneous and customizable in a way unimaginable just one generation ago. Local stations were once the sole gatekeepers, and now they survive by fitting themselves into those niches in which they can be competitive.

Despite the fears of media Cassandras who prognosticate the end of broadcasting, however, history tells us otherwise: Television did not kill off the movie industry, FM radio did not eliminate AM, cable did not eliminate local broadcast, and satellite-delivered television did not defeat cable. Instead, each industry had to adapt itself to the new challenge. Like many businesses, broadcasting is organic: It expands, contracts, mutates into different forms. Unlike many businesses, broadcasting is a fascinating mix of technology, creativity and commerce. The cumulative impacts of computers, digital technology and regulatory changes will be strong but not fatal.

Notes

1. This disproportionate amount of discussion of FOX's raid indicates the level of root-and-branch disruption that FOX caused in the relatively calm of an oligopoly network landscape. It was as if a starter's gun had fired, and all networks and affiliates scrambled for new partners. Murdoch's audacity created turbulence, which distracted his competitors, thus leveling the playing field for him. The raid gave FOX a chance to be sampled by new viewers and, not incidentally, to deeply wound a major competitor. If there was any doubt about Murdoch's intentions when he started his network in the 1980s, it was now clear that the game was being played for keeps. And he did it again after CBS and Time Warner closed UPN and the WB and cozied up to form the CW. FOX's left-out stations got their own competing network, MNTV.

2. NSI, 2/14-2/20/11, as cited in TV News Check (*tvnewscheck.com*).

3. For an unsurpassed anthology of hilarious, believe-it-or-not stories of television during its first decades, read *The Box: An Oral History of Television 1920–1960* by Jeff Kisseloff (Viking Press, 1995). The book is currently out of print, so try a library.

4. Murrow (1908 to 1965) was one of the earliest broadcast journalists to achieve professional notoriety and, later, celebrity. Murrow joined the CBS Radio Network in 1935 and was sent to Europe in 1937. He is most remembered for his on-scene reporting of harrowing Nazi Luftwaffe bombing raids in London during World War II. Murrow moved to television after the war. His onscreen news career notched highs (with his award-winning documentary series *See It Now*) and lows (he hosted *Person to Person*, an early personality-interview program, during which Murrow often looked physically stricken to be interviewing celebrities rather than newsmakers).

5. *Federal Communications Commission, Information Needs of Communities: The Changing Media Landscape in a Broadband Age, 2011.*

6. Information from *2011 Ownership Survey and Trend Report*, as cited in TV News Check, June 6, 2011.

7. In their affiliate incarnations, however, stations are somewhat hamstrung because they are legally committed to air the programs their networks distribute and must work around those. Moreover, when stations are located in more socially traditional parts of the country, and a network program is "too cool for the room" (that is, has content inappropriate for the audience), the stations still must clear it—in the absence of an overwhelmingly compelling reason that justifies preemption (and the outlay for a substitute show).

8. See *http://en.wikipedia.org/wiki/OprahWinfrey*, p. 2, for these quotes.

9. Early fringe is outside prime time, so the networks technically could fill it like the other parts of daytime, but good luck getting this profitable time back from the stations!

10. *http://mediamatters.org/items/200610240003*, 17 October 2006.

Basic and Premium Subscription Programming

Susan Tyler Eastman and Douglas A. Ferguson

Chapter Outline

Cable content networks are popping up everywhere. Once exclusive to cable systems, cable networks are now carried not just by satellite and telephone companies, but also appear online. You can watch MTV on your tablet, if you spring for the app. Many companies that own cable program networks first operated local cable systems in the United States but moved into content ownership as the cable installation business matured. Now the owners of content networks sell the carriage rights to competitors. Why would they do that? The answers are *channel proliferation, government regulation* and *need for revenue.*

Competing Content Networks

Subscription content networks is an overall term that encompasses all kinds of television program services requiring fees to subscribe and distinguishes them from the media distribution services (MVPDs). The subscription networks traditionally provide programs organized in 24-hour channels that come by satellite to the MVPDs who in turn put them onto their wires or beam them out wirelessly. Those structured networks are usually accompanied by access to unstructured on-demand programming. The MVPDs pay monthly fees to include specific subscription networks on their services and charge their subscribers enough to cover those fees (see Chapter 3). The subsets of *basic cable networks* and *premium cable networks* refer to those with and without advertising, respectively (although a very few "basic" networks don't have ads), plus premium networks usually require extra subscription fees.

Commonly called *cable networks* to distinguish them from *broadcast networks* (a distinction largely irrelevant to viewers but crucial to owners), a huge-seeming variety of subscription networks appear on the two satellite services, on the various teleco services, and online sites carrying web series and movies, as well as in very different arrangements and selections on the hundreds of U.S. cable systems. Many also appear in some variation on distribution systems in other countries. Of course, the 8 percent of U.S. households still receiving only over-the-air signals (if without internet access) cannot see any subscription networks—only local broadcast stations.

Some companies that provide nationwide subscription programming have adopted the word *network* in their names, trumpeting that they possess the primary characteristics of a big network and likening themselves to the long-familiar broadcast networks. Being a network lends prestige while invoking images of great size and the likelihood of subsidiary services. Others use the word *channel.* Such program services are saying that they occupy a full channel on television sets (no sharing) and that they are centralized; that they distribute simultaneous programming, carry advertisements and sell adjacencies (if advertiser-supported), and that they are retransmitted to homes via MVPD services. Whatever a content service is called and however it is delivered, all are generically *subscription* (or *cable*) *content networks.*

Totaling maybe 100 in the 1990s, the number of distinct subscription networks had expanded to more than 200 (or perhaps 300) by first decade of the 2000s. Enumerating networks, however, depends on what you include and exclude (see 9.1). *One problem is differentiating between parent companies, networks and channels.* NBCUniversal (itself owned by MVPD Comcast) owns the NBC broadcast network as well as Telemundo, and they both appear on cable systems, but NBC appears via a local affiliated station and so may Telemundo (and thus their carriage as stations is legally required), but in markets with no local Telemundo affiliate, the network can appear as a cable channel. (Generally, broadcasters avoid the term "cable networks" because they come under different FCC rules than those applying to broadcast networks). But that's not the whole picture: NBCUniversal owns all or part of several subscription channels, including USA Network (which is solely a cable network), Bravo, Syfy, Chiller, Oxygen and Sleuth, while parent Comcast also owns E!: Entertainment and FEARNet. Comcast systems may also carry a dedicated "Comcast Channel" that promotes the network itself. In addition, NBCUniversal also owns Universal HD, a hi-def only channel. The industry counts all these channels separately for purposes of Nielsen ratings. But then there are other kinds of *channel multiplication*.

The Proliferating Nonbroadcast World

Technical advances make possible both *duplication* and *splintering* of various kinds. First, fiber technology has such great capacity that it readily permits simultaneous distribution of the same channel three ways: *analog, digital* and *HD*, so all established broadcast and cable networks were duplicated in three formats until recently. Even digital-only cable networks can exist in both standard digital and HD. And 3D is coming, necessitating another feed of each network, although analog will soon drop away completely. Are TNT and TNT HD one or two networks? Technically, they take up two bandwidth channels.

Second, fiber's immense capacity has led established networks to create or buy up *digital niche channels* to see what attracts audiences. A&E Television Networks, for example, owns the classic Bio (formerly Biography) and History channels, but acquired or invented the digital Crime & Investigation Network, History en Espanol and Military History Channel. Many digital niche channels, such as Jewelry TV, Cooking Channel and Military History Channel, do not yet exist in HD, so some have two versions and others just one.

Third, digital fiber can easily carry multiplexed signals, so several digital networks split their programming into separate virtual channels—each carrying a rotating sliver of programming such as thematically chosen movies—called *splinter channels*. Did you know there are 17 versions of Showtime? Not only are there separate channels for Showtime, Showtime 2, Showtime Showcase, Showtime Beyond, Showtime Extreme, Showtime Family Zone, Showtime Next and Showtime Women, but each comes in East and West (time zone feeds). Plus there is Showtime On Demand. And all or some feeds can be available on a single MVPD (FiOS carries all 17). Do 17 channels comprise just a single premium

network—or should they be counted as 17 separate ones? The industry usually counts Showtime as one, because it doesn't care: there's no advertising. Non-movie channels also split into multiple content channels targeting different audiences: National Geographic Channel also comes with National Geographic Wild, but they are usually counted as two.

Fourth, there are East and West *time zone feeds* for the premium networks, and on some MVPDs subscribers can watch either feed, such as Starz Edge and Starz Edge West or HBO Signature or HBO Signature West. In Washington, D.C., politicians like to be able to see what is being fed in their home towns so all feeds appear there.

Fifth, there are *foreign language feeds* of American channels for citizens who want their U.S. television in another language (as distinct from all the imported foreign-language networks from other countries). CNN comes in Spanish, as does Fox Sports, Discovery, Playboy, Toon Disney and others. Some foreign language feeds consist of audio overlays and subtitles; others are separate splinter channels.

And finally, some smaller *broadcast networks duplicate themselves* as cable channels, even though one of their broadcast affiliates may also appear as a station filling a channel on the same MVPD. Ion Television does this, presumably to increase national viewing of its infomercials.

Subscribers by Channel

At least 200 subscription television networks exist, and of those, nearly half reach a minimum of 50 million U.S. homes, making those the ones on which most advertisers will pay to place commercial spots. The top 30 of those networks, such as TBS, ESPN, USA, The Food Network, The Weather Channel, Discovery, Nickelodeon and the others listed in 9.1, have become household words because they appear on virtually every cable system in the United States and on both satellite and the main telco systems. Each of the top 30 has more than 100 million U.S. subscribers, and many are closing in on 200 million worldwide. *Since there are only about 116 million TV households in America and of those, 107 million (92 percent) subscribe to some kind of multichannel system, reaching 100 mil-lion is not far from reaching nearly everybody.* Moreover, the numbers in 9.1 are for both cable and satellite but do not include telco subscribers or other small services (see 9.2).

9.1 Top 30 Cable Programming Networks, 2012 (cable and satellite only)	
Services	**Subscribers**
TBS	105,400,000
ESPN/ESPN HD	104,400,000
USA	104,400,000
Food Network	104,200,000
HGTV	103,900,000
ESPN2	103,800,000
Weather Channel	103,900,000
TLC	103,800,000
CNN	103,800,000
Discovery Channel	103,700,000
Nickelodeon/Nick	103,600,000
FOX News	103,600,000
TNT	103,600,000
Spike TV	103,600,000
MTV	103,400,000
VH1	102,800,000
Lifetime Television	102,700,000
Disney Channel	102,700,000
TV Land	102,600,000
A&E	102,300,000
CSPAN	102,100,000
E! Entertainment	101,900,000
FX Network	101,800,000
Syfy	101,500,000
Comedy Central	101,400,000
Cartoon Network	101,200,000
History	101,100,000
CNBC	100,900,000
ABC Family Channel	100,900,000
Travel Channel	100,200,000*

*Animal Plant, AMC and MSNBC are close behind with 99 million and 98 million subs.

2012 Estimates from SLN Kagan, 2011, and Nielsen Media Research, Inc., 2011.

9.2 Multichannel Reach

The cable industry no longer publishes the precise percentages of viewers who receive the cable networks over *alternate delivery systems (ADS)*, perhaps because terrestrial competitors to cable are growing while cable system penetration has halted expansion. Other published sources, such as the FCC, tend to be somewhat out of date. As a consequence, the most accurate subscriber information (as in 9.1) comes from Nielsen ratings and combines cable and satellite but omits AT&T and Verizon, other smaller competitors and online subscribers.

As was pointed out in Chapter 3, overall cable penetration of the U.S. TV households has stayed almost stable for a decade at nearly two-thirds (close to 66 percent) of multichannel households: that's 70 million households subscribing to cable. Penetration from services such as DirecTV and DISH has levelled at about 30 percent of multichannel homes (another 32 million subscribers), and AT&T and Verizon currently account for about 5 percent more (another 5+ million subscribers).

Foundation and Niche Subscription Services

National subscription networks can be differentiated in terms of how established they are and whom they target. *Foundation networks*—generally the earliest, most firmly established, and most popular entries in the field—reach about a 100 million U.S. subscriber homes each via cable/satco/telco or other MVPDs. The very largest (TBS, the Weather Channel, Discovery, Nickelodeon, CNN and ESPN) are in hundreds of millions homes worldwide. *About 25 subscription channels are considered the foundation networks.*

The second broad group consists of the *niche* or *theme networks.* Some of major networks began life as theme networks and grew into channels that serve more than a niche. Comedy Central is an example of a theme network that became a foundation network. When a cable network gets into that Top 25 list year after year, it is firmly established. If a new cable, satellite or telephone system wants to offer potential subscribers at least one of every kind of channel, it will begin by seeking to license all the foundation networks.

True *niche networks* usually either have a *single program content type* (all music, all shopping, all travel) or target a *defined demographic group* (just children, just Spanish speakers—groups numbering in the tens of millions) using a mix of program types. SOAPnet, Golf Channel, VERSUS, SPEED, Sundance Channel, the Travel Channel and BET are niche networks.

Currently, the hot type of niche network is the *branded subniche network*, which is the product of further *specialization within a theme network* by a well-known media company. Investigation Discovery is a clear example. Subniche channels are managed as a group and owned by one parent company or network. Most notably, Discovery Communications, which operates the Discovery Channel (foundation) and TLC (formerly The Learning Channel) launched several branded subniche services (Discovery Health, Discovery Science, Discovery Kids, Discovery Times, Discovery Home, Discovery Wings and so on), all using the Discovery name. Other networks, such as A&E and Nickelodeon followed Discovery's lead, developing additional channels. To Lifetime, A&E added Lifetime Real Women; to the classic Nickelodeon, the company added Nick Jr., Nick 2, Nicktoons and TeenNick. (Once sufficiently established, instead of more splintering, Discovery changed several channel names to broaden or clarify content: Wings became The Military Channel; Kids became The Hub for teens, Science lost the word Discovery in its name, Health became Fit & Health and so on.)

Subniche services are made possible by cheaper satellite time resulting from digital compression. As outlined in Chapter 3, digital compression encourages a process called *multiplexing*, distributing several different channels simultaneously, usually 12 digital channels squeezed onto the bandwidth formerly used by one old analog channel. In some cases, the "new" services run the same programs as the main network; they are merely scheduled at different times. In other cases, programs are subdivided by target audience, and each channel focuses on one target audience. The *splintering phenomenon* occurs particularly in premium services: HBO now provides programming for nine subniche channels: HBO2, HBO Signature, HBO Family, HBO Comedy, HBO Zone, HBO Latino, HBO on Demand, HBO Home Satellite and HBO HDTV. In addition to the 17 Showtimes and 9 HBOs, there are 14 different Encores.

As the spread of newer technologies permits greater proliferation of channels, the strategy of channel *spinoffs* (into subniches) is becoming more commonplace. For example, in addition to FX, Fox spun off a new branded business news channel called Fox News Channel (digital and HD) and a movie spinoff, Fox Movie Channel. Even more widely known are its multiple sports channels (Fox College Atlantic/Central/Pacific, Fox Soccer Channel and FSN Prime Ticket).

Microniche networks target even more specialized population subgroups, including the hearing-impaired viewers and foreign-language speakers. Some of these have the same content as another channel but include sign language and subtitles or are in another language. Others have a lot of original programming. While Spanish-language itself is hardly a subniche these days, channels appealing to viewers with a Latino, or Columbian or Mexican or Caribbean orientation constitute microniches. For example, Sur Mexico, Sur Peru, ESPN Deportes, Canal Sur, Bandamaz and others appear on U.S. cable systems. In Chicago and Detroit, channels in other language groups such as Polish or Armenian require microniche channels. Satellites and cable carry the Filipino Channel and AZN (targeting Asians). Then there's Kung Fu HD, MOJO, Rave HD, Rush HD, Treasure HD, and Water Channel. All this is probably more than you wanted to know!

Some microniches provide programming that is a further differentiation of a niche service (women's sports, independent films) and thus are both narrow in content and targeted in audience. As streaming video opportunities expanded via broadband internet connections (see Chapter 4), a few of these microniche channels (in particular, TRIO and Lime) shuttered their cable/satellite channels and moved onto the web.

Virtually all basic subscription networks carry advertising; the smaller ones carry as much as they can get. A very few services, notably C-SPAN, C-SPAN 2 and C-SPAN 3, are basic cable networks but without advertising. Because their content consists largely of government meetings, hearings and discussion shows on which elected and appointed government officials appear, they are offered as a noncommercial public service on the lowest level of subscription services (in hopes of forestalling government regulation of commercial programming). The C-SPAN group is owned by the parent companies of several large cable networks, but also carried by the satcos and telcos.

Types of Premium Subscription Services

Premium services is an umbrella term for a group of specialized entertainment services that provide special or "premium" programming to about 70 million U.S. cable, satellite or telco subscribers who pay additional fees above the basic MVPD service cost. Premium services primarily offer unedited movies and original productions in a commercial-free format.

Premium movie and sports channels number about 15, not counting their splinter services. The five with the largest number of subscribers are HBO, Encore, Showtime, Starz!, Max (Cinemax) and The Movie Channel. Another five, HDNet, Flix, Epix, Turner Classic Movies and The Sundance Channel, also reach large audiences. Still others are mostly on-demand channels or in limited distribution. Then there's Netflix, described in detail in Chapter 4, which is certainly a direct competitor to all pay television channels.

Details on the number of premium subscribers are generally not available, largely because the absolute number of pay subscribers also began declining in the early 2000s (so the companies keep the totals secret). We do know that the total number of subscriptions to the collective top five had reached 70 million by 2008 and has stayed largely flat since. Of those, HBO has about 30 million. Its problem is that competitor Netflix had about 23 million subscribers as of 2011, but its subscribership was continuing

to grow. (At any rate, not even HBO has the penetration of any of the top 25 basic cable networks who reach around a 100 million subscribers each.)

The premium television field has long had three distinct components:

1. **Pay-cable networks,** which charge viewers a monthly subscription "premium" (traditional pay)

2. **Pay-per-view (PPV) services,** which charge on a program-by-program basis

3. **Video-on-demand (VOD) services,** which usually charge per-program-viewed, similar to PPV, and are available in several subvarieties or formats, but that offer more viewer control and often DVR-like functionality

The key difference to consumers is that classic premium cable means buying a *group of movies* over a month (*pay-per-month*), whereas PPV and VOD mean purchasing *just one program* at a time (*pay-per-use*). One difference is that PPV normally consists of movies while VOD includes a huge body of television programs of all kinds.

This chapter differentiates the services by payment method (by month or by use), but at the time of this writing, the distinctions among them are becoming very fluid. Many premium services of the pay-per-month variety are being relabeled *subscription-video-on-demand (SVOD)*, and many pay-per-view services have switched to VOD as systems digitized.

Video-On-Demand

PPV was once thought to be the "killer application" of cable, but the industry had turned to video-on-demand in the early 2000s, and VOD households have grown along with digitalization. Just to confuse us all, the video-on-demand name is currently applied to four somewhat different formats:

1. **VOD,** the true digital kind, which delivers movies or programs as the consumer asks for them, for a per-program fee

2. **FVOD (Free-VOD),** where some content is available without charge to entice subscribers to become more comfortable with the idea of on-demand programming

3. **SVOD (Subscription-VOD),** where a separate monthly fee is charged (for example, Showtime on Demand and HBO on Demand) but the movies come as requested over the month

4. **Download-to-own,** an internet venue that relies on broadband connections but offers the same programming as basic and premium cable channels

One important limitation to on-demand is that neither all movies nor all TV programs are available. The movie studios and television program distributors hold back many shows, requiring each MVPD to negotiate a selection of programs for its VOD service. If a show originally had advertising in it, those ads transfer to VOD, expanding the reach of those messages. While shows from all four networks may appear on the largest on-demand services, only some of their programs are included. For three reasons, major MVPDs constantly seek to expand and update their television and movie listings. First, an attractive on-demand lineup forestalls DVR use, and second, carrying the current hits keeps viewers from turning to competing online streaming services. A third reason is that MVPDs are able to insert different commercials into television program breaks. This is a valuable source of revenue because the ads can be targeted to specific groups of subscribers. One programming problem is that many network executives fear that feeding strong product to VOD will cannibalize their main networks and give them little in return. At the same time, MVPDs press hard to persuade networks to move hit series to their VOD menus, thus competing with Netflix for the valuable replays.

Systems that charge for VOD find subscriber resistance to paying twice for the same program. Digital and HD subscribers already pay for all channels in their monthly bills. For example, the cable operator charges about $.50 per month for MTV (hidden in the total bill), which includes *The Real World*, so why would viewers want to pay again for that show on VOD?

Convenience, however, is the real selling factor because on-demand comes whenever the subscriber wants it. Free VOD has great appeal for children and teens who like watching many episodes of favorite series or some sport at one time and don't care if they are "old" or repeats. Cable operators expect VOD to be the kind of service to which viewers are strongly attracted, once they try it.

From the standpoint of the end-user's experience, true VOD operates largely the same as most MVPDs: recorded programs are stored in DVRs, with play, pause, stop, fast-forward and rewind capabilities, but fast-forward may be disabled in key VOD shows to prevent skipping commercials. Usually viewers can watch all or part of any movies as often as they wish during a 24- or 36-hour period.

One of the major reasons for implementing on-demand is to cut down on *churn* (subscribers who start and stop their premium subscriptions faster than the network would prefer, a process that adds to the business costs). *The industry's assumption is that if more options and more conveniences are available to consumers, they will be more likely to continue paying for a service.*

Internet services such as CinemaNow and Movielink offer internet-based VOD services, as does Netflix (see Chapter 4). The days when VOD meant only "cable" are long gone, and the internet may win this battle eventually, as consumers learn to turn to their computer or tablet screens for television as readily as to large HD screens.

Comcast has been able to leverage its full or part ownership of such niche networks as Home & Garden Television, Food Network, Cartoon Network, the History Channel and E! Entertainment Television to create demand for VOD. Even sports networks associated with the NBA and the NFL make older game replays and highlights available on VOD, and multicultural programming is particularly popular, especially Hispanic programs (see Time Warner's FVOD in 9.3). FVOD is now viewed enough that Nielsen already measures aggregate linear cable networks separately from VOD viewership of individual programs. VOD revenue today is in the billions.

With SVOD, subscribers may get the best of both worlds for the same subscription price. They get (1) a packaged "live" service for watching highly promoted first telecasts of premium programming

9.3 Time Warner Cable's "Start Over"

Time Warner Cable has its own FVOD feature called Start Over, an on-demand application that allows customers to jump to the beginning of a program in progress without any preplanning or in-home recording devices. When tuning to a Start Over–enabled show in progress, customers are alerted to the feature through an on-screen prompt. By pressing "Select" on the remote control, the program is immediately restarted from the beginning (but without the ability to skip commercials). Recently, some HD channels have become "start over' enabled. About 70 percent of Time Warner's digital subscribers use Start Over, and the idea was awarded an Engineering Emmy at the 2007 Consumer Electronics Show.

and (2) using a different distribution system, a video-on-demand version of the same programs. The packaged service is like a conventional real-time linear network where scheduling is important. The VOD version has two methods of delivery, depending on the cable operator. The first method warehouses the programs on a central video server located at the headend building of the cable provider and makes the content available whenever the viewer requests it. Niche or "lightly viewed" networks are considered the best for early implementations of *switched digital video*, a relatively new technology that directs channels only to customers who want to view them at that time. The second system relies on decentralized storage, housed in set-top boxes equipped with high-capacity disk storage, if viewers have DVR equipment. The operator downloads the material, where it can be retrieved on demand. Either way, viewers can watch what they want, when they want it, for only a monthly fee. They choose to watch the first-available "live" version or choose another time to view a replay.

If all these kinds of VOD sound complicated, it is because this decade is the shakeout period in which new delivery and reception technologies are *battling to win.* Because cable subscribers are more accustomed to paying monthly for tiers of services than paying for each use, SVOD successfully bridges the two models. Anyone who has had the option of paying a single price for entry to all amusement rides at a county fair versus a per-ride cost understands the appeal of SVOD over VOD, even when it is called "free."

Services such as HBO that cling to the premium pay-per-month model use SVOD as a way to enhance the value of their programming. Disney (which owns ABC Family, ESPN, the Disney Channel and other services) is reluctant to give away the added value of its programs by making them available on demand, so it has resisted SVOD. At the other end of the spectrum, World Wrestling Entertainment launched WWE 24/7 as an SVOD service to leverage its 75,000 hours of professional wrestling. As long as subscribers are willing to pay an additional $4.95 or so a month for SVOD access to basic channels, such channels will resist the trend toward pay-per-use, the true VOD. Having unpredictable amounts of revenue is what understandably scares content suppliers.

Furthermore, on-demand is not limited to cable, satellite and telephone television. Even conventional broadcasting stations can be part of this brave new world through online services, second channels negotiated from cable operators in return for retransmission consent or, they hoped, multiplexed digital channels using a spectrum set aside for HDTV (but Congress soon put an end to this practice: HD spectrum is only for HD). Starting in 2005, CBS-owned stations offered CBS on Demand service to compete with HBO on Demand and TBS on Demand. The internet variety, *download-to-own VOD*, is more suited to the type of streaming distribution described in Chapter 4 but offers programming identical to that offered on basic and pay services.

Competition among Program Services

When considering advertiser-supported services, what real difference exists between CBS and USA networks? Both target a broad audience, both carry a mix of rerun and original shows, both carry live sports, both have theatrical and first-run movies, and both have sitcoms and game shows. The obvious difference is the presence or absence of news programming, but another modest difference lies in the better than 98 percent reach of a broadcast network versus the 92 percent reach of the top subscription networks (and much smaller reaches for smaller ones). But most important, broadcast networks still outspend the cable networks, with each of the Big Four networks spending far more on content than any subscription program services. Broadcast network programs garner the most press and social network attention individually and as a group.

One way to understand the multichannel programming business is to consider the wholesaler–retailer analogy: National cable networks are like coast-to-coast wholesalers in that they sell their product—*programming*—to regional and local outlets, the wired (or wireless) cable system program operators, satellite services, telcos and others. MVPDs are like retailers because they sell their product—*television programming services*—to consumers, home by home and subscriber by subscriber. The wholesalers have four functions:

1. **Licensing** existing shows or financing original programming created by Hollywood's studios or independent producers, or in conjunction with international joint-venture partners

2. **Packaging** programming in a form acceptable to consumers (by providing interstitial promotions such as wraparounds, titles, on-air hosts and graphics)

3. **Delivering** programming by satellite to MVPDs

4. **Supporting** their products with national advertising and promotion and by supplying advertising materials and co-op dollars at the local system level

Program content services actively compete for fresh content; there are more outlets than top quality new programs. *The licensing of many American television programs and movies follows a pattern beginning with the most profitable U.S. markets and ending with international distribution.* Basic cable

networks bid directly against local broadcast stations (and each other) for the rights to movie packages and hit off-network television series. Because of the way original contracts for most series are written, most basic cable networks pay much lower residuals than broadcast stations do. *Residuals*, as discussed in Chapters 2 and 6, are payments to the cast and creators every time the program is reshown. Licensing fees for cable networks can be several hundred thousand dollars per episode (which may seem expensive but is far lower than for big broadcast stations). As a result, basic cable television has become a key *aftermarket* in the progression of sales of movies and serial programs, generating hundreds of millions of dollars in profits for U.S. and foreign program distributors.

In addition, the largest cable networks have consistently outbid broadcasters (stations and station groups—as explained in Chapter 6) to get first rerun rights to newly available hour-long adventure and drama series and even some half-hour situation comedies. (As discussed in Chapter 2, hour-long series are less useful in rerun to broadcasters, and even such a hugely successful action series as *CSI* has underperformed many half-hour sitcoms in station reruns.) All this heavy-duty competition for content has driven the top cable networks into producing their own *signature series*. Although production costs are very high, the reward comes from having promotable content ("See X here and nowhere else!"). Such series are normally produced in conjunction with advertisers so costs are underwritten. Putting out a new series without underwriting commonly means that producers have to wait for a ratings track record to develop, a long process that demands very deep pockets.

A few theatrical films have gone straight from theaters to cable networks, and many European television series go directly to cable. Spike TV imports Japanese shows dubbed in English or cloned. Cable also has become a *foremarket* for some programs that later appeared on U.S. broadcast stations. For example, *Politically Incorrect* migrated from Comedy Central to ABC in 1996 (although Bill Maher eventually took his show to HBO to escape censors and controversy).

The battle for movies after their theatrical appearance rages on. The established premium channels get access to theatrical movies long before they are offered to most basic cable networks (and broadcasters), but the window for the hottest movies doesn't come soon enough to suit HBO and Showtime. Because video sales and rentals have been a cash cow for the major studios, the popular movies exhaust the DVD market before the premium networks are given access to them. The pay-per-use services, being the newest guys on the block, would be low on the totem pole in the bidding for Hollywood's movie output except for the fact that most are owned by the same parent companies as the established pay channels, so most deals are packages for all channels owned by one company.

Of all the problems associated with on-demand, the *delayed release windows* (for movies and broadcast TV series), as well as a general lack of fresh content, are especially frustrating for programmers because they have no control over them. Delayed windows helped prevent pay-per-view from taking off a decade ago, and they hamper VOD growth now. Most movies currently have VOD or PPV release windows about 45 days after a film goes to DVD (and the video stores). Many movies that are highly popular in rental and sales are completely withheld from premium networks, sometimes for decades. Currently hot TV series tend to be released in just a handful of episodes, the rights to older episodes expiring (to go into syndication) and the rights to the newest episodes protected and not yet available. Rights owners have to find a balance between availability to maintain interest and the highest revenue streams.

As media conglomerates grow larger, competition favors the giants. Vertical integration in combination with digitalization of cable systems has eliminated the shelf space shortage and created content shortage instead. The clout that comes with enormous size has improved the owned channels' ability to license top programs and produce original shows, but movies are the lifeblood of the premium services, and rapid access to them continues to be a barrier to growth.

Selecting Strategies

To fully understand programming strategies, it is first necessary to grasp the economic fundamentals of multichannel service as described in Chapter 3 and expanded here. *Unlike the broadcast model of maximizing the audience size, the multichannel model seeks to maximize subscriber revenue.* On one hand, VOD programmers need not choose their content carefully because there's room for so much programming. On the other hand, selection of programs for most subscription networks is far more constrained (see 9.4). And in both cases, only so many programs can be actively promoted.

Economics and Technology

The programming side of the business has matured to the point that selection decisions related to the subscription networks have become secondary to many MVPDs. All carry as many content services as they can manage, including every foundation network and the main theme channels and as much VOD as is available. Their focus has turned to expanding HD subscriptions with the long-term goal of shifting all channels to hi-def and turning off mere "digital" service. At the turn of the century, the MVPDs' primary concern was expanding their media dominance via high-speed internet service and Voice-over-Internet (VoIP) phone service; now it is upgrading subscribers to all HD and even 3D, while enhancing for-pay VOD.

For multichannel network programmers, the key to maximizing revenue in the programming realm is to generate the greatest value for the bread-and-butter subscriber who probably wants choice and convenience—but who may not need phone or broadband services and may feel unable to afford HD service right now. Although pressure to upgrade to HD surrounds the business, this programming textbook focuses on the traditional two *revenue streams* (subscriptions and advertising) in media.

Advertising is one of the two main revenue streams for virtually all basic cable networks. Agencies base their buying decisions on reach, frequency, selectivity and efficiency. Subscription channels are

9.4 Ted Turner and CNN

Cable, satellite and telco subscribers have a healthy selection of news channels today. Fox News is the ratings leader, but viewers can also choose among MSNBC, HLN (Headline News), the business news channels CNBC and Fox Business, and even the sports news specialist, ESPN News. The grandfather of cable news, of course, is CNN. Launched in 1980, CNN was critical in helping bring viewers to cable television in the 1980s, and before the advent of Fox News, it was an influential and well-respected monopoly position in the field. Ted Turner, who created CNN, has been honored as a visionary, in part for his effort in developing a 24-hour television news service—which many at the time said "couldn't be done."

In fact, Turner's vision had a great deal more to do with economics than public service. Turner, ironically, never liked television news. He built his early success in Atlanta broadcast television by counter-programming local news, offering viewers re-runs of old network sitcoms like *Gilligan's Island*, and was once quoted as saying, "I hate news. News is evil. It makes people feel bad."

But Turner was an exceptionally astute businessman. He surveyed the available niche markets in cable programming at the time and concluded that all the lucrative genres had been tapped. He told his new CNN President, Reese Schonfeld: "There are only four things that television does, Reese. It does movies, and HBO has beaten me to that. It does sports, and now ESPN's got that. There's the regular kind of stuff, and the three networks have beaten me to that. All that's left is news! And I've got to get there before anybody else does, or I'm gonna be shut out." In later years Turner would also create the Cartoon Network and subsequently comment that while CNN received most of the accolades, the Cartoon Network was always more profitable.

Patrick R. Parsons, Ph.D.
Pennsylvania State University

slowly approaching universal reach, and they offer tremendous format selectivity. It is ironic that cable and satellite networks have stolen away much of the broadcast audience by offering a proliferation of choices because the huge constellation of channels now works against the kind of mass audience viewing that supports big-dollar advertising. In turn, online media services threaten cable's revenues. Targeting specific audiences is great, but efficiency gets lost as smaller and smaller groups of viewers produce diminishing returns in selectivity. As more nonbroadcast networks splinter and launch, find distribution and ultimately, acquire broader household penetration, subscription program services have begun to feast on themselves in the same way they consumed broadcast network share.

Carriage fees are the other main support of subscription networks. In most arrangements, the cable operator pays a monthly license fee to the program supplier, and these fees normally expand in each contract renegotiation. In order for large systems with more potential viewers to pay more than small systems, *cable network license fees are usually*

structured as per-subscriber, per-month charges to the cable operator. The typical fees range from about $.15 per subscriber for services such as Country Music TV to about $1.00 per subscriber for more popular services such as CNN. *For advertising-supported networks, a tension exists between getting the national penetration necessary to attract advertisers and keeping the carriage fees high enough to pay the bills.* At $.40, A&E's license fee is about on par with that of Lifetime Television, which is way below that of TNT. The high price of sports contracts has driven up the cost of all channels that bid high for telecast rights, driving TNT's carriage fee above $1.00 per subscriber. Fox Sports Network 1 carries a rate of $2.25 per subscriber, per month, while its second regional network charges around $1.00. ESPN charged between $4.50 and $5.00 per month by 2012.

Many new channels pay one-time-only *launch fees* and offer *free carriage* to appeal to potential cable operators. For example, E! Entertainment paid operators $7 per subscriber and gave free carriage when it launched the Style Network. Originally, the

Fox News Channel paid $10 per subscriber to be added to DirecTV's lineup. By the late 1990s, paying launch fees was such an established inducement system that DBS providers were charging new networks an average of $6 per subscriber.

On the premium channels, feature films are licensed to networks in one of two ways: *per-subscriber* charges or *flat fees*. *Per subscriber* means that the film's producer or distributor negotiates a fee per customer for a specific number of runs within a fixed period, the number varying with the presumed popularity of the film. Such a fee is based on the number of subscribers who had access to the film (though not necessarily the number who actually saw it). In a *flat-fee* arrangement, the parties negotiate a fixed payment regardless of the number of subscribers who have access to the film.

Once the premium cable networks grew large enough that the amounts for movies were substantial, they usually abandoned the per-subscriber formulas and negotiated flat-fee arrangements with the program suppliers. The flat-fee method is also used for acquiring original programming. In PPV and VOD, however, the cable operator pays a per-subscriber fee to either the studio or service provider, necessitating large enough fees to users to cover their costs. By 2012, the big concern in the industry was how to configure and reimburse costs for multiple media use of the same movie by a single user. If subscribers pay over and above their MVPD service fees to get HBO (most of which goes back to HBO to cover the cost of licensing the movies it airs), should those subscribers have to pay again for the same movies if they choose to watch them on tablets or online? Generally no, IF the MVPD has the hardware and software to track individual movies and IF the online or tablet viewers can identify themselves as the MVPD's subscribers. (Another ID number for all of us to carry around?)

Program Types

Although the subscription networks license many off-network shows and air movies already shown on the broadcast networks, they also carry unique multi-channel programs. Signature programs and vignettes

characterize specific networks and are often produced by them to play only on those networks. In addition, subscription networks increasingly choose to license first-run series, keeping them out of station syndication and away from other subscription networks. (At the same time, a broadcast network may replay episodes of its hit series on a sister cable network; total exclusivity has gotten so pricey that sharing programs makes economic sense.)

Signature Programs

Tough competition for viewers drives most subscription networks to strive for signature programs, unique programs or a pattern of programs that distinguish a network from its competitors. *Signature programs create a well-defined image for the network and breed a set of expectations for both audiences and advertisers.* These expectations, whether positive or negative, help viewers select which channels to watch and lead advertisers and their agencies to expect that advertisements on some channels will or won't be effective. A lack of program definition, or an absence of signature programs, killed off several early cable services.

Four major types of signature programs appear on cable program services. The first consists of *original movies or series* not shown elsewhere, also called *made-for-cable* movies and programs. Although they are expensive to produce, they are highly promotable and attract new viewers more than repeat programming does. A second type of signature programming consists of *narrow theme genres*, such as all live nightclub comedy or all shop-at-home or all cooking shows. BET's *Comic View* is an example of the comedy nightclub genre. A third type consists of programs for a *niche audience*, or viewers with a narrowly defined set of interests or within a targeted demographic group. For example, Spike TV sought a young male audience with *Maximum Exposure*. The fourth and least common type of signature programming consists of the *cable exclusive*, programs shown once or twice on the broadcast networks but not shown before on cable. A fifth type consists of long-running popular programs whose hosts or personalities have become household names. See 9.5 about CNN's Larry King.

9.5 Larry King

Until his retirement in late 2010, *Larry King Live* was CNN's top-rated and most-visible program for more than two decades. Airing in the peak viewing hour (9:00 P.M. EST), King was known for his high-profile guests (including the last six U.S. presidents) and his "soft" questioning style. Some argue that Larry King's ability to book big names was directly a result of his one-sentence questions and jovial nature. King contends his show was not journalism but "infotainment," pointing to his wide range of guests (ranging from Marlon Brando to Pete Rose to J. K. Rowling), encompassing a considerable swath of American interests. Critics maintain that the rise of King's program represents a notable shift from hard news to soft news stories on television. Many of his programs in later years featured animal guests or explored perceived non-issues such as paranormal activity.

Initially trained in radio broadcasting, King's CNN program premiered in 1985, with peak interest occurring in 1993 when a debate on free trade between Ross Perot and Al Gore reached the largest cable TV audience in history, a record that held for more than a decade (until ESPN acquired the *Monday Night Football* contract in 2006 and routinely surpassed it). King's show was also different from most other television talk programs in that it allowed for live call-ins from viewers at home, encouraging a conversational and easygoing format. Larry King's work was been richly rewarded; he is one of the few people to receive Peabody Awards for his work in both radio and television.

Andrew C. Billings, Ph.D.
Clemson University

Sometimes signature genres cut across various networks. For example, such channels as the Travel Channel, ESPN2 and Bravo all caught poker's wave of popularity in the early 2000s with *Celebrity Poker Challenge* and *World Poker Tour*. The Travel Channel and Bravo temporarily diverged from their central programming mission to boost short-term ratings because of pressure from advertisers to attract larger audiences, and the result was far greater than anticipated.

Less temporary overhauls in signature programming occur, too. American Movie Classics switched from pre-1980 classic movies to modern-day classics, to the consternation of some system operators who wanted the movie content to stay different from mainstream movie channels (but, doubtless, to the joy of Turner Classic Movies). Another major change took place in 2004, when the Game Show Network condensed its name to GSN and got rid of classic and neoclassic game shows in favor of interactive gaming and reality-based content. Probably the most dramatic makeover for a cable channel was in 2003 when the National Network (TNN, formerly the Nashville Network) rebranded itself a second time as Spike TV, the first network for men

(or so it claims). Then Spike TV dropped the "TV" in order to project an image suited to online and tablets as well as traditional television (although listing companies retain the "TV").

House-remodeling and room-makeover programs gradually became signatures for HDTV and TLC, including *House Hunters, Property Virgins, My First Place* and *Curb Appeal: The Block*. Then cake and cupcake baking shows led to the rise of Food Network; programs about muscle cars and fancy car values (e.g., *What is My Car Worth?*) became signatures for Spike TV. Spike TV even managed to turn car interest into a game show with *Repo Games*.

And some prime-time successes on the major broadcasters have transferred effectively to cable networks. ABC's hit with personal makeover shows such as *Extreme Makeover* led TLC to signature programs of *What Not to Wear* and *Say Yes to the Dress*. PBS's success with *Antiques Roadshow* morphed into *American Pickers* on History, Lifetime's *Pawn Stars*, TLC's *Hoarding* and *Pawn Queens* and others, some of which will doubtless fade away, but a few will weave themselves into defining channel images.

Vignettes

Another common cable genre consists of vignettes, also called interstitials, meaning the programming bits between the regular programs. Traditionally a staple of premium services, this type of short-form filler programming appears between movies that end at odd times, and vignettes have also found their way onto basic program services. The Hallmark Channel offered a "Tell Us Your Story" campaign in association with Valentine's Day one year, featuring the best viewer-submitted stories of romance and love on its subscription network and online platform. *Although the primary purpose of vignettes is to promote branding, they also serve as backdoor pilots or ways to push viewers to online programs and websites.*

Many basic networks use interstitials even though the airtime could be sold to advertisers. For example, *Perspectives on Lifetime*, a series of editorials and interviews tied to issues such as breast cancer awareness or events such as Black History Month, contributes to the overall mosaic of the channel. Lifetime has even experimented with live hosting between programs to achieve a seamless look with no commercials on the hour or half hour, thus keeping viewers away from their remote controls. Turner Classic Movies shows vintage filler called *One Reel Wonders* between featured movies.

Movie studios also use interstitials to promote theatrical films by showing the first several minutes of the film to tease the audience into going to the box office. Universal Pictures paid USA to show the first 10 minutes of the movie *Dawn of the Dead*. In a similar move on the internet, Warner Brothers showed the first nine minutes of *Taking Lives* online at Yahoo! Movies to whet potential moviegoers' appetites.

The growing popularity of the *clip culture* (see Chapter 4) on websites like YouTube and Revver may add to the importance of vignettes. As online videos further shorten the attention spans of many viewers, cable networks can be expected to expand the use of interstitials for content or promotional purposes.

Originals

Despite the continued use of off-network programming, the dominant trend for subscription networks (and superstations) is toward more commissioned, coproduced or solely produced original programming (*Monk* and *The Closer* are two broadly popular examples). With the exception of signature reruns like *Law & Order: SVU* on USA, *Without a Trace* on TNT, *Everybody Loves Raymond* on TBS, and *CSI: Miami* (plus *The Sopranos*) on A&E, off-network programming has largely migrated from prime time to other dayparts. It appears especially in daytime and access.

With few exceptions as mentioned above, original series are what successfully brand a network by defining and distinguishing it from competing services. In the last decade, such networks as A&E, Syfy, USA, Lifetime Television, FX, TLC, Bravo, MTV and even ESPN have dramatically increased their budgets for original programming, especially creating programs for Friday and Saturday nights when the broadcast networks offer weaker shows than usual. USA, for example, has a big investment in the series *Silent Partners* and two comedies, *On We Go* and *We the Jury*. A&E has followed its successful *Intervention* with *Obsessed*. TBS plans original shows every night of the week as lead-ins to late-night *Conan*. Syfy carries originals such as *Being Human*, *Face Off* and *Alphas* to support its original ongoing successes of *Warehouse 13*, *Eureka* and *Haven*. Netflix has its own signature series *House of Cards*. And even YouTube and PlayStation are investing big dollars in original programs.

Collectively, the subscription networks spent about $15 billion for original programming in 2006, and that amount is expected to grow, but with total pay subscribership flat or declining, it may not grow quickly. As with previous Summer Games, in the winter of 2012, NBC heavily cross-promoted live Olympic coverage on co-owned Bravo, CNBC, MSNBC, Telemundo and USA. Although the segments of the Games appearing on the basic cable networks were noncompetitive with NBC because they occurred outside prime time, carrying such a high potency mega-event live improved the channels' international visibility as well as their domestic viewing (and advertising sales), and the original nature of the content contributed to their positive branding.

Genres on Advertising-Supported Channels

Some basic services such as USA, TBS, TNT and ABC Family consist of a broadly appealing mix of program forms (*full service*) similar to those of broadcast television, scheduled by daypart. Along with the superstations WGN America and WWOR,[1] they are among the most popular cable networks. Nearly every genre of program seen on a broadcast network has been tried by full-service cable networks, although not all have proved equally successful. Despite the shift to more original programming, hit off-network syndicated hours such as *Law & Order* and its spinoffs persist in popular with the audiences of broad-appeal networks. Because these cable networks generate most of their income from the sale of commercial time, they must select programs that will appeal to the same mass audience sought by the broadcast networks. Most subscription networks, however, especially the newer services, are niche (or theme) and subniche services. They must select programs that have a particular type of content or that target a specific psychographic group.

ESPN's signature program, *SportsCenter*, is a flexible sports-talk program that can appear live a dozen times a day or be cut back or rerun when live sporting events take up center stage (see 9.6). After obtaining live NFL games, ESPN became a major network competing (alongside ABC) for such megasports events as NBA, NHL and MLB games; soccer; boxing; and NCAA college football. The network has had limited success with such series as *Playmakers*, *Tilt* and *SportsCentury*. It has also begun producing under the umbrella of ESPN Films, which is known for such documentaries as *30 for 30*.

Once the home of all-day/all-night music videos, MTV now combines signature programs (for example, *Punk'd*, *Teen Mom*, *Sun of a Gun*) with reality

shows (*Real World*, *I Used to Be Fat*) and music-based favorites (*America's Best Dance Crew*). Writing about signature programs on MTV is difficult because the trend has been for its shows to move very quickly, often within a year, from being a phenomenal success to being yesterday's news (for example, *Jackass*). A similar situation exists on Comedy Central, another favorite of fickle youth, where only *South Park* and *The Daily Show* with Jon Stewart have much staying power. MTV and VH1 have a hot new competitor, Palladia (formerly MHD), carrying mostly live rock concerts and replays, along with the weekly music performance series *Uncompressed*.

On Lifetime, romantic made-for-cable movies predominate, mostly about relationships and the "woman-in-danger." Its prime-time schedule has reruns of *Reba*, along with a full slate of successful original series, including *Army Wives*, *Drop Dead Diva* and *Project Runway*. USA wins awards for *Monk* and *The Closer* and has some success with *Fairly Legal*, but also schedules regular reruns of NBC shows like *JAG* and *Law & Order: SVU*, supplementing them with half hour comedies (*We the Jury*, *TGIM*) and original series (*The Enclave*, *The Exceptions*). History, formerly The History Channel, is characterized by older documentaries about battles, airplanes and ships in past wars, as well as by colorful hosted documentaries that investigate the warfare, art and other remnants of ancient Roman, Greek or other civilizations, although some of that material has moved to The Military History Channel, which competes with Discovery's Military Channel. One recent two-hour original special surveyed the entire 600 years of the Dark Ages.

Syfy has filled its early-evening schedule with reruns of hour-long series such as *Stargate SG1*, *Eureka*, *Sanctuary* and *Star Trek: The Next Generation*, using an uncommon scheduling twist: Starting in mid-afternoon, it airs five or six previous episodes in a row, culminating in one new episode in prime time (if any are available). The popular *Stargate* series eventually spawned *Stargate Atlantis* and then *Stargate Universe*. *Battlestar Galactica* and *Andromeda* were also highly successful with scifi fans, but after a couple of years or so, these limited

9.6   The Sports Fan's Program: *SportsCenter*

ESPN's venerable *SportsCenter* has aired continuously since the sports channel's inception in 1979, and had reached more than 36,000 unique episodes by 2012. The program currently appears over 24 hours each day, (thanks to replays on ESPN's ancillary station, ESPNEWS), providing a mix of game highlights, recaps, top stories, commentary, analysis and predictions. At its start, many television experts claimed that an entire program devoted to sports was too narrowly defined and doomed to cancellation, but the joke was on them. *SportsCenter* evolved into a national and international phenomenon, part of not just one but several television channels of all-sports news, talk and events from ESPN, Fox Sports Regional and other networks.

When fresh game news is scarce, *SportsCenter* fills slow days with such attention-grabbers as Chris Berman's "2-Minute Drill," which looks forward to the weekend's NFL games with analysis and predictions. Other examples of *SportsCenter*-specific formats have included the "Budweiser Hot Seat," in which a guest is asked some particularly probing/interesting questions; "Contender or Pretender" where analysts determine whether a currently successful team or player can continue to excel; and "Top 10 Plays," which can range from the best plays of a particular day to the worst plays of the week to the 10 best catches by a centerfielder.

SportsCenter not only analyzes games but has influenced the way games are played in small ways. For example, the number of slam dunks has increased in professional basketball because they are more likely to make ESPN's highlight reel. The same can be claimed for spectacular dives to catch baseballs. The program has also had an impact on vocabularies ranging beyond sports. Most fans know that "going yard" is a home run and that

"boo yah" is host Stuart Scott's catchphrase when describing the action. *SportsCenter*'s Chris Berman gave a twist to the long tradition of nicknaming athletes, as with his Bruce "Eggs" Benedict and Jose "can you see" Cruz.

SportsCenter has become the broadest brand of sports news and is sometimes referred to as "The Big Show"—handling the most important sports, with niche sports interests being served by complementary ESPN news shows, such as *Baseball Tonight* and *College Football Gameday*. Starting first on *SportsCenter*, these shows all now include a scrolling "Bottom Line" ticker to supply ongoing and just-past game scores for several sports. *SportsCenter* incorporates other ESPN programming into the show by having commentary from Tony Kornheiser and Michael Wilbon from *Pardon the Interruption* and integrates itself into ongoing games with a "*SportsCenter* 30 at 30 update," in which fans get 30 seconds of the top headlines within a college basketball telecast, for instance.

While *SportsCenter* had dozens of solo and paired anchors in its earliest days, ranging from George Grande to smooth Bob Ley and chatty Chris Berman—today it has roughly 30 anchors, supported by a large team of reporters. Some notables, such as former *Late, Late Show* host Craig Kilborn, moved into non-sports television, and others, such as *Good Morning America*'s Robin Roberts, moved to broader news formats. No single sports program wields the international influence that *SportsCenter* does. With its clever animated graphics, it is now offered in multiple versions ranging from a Canadian-oriented show to Spanish-language offerings on ESPN Desportes.

Andrew C. Billings, Ph.D.
Clemson University

series completed their storylines, so many old disaster movies are slotted in, and Wednesday nights filled with *Ghost Hunters* or other paranormal shows. Later in prime time and weekends, Syfy airs a plethora of horror films, full of monsters and death in scary varieties. In another twist, it has an original series called *Hollywood Treasures* where hosts hunt for artifacts and memorabilia from old

movies (especially old science fiction) and 1960s TV series, which are then auctioned off on Hulu.

Three Scripps' owned channels, The Travel Channel, the Food Network and Cooking Channel, seem to interweave some of their programming. The Travel Channel now goes beyond travelogues, having hit it big with *World Poker Tour*, but also carries *Man v. Food*, *Triple Rush* (about bicycle messengers in NYC) and *Ghost Adventures*. Food Network has a winner in *Emeril Live* and *Tough Cookies*, but also carries a show called *Have Cake, Will Travel*. Cooking Channel gets some Emeril magic via *The Originals with Emeril*, along with *Unique Sweets* and *Eat St.*

HGTV (Home & Garden Television) has found several hits in its schedule of home redecorating and fix-up shows, including *Property Virgins, My First Place, For Rent, Holmes on Homes, Selling New York* and the parallel *Selling LA*. If you like these shows, you tend to watch them all, day after day. In some contrast, Spike TV features police videos and movies about men doing dangerous (but heroic) things, such as in its hit *Blue Mountain State*.

The Discovery Channel has drifted away from stories about pivotal inventions (for example, *Industrial Wonders*) into motorcycle shows (*American Chopper* and *Gut Busters*), along with *Cops & Coyotes*, and an New Yorkers-only game show called *Cash Cab*. Meanwhile, much corporate attention shifted to its two Spanish-language channels, Discovery en Espanol and Discovery Familia, and the newer Investigation Discovery. The latter debuted a sort-of documentary called *I Married a Mobster* (probably not to be confused with VH1's fictional series *Mob Wives*). Discovery's other sister service, TLC, has had its own signature shows for several years, entitled *What Not to Wear* and *Say Yes to the Dress* (in various sizes), and followed them with *Pawn Queens* and *Sister Wives*. Bravo has come a long way from its days as a fine arts channel. It has captured the reality contest genre with its signature competitions in *Project Runway, Top Chef* and *Top Design*.

Genres on Premium Channels

In the days of analog television, every cable system in the United States offered at least one premium service. And if a system had only one pay channel, the odds are very high that it was HBO (formerly, Home Box Office). HBO achieved its leading position through its early entry into pay television in 1972 and early adoption of satellite delivery in 1975. (Showtime began in 1976 and moved on the bird in 1978, but never quite caught up.) HBO then consolidated these early leads through aggressive national marketing

campaigns in the 1980s that competitors could not afford because of their smaller audience bases. Relatively few systems carried just Showtime, Flix, Encore or one of the other pay services.

With HBO in the primary role for many years, the competition among the others focused on securing shelf space as the second or third (or even fourth) service provider on the local cable system's menu of premium offerings. And then cable became all-digital like the satellite services, with room for all, especially in various kinds of VOD. Today, HBO's main competition comes from co-owned Cinemax, The Movie Channel, Showtime, Flix, Starz and Encore, and all of these services, including HBO, have taken advantage of compressed video delivery and spun off handfuls of additional channels, ranging from just four to dozen or more, with a high of 17 variations of Showtime.

Selection strategies for premium networks differ from those for basic networks. Because viewers pay extra per channel (or per sets of channels, such as 8 to 12 Encores), they have higher expectations of the programming on premium channels, which leads to enormous investments in such original series as the award-winning *The Sopranos*, followed by *True Blood, Entourage, Treme* and *Game of Thrones*. In addition to original series and movies, HBO carries large quantities of more or less successful entertainment specials. Those networks competing with HBO—particularly Showtime—target their movies to more carefully defined audiences and directly counterprogram HBO's lineup, at least on the main channels. Differentiating themselves through acquisition of exclusive rights to hit movies and developing appealing and promotable original shows has become key to the premium services' competitive strategies. Besides *spinoff channels, differentiation* via promotion, and *original content* strategies, some premium networks have adopted *time-shifting* as a strategy by using staggered start times (see the discussion of *bridging* in Chapter 2).

Nonetheless, both Netflix and VOD threaten these pay movie channels. People's lives vary so much that one month they might watch several movies and another none at all. So much is available for free and much more on premium VOD that subscribers wonder why they need also pay an extra monthly fee for one or a group of premium channels that they might or might not watch. However, its original series might save HBO, in one form or another—perhaps as an online service.

Movies

The staple of premium cable networks, including PPV and VOD, remains the Hollywood feature film, aired soon after theatrical release. The rapidity with which a film can be offered to subscribers is central to establishing a premium service's viability and value. While the pay-per-use services generally present top movie titles a few months after their initial domestic theater distribution, by contrast, the usual exhibition window for the monthly premium channels is 6 months after theatrical release (with the broadcast networks following at 18 months). VOD distributors are very eager to get their windows earlier than home video, but Hollywood worries about piracy and lost revenue.

None of the national premium services as yet carry commercials. With rare exceptions, films are shown unedited and uninterrupted, including those rated PG-13 and R (containing strong language and behavior normally censored on broadcast television). The VOD services and at least Cinemax on the pay side also run films in the NC-17 category (formerly X-rated).

Entertainment Specials

Selecting performers to star in original specials for the pay-per-month channels and choosing properties to adapt to the television medium requires an in-depth examination of subscribers' expectations. Because the major broadcast networks can offer opportunities to see leading entertainers, either on specials or late-night talk shows, premium programmers are forced to seek fresher, more unusual entertainers and material. They have several options, especially the following:

1. Using performers who are well known but who appear infrequently on broadcast network television

2. Using performers often seen on broadcast television but who rarely headline their own programs

3. Developing programs and artists unavailable on broadcast television

For performance specials, every effort is made by premium producers to preserve the integrity of a complete performance—without the guest stars, dance numbers and other window dressing sometimes used by to widen the audience base. At their best, these shows are vivid reproductions of live performances (and the practice has been copied by Palladia and other music channels). Premium cable's time flexibility also permits nightclub acts and concerts to run their natural lengths, whether they are one hour and 11 minutes or one hour and 53 minutes. The private nature of pay viewing also allows for telecasting "edgy" adult-oriented comedy (for example, Dennis Miller, Chris Rock) and dramatic material unsuitable for airing on broadcast television (*The Sopranos*).

Sports

The third major component in pay programming is sports. ESPN offers six ESPN-PPV channels on most cable and satellite systems, along with five other channels, with competition from four Fox sports channels, and another ten or so specialized sports channels (Tennis Channel, Speed Channel, Versus, NFL Network, The Golf Channel, Big Ten Network and suchlike). HBO and Showtime traditionally scheduled major, big-ticket, national sporting events in prime time. Indeed, HBO was long known to carry the top boxing matches until economics drove them to PPV. Premium programmers are divided about the value of sports to premium channels, because sports blur a movie network's image. In consequence, neither The Movie Channel nor Cinemax ever carried sports. Because of the broadcast networks' financial strength and audience reach (and a general consensus that certain events like the Super Bowl should stay on over-the-air television), ABC/ESPN, Fox, CBS, and NBC still manage to acquire the rights to most major sporting events. Thus the pay-per-month premium networks often have to settle for secondary rights or events of lesser national interest (and the old ones go to Versus and other sports channels). Nevertheless, an audience can be found for some sports that broadcast television does not adequately cover, such as middle- and heavyweight boxing, regional college sports, track and field, swimming, diving, soccer and equestrian competitions.

Big-ticket boxing and wrestling have been programming staples for pay-per-view packagers for many, many years. For some years, the relatively small universe of pay-per-view-equipped homes took PPV out of contention for major events. But digitalization brought PPV and VOD to all homes so they gobbled up major boxing matches (generating over $100 million for a single high-profile match), and DirecTV began carrying live NFL and NHL games. These sporting events continue to achieve record **buy rates** and revenues, and they fuel subscriptions to PPV, which caused ESPN to enter the PPV competition in a big way. *The key to success in sports now lies in having strong branding, along with extensive local and national marketing efforts.*

PPV Specialties

Interactivity is one way to enhance original PPV offerings. For example, Playboy TV has had much success with its call-in show *Night Calls*, which generates significant revenue (and thousands of phone calls). Cable operators get 70 to 80 percent of the $8 to $10 per-program-viewed cost of adult PPV programming (compared with 50 percent of the $4 cost of typical movies), so adult programming is their most bankable asset.

Launching a Network

As the digital tiers have filled, cable, satellite and telco providers are no longer eager to bring on new services unless they can be bundled with existing services from the subscription content networks with big muscle, such as Disney, Viacom or Comcast. By 2003, observers had declared the end of the era of new network launches. Still, some new channels have emerged since that year: Versus (a Fox-owned sports action channel), G4 (a Comcast-owned video

gaming network), NBATV, TV One (targeting African-Americans) and a few others. But compared with the 25 channels that launched between 2000 and 2005, only one network (Sleuth) launched in 2006, only one in 2007 (Chiller, dedicated to the horror genre), two in 2009 (MLB Network and TV One from Time Warner), for example. Maybe the declaration was only a little early.

More typical is the big name launch in 2011 of OWN, Oprah's channel, and the two-channel merger and fine-tuning that produced Discovery's Fit & Health. Most new introductions now occur on the internet and presume a substantial wait until the interest and revenue build before any shift to cable.

To get on the MVPDs, the first element in strategy for a start-up network is to pay *launch fees* to cable/sat/telco providers, typically $10 to $12 per subscriber. A related approach allows such large MSOs as Comcast and Viacom to become partners in the venture. With the periodic megamergers of media industries, fewer players are controlling larger and larger pieces of the multichannel universe. Another way to facilitate distribution of a new channel is not to charge cable systems for carriage for a few years. As was pointed out in Chapter 3, some cable networks have launched by reversing the traditional model of carriage; in other words, by paying MSOs a monthly per-subscriber fee for carrying them. Because of excessive start-up costs in the range of $40 million to more than $100 million, there have always been difficulties launching a new cable network.

Nonetheless, certain *incubation strategies* have become traditional for gaining shelf space for new cable networks. One is *sheltering* launches to help new networks establish themselves before moving full speed ahead. Americana Television, a 24-hour country lifestyle channel, got its start as a part-time service on Nostalgia Television. Viewers could watch a *BET on Jazz* program on BET before Jazz Central launched. Turner Classic Movies showed up on TNT, and Cable Health Club was initially part of the Family Channel—the pattern Discovery Channel followed with its health channel, that later merged with FitTV. NewsTalk Television launched with 4 million part-time homes as well as 3 million full-time homes. Of course, big names such as MLB don't require any shelter.

To gain sampling, newer networks have also turned to satellite for distribution, because DISH and DirecTV offer many more channels than many cable systems. One final strategy, and a solution to the low distribution problem for new networks, is *piggybacking* or sharing a channel with another service. American Movie Classics gave Romance Network a slot on Sunday afternoons and incubated American Pop on Saturday nights.

Regardless of shelf space, and regardless of whether a cable or online launch, a high mortality rate will continue among new services. No matter what a network's programming entails, limited distribution into America's subscription and broadband households make it difficult to cover operating costs. Thus, three basic ingredients are needed in order for a network to survive: *a good programming idea, smart people behind the idea* and *money*. In addition, new program services need to be flexible with regard to tiering, pricing and packaging.

Overcrowding in the subscription cable environment will inevitably have two outcomes. First, cable operators will remove (or displace to less desirable locations) older foundation services that have become stale in favor of new services; and second (and more common), start-up services will sell out to other (larger) networks, thus merging their top content or serving as a splinter version of the key network. In addition, because of the high cost of maintaining a single network's infrastructure and purchasing or producing programming, a service that is co-marketed (and usually co-branded) simultaneously with several other networks reduces sales, marketing and engineering/production costs. Further, it helps to be able to lose money through sister companies.

Scheduling Strategies

Subscription networks come in two broad types: *advertiser-supported basic cable networks* (CNN, ESPN) and *premium networks*, those that require an extra fee above the regular monthly MVPD subscription. But as Chapter 3 explained, and you

probably know only too well, MVPDs now offer a dozen or more packages with fees determined by whether the channels are merely digital or HD or 3D and how many and which channels are included. Moreover, some packages mix basic and premium digital services and then repeat the same channels at a higher price levels in various HD groupings.

Nonetheless, most MVPDs reserve some channels for *pay-per-use* (PPV, VOD). Many experts expect all channels (excepting the lowest level carrying local television stations) to become on-demand offerings eventually.[2] As more and more consumers get their television from apps on tablets or pay for special internet content, it is expected that they will become accustomed to paying for each "use" (viewing) of a content channel. However, the total-VOD-day isn't here yet, and most subscribers accept the pattern of many channels for a single package fee, even if they don't watch all or many of them.

Basic and premium cable networks need to follow the same general practices outlined in Chapter 1: conserve resources, form habits, control audience flow, schedule shows to be compatible with viewer lifestyles and maximize breadth of appeal. Until the day when viewers truly can choose anything, anytime—when VOD and DVRs make scheduling irrelevant—the linear scheduling aspect of the programmer's job will be crucial to the success of a program service.

Basic Channel Scheduling

The advertiser-supported networks have adopted several program scheduling ideas that have appeared for a short time on broadcast services but better suit the special needs of subscription program suppliers. These include program marathons, blocking, zoning and other alternatives to ratings that build the networks' appeal to advertisers.

Marathons

Subscription networks often use marathons—all-day, all-night, continuous program scheduling of the same series—to counterprogram major broadcast events like the Super Bowl. Marathons are also scheduled during holidays, protracted bad weather periods, or any time viewers are likely to turn into "couch potatoes." There have been plenty of examples: Leading up to and on Mothers' Day, TBS gave viewers a *Leave It to Beaver* marathon with Barbara Billingsley, the actress who played Beaver's mother, as the host; Nick at Night provided a *Coach* marathon starting after the end of the Super Bowl in hopes of snaring football fans who liked the old ABC sitcom about a college athletic director. During the 2007 Super Bowl, TNT ran 13 hours of *The Closer*, which performed well during the actual game. Marathons can generate exposure for a newly acquired show as well as remind viewers that a popular show appears on the network.

Because the networks promote marathons heavily, they usually perform well—even better than the average programming—which can lead to increased advertising sales. In one case, a marathon briefly generated a signature program for VH1 when *I Love the 70s* devoted an hour to each year of the decade; this resulted in the nostalgia sequels *I Love the 80s* and *I Love the 90s*. VH1 previously enjoyed marathon success with its *Behind the Music* series on defunct or controversial music groups.

Blocking

Some networks have adopted blocking strategies to lure mainstream audiences away from network affiliates. TNT's daytime programming is called "Primetime in Daytime" and features reruns of such off-network programs as *Charmed, ER, Judging Amy* and *Law & Order*. At one time, these shows were syndicated only to broadcast stations. Now such scripted dramas go to subscription networks, while broadcast stations concentrate on first-run syndication and off-network sitcoms.

In another variation, several basic cable networks schedule multiple episodes of a single series in one block starting in early evening and going on for several hours. Spike TV has blocked as many as three or four episodes of *CSI* on some evenings, and USA has put several episodes of *Law & Order: Special Victims Unit* in sequence on an evening. Other channels repeat a single episode all day to be convenient for all kinds of viewers. A&E, Syfy and History, among others, follow these general patterns. And amusingly, Syfy varies the season of *Stargate SG-1* in such blocks, mixing up first-season to sixth-season episodes (so the characters' hair is first long and then inexplicably short and then long again, and costumes change without rationale).

Homogeneity, Zoning and Roadblocking

Cable has developed criteria other than ratings for selecting and scheduling national and local services and for attracting advertisers. Cable executives generally emphasize the demographic or psychographic homogeneity of viewers of a particular service. MTV viewers, for example, are alike in age and interests; Lifetime viewers are mostly women; Spike goes after men. Viewers of cooking shows, house fixing-up shows, historical or science programs and so on probably share several interests (that advertising can appeal to). A second and related strategy is zoning, dividing an interconnect into tiny geographic areas to deliver localized advertising, which permits local businesses to purchase low-cost ads that reach only their neighborhoods.

Another strategy is *roadblocking*, scheduling the same ad (or promotional message) on many cable networks at the same time so the advertiser's message blankets most cable channels (and sometimes broadcast networks, too). This practice occurs at the national level (so all viewers might see the same spot at the same time) and at the regional level (using inserts on a single cable interconnect). Roadblocking, in theory, keeps grazers from using their remote controls to avoid commercials because many viewers quickly give up surfing when the same commercial message appears on channel after channel. But the strategy works for program promotion, too. For example, on one June day at 9 P.M., all nine of NBCUniversal's broadcast and cable networks ran the same the two-and-a-half-minute teaser for the movie *King Kong*. Similarly, in 2010, all Nickelodeon channels simultaneously ran a promo for *The Last Airbender*.

Cable networks are analogous to radio stations in a single large market—both numerous and fragmented. No one can deny their collective media reach, but few can figure a way for each individual program service to compete with any of the individual broadcast networks. Only the biggest MVPDs can buy up very large numbers of cable networks and market them as a group to advertisers but individually to viewers. Most cable programmers must focus their strategies on *hard-to-reach audiences*, just as radio programmers do.

Premium Channel Scheduling

The need to schedule movies is likely to be the first aspect of traditional programming to succumb to the advent of the widespread availability of PPV or VOD. Nevertheless, some viewers would rather choose a channel and see what's there than pick from a menu, so some pay channels will stay with a schedule for the foreseeable future.

Rotation

Preplanned multiple reuse of content used to be a major difference between traditional premium and broadcast television; now both broadcasters and large cable networks lay out a multiplatform design before a new show goes on the air. As pointed out in Chapter 2, *only when a show becomes a hit or develops a cult following are such plans actually implemented.*

Most pay services offer a range of 20 to 100 movies per month, some first-run and new to the schedule (*premieres*), some repeated from the preceding month (*carryovers*), and some returning from even earlier (*encores*). In the course of a month, movies are typically scheduled from three to eight times on different days and at various hours during the daily schedule. Different movie services offer varying numbers of monthly attractions, but all services schedule most of their programs more than once. (Programs containing nudity or profanity, however, rotate only within prime time and late night on most networks.) The viewer, therefore, has several opportunities to watch each film, special or series episode. *These repeat showings maximize the potential audience for each program.* The programmer's scheduling goal is to find the various complementary time slots

that deliver the greatest possible audience for each attraction during the course of a month—not necessarily in one showing.

Unlike the monthly pay-cable networks, pay-per-view services rotate *rapidly* through a short list of top-name Hollywood hit films. The same movie may air as few as four or as many as ten times in a day. This occurs because PPV, like VOD, markets "convenience viewing." PPV networks either rotate two to four major movie titles a day, some across multiple channels, or run the same movie continuously all day. As the number of channels available to pay-per-view increases, the trend is to assign one movie per channel, thus emulating the "multiplex" theater environment.

Title Availability

Balancing the number of major films and lesser-known but promotable titles every month, then adding a handful of encore presentations, is one of the key challenges a premium movie programmer faces. A crucial factor in preparing the lineup is title availability. Most films with good track records at the box office are obtained from major film distributors, but an increasing number can be purchased from independent distributors and producers.

Usually it does not make economic sense for studios to hold a film in theatrical release for more than a year, but occasionally video sales disrupt the pattern and delay a film's availability as already explained. Hot Disney movies for children usually do well in DVD sales, as do some cult films that bomb in theaters but appeal to DVD buyers. The home video *sell-through* is a film priced to be bought rather than rented by consumers. (For rentals, the studios receive revenues only from the initial purchase of each tape by the retailer.) Successful sell-throughs of extremely popular films, even at much lower wholesale prices, are a distributor's dream—and the studios maximize revenues by delaying premium television release until the first stage of video sales has passed.

Time constraints on the use of films also affect steady product flow, including *how long* and *when* a film is available to pay services. Commercial broadcast television buyers, for example, traditionally had the financial clout to place time limitations on distributors' sales of films to premium services. The broadcasters would seek early telecast of key films to bolster their ratings during Nielsen ratings sweeps, shortening the period of time during which the films were available to premium networks. The number of such key films of interest to the broadcast networks has been dropping, however, as their ratings deteriorate because of increased home video and premium penetration.

Some desirable films are unsuitable for broadcast sale altogether, increasing their pay-television staying power. Films such as the *Emmanuelle* series, although not recent, crop up again and again because they never enter *broadcast windows*. Therefore, distributors allow premium networks to schedule them as many times as they like for as long as they like.

Occasionally, the major pay-per-month services disagree about whether to schedule a movie *after* it has already had a commercial broadcast network run. HBO and Showtime have found a following for these movies when they are shown unedited and without commercials. Some survey research even demonstrates viewer support for reshowing films that have been badly cut for commercial television presentation or that have exceptionally strong appeal for repeat viewing. Almost all premium services also show selected off-network movies, often drawing sizable audiences.

Exhibition Windows

As explained earlier, distributors create a distribution window for a film's release when offering it to the premium services. The programmers negotiate for a certain number of first-run and second-run plays during a specific time period, generally 12 months. For example, a given film may be made available to a pay-cable service from April to March. It might premiere in April, encore in August, and then play again the following March to complete the run. Programmers must project ahead to see that the scheduled play periods for similar films from different distributors do not expire at exactly the same time. Generally, premium services don't want to waste their scarce resources by running

five blockbusters, four westerns or three Kevin Costner films in the same month. Such clustering can be advantageous, however, when older films can be packaged and promoted as special "festivals."

Broadcast television's scheduling practices, organized around the delivery of commercial messages, differ broadly, resulting (mostly) in the once weekly series in prime time and stripped programs and nightly newscasts outside of prime. It used to be the pattern that in broadcasting, an episode was shown only twice in one year, and the largest possible audience was sought. As already explained in Chapter 2, episodes are now repeated on the networks more than twice (even tripled or stripped) and on associated cable channels, plus may be available online.

Some premium networks have adopted the short-length formats of broadcast television, such as episodes of *Weeds* on Showtime and *Six Feet Under* on HBO. The shorter lengths (not to mention the sometimes provocative content) help these first-run shows get sold internationally and to move later into domestic syndication. Most pay programs, however, run to their natural lengths, ending when and where the material dictates rather than running in fixed segments to accommodate commercials. Even with series programs, frequent repetition and rotation throughout the various dayparts set premium program scheduling apart from broadcast scheduling. Also, *broadcasters set their schedules for an entire season—pay-per-month and pay-per-view set them one month at a time.*

Monthly Audience Appeal

Another major contrast between broadcast and premium programming services lies in their revenue-generating strategies. As already noted, to maximize ad revenues, commercial networks and broadcast stations program to attract the largest possible audiences every minute of the programming day. Premium cable networks, in contrast, try to attract the largest possible cumulative audiences over the period of a month.

The lifeblood (read *daily operating revenues*) of a pay service is its direct subscriptions. Pay-per-use services must satisfy their customers movie by movie, event by event, or night by night. Pay-per-month services must satisfy their subscribers month to month, throughout the year, forestalling disconnections. A premium service's success is not determined by the audience ratings of its individual programs but by the general appeal and "satisfaction levels" of its overall schedule. Insofar as quantitative measures such as ratings reflect that appeal (especially for one-shots like boxing matches or a live Sheryl Crow concert), they are useful in gauging response. In cable and satellite service, however, where subscribers must be persuaded to pony up month after month, qualitative measures take on greater importance.

One important qualitative measure is subscriber turnover. Because both schedules and subscriber billings are arranged by the month, viewers tend to evaluate programming in month-long blocks. Subscribers will most likely continue the premium service for another month if:

- They use their pay service two or three times a week.

- They see benefits in its varied viewing times or on-demand availability.

- The service runs commercial-free, uninterrupted program content.

- The service runs unique entertainment programs and theatrical feature films.

The pulse of PPV and VOD success is measured by *buy rates*. Careful matching of buy rates and titles offers both the pay-per-view or on-demand distributor and the system operator a tool for fine-tuning scheduling and promotion plans. Providing viewers have plenty of PPV or VOD choices, they can always find something to watch. In contrast, month-to-month services have different problems. While discontinuing a month-to-month pay service seldom reflects dissatisfaction with one or two individual shows, viewers disconnect when they feel that the service *as a whole* is lacking. Customers repelled by violence, for example, may disconnect a movie service if a large number of a particular month's films contain a great deal of violence. A family may determine that its desire for wholesome, G-rated fare is not being filled by the programming

mix of one particular movie service and so will cancel after a trial month or two.

Movie Balancing Strategies

Selecting programs that will appeal to different target audiences through the course of a month becomes the challenge for most pay-per-month programmers. For example, if a particular month's feature films have strong appeal to teenagers and men 18 to 49, the obvious choice for an entertainment special is a show that appeals to women. Premium programmers break down their audiences as follows:

1. Urban-rural classifications

2. Age groups of 18 to 24, 25 to 49, and 50+

3. Gender

By scheduling programs each month that will appeal to all these groups, the premium programmer theoretically creates a "balanced" schedule.

Films subdivide into several groups with overlapping appeals and are usually scheduled by considering either their timeliness or their appeals. The major audience attractions for monthly schedules are the premieres—that is, the films that were recent box-office hits and are being offered for the first time on that premium service. These films may be rated G, PG or R by the movie industry. The second sets of films placed in a pay-per-month channel's schedule are the major G- and PG-rated films. This establishes a strong pattern of family and children's appeal in the schedule. The third group of films has varied adult audience appeals. Films without notable box-office success usually fall into this category. They are repeated slightly less frequently than premieres and G-rated hits.

Other films that were not major theatrical hits may still rate as important acquisitions for premium services. Viewers may value seeing a film on television that they might not be willing to pay $8 to $10 to see in a movie theater. Foreign films fall into this group. Also, if a premium network feels that a particular film has appeal to a segment of its audience, it doesn't matter whether it was originally made for home video or made for broadcast television; films in both categories increasingly show up on premium schedules. Another growth category is film classics.

Film Placement

On the pay-per-month channels, the general rules of thumb for film scheduling include beginning week-night programming at 7 or 8 P.M. and starting final showings (of major offerings) as late as 11:30 P.M. to 12:30 A.M. Those networks concentrating on the over-night daypart employ still later final showing schedules. For most of the premium movie services, an evening consists of three to five programs, depending on individual running lengths. Entertaining short subjects, elaborate animated titles and promotional spots for other attractions fill the time between shows. All-movie networks especially favor movie-oriented shorts, such as interviews with directors or location tours. Using 16 or more new films each month (not counting carryovers of the previous month's late premieres) usually means scheduling *four premieres each week*, gradually integrating first-, second-, third- and up to sixth-run presentations week by week. This pattern gives viewers a constantly changing lineup of material from which to choose—and new movies appear every week on the pay-per-month channels.

Counterprogramming broadcast network schedules is another strategic consideration. For example, on Tuesday nights when CBS scheduled a string of male-appeal dramas (*NCIS, The Unit* and *Without a Trace*) and NBC carried *Dateline NBC* and two *Law & Order* shows, premium networks tended to schedule female appeal films. Taking another tack, preceding or following a popular broadcast network show with a program of the same genre on pay cable creates a unified programming block for viewers (requiring channel switching, an easy move with remote controls). Beginning programs on the hour as often as possible—especially during prime time from 8 to 11 P.M.—makes it convenient for viewers to switch to and from pay cable.

Films and specials containing mature themes are usually scheduled at later hours than G-rated films, even though pay television is not bound by broadcasting's traditions. PG features are offered throughout premium schedules. Magazines and program guides encourage parents to prescreen all films rated PG, PG-13 or R early in the week to decide which are appropriate for their children to watch on subsequent airdates. This presumes several silly things: that parents have the time to pre-watch movies, that web-adept children cannot defeat channel safeguards, and that they do not watch anything they want at other people's homes or online.

Evaluating Apples and Bananas

Audience evaluation remains iffy in the cable industry. Inadequate viewing data hampers many national advertiser-supported networks in selling time—especially the newer niche services. Although *the total number of a system's subscribers is always known more or less accurately*, and the most popular services are rated by Nielsen, determining how many subscribers view the less popular nonpay channels has traditionally been a problem on most systems.

Comparison Problems

Cable penetration stands at about 60 percent of U.S. homes. In addition, another 27 percent or so of homes are connected to the subscription networks via direct satellite service, and 5 percent get the same channels from telcos, wireless cable or some other small business. (Collectively, 92 percent of homes get service from MVPDs.) Individually, however, *audience ratings* for most cable/satellite networks (excluding the top-10 services) have only occasionally exceeded 1 or 2 million television households at a time. In fact, the top five or so cable networks garner 3 to 4 million households each in prime time (about the same as a 3 or 4 rating among all 116 million television households). *Although the combined audience for ad-supported subscription networks regularly exceeds that of all commercial broadcast networks, the broadcast business is still very healthy.* Because many advertisers continue to buy spots one channel at a time, the combined cable network ratings are not much comfort to them.

Nonbroadcast Audience Measurement

As is explained in Chapter 5, ratings for subscription networks really represent three audience measurements. One measure is the audience watching a *particular program at a given time*, measured by average quarter hour (AQH) ratings and shares as in national broadcast ratings. A second measure is the cumulative audience that watches a *given program in all of its showings* because some program services repeat shows. When all viewers of repeat showings of a program (such as a movie) are summed, the audience for that one program may exceed a competing broadcast station's audience in one market. The third and perhaps most important measure to subscription networks is the *cumulative audience for a channel*. Although people meters have benefited the established cable networks by increasing their reported share of prime-time viewership, they reveal little about the viewing of less popular advertiser-supported services. Subscription networks must commission their own research to understand viewing by such demographic subgroups as children, teens and ethnic minorities.

Measuring Cable / Satellite Viewing

The overriding problem in evaluating cable program audiences is that local audience shares cannot be compared directly with local over-the-air audience shares. As 9.7 shows, cable franchise areas differ in size and shape from markets defined according to broadcast station coverage patterns (DMAs). This type of map prevents advertisers from comparing cable's effectiveness with that of broadcasting and other media in one market.

To be measured on a national level, Nielsen currently requires a subscription network to be available in about 3.3 percent of U.S. TV households (about 3.7 million homes) to qualify for its national cable TV ratings report, the *Nielsen Cable Activity Report (NCAR)*. Further, to show up in the report, the network has to generate at least a 0.1 rating in its coverage area (the number of households a channel reaches).

Although in total the programs on all subscription networks have averaged more than a 25 Nielsen prime-time rating in the last several years, most viewers apparently watch the established broadcast services. The weekly cumes still favor the broadcast channels despite gains in subscription network viewing (see 9.8). Further growth in the number of channels will make increases in individual network ratings difficult.

Programmers and consultants are divided over how to best increase audience size: Some believe that heavy series production is necessary (USA); others argue for original movie production, heavy promotion and more effective scheduling (TNT).

The cable industry reports its own ranking of top shows, which are based on multichannel homes, not all television homes. The *rankings* in 9.9 come from these so-called cable ratings, but the *ratings* shown in the table are based on household ratings. In 2004 Nielsen changed the way it measures multiplexed premium channels, no longer aggregating the different channels showing the same program (for example, *Entourage*) on cable and satellite systems. Instead, Nielsen began reporting ratings for each "plex" separately.

The goal for basic and premium programmers is to count the number of people who make a return visit to their channels on a regular basis. Perhaps because of the influence of measuring the enduring appeal of web pages, the cable industry has borrowed an internet term to describe the viability of a channel: *stickiness*. A website that holds its viewers is said to be sticky, like a real spider web, and now programmers discuss the stickiness of their channels. It's a new word for an old concept: giving the target audience what it wants so it will come back for more.

Measuring VOD Use

Surveys and audience sampling are unnecessary for gauging on-demand programming. Two-way capabilities in most cable systems allow accurate tracking of buy rates, and the satellite and telephone services have their own usage records. However, this is proprietary information, compiled by each separate MVPD system. No combined measures exist, and estimates of all VOD and PPV use are not wholly reliable.

The Many Channels

This section looks at content of the various kinds of subscription services widely available in the second decade of the twenty first century. It divides them into 15 general types of advertising-supported

9.7 Map of Broadcast Market Showing Cable Franchises

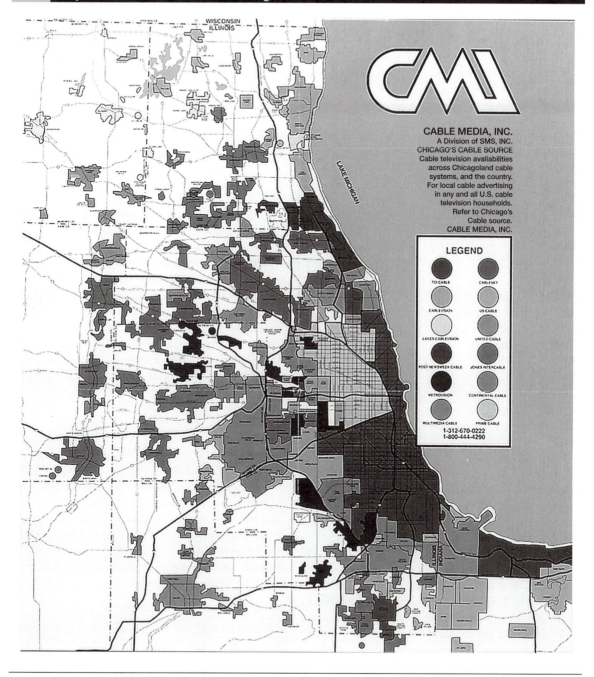

Courtesy of Cable Media, Inc. Used with permission.

9.8 Nielsen Television Activity Report

Broadcast Affiliates	Average Weekly Cume %
NBC	75.7
CBS	74.9
ABC	74.6
FOX	70.1
WB	44.7
UPN	37.2

Cable Networks	Average Weekly Cume %
TBS	39.0
USA	38.3
TNT	38.2
FX	29.6
A&E	28.3
DISC	27.6
SPIKE TV	27.5
ESPN	27.2
NICK	26.8
LIFE	26.5
COMEDY	26.5
AMC	26.4

Nielsen Media Research Television Activity Report, NHI, first quarter, 2006. www.tvb.org/rcentral/MediaTrendsTrack/tvbasics/10_Reach_BdcstvsCable.asp.

services and two kinds of premium services by adapting grouping patterns used by FiOS, U-verse and Comcast, and supplemented by Wikipedia! Of course, the list is incomplete (we don't want you to fall asleep!), but you will find most you know here.

Major Subscription Networks

Foundation

As already described in 9.2, these channels are found on nearly every multichannel service in the United States, so most people are probably quite familiar with their content. There are the long-established channels that appear on virtually every MVPD's lineup: TBS, ESPN, Food Network, USA, ESPN2, HGTV, The Weather Channel, TLC, Discovery

Channel, MTV, Fox News, Nickelodeon, Spike TV, TNT, Disney Channel, A&E, CNN/HLN, Lifetime Television, C-SPAN and VH1. Of these, only the Food Network is a relative newcomer. These 20 networks capture the largest audiences, spend the most money and have the most visibility in the United States and abroad. (Cutting off the so-called foundation networks at 20 instead of 25 or 30 is entirely arbitrary and based solely on one year's subscriber rolls. Some networks in the next dozen are equally well known and may swap places in any given year.)

Children's

For a while, only one or two channels targeted to children found their way onto the cable/satellite lineups. Nowadays, several choices are available—some more family-oriented than purely for kids. Nickelodeon has added Nick Jr., Nicktoons and Teen Nick (Noggin seems to have been swallowed). After Nickelodeon and Disney Channel, the best known are Cartoon Network, Discovery Kids, TeenNick.com, Boomerang, FUNimation, PBS Kids Sprout, plus HD versions of Disney XD (see 9.10). There's also Anime Network, BabyFirstTV, Cbeebies, Familyland, Hallmark Channel, the Hub, qubo, pets.tv, Sorpresa and TV Land.

Documentary/Educational

In addition to TLC and Discovery in its various forms, Animal Planet fits here, along with Crime & Investigation Network, History, Military Channel, Military History Channel, National Geographic Channel and National Geographic Wild, Science Channel, PBS World, and Bio (formerly Biography). Some university towns have local cable channels they support, often of this educational sort (for example, UCTV by the University of California and BYU TV by Brigham Young University).

Entertainment

This broad group varies from very adult programming down to comedy and over to science fiction. A&E, generally considered a foundation service, fits here, as does Adult Swim, BBC America, BET, Bravo,

9.9 | Top Cable Shows, February 2007 Top 10 Cable TV Programs (Total Day)

Rank	Program	Network	Total U.S. Household Rating	Total Viewers
1	WWE Raw	USA	3.4	5,975,000
2	WWE Raw	USA	3.3	5,706,000
2	Prime Movie (Montana Sky)	LIF	3.3	4,767,000
4	SpongeBob	NICK	3.1	4,809,000
4	Monk	FX	3.1	4,856,000
6	Fairly Odd Parents	NICK	2.9	4,431,000
7	SpongeBob	NICK	2.7	3,916,000
8	SpongeBob	NICK	2.6	3,838,000
8	Fairly Odd Parents	NICK	2.6	3,871,000
10	Fairly Odd Parents	NICK	2.5	3,404,000
10	Fairly Odd Parents	NICK	2.5	3,459,000
10	Drake & Josh	NICK	2.5	3,432,000
10	Hannah Montana	DSNY	2.5	3,695,000

Nielsen, *www.nielsenmedia.com* (retrieved for February 2007). Consult *http://tvbythenumbers.zap2it.com for any week to get current numbers.*

9.10 | Are Kids (Still) Watching TV?

With MySpace, Neopets, Gaia, YouTube and blogging, it's not surprising if one wonders whether kids have time to watch plain old television, whatever service it comes from. A recent study by the Kaiser Family Foundation found that "new" media such as computers and video games have not displaced the use of "old" media such as television and music. In fact, for better or worse, the amount of time spent viewing TV per day was three times greater than the time spent with any other medium. So, yes, kids are still watching TV, and they are watching cable, Nickelodeon and Disney in particular. Despite the broadcast network's efforts, these two networks garner the lion's share of kids and tweens. With kids ages 2–11, Nick's *Sponge Bob SquarePants* gets top ratings, and its *iCarly* and *Drake and Josh* are popular with teens. Disney also captures tweens 9–14 with such live-action series as *Jessie* and *Wizards of Waverly Place*. But television for kids is not all escapades and cartoons.

Concerns about children's health and wellness have not gone unnoticed by cable programmers. Nickelodeon's 2006 "Let's Just Play" campaign centered on a five-month miniseries that documented real kids' efforts to make their lives healthier, and the "Let's Just Play" website encourages kids to join the challenge and implement an action plan for living a healthier lifestyle. In honor of the Worldwide Day of Play, Nickelodeon goes dark for three hours to encourage kids to "get up, go out, and go play." "Rescuing Recess" is part of Cartoon Network's "Get Animated" initiative to get kids active, healthy and involved. The network introduced the first annual National Recess Week in 2006, concluding with a new "Operation R.E.C.E.S.S" episode of the network's series, *Codename: Kids! Next Door*. The "Get Animated" website features information on how to eat like a superhero and games that kids can play both inside and outside. Whatever the broadcast networks are doing has so far not made much of a dent in the distribution of ratings.

Nancy C. Schwartz, Ph.D.
The Academic Edge, Inc.

Chiller, Comedy Central, E! Entertainment Television, FEARnet, FX, FSN, here!, Lifetime, Logo, Oxygen, ReelzChannel, Sleuth, SOAPnet (if it's still alive), Spike, Syfy, TBS, Telemundo, TeleFutura, truTV (formerly Court TV), TNT, Univision, WE tv, Wedding Central, and others. In fact, it's hard not to think of virtually all television as entertainment, especially if you have a dry sense of humor.

An almost singular channel, MTV's Logo debuted in 2005. Devoted to gay and lesbian programming,

Logo carries mostly series and films that previously aired on other broadcast and cable networks or appeared only in movie theaters (see 9.11).

Foreign

Until the availability of digital channels, the only way to receive foreign-language channels was to live in a very large city or stay at a Disney hotel. Nowadays, dozens of options have found their way

---

9.11 | **Narrowcasting to the Gay Community**

The 8-year run of NBC's hit *Will & Grace* (1998 to 2006) brought a successful gay title character to the prime-time landscape for the first time. The Emmy-winning show in turn spawned other programs on cable featuring gay or lesbian characters. Showtime followed up with an adaptation of the British hit *Queer as Folk*, which ran for five years in the early 2000s. Overlapped by another long-running series *The L Word* (2004 to 2009), these shows brought the premium network some of its highest Nielsen ratings. Bravo found similar rating success with the makeover show *Queer Eye for the Straight Guy*.

The popularity of these programs was convincing evidence that a niche audience existed for gay-, lesbian-, bisexual- and transgender-themed (GLBT-themed) programming, and soon whole cable networks with programming targeted to gay and lesbian viewers appeared. The first network, here!, began in 2002 as a video-on-demand service or a premium subscription channel on most cable and satellite systems. Its biggest hit is *Dante's Cove*, a dramatic series that mixes the soap opera and horror genres. Movies and documentaries are the other popular staples of here!'s on-demand programming.

Q Television Network (QTN) was the second cable network to target a GLBT audience. Begun in 2004, the short-lived QTN aired primarily in such urban markets as New York, San Francisco and Seattle, carrying a range of variety, talk and music programs. The most popular of its original shows, *The Queer Edge with Jack E. Jett*, was a variety show that mixed music and comedy. QTN was unable to gain carriage outside the largest urban markets, and after being plagued by rumors of financial problems and impropriety by its executives, it went dark in May, 2006.

Launched in 2005, the Logo channel became the third channel targeting GLBT (or LGBT) audiences. Owned by media giant Viacom in its MTV Networks division, Logo found a secure place with most cable providers across the country. Carriage came easily because the channel was swapped for Viacom's fading VH1 Mega Hits, a digital channel already slotted on hundreds of cable systems. Logo's programming is a mix of original and syndicated programming, including documentaries, music videos, reality television and travel programming. Its successes include the reality series *Coming Out Stories*, the African-American themed *Noah's Arc*, and the animated series *Rick & Steve: The Happiest Gay Couple in All the World*. Logo has captured its greatest Nielsen ratings success with *RuPaul's Drag Race*, a competition reality program launched in 2009 in which contestants vie to become the next "drag superstar." As a result of *RuPaul's Drag Race*'s huge popularity, Logo has spun off two related programs which have, in turn, become ratings winners: *RuPaul's Drag Race: Untucked* and *RuPaul's Drag U*. Logo partners with CBS News to bring coverage of gay-themed news topics to the cable network. Logo has also become an internet presence by providing three LGBT-themed websites and by having its programming downloadable from iTunes. Logo programming is also available via video-on-demand, and it provides a wireless platform for Sprint and Verizon. Reaching beyond television, Logo has also been in part responsible for the theatrical release of two motion pictures, including the film version of its hit series *Noah's Arc*.

James Angelini, Ph.D.
University of Delaware

onto the lineups of both satellite services and some cable MSOs in very large metropolitan areas (FiOS concentrates more on very local news channels). Many world networks have high production values and serve two functions: They bring homeland comfort to ex-patriots while also providing native-born Americans with chances to learn about other cultures. The best-known channels include ART (Arab Radio & Television), Asian American Satellite TV, BBC America, TV Asia and TV Japan. Then there are a slew of Spanish-language channels appealing to Spanish-speaking immigrants and to people who want to keep up or improve their language skills, as already described.

Lifestyle

Lifestyle channels are the niche and subniche channels that instantly remind viewers they are not watching regular broadcast television. The content is very specialized, but so are the advertising and viewers. A few examples are DIY (Do It Yourself) Network, the Outdoor Channel, the Cooking Channel, as well as The Africa Channel, Planet Green, Recipe TV, Style Network, Travel Channel, Wealth TV, Casa Club TV, Discovery Fit & Health, Fashion TV, HGTV, Halogen, Ovation, and Oprah's darling OWN.

Movies

Then there are a seeming excess of movie channels. A double handful of advertising–supported movie channels appear on some basic cable and satellite services. These include AMC (used to be American Movie Classics), Hallmark Movie Channel, Lifetime Movie Network, Fox Movie Channel, Turner Classic Movies, Reelz Channel, HD Net, HD Theater and, maybe on some systems, the Sundance Channel, VeneMovies, Cine Latino, Flix, Epix, plus IFC (Independent Film Channel). Most of the really big name movie channels require paying a premium.

Music

Channels that offer different music formats have grown beyond the limited MTV/VH1/CMTV

options of the early 1990s. Now six different variations of the trailblazing MTV service coexist and two VH1s have survived. Defeated by the popular CMT (Country Music Television), TNN morphed out of music into Spike TV. Some of the other widely-distributed music channels are Centric (formerly BET Jazz), BET Hip Hop, BET Gospel, Z Music Television, A3 Network (a dance and nightlife channel), Fuse, Great American Country, Harmony Channel and Palladia. Then there's DMX, the digital audio service that comes with DirecTV, Sirius that comes with Dish, and Muzak and Music Choice. Music, music, everywhere, even on TV!

News

What were once just CNN and CNN Headline News have now expanded to several options. Fox News battles head to head with MSNBC, each taking the opposing political slant. CNBC, The Weather Channel and three channels of C-SPAN are available nearly everywhere. Sports news comes from ESPNews, of course. In addition, two channels vie for the business-news market: Bloomberg Television and Fox Business Network. U.S. distribution of foreign-owned news channels has also expanded over the years, ranging from BBC World News to the controversial Al Jazeera (see 9.12). In addition, there are hundreds of local public, educational and governmental (PEG) channels, especially in and near major cities and college towns. In the Washington, DC, area, for example, FiOS carries at least 27 hyperlocal PEG channels.

Religion

Depending on where you live, you may think the number and variety of religion channels has increased greatly in the past decade; digital shelf space made this possible on cable, and still more variants exist only online. Current cable examples are Church Channel, EWTN (Eternal Word Network), Shalom TV, TJC (the Jewish Channel), Gospel Music Television, JCTV, the Word Network, TBN (Trinity Broadcasting Network), I-Life, INSP (Inspiration), Smile of a Child and Three Angels

9.12 The Phenomenon of Al Jazeera

Since its start up in 1996, Al Jazeera has had difficulty in shaking the public perception that it sympathizes with Al Qaeda and provides favorable treatment to extremist and terrorist groups. Started by the Emir of Qatar, Sheik Hamad bin Khalifa al-Thani, Al Jazeera was envisioned as a means of encouraging democracy in the Arab world through the introduction of controversial views on an independently-run 24-hour television news service. Despite its pledge to bring objective news reporting and a freer news media, in many countries the public perceived Al Jazeera as a propaganda vehicle for Al Qaeda and similar extremist groups. This view stigmatized the network, ultimately forcing temporary shutdowns of its field offices in many Arab countries. Indeed, two of its offices were bombed by American troops.

Over time, however, Al Jazeera expanded beyond Arabic news reporting to include Al Jazeera Sports 1 and 2, Al Jazeera Children's Channel, Al Jazeera Documentary Channel, Al Jazeera Mobasher (a channel similar to C-SPAN) and a pan-Arab newspaper. It even spawned several Arabic-language television competitors: Al Arabiya out of Saudi Arabia, Al Kawthar from Iran, and German and French Arabic-language news and entertainment satellite channels, along with BBC programming in Arabic. CNN now sponsors an Arabic-language website in the Near East, with others in Russian and Spanish, but other American efforts to compete in Arabic via Al Hurra have been unsuccessful.

In order to change its image, in 2006 Al Jazeera added Al Jazeera English, an English-language news channel made available around the world. This channel provides international news coverage 24-hours a day, drawing on news offices in Qatar; Washington, DC; London; and Kuala Lampur. Twelve hours of its daily programming originates in the Qatar offices while four hours come from Al Jazeera's other news offices. By hiring experienced journalists away from such established world news providers as the BBC and CNN, Al Jazeera English sought to give a credible voice to underrepresented parts of the world. Its stated goal is to cover controversial stories not always fully reported by the Western news media. Al Jazeera English provided unprecedented English-language coverage within both Gaza and Israel during their 2008–2009 conflict as well as during the turmoil in Egypt in 2011. It is estimated that, as of 2012, Al Jazeera English can be accessed in every major English-language market, is available as a television channel in over 100 countries worldwide, and appears in more than 130 million homes. It is live-streamed online and available on Android phones and tablets.

Because its public profile in the United States has been persistently negative, penetration into this country has been poor. Only one satellite service (DISH) and only three local cable providers in the United States carry Al Jazeera English (no major cable operators have it). The network is available as a television channel in Toledo, Ohio; Burlington, Vermont; and Washington DC.

However, public perceptions of Al Jazeera (and Al Jazeera English) seem to be evolving. Testimony provided by U.S. Secretary of State Hillary Clinton to the Senate Foreign Relations Committee in 2001 took a broader view. Clinton stated that "viewership of Al Jazeera is going up in the United States because it is real news...you feel like you are getting real news around the clock instead of a million commercials and, you know, arguments between talking heads and the kind of stuff that we do on our news that is not providing information to us." Because journalists as a group make considerable use of the internet to gain background and perspectives, a more positive view of Al Jazeera English is emerging.

James Angelini, Ph.D.
University of Delaware

Broadcasting Network. Sometimes MVPDs group a few religious channels with TV Land, ABC Family and the Hallmark Channel, creating a "Family" section of service. This is probably an unhappy linking for Hallmark and ABC as well as for the more formally religious networks.

Sex

Soft-core pornography still abounds on multichannel services. Social norms that used to discourage the proliferation of such services are eroding, especially with reformers' attention focused on hard-core internet pornography. Another key to the popularity of soft-core porn is a very relaxed view of "porn" by twenty-somethings, who no longer see social stigma associated with viewing pornography. Not counting all that is available online, the widely available cable choices include Adult Swim, Hot Choice, Playboy TV, Pleasure, Spice and TeN (The Erotic Network). In some locations these are restricted to PPV.

Shopping

Home shopping channels continue to attract viewers, but the number of services has leveled off since 1990, largely because competition from the internet has drawn away many customers. The long-surviving options include HSN (Home Shopping Network), Home Shopping Spree (Spree!), QVC and Shop at Home. In addition, channels linked to department store chains appear on some MVPD's outlets, such as JCPenney shopping channels on Time Warner Cable.

Spanish-Language

Unlike the "foreign" category, this programming reflects the mainstream of Hispanic and Latino viewers in the United States. Advertisers are keenly interested in this growing population segment. Latino or Hispanic programming is found on Galavisión and three hybrid broadcast/cable networks, Univision, Telemundo and TeleFutura. Univision regularly often outdraws the English-language broadcast networks in many markets. There are also Spanish-language versions of some foundation services, such as Discover en Espanol and History en Espanol, plus such Spanish-only channels as Azteca America, HITN (Hispanic Information and Telecommunications Network), Mexicanal, Mega TV, WAPA America and Cine Latino. In addition, many channels come with the option of an English or Spanish audio feed.

Sports

ESPN, ESPN2, ESPNU and ESPN Classic are still the top purveyors of cable sports, but they get plenty of competition these days from Versus, NFL Network,

NHL Network, NBA TV, Big Ten Network, Fox College Sports, CBS Sports Network and MSG Network, plus all the regional sports channels operated by Fox. The most recent trend is to differentiate each channel by the sport itself, rather than solely by league or channel owner, although branding from NFL or Fox always helps. Because men are a difficult-to-reach advertising target, the revenue potential is very high. On the other hand, sports rights fees continue to skyrocket (see Chapter 7). Besides the ESPN, Fox and major league channels named above, the Tennis Channel, FUEL TV, the Golf Channel, the Speed Channel, the Sportsman's Channel and Yes HD attract sizable audiences of fans.

Superstations

Local stations with sports and movies can get national attention when distributed by satellite to distant cities. As mentioned in Chapter 3, the FCC has called a halt to the proliferation of superstations but grandfathered the biggest ones: KWGN, WGN, WPIX, WSBK and WWOR. These originate in very large cities and bring urban news and big-time sports. WTBS in Atlanta is now considered a local station, and its sister network, TBS (once a superstation), became a foundation network.

Premium Networks

The number of pay-per-month channels leveled off when the two kinds of pay-per-use were fully rolled out, and then froze or even shrank when Netflix and other online movie services gained users. Each premium channel has worked hard at establishing a signature program and pushing its brand images, while fighting to maintain market share.

HBO/Max

Owned by Time Warner, HBO encompasses seven pay-per-month channels already mentioned as its sub-niche services (HBO, HBO2, HBO Signature, HBO Family, HBO Comedy, HBO Zone and HBO Latino) plus HBO On Demand. Time Warner also owns HBO's sister service Max (formerly Cinemax) and its subparts, MoreMax, ActionMax, OuterMax, 5Star-Max, ThrillerMax, WMax, plus @Max and Max On Demand. (The sole focus of Cinemax is movies.) HBO has moved far from the movies-only channel that began in the 1970s. It differentiates itself from other "movie" channels by scheduling original programming in drama, comedy and sports that is much acclaimed by critics and viewers. HBO has won many dozens of Emmys, Golden Globes and Oscars for such programs as *The Sopranos, True Blood* and *Sex and the City*, stealing the limelight from the Big Four broadcast networks. Most recently, its drama *Game of Thrones* seems headed to a new raft of awards. HBO appears on virtually every cableco/satco/telco system in the United States, as does Showtime, and HBO is distributed internationally to more than 170 countries, including HBO Canada, HBO en Español, HBO Ole, HBO Brazil, HBO Asia, HBO Central Europe and dozens more place-related names.

Showtime / The Movie Channel / Flix

CBS Corporation owns Showtime and its movies-only channels Flix, The Movie Channel and the Sundance Channel. Showtime's strategy is to make major studio deals, having learned a tough lesson in the 1990s when other premium channels kept it from getting new, big-draw theatrical movies. The channel's other strategy is to compete with HBO for the top-boxing draws. Showtime won several Golden Globe Awards for its original series *Weeds*. Showtime's subniche channels are Showtime 2, Showtime Showcase, Showtime Beyond, Showtime Extreme, Showtime Next, Showtime Women, Showtime FamilyZone, along with The Movie Channel and TMC Xtra. In addition, three on-demand/PPV channels (Showtime on Demand, The Movie Channel on Demand, and Showtime PPV) appear on many cable and satellite systems. In 2007 Showtime introduced Showtime Interactive 2.0 on the DISH Network.

Encore, Starz and MoviePlex

Liberty Starz owns Starz Encore, which comprises 17 channels of cable- and satellite-delivered premium movie channels. The cornerstone of Starz

Encore's programming strategy is to lock in studio releases of theatrical movies for several years, although the associated costs of this strategy had put the company in financial jeopardy in the early 2000s, causing subsequent rebranding efforts to gather more subscriptions. Like most other premium movie channels, Encore added the Encore name to all of its six channels, ending up with the basic Encore plus Encore Action, Encore Drama, Encore Love, Encore Mystery, Encore Westerns—all with East and West feeds—and an on-demand channel. Encore is distributed even more widely in the United States than HBO because some subscribers can get it as part of a digital tier as well as a premium stand-alone or packaged with Starz. However, only the main Encore channel is HD; the others are digital only. On the other hand, most of the movies they show are in older formats anyway.

Starz's makeover was more dramatic, opting for cohesive graphics packages across all channels, dropping the annoying exclamation point, and eventually shifting all channels to HD. Starz Theater became Starz Edge that focused on young men by showing four films at fixed times all week. Two channels were merged into Starz Kids and Family to make room for a new channel called Starz Comedy. And to fit in with the new look, Black Starz was renamed Starz InBlack, leaving Starz Cinema as the only Starz channel to keep its original name. Unlike other premium movie channels, Starz carries some banner advertising across some of its programs, a practice that stirs criticism and contradicts its all-movie promotion.

MoviePlex replays one of Encore's seven channels each day in the week (all Encore Western one day, All Encore Love the next and so on), but accompanies them with interstitials and a lot of promotion. The Plex idea gave rise to two simulcast channels—IndiePlex that carries only independent films and RetroPlex that carries only older movies. MoviePlex's distribution is limited largely to DISH and Comcast systems. In contrast, both Encore and Starz appear on all the major MVPDs, including DirecTV, DISH and FiOS, but unlike HBO and Showtime, Starz and Encore are distributed almost exclusively in the United States.

Pay-Per-View/Video-On-Demand

At one stage, PPV and VOD channels were considered separate and discrete companies, but all have been folded in as arms of the main channels. Unlike VOD, PPV services show the same movie or event to all subscribers at the same time and charge an extra premium for these events. Besides movies as on Starz On Demand, PPV carries primarily major boxing, wrestling and other fighting events (specifically UFC, Ultimate Fighting Championship). HBO has had the most success with PPV, generating huge revenues for top matches. Every MVPD now includes some VOD channels where subscribers choose among the available episodes of recent and older television shows and movies. The selection is limited by the rights holders so as not to undercut their main broadcast and cable channels and DVD sales.

Hyping Subscription Networks

Like the broadcast networks, basic and premium networks require sophisticated marketing. Although some newer networks naturally focus on acquiring new viewers, the usual strategy is to retain existing viewers while developing new services. Above all, promoting *brand identity* is the key marketing goal, as in such phrases as "Lifetime—Television for Women" and "Spike TV! The First Network for Men."

All subscription services use on-air *tune-in* and *cross-channel promotion*. Tune-in promotion encourages viewers to stay with the channel for upcoming programs. Cross-channel promotion allows regular viewers of one cable channel (or website) to learn about the shows on another program service. Most of these efforts are accomplished using automated equipment with *insert capability* that can introduce one channel's promos into another channel's program lineup in predetermined time slots. In addition, automated *flow-titling* has been adopted by many channels. This form of on-air promotion places an overlay on one side at the bottom of the screen naming the next program coming up. To the annoyance of viewers, such overlays sometimes obscure a crucial part of the story content and certainly draw

the viewers' attention away from the ongoing drama. Nonetheless, like network identification *bugs* (logos in the corner on live programming), automated advance titling is probably here to stay.

Over the years, the premium channels have developed especially sophisticated, big-budget campaigns for marketing their programs year-round using slogans, giveaways and special package rates. The actual promotion vehicles include mass media advertising, reminders in monthly bills (*statement stuffers*) and coupons in mailers. When trying to expand subscriptions in a local area, they may temporarily unscramble their signals to give cable viewers a taste of what they are missing. Premium channels seek greater *buy rates* by broadly (and loudly) promoting specific events or signature programs (such as *Game of Thrones* on HBO) through all available promotional vehicles. They also send a deluge of special mailers to those who have discontinued their pay channels. *When successful, anticipating and meeting customer expectations creates brand loyalty that is difficult to dislodge.* Just how this principle will apply in some future all-demand age is an interesting question.

Regardless of the method, subscription network programmers must get closely involved with the promotional and marketing efforts on the air, in print advertising and on related websites. These days, *the job of acquiring and scheduling content is tied to making sure that an audience will be there when the program is shown.* Launching a new program sometimes calls for innovative methods. One event that backfired on Turner was its promotion of an "Adult Swim" program called *Aqua Teen Hunger Force*. A few fake devices that looked a lot like bombs were placed under bridges in Boston, causing a mild panic. Naturally, the promotion chief lost his job over that stunt.

Audio Services on Cable

In addition to video programming, cable and satellite systems provide subscribers with radio and audio services. Like video services, radio and audio come in both basic and pay forms and are mostly nationally distributed. Above all others, in the U.S. satellite radio means Sirius XM, a pay service which can be received by mobile receivers in cars or hand carried and by personal computers. It also has competitors such as Music Choice (12 channels), DMX (100 channels), WFMT Radio Network and Yesterday Today.

Big cable companies such as Comcast provide several channels of national digital audio, mostly as part of a package of cable services. Some of these channels carry advertising, and some do not. There are also pay services that charge subscribers a monthly fee for a series of specialized music channels, which are collected by the local cable or satellite operator and shared between the two entities. If people want to hear the king of shock jocks on satellite radio, for example, they'll have to pay (see Chapter 12).

Cable operators are understandably skeptical about the size of pay audio's potential as a revenue stream for wired distribution. The buy rate for all digital audio services runs about 15 percent of basic cable television subscribers, and marketing plans generally target cable subscribers who have high-end CD units. On the positive side, newer surround-sound and other receiver advances have much improved reception, making more consumers more sensitive to audio quality. This new awareness and appreciation of audio spurred the digital audio business, but cable audio now has plenty of competition from internet downloading, iPods and even cell phone aps (see Chapters 11 and 12).

Twisting Paths for the Future

The last five years have brought dramatic changes in subscription cable networks—largely resulting from television's digitalization and broadband growth. Advertiser-supported cable networks have proliferated into families of niche, subniche and microniche program channels serving subgroups of Americans. At the same time, the subscription services feel pressure toward online distribution and VOD while trying to maintain their paying cable and satellite customer bases. Finding profitable internet and

on-demand models for subscription television networks that will be profitable remains the active goal.

As digitalization permits greatly increased channel capacity—and impulse technology becomes standard for cable converters—a wide range of possibilities opens up for cable operators and programmers alike. Increasing numbers of cable subscribers can now order a movie, concert or sporting event in an instant, and, increasingly, they avail themselves of the opportunities. The quantity of options increases daily, many of which are free, not pay, at this time. Projections of 90 million VOD homes in just a few years may entice Hollywood's studios to release movies to pay-per-view services closer to their theatrical release date, truly creating a "home box office" bonanza for movie makers and event organizers. The key obstacle is that Hollywood and the big program producers receive much of their revenue from domestic and international syndication and are reluctant to gamble with anything that threatens that honey pot.

One caveat lies in the rapid spread of online programs that allow viewers with high-speed online connections to watch pirated movies. Hollywood studios that invest $150 million for a feature film have more to lose from pilfered content than a music company whose product costs a fraction to make. A digital copy is a perfect replica of the original, and faster connections and larger hard drives encourage pirates to defeat the copy-protection schemes designed by the content providers. The curse of pirating generates big headaches for producers.

In the midst of rapidly changing technologies, programmers hunt new methods of cutting program costs while recycling and reusing what they have in exciting ways. Basic service strives to identify programming with appeal to narrow slices of subscribers in order to carve out unique services, while premium channels adopt a *low-price, high-volume* strategy of splintered services. Meanwhile, hundreds of millions of potential subscribers in such countries as India and China have become a powerful lure for U.S. cable program suppliers, who can clearly see the pie at home being split into smaller portions by increasing numbers of hungry new services. Increasing access to potential viewers in the once-inaccessible countries, however, is fueling experimentation with new types of niche services and providing hope to wannabes who envision a world market of sufficient size to support their programming.

Nearly all newer and proposed program services fit into the niche, subniche and microniche categories. Very few seek broad appeal. These newer services function like radio station formats, targeting a specific audience segment with demographically-tied programming, talent and promotion. More niche program services mean greater competition, however, and in almost every category or genre, the dominant service now has many challengers ... including the monster Netflix who directly challenges HBO and indirectly challenges all of cable.

Because of efficiencies in cross-promotion and the reuse of original programming in multiple media, the clearest direction for the future is that—joint ventures, mergers and buyouts will increasingly integrate cable program suppliers with both the companies that distribute their wares and with broadcast services. The trend toward building

media conglomerates that reach across media technologies and once-rigid legal boundaries, as well as across international borders in distribution, is undeniably accelerating, and Comcast is leading the way.

Notes

1. Because of conflicts over program distribution rights, the FCC grandfathered five satellite-distributed broadcast stations but banned others from wide satellite distribution. The five remaining superstations are WGN (now called WGN America), WWOR-TV, WSBK-TV, WPIX-TV, and KTLA-TV. KYUR-TV in Alaska calls itself a superstation but is actually an affiliate of ABC and CW.

2. Camcast and Disney have bet on the monthly subscription model for the next decade. In 2012, they reached a 10-year agreement for Camcast to distribute all Disney television content (about 70 ABC, Disney and ESPN services). This extraordinary deal includes VOD and streaming for tablets, phones and other (perheps not yet invented) devices, and it bolsters TV Everywhere as the business model of the future. Amy Chozick and Brooks Barnes, "If Disney Owns It, Comcast Will Soon Be Streaming It." *New York Times*, Jan. 5, 2012, p, B2.

Public Television Programming

Glenda R. Balas

Do you sometimes say "I never watch public TV"? Are you sure you didn't devour *Sesame Street* as a kid? Did your teacher make you watch *NOVA* when you were in school? Don't you sometimes find yourself watching *Curious George* with a sibling or *Antiques Roadshow* with some older adults? Did you watch part of Ken Burns' *Baseball*? A lot of people think they never see public television, but they occasionally do. In fact, about half of Americans watch something on public television at least once a week.

A Special Kind of Television

Public television, its mission and its public service objectives occupy a unique position in American broadcasting. Generations of children have grown up with *Sesame Street* and *Mister Rogers' Neighborhood* in this country and abroad, and adults have sampled *Masterpiece*, *NOVA* and *PBS NewsHour* for decades. Public TV, once known as educational television, has become a staple among the informational and cultural offerings in the United States, taken for granted in many households and schoolrooms.

Public television didn't develop overnight or without a struggle. Critics have argued that public broadcasting presents a left-leaning ideological stance, caters to an elite audience, or has become unnecessary in an age of large-capacity cable and satellite systems, DVD distribution and internet television. Many have questioned public funding for public TV, maintaining that the marketplace—not taxpayers—should provide the specialized programming available on the noncommercial service.

Even U.S. presidents and members of Congress have entered the fray, seeking to eliminate federal funding for public television stations, PBS (Public Broadcasting Service) and NPR (National Public Radio). In 1972, President Richard Nixon—angered by programming he viewed as left of center—vetoed the system's three-year federal appropriation and sent word that he wanted PBS out of the "public affairs business." Nine years later, in 1981, President Ronald Reagan also tried to cut the system's funding entirely, this time in an effort to balance the federal budget. In

both these cases, the U.S. Congress (thankfully) overturned the executive mandates and authorized funding. Within 14 years, however, conservatives in Congress would take the lead to defund public broadcasting once again, an effort repeated yet again in 2011. Ultimately, in both 1995 and 2011, late night negotiations prevailed and saved the day for public television. Even though public broadcasting maintained level funding in 1972, 1981, 1995 and 2011, these battles were fierce and the outcomes uncertain. (And of course, "level" means "less" as costs rise.) These struggles speak to the tenuous and fragile qualities of public broadcasting's financial position.

Other facets of public broadcasting also point to a less-than–rosy future for the national service. PBS went from an average 2.0 rating overall in the 1999–2000 season to 1.5 nationally in the 2004–05 season and 1.2 in 2009. Underwriting support for national programming has seriously slumped since 2001, resulting in the loss of more than a third of all corporate support by 2004 and the withdrawal of several major donors for primetime programs, including ExxonMobil, long-time supporter of *Masterpiece* (that was a biggie). By 2009, underwriting for the PBS core schedule had dropped by 50 percent.

In addition, other forms of giving have decreased, resulting in shrinking state, university and foundation support, as well as smaller member contributions. These broad-based cuts to national underwriting revenues were due, in part, to decisions by some sponsors to migrate to networks and basic cable, where they could buy call-to-action advertising. Some major-market stations, including WTTW-Chicago, also blamed PBS, which has not, they charge, been active enough in securing "what we most need—powerful, successful, innovative programming."[1]

Finally, if funding is shrinking, so too is public television, as stations either "go dark" or choose, like KCET-Los Angeles, to leave the system entirely (see 10.7). Analysts suggest the problems confronting public television are not new or unique to PTV and range from financial woes in a down economy to the persistent programming challenge of having enough content of quality and variety to attract a broad audience.

Even with these sometimes crippling problems, public television stations persist, broadcasting multiple streams of content 24 hours a day, seven days a week, in all regions of the country, expanding into HD and online, and continuing to serve schools in essential ways. On the more than 350 public television stations that cover 99 percent of the country, public television provides local programs and a nightly core schedule in HD of quality arts, education and public affairs series, supplemented by informational websites. Even though many Americans view public television as alternative service, watching it only part of the time, more than half of the country uses public broadcasting each month, generating a monthly broadcast audience of more than 121.9 million people. *Researchers report that Americans rate public television as one of the most trusted of all American institutions.*

The following sections trace out the history, philosophy and practices of this uniquely American broadcast service, focusing on programming strategies and current challenges confronting public broadcasting. Some of these issues also resonate with public service broadcasting in Europe (see 10.1).

10.1   **Public Broadcasting in Europe**

European public broadcasting has long been seen as the ideal by a number of U.S. public broadcasters. *Public service broadcasting* (as public broadcasting is known in Europe) has historically enjoyed adequate funding, editorial autonomy and broad acceptance and support of its educational and cultural purpose throughout Western Europe, though times got tougher during the recent global financial crisis. As one might guess, the establishment of successful public broadcasters in Eastern and Southern Europe has been more difficult. While all broadcasting services faced severe budget cuts over the past few years, stations are also threatened by national and regional governmental agencies that seek to use the public airwaves as mouthpieces for their own political agendas and policies.

Newly established public broadcasting services in Bosnia, Kosovo, Croatia, Herzegovina and Hungary seem particularly at risk from political interference. For example, in 2009, the Prime Minister of Kosovo suspended the public license fee for RTK (*Radio Televizija Kosova*), virtually eliminating the funding base for the Kosovo public broadcaster. The suspension of this monthly fee (which had been added to all electrical bills in Kosovo) caused the European Broadcasting Union, which represents all public broadcasters in Europe, to issue a public letter charging that this decision endangers the broadcaster's independence. Further, the new Media Law established in Hungary in January 2011 has seriously undermined the independence of that country's public broadcaster, *Magyar Televizio* (MTV).

Under this law, adopted after the 2010 national elections, Hungarian public broadcasting has been forced to alter its editorial policy based on the composition of the Hungarian parliament. Finally, changes in mid-2011 to the governing statutes for BHRT (Radio-Television of Bosnia and Herzegovina) have granted broad powers to a governmental Steering Committee to interfere in the public broadcaster's editorial and managerial issues.

Public broadcasters in Western Europe view these political threats to public broadcasting in Eastern and Southern Europe partly as a result of the region's lack of internalization of democratic process. Concerned that public broadcasting in these countries could disappear in the next few years, the European Broadcasting Union stepped in to provide more than 500 hours of high quality content each year to public service broadcasters in Eastern and Southern Europe.

Further, as reported by Eric Pfanner,* public broadcasters in France, Germany, England and Italy have agreed to provide consulting and technical assistance with their neighbors' transition to digital broadcasting. Importantly, the Vienna-based South East Europe Media Organization (SEEMO) has issued public statements demanding broad respect for the social purposes of public broadcasting and its role as the bedrock of democracy and public information throughout Europe. Attitude change is likely to come slowly and in fits and starts.

---

*Eric Pfanner, "Public Radio and TV Get Peers' Help in Europe," *New York Times*, 5 December 2009.

Program Philosophy

Officially established in 1967 as a national broadcasting service, public television's 125 original stations were all committed to education and community. As descendants of educational radio—which had its own origins in the broadcast reform movement of the late 1920s and early 1930s[2]—*these stations were united by beliefs that broadcasting should not only be a positive force in society, but that it should also reside outside the capitalist funding model that has defined U.S. broadcasting since the mid-thirties.* These foundational tenets have driven public television's programming philosophy and ideas about audience and purpose since the founding of public broadcasting as a part of President Lyndon Johnson's Great Society in the 1960s, but they are getting a sore test today. Nonetheless, these concepts continue to frame public broadcasting's struggle for adequate funding and, as discussed in the following sections, ongoing debates about programming.

In fact, arguments over content have persisted within the industry since public television began. For stations, the debate centers on the meaning of *noncommercial educational broadcasting*, which is what the Communications Act of 1934 and the FCC call public television's program service. Noncommercial television service came into existence in 1952 when educational interests lobbied the FCC into creating a special class of reserved channels within the television allocations exclusively dedicated to "educational television."

One argument defines *educational* in the narrow sense of *instructional*. From that viewpoint public television should teach—it should direct its programs to school and college classrooms and to out-of-classroom students. The last thing PTV should do is to compete for commercial television's mass audience. Others define *educational* in a broader sense. They want to reach out to viewers of all kinds with programs that enrich lives and respond to needs. This group perceives "instructional" television as a duty that sometimes must be performed, but their devotion goes to the wide range of programming the public has come to think of as public television.

The Carnegie Commission on Educational Television introduced the term *public television* in 1967. The commission convinced many in government and broadcasting that the struggling new service had to generate wider support than it had in its fledgling years. One of the impediments to such support, the commission felt, was the word *educational*, which gave the service an unpopular image. They suggested *public television* as a more neutral term. Thus, a distinction has grown between *instructional television (ITV)*[3] and *public television (PTV)*.

Lacking a truly national definition for public television's program service, a PTV station's programmer must deal with the unresolved, internal questions of what it means to be a noncommercial educational broadcasting service. The PTV programmer must come to grips with a station's particular program philosophy. Philosophies vary widely from one station to the next, but two common themes persist: being educational and being noncommercial. These terms imply that *public television must directly serve "the people"; it must be educational and different from commercial television.* One of the implications of such a fundamental difference is that public television programming need not pursue the largest possible audience at whatever cost to programming. Public broadcasting has a special mission to serve audiences that would otherwise be neglected because they are too small to interest commercial broadcasting. This difference in outlook has great programming significance. It means that the public station programmer is relieved of one of the most relentless constraints inhibiting a commercial programmer's freedom of choice.

At the same time, public television cannot cater only to the smallest groups with the most esoteric tastes in the community. Broadcasting is still a mass medium, whether commercial or noncommercial, and can justify occupying a broadcast channel and the considerable expense of broadcast facilities only if it reaches relatively large numbers of people. Public broadcasting achieves this goal cumulatively by reaching many small groups, which add up to a respectably large cumulative total in the course of a week. Remember, roughly 50 million U.S. television households tune in to something on PTV each week.

Moreover, on the commercial side, PBS continues to move toward practices consistent with for-profit media. For example, to appeal more powerfully to large underwriters, PBS has expanded the time devoted to underwriting credits and changed their formats so they now resemble commercials. It is telling that some corporate underwriters now use the same spots on public television that they air on the commercial networks and cable. PBS has also formed partnerships with commercial entities (DirecTV, Comcast and others) to generate income and has commercialized its online site (*pbs.org*) by selling advertising on the webpage itself and throughout some of the programs streamed on the site. Finally, as discussed later in this chapter, PBS is exploring the option of creating internal program breaks for placement of its own promotional spots, a move seen by many as a first step toward within-program underwriting content. It seems clear, then, that PBS is not as completely "noncommercial" as it once was ... in attitude or practice.

The Network Model

Programming the national Public Broadcasting Service is a little like trying to prepare a universally acclaimed gourmet meal. The trouble is that a committee of 177 plans the menu, and the people who pay the grocery bills want to be sure the meal is served with sufficient regard for their images. Some people coming to the dinner table want the meal to be enjoyable and fun; others want the experience to be uplifting and enlightening; still others insist that the eating be instructive; and the seafood and chicken cooks want to be sure the audience comes away with a better understanding of the problems of life underwater and in the coop.[4]

The analogies are not farfetched. A board of appointed and elected representatives governs PBS during three-year terms. The PBS Board of Directors includes both professional directors, who lead public television stations, and general directors, who represent the general public. The membership of public television elects the professional directors, while the general directors are selected by the PBS board,

which also appoints the PBS president and CEO. The directors are responsible for governing and setting policy for PBS. In total, the PBS Board of Directors is comprised of 27 members, including 14 professional directors, 12 general directors, and the PBS president. The board is expected to serve 168 public television licensees operating 354 public stations all over the country and in such remote areas as Guam, American Samoa and Bethel, Alaska.

Because PBS produces no programming, it uses a host of program suppliers and tries to promote and schedule their programs effectively. In addition, constituencies ranging from independent producers to minority groups constantly pressure public television to meet their special needs. And, of course, the program funders have their own agendas too.

In *commercial* television, programming and money flow *from* network headquarters *to* affiliates. Production is centrally controlled and distributed on a one-way line to affiliated stations, who are paid compensation to push the network button and transmit what the network feeds. Most of the economic incentives favor affiliate cooperation with the network, placing tremendous programming power in network hands.

In *public* television, money flows the opposite way. Instead of being paid as loyal affiliates, member stations *pay* PBS, which in turn supplies them with programs sufficient to fill prime time and many daytime hours. Stations pay membership dues to cover PBS's operational budget and, entirely separately, fees to cover part of the program costs. PBS is both a not-for-profit network and a membership organization responsible for developing, maintaining and promoting a schedule of programs while also providing services to its dues-paying members. None of the stations are owned by the network. A public station's remaining broadcast hours are typically filled with leased syndicated fare (movies; off-network reruns; made-for-syndication series; and instructional programs for local schools), local productions and programs supplied by other public television networks.

Four noncommercial networks also distribute programming to public stations. Once thought of as a regional network, American Public Television (APT, formerly Eastern Educational Network) is the second-largest national program supplier for public stations after PBS, and it distributes such favorites as *Globe Trekker, The Victory Garden, Agatha Christie's Poirot, Simply Ming, Baking With Julia* and *The Seasoned Traveler* on digital and HD channels. As with PBS, *member stations pay APT for the programs*, which then delivers the requested content to them during off hours via satellite for local recording

and scheduling, more like syndicators. *PBS, however, delivers its programs in a prearranged schedule.*

An entire week of daytime PBS programming in 2011 appears in 10.2, covering the hours from 6 A.M. to 7:30 P.M. The daytime schedule emphasizes programs for preschool children early in the day and for older children after school gets out. Many of these series have run for decades and are award-winning.

10.2	**PBS Daytime Programming (September 12–18, 2011)**		
	Monday–Friday Schedule HD01	**Saturday**	**Sunday**
6:00 A.M.	Clifford the Big Red Dog	Mister Rogers' Neighborhood	Sesame Street
6:30 A.M.	Wild Kratts	Bob the Builder	
7:00 A.M.	Arthur	Curious George	Curious George
7:30 A.M.	Martha Speaks	The Cat in the Hat Knows a Lot About That!	The Cat in the Hat Knows a Lot About That!
8:00 A.M.	Curious George	Super Why!	Super Why!
8:30 A.M.	The Cat in the Hat Knows a Lot About That!	Dinosaur Train	Dinosaur Train
9:00 A.M.	Super Why!	Thomas & Friends	Sid the Science Kid
9:30 A.M.	Dinosaur Train	Angelina Ballerina	Martha Speaks
10:00 A.M.	Sesame Street	This Old House Hour	Arthur
10:30 A.M.			WordGirl
11:00 A.M.	Sid the Science Kid	Antiques Roadshow	Wild Kratts
11:30 A.M.	Word World		Electric Company
12:00 P.M.	Super Why!	Baking With Julia	CyberChase
12:30 P.M.	Barney and Friends	The Victory Garden	Fetch! With Ruff Ruffman
1:00 P.M.	Caillou	This Old House	Need to Know
1:30 P.M.	Sid the Science Kid	This Old House	PBS Previews
2:00 P.M.	Dinosaur Train	Ask This Old House	Religion & Ethics
2:30 P.M.	The Cat in the Hat Knows a Lot About That!	Hometime	To the Contrary
3:00 P.M.	Curious George	The Woodwright's Shop	This Old House Hour
3:30 P.M.	Martha Speaks	MotorWeek	
4:00 P.M.	Arthur	History Detectives	(Specials)
4:30 P.M.	WordGirl		
5:00 P.M.	Wild Kratts	American Masters	
5:30 P.M.	Electric Company		
6:00 P.M.	Fetch! With Ruff Fuffman		History Detectives
6:30 P.M.	Nightly Business Report		
7:00 P.M.	PBS NewsHour	Antiques Roadshow (repeat)	NOVA
7:30 P.M.			

Courtesy of PBS.

Station Scheduling Autonomy

In public television, much clout rests with the stations. They spend their revenues as they see fit, expecting to be treated fairly and with the deference due any consumer. PBS, as a consequence, has a limited ability to get stations to agree on program scheduling. Citing the principle of *localism* as public television's community service bedrock, station managers display considerable scheduling independence, ostensibly to make room for station-produced or acquired programs thought to meet some local need.

After the nationwide satellite system was phased in (1978) and as low-cost recording equipment became available in the 1970s, stations carried the PBS schedule less and less frequently than originally programmed. Until a networking agreement was worked out with the stations, no two stations' program schedules were remotely alike. National promotion, publicity and advertising placement were,

if not impossible, extremely difficult to achieve. Nor were corporate underwriters pleased at the scheduling irregularity from one market to the next.

Even though more and more stations increasingly mirror the national schedule, decision making about program content remains complicated at the local level. The public broadcasting climate supports multiple layers of choosing what gets on the air, which fuels an often-animated conversation about what audiences need and what stations should broadcast. Those who work in programming within the local stations consider their relative autonomy (even from PBS) and freedom from powerful commercial interests to be worth the extra effort of collaboration. The culture at most stations fosters consultation among programming, development, promotion and operations personnel, but the chief programmer typically has final say in developing programming strategies and the schedule (see 10.3).

10.3 What Do Programmers Do?

Franz Joachim is director of content at KNME-Albuquerque. A 35-year veteran of public television, Joachim got his start as a member of the student crew at KUAT-Tucson in 1976. In subsequent years he also freelanced at KUAT as camera operator, editor and director, until becoming student crew supervisor in 1984. In 1995, he moved to WUSF/WGCU-Ft. Meyers, Florida, to take the position of Senior Editor. Joachim joined the professional staff of KNME in 1999 as Production Manager, a position he held until 2010 when he become director of content at the Albuquerque station.

Joachim sees this career path, which originally focused on production and technology management, as particularly appropriate to his job as chief programmer at KNME. Acknowledging that most programmers come up through the ranks as assistant programmers, schedulers and traffic managers, Joachim sees the PTV programming function as becoming more complicated and demanding. "The job is no longer just about programming, per se. It's now about *content*—content on air, on the web, on the phone, and during Pledge," he says. KNME, a

joint licensee of the Albuquerque Public Schools and the University of New Mexico, holds two licenses, which allows the station to broadcast four streams of content on air and over the internet. Long committed to local public affairs and cultural programming, the station also produces weekly series about New Mexico politics and culture.

KNME pulls programming from a range of sources (including NETA, APT and PBS, as well as local programs) to build its schedule. Selection of content and the schedule grid are typically developed three months out by the programming team, which includes the station's CEO. Once approved, the schedule goes forward then to promotions, operations and development units, where on-air promos are produced and scheduled and underwriting is finalized.

Joachim reports that KNME's programming is generally consistent with the PBS core schedule, rarely deviating from the PBS feed by more than 5 percent over the course of the year. When the PBS schedule conflicts with programs seen as important to local needs, however, like all PTV, KNME invariably chooses the localized option.

The Carriage Agreements

A 1979 common carriage agreement gave some order to this networking chaos, at least from the national perspective. *Common carriage* refers to a nonbinding agreement among stations that, in this case, established a core schedule on Sunday, Monday, Tuesday and Wednesday nights. During the hours of 8 to 10 P.M. (with time zone delay feeds), PBS fed those programs most likely to attract the largest audiences. In turn, stations committed themselves to airing the PBS core offerings on the nights they were fed, in the order fed, and within the prime-time hours of 8 to 11 P.M.

For several years the common carriage arrangement worked well. The typical *core program* received same-night carriage on more than 80 percent of stations. Core slots thus took on a premium quality; underwriters and producers, looking for favorable treatment for their programs, began to insist they be assigned a time slot within the core period. Maximum carriage was thought to mean maximum audience size. With more core-quality programs on their hands than available hours in the eight-hour core period, PBS programmers were forced in the early 1980s to move some long-standing core programs (*Mystery!* and *Great Performances*, for example) outside the core period to make room for other programs in the hope that the stations would still carry the moved shows on the feed night.

This move was partially successful; even though same-night carriage for the rescheduled programs

fell, it was only to about 55 percent for these non-core programs. Station programmers, however, soon took these moves by PBS as a sign that core programs could be moved around at will, and station independence began to reassert itself. By the 1985–86 season, same-night carriage of the core itself had slipped to 73 percent overall. PBS, concerned with complaints from national underwriters that "their" programs were not receiving fair treatment, moved to bolster same-night carriage. In fall 1987, PBS began a new policy of *same-night carriage* by which selected, broad-appeal programs would be designated for carriage the night they were fed. This policy had little effect, however, because PBS did not strictly enforce it.

In 1995 PBS once again attempted to get control of unpredictable station scheduling. Wanting to encourage new corporate underwriting because Congress had reduced its federal funding, a committee of the PBS board presented the stations with a *new common carriage agreement*—this time with financial penalties. Some 40 stations refused to sign the agreement until the penalties were removed. The new agreement went into effect in September 1995, requiring stations to carry certain programs within prime time on the feed night (see the programs identified in 10.4). The agreement promised that PBS would designate no more than 350 hours per year for common carriage, of which stations could choose up to 50 hours *not* to carry on feed night, a

10.4 | **Typical PBS Prime-Time Schedule (September 12–18, 2011)**

	Monday	Tuesday	Wednesday	Thursday	Friday	Saturday	Sunday
8:00 P.M.	Antiques Roadshow	Tavis Smiley	Nature	Antiques Roadshow (repeat)	Washington Week in Review	Tavis Smiley	Nature
8:30 P.M.					Need to Know	PBS Previews	
9:00 P.M.	(Specials)	Frontline	NOVA	PBS Previews	American Masters	POV	Masterpiece
10:00 P.M.	(Specials)	POV	NOVA	This Old House Hour	(Specials)	Austin City Limits	

Courtesy of PBS.

provision allowing local programming flexibility. Within these limitations, the agreement stated a goal of 90 percent carriage or better for designated programs.

Most programs designated for common carriage were receiving the requested carriage by at least 90 percent of stations by 2005, and the maximum number of designated hours had risen to 500 per year. As for shows not designated, program managers often tape-delay them outside of prime time, using the vacated evening slots for other programming. As budgets at the local and state levels tighten up, however, stations are expected to use even more of the PBS feed, finding it more cost and time effective than local production and tape delay. As KNME's Joachim notes, "At Channel 5, we now have 50 people doing what 80 used to, plus we're now programming four channels, not just one. We're working to be as efficient as possible, and we're finding that PBS is recognizing that and making efforts to work with us."[5]

Multicasting

Digital TV broadcasts are described as long streams of digital information or bits that can contain any data the broadcaster wants to add to their signals. Public broadcasters, many of whom began with single over-the-air channels in the 1950s and 1960s, are now able to send multiple streams of video through the same channel's "pipeline." Working with compressed content, some public broadcasting stations now choose to "push" four streams of lower-definition programming to air, while others elect to maintain higher signal quality by broadcasting two streams at one time, one of which is always HD. Those stations that are duopolies, holding two licenses, are able to broadcast four programming lines at one time, without compromising quality.

Although some public stations have developed their own local or regional content to fill multiple channels, many have elected to work with four packaged feeds developed by PBS, public stations and established syndicators, and then transmitted to participating public television stations via satellite. These channels include PBS World and Create,

both produced by PBS, WNET-New York, WGBH-Boston, APT and NETA. V-me is a Spanish-language channel developed in partnership by V-me Media, Inc. and WNET-New York with offices in the same building. The fourth channel is MHz Worldview, which has studios in Falls Church, VA, and Washington, DC. This network pulls from a number of international channels and aggregates a feed of public affairs programs, documentaries, dramas, music and sports from Japan, Germany, China, Vietnam, South Africa, France and Nigeria, among others. Although stations pay a tiered price for Create and PBS World, depending on market size, both V-me and MHz International are free, as long as stations abide by stated rules of carriage. (V-me, for example, requires a ten-year commitment.)

It's clear that the technology is in place for stations to provide multiple streams of diverse programming for multiple constituencies. Even so, public television's multicasting efforts generally involve broadcasting more of the same. A review of their schedules reveals that most stations look to older programs and successful PTV trends in developing their streams of content. These decisions are based in no small part on the enormous costs related to new production. As costs rise and revenues flatten and fall, it becomes increasingly difficult to produce or acquire large amounts of new content. Critics also suggest that PTV caters to a "preferred viewer" that is largely upscale, older and well-educated. This institutionalized notion of (much of) the public television audience leads naturally, says scholar Patricia Aufderheide, to PTV programs that are predictable and "safely splendid."[6]

Multiple Platforms

If multicasting is the "push" of PBS content to audiences through multiple streams of programming, multi-platforms are the numerous technologies that allow reception. Your television set is one of these platforms and is clearly the oldest. (In fact, color television sets came to U.S. consumers in the early 1950s at about the same time as "educational, noncommercial" television.) But increasingly, PBS viewers also get their programs on hand-held devices (cell phones and digital tablets), as well as the internet. Sometimes, they use all these "platforms" at the same time, so it may not be uncommon for a dad to watch *Sesame Street* with his children, while also (simultaneously) viewing *PBS NewsHour* on his cellphone and last week's episode of *NOVA*, "on demand," on his laptop. A teenaged daughter, also sitting in this family living room, might be using her tablet to pick up the *American Masters* interview with Pearl Jam's Eddie Vedder on PBS-YouTube.

Viewers can also follow PBS, as well as many of their favorite shows and celebrities, on Facebook and engage directly on Twitter with Jim Lehrer (*PBS NewsHour*) and Gwen Ifel (*Washington Week in Review*). If you're into collectibles and old furniture, you can stay up to date with *Antiques Roadshow* by subscribing to its e-newsletter, which is dropped into your email box each month.

Even young kids can stay in touch with their favorite children's shows (*The Cat in the Hat Knows a Lot About That!*, *Dinosaur Train* and *Super Why*) by downloading PBS apps to their phones and tablets and watching programs on demand. PBS has produced at least 14 different apps for mobile devices, and by early 2011 more than 1 million people had downloaded the apps for iPad and iPhone. Additionally, PBS has more than 600,000 Facebook fans and more than 700,000 followers on Twitter. Public TV's interactions with new media demonstrate its exceptional desire to connect with—and serve—its audiences.

PBS Responsibilities

Since its founding, PBS has had two key responsibilities: *to accept or reject programs* and *to schedule those accepted*. The program acceptance/rejection responsibility is grounded in technical and legal standards established by PBS during the 1970s. The technical standards protect stations from FCC violations and maintain high levels of video and audio quality. By their very nature, they can be applied with reasonable consistency. As the steward for underwriting guidelines, PBS maintains rules for

on-air crediting of PBS program funders to prevent violations of FCC underwriting regulations and to ensure against public television's appearing too "commercial." The legal standards protect stations from libel and rights infringements and alert them to equal time obligations that may result from PBS-distributed programs.

Underwriting and advertising are fundamentally different, although they both share some elements. The key difference is that advertising in the form of a paid commercial usually contains a *call to action* (for example, "Stop by our showroom today"). Underwriting presents the name and makes neutral statements (for example, "Funding provided by Kellogg's, makers of quality breakfast cereal") that serve to reinforce brand awareness. Over time, the length and kinds of supporting content permitted by PBS rules have become less restrictive, and now on-air crediting is both longer and more detailed but continues to lack action statements, so far.

Even as public television strives to adhere to the tenets of its early noncommercial roots, the broadcasting service has continued to move toward a for-profit model, particularly in its online content. The periodic Congressional threats of defunding make this essential. In 2006 PBS announced a newly-developed online sales division charged with web advertising on public TV's national website, noting that it would ban ads from broadcasting competitors and be cautious about display ads and commercials for prescription drugs and R-rated movies. Advertising on its children's sites was to be limited, a vague commitment.

Well, five years later, an examination of Kids Sprouts Online revealed a site tab dedicated to advertisers, carrying the slogan, "With so many engaged parents, there's no better place to advertise. Live Sprouts!" Further, PBS continues to feature sponsorship banners on its six major web categories—Arts, News & Views, History, Science & Technology, Business & Finance and Home & How-To—and allows banners, aimed at parents rather than children, on PBS KIDS and PBS KIDS GO! Most disconcerting to some viewers has been the insertion of ads in programs that are streamed online.

10.5   Boon or Bust? KCTS, Early HD Pioneer

High definition television (also known as HD or high def) is characterized by video resolution that is much higher than that of standard definition (SD). In fact, HD has between one and two million pixels per frame, which is roughly five times the resolution of SDTV.

Since U.S. broadcasting officially "went digital" in 2009, we've come to expect very high image quality in the television programs we watch. At least one channel on all PBS stations is now broadcast in high definition, and today much of the programming on PBS is created—through videography, editing, graphics, sound and special effects—in high definition format, which inherently raises video quality even on a non-HD digital channel.

Even though several PBS stations (most of them large community stations in major markets) were innovators in digital transition, one station—KCTS-Seattle—stands out as a leader. The station not only took steps in 1998 (eleven years before the mandated transition!) to broadcast some of its schedule in digital format, but also pioneered production in high definition. Because of a long-standing, collaborative relationship with NHK, Japan's public TV network, KCTS was able to borrow the HD gear required to shoot several shows, including *Over California* (1994) and *Chihuly Over Venice* (1998). This extremely scarce HD equipment included not only a 40-pound SONY camera—called the "best video camera in the world"—but also a 300-pound recorder that required its own power supply.

These early HD programs, which were shot mostly by a videographer hanging out the side door of a noisy helicopter, were lush "travelogues" of the countryside below. Viewers likened the experience, with its sweeping visuals and orchestral soundtrack, to the immersive dome technology present in many planetarium shows.*

KCTS offered the programs (and other similar shows that followed) to public stations as fundraisers and thus established itself as the PBS market leader in digital broadcasting. This reputation did not come without a price, however. Local newspaper reports later made the case that the expense of high-end digital production and distribution contributed to KCTS's massive debt and the layoffs of staff beginning in 1998. Members of the management team that had pushed KCTS to pioneer in digital broadcasting retired early in 2003 in the face of widespread staff upheaval and a station deficit of $2.5 million. Not only was KCTS unable to pay its rent to the city of Seattle in 2002, but the Corporation for Public Broadcasting withheld nearly $750,000 in funding in 2003 because the station's financial reports were late.**

How much of the KCTS financial downturn can be traced to its early and aggressive push to "go digital" is debatable, but it seems clear that the station's deficits, which began as early as 1996, were linked to early explorations and adoption of expensive digital production and upgrading initiatives. At the same time, it also seems clear that the public system as a whole benefited from KCTS's pioneering forays into the digital realm, using the Seattle station's high-def programs in fundraising, taking cues from its digital transition and learning from its mistakes. This case study illustrates the risk of being a technological pioneer, particularly in such high-stakes innovation as the digital transformation of a television network. Was it worth the cost to KCTS, its staff, and the management team that put the plan in place? You decide!

---

*Although PBS stations have not experimented broadly with digital dome technology, as it is tied to a particular classroom or theatre space and not broadcasting, PTV stations and producers have entered into educational partnerships with air and space museums and planetariums to share programming.

**"Trouble on Channel 9," *The Seattle Times* 22 May, 2003, retrieved at *http://seattletimes.nwsource.com/news/local/links/kcts.html*.

These decisions to commercialize part of the PBS website are also reflected in efforts to satisfy the needs of corporate sponsors by changing on-air guidelines for underwriting credits to more closely resemble those of commercial broadcasting. Public television underwriters increasingly are using the same spots they place on commercial venues. Further, in the past, most public TV underwriting opportunities have been limited to a year. Now, stations and PBS are offering shorter sponsorship stints, including some as short as a week for children's programs such as *Clifford* and *Arthur*. Critics and proponents alike maintain the effort is to create a more "sales-friendly" environment for companies hard-hit by financial woes. Of course, at the same time, it also generates more advertising receptivity in children.

Finally, PBS announced at the PTV annual meeting in 2011 that it was experimenting with placement of internal promotional material in PBS programs. The proposal was met with such outcry that PBS underwriting and programming executives agreed to back off and just continue their research about ramifications of such a plan. Critics suggest that internal promotion not only violates public TV's long-standing commitments to uninterrupted programming, but also opens the doors widely to in-program advertising breaks.

Old-timers remember the days when an underwriting credit was a corporate name on a slide, featured at the beginning and close of the underwritten program for 15 seconds. Many join contemporary critics in suggesting that program interruption and increased commercial content may damage public television's already weak support in Congress and lead to even more reduced allocations during the next funding cycle.

Another PBS function is warning stations in advance of programs that contain offensive language or sensitive scenes (nudity or violence). It makes edited versions of programs that contain extreme material available to stations. In rare cases, such controversial programs as *It's Elementary* (a documentary on gay issues in grade school) have been canceled or postponed, but in general PBS tends toward airing programs as produced.

Day-to-Day Management

An executive vice president heads PBS's National Program Service (NPS). This senior executive sets policy for and oversees the content and array of formats within the program schedule, directing long-range development of major programs. Other managers assist in the day-to-day activities of program development, scheduling management and acquisition of international programs, while content departments within the NPS concentrate on the development of news and public-affairs, children's, cultural and fundraising programs.

PBS Plus offers a menu of "user-pays" programs to supplement local schedules. Other departments deliver programs for adult at-home college education and in-school instruction for children. Interactive and online services, extensions of PBS's programming, were introduced in the mid-1990s—including *Mathline* for students and *PBS Online* on the internet (*www.pbs.org*). Thus, programming for the station broadcasts is only part of PBS's activities.

Satellite Distribution

The broadcast operations department manages the daily details of the national schedule much as a traffic department would at a commercial network. All the pieces of the jigsaw puzzle must be plugged into place across an array of satellite schedules, ensuring, for example, that (1) the end of a 13-episode series coincides with the start of another ready to occupy its slot; (2) dramas with profanity or nudity have an early edited feed available on another transponder; and (3) replacement programs are available when, for example, the Saturday morning schedule of how-to programs runs short in the summer.

PBS now delivers instructional and general audience services via direct-to-home satellite channels (TVRO) as well as the regular national programming feed provided to PBS member stations retransmitted by DirecTV and DISH Network, but delayed by 24 hours to allow member stations the opportunity to air the programming first. In 1999, PBS initiated two other satellite program services, PBS Kids Channel (children's programming) and PBS U (adult learning service for college credit) carried on DirecTV. (See 10.6 for the story of the adult educational services.) In March 2004, PBS also launched PBS HD, making public broadcasting first to provide a fully-packaged 24/7 channel consisting entirely of high definition and widescreen content.

PBS HD was available from local PBS stations that had already transitioned to digital broadcasting, as well as digital cable systems that agreed to retransmit the digital signal of their local public television stations. By the mid-2000s, 236 PBS stations were on the air with digital signals, reaching more than 85 percent of U.S. TV households. The PBS HD channel featured a mix of new and library HD and widescreen programs, providing around-the-clock high

---

10.6 | **The Demise of the Adult Learning Service**

PBS began its Adult Learning Service (ALS) in the early 1980s, offering over-the-air instruction leading to college credit for more than two decades. With over 100 telecourses, the ALS was the largest source of such programming in the world. Enhanced by the web and then programmed as a network (PBS U), the service supplied college credit to more than 5 million students in academic areas including arts and humanities, business and technology, history, professional development, science and health, and the social sciences.

Shortly after its launch, ALS received a significant boost from Walter Annenberg, then owner of *TV Guide*, who established the Annenberg/CPB Project. For this project, the Annenberg School of Communications gave $15 million to CPB each year for ten years (1983 to 1993) to fund college-level instruction via television and other new technologies. The project resulted in such high-visibility public television series as *The Constitution: That Delicate Balance*, *French in Action*, *Planet Earth*, *The Africans*, *War and Peace in the Nuclear Age*, *Art of the Western World*, *Discovering Psychology* and *Economics USA*, with subject matter ranging from the humanities to science,

mathematics, and business. The net result of Annenberg's entry into this field was not only an increase in the number of adult instructional programs available through ALS but also, thanks to their above-average budgets, an increase in production values (quality).

Colleges and universities that wanted to offer credit for these telecourses normally arranged for local public television stations to air the series, and all registration, fees, testing, and supplementary materials were handled by the school. Some of the courses used computers, and all were keyed to special texts and study guides. ALS offered programmers one of the most challenging additions to their program schedule. Because such programs required close cooperation with the institutions offering credit, they required a reliable repeat schedule that would permit students to make up missed broadcasts. In time, however, the wide availability of internet access ended the need for PBS to act as distributor. Universities could email course materials and video directly to individual students, irrespective of the number taking a particular class, and now with Wi-Fi on campuses and larger towns, people can take courses whenever and wherever they like.

---

quality content to those "early innovators" who owned high definition receivers. This channel evolved into HD01 (the PBS high definition feed), as all PBS stations eventually proved capable of providing HD programming on at least one of their channels.

By 2002, PBS Kids Channel wasn't doing well in competition with Viacom's Noggin, a digital cable/satellite channel that featured *Sesame Street* reruns and other satellite channels targeting children. Withdrawal of DirecTV's support in 2005 led to the formation of PBS Kids Sprout and PBS Sprout On Demand, digital commercial channels on cable owned by Comcast, HIT Entertainment, PBS and Sesame Workshop. They carry such shows as *Angelina Ballerina*, *Curious George*, *Barney & Friends*, *Bob the Builder*, *Teletubbies*, *Thomas & Friends*, *Dragon Tales*, *Zoboomafoo* and of course, the so-essential *Sesame Street*. The term "PBS Kids" returned to the main network as an umbrella brand

for preschool children's programming (offering *Arthur*, *Clifford the Big Red Dog* and *Curious George*), along with PBS Kids GO! for early elementary kids (which provided such shows as *Kidsworld Sports*, *Arthur*, *Maya & Miguel* and *Wishbone*). Although not in HD as yet, all these over-the-air and digital services are supported with clever online sites, *www.pbskids.org*, *www.pbskidsgo.org* and *www.sproutonline.com*. In most markets, households that subscribe to Comcast or DirecTV get most of these channels; other cable, satellite and phone service providers offer some, but not all, of the PBS channels. The internet remains a reliable source of all PBS content.

Fundraising Assistance

The Station Independence Program (SIP), a division in PBS's National Program Service, is big hit with stations. The SIP schedules and programs three main on-air fundraising drives a year, called *pledge drives* (a 16-day event held annually in March and two 9-day drives held in August and December). Stations wishing to avail themselves of the SIP service (and most do) pay PBS additional fees for it. A key SIP function is acquiring, funding and commissioning special programs for use during local station pledge drives.

Programs with emotional payoff, not necessarily those programs with the largest audiences, tend to generate more and higher pledges. Self-help programs and inspirational dramas, for example, generally make money for stations, but documentaries on topics such as world economics do not do well. In general, such performance events as *Yanni* and *Three Tenors* do very well in pledge drives. As baby boomers age and edge closer to the typical demographic of "donor," pledge programmers also rely increasingly on concerts (live and on tape) by music icons of the 1960s and 1970s, including Joan Baez, James Taylor, Chaka Khan, Billy Joel and the folk trio Peter, Paul and Mary.

Types of Station Licensees

One of the difficulties in describing PTV programming strategies is that the stations are so diverse. The 168 *licensees* operating 354 *stations* (lots of which are unstaffed transmitters) represent varied management viewpoints. More stations (that is, transmitters) than licensees exist because in 20 states a legislatively created agency for public broadcasting is the licensee for as many as 16 separate transmitters serving the whole state. Also, in several communities, one noncommercial educational licensee operates two television channels. In these cases (San Francisco, Boston, Pittsburgh and Milwaukee, among others), one channel usually offers a relatively broad service of PBS programming while the second channel is used for more specialized programming, often instructional material. In addition, a handful of noncommercial television stations are not members of PBS because of signal overlap with other PBS stations or because they dropped their membership.

Much of public television's diversity is explained by the varying auspices under which its stations operate. Licensees fall into four categories: *community, university, public school* and *state agency*, and each approaches programming in different ways.

Community Licensees

In larger cities, particularly those with many educational and cultural institutions but without a dominant institution or school system, the usual licensee is the nonprofit community corporation created for the purpose of constructing and operating a public television station. Because the governing board of such a station exists solely to administer the station (as compared with university trustees who have lots of other concerns), many feel that community stations are the most responsive type of licensee. With the separation of community licensee KCET-Los Angeles from PBS in early 2011, 85 such licensees still operate in the United States (see 10.7).

Compared with other licensees, community stations have traditionally derived a higher proportion of their operating support from fundraising activities (including on-air auctions). As a result, their on-air pledge-drives reflect their so very urgent need to generate funds from their viewers. Programmers at these stations are thus more likely to be sensitive to a proposed program's appeal to donors. Certainly, they will lean toward high-quality production values to attract and hold general audiences. Within the community category, several stations stand apart because of their metropolitan origins, their large size and their national impact as producers of network-distributed programs.

The flagship stations of PBS are located in New York, Boston, Los Angeles, Washington, Chicago, Baltimore, Seattle and Pittsburgh. The first four are particularly notable as production centers for the nation, originating such major programs as *NOVA, Nature* and *PBS NewsHour* (see 10.8). Although other public stations and commercial entities often participate in their productions and financing, these large, community-licensed producing stations generate most of the PBS schedule.

10.7 Stations Withdraw From PBS

In 2008, public broadcasting licensees included 86 community stations, 6 local public school facilities, 20 state government stations or networks, and 56 college or university stations. Three years later, those numbers had dropped by three, and other stations and their boards were considering leaving PBS. KWBU-Waco, a university station licensed to Baylor University, was the first of the three to close. Having exhausted a $1 million line of credit, KWBU was unable to secure additional funding from Baylor and subsequently severed all ties with PBS, going "dark" in 2010. Within a year, KCET-Los Angeles and WMFE-Orlando had also decided to leave PBS. Like KWBU (which had limited community support and only 1,600 members when it closed), the stations cited financial woes as the reason for dropping the PBS affiliation or closing altogether.

The case of KCET is chilling. After learning that its PBS dues would increase by more than 40 percent, ironically because of the station's success in generating $50 million in donations, KCET-TV split from PBS in 2011, becoming an independent community station. One of the country's oldest public stations and the PBS flagship of the nation's second-largest media market, KCET pioneered productions in the arts, Spanish-language programming, education and public affairs, so it was an enormous loss to the system.

KCET sold its historic 105,000 square-foot Sunset Boulevard facility to the Church of Scientology and moved into quarters half that size in Burbank. Initially programming its "independent" schedule with local talk and re-runs of classic films, the station adopted an eclectic international stance by airing a range of worldwide news programs. These daily broadcasts included *IBA News* (Tel Aviv), *NHK Newsline* (Toyko), *Russia Today* (Moscow) and the *Al Jazeera English News*, and the ratings are looking good. Happily for PBS and the former KCET audience, public stations KOCE-Orange County and KVCR-San Bernardino enlarged their coverage areas to serve PBS viewers in the Los Angeles area.

The fate of the huge New Jersey Network (NJN) rings another warning bell. The 40-year-old PTV network in New Jersey was closed by the state's budget-cutting efforts. PBS service to New Jersey had to be picked up by New York and Pennsylvania stations WNET and WHYY as best they could. Similarly, the University of Central Florida and Brevard Community College teamed up to jointly provide PBS services to Central Florida, when WMFE-Orlando closed its PBS station in 2011.

Change is here. Another giant in the system, WTTW-Chicago suggested that it might withdraw from PBS, while Indiana's eight public television stations are working on a merger that would not only share content but also facilities (including master control) among the stations. The stunning losses to the PTV system help explain why PBS is altering its policy toward commercials. *Programs continue to cost what they cost even when there are fewer (and smaller) stations to split the expense.*

Because of comparatively high levels of community involvement, community stations have tended to attract larger local audiences than other types of noncommercial licensees. Most of these stations adopted HD technology at a rapid rate at the turn of the twenty first century, largely because their membership tends toward the high-end viewers of interest to underwriters. For example, Nielsen reports that about half of the households in San Francisco, one of the nation's largest media markets, tune weekly to community-operated KQED. With such a high audience level, more of its viewers see its fundraising appeals and thus contribute money to the station. WNET, New York's largest public television station, is an exception among community stations. It receives a portion of its funding from state government.

University Licensees

Many colleges and universities have activated public television stations as a natural outgrowth of their traditional role of providing extension services within their states. As they see it, "the boundaries of the campus are the boundaries of the state,"[7] and both radio and television can do some of the tasks

10.8 *PBS NewsHour*

In 1973 Robert MacNeil and Jim Lehrer joined together to cover the Watergate hearings for PBS. The results were an Emmy and a new news program for Public Broadcasting. Unlike the commercial nightly newscasts, MacNeil and Lehrer were actually throwbacks to Edward R. Murrow and *See It Now*. Instead of doing many two-minute stories, they concentrated on one major story and went in-depth. They let people tell their own versions of the story in interviews that lasted several minutes; they also avoided sound bites and ran extended portions of news conferences. These were usually followed by nonjudgmental cross-examinations that questioned what had been said.

In 1983, the program, then called *The MacNeil/Lehrer Report*, saw its only major format change as it went from 30 minutes to a full hour. It added a news summary of major stories at the start and increased the number of in-depth stories from one to three or four, each running 10 to 15 minutes. Because the show airs on PBS, it currently has no interruptions (except during pledge drives). Mondays through Thursdays, the program often wraps up with a "reflective essay."

When Robert MacNeil retired in 1995, the show became *The NewsHour with Jim Lehrer*, and in 2006, acquired new graphics and a new version of the show's theme song, but otherwise stayed about the same. In 2009 PBS added rotating anchors and renamed the show *PBS NewsHour*. The most recent change, instituted in 2011, remains the most significant. After 36 years with PBS, Lehrer stepped down as a daily anchor of *PBS NewsHour*, electing instead to cover specific stories and to moderate the highly-popular Friday weekly analysis segment with Mark Shields and David Brooks.

PBS NewsHour is one of PBS's most successful programs, reaching over 8 million people during a week in the United States and averaging 2.7 million viewers each night. The program also airs in Australia, Japan and New Zealand and is broadcast by Voice of America and Armed Forces Radio. Keeping up with the PBS tradition of trying new technologies, the program has archived all broadcasts on the web since early 2000, and they can be accessed as streaming video. In addition, audio segments are also released in podcast form.

Strangely enough, on a network often criticized for its left-leaning shows and a tendency to slant the news, *PBS NewsHour* has been attacked for being too "mainstream" and for having a "pro-establishment bias." Several studies released by Fairness and Accuracy in Reporting, a "left-oriented" media watch group, have accused the show of being too balanced, of favoring Republicans and business, and of not having enough minorities. One of the group's major objections in 2006 was "not one peace activist" had appeared on the show during the six months analyzed. The 2011 critique took similar issue with the lack of diversity of viewpoint about the war in Libya, leaving "little room for antiwar voices" and critics of U.S. foreign policy.

The PBS Ombudsman, Michael Getler, agreed, saying: "These are perilous times. As a viewer and journalist, I find the program occasionally frustrating; sometimes too polite, too balanced when issues are not really balanced, and too many political and emotion-laden statements pass without factual challenges from the interviewer."* In this day and age, *PBS NewsHour* may have a unique distinction in being criticized for being too fair.

William J. Adams, Ph.D.
Kansas State University

---

*www.pbs.org/ombudsman/2006/10/a fair analysis.html.

extension agents formerly did in person. Fifty-five licensees currently make up the university group.

Here, too, programmers schedule a fairly broad range of programs, largely in HD as well as digital, often emphasizing adult continuing education and culture. Some, typically using student staff, produce nightly local newscasts, and many produce a weekly public-

affairs or cultural program. But these stations rarely produce major PBS series for the prime-time schedule, lacking both budget and permanent staffing. University-licensed stations such as WHA (Madison, Wisconsin) and KUHT (Houston, Texas) contribute occasional specials and single programs to the PBS schedule. WUNC-TV at the University of North Carolina in Chapel Hill produced *The Woodwright's Shop* series, and other university-licensed stations have supported short-run series aired in the daytime PBS schedule.

As operating costs mount and academic appropriations shrink, some university stations turn to over-the-air fundraising to supplement their institution's budgets. In doing so they use tactics similar to those of community stations, including airing programs specially produced for fundraisers. Expanded fundraising efforts are generally accompanied by broadening program appeal throughout the station's schedule, although the shows target a wide range of small, niche audiences.

Public School Licensees

Local school systems initially became licensees to provide new learning experiences for students in elementary school classrooms. From the outset, some schools augmented instructional broadcasts with other programming consistent with the school system's view of its educational mission. By 2008 only six of these school licensees remained. Most of them have organized a broadly-based community support group whose activities generate wider interest and voluntary contributions from the community at large. As a result, the average local-school licensee now draws only about 7 percent of its income from subscriber contributions.

Naturally, programmers at these stations are heavily involved with in-school programming—but because they desire community support, they are also concerned with programming for children out of school and for adults of all ages. All of these stations transmit a digital signal but, depending on station resources, may not yet have full HD production capability. Due to the significant costs of converting all studio, editing and field equipment to high definition, some stations still produce programs in standard definition and "upconvert" the video to HD.

Other than ITV series, most public school stations rarely produce original programs for PBS, and they obtain most of their schedules from national, state and regional suppliers of instructional programming. Of course, they usually carry such general (non-ITV) PBS educational children's programs as *Sesame Street*, too.

State Television Agencies

About 186 of the nation's 354 public television transmitters are part of state networks operated by legislatively created public broadcasting agencies. Networks of this type exist in 20 states (or did until New Jersey faded away). Most of them were authorized initially to provide new classroom experiences for the state's schoolchildren and have usually succeeded admirably in this task. Then they augment their ITV service with a variety of public-affairs and cultural programs furnished to citizens throughout their states, but rarely in HD.

State networks, such as those in South Carolina, Maryland, Kentucky, Nebraska and Iowa, are very active in the production and national distribution of educational programs. Their efforts range from traditional school programs for primary and secondary grades to graduate degree courses offered in regions where colleges and universities are few. These production efforts are thus counterparts to the national production centers of the community-based licensees. Although state networks hardly ever produce prime-time PBS series, they frequently join consortia generating specific programs for series such as *Great Performances*. Moreover, the Maryland Center for Public Broadcasting does produce the long-lived PBS series *Wall Street Week*.

Although in recent years these state network stations have gotten more foundation, underwriter and even viewer support, state legislatures still appropriate more than three-fifths of their budgets. This fact, plus the perception of their "community of service" as an entire state rather than a single city, gives programmers at these stations a different perspective ... and keeps them at risk as state budgets shrink.

Similarities and Differences

It should be quite evident from these brief descriptions that each category of public television station has distinctive problems and singular opportunities for programming. Each station type is ruled by a different type of board of directors—community leader boards, university trustees, local school boards, state-appointed central boards. Each board affects overall strategy and program personnel differently:

- Community representatives try to balance local power groups and foster underwriting.

- University boards, preoccupied with higher-education programs, tend to leave station professionals free to carry out their jobs within broad guidelines.

- School boards, similarly preoccupied with their major missions, may pay too little attention to their responsibilities as licensees.

- State boards try to protect their stations from inappropriate political influences and drastic budget cuts.

All licensees in both public TV and public radio struggle to function with what they regard as inadequate budgets, but there are wide funding discrepancies between the extremes of a large metropolitan community TV station and a small public-school radio station. Significantly, all types of stations have been forced to broaden their financial bases in recent years to keep up with rising costs and funding while improving program quality and quantity.

Licensees having the greatest success in securing new funding have, in general, made the strongest impact on national public television programming. In turn, successful public television producer-entrepreneurs working through their local stations are highly motivated to create new public television programs with broad audience appeal in the hope of securing still more underwriting. Such programs increase viewership and draw more support in the form of memberships and subscriptions.

Public-affairs programs and those of interest only to specialized smaller audiences—the "meat and potatoes" of public television—do not always appeal to corporations (who usually want to avoid controversy) and must be funded by CPB, PBS or foundations (see 10.9). Public radio operates differently but still shares some of the same problems (see 10.10).

Program Production

Early in its history, PBS developed a characteristic schedule of dramatic miniseries and anthologies; documentaries on topics in science, nature, public affairs and history; concert performances; and a few other types of programs, none of which ABC, CBS, FOX or NBC offers on a regular basis. PBS's marketplace position has thus historically been that of an alternative to the commercial networks. Today, however, several cable networks (including the Discovery Channel, A&E, the History Channel, The Learning Channel, the Food Channel, House & Garden) offer some programs similar to PBS's.

From time to time, some members of Congress—important critics because of CPB funding and grants: Congress supplies public television with about 16.4 percent of PBS's annual revenue—argue that PBS has become superfluous because it duplicates programming available on cable. The argument lacks merit because about 8 percent of U.S. TV households don't subscribe to either cable or satellite, while 99 percent can receive PBS. Moreover, fewer cable subscribers actually watch the cable networks that have PBS-like programs; PBS's ratings are two to four times larger.

Program Financing

How a program gets into the PBS schedule contrasts dramatically with the process at its commercial network counterparts. At ABC, CBS, FOX, NBC and most cable networks, program chiefs order the programs they want, pay for them out of a programming budget, then slot them into the schedule. To minimize ratings failures, the networks first pay for the production of pilot programs each year. Additional episodes of the most promising pilots are ordered, and each of these series receives a place in the schedule (see Chapter 2 for more details).

At PBS, however, program funding is far more complex. A program may have a single financial backer or several. More frequently than not, funding comes from a combination of sources, especially when the project runs into millions of dollars. PBS will partially fund and, on occasion, fully fund a

10.9 Corporation for Public Broadcasting

Although largely invisible to most people, the Corporation for Public Broadcasting is the largest single source of funding for public television and radio programming in the United States. This private nonprofit organization was established with the passage of the Public Broadcasting Act in 1967 to support and fund the development of educational, locally relevant and culturally diverse programs for public broadcasting. It created the Public Broadcasting Service (PBS) in 1969 and National Public Radio (NPR) in 1970. Most of CPB-funded programs are distributed through PBS, NPR, Television (APT) and Public Radio International (PRI).

Though it awards federal grants, CPB has a legal mandate to be nonpartisan and ensure objectivity on public programming. Yet controversies continue to plague CPB. In the mid-2000s, Democrats called for an investigation into whether CPB violated federal law when its former chairman Kenneth Y. Tomlinson, a Bush appointee, commissioned a review of several PBS and NPR programs in order to investigate liberal bias. Programs under review included the *Now With Bill Moyers* show, which had been criticized for being left-leaning. Tomlinson resigned in 2006 after investigations by CPB's inspector general revealed he "had made improper hires, had tried to tamper with PBS's TV programming and appeared to show political favoritism in selecting CPB's president while he was chairman."*

In 2011, the Republican-controlled U.S. House of Representatives passed a bill to ban government funding for NPR and affiliated public broadcasting stations. Conservatives claimed this would cut and control federal spending, but critics say it was in response to earlier fallouts with NPR. These notably include the firing of NPR news analyst Juan Williams

for remarks he made on Fox News Channel's *The O'Reilly Factor* (see 10.10) and a sting video showing NPR's then senior vice-president for fundraising Ron Schiller describing the Tea Party political movement as "xenophobic."

In the end, Congress spared the basic appropriation for CPB, which included $430 million annually for 2011 and 2012, plus another $445 million for 2013. CPB also retained $6 million for digital projects, which was the balance of a fund that had previously been set at $36 million a year. Journalist Steve Behrens reported that "the late night negotiations" also saved NPR from a Republican-led effort to ban federal funding for public radio.**

What did not survive in the budget deliberations was the 49-year-old Public Telecommunications Facilities Program, a $20-million line item in the Department of Commerce. This longstanding public broadcasting program had been used successfully for years by public broadcasters for start-up funds for new stations, to replace failing transmitters or to convert to HD. In 2010, even though more than 90 percent of the country was covered by both public TV and NPR, the facilities program awarded grants to 30 new public radio operations and one new PTV station.

Debbie Goh
Nanyang Technological University

---

*Paul Farhi, "Tomlinson Cited for Abuses at Broadcast Board: CPB Ex-Chief Puts Friend on Payroll, State Dept. Says." *Washington Post*, 22 January 2007, p. C1.

**Steve Behrens, "CPB Survives, But Not the Facilities Program," *Current*, 18 April 2011. http://www.current.org/federal/fed1108 ptfp.html.

---

project out of its station program assessment funds, but many programs must find their own backing. Of course, producers would prefer to walk away from PBS with a check for the full amount. But owing to PBS's limited purse, they must usually "shop" a project from one corporate headquarters to the next, perhaps even to foundations and CPB. Given the daunting process, producers have been heard to say that they spend more time chasing after dollars than making programs.

Program assessment fees, now levied on PBS member stations, were begun in the early 1990s. They represent public television's response to expanding cable network competition for the limited supply of programs to buy (see 10.11). Stations voted to streamline the program funding process so that newly offered productions could be snapped up without delays. The chief program executives now handle selected program funding as a centralized responsibility (in contrast to the long-beloved

10.10 Financing NPR

NPR's firing of analyst Juan Williams in October 2010 set off a firestorm by both the right and left, who variously charged that the radio network had denied Williams his right to speak. In an appearance on Fox Channel's *The O'Reilly Factor*, Williams said he got "worried" and "nervous" when he saw people in Muslim dress on airplanes. Maintaining that Williams' comments were inconsistent with NPR's editorial standards, Ellen Weiss, NPR Director of News, promptly called Williams and told him his contract was being terminated.

Even though NPR chief executive officer Vivian Schiller agreed that Williams' dismissal was appropriate, the termination evolved into a public relations nightmare for NPR. The radio network received more than 23,000 emails about the incident, almost all of them negative. Williams, a black man working in a largely white organization, was perceived by many conservatives as a target of liberal bias. Eventually, Weiss, a 30-year veteran of public radio, resigned her position. Ironically, Williams went to work for FOX, with an annual contract of $2 million.

Five months later, public radio suffered another embarrassing set-back, when a conservative sting video captured NPR's chief fundraiser disparaging Tea Party supporters as "seriously racist" and asserting that NPR would be better off without federal funding, "although some stations would go dark." Both Ron Schiller, vice-president for NPR's Foundation, and CEO Vivian Schiller (no relation to Ron Schiller) subsequently (and immediately) resigned amid questions about NPR's management and calls to de-fund the radio network.

Ultimately, both Williams' termination and the sting video had negative ramifications for both public television and NPR. Conservative media commentators and Republican lawmakers, in particular, used the incidents to claim that public broadcasting was partisan and undeserving of public funding. House Republicans passed a bill in March 2011 to ban government funding for NPR and affiliated public broadcasting stations, and though defeated at the eleventh hour, the budget bill posed a genuine threat to federal funding for public broadcasting. Several states—including New Jersey, Virginia and Florida—followed the lead of the House bill to implement deep cuts in their states' funding for public stations.

10.11 PBS Competing for Kids

Cross-platform initiatives are not restricted to the commercial networks. *PBSKIDSGO.org* introduced *Kids-World Sports*, a website based on an international documentary series that profiles kid-athletes who have the talent and drive to succeed in various sports. On the site, kids can watch short clips from the series, learn about different sports from videos featuring real kids, send video e-cards and compete in sport-related games.

News Flash Five, another PBS effort, is a current events website aimed at tweens aged 8–11. It features a cast of five kids, rendered in flash animation, who report on

national and world news, technology, entertainment, sports and weather. On the site, kids are able to play games such as Just the Facts (news quiz), Pin Point (finding places in the news on a map), Match It (connecting photos to newsmakers) and Get the Scoop (news gathering and writing). PBS's efforts match those of Nickelodeon, the top commercial channel for kids, and are far beyond the efforts of the broadcast networks.

Nancy C. Schwartz, Ph.D.
The Academic Edge, Inc.

notion that program decision making should be tightly controlled by public television's 168 station program managers—who usually had 168 opinions).

To form this fund, stations are assessed in proportion to their market size (and the loss of major-market member stations hurts badly here). Programs produced either wholly or in part from this fund carry an announcement crediting "viewers like you" because station money is involved—a large part of which comes from viewer contributions.

A program on PBS can—and usually does—have multiple producers. Typically, separate production units shoot film for partners in a coproduction deal, as when PBS joins with the BBC to produce a science or nature program. In such an arrangement, both have usage rights. Rather than share a program with a U.S. competitor, such as a cable network, public television prefers foreign coproduction over domestic coproduction.

The Major Producers

As already pointed out, a very large portion of PBS's schedule comes from series produced by or in conjunction with three major producing stations—WGBH in Boston, WNET in New York and WETA in Washington, DC. In most years, these producing stations account for well over half of PBS's new shows (see the list in 10.12). Other stations

10.12	**Major Producing Centers**
Stations	**Program Series**
WGBH, Boston	*American Experience*
	Antiques Roadshow
	Arthur
	Frontline
	Masterpiece
	Mystery!
	NOVA
	This Old House
WNET, New York	*American Masters*
	Charlie Rose
	Great Performances
	Live from Lincoln Center
	Metropolitan Opera Presents
	Nature
WETA, Washington, DC	*In Performance at the White House*
	PBS NewsHour
	Washington Week in Review

contribute an occasional series or special to the PBS schedule, but most local efforts either focus too narrowly on a topic to be of wide national interest or fall short of national standards for writing, talent and technical characteristics because they lack a sufficient budget. PBS seeks programs on a par with commercial efforts in terms of content and production quality.

British programs such as *Masterpiece* and *Mystery!* have become staples of U.S. public television because they are high-quality programs available at a small fraction of the cost of producing comparable fare in the United States. But they, along with other foreign productions, occupy only a fraction of all PBS airtime. Beside a mix of foreign producers, international coproductions, commercial independent producers and the three producing stations, such producing organizations as Sesame Workshop (formerly Children's Television Workshop) have traditional ties to PBS.

This pattern of multiple sources has been consistent over decades, although increased competition from cable networks for foreign programs has further squeezed PBS's options. The greatest change in programming in recent years has been the acquisition of funds by means of station program assessment, not in the actual program sources.

Balance in Selection

Responsibility for acquiring programs falls to one of several "content" managers, including the directors of Factual Programming, Fiction and Performance Programming, and Children's Programming. They must view sample tapes (demonstrations) and sift through many hundreds of proposals each year. Based on these written proposals or sample tapes (pilot episodes are very rarely made), the manager decides whether to purchase the program or provide some portion of production funding.

Happily, in the case of foreign productions, a program can be purchased ready for broadcast because it's already "in the can" (produced). If the decision on a proposal for a new production is favorable, a small research and development grant is usually the first step, perhaps with a promise of larger amounts to follow. Once production is under way, the content manager will consult with the producer during the production process to guide the outcome toward a mutually satisfactory result. It is important to note that, by law, *PBS can order programs to be produced, but it does not itself produce them.*

Through all this, National Program Service executives attempt to maintain balance in the national schedule so that the network doesn't find itself one season with, for example, too many symphony concerts and too few investigative documentaries in the schedule. To better regulate the flow of new productions into the national schedule, PBS established the Public Television Pipeline, a management system for monitoring and coordinating all program development activity from the proposal stage through delivery to PBS.

Throughout the year, the Pipeline sends signals to producers about PBS's overall schedule surpluses and shortfalls as well as specific content needs. Proposals are submitted and approval (and perhaps seed money) obtained from PBS, and the final selection process is under way. Pipeline 2011, published in *Current* in December 2010, included 140 projects scheduled for production within the public television system. A lot of juggling goes on to get something new in the Pipeline.

Corporate Pressure

Corporate underwriters of programs invest not only prodigious sums from corporate treasuries but also personal effort and reputation, and they feel entitled to choice slots in the prime-time schedule. Of course, PBS can't always fit a program in the time slot the underwriter wants and still maintain a balanced schedule.

Corporate fiscal needs can also affect scheduling. Often, the underwriting corporation requires that a program be played within its fiscal year—irrespective of audience and schedule needs. PBS program executives attempt to accommodate such cases, knowing that if they do not, the corporation in its pique may refuse future requests for support.

The major producing stations also attempt to influence program decisions at PBS on behalf of their program underwriters. For those stations, financial health depends on corporate support, which pays for salaries, equipment loans and other production expenses. Were just one major underwriter to withdraw support, the financial effect on a producing station could be devastating.

Station Pressure

Other programming pressures occur. Many stations, for example, *refuse* to telecast a program at the time fed because their programmers decide it

1. lacks prime-time quality.
2. contains too much profanity or violence to air in early evening.
3. occupies a slot the station wants for its own programs.
4. has little appeal for local viewers.

Although each of these reasons has merit at times, the combined effect of 168 station program managers exercising 168 independent judgments has often left portions of the PBS schedule in a shambles. PBS program executives assembling a schedule must anticipate these concerns to minimize defections.

Program Rights

PBS programmers must also wrestle with program rights. In public television as in commercial television, standard program air-lease rights are set by contract with the producer, who owns the rights. PBS has traditionally negotiated with producers for as many plays as possible so that by airing the same program several times, the typically small (per airing) PBS audience snowballs. Extra plays also fill out the program schedule.

At the same time, the program syndicator seeks as few airings as possible over the shortest time period to retain maximum control and resale potential for a program. A compromise between various producers and PBS that permits *four program plays within three years is now the standard rights agreement in public television.*

Syndicated and Local Programming

American Public Television (unrelated to American Public Media which is radio) licenses a large number of programs to PBS and public radio stations, programs such as British sitcoms; documentaries; travel, cooking and music programs; how-to series; and movies from Warner/Turner and 20th Century Fox (for a more complete listing, see *www.aptonline.org*). This company is a significant player in public television programming and a prime source of entertainment programs for public stations.

In addition, because of its role in formal education, public television has had to develop its own unique body of syndicated material to meet instructional television needs. A number of centers for program distribution have been established to perform the same function as commercial syndication firms, but on a noncommercial, cooperative basis (see 10.13 for more on these centers).

Noncommercial Syndication

The abundance of ITV materials means that it is no longer necessary to produce instructional programs locally, except where desired subject matter is unique to a community. Local school authorities are usually in charge of selecting instructional materials for in-school use, although the public television station's staff often serves as liaison between sources of this material and users. In addition, the state may appropriate funds for instructional programs, giving them to its public stations, or school districts may contract with a local public station to supply particular ITV programs at certain times.

Noncommercial Adult Education

Quality programming for adult learners is also now available in quantity to public stations. Beginning in the late 1970s, various consortia began to turn out *telecourses* (television courses) for integration into the curricula of postsecondary institutions. These efforts have centered particularly in community

---

10.13 **Noncommercial Syndicators**

The Agency for Instructional Technology (AIT) in Bloomington, Indiana, produces series for primary grades, high school and postsecondary students. Among the best known are *All About You, Math Works, Assignment: The World* and *Up Close and Natural*. AIT took the lead in developing innovative classroom programs that operate in conjunction with desktop computers, creating the first interactive lessons on DVD.

Great Plains National (GPN) in Lincoln, Nebraska, offers dozens of series for elementary and junior high use along with a great many materials for college and adult learning. Titles in its catalog range from *Reading Rainbow* (for first graders) to *The Power of Algebra, Tombs and Talismans* and *Truly American* (for high schoolers and adults).

Western Instructional Television (WIT) in Los Angeles offers more than 500 series in science, language arts, social studies, English, art and history. TV Ontario also supplies U.S. schools with dozens of instructions series,

especially in science and technology, including *Read All About It, The Landscape of Geometry* and *Magic Library*. Even PBS, through its Elementary/Secondary Service, offers a slate of ITV programs, such as *The Voyage of the Mimi, Amigos* and *Futures with Jaime Escalante*.

These not-for-profit companies fund their operations in a variety of ways, including leasing programming they own to stations and PBS for broadcast, selling DVDs to the general public, and acquiring contracts from private foundations and state and national agencies. For example, in 2011 AIT (for the fifth year) secured the fulfillment contract for Jumpstart's "Read for the Record" campaign. This national program, funded in part by the Pearson Foundation, was an effort to close the early achievement gap for some children living in lower economic environments. Similarly, AIT has partnered for years with the Kettering Foundation and local and state organizations dedicated to literacy and childhood education.

colleges, led by Miami-Dade (Florida), Dallas (Texas), Coastline Community College (Huntington Beach, California) and the Southern California Consortium. With budgets ranging from $100,000 to $1 million for a single course, they have proven to be sufficiently well produced to attract casual viewers as well as enrolled students.

Meanwhile, faculty members at other leading postsecondary institutions began developing curriculum materials to accompany several outstanding public television program series distributed nationally through PBS for general viewing. The first of these was *The Ascent of Man*, with the late Dr. Jacob Bronowski, a renowned scholar as well as a skillful and effective communicator on camera. More than 200 colleges and universities offered college credit for that course. Others quickly followed (*The Adams Chronicles, Cosmos, Life on Earth, The Shakespeare Plays*) as programmers discovered that such series furnished the casual viewer with attractive public television entertainment and simultaneously served more serious viewers desiring to register for college course credits.

This experience led many public television programmers to realize that too much had been made of the supposed demarcation between ITV and PTV. Too often during earlier years, many program producers would not even consider producing so-called instructional television. The first Carnegie Commission in 1965 strengthened this presumed gap by not concerning itself with television's educational assistance to schools and colleges and by adopting the term *public television* to mean programming for general viewing. The narrowing of the distance between instructional and general interest programming has been highlighted by the broad use of such public TV documentaries as *Baseball* and *The Civil War* by Ken Burns in the classroom setting (see 10.14).

The lesson for public television has been that ITV and PTV programs can appeal to viewers other than those for which they were especially intended. The Annenberg/CPB series is only one example. Another is *Sesame Street*, which was initially intended for youngsters in disadvantaged households—yet the in-school use of *Sesame Street* has been one of the significant occurrences in kindergarten and lower elementary classrooms throughout America, leading to new and more complex attitudes toward television in and out of the classroom (see 10.15). Ironically, *Sesame Street* may also contribute to the gap in knowledge between advantaged and disadvantaged children because it is widely watched (and learned from) by already advantaged children, perhaps making the disadvantaged more disadvantaged.

Commercial Syndication

More extensively tapped than noncommercial sources, however, are such commercial syndicators as Time-Life, David Susskind's Talent Associates, Wolper Productions, Granada TV in Great Britain, and several major motion picture companies including Universal Pictures. Public television stations sometimes negotiate individually for program packages with such syndicators; alternatively, they can join with the public stations through regional associations to make group buys.

Commercially syndicated programs obtained in this way by PTV include historical and contemporary documentaries, British-produced drama series and packages of highly popular or artistic motion pictures originally released to theaters. Such programming, because it was designed for general audiences, is thought to bring new viewers to a public station. Many programmers believe those new viewers can then be persuaded, through promotional announcements, to watch more typical PTV fare (and maybe, just maybe, become members).

The proportion of commercially syndicated programs in public television station schedules, nonetheless, averages less than 5 percent of broadcast hours. The number stays small partly because those syndicated programs that public stations find appropriate are relatively *expensive;* unless the station secures outside underwriting to cover license fees, it usually can't afford them. Stations now pay as much as $100,000 for an hour of British television that cost as little as $50,000 a few years ago. Another reason is *philosophical:* Although much commercially syndicated material has strong audience appeal, its educational or cultural value is arguable.

10.14 **Ken Burns and PBS: A Match Made in Broadcasting Heaven?**

There is probably no single person more closely identified with the Public Broadcasting System than Ken Burns. Hailed for over 30 years as the most prolific, most influential, and most awarded documentary filmmaker in the United States, Burns has produced virtually all of his groundbreaking films with and for PBS. And while some of his earliest pictures were produced for theatrical release, it's PBS that made Burns who he is, and he's returned the favor many times over.

Burns is best known for his epic PBS documentary mini-series *The Civil War* (1990), *Baseball* (1994 and 2010) and *Jazz* (2001), all of which were nominated for—and in the cases of *The Civil War* and *Baseball*, winners of— multiple Emmy awards. But Burns's vast filmography also includes docs on topics as diverse as the U.S. park system (*The National Parks: America's Best Idea*, 2009), women's suffrage (*Not for Ourselves Alone: The Story of Elizabeth Cady Stanton and Susan B. Anthony*, 1999), American landmarks (*The Statue of Liberty*, 1985), and individuals as different as Huey Long (1985), Thomas Jefferson (1997), Frank Lloyd Wright (1998) and the first black heavyweight boxing champion (*Unforgivable Blackness: The Rise and Fall of Jack Johnson*, 2004). These and Burns's other acclaimed films skillfully interweave archival still and motion photography, period music, interviews with experts and voice-over narration by respected actors and historians to create what has become a trademark Ken Burns look and feel.

Like many documentarians, Burns plays a variety of simultaneous roles in the production of his films, serving as not only director but also, almost always, as producer, writer, cinematographer and even music composer. For his troubles, he's taken home a slew of Emmys and two Oscar nominations and has been a nominee or winner of awards bestowed by organizations as diverse as the Directors Guild of America, the International Documentary Association, the Sundance Film Festival, the George Eastman House Museum of Photography and Film, the Western Writers of America and the Organization of American Historians.

But perhaps the honor (if it can be called that) most closely associated with Mr. Burns in the minds of filmmakers and editors is as the inspiration for the so-called Ken Burns Effect, a panning and zooming technique that can be found in just about every one of Burns' films as well as those of documentarians he's inspired. (Burns didn't invent the technique, but he's used it so often and so consistently that, for better or worse, it's come to bear his name.) Since Burns in his PBS documentaries uses so many still images—archival photos mostly, but also paintings, illustrations and clippings from old newspapers and other stationary two-dimensional visual materials— he's found that he can bring his movies to life by, for example, having his camera zoom in on one individual in a photo, then panning across the width of the picture

Local Production

The percentage of airtime filled with locally produced programming has gradually decreased over the years as both network and syndicated programming have increased in quantity and quality. Owing mostly to its high cost, the percentage of total on-air hours produced solely *for local use* by public television stations had declined from 16 percent in 1972 to much less than 5 percent by the mid-2000s. Moreover, production quality expectations have risen. More time and dollars and better facilities must now be used to produce effective local programs.

Locally produced programs, nonetheless, are far from extinct in public television. A survey of station producers found that, among the 79 licensees responding, more than 3,000 programs had been produced during the past year. Among them were weekly and occasional nightly broadcasts devoted to activities, events and issues of local interest and significance.

Also, many stations regularly cover their state governments and legislators. Unlike commercial stations, which concentrate on spot news and devote a minute or less to each story, public stations see their role as giving more comprehensive treatment to local matters. But news and public-affairs programs aren't the only kinds being produced. The survey found stations turning out a spectrum of arts and performance, documentaries, sports events and sports talk, before coming to rest on the face of another person in the photo, and then zooming in on or out from that second person.

The popularity of Burns' films has been a boon for PBS. In fact, the initial (1990) airing of the 11-hour *Civil War* mini-series attracted more than 40 million viewers, a public television ratings record that still stands some two decades later. (The PBS network and its member stations, recognizing the continuing appeal of *The Civil War*, repeatedly trot it out during fundraising drives.) Because Burns' work is so well respected—and is such a reliable audience draw—in 2008 the Corporation for Public Broadcasting committed to a 10-year agreement with Burns and his production company, Florentine Films. Under the agreement, CPB provided funding for the development of new Burns projects, including *Prohibition* (2011) as well as *Vietnam* (targeted for 2016), biographies of the Roosevelts (Teddy, Franklin and Eleanor) and a look at the history of country music.

Given the continual threats of budget reduction and even elimination that public broadcasting perennially faces, the fact that the CPB has made such a long-term commitment to the development of new Ken Burns films is encouraging. Indeed, Burns himself is all too familiar with funding problems; in 2009, his long-term supporter General Motors publicly announced that it would no longer be able to underwrite Burns' work. (GM, of course, is far from the only major corporation to cut back on its financial support for PBS and its programs.)

Indeed, the threats to public broadcasting—and, as a result, to the continued viability of his own career—thrust Burns into the political spotlight in early 2011. As Congress yet again debated the desirability of funding PBS during a recession, Burns wrote an op-ed piece for the *Washington Post* entitled "Public Broadcasting: A 'Luxury' We Can't Do Without." In his article, Burns defended the quality of PBS's work, contrasting it with the content of commercial broadcasting. "With minimal funding," Burns wrote, "PBS manages to produce essential (commercial-free) children's programming as well as the best science and nature, arts and performance, and public affairs and history programming on the dial— often a stark contrast to superficial, repetitive and mind-numbing programming elsewhere." Burns not only stood up for PBS's mission; he also unambiguously gave public television credit for the existence and success of his own work: "Many say that what can't survive in the marketplace doesn't deserve to survive. Not one of my documentaries, produced solely for PBS over the past 30 years, could have been made anywhere but on public broadcasting."

Davis Weiss, Ph.D.
Montana State University Billings

history, comedy, science, nature and even (surprise) original children's programs.

Scheduling Strategies

Nowadays, PBS programmers want to maximize audiences. Gone are the educational television days when paying attention to audience size was sneered at in public television. The prevailing attitude at PBS recognizes that a program must be *seen* to be of value and that improper scheduling prevents full realization of a program's potential. Member stations now recognize that bigger audiences also mean a bigger dollar take during on-air pledge drives.

Counterprogramming the Commercial Networks

Competition, of course, is a key consideration. There are three ways to respond to it:

1. Offensively, by attempting to overpower the competitor
2. Defensively, by counterprogramming for a different segment of the audience than the competitor's program is likely to attract
3. By ignoring the competition altogether and hoping for the best

PBS has never been able to go on the offensive; its programs lack the requisite breadth of appeal.

10.15 Remembering *Sesame Street*

Generations of preschoolers, probably including you, learned the alphabet—and a whole lot more—from watching the Muppets. *Sesame Street* premiered in 1969 on National Education Television Network, now called the Public Broadcasting Service. After 43 seasons and nearly 4,500 episodes, it's one of the longest-running shows in television history. Created by Jim Henson, *Sesame Street* is probably the most respected educational program in the world.

The original U.S.-produced show currently airs in 120 countries, and more than 20 international versions are produced in such countries as Brazil, Mexico, France, Turkey, China and Russia. More than 77 million Americans watched *Sesame Street* as children, as well as millions more worldwide. One survey reported that 95 percent of all American children watched *Sesame Street* by the time they were 3 years old, and based on Nielsen ratings, the show continues to appear among the top 15 children's programs on television.

Sesame Street teaches letters and numbers, as well as basic word recognition, mathematics and science, but its goals include basic social skills. *Sesame Street* has worked toward teaching children about how to make friends, practice good hygiene and eat healthfully. Known for its rigorous ongoing research, the program's overall curriculum has changed over time to reflect the problems of growing up in America. At the same time, using witty humor and fast pacing, the show tries to appeal to parents and older siblings as well as preschool children.

While the elaborate hand-held puppets called the Muppets are central to *Sesame Street*'s broad appeal, its live actors keep the show grounded, and the program has led the way in portrayals of minorities on television. The program has been praised for its multicultural cast, as well as for the actors' overall longevity. *Sesame Street* boasts the longest-running Hispanic character in the history of television (Luis) as well as the longest-running character with a disability (Linda, who is deaf) and what are believed to be the longest running African-American characters (Gordon and Susan).

The changing relationships among the people who act the characters also get incorporated into the program. For example, Luis married Maria, the owner of *Sesame Street*'s Fix-It-Shop, and Maria later gave birth to Gabby; Maria's pregnancy became part of the show's storyline. Gordon and Susan's story included the adoption of their son Miles. When original cast member Will Lee, who had played store owner Mr. Hooper, died, producers chose to include the death of Mr. Hooper into *Sesame Street*'s story. The producers believed that the inclusion of Mr. Hooper's death would educate children about the death of a loved one.

By the late-1990s *Sesame Street*'s producers had come to the realization that the modern child had different viewing habits than the child of the past. At the same time, the explosion of more programming—on cable television, on the internet and on DVDs—led to an increased level of competition for *Sesame Street* and wee-bit-of-a-drop (!) in the ratings, so the producers took steps to make structural changes. First was the inclusion of *Elmo's World* as a miniseries during the final fifteen minutes of every episode of *Sesame Street*. This segment follows the adventures of *Sesame Street*'s most popular Muppet monster, 3½ year old Elmo. In the early 2000s, *Sesame Street* began including more narrative and more storylines in its modular episodes.

The popularity of the Muppet characters and the show's overall success turned *Sesame Street* into one of the earliest and most enduring multiplatform brand names. It may also deserve an award for being the most studied program in history: Decades of scholars have poured over it, trying to assess its influence and efficacy. Comic writer Michael Davis has been quoted as saying: "Sesame Street [is] perhaps the most vigorously researched, vetted, and fretted-over program on the planet. It would take a fork-lift to now haul away the load of scholarly paper devoted to the series…"*

In addition to its 118 Emmy award wins (more than any other series in the entire history of television), including a Lifetime Achievement Emmy in 2009, the show has won 11 Grammys, has its own theme park (Sesame Place), publishes magazines on five continents and generates movies, toys, books, DVDs and video games. The clever use of Muppets, animation, music and live actors in brief modular segments results in a broad-appeal program capturing the imagination of millions of children while involving them and their parents in the learning process.

James Angelini, Ph.D.
University of Delaware

---

*Davis, Michael. *Street Gang: The Complete History of Sesame Street*. New York: Viking Books, 2008.

Prime-time PBS shows average around a 1.2 household rating. ABC, CBS, FOX and NBC regularly collect ratings of 4.5–6 (although their figures are much smaller than a decade ago—the result of audience defections to the many cable networks and online services).

PBS, then, must duck and dodge, a strategy called *counterprogramming*. By studying national Nielsen data, programmers learn the demographic makeup of competing network program audiences so they can place their own programs more advantageously. For example, a symphony performance that tends to attract well-educated women older than 50 (*upscale* in socioeconomics) living in metropolitan areas would perform well opposite FOX's *The Simpsons*, NBC's *Deal or No Deal*, or CW's *WWE Friday Night Smackdown!*, all having *downscale* (lower socioeconomic) audiences. Similarly, in searching for a slot for the investigative documentary series *Frontline*, PBS did not consider for a moment the 8 to 9 P.M. slot on Sundays because football overruns often push 60 *Minutes* into this slot.

PBS tries to avoid placing a valued program against a hit series in the commercial schedules, although there aren't enough such slots. The network also has traditionally avoided placing important programs during the three key periods of all-market audience measurement (sweeps) in November, February and May—times when commercial television throws its blockbusters at the audience.

But because the commercial networks have cut back on sweeps blockbusters in recent years (especially costume-drama miniseries, which lure away many PBS viewers), PBS has grown more willing to run an important series through a sweeps month. This is clearly a calculated risk, a kind of TV "minefield"; a powerful commercial network special could draw off so many viewers from a weekly PBS miniseries that few would return to see its continuation and concluding episode.

Further, because public as well as commercial stations are measured during the sweeps, PBS's stations demand a "solid" schedule, with a minimum of "mission programs." This is a mildly pejorative reference to public television's mission to serve all Americans, specifically referring here to narrow-appeal programs of interest only to some very small groups of viewers. Many programs are "good for the mission" but earn small ratings. Thus, during the sweeps, PBS now displays many of its strongest—not weakest—programs.

By the mid-2000s the top programmers at PBS had decided to stop using ratings as a "rear-view mirror" and had begun to state goals for their programs, using a formal process that judges prime-time programs according to predetermined goals. Some stations continue to be nervous about the transition to objective standards, preferring to balance critical acclaim and awards against audience size. Nevertheless, PBS must be accountable to an ever-shrinking number of underwriters who want their programs to be seen, really seen.

Stripping and Stacking Limited Series

A standard among PBS's offerings, the *limited series* includes both nonfiction and fictional miniseries (as explained in Chapter 2, limited series have continuing topics with a fixed number of episodes, usually ranging from 3 to 12 or more). Some notable examples in recent years include *Texas Ranch House; Jean-Michel Cousteau: Ocean Adventures; African-American Lives;* and Ken Burns' *The War*. Most limited series appear once a week in prime time, much as weekly series are scheduled on commercial television.

Because short-run series lose viewers across the first few weekly telecasts, however, PBS schedulers have experimented with alternative play patterns in the hope of staunching the dropoff. Borrowing jargon from computer technology, they asked whether limited series scheduling could be made more "user friendly." Experiments with the *Holocaust* series and *Shoah* in 1988 showed that limited series that have sufficiently engaging material lend themselves to airing on consecutive nights, a practice known in commercial television as *stripping*. This ploy not only attracted at least as many viewers as tuned in to similar programs on a weekly basis but also encouraged viewers to spend significantly more time watching the series. Moreover, the episode-to-episode ratings dropoff disappeared.

Which limited series receive special treatment and which must air in the usual once-a-week way has hinged on a decision about what "sufficiently engaging material" means. This is in part a function of production budget, advance promotion, casting, subject matter and less well-recognized variables such as timing, quality and appeal to the public television audience. Such decisions cannot be supported by audience research alone; the programs must be screened (watched) as well. Ultimately, the chief program executive now makes the call.

When a limited series has too many episodes for convenient stripping, PBS bunches episodes together, *stacking* two episodes per evening. Ken Burns's epic on World War II, *The War*, for example, was scheduled in this pattern, thereby limiting the magnitude of nightly commitment on the part of viewers. PBS's practice is to schedule limited series on a maximum of five consecutive nights (although *The War* required seven evenings).

Audience Flow

Certain PBS series are especially dependent on audience flow from a strong lead-in. New, untried programs especially need scheduling help. *The Ring of Truth*, a six-part series on the scientific method, for example, was not expected to build a loyal following the way a predictable series such as *Washington Week in Review* has. Thus it was placed following an established, successful science series, *NOVA*, which regularly draws large audiences (large, that is, for public television) and itself has no need of a powerful lead-in.

Particularly in need of a lead-in boost—on a regular basis—is another PBS staple, the *umbrella series*. These are anthologies of single programs with loosely related content that appear under an all-encompassing title (or umbrella) such as *American Experience* (history programs) or *Great Performances* (ballet, plays, operas, orchestral music, Broadway shows and so forth). Because the material offered under the umbrella changes from week to week, the audience never knows what to expect. Clearly, the format works *against* habit formation. Thus, it is essential that a strong audience be introduced to each week's episode, if not by costly media advertising (usually out of public television's reach), then by a substantial lead-in.

Considerations at the Station Level

A public television program schedule is notable for its variety; it is meant to serve the total population over time but not the complete needs of the individual viewer. Although this is also true of commercial stations, it especially applies to public television schedules. Because they usually are so focused in content, PTV programs tend to be watched by small, often demographically-targeted population segments. Seeking the most opportune time slot for reaching those target groups is the local program manager's challenge.

No U.S. PTV programmer ever builds an entire schedule from scratch nowadays. Rather, the manager's ongoing responsibility is to maintain a schedule while considering the following factors:

1. Licensee type, as each carries its unique program priorities

2. Audience size and demographics

3. Competition from commercial stations, other public television signals and cable networks

4. Daypart targeting, such as daytime for children's programs and instructional services, and early evenings for older adults

5. Program availability

No single element overrides the others, but each affects the final schedule. Public television programmers seek programs that meet local audience needs and schedule those programs at times most likely to attract the target audience. Because all audience segments cannot be served at once, the mystery and magic of the job is getting the right programs in the right time slots. High ratings are not the primary objective; serving the appropriate audience with a show they will watch that adds to the quality of their life, is.

National Promotion

Still another consideration is the importance of national promotion. Fledgling programs and episodes of an umbrella series need extra help for viewers to discover them. Although an effective lead-in program is essential, advertising and promotion can alert other potential viewers to a new program and persuade them to try it. Unfortunately, public television budgets permit little advertising, sometimes none. Sadly, only a few underwriters include some promotional allotment in their program budgets.

Still another PBS practice is to carefully schedule on-air promotion announcements for a particular program in time slots where potential viewers of that program (based on demographic profiles) are likely to be found in maximum quantity. Such on-air promotion is crucial because it reaches known viewers of public television, but its effectiveness is somewhat hampered by public television's limited prime-time reach. In one week, a massive on-air campaign promoting one program could hope to reach at best only 20 to 25 percent of all television households, and far fewer would actually watch.

Audience Ratings

Public television must constantly demonstrate its *utility*. Many have contributed to its continuance— Congress, underwriters, viewers. If few watch, why should contributors keep public television alive? Programmers have come to realize that critical praise alone is insufficient; they need tangible evidence that audiences feel the same way. That most convincing evidence comes from acceptable ratings.

Nielsen Data

PBS evaluates the performance of its programs with both national and local viewing data, each having its own particular usefulness in analysis. National audience data are provided by the Nielsen People-Meter service (NPM), and the Nielsen Station Index (NSI) provides the individual market data. In the past, PBS's limited research budget permitted the purchase of only *one* national audience survey week *per month*. Forty weeks therefore went unmeasured. (The commercial networks, as described in previous chapters, purchase continuous, year-round national data.) Even though restricted, NSI's Metered Market Service provided PBS with a comparatively inexpensive proxy for daily national ratings because 66 percent of the

country's TV households were within measured markets.

Beginning in 2010, however, PBS finally began a fulltime ratings subscription with Nielsen. The subscription has provided ongoing and detailed viewer information about such programs as *Frontline*, *Antiques Roadshow*, *Masterpiece*, *NOVA* and even *Sesame Street*. PBS apparently moved to more frequent and in-depth information about its viewers to supply more and better data to corporate underwriters (as well as help PBS programming).

Commercial network programmers, to the irritation of advertising time-buyers, have traditionally inflated affiliates' ratings by *stunting* with unusually popular specials and miniseries during the sweeps weeks. These higher ratings provide the local affiliates with an opportunity to raise advertising rates. PBS programmers schedule some new programs during sweeps but rarely stunt for an entire four-week period. PBS does, however, try to schedule a *representative mix* of PBS offerings during each of the national survey weeks. No more than one opera is permitted, for example, nor are too many esoteric public-affairs programs scheduled during that week.

Not being entirely "holier than thou," PBS does practice some stunting during its pledge drives. Just as networks stunt for economic reasons, so too does public television. The difference is structural: Rather than raise revenue by selling advertising time on the basis of ratings, PBS stations raise revenue by direct, on-air solicitation of viewer contributions. Programs specially produced for the drives are scheduled alongside regular PBS series. To an extent, larger audiences mean larger contributions, but a low-rated program may find a small but appreciative audience and prove a lucrative fundraiser. At the same time, high ratings (relative to the whole schedule) have considerable appeal to uncommitted funding agencies and potential underwriters.

Audience Accumulation Strategy

PBS strives for maximum variety in its program schedule to serve as many people as possible at one time or another each week. Unlike commercial network programs, not all public television programs are expected to have large audiences. *Small audiences are usually acceptable so long as the weekly accumulation of viewers is large, an indication that the "public" is using its public television service.* And so, an important element in assessing PBS's programming success is its weekly cumulative audience, or *cume.* This statistic, along with *time-spent-viewing,* comprises the two basic elements of audience data.

The most important data come from the cumes. Nielsen defines a cumulative household audience as the percentage of all U.S. TV households (unduplicated) that have tuned in for at least six minutes to a specific program or time period. (Six minutes is a minimum figure, the "ticket" for admission into the cume. Even if the viewer watches for 50 minutes, or leaves and rejoins the audience five or six times during a telecast, that person is still counted only once in the cume, provided the six-minute minimum has been met.)

A more typical statistic for public television than cumes are *average audience ratings.* For the major ongoing series in 2010, the composite average ratings were as follows: nature and science programs, 2.3 rating; dramas, 1.8; musical performances, 1.1; news and public affairs, 1.2. Based on prior experience, PBS programmers apply informal guidelines for what rating levels constitute adequate viewing. Because ratings are not the sole criterion by which PBS program performance is evaluated, however, failure to meet predicted levels never triggers a cancellation. Repeated failure to earn the minimum expected cumes, though, could eventually result in nonrenewal.

Loyalty Assessment

PBS researchers also study *audience loyalty* (tenacity) as a way to evaluate a program, something commercial entities pay little attention to. Using ratings from Nielsen's metered markets, it is possible to plot an audience's course across a single program or across an entire multiweek series. If the audience tires quickly of a program, the overnight ratings will slip downward during the telecast (a fate to which lengthy programs are especially susceptible). If the audience has weakened in response to the

appeal of competing network programs—such as when a special starts a half hour after a PBS show—the overnight ratings will suddenly drop at the point where the competing special began.

This information tells the programmers (roughly, to be sure) the extent to which their program has engaged viewers. Noncompelling programs are vulnerable to competition. Shows failing this test have to be scheduled more carefully when repeated, preferably opposite softer network competition (like in the middle of the night).

The National People-Meter Service, in addition to TV ratings and cumes, provides a different but equally valuable analytical statistic: the number of minutes spent by people (or households) viewing a single program or even a whole multi-episode series. This time-spent-viewing figure reveals how *much* of a production was actually watched, in contrast to the cume, which simply tells how *many* watched. As mentioned previously, some miniseries earn higher time-spent-viewing figures when stripped on consecutive nights than when scheduled weekly.

Demographic Composition

Another useful way to evaluate a program is by observing exactly who is watching. If a program is designed for the elderly, did the elderly in fact tune in? When African-Americans were the goal, did sufficient numbers switch on the program? Although households tuning to public television each week are, as a group, not unlike television viewers generally, audiences for individual programs can vary widely in demographic composition. Programs such as *NOVA* and *Masterpiece* attract older, college-educated, professional/managerial viewers because these programs can be intellectually demanding. Demanding shows are numerous on PBS, thus its cumulative prime-time audience composition reflects this tendency. Many programs, though, have broader-based followings, among them *Nature* and *This Old House.*

PBS's evening programs have also been found to have an age skew (tendency) favoring adults 35 years of age or older. Few young adults, teenagers or children watch in prime time. The reason for this skew probably lies in the nature of the evening schedule, which, despite the occasional light entertainment special, consists largely of nonfiction documentaries. According to CBS's top research executive:

> *Our analysis shows that over age 35, you get an adult programming taste. Under age 35, you still have a youth orientation. It is only when people reach their mid-30s that their viewing tastes become more like older adults'.... And their appetite grows for news and information programming.*[8]

Still, public television's overall (24-hour-a-day) cumulative audience demographically mirrors the general population on such characteristics as education, income, occupation and racial composition. That is partly because it is a large audience, with more than half of all U.S. TV households tuning to public television each week and about four-fifths tuning in monthly. Another reason for PBS's broad profile is that the overall audience includes the viewers of daytime children's and how-to (hobbies and crafts) programs, many of whom are not frequent users of the prime-time schedule.

Public television representatives frequently are called upon to explain a seeming paradox: How can public television's audience duplicate the demographic makeup of the country when so many of its programs attract the *upscale* viewer? The question is second in importance only to that of how many people are watching; it is often tied to charges of elitism in program acquisition, implying that PBS is not serving all the public with "public" television.

PBS replies that it consciously attempts to provide *alternatives* to the commercial network offerings; to do so, the content of most PBS programs must make demands of viewers. Demanding programs, however, tend to have less appeal to viewers of lower socioeconomic status (as well as to younger viewers). The result is *underrepresentation* of such viewers in certain audiences. This underrepresentation is, however, on balance, only slight and limited largely to prime time, being offset in the week's cumulative audience totals for other programs having broader appeal.

Critics often overlook the fact that underrepresentation does not mean no representation. *NOVA*, for example, is watched each week in some 900,000 households headed by a person who never finished high school. Even operas average nearly 300,000 such downscale households in their audiences.

Audience statistics serve a unique function: *justification of public television.* Commercial broadcasters and cable operators justify their existence when they turn a profit for their owners and investors; public broadcasters prove their worth when survey data indicate the public *valued* (that is, viewed) the service provided.

Developments Ahead

Some people in the noncommercial field believe the public television station of today will become the public telecommunications center of tomorrow—a place where telecommunications professionals handle the production, acquisition, reception, duplication and delivery of all types of noncommercial educational, cultural and informational materials in all kinds of media and stand ready to advise and counsel people in the community. In this scenario, existing public television stations will transmit, stream or podcast programs of broad interest and value to relatively large audiences scattered throughout their coverage areas; and they will also feed these and other programs to local cable channels and transfer programs of more specialized interest via the internet for use in schools, colleges, libraries, hospitals, industry settings or in use on homes.

Clearly this is a view that has vision and purpose. It describes a project that could excite Americans and provide genuine informational service for a range of populations. Currently, however, little political or industry will exists to take on such an ambitious project. Rather, public broadcasters will continue to struggle to "keep up" with the industry's digital advancements and to maintain the status quo in corporate, member, foundation and governmental support.

In coming years, emphasis will likely be placed on maintaining most of public television as it is, rather than expanding stations into centers of large public telecommunications complexes. To this end, we will likely see limited growth—probably even more shrinking in overlapping markets—of the quantity of noncommercial television stations, even in areas of minority broadcasting (think Alaska, Indian concentrations, islands, as well as under-served rural areas). Analysts also predict that more stations will either close or separate from PBS in the coming decade. Public television, they suggest, is "overbuilt," characterized by a redundancy that seemed helpful in past years when individual stations provided just a single stream of programming and the internet wasn't a part of television viewing. With the loss of funding provided by the Public Telecommunications Facilities Program (see 10.9), fewer avenues will exist for funding upgrades, making digital catch-up the main focus of effort. And finally, industry insiders look to increased commercialization of the entire system, as stations seek out new ways to fund existing services.

The coming years, then, will pose multiple challenges (a polite word for threats) to those who hold public television licenses across the country. Even as these dilemmas surface, however, public broadcasters are expected to embrace HD, online, on demand and eventually 3D, seeking ways to extend their stations' public services for PBS audiences. As the digital age advances, at least the major public broadcasters will be able to offer even more streams of programming through multiple digital platforms, squeezing smaller stations that cannot follow suit. Nonetheless, an increased amount of content will be provided on-demand; and stations will be encouraged to follow the lead of WNET-New York and Spanish-language channel V-me in offering specialized services for specific populations.

In order for public broadcasting to achieve its public service potential and move beyond the limitations imposed by broadcast towers, the social value of noncommercial, educational video service must be continually reaffirmed by policymakers, public broadcasters and the American public. Public television cannot advance into the new media environment of the mid-twenty-first century without such affirmation. *The public service, and particularly the educational value of this institution, is founded on the principle that a certain portion of the public's airwaves should be reserved for noncommercial, educational use.*

Public financing was a key element of that founding assumption, and billions of dollars have been invested in making public television available to the entire nation. To continue as the national resource that it has become in broadcasting, *public television must further extend its mandate to additional media technologies.* The educational, informational and cultural functions of public television are certain to play a key role in achieving that objective (see 10.16).

A renewed focus on its educational mission will guide PBS's program selection and fundraising efforts in the future. One of its successes, *Arthur*, targets school-age children on weekday and Sunday mornings and is the most watched children's program in all of television, among young children. PBS usually has six of the top-10 preschool programs on U.S. television, including *Barney and Friends, Dragon Tales, Teletubbies* and others.

On the other side, public television is seeking wide-appeal programs, much like commercial networks, that can attract underwriting. One such effort was *Slavery and the Making of America*, a four-part documentary produced by WNET in New York, which was underwritten almost entirely by the New York Life Insurance Company. These programs may signal directions for the future. As with all broadcasters, however, the operative strategy for public networks and stations is *alternative means of program distribution* via the internet, mobile media, and interactive CD- and DVD-ROM.

By 2020, PTV will still be around but may be a smaller collective force on the national and local scenes because it faces daunting competition for product and funds. On the hopeful side, additional digital and online channels along with exciting program ideas, coupled with digital compression and HD pictures, may revitalize the noncommercial television industry. You never know. In the late seventies, PBS President Hartford Gunn advocated three network services for public television, each targeting different audiences and purposes. Video technology—with digital compression capabilities

10.16 KUED's Digital Asset Management—A Case Study

As early as the mid-1990s, former PBS president Bruce Christensen was advancing a compelling argument that the future survival of public television would be determined by the system's ability to return to its roots—*educational* television. Envisioned by its founders as an educational institution that deserved a place beside the public library, public schools and the system of higher education, the local educational television station was seen as a learning resource for the communities they served.

By the late-1990s, the multichannel media landscape contained an enormous array of new delivery systems, and new niche television channels within the commercial sector were successfully attracting television viewers away from what had become known as public television. The arrival of the internet made the situation even more complicated as television programmers scrambled to understand the changing viewing patterns and preferences of the television audience. However, the transition of television from analog to digital production and transmission afforded public television stations with an unprecedented opportunity to reconceptualize the entire television program production process, and some stations did so effectively.

At public television station KUED in Salt Lake City, the transition to digital and HD meant a complete technical rebuilding of the station from the ground up. But this enormous challenge also created the opportunity for station personnel to rethink how programming was produced and the multiple audiences that the station could serve beyond its regular digital television channels. According to KUED's Director of Production, Ken Verdoia, the conversion to digital HD totally revolutionized the way the entire staff defined their mission—seeing KUED as much more than a television station, but rather as a genuine educational institution in service to a worldwide audience.

As one of the nation's leading producers of long-form documentary programs, KUED prides itself in its reputation as "Utah's best storyteller." Today, from the moment a program is conceived, KUED producers begin imagining the documentary program not only as it will be broadcast as a finished television program, but also the multiple educational objectives the program content might fulfill and the media that might best serve them. Since mid-2009, the KUED production staff has been systematically categorizing and archiving program content for delivery online. The station's commitment to Digital Asset Management has completely revised the way production teams perform both in the field and back in the studios and editing suites, as the cataloging of raw footage from every production is now standard practice.

As part of the CPB's American Archive Inventory Project, KUED is not only cataloging and archiving every new program segment it produces, but has undertaken the challenge of cataloging and archiving all finished programs and raw footage that still exists from the station's 53-year production history. The goal is to deliver the station's entire digital library to the viewing public online, around the clock.

While the completion of this ambitious project is still several years away, when finished it will provide an extremely invaluable demonstration of the educational potential of the local public television station in the lifelong learning of humans around the globe.

Robert K. Avery, Ph.D.
University of Utah

and new distribution opportunities—may finally have caught up with his vision.

Notes

1. June-Friesen, Katy, "Surge of Channels, People Meter Chaos Depress PBS Ratings," *Current*, 8 Dec 2008, retrieved at *http://www.current.org/audience/aud0822pbs.shtml*.

2. The broadcast reform movement was an effort by a loosely-organized coalition of not-for-profit broadcasters to maintain a large portion of the radio spectrum for public, not commercial, use. The movement—begun in the late 1920s—generally disbanded after the Wagner-Hatfield Amendment (which would have set aside a fourth of the spectrum for non-profit use) failed in 1934.

3. *ITV* in this now old-fashioned usage should not be confused with *ITV* meaning "interactive television" or "internet television."

4. Credit for this analogy and other portions of the chapter goes to S. Anders Yocum, Jr., who was at that time director of program production for WTTW in Chicago and an early contributor to this chapter, as published in *Broadcast Programming* (Belmont, CA: Wadsworth, 1980).

5. Joachim, Franz, "Personal Interview," 20 June 2011, Albuquerque, NM.

6. Aufderheide, Patricia, *The Daily Plant: A Critic on the Capitalist Culture Beat*. Minneapolis: University of Minnesota Press, 2000.

7. This particular expression was coined by President Charles Van Hise of the University of Wisconsin in the early 1900s, but all land-grant colleges espouse similar traditions.

8. Quoted in Townsend, Bickley, "Going for the Middle: An Interview with David F. Poltrack," *American Demographics*, March 1990, p. 50.

PART

5

Audio Programming Practices

Music Radio Programming

Gregory D. Newton and Matthew T. Kaiser

I s radio dead? Googling that phrase turns up well over 100,000 results—ranging from newspaper and magazine articles to blogs to song lyrics. In fact, radio has proven to be a very hardy survivor. Its history is one of continual adaptation and innovation, driven by changes in technology, audience tastes and lifestyles and the industry's economic structures. Successful programmers have reinvented "radio" every generation (or even more often), and stations continue to be a vibrant part of the media landscape for many listeners.

The Shifting Ground

Indeed, radio listening is still substantial—attracting more than 90 percent of the U.S. population in every age demographic each week.[1] Radio revenues actually increased in recent years, and industry experts project continued increases in the years ahead (through 2015). Although listeners may spend a bit less time each day with their favorite stations, in part due to the sheer number of alternative audio and other media choices, radio remains a central portion of the daily media diet for most people.

Nevertheless, changes that rattle radio's foundations erupt more frequently. It's hard to overstate the impact of media consolidation that came out of the 1996 Telecommunications Act. For station groups, who the competition is has altered. It used to be that a *program director (PD)* was responsible for one or maybe two stations, and the competitors were the other stations in the same local (geographic) market that were broadcasting in a similar (or identical) format, or that were targeting the same demographics. The competition was owned by somebody else, and disc jockeys worked for a single station (or maybe were heard on-air on co-owned AM and FM stations). But a single owner can now control five, six or even eight stations in a single market. Most of the listening in a market is typically controlled by two or three owners. The most direct "competitor" may be across the hall rather than across town, and the on-air talent is likely working for several stations during each day, in the local market and perhaps also far across the country.

PDs working with station *clusters* need to understand their company's vision of the radio market and the roles of their particular stations in their company's overall strategy. In other words, programmers are brand managers—responsible for all of the elements that *position* each co-owned station and with the strategic goal of dominating listening within a demographic category or a set of formats. Most major group owners specialize in one or more formats. These specialties may be in one or two related formats that nearly always appear in any market they participate in—even though they may have a dozen or more formats across all of their stations. Alternatively, the owners may have a true format specialization strategy in which all their properties are programmed in a very narrow format range. For example, Clear Channel dominates the contemporary hit radio market whereas Cumulus is a country music leader, although both owners have stations programming many other formats. Taking a more audience-focused approach are companies like Univision Radio, the largest operator of Hispanic-oriented stations, and Radio One, the country's largest owner of stations targeting African-American and urban audiences.

Two factors, the superfast growth of digital media platforms—particularly internet streaming and mobile phone applications—and the convergence of various media forms, make it essential to now take a broad view of the elements that make up successful radio programming. First, the audience now has a plethora of new listening choices that did not exist just a few years ago or were not generally available in the car, radio's most important listening location. Second, mobile apps have dramatically expanded the range of listening options for anybody with a smartphone (and an adequate data plan), although broadcast radio retains some inherent advantages.

Despite the fragmented, complex and rapidly changing landscape of contemporary radio programming, the more things change, the more we see that (at least some) things stay the same. Key elements of the tried-and-true programming formulas that worked in the past remain successful (not only for broadcast stations but for many of their competitors and imitators). Thus, programmers need to understand the history of the industry—what worked, what didn't, and how radio has survived by continually reinventing itself—as well as the new elements in the competitive environment that also shape their opportunities to build and serve an audience.

A Little History

In the beginning, there was broadcasting, and broadcasting consisted of AM radio stations. There were fewer stations (and far fewer competing media) than now, and it was possible to appeal to an extremely broad audience through a strategy of providing a little of something for everybody. Stations typically programmed not only some live music but also comedies and dramas, news and talk programs, farm information, game shows, soap operas and a great variety of other programs for people of all ages. Some of the programming was produced locally, but much of it came from local and regional network sources that sprang up to serve the growing new medium. The industry quickly recognized the economic advantages of producing one program for many stations versus many programs for many stations; and the first stars of the new medium were created as successful programs were carried on more and more stations.

Then came television. Television took many of radio's entertainment programs, and much of radio's audience followed their favorite stars to television. "Radio is dead," said some. "It is old-fashioned. Who wants just sound when you can also have pictures?" But radio was not dead. Instead, a new style of programming emerged. The local radio station no longer tried to supply all types of programming to all people some of the time but instead offered the most important programming to some of the people all of the time. The *format* approach created a new golden age for radio.

The first music format was top 40 radio. It is difficult to say with certainty who really invented top 40, but Todd Storz and Gordon McClendon are the two programmers who are generally believed

to have respectively created and perfected the approach. Rick Sklar and Bill Drake are other leaders among the early programmers who significantly advanced the elements of the format. The original top 40 format was not music genre specific. From pop to country, a top 40 station played a little bit of everything, as long as it was a hit, and adjusted the music rotation by times of day (*dayparting*) to cater to the available audience. Music fans now had a place to hear the most popular songs of the day, any time they wanted to tune in. There was, of course, also some regional variation—the most popular songs in Nashville were likely to be somewhat different from the most popular songs in Chicago or New York City.

Over time, the number of stations and the competition for listeners increased. FM stations developed in a different part of the spectrum and offered better audio quality. And some programmers asked whether it was a bit strange to have a country song alongside a rock song followed by a jazzy ballad. Radio stations soon found it necessary to fine-tune their formats to target a specific audience (*segmentation*)—fans of particular types of music. Thus, top 40 radio stations focused increasingly on the most popular pop (and rock) songs but still kept room in their playlists for the occasional crossover country or rhythm & blues song, while other stations adopted different niche formats. At first, there were four: country, album-oriented rock (AOR), urban or R&B, and middle-of-the-road (MOR). Now, fans of particular broad types of music could find what they wanted on the radio any time they wanted to listen. Those with wide-ranging tastes still had top 40 stations.

Radio continued to thrive, and because it looked like a good business, still more stations came on the air through the 1980s as the number of FM listeners surpassed AM. As more and more stations competed for listeners, they needed to find new ways to attract audiences. Thus, the four niche formats produced offspring, alone or sometimes in tandem, while the "mainstream" parents also continued to thrive. From country came traditional country and "young country." AOR spun off classic rock, active rock and alternative. MOR led to adult contemporary (AC), oldies, soft (or Lite) rock, beautiful music/easy listening and adult standards (the old middle-of-the-road, or MOR). Then programmers began merging elements of existing formats into new hybrids. Urban and top 40 (now known as contemporary hit radio, CHR) combined created a format originally referred to as "CHurban" but that is now known simply as rhythmic CHR. Urban plus AC can be divided into urban AC, smooth jazz/new age, and urban oldies formats. AC and CHR? That's hot AC and adult CHR.

Stations and formats continued to multiply through the 1990s, fragmenting the audience even further. Programmers responded by further subdividing and combining musical genres and other programming elements into new niche formats in the larger (and some of the smaller) markets. Rock, alternative and AC playlists were merged into an adult album alternative (AAA) format. In turn, pop songs from alternative artists and hot AC were combined into modern AC. Alternative plus some programming elements that are more CHR than AC leads to modern rock. Once alternative existed for a decade or so, it was obviously time for alternative with a classic rock approach, thus classic alternative (or modern gold). Pop mixed with a little classic rock and an AC presentation style creates classic hits ("the best

music of the '80s, '90s and today"). Oldies multiplied into specific '50s, '60s, '70s and '80s formats (or '50s/'60s and '70s/'80s in some markets). Contemporary Christian, and then Christian AC and Inspo emerged from traditional gospel, AC and CHR elements.

American radio's family tree also became more global as various Hispanic formats appeared, similar in their structure to existing CHR, AC and country. Latin music formats (including regional Mexican and Caribbean music as well as contemporary and gold-based Spanish-language) appeared in niche variants, and Spanish-language news/talk formats grew rapidly—leading the market in some areas of the United States. Formats have exploded in the past few years. *Billboard* lists four separate Spanish-language charts, reflecting the diversity of cultures and music often lumped under the umbrella terms *Hispanic* and *Latin*. And as with Anglo formats, there is frequently some crossover between particular formats (see 11.1).

To get some idea of the musical artists that are characteristic of each format (or who cross over format boundaries), consult the charts in trade publications such as *Billboard* (*www.billboard.com*), *Radio Info* (*www.radio-info.com*), *Friday Morning Quarterback* (*www.fmqb.com*) or *All Access Music Group* (*www.allaccess.com*).

11.1 **Spanish-Language Radio Formats**

Spanish-language radio formats are found in large regions of the United States, especially the West, Southwest and Southeast, as well as in most major cities. Four of the most common formats are the following:

- **Tejano.** The term itself refers to Texans of Mexican descent; the music is native to South Texas. The music and the instruments reflect not only traditional Spanish and Mexican influences but also the presence in South Texas of other European immigrants in the nineteenth century, particularly Germans, Czechs and Poles. Thus, Tejano music draws on Mexican folk, polkas and waltzes, as well as on contemporary Latin and rhythm and blues influences.

- **Regional Mexican.** This format features the traditional music of Mexico from the past 100 years. It embraces several specific styles, including ranchero, banda and Norteña (a musical cousin of Tejano historically rooted in northern Mexico).

- **Tropical.** The music is primarily from (or influenced by) Spanish-speaking cultures in the Caribbean. It also has influences from some northern countries in South America as well as Central America. Music styles include salsa, cumbia and merengue, among others.

- **Latin pop and Latin rhythmic.** These are the Spanish-language versions of the standard CHR formats, drawing on the most popular music in many Latin styles.

The past three decades also brought additional competitors to the music and audio marketplace, including cable radio, satellite radio, HD radio, streaming audio, mobile applications, and such social media as MySpace and Facebook. The major differences between these media and what have been traditionally called radio stations are that broadcast radio and HD radio retain a *local* focus, even if they incorporate national news networks and syndicated music and information; and they are available to the audience at no additional cost beyond a receiver. Cable radio and satellite radio, on the other hand, require a subscription fee and are essentially *national* services available in identical form all over the country. Streaming audio and mobile applications for devices like the iPad and various smartphones are a mix, with connections to local stations' content as well as possible programming from all over the country (and the world).

The thousands of audio services available online run the gamut from simply repeating the programming of local radio stations to offering web-only broadcasts of every imaginable sort, all with a potentially global audience. Along with all of the formats offered by broadcasters, these services provide other music not widely available—traditional jazz, blues, world beat, reggae, show tunes, bluegrass, folk, classical, kids. There is even a satellite channel and other services dedicated to unsigned bands. Some services, like Pandora, use complex algorithms to customize music rotations for listeners (much like various consumer web sites "suggest" other products you might like based on past customer behavior). Streaming audio content is best conceived as "all of the above."

Good programming is carefully designed to appeal to particular listeners, and tastes vary from region to region and among markets in a region. For example, the top-rated station in New York City has an adult contemporary format, with classic hits, two CHR rivals and a tropical station rounding out the top five. In Chicago, meanwhile, news and talk are more dominant—occupying three of the top five slots—while the top music formats are urban AC and hot AC. Just 90 minutes north in Milwaukee, on the other hand, the top five stations are news/talk, country, oldies, CHR and either classic rock or mainstream AOR (depending on just how one chooses to view recent ratings). If you head south to Memphis, gospel appears among the top five or six stations along with urban, urban AC and country. In Dallas, regional Mexican and contemporary Christian are among the top formats along with CHR, country and classic hits. *Such strong differences mean that a smart program director always tailors a station's programming to the available target audience within the market it serves.* The advertising value of different audiences (or, for some services, the audience's ability and willingness to pay a subscription or software fee), the station or service's technical facilities, and the existing competition in the market also affect programming choices.

Terrestrial Radio

Since the turn of the century, *digital audio broadcasting (DAB)* has been supplementing both terrestrial AM and FM analog broadcasting, improving the sound quality of each. Although most other countries have adopted a digital radio system that uses a different portion of the spectrum—and that therefore makes digital broadcasting incompatible with existing radio (such as the Eureka 147 system used in much of Europe) in those countries—the United States has chosen to create an *in-band-on-channel (IBOC)* system that operates within the current AM and FM spectrum allocations and is totally compatible with existing AM and FM systems. Thus, unlike with broadcast television, no date for ending analog AM and FM broadcasting in the United States has been established.

The U.S. IBOC technology is licensed to equipment manufacturers and stations by iBiquity Digital (*www.ibiquity.com*), and stations broadcasting a digital radio signal have to pay annual royalties to iBiquity. Referred to as *HD radio* (note the parallel to high-definition television in the name—something already familiar-sounding to consumers), it is multiplexed along with the primary analog FM or AM signal and requires a special HD receiver. Digital FM allows for inexpensive *simulcasting* (repeating the main signal, ads and all) at startup. This can be followed by the creation of specialty signals for local news, sports and other content for narrow niches, or the use of content from other co-owned stations, perhaps from other markets (*multicasting*) on secondary (HD2, HD3 and HD4) channels if the broadcaster has the desire to split the bandwidth.

As of mid-2011, fewer than one in five U.S. stations were broadcasting a digital signal (see 11.2). Digital authorizations from the FCC amounted to:

1646 FM stations

297 AM stations

2 FM translators

1 Low Power FM

Cable Radio

Many U.S. cable systems and DirecTV and Dish (the two TV satellite services) offer dozens of digital audio channels alongside digital television. These are large packages of nationally syndicated channels from such companies as DMX (formerly Digital Music Express) and Music Choice. In addition, DirecTV and DISH offer satellite radio programming on some of their programming tiers. Cable audio thus comes in a dizzying array of formats, ranging from bluegrass to rap to salsa to gospel to pop Latino, just as internet audio does.

The disadvantage of cable radio for most people is that reception requires a wireline (or satellite dish) in a house or office. The advantages are that these audio services come automatically along with certain tiers of television service and are available all the time, although some, such as DMX, are pay services. MusicChoice also provides many of the same channels both on cable and online. The online availability of the service thus makes music available to subscribers not only at home but also anywhere they can access a broadband connection.

11.2 | **The Slow Adoption of HD Radio**

Stations broadcasting HD radio were mostly the members of the "HD Radio Alliance" that formed in 2005 to promote the service—CBS Radio, Clear Channel Radio, Greater Media, Emmis, Entercom, Bonneville International, Beasley Broadcasting, Buckley Radio and WBEB- FM Philadelphia. With relatively few stations and thus little compelling programming incentive beyond the already available analog choices, it's not surprising that few consumers have purchased digital receivers, although there are several choices available for consumers.

One other major factor slowing the adoption has been the slow pace with which the automotive industry has added receivers with HD radio as either standard or optional equipment in their new car lines. As of 2011, HD radio was available from 17 auto manufacturers, representing 109 car models. That may sound like a lot—but represents no more than one-third of the models available (GM and Honda are most notable among those completely absent). More important, HD capability was included in the standard receiver in just 54 of those new car models.[2]

One additional concern that delays a shift to HD Radio by both AM and FM broadcasters has been the inability to maintain their existing *coverage areas* (the geographic areas where listeners can receive an adequate signal). With analog broadcasting, a station's signal gradually fades in quality farther away from the transmitter, creating a fringe area at the outer reaches where some listening is still possible. However, a digital signal is subject to a *cliff effect*—the signal is either of sufficient quality for the receiver to reproduce or it is not. The FCC tried to address this problem through a rule-making that resulted in a 2010 order that permitted greater power levels and improved coverage for digital transmissions. But so far, this has had little effect. Broadcasters are a stubborn group, it seems.

There are other problems for radio programmers considering a move to digital. The processing required, at both the transmitter and receiver, creates a delay of several seconds compared to analog signals—no small concern for stations who regularly broadcast live promotional events or sports. The delay means talent on location (in the field) monitoring the on-air signal for cues would be several seconds behind what was happening back in the studio. Slotting in commercials without accidentally covering up reporting sometimes becomes next to impossible.

Satellite Radio

DARS (digital audio radio service) refers to high-powered national satellite signals that require only a small receiving antenna that is especially suited to cars and mobile media. At the start of the 2000s, Sirius and XM were two competing satellite-radio providers licensed by the FCC. Each provided more than 100 channels of audio service nationwide to a combined total of nearly 14 million paying subscribers (for $12.95 a month). Like most large radio companies today, both were publicly traded corporations and eventually were forced by economics to merge in 2008, becoming *SiriusXM*.

Although their individual subscriber bases had grown rapidly by 2007, a great deal of subscriber churn had also occurred. The two services had tried to distinguish their programming by introducing original live talk and sports, and to make things worse, both had marketed themselves as different not only from terrestrial radio but from each other. Moreover, each had signed deals with substantial rosters of cable networks that supplied news, sports, music and other content, and each had various exclusive agreements with consumer electronics manufacturers and retailers and with specific car manufacturers. In addition, XM provided Major League Baseball games, and Sirius had the infamous Howard Stern (see Chapter 12).

But by 2007 it had become clear that the national market could support only one service. Because their receiving equipment was not compatible, the two combined companies had to juggle various programming options for current subscribers by repurposing channels on each system and creating a dizzying array of tiers of service. Depending on their receivers and interests, subscribers can choose from packages delivering between 120 and 180 channels for a monthly charge ranging from $12.95 to $16.99. Over half of the channels are dedicated to various music formats, most of which are commercial-free; the rest offer news, information, sports, foreign language content and other special programming from former terrestrial radio stars like Bob Edwards, Howard Stern and Opie & Anthony as well as multimedia stars like Oprah and Martha Stewart. Access to the content from the featured stars is the primary cost difference among most of the tiers. SiriusXM programming is also available online, either as a value added bonus of a satellite subscription or as a stand-alone offering.

Online Audio

Widespread adoption of broadband internet service has opened several opportunities for online distribution of audio content. These can generally be grouped into two categories. The first, *streaming* or *webcasting*, is akin to traditional radio programming because content is delivered in real-time over the network to a computer. Some of the streams available are the programming of terrestrial radio stations, but there are also many, many online-only services ranging from professionally formatted channels from big companies like AOL to offerings that could be fairly described as hobbies. Those providers have the advantage of not needing a license from the FCC and are happily without content oversight by the government other than that imposed by defamation or obscenity statutes. However, as with all digital audio services (including satellite radio), online services pay music performance royalty fees to the record labels and recording artists beyond those that apply to analog terrestrial radio, making the economic structure of this market more difficult.

The issue of copyright has limited some of the potential of online music. However, a more open online space is taking form. In particular, the British service Spotify launched its U.S. service in 2011 with a library of over 15 million songs. The service presents listeners with the closest thing yet to "any song, anytime, anywhere" (or any song anywhere for the 10 percent or so of Spotify users willing to sign up for the service's paid version that grants full library access from any device). While it's clear that personal, portable music devices from the Walkman to the iPod have cut into the amount of time listeners spend with radio (and have limited the ability of radio stations to stake out musical turf to call their own), the bandwidth costs of mobile data plans and the requirement to purchase a premium subscription to use Spotify on a mobile device may yet limit how much additional damage a service like Spotify—where the music resides in the cloud—can do to radio.

While that online audio market is growing, only about one-third of the U.S. population 12+ reports listening to streaming audio in the past month as of 2011.[3] Most online listening occurs on desktop or laptop computers in offices or homes although interest in, and access to, audio on mobile devices (smartphones, tablets) is increasing. Compared to broadcast or satellite coverage, wireless broadband internet connections are less widely available. However, wireless providers continue to expand the networks. When wireless broadband is ubiquitous for subscribers, the "radio" marketplace potentially expands from a few dozen or scores of choices within a local market to tens or hundreds of thousands.

Nonetheless, limits on mobile subscribers' data plans may check their willingness to devote large blocks of listening time to online radio on smart phones. That will, in turn, curb the short-term growth of online listening as people increasingly move their overall online use to mobile platforms and have to make choices about how to allocate data usage. Although audio doesn't consume as much data as video, a heavy listener could easily run over the allotments of many carriers' lower tiers of service, and that'll hurt when the bill comes in.

The second type of online audio service, colloquially known as *podcasting* (the result of the Apple iPod's early dominance of the audio player market), is archival in nature. Prerecorded content is downloaded from a provider's website to a computer and can then be transferred to another listening device. Podcasts are therefore more mobile at this time than streaming services. However, because of licensing problems, podcasts seldom include popular music and are primarily filled with the spoken word… lots of them.

Broadcast Radio and the Internet

It is absolutely imperative that a radio station have a strong presence online. While this may seem like common sense in today's environment, some broadcasters still shun online, seeing it as a distant second to their terrestrial signal. Such operators have a deeply entrenched "old school" mentality that makes digital integration a struggle if not downright impossible. They argue that it's the over-the-air station that pays the bills and efforts to put in place 'secondary media' would cannibalize their listening audience. Incredibly shortsighted, these broadcasters will quickly find that they face the very real problem of becoming irrelevant to listeners and, in the not so distant future, obsolete. *The changing digital landscape is making such traditional concerns as market size and geographic location into afterthoughts.* After all, with an internet connection, you can be a part of the CHR community on Z100 in New York or KISS-FM (KIIS are the actual call letters) in Los Angeles just as easily as you can KTRS-FM in Casper, WY, or Q-102 in Albany, GA, even if you live in Indiana or Texas.

As its history shows, radio stations have repeatedly been forced to adapt to technological changes and increased competition for the audience and advertisers. The internet is quite literally the latest in a long line of challenges facing programmers searching for a big enough piece of the audience pie. In the 1990s, radio still enjoyed several advantages, particularly portability, over early attempts to distribute programming online. The development of wireless internet services (Wi-Fi) and small portable audio players (like the iPod Nano which also contains an FM tuner) are removing the portability advantage of traditional broadcasting. *To maximize their audience and the value of their programming, smart programmers leverage their existing audience goodwill and brand recognition in order to aggressively court the online and mobile audiences while not forgetting the traditional (and larger) broadcast audience.* Indeed, this symbiotic relationship between on-air and online is one of the most difficult for programmers to figure out. *The problem facing all of them, from the smallest local markets to largest national groups, is how to best compete effectively.* And that often means competing for every available listener, including the relative fewer online, in the increasingly fragmented market.

Oddly, for an industry whose past norm was change and adaptation, radio has been extremely slow to accept the online world as a viable extension of a station's brand. The current problem may stem from the fact that there continues to be no clear right or wrong answers as to how to approach digital integration. Consolidation in the 1990s further clouded the situation. Many utility players and younger staff members who would previously have been given the reins of digital media were instead eliminated to maximize profits. Certainly another consideration is the financial risk; many managers were hesitant to be innovative with no guarantee of a return to the bottom line (see 11.3).

Finally, by 2000, radio stations and associated companies like Arbitron and Nielsen seemed to sense the changing environment and began a furious game of catch-up. The farsighted feared that the window of opportunity for attracting and profiting from the new media audience might close before they could develop a serious presence in that environment.

At first, the stations that did have an online presence did little more than put up rudimentary websites that, at their most technically advanced, offered listeners the ability to email requests to the station or possibly provide screen names so they could instant message the jocks in the control room. The majority of these sites were often the product of one poorly equipped and already over-loaded staff member at the station or done as *trade* (a service or goods provided in return for advertising time on the station) by the station's internet service provider (ISP). The results generally gave listeners little reason to visit once, let alone return for subsequent visits. Moreover, stations and listeners alike were often frustrated by the technological problems that made it difficult to deliver high-quality content, usually stemming from insufficient bandwidth. The bad news was that stations actually offering programming online found that it an expensive way to reach only a few listeners.

However, as bandwidth became a more affordable commodity to the average broadcaster, and as online content became an increasingly important portion of the average consumer's media consumption, it became clear (to most insiders) that radio would have to adapt once again if it expected to

remain a viable option in a sea of ever-increasing choices. The stations that were most successful in the mid-2000s realized that by offering compelling original content, they were able to *attract* audiences that actually helped *increase* traditional station listenership and as a bonus, online provided an additional outlet for revenue to advertisers. During this time, the added revenue streams from digital properties and station events became known as *Non-Traditional Revenue* or *NTR*.

It is important to remember, however, that for each additional stream a station puts online, there are additional royalty costs associated with their broadcast. Currently, there is a "per performance" royalty rate scale in place with varying rates for broadcasters, statutory webcasters and pureplay webcasters that is approved for modest yearly increases through 2015. Each time a song "airs" in a digital stream in 2012, broadcasters are expected to pay $.0020 per performance per listener, with that rate increasing to $.0025 by 2015. While a fraction of a cent per play per listener might not seem like a tremendous amount, those costs easily (and quickly) add up, leaving some broadcasters feeling that online streaming is not a financially viable business decision.

Some larger companies not only support online streaming, but actively promote mobile phone applications (apps) that provide easy access to a station's content. Some individual stations have launched their own branded apps, but apps that aggregate many stations and other audio content nationally or even globally dominate the market. Clear Channel Communications, one of the most aggressive companies in the mobile environment, released its *I Heart Radio* app, which provides access to a stable of more than 750 stations from coast to coast. Listeners have the ability to select by market or format and to stream the station's online content. *CBS Interactive's radio.com*, *TuneIn Radio* and *Public Radio Live Stream* are other widely used apps, each offering access to hundreds or even thousands of audio streams.

Many barriers to expanding a station's reach in a crowded terrestrial environment disappear in the digital world, but going digital is not without new dangers for broadcasters. A question raised briefly earlier in this section is the idea of geography, more specifically

11.3　Online Strategy

As radio's attitude towards digital media changed and the right technology became more accessible, broadcasters were forced to develop strategies for programming in a new environment. The simplest was to merely rebroadcast the over-the-air signal in an online stream—commercials and all. The *streaming audience remains largely popular among at-work listeners.* As more people accessed to audio through their computers, cell phones and music players, streaming audio became a viable competitor to broadcast radio. Happily, when a station streams itself, the online version can be jointly marketed as a sister-service to advertisers. For more information on the streaming audio market, consult *Radio and Internet Newsletter* (updated five days a week at *www.kurthanson.com*).

Simply rebroadcasting a station, though, can cause big trouble because not all commercials are licensed for streaming online. This seems counter-intuitive; you might think that any opportunity to put a commercial in front of more ears would be a clear advantage to the advertiser. And while that may be the case, many national spots use union talent to voice and produce their commercials, and under union regulations, the spots are only licensed for use at the specific over-the-air times and dates that were purchased by an advertising agency or via a station barter agreement. While obviously not the best-case scenario both legally and ethically, some stations elect to broadcast these commercials on their internet stream anyway until presented with a cease-and-desist order.

Savvy broadcasters contract with an *ad insertion service,* which allows selective online preemption of commercials. Companies like Ando Media provide software that allows stations to target certain streamed commercials and replace them with other inventory. Public Service Announcements (PSAs), other local spots (say, for a local car dealer sold in addition to their on-air advertising schedule), and streaming exclusive content can be used as filler. Web exclusive songs, for example, that are not available in any other format—including the over-the-air broadcast—provide an exclusive audio element to promote and to reward listeners.

A more complex strategy for programming radio online goes far beyond rebroadcasting the terrestrial signal to offer a wide-array of additional content. This includes on-demand content, video and additional audio streams. Such aggressive strategies seem to win with consumers and give listeners a definitive source for "discovery" of music, which has always been a strong suit of terrestrial radio. Content-rich websites should include numerous features of use or of interest to audience members. Some stations integrate online playlists within their websites and give answers to most-common-listener-questions like "What song are you playing right now?" or its more frustrating variation, "What was the song you played last Thursday right after the weather forecast?" In addition, websites can showcase local community information, coupons from local merchants and online-only promotions. Advertisers who choose to participate in online-only campaigns find they are typically more affordable than their over-the air counterparts. They also give the advertisers the ability to provide more information about their products than can fit into traditional :30 or :60 commercials. Some stations will go so far as to create an online "virtual mall" in which many local retailers feature their products (for a fee, of course) or where they hold "half-off" promotions that give the station's listeners the chance to purchase gift cards or restaurant certificates for half price. These ideas provide more affordable opportunities for advertisers, as well as another NTR revenue stream for stations.

Online sister-stations can take several forms, including subniche formats designed to superserve one or more fragments of the broadcast station's audience. For example, a "new country" station can offer an online stream of "classic country" to serve the audience portion that prefers the classics, but which may not be large enough to sustain the ratings needed for a terrestrial station.

"who really is the audience of our station?" This used to be much clearer before the internet: *"Our audience is anyone who listens to country music as far as our signal travels,"* and that answer sufficed for decades.

However, broadcasters streaming online have the potential for national and even global reach. As wireless internet access expands around the world, the number of consumer devices capable of accessing

U.S. radio services multiplies, along with analytic programs that track online listenership down to the second. These virtually limitless possibilities have become very real for broadcasters.

But here's the kicker: *Even in the online world, success for broadcasters is tied to a conscious decision to target content to a specific group at the sacrifice of being "all things to all people."* Where on-air and streamed online traffic reports in Dallas are invaluable to someone trying to make it to work on time in that city, someone listening online from Raleigh or even London is necessarily alienated by the unfamiliar and useless information. One of radio's inherent strengths continues to be localism, which means keeping people informed of what is going on in a specific community or group of communities, however defined. Broadcasters cannot turn their back on the communities in which they exist simply to cater to the global population. Indeed, many now impose geographical boundaries on their content while still making it accessible from anywhere in the world. For stations that want to put in the effort and target a broader audience, it is technically feasible to separate purely local content out of online audio and fill the time with something more global in nature.

Currently, there are more than 13,000 radio stations on the air in the United States alone, with countless more in every country on Earth. While online presence is a part of the larger picture, the remainder of this chapter tightens its focus to terrestrial broadcast radio. The storyline consists of a proposed scenario about whether or not to buy and program a station in the hypothetical market. The problems and the principles for finding solutions discussed here, however, are fully applicable to the programming decisions of today's cable, satellite and online audio services because they compete in the same or similar marketplaces (see 11.4 and 11.5).

11.4 Dominant Players

There has been a lot of commentary about consolidation in radio, but how dominant are the top radio companies? There are different ways of measuring that, but in 2009, only Clear Channel and CBS reported more than $1 billion in revenue ($2.35 billion for Clear Channel, $1.2 billion for CBS). The top three groups generated revenues totaling $4.4 billion (if one combines the revenue generated by the now merged Cumulus and Citadel stations). The remaining six companies in the top ten accounted for $1.6 billion ... or about 72 percent of what Clear Channel alone did in the last full reported fiscal year before work began on this chapter (see 11.5).

Dominant Content Providers

Clear Channel

Clear Channel Communications, founded in 1972, has two operating divisions—Radio and Outdoor Advertising. Of primary interest here, the radio division is the largest group owner in the U.S., currently operating more than 850 stations in approximately 150 markets (including 89 of the top 100). That figure is substantially reduced from its post-Telecommunications Act peak of more than 1,200 stations, however. Economic factors and other strategic considerations led the company to sell a number of stations, primarily in smaller markets, between 2007 and 2010.

Although Clear Channel's stations run the full gamut of formats, they have particular strengths in CHR, AC and News-Talk. In addition to the stations and their companion websites, the company's assets also include a leading smartphone app, iheartradio. It also owns about 140 stations in Australia and New Zealand (owned in partnership with local entities); Premiere Radio Networks, which syndicates approximately 90 radio programs including Rush Limbaugh, Ryan Seacrest, Steve Harvey and Delilah. Besides all that, it owns Katz Media Group, a leading advertising rep firm with more than 3,000 radio and TV clients; RCS, a leading provider of broadcast software including the most popular music scheduling application—Selector; Inside Radio, a radio industry trade publication; and Clear Channel Total Traffic Network and CCC News Networks.

Cumulus

In 2011, Cumulus Media, the country's second largest group owner by number of stations, acquired Citadel

(Continued)

11.4   Dominant Players (*Continued*)

Broadcasting, the third largest radio group in the U.S. The combined group has more than 550 stations reaching 120 markets, including 8 of the top 10. Ranked by number of stations, there is now a very big gap between the top two radio companies and everybody else. The new Cumulus combined Citadel's format strengths in Country with Cumulus' larger station roster.

The company also includes all of the former Citadel Media (and former ABC Radio Networks), a major syndicator whose offerings include *Imus in the Morning*, *American Country Countdown*, ESPN Radio, ABC News and Sports, and ESPN Deportes as well as other Spanish-language programming (some in partnership with Hispanic digital content provider Terra).

CBS

In contrast to Clear Channel and Citadel, CBS has focused almost exclusively on large market stations—of their 130 properties, 129 are in markets among the top 50 DMAs (the exception is KEZN in Palm Springs, CA). As a result, even though the number of stations owned is much smaller than the totals for Cumulus or Clear Channel, CBS is a solid number 2 in radio revenue.

In addition to the stations, the company also has its own mobile app (*radio.com*) which includes a number of channel offerings from outside the CBS group. Although late entering the online universe under former head Mel Karmazin (who didn't see streaming as important to the business), all CBS stations now offer live streams of their programming as well as a multitude of other digital offerings. Perhaps best known for their flagship News and News-Talk stations such as WCBS (New York), WBBM (Chicago), KMOX (St. Louis), WCCO (Minneapolis-St. Paul) and KCBS (Los Angeles), the company also has significant programming strength in various adult-leaning pop and rock formats—classic hits, AC, Hot AC, adult hits and alternative/AAA.

Univision

Univision Radio was created in 2003 when television company Univision completed its acquisition of Hispanic Broadcasting Corporation. The radio unit, part of Univision Local Media, is now the largest Spanish radio network in the U.S., operating 70 stations in 17 markets, including all of the top 10. Their primary growth since 2003 has come

through the acquisition of English-language stations in the largest Hispanic markets in the U.S. Those stations are then reformatted and launched as Hispanic.

The formats include the following: Adult Contemporary (in the Hispanic version, some combination of Romántica, ballads, international pop hits and top 40); Regional Mexican (Banda, Ranchera, Mariachi and Norteña music); Tropical (a "Latin beat" music format from the Caribbean that includes salsa, merengue, cumbia and reggaeton genres); Tejano (music performed by Tex-Mex/Chicano groups (*conjuntos*) that is a cross between contemporary Rock/Ranchera/Country, with lyrics in both Spanish and English and potentially appealing across ethnic boundaries); *Hip-Hop* (Hip-Hop music culture today has obviously grown far beyond its urban roots, reaching all segments of American society); and *RadioCadena Univision-News/Talk/Sports AM Network*.

In addition to their own stations, Univision syndicates a number of their personalities and shows to Spanish-language stations in other markets, including Eddie "Piolín" Sotelo, whose *Piolín por la Mañana* originates weekday mornings on KSCA and is syndicated to approximately 50 markets; Javier Romero, who hosts a music-intensive morning show that also features lots of interviews in Miami, *El Desayuno Musical*; Raul Brindis, whose morning show originates at KLTN in Houston; and New York's Luis Jimenez, host of a morning show that is stylistically similar to many English-language morning offerings, with prank calls, musical parodies, comedy characters and sketches and listener telephone calls.

Westwood One

Also in 2011 (a busy year), Westwood One merged with Triton Media Group, the parent company of Triton Radio Networks (which included Dial Global), Triton Digital Media and TM Studios. The merged company created the largest provider of radio content in the U.S. Its services include the following:

- Thirteen format offerings are available as 24/7 "turnkey" programming or in more customized structures.

- More than 200 syndicated programming choices available for almost any programming hole, from short features lasting no more than a couple of minutes (e.g., *Ask Dr. Phil*, *Late Show Top Ten*, *Talking Points with Bill O'Reilly*, *Weather Channel Radio Network*)

(*Continued*)

to weekly one- to two- hour programs (such as *Beatle Brunch, Dave Koz, House of Blues Radio Hour,* countdown shows for country, CHR and AC formats, and MTV Tres, a Spanish-language countdown) to syndicated personalities for Monday–Friday dayparts (*Kevin & Bean, Bob & Sheri, Rocsi on the Radio, The Billy Bush Show*).

- Special programming built around several entertainment events such as the Grammy Awards, the Academy of Country Music Awards and the BET Awards, with packages tailored to particular formats.

- National broadcast rights for a number of top sports, including the NFL, NCAA football and basketball, and the major PGA tournaments.

- A range of digital services and products provided by Triton Digital Media, including content management system (CMS) architecture, streaming management, web analytics, mobile apps, texting and email services, game and audience loyalty elements, and ad insertion.

- A rep firm.

- And all of TM Studios' services include commercial jingles; radio, TV and online imaging packages; music libraries; production music; and show prep and comedy services.

NPR

National Public Radio (NPR) is the largest producer and distributor of public radio programming in the U.S., but it differs in significant structural ways from its commercial counterparts. NPR is not a network with affiliate stations, but rather a membership organization that provides programming and other services to its member stations. And its business model is very different. Unlike commercial networks or syndicators, NPR carries no advertising in its broadcasts (although like other public media, it can—and does—include advertising on its non-broadcast platforms such as the website).

Instead, broadcast revenue comes from a combination of philanthropic grants, government funding, program fees from member stations and underwriting (as explained in relation to PBS in Chapter 10). Underwriting is a form of support where businesses make donations to NPR (or local public radio stations) to support either the general operation of the service or, more often, a specific program. In return, they receive brief statements on air thanking them for the support and, one assumes, the goodwill of listeners to the program. These "thank you" announcements are called underwriting spots, not commercials; and, unlike commercials, they are governed by specific FCC restrictions limiting what can be said about the business in several ways.

While music is a relatively minor element of the programming offered by National Public Radio (although this varies among public radio stations), NPR is notable for a number of the shows they produce and/or distribute. These include *All Songs Considered* (and the All Songs Considered 24/7 Music Channel online and mobile service); long-running favorites like Marian McPartland's *Piano Jazz, Mountain Stage, The Thistle and Shamrock* and *World Café*; and various concert recordings from South by Southwest, Bonnaroo, the Village Vanguard and other locations.

NPR has also been a technological pioneer in radio. They were among the first to develop satellite distribution of programming to stations in the 1980s and, more recently, have been leaders in the rollout of various online and mobile applications for getting audio content to audiences.

American Public Media

American Public Media is the parent organization for Minnesota Public Radio, Southern California Public Radio and Classical South Florida. Beginning with the launch of a single classical music station in Minnesota in 1967, they have grown to operate 43 radio stations and 32 translators in Minnesota, Iowa, Wisconsin, Michigan, South Dakota, North Dakota, Idaho, California and Florida (making them the largest owner and operator of public radio stations in the U.S.).

The second-largest producer and distributor of public radio programming, American Public Media is the largest producer and distributor of classical music programming in the country, offering a full-range of content for classical stations from a 24-hour, seven-day-a-week classical music service to *Performance Today*, a daily two-hour classical music program, to weekly programs and specials. They also provide a number of other prominent programs including that all-time favorite *A Prairie Home Companion, The Splendid Table, Marketplace* and *Being*.

Like NPR, it is considered an innovator. In addition to developing a wide range of new media platforms and content, APM was the recipient of the first Knight News Innovation EPpy Award for their Public Insight project. This project, which has been rolled out to many other major

(Continued)

11.4   Dominant Players (*Continued*)

public radio and TV stations, develops and applies social media techniques to engage the public and tap its insight with the goal of producing significant journalism featuring stories and perspectives from every facet of experience.

PRI

Public Radio International is the third major distributor of noncommercial radio fare in the U.S. Established in 1983 as American Public Radio, PRI understandably changed its name to Public Radio International in 1994 (it was constantly confused with APM). It distributes over 400 hours of programming weekly to approximately 800 stations in the U.S., as well as across other media platforms—including SiriusXM's Public Radio Channel. Although its best known programs are talk-based (including *This American Life, Michael Feldman's Whad'Ya Know, BBC World Service* and *Bob Edwards Weekend*), it also produces and/or distributes a number of music and music-oriented talk programs. These include *Echoes* (a mix of instrumental, world music and impressionistic jazz recordings along with *Living Room Concerts* recorded in artists' homes), *Afro-Pop Worldwide* (the music of Africa, the Caribbean and the Americas), *Soundcheck* (covering music of all genres, featuring interviews, listener phone calls and studio performances), *Jazz After Hours* and the *Pittsburgh Symphony Orchestra*.

Ancillary Services

Arbitron

For most stations, networks, syndicators and advertisers, Arbitron is *the* provider of radio audience information in the U.S., in both local markets and nationally. Local radio ratings are available both in local station/advertiser form and for networks (Arbitron Nationwide). The national network rating service is known as RADAR. The company was also the developer of the Portable People Meter (PPM) device that has replaced diaries as the primary means of gathering radio ratings data in many markets (see Chapter 5 for a full discussion of PPM), and that has led to various forms of cross-media audience measurement. The company also provides consumer behavior research (such as such as lifestyles, shopping patterns and media behavior) through their

Scarborough Research division. Its methods enable marketers and media companies to develop much more complex profiles of their consumers on a local, regional and national basis.

Billboard

Billboard Magazine, part of the Billboard Information Group (a division of Nielsen Business Media) is published weekly. Following its acquisition of *Radio & Records*, its became the leading trade publication for the music and radio businesses, although the scope of its coverage extends beyond pure music to include much of the entertainment industry. Along with news, analysis and trend reporting, it features widely-watched charts of music sales, airplay and downloads developed with data from Nielsen SoundScan and Nielsen Broadcast Data Systems. The company has separate online presences for industry pros (*billboard.biz*) and consumers/fans (*billboard.com*).

Billboard.biz houses the full collection of weekly charts and all of the articles printed in each week's magazine, a database of all *Billboard* articles, reviews, features and special reports dating back to 1991, as well as weekly album, singles and video charts dating back to 1984 and year-end charts dating back to 1946. *Billboard.com* is more of a typical consumer entertainment news site, with music news, videos and a limited selection of weekly charts.

Jacobs Media

Jacobs Media is a Detroit-based media research and consulting firm. Although there are many prominent radio consultants, Jacobs Media stands out in a couple of ways. First, in addition to its status as the preeminent rock radio consultancy and creator of the Classic Rock format, its staff has also worked extensively with public radio stations and NPR—likely the only major consultant to have a significant client base in both the commercial and noncommercial sectors. Second, its was one of the earliest voices in radio to recognize the importance of mobile applications, and the JacApps service that Paul and Fred Jacobs began has developed hundreds of mobile apps for both commercial and noncommercial stations, groups and networks, as well as other companies.

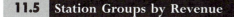

11.5 Station Groups by Revenue

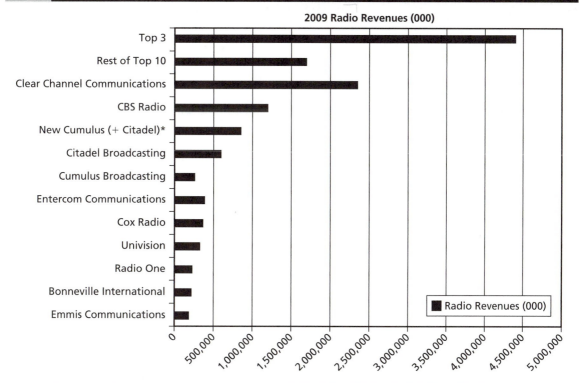

2009 Radio Revenues (000)

Radio Revenues (000)

Choosing a Format

The heart of most radio stations continues to be their music, however distributed, and the principles guiding on-air have counterparts for cable, satellite and online-only radio. In all cases, the program director's job is essentially a continuous cycle of *analysis, design* and *implementation.* The first step in analyzing a market is a thorough evaluation of all stations (or competing services) and their current programming. This information can then be used to modify or replace existing program formats or to decide which property to buy and what to do with it after purchase. Such an evaluation, in the context of the company's overall strategy, takes into account the following factors: (1) the technical facilities of each station or service, (2) the character of the local or national market, (3) the delineation of a target audience, (4) the available budget and (5) the

potential revenue. Once completed, this evaluation will determine which music format is commercially viable and which can best help the station or service succeed in a given market.

Comparing Technical Facilities

Unlike television, radio isn't going fully digital anytime soon. Industry deals still focus on traditional AM and FM analog technology. Therefore, the old rule holds for now: *The best over-the-air facility has the best chance to succeed.* Going head-to-head with a similarly formatted competitor that has better facilities is almost always a big mistake. For AM stations, *power* (strength of signal), *frequency* (lower in the band is better) and any *license limitations* (reduced power or eliminated night service and directional requirements) are the key factors. For FM stations, *power* and *antenna height* are the crucial considerations. Generally, these elements determine signal quality.

A clear, undistorted signal is less tiring to the listener than one that is distorted, faint or accompanied by natural or artificial interference. *All other qualities of similar formats being equal, the station or service with the best signal will be the listener's choice.* Emotional fatigue unconsciously sets in after a period of straining to hear a program with a noisy, uncomfortable signal.

An FM station with 100,000 watts of effective radiated power (ERP) and that has its antenna assembly mounted on a 1,000-foot tower is a much better facility than a station with the same power but with the antenna mounted on a 500-foot tower. An AM station with a power of 50,000 watts on a clear channel (820 kHz) is a much better technical facility than a station with 5,000 watts of power at 1570 kHz. *Usually the low-power station is at the mercy of the higher-power station.* A 5,000-watt facility with a talk or news format may be very vulnerable to a same-format station broadcasting at 10,000 or 50,000 watts because the more powerful station will provide a listenable signal over a larger area.

This rule of thumb does not hold in all cases. For example, a 5,000-watt facility at 1600 kHz might easily fall victim to a 1,000-watt station at 710 kHz. *In AM, both power and dial position are important. The lower the frequency, the greater the range of the AM signal.* A 1,000-watt AM station at 710 kHz might easily reach a bigger population than a 10,000-watt station at 1600 kHz.[4]

In FM, tower height and power are the principal considerations, and antenna height is generally the most important (a station with a higher antenna using lower power will generally cover more area than a station with more power but a much lower antenna). However, the terrain is also an important factor; hills can block FM signals. Three classes of FM have been developed (see 11.6).

Defining the Competitive Market

Before any discussions of the opportunities that exist within a market can take place, it is absolutely essential that a complete and thorough market analysis be

11.6 Classes of FM Stations

There are three broad classes of FM stations, although there are also subclasses, and not all stations use the class maximums. Class A stations are permitted a maximum of 6,000 watts—or 6 kilowatts (kw)—ERP with a maximum antenna height-above-average-terrain (HAAT) of 100 meters, which provides a signal radius of approximately 18 miles. Class B stations (located in the more densely populated eastern United States) have a maximum ERP of 50 kw and a HAAT of 150 meters. Class C stations are located primarily in the flat parts of the western United States and are permitted up to 100 kw and a maximum HAAT of 600 meters. These stations may have a signal radius of 60 miles or more. Dial position is much less technically important in FM, although stations at the center of the dial get more sampling. An FM station at the upper fringe of the band (the lower portion from 88 to 92 MHz is reserved for noncommercial stations) needs an advertising and promotional blitz when altering its format.

For many years, AM was the king of radio. AM stations were tops in ratings, regardless of format. Beginning in the 1970s, FM replaced AM as the music format champion. Music simply sounded better on FM because of the technical differences between the two bands. Furthermore, FM doesn't fade under bridges or inside urban skyscrapers and doesn't suffer from weather interference the way AM does. To survive, AM turned toward full-service programming, including elements of news, talk, sports, satellite or syndicated programming, ethnic (non-English-language), and religious (preaching and gospel music) content. The station's technical facility plays an important part in the initial decision about whether to enter the music programming competition. It would be aesthetically foolish and economically disastrous to pit, say, an AM station against a full-power FM station in the contemporary rock field. *Always—having the best or one of the best facilities in the market is crucial to beating the competition.*

completed. As discussed in Chapter 5, Arbitron (*www.arbitron.com*) data is an invaluable resource in this process that provides an immense amount of information ranging from demographic breakdowns of current stations to format performance and critical reception in the market. All of this data compiled together will paint a clear picture of the competitive landscape—what competition exists in the market, what formats are present, and where the format holes or underserved demographics may be. Further, it will identify the key players in the market and identify the strengths of each.

The first step is identifying geography: *"Where will the radio station in question exist?"* Although the internet makes it possible to hear programming almost anywhere, most of the audience will be from the local area, and so that area is generally the first concern of programmers. However, this process is not as simple as merely identifying the city. Arbitron makes clear distinctions among radio markets across the country, and nearly every viable radio station falls into more than one geographic category. Note that Arbitron reviews, and sometimes changes, these market definitions on an annual basis.

To review the relevant material from Chapter 5, the **Metro Survey Area** (often referred to simply as "metro" or "the metro,") is defined as counties where the sum of the percentage of listening and the percentage of commuting is 70 percent or more, provided that a minimum of 55 percent of the listening in the county is credited to stations that are home to the existing metro radio market. The **Area of Dominant Influence**, or **ADI**, includes all counties adjacent to the Metro where measured listening is predominantly to the stations from that metro. All counties are exclusive to one ADI (in other words, are assigned to one, and only one, ADI). However, the assignment can change over time if listening patterns change. The **Total Service Area** (TSA) includes the outlying counties that often directly border the counties in the ADI that have significantly less total listening to stations in a market but are still served by the stations in that area. The **Designated Market Area** (DMA), similar to the ADI but defined by Nielsen and not Arbitron,

is the area that makes up the television viewing market, and will often contain counties well beyond the reach of a terrestrial radio station but served by television stations in the market. Once these areas are all identified on a map, a **Coverage Map** (how far a station's signal will travel from its tower) of the station should be placed over top of the market map to identify how the station in question relates to the different categories. These will be important not only in understanding what areas the station will cover, but also in estimating potential revenue, which is covered later in this section.

Because these are man-made geographic boundaries, it is likely that a station may service areas that fall in more than one ADI or TSA (or, in some densely populated areas, even more than one metro). For example, the Brunswick market on the coast in Southeast Georgia is at the far north end of the Jacksonville, Florida DMA. The signals of the stations based in the metro (a one-county metro, Glynn County) do not simply stop at the county line, but broadcast into areas north toward Savannah, areas that are outside of the DMA. In this case, the TSA actually straddles two different DMA's: Savannah, Georgia, and Jacksonville, Florida. To see the market breakdown in the city you live in, or in the geographic area you are most familiar with, look for the most recent Arbitron map in the radio reference library at *http://www.arbitron.com/ radio_stations/reference_metroinfo.htm.*

The next step in completing the radio market analysis is to compile a list of all of the radio stations that currently exist in the metro, any *construction permits (CPs)* that may have been granted or are pending with the FCC, and those stations in both the TSA and DMA that may provide fringe competition. This list should include important statistics for *each* station that include but are not limited to: service (AM or FM), frequency (98.7 Mhz, for example), signal strength (in watts), antenna height above average terrain (for FM stations), format, owner and ratings.

One common methodology helps to represent some of this data in graphic form to make the analysis easier. A demographic profile of each station and each ownership group is represented in a set of bar graphs to show what percentage of listenership a station has in each of the six standard demographic groups. The bars in such graphs display the age "leaning" of a station's audiences, suggesting the industry name of **skew graphs**. Arbitron is the principal source of these data. If using a hard copy of the Arbitron ratings book, this information can be found already completed in the 6 A.M. to midnight, Monday through Sunday page. This information can also be obtained online through Arbitron's TAPSCAN software (by subscription only) that will create these or any other reports on demand. While Arbitron is the preeminent source, any audience analysis service that provides demographic separation will have the necessary information. Skew graphs for two stations in the hypothetical market that is considered in this chapter are shown in 11.7.

Once the market is identified, coverage maps are created, and demographic profiles are assembled, program strategists can begin the work of identifying what opportunities exist in the market. They can quickly decide what demographic groups are best served by which stations and groups, and therefore which stations will represent major competition. Compare the examples from the hypothetical market in 11.7. KAAA, a rock station, is skewed male (nearly 70 percent) and young (more than half the audience is younger than 35 years of age). KIII, a soft AC, is nearly the opposite. Their audience is nearly all female and older (almost 60 percent between 35 and 64 years of age).

Graphs for the Big Sky and RadioEast station clusters appear in 11.8. Although the individual stations vary, group patterns emerge here. Both groups skew male overall, but Big Sky more so. There are also significant differences in the age breakouts. RadioEast is strongest for ages 35 to 54, while Big Sky's stations appeal to younger listeners. These differences reflect the existing formats of the stations in each group, but more important, they provide important strategic information about the marketplace for a potential new entrant (including any reformatted station within one of these groups). In order to maximize the advantages of group ownership, it is essential not only to look at the formats of individual stations but also to consider how the programming and audiences for each station fit together in the group. Different groups try to leverage different audience segments. One may focus on capturing the female audience across several age categories; another may try to dominate a specific age demographic for both men and women. It cannot be overstated that most such decisions are based on financial considerations relating to potential revenue, as well as how likely programming decisions may or may not attract advertisers.

Identifying Target Audiences

It is not enough to study population graphs and other research data about a market's radio listeners. *Radio is essentially a lifestyle medium.* Listeners choose stations, at least in part, because the station's image reflects their self-image: their tastes, their values and their interests. It is important to go into the community to find out specifically what people are doing, thinking and listening to. It is helpful to observe lifestyles by visiting restaurants, shopping centers, gas stations, nightclubs, bars, parks, sports arenas and other places where people go to have a good time.

Don't think of observation as a task reserved for times of change, however. Being active in the community, and especially in the areas of most importance to the audience, is not a one-time or occasional effort but an ongoing process to keep programmers in touch with listeners and all aspects of their lives. *Street presence, as both a promotional exercise and a research tool, is critical to the success of most music stations.*

Personal interaction with the members of the audience and community is important and can provide valuable insights, but programmers should be careful not to generalize too much from that kind of anecdotal evidence (and should *never* assume that *their* personal tastes reflect the target audience's taste). Therefore, formal research using careful sampling procedures should supplement personal investigation. Most cities have research firms that can be hired to make special studies, and many national firms specialize in broadcast station research. Psychographic profiles (listener lifestyles and values)

11.7 Station Skew Graph Samples: KAAA-FM and KIII-FM

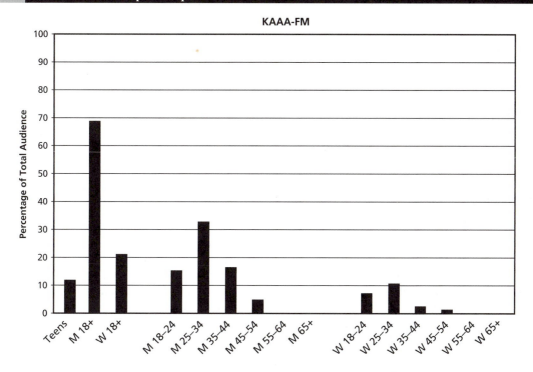

KAAA-FM

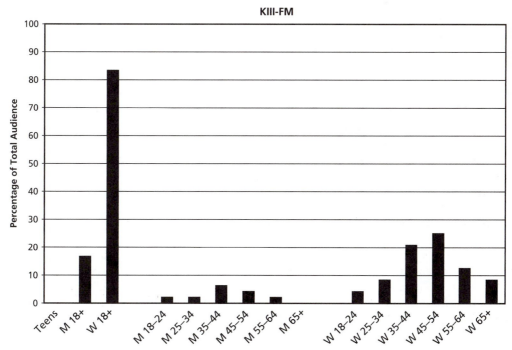

KIII-FM

11.8   Station Skew Graphs for RadioEast and Big Sky

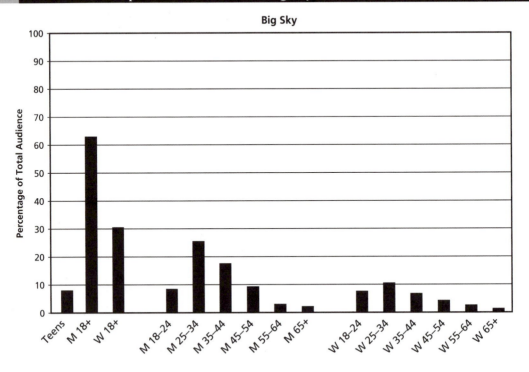

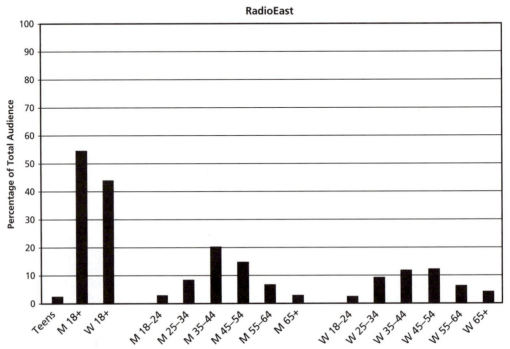

can provide additional invaluable information for programmers about target audiences.

A study assessing current formats in the market using lengthy, in-depth interviews might get interesting responses: too many commercials, bad commercial production, too much unfamiliar or repetitive music, obnoxious contests, can't-win contests or DJs who talk too much. A station getting answers like these is ready for a major overhaul (or is vulnerable to new competition). However, research is merely one tool in the programmer's arsenal. Any study should be carefully weighed before being used to make important decisions.

As an example of the kind of findings that prove useful, a broadcast station may identify its typical over-the-air listener as a male, 30 to 40 years old, in a professional career who earns $75,000 to $100,000 a year, drives a Lexus or other upscale car, drinks imported or craft beer, goes out at least twice a week to a good restaurant, and plays golf. The station can sell this audience to advertisers that have the same target. Station promotional efforts, from contests to events, would tie in elements of lifestyle with the programming on this particular station.

Knowing the Available Budget

In addition to a program director, the usual hit music operation requires one or more *air talents* along with a production director and, perhaps, a music director. Salaries vary widely, even within market classes, and are a function of the station's results (ratings and ad revenue), the individual's job history and the individual's negotiating skills. In a medium market of 500,000, the program director may earn as much as $50,000 a year—more if she or he also handles an air shift. The morning DJ probably gets $50,000 to $80,000, and a popular afternoon drivetime DJ may get up to $40,000. The production director's salary is probably between $30,000 and $50,000 per year, and the other five or six jocks fall in a somewhat lower range.

In the top-10 markets, stations would likely have to double or triple these salary figures to get the required talent. Top morning show talent for a large market can easily run well into six figures, with superstars earning a million dollars or more annually. Successful PDs can likewise command six-figure salaries in a major market. But talent is often expected to do more for that money than they used to have to do, in every market. The afternoon drive jock is probably also recording midday, afternoon or evening shows (*voice tracking*) for as many as five or six other stations in addition to making a promotional appearance or two for the station each weekend. In smaller markets, they may also be doubling as sales personnel.

In addition to staff salaries, management must expect substantial ongoing costs for promoting and advertising. Moreover, a station often employs various consultants to help with specific areas of the operation—legal, technical, management, personnel, marketing and sales as well as programming—and all of these consultants are useful or even essential at one time or another. Some consultants are practically required on an ongoing basis—for example, a communications law firm in Washington, DC, should handle proceedings with the FCC and keep the station advised of changes in the requirements for operation or of any licensing changes pending before the commission for stations in their market.

Engineering consultants with experience in going before the commission are necessary when the station is applying for a new license or at any subsequent time when the station makes a change to its facilities that requires FCC approval. Programming consultants can provide important insights on a regular or occasional basis by finding market voids and spotting competitors' weaknesses (or your own). They may even assemble a staff to work up a specific format.

Consultation is (Whew!) expensive, however. An engineer may charge $700 a day plus expenses; a programmer may charge $3,000 a month on a three-to-six-month contract. For a complete station overhaul, consultants range from $400 to $1,000 a day. A neophyte licensee may be literally unable to start up without using one or more consultants, and even experienced operators will frequently rely on the expertise consultants provide. (As you can imagine, sharing such expertise has been one pressure toward or byproduct of consolidation.) A great deal of highly specialized knowledge and experience must be brought to bear immediately once the FCC has given the licensee authority to operate the station following construction or, more commonly, a license transfer.

Estimating Potential Revenue

It's a cold, hard reality, but programming decisions are based primarily on their revenue potential. Maximizing advertising revenue is normally the goal of the station's owners, and the value of a station and its programming is found in the value of the audience to advertisers. Program directors need some understanding of basic business principles in order to be effective. Good programming (along with good promotion and a few other factors) should deliver a good, salable audience. That is what determines the success (or failure) of a station (unlike commercial-free services).

In addition to cable, satellite and online radio competing for audiences, television, outdoor, direct mail and those few remaining newspapers compete with radio for many of the same advertising dollars. The increasing number of stations and audio services has fragmented the available audience more than ever, making survival even more difficult. Broadcast radio is generally viewed as a mature medium, demonstrating little revenue growth.

Although total revenues for the industry have gone up in recent years despite the recent recession, this factor is rapidly affected by dips and rises in the overall economy. Radio's percentage of total advertising dollars has been around 6 to 8 percent for decades, and consolidation did not improve that figure as many had hoped it would (leading many of the largest groups to divest some of the stations they perceived as less important, often in smaller markets).

On the other hand, the new competition hasn't particularly hurt it, as yet—largely because most services are supported by subscriptions rather than by advertising, or they have limited availability to audiences compared with broadcast radio, or because they don't accept advertising (or only very limited amounts). The picture may not stay this way.

It is important to keep in mind that commercial media compete intensely for local advertising revenues. In any area, advertisers most desire the 18- to 49- or 25- to 54-year-old audience (although as the baby boomer generation ages past 60, some advertisers and programmers are beginning to target those older demos). In radio, the audience subdivides into 10- to 15-year segments that specific formats target.

Following Arbitron's pattern, most radio audience segments end in a 4. *If particular advertisers are not seeking all listeners 25 to 54, then they generally want a subset of that market;* some seek subgroups of 25 to 34, 25 to 44, or 35 to 54. For example, many nightclubs and other entertainment venues target audiences aged 18 to 24 or 18 to 34.

Selected advertisers, such as banking, financial institutions and packaged vacations, may seek listeners aged 55 to 64. For the most part, though, older people are seen as set in their buying habits, and regarded as saving money rather than spending it; it is presumed that they have probably bought just about everything they are ever going to buy. This perception is not necessarily accurate, however, because people are living longer, healthier, more active lives.

Many advertisers are most interested in the large population bulge represented by the baby boomers. They see that market as having money, responding to advertising and receptive to buying, even if it means going into debt. Stations have tended to track the boomer generation and adjust their music formats to continue to appeal to this group as it ages. This has resulted in continued heavy play of late '50s, '60s and '70s music (oldies or classic rock, as well as AC formats that feature plenty of songs from that era), which capitalizes on the hit songs of the baby boomers' teens-through-20s years. The next largest population bulge, the boom echo, were teens and 20s themselves from roughly the mid-80s to shortly after the turn of the century. Their music is also well represented, in various alternative and rock formats as well as contemporary country and Hot AC.

Step-by-Step Selection Process

Format strategy can be examined by working through a hypothetical market—say, a metropolitan area of slightly more than 1 million people, with 19 commercial stations licensed to the city or to nearby suburbs. The market also includes four noncommercial stations: three public radio stations affiliated with colleges and a contemporary Christian station. (The different nature of noncommercial operations is discussed in Chapter 10.) See 11.9 for a list of commercial stations in this

11.9 **List of Stations, Formats, Facilities, Owners and Ratings in the Hypothetical Market (6 A. M.–Midnight, Monday–Sunday)**

Station Format	ERP/HAAT Frequency	Owner	Share 12+ Cume (00)	M 18–34	W 18–3	M 25–54	W 25–54
KAAA-FM	97 kw kW/375m	Big Sky	**8.2**	**24.6**	8.4	**12.6**	3.9
Rock	100.7		1475	559	329	558	309
KBBB-FM	6 kw kW/100m	Big Sky	2.3	0.8	0.8	2.7	2.7
Smooth jazz	98.1		446	41	39	147	156
KPPP-FM	100 kw/325m	Big Sky	5.6	7.6	10.7	5.6	6.7
Hot AC	99.1		1423	329	409	379	465
KSSS	1 kwD/1 kwN	Big Sky	1.5	2.9	0.1	3.2	0.4
Sports	620		386	89	9	217	39
KSSS-FM*	6 kw/90 m	Big Sky	1.7	3.8	0.4	4.0	0.4
Sports	105.1		401	120	31	263	52
KCCC-AM	1 kwD/1 kwN	HugeCo	1.3	1.4	2.0	1.1	1.2
Variety	1320		309	63	79	70	97
KDDD-FM	100 kw/300 m	HugeCo	**10.9**	10.5	**18.5**	5.4	**11.6**
CHR	102.9		2268	443	575	434	692
KIII-FM	100 kw/425 m	HugeCo	3.9	1.3	3.8	2.6	7.1
Soft AC	94.9		918	97	174	219	389
KKKK-AM	5 kwD/5 kwN	HugeCo	**6.5**	2.0	1.4	5.3	3.5
News/talk	1010		1207	77	65	329	254
KLLL-FM	100 kw/425 m	HugeCo	6.1	6.6	11.1	4.6	7.9
Hot country	102.1		1249	223	334	301	412
KOOO-FM	98 kw/350 m	HugeCo	**7.6**	5.0	6.6	6.8	**8.1**
Country	96.3		1401	162	256	326	441
KRRR-AM	5 kwD/5 kwN	HugeCo	1.1	0.1	0.1	1.3	0.5
Talk	910		359	10	11	90	43
KFFF-FM	100 kw/400 m	RadioEast	5.4	3.4	7.9	4.0	9.2
AC	104.3		1201	149	268	285	500
KGGG-AM#	50 kwD/50 kwN	RadioEast	1.4	0.2	0.1	1.4	0.6
Oldies	1490		392	21	14	92	67
KGGG-FM#	100 kw/275 m	RadioEast	5.8	1.4	2.4	6.2	6.9
Oldies	92.7		1156	86	82	351	387
K J J J-FM	100 kw/300 m	RadioEast	**6.5**	7.7	4.3	**12.4**	6.1
Classic rock	107.7		1199	258	180	584	359
KNNN-AM	1 kwD	Hometown	3.7	4.1	5.5	2.5	4.5
Urban	1110		513	90	129	104	166
KHHH-AM	2.5 kwD/.5 kwN	Faith	0.9	0.2	0.5	0.8	0.8
Religious	780		252	21	11	69	63
KEEE-FM	100 kw/250 m	OK Ltd.	4.4	3.3	1.7	4.1	2.9
Classic country	93.5		730	86	78	186	174

*Simulcast approximately 75%.

#Simulcast approximately 90%.

hypothetical market. **Boldfacing** shows the leading station in each demographic group.

The market is typical of many medium and large markets, with three significant group-owned station clusters. The remaining commercial stations in the market are owned by small groups, with additional properties located in other markets. Of the three groups, HugeCo controls the most stations in the market and is one of the biggest national station groups, with several hundred stations covering all market sizes. Big Sky is also a major group with around 200 stations nationally, primarily in medium and a few large markets. RadioEast is a relatively small company, family controlled with fewer than 20 stations, most in medium and small markets. This is their largest cluster and second-largest market.

After a period of rapid consolidation, programming and station rankings in the hypothetical market have been fairly stable for the past couple of years. The last station acquisition took place two years ago when RadioEast bought into the market. The last format change (KIII's move to soft AC from alternative) took place at about the same time. There is relatively little competition within formats; KDDD-FM, KAAA-FM, KOOO-FM and KKKK-AM have generally been the ratings leaders for quite some time.

Station facilities are remarkably equivalent. Of the AMs, only one station is a daytimer (KNNN), although KHHH does have a restricted nighttime pattern. In the FM band, all are high-powered class Cs with the exception of Big Sky's KBBB and KSSS, both of which are class A stations licensed to nearby suburbs of the metro city. Most of KSSS's programming is simulcast on KSSS-AM as well as on four other AM stations around the state (billed as the Sports Monster Radio Network). Big Sky recently added a translator for KBBB on the opposite side of the metro area to improve coverage.

Even taking into account the relatively poor nature of its facility, Big Sky believes KBBB is underperforming in its present/smooth jazz format and is considering a format change. *Given the makeup of the market, what are the best options? Is there a format that could improve Big Sky's overall competitive situation? What groups are unserved in the population?* See 11.10 for a description of the population distribution in the hypothetical market.

First, let's look at the competitive structure of the market. Big Sky's existing primary strength is in the male demos; it has the number-one station (KAAA) among men aged 18 to 34 and 25 to 54. Between the rock and sports stations, it has nearly 35 percent of the 18 to 34 male demographic and a 20 percent share of men aged 25 to 54. With classic rock and oldies formats, RadioEast is also strong in the male demographics, but has primarily an older audience (remember the skew graphs?). Meanwhile, because of its size, HugeCo has effectively covered the full age range on the female side. Big Sky has only one female skewing station, hot AC KPPP, which is a distant third among women aged 18 to 34 behind HugeCo's CHR KDDD and hot country KLLL. Among women aged 25 to 54, KPPP is seventh, also trailing HugeCo's mainstream country KOOO, RadioEast's AC KFFF, and oldies KGGG.

Given that overview, let's look at potential format holes in the market. We can eliminate the news

11.10	Selected Population and Demographic Estimates

Total metro population: 861,000

Total DMA population: 1,300,000

DMA Racial/Ethnic Population Estimates

White	77.0%
Black	10.0%
Hispanic	5.0%
Asian	3.0%
Native American	5.0%
Women	51.4%
Men	48.6%
Teens 12–17	10.5%
18–24	11.3%
24–34	16.5%
35–44	18.7%
45–54	16.4%
55–64	10.6%
65+	16.0%

and talk formats right away. They're expensive to program, requiring large staffs unless you offer primarily syndicated or network fare; and with two stations covering that territory, there are already enough stations in the market providing that programming.

We can also eliminate country off the top. Although this is a strong market for county music, there are already three stations in the format, with a combined 18 share of persons 12+. Each station has carved out its own audience niche, and no single station seems to have a segment large enough to further subdivide. Moreover, the two most successful country stations are owned by HugeCo, and their combined promotional and programming strength would represent a substantial barrier for any new competitor to overcome. Big Sky should look elsewhere.

The situation in AC is similar, except that no owner has more than a single station in the format. KFFF, KIII and KPPP represent a combined 15 share (and a whopping 23 share among the primary target audience, women aged 25 to 54), and their formats are spread across the range of AC programming. A fourth station would be competing head-to-head with one—and, to some extent, with all three plus CHR KDDD (which, like many CHR stations, sounds more like an AC format during weekdays in order to better capture at-work adult listeners). There could be some small niche available, but the competition in this segment, although indirect, is most likely a significant factor in KBBB's current low ratings. Moreover, we certainly want to avoid potentially cannibalizing our existing female audience on KPPP.

In the rock category, Big Sky is dominant (KAAA). Oldies and classic rock belong to competitors, but those are generally one-to-a-market formats (although an oldies hybrid might be a possibility). Combining the sports stations (KSSS-AM and FM) with KAAA, Big Sky has very strong male numbers. *Perhaps it would be possible to further increase our younger male demographic power with an alternative format or add some older listeners with a AAA format?* The rock audience will generally accept alternative music on their station,

although the reverse is often not true, and KAAA plays some alternative music. Most likely, moving KBBB to alternative would simply take audience from KAAA, leaving little or no net gain.

There are several possibilities, however. One option would be an older-skewing music format like adult standard. This audience is not well served by existing programming, but that is because an older audience (55+) is often difficult to sell to advertisers. Another possibility is urban or urban oldies, currently available only on an AM daytimer with poor facilities. According to the U.S. census data, the market has a substantial minority population (approximately 10 percent black and 5 percent Hispanic), and the urban format can also have substantial appeal for white ethnic audiences. One of the Hispanic formats might succeed if it had that market all to itself, although implementation is difficult for a company without previous experience in that marketplace because of language and cultural barriers.

Finally, there's CHR, currently represented by the 12+ market leader KDDD with a share of 10.9 percent. That big share of the audience is a tempting target, and the opportunity for Big Sky to strike at the market's biggest group is a battle many program directors would relish. Moreover, the CHR (or the urban) audience would be a good fit for KPPP if there were some minor tweaking of its format, and this could potentially strengthen Big Sky's relatively weak overall female numbers without Big Sky having to simply steal from KPPP's existing audience (although there would undoubtedly be some audience sharing).

Thus, an urban hybrid (rhythmic CHR or urban AC) looks to be the best opportunity in the market. Census data indicates a substantial younger population—57 percent—within the target age range for contemporary music (28 percent in the core demographic between 18 and 34 years of age, plus 11 percent aged 12 to 17, and another 18 percent aged 35 to 44; slightly more women than men in all ages). Most of this audience is currently served by relatively few stations because the majority of stations chase the mid-adult demos. The existing urban station would not be a significant competitor because of its facility. In addition, picking rhythmic CHR rather than true urban would allow the new KBBB to attract listeners from the large KDDD audience and potentially turn them into listeners whose first preference is KBBB (**P1s** in rating terminology—the core listeners of a station).

Implementation

A format change will necessitate a new station identity (new call letters, which would require an FCC application, and a fresh slogan), new music and probably new air talent. Moreover, the work will have to happen quietly, behind the scenes, in order to avoid tipping off the other stations (and media reporters) in the market. That means some (or even all) of the work must be done away from the station or at times when few, if any, other staff are around. The program director's first step is to settle on the station's target audience and identity.

Branding and positioning are complicated matters, but in simplest terms, *the station needs to create an image in the audience's minds that matches the audience's self-image. In other words, the station should fit into the listeners' desired lifestyle in all regards, from the music to the logo and slogan to the DJ patter between songs.* Who is the typical listener, the highly valued P1? In this case, imagine a young (20- to 30-year-old) adult, most likely female, who works in a professional or technical field; she enjoys music (with a danceable beat), clubs, movies and sports; drives a small, sporty car; is interested in fashion; dines out several times a week; exercises regularly; and enjoys traveling.

Next, we'll need to consider, in consultation with the general manager and other corporate executives, whether current Big Sky personnel (at KBBB or perhaps KPPP, or at another station outside the market) are suited to the new format. If so, those people may be quietly brought into the process as needed. If not, there will be that much more work for the PD and the one or two other managers who are aware at this point of the impending change. The air staff can be hired prior to the debut but doesn't have to be. Some stations change format, then

gradually add air talent as they can be located and hired. In the interim, the station operates either without DJs or by utilizing voice tracking.

Some stations have used the initial launch period to make a splash in the market by offering extended commercial-free stretches or other special programming that lasts a few hours to a few days. But beware of setting up inappropriate audience expectations with this strategy. *Whatever management does needs to both encourage the target audience to sample the station and begin the process of building an affinity with that audience.*

Building the station's music library is another task to be accomplished before the format goes on the air. Developing rapport with record company promoters is one way to receive music (see 11.11 to get a sense of the risks). When the music director or program director makes contacts with friends in the music business, the station gets on their call schedules and mailing lists. This ensures that the station will receive all the current material promptly, in many cases prior to the actual release date. Most important, however, is becoming a reporting station for trade journals. Getting current CDs is fairly easy for stations in larger markets and others that report their airplay to major trade outlets because the record labels will happily provide them. There are also more specialized trade journals, such as *CMJ* (*www.cmj.com*), and reporting airplay to those magazines can also be a way to ensure music service (see 11.12).

To prepare a new contemporary format, the station needs the previous 6 to 12 months of releases. Performance licenses (requiring annual royalty fees) should be obtained from each of the three traditional performance rights organizations (PROs): **ASCAP** (*www.ascap.org*), **BMI** (*www.bmi.com*) and **SESAC** (*www.sesac.com*). The licenses grant the station the right to play nearly all popular music, a necessary expense for music stations. The PROs then distribute most of the money to the music's copyright holders (music publishers and songwriters), based on surveys reporting the amount of airplay.

If the station plans to stream its signal online, separate licenses are required from ASCAP, BMI and SESAC. More significantly, streaming requires paperwork to be filed with the U.S. Copyright Office

11.11 Pay-for-Play

Record companies rely on about 1,000 radio stations in the largest markets to expose their records and thus influence music sales, although online exposure is now also significantly influencing sales. Dozens of songs are released weekly, but only a handful of slots open on most radio station playlists. To call attention to new releases, the record industry enlists promotion specialists who introduce the product to radio programmers. Some of these promoters are label employees; others are independent contractors, often called "indies."

One promotion strategy used to be called "Pay-for-Play" but that term (and the associated practices) are in bad odor. Some indies were paid by major labels to get songs on major station playlists, and payments varied based on the station's market size. Bonuses were paid when songs were added during a desired week, a song's rotation increased or a song reached a certain position on the playlist. Indies paid the *station* for the right to "represent" them by getting the station exclusive releases, prizes or other promotional considerations. The indies guaranteed promotional payments to the stations, then billed the record companies.

This sounds smelly, but the "Pay-for-Play" strategy was *technically not payola* because indies didn't pay DJs to play specific songs; they wrote their contracts with participating stations. However, the word *indies* has been tarred because it has been used for both highly questionable "Pay-for-Play" promotion (read *payola*) as well as legitimate promotion by independent contractors.

In genres that don't rely on mass audiences, independent promoters are effective and generally work fully within the law. Texas, for example, has its own blend of roots country music, and about a dozen promoters target radio stations in the state. The Americana format—a hybrid of country, roots and folk—has promoters dedicated to its stations. Christian and college broadcasters have their own cadres of indie promoters.

Some indies are paid by artists and smaller labels to represent them in small markets in the hope of gaining notice by larger stations. Money is not usually passed on to stations at this level (though one wonders where it goes …). Labels can also bypass promoters and programmers to deal directly with big station groups at the corporate level. Fees are considered "sponsorship" when songs are previewed by corporate programmers or "showcases" when new talents perform.

The internet has certainly facilitated the success of local artists and bands by giving thousands of groups a chance to find an audience. Artists are creating their own promotions via websites, and of course social networks can build fan support and regional popularity. Moreover, the enormous impact of videos going viral on YouTube can't be overestimated.

Frank Chorba, Ph.D.
Washburn University

(*www.copyright.gov*) along with a small fee, and additional performance royalties are due to the record labels and musicians. That separate performance right is acquired from SoundExchange (*www.soundexchange.com*), an organization formed to manage those digital copyrights for the record labels much as the traditional PROs track airplay and collect and distribute money for songwriters.

When assembling the music library, someone will have to dig for the recurrents and the gold—especially the latter. Because of their age, physical copies of these recordings may be scarce. Promoters and distributors are often out of stock and in some cases, discs are simply out of print. In a pre-digital world, it could have taken months to build the gold library, and these recordings would have been kept under lock and key to forestall avid collectors among staff members. This remains true today for the few stations that still play compact discs on the air, use carts (audio cartridges), reel-to-reel or even on special occasions, actual vinyl records. While certainly not commonplace for everyday use, many facilities still possess the ability to use one or more of these now antiquated technologies.

If nothing more than for ease and sound quality, most radio stations' audio functions are completely digital. This is especially true for the music library if the desired format is already in use by the company

11.12 Measuring Airplay

Disagreements about airplay decisions and how the quantities of spins are reported have been an onoing problem for both radio and the music industry. Because of flagrant abuses in the past when stations and local retailers individually reported figures, nowadays sales figures and airplay (spins) are monitored by such independent tracking organizations as Nielsen Broadcast Data Systems and Mediabase Research. Outside monitoring presumably prevents unscrupulous programmers from reporting that they played certain songs more or less frequently than they really did. Subsequently, station play figures are compiled into charts for various formats, and reported in trade magazines like *Billboard*.

Frank J. Chorba, Ph.D.
Washburn University

in another market. Online file transfers, flash memory devices and cheap digital storage make compiling an initial music library a process that may take only a day or two as opposed to months. It should be noted, however, that a music library is never "complete," but rather is continually changing with music being added and removed almost daily.

Some stations employ the use of *gold services* such as TM Studios' Gold Disc™ Library, a complete oldies library available on compact disc. Although it is an additional programming cost to the station, a purchased library offers savings in time and convenience. Each disc contains upwards of 20 songs, and provides an expansive collection of "the hits." In a newer incarnation, TM Studios (*tmstudios.com*) provides various catalogues of oldies and currents in both compact disc and on demand formats, including the popular *Prime Cuts* discs that are mailed weekly to the station. TM Studios also provides a comprehensive collection of online services that provide on-demand download capabilities. Depending on how far back a station will need to go for music, another online service may provide all of the necessary audio needed for the library. A straight-ahead CHR whose gold category may only go back three to five years would likely find everything

needed to complete the library in a service (or combination of services) like Play MPE (*plaympe.com*), New Music Server (*newmusicserver.com*) or Radio Currents (*radiocurrents.com*). These services are available to program directors music directors and operations managers through an agreement between the station and the service for providing digital audio licensed for broadcast use, and may contain audio in all categories from gold to currents.

Another option that may be preferable when putting a station on the air with brand new facilities is to simply purchase a digital automation system with a complete (or nearly complete) music library pre-loaded in the system. Wide Orbit (*wideorbit.com*) is one such company. In addition to WO *Automation for Radio*, they also own the rights to automation software like *Scott Studios 32* and *Maestro* (products formerly owned by dMarc and Google). Another major provider is RCS (*rcsworks.com*), owned by Clear Channel, which offers automation products like *Zetta* and *NexGen* in addition to the widely used music scheduling software *Selector*. They can include the music itself (for an additional charge, of course).

Digital automation systems are dedicated computers that are used solely for running the radio station, and often contain a central server with hard-drive audio storage and a separate machine that acts as the user interface and playback machine in each of the station's control rooms. All of the music, station imaging, promos and commercial inventory can be first hosted on the server, and are streamed over the local network to the computers in the control room for storage and playback on air. This is especially efficient in the case of audio files that are used on more than one station in the cluster. Take, for example a commercial for a local car dealer: Rather than loading the car commercial on to each of the station's machines individually, the spot can be placed on the server and then distributed to one or all of the on-air machines in the building (or maybe be sent farther away). This double redundancy can also be a lifesaver in the event of a catastrophic failure of one of the local machines in a control room. *In a digital environment where no physical copy exists, backups (and backups of backups) are essential.*

Initially, the program director will need to temporarily act as the music director in order to structure the music when revamping a station or flipping formats. Later, those duties can be transitioned to one of the jocks who will act as the music director (MD). In a typical setup, the music director works for the program director, overseeing music research, taking calls from record company promotion reps and independent promoters, and preparing proposed additions and deletions to the playlist. The program director has the right to make the final call, but the music director does the background work.

The Station Sound

As you might guess, the four main elements that go into creating the sound of a radio station are *the music, the jocks, the imaging* and *the commercials* (spots). The art of radio programming is finding just the right balance as these elements come together, and that balance in turn determines whether the final product is great, mediocre or downright terrible. Clearly, no *one "right way" to program a radio station exists* (or we'd all listen to the same stations). Rather, each PD has his or her own style that influences the overall sound and gives each station its own unique personality. Most programmers will specialize in one specific format, or at most a handful of formats, but what works in one format probably doesn't work in another, and the same problem exists from market to market. One common key, however, to programming success in all formats is good research, driven by the listeners. Ultimately, the listeners decide the success or failure of a PD each time a new ratings book is released (and a lot of tension precedes the release of each book!).

To illustrate how the basic process works, this chapter presents a model that combines aspects of systems used by radio stations across the country. This system represents one plan for programming a rhythmic CHR station that is designed to achieve maximum attractiveness to the target demographic of Adults 18-34.

The Anatomy of the Clock

One of the program director's major responsibilities is to construct one or more clocks that serve as templates for each hour of a station's programming. So called because it resembles the face of a clock, it creates a graphic representation of the formula by which the station is built to achieve the desired "sound." A clock will divide any given hour of programming into portions for music (by category), station elements (jock chatter, weather, news, imaging and promos), as well as commercials. It will also provide specific placement (in minutes) for each of the elements that make up the hour. For instance, commercial breaks may be scheduled to always fall at 20 and 50 minutes after the top of the hour, with weather being the last element in the 20 break.

The PD also will create as many clocks as are needed: one for an hour with no news, another for an hour with two newscasts, another for an hour with one newscast, another for an hour with 10 commercial minutes (or 12 or 16 or however many the station allows and could sell). Clocks are a way to effectively manage dayparting—that is, estimating who is listening at a particular time of day and what their activities are, and then programming directly to them.

The most common dayparting strategies use Arbitron-defined standard dayparts: **Morning Drive** from 6 A.M.–10 A.M., **Middays** from 10 A.M.–3 P.M., **Afternoon Drive** from 3 P.M.–7 P.M., **Evenings** from 7 P.M.–Midnight, and **Overnights** from Midnight–6 A.M. Each daypart may have its own clock or multiple clocks. Conversely, there may be one clock for morning drive, and the same clock may be used throughout the rest of the day.

The Music

Our hypothetical rhythmic CHR will use five major music categories: power, current, recurrent, power gold and gold, though other stations or formats might employ additional categories. Some programmers might also further divide the categories by tempo, style, genre or—in the case of formats with substantial gold libraries—by era.

The Model

Any contemporary music station can use this basic formula ranging from CHR to rock and AC, country or urban. It would require significant modification, however, to work for an oldies or classical format.

Power. This category contains approximately ten top songs, played at the rate of four to eight each hour. (The rotation would be slower, one to three each hour, in most non-CHR formats.) Rotation is controlled so that the same song is not played at the same time of day on consecutive days. Rotation time, or the time that elapses before the cycle of ten songs begins again, will likely vary by daypart ranging from as little as 75 to 90 minutes in the late afternoon and evening in our rhythmic CHR format to as much as six or eight hours in some AC or rock formats. The exact rotation is decided by the program director. The songs in this category are the most popular of the day and receive the most airplay. They are selected weekly based on the following:

- How they test during call-out research with the station's audience

- Their national airplay rankings and audience test scores from services like BDS Radio (*bdsradio. com*, airplay charts available at *radio-info.com*)

- Local sales (to a lesser degree, but still may produce "local hits")

Area record stores can be contacted weekly for sales information, which they record by bar code. In smaller markets, rankings of sales and airplay in trade magazines often play the biggest part in determining playlists (see the "Music Research" section of this chapter). In bigger markets, telephone testing was traditionally used to measure popularity, but the popularity of cell phones among young listeners and restrictions on calling out have diminished the use of this option. In a call-out, a sample audience hears part of a song, almost always "the hook," and is asked to evaluate it. Many stations also now use online panels of listeners to evaluate songs.

Current. This category contains the remaining 20 or so currently popular songs. They are played at the rate of three or four per hour (in an hour with no

commercials, five might be played). Some stations subdivide this category by tempo or mood, placing slow songs in one group and fast, upbeat ones in another; other programmers subdivide by popularity, grouping those moving up in the charts separately from those that have already peaked and are moving down in the charts. The same research methods used to determine the power songs determine those in the current category. Together, the powers and currents form the station's current playlist of about 30 songs.

Recurrent. This category contains songs that are no longer powers or currents but have been big hits within the last two years. (Some rock and AC stations may keep songs for up to three years in the recurrent section.) These songs get played at the rate of two to four per hour, depending on commercial load and desired rotation time in the first two categories. Some stations limit this category to 30 records played at the rate of one an hour; others may have as many as 100 songs, playing them twice an hour. Songs usually move into this category after being powers or currents, after a short "resting" period (where the song is not played on the station at all) of anywhere from one to four weeks depending on the song. A few songs will be dropped from the library and never make it to the recurrent category, predominantly novelty records that are burned out (listeners have tired of them) and records that *stiffed* (failed to become really big hits). These songs should be tested periodically for audience burnout by telephone call-out or web-based research.

Power Gold. This category contains records that were very big hits in the past three to ten years. There may be anywhere from 100 to 300 of these classics, and they are played at the rate of one to three per hour, depending on commercial load and format. The songs are recycled every few days with a few "new songs" from the library of power golds being added, and others being removed ensuring this category always stays fresh. These are the "never-die" songs, often by core artists in the format, that will *always* be recognized by the target audience and *immediately* identified as classics. They greatly enhance the format because listeners get the impression that the station airs a broad range of music. Because there are so many of them, auditorium research is the best way to test these songs for desirability, recognizability and burnout, but they may occasionally also be rotated through call-out or web tests.

Gold. The gold category contains the "best of the best" from the past 10 to 15 years that are not in the recurrent or power gold categories. This group of 200 or so titles is played at the rate of maybe one an hour, depending on format and commercial load. In some formats, they may disappear entirely for certain dayparts (in the case of our hypothetical rhythmic CHR, we probably would not schedule many, if any, in afternoon drive and evenings). Songs in this group are carefully researched, usually with auditorium tests, to make sure they appeal to the station's target demographic group and are not suffering from burnout. Stations can extend their gold categories by not including in the active library every song that meets their criteria for airplay. Rotating songs in and out of the active gold library every few weeks—or creating subcategories that rotate at different speeds—can increase the audience's sense of musical variety on the station—while maintaining a consistent sound.

A final category, **oldies**, may complete the record library for some formats (although CHR stations omit it entirely). Oldies comprise the largest group because it covers the greatest span of time—all the hit songs from the 1950s up to 10 or 15 years ago. As many as 600 songs may be in the group, and they are played at the rate of one to two per hour in some formats. The commercial load and the number of older listeners the station wants to attract will determine how many oldies get played. Songs in this group had to be hits at the time they were released and must continue to be popular. Programmers for AC and oldies stations subdivide songs in this category according to the dates the songs were originally hits. The year categories listed here roughly parallel major historical shifts in the style of popular music:

- Mid-1950s to 1964
- 1965 to 1972
- 1973 to 1980
- 1980 to the early 1990s

It is important to manage the rotations carefully within gold, power gold and oldies categories, because there is never any "new" music from these periods; that is to say, you can't go back in time ten years and release a new song. There are only a certain number of songs that will exist in these categories, which is why program directors will hold some of them back, playing only 30 to 50 at a time when the library has more than 200 titles. This little trick enables the listener to still find discovery (or the "man, I haven't heard this song in forever") factor that exists with older songs. There are no "new oldies," so programmers have to be smart about their use.

Finally, it is important for programmers to realize that a song that is a huge hit in one market can be a dismal flop in another. This is especially important for a PD to remember when moving to an unfamiliar city.

The Research

In case we haven't said this often enough, *the key ingredients in designing a successful format are careful planning, ongoing local research and a willingness to adapt to changing audience tastes and competition.* Although music tastes within a format tend to be more homogenized nationally today than in the past, because of video music channels on cable, the mobility of the population and consolidation in the music and radio industries, successful programmers are always aware of—and take advantage of—market-specific variations. Music stations may employ one or more people to handle call-out or web-based research and to assemble statistics, or the music director may work with specialized consulting services.

The *more* objective information that the researcher gathers, the easier it is for the programmer to evaluate the record companies' advertising and sales. Record promoters naturally emphasize their products' victories, neglecting to mention that a record died in Los Angeles or Kansas City. The station must depend on its own research findings to rate a piece of music reliably.

As explained in Chapter 5, call-out and web-based research gets reactions directly from radio listeners. Two versions of the technique are used—active and passive. In active call-out research, the names of active listeners are obtained from lists of contest entrants or regular listeners who volunteer to be part of a web panel. The passive version selects names at random from the telephone directory (see 11.13).

Another method of radio research, primarily for the gold and recurrent parts of the library, is auditorium testing. Several companies specialize in this kind of audience research. Typically, they bring a test group to a large room and ask them to evaluate music as excerpts are played. As many as 300 songs may be tested, with the audience writing their responses on special forms or punching in responses

electronically. The tabulated results will be broken down demographically and usually provide valuable information to programmers about which songs to play in which dayparts and which songs may be wearing out for the target audience. Additional questions can be asked; for example, "What station do you listen to most?" "Second most?" "Who has the best news/the best sports/the best personalities?" "What is the most irritating?" and so on.

Web-based systems have made research more accessible to small- and medium-market stations than traditional telephone or auditorium testing because web testing is less expensive. The process begins similarly to that of active call-out telephone testing. A station recruits a sample of audience members willing to participate in testing (in this case, via on-air announcements or the station's website). Once the panel is assembled, the program director uploads the song hooks to the website weekly (or

---

11.13 Call-Out Research

When calling randomly selected people out of the telephone book, the first step in an interview is to qualify the person—that is, to make sure the person is in the target demographic and listens to, or prefers, the kind of music the station plays. In either case, respondents are asked to listen to excerpts (*hooks*) from the songs being researched and to rate them on a scale from 1 to 5 as follows:

1 = "Hate it."

2 = "Dislike it."

3 = "Don't care."

4 = "Like it."

5 = "My favorite record."

Research will also assess the extent to which a record might be burned out by asking listeners whether they are "tired" of hearing the song. (A high burnout percentage tells a PD that the song might need to be retired from the active library, either temporarily or permanently.) When a sample is completed (100 calls is typical), the votes for each number on the scale are tabulated. The various totals are then manipulated to obtain interpretations in terms of ratios or percentages.

For example, assume 100 listeners are called within a week, and 30 records are discussed. Twenty-four listeners say they like song number five, and 36 say it is their favorite record; 11 said they didn't like it, 6 didn't care, and 9 hated it. Fourteen had never heard it before (a very high recognition rate of 86 percent). Song number five thus has a total score of 325 and an average response of 3.78—this song is scoring very well with that core audience. It should definitely be high in the playlist, and depending on its age, trend and the scores of other current songs, it might qualify for the power category.

When doing call-based research of any kind, it is crucial that the questions be asked in the right manner. It is important to make the respondents understand that they are being asked to help determine the station's music selection. Because the station is their favorite, they should be pleased to have the opportunity to shape its programming even more to their liking. During a music interview, respondents can also be asked to comment on other things they like or dislike about the programming. This requires a sympathetic ear on the part of the researcher. No arguing back allowed.

even more frequently if needed) and then sends out an email to the sample group announcing that the music is ready for their assessment. The listeners then complete the testing at their convenience, and the results are made available immediately to the program director and music director.

The Rotation

Regardless of format, music stations must control rotation, or the frequency of play of different kinds of songs. For many years, stations used a flip card system (really!). Each song was placed on a 3 × 5 index card in a file box, sometimes separated into different categories of music. DJs were instructed to play the next available and appropriate song and place the flip card at the back of the stack.

Surprisingly, the basic system hasn't changed much, but music scheduling software allows for a much more sophisticated means of tracking what song is played, and where it is played in regard to the other elements surrounding it. By placing "restrictions" on songs, the music director and program director create exactly the flow they want. By combining airplay data with ratings information, programmers can track how the music flow impacts audience flow as well as how frequently the audience is really hearing a song. Computers can be used to do the following:

- Follow a category rotation
- Restrict some songs to particular dayparts
- Balance up-tempo and down-tempo songs
- Avoid the scheduling of two songs by the same or similar artist too closely together (for example a power gold by Justin Timberlake followed by a gold from NSync)
- Prevent songs from playing too close to the same time every day
- Prevent adjacent songs of the same type (such as two "old school" songs or two rhythm-and-blues songs)

Adherence to such restrictions leaves most of the control in the hands of the program director rather than in the hands of the on-air personality—whose focus should be on his or her performance between songs rather than on selecting music. The

jocks as well as the program and music directors can get printed lists (paper logs) of all the songs to be played, although it is far more common to display the log on a computer monitor in the studio. Experienced talent with a good understanding of the format may sometimes be given the flexibility to make alterations to the schedule, but not all PDs are comfortable giving up that control. Similarly, freehanded jocks who think they may be able to skirt the system and add or delete songs at their leisure are often caught when the program director runs *reconciliation reports* that compare what was *supposed* to play with what *actually did* play.

When setting up the rules for the format, the PD must balance concerns about the sound of the station with the ability to schedule music. The more rules that are in place, the more difficult it becomes to schedule each day without breaking one or more rules. In setting up the rotations for various music categories, *it is especially important to watch the relationship between the number of songs in the category, the rotation speed and the clock structure.* The program director must make sure the categories are not cycling in time frames that are multiples of each other, which would lead to categories synchronizing and the same songs playing together in a pattern. In the example of our hypothetical station, the power category is set to turn over every 90 minutes. Thus, the current category should be rotated at a pace to *avoid* turning over at 3 or 4.5 hours (which would synchronize to the second or third power rotation at 90 minutes). Good choices would be 3.5 or 5.5 hours, keeping given songs in the categories out of sync for substantial lengths of time. Gold and recurrent categories generally have enough titles and slow enough rotation that synchronization is not a major issue, but programmers should still be aware of unintended patterns.

Superior program directors will manually "massage" the log prior to its final approval, personally reviewing the music song by song to catch any of the above-mentioned unintended patterns. While scheduling software usually eliminates these, the computer only knows to do what you tell it to do. Even with sufficient restrictions and rules outlined in the software, different songs by the same artist may unintentionally be scheduled as the first song out of a commercial break. Should this happen three times in a five-hour airshift, it may seem to the listener that an abnormal amount of music is being played by that artist, especially if the jock calls it to their attention. By personally reviewing the log, the PD can almost completely eliminate such errors.

The Jocks

Station personalities make up a large portion of the overall "sound" of the radio station, and along with the imaging, is what truly gives a station its own identity. Once there was the big-voice boss who told the listener this was a Big Announcer, but this style faded in the early 1970s. Now there are SCREAMERS!!! (sometimes derogatorily referred to as pukers) who try to wake the very young. Then there are the shock jocks, the adult-male-oriented personalities who court FCC retribution daily (see 12.5 in Chapter 12, which discusses indecency in radio programming). But most contemporary stations rely on conversational jocks who just talk normally, as they would with any friend, when they open the microphone switch. What they talk about, and the attitude with which they convey the information, is what makes each talent and format distinctive.

Typically jocks will work in shifts following (or on a slight variation of) the standard daypart schedule: **Morning Drive** from 6 A.M.–10 A.M., **Middays** from 10 A.M.–3 P.M., **Afternoon Drive** from 3 P.M.–7 P.M., **Evenings** from 7 P.M.-Midnight and **Overnights** from Midnight-6 A.M. The challenge for the PD is to make each daypart its own distinct entity, appropriate to the audience's characteristic activities at that time, while simultaneously keeping the station's sound consistent across all dayparts. The most important ingredient in making daypart distinctions is the personality of the jock assigned to each time period, followed by the appropriate adjustments to the music rotation and other programming elements. *Neither the PD nor the air talent should ever lose sight of the fact that consistency is the primary goal.* For key attributes of each daypart, see 11.14.

Under the direction of a strong PD, a kind of "sameness" will develop among all the jocks in a specified format without the drabness or dullness normally associated with sameness. In this context, *sameness* means consistency and not predictability. A listener who tunes in to the station at odd hours should always hear the same *sound* and get the same feeling from the station that they get when tuning into the station driving to work in the morning or on the way home in the afternoon. The listener should know what kind of programming to expect, and a well programmed station will deliver no matter the day or daypart.

The best air talent offers enough of herself or himself to the audience that a relationship develops, and the kind of familiarity translates into more regular listening. Listeners should feel as if they have a trusted friend with them in the car or at work when listening to the station. This relationship is especially true on country and adult contemporary stations, and while still a factor is less of a consideration on CHR stations. The true test is when jocks have the opportunity to interact with listeners at station events: Do the listeners initiate conversation recalling intimate details or things that were said on air weeks ago, or do they think it's just a person wearing a polo shirt with the station logo on it? Jocks are *station personalities* and should have personalities that are funny, informative, trustable and most of all likeable. Without these characteristics, the jock is nothing more than an announcer, and announcers are a dime a dozen.

The ever-increasing demand from owners to cut expenditures and post higher earnings at radio stations nationwide leads some programmers to consider going as far as eliminating some, most or all local air talent order to pass those savings to the bottom line. While this obviously would save money in the short term, a successful station can't survive for long playing just music and commercials. Radio needs personality to succeed—otherwise, the listener is more likely to plug in an iPod or fire up a service like Pandora so as to skip the commercials altogether. Technology has provided one partial solution to this dilemma: the invention of a process known as *voicetracking*, or the pre-recording of some or all of a jock's talkpoints during a shift. One or two people can voice track an entire day's programming on a station before going off to do production, engineering or sales; or one air staffer can provide voice tracks for many stations in a local or regional group, perhaps in addition to a live shift on one station.

Using the internet, it is technically easy for the air talent to be in Dallas and upload voice tracks to stations in Michigan, Florida and Oregon. (But beware the accent … People in Oregon don't talk like people in Dallas.) Not only can this provide budgetary savings for the local station, but it also offers the opportunity to use better-quality air talent than would otherwise be affordable in many small and medium markets. Large-market talent may be available to voicetrack stations for as little as $100 per week.

The downside is the potential for losing what radio is best at—*being live, local and immediate.* If a station is voicetracked from a distant source and has competition that is well programmed, live and local, history says unequivocally that the nonlocal station will lose. If management decides to voice-track, it would be best to limit it to off-peak hours like overnights, weekend mornings and nights if possible and to make every effort to ensure the talent localizes the content. Ideally, the voicetracks should be recorded as close to the actual airtime as possible in order to provide the most up-to-date information.

The Imaging

The first step in positioning the station in the listener's mind is establishing a name and call letters, which will then be used in the *imaging* or audio vignettes placed throughout the hour to establish the identity of the station. Often this will employ a mix of dial position and call letters, as well as a tag line or slogan that further establishes the station's image such as "Jacksonville's #1 Hit Music Station," or "Today's Best Country." The name should reflect the lifestyle and attitude of the target audience, and the call letters should be easily recognizable and easy to recall.

Gordon McLendon, an early innovator of the top-40 format, was one of the first broadcasters to recognize the value of sayable call letters. His first big station was KLIF, Dallas, originally named for Oak Cliff, a western section of the city. The station call was pronounced "Cliff" on the air. Then there is

KABL ("Cable") in San Francisco, KOST ("Coast") in Los Angeles, and KEGL ("Eagle Radio") in Fort Worth. These call letters are memorable and distinctive brand identities and get daily usage.

Other call letters may not stand out as much, but have a history or geographic tie-in to their metro service area. WCOL in Columbus, Ohio, employs the first three letters in the city's name, and WPTI in Greensboro, North Carolina takes its calls from the region known as the Piedmont Triad. Other times, the calls will give clues to the station's history: In Charleston, West Virginia, WVSR's calls recall the day when the station was known as "Super 102," and the calls stood for the Valley's Super Radio.

Today, nearly every city has a "Magic," a "Kiss" and a "Mix." More recent variants include names like "Alice" (KALC, a Hot AC station in Denver) or the Jack/Bob/Mike/Dave/Tom "anti-radio" or "we play everything" formats that originated in Canada and have spread to other countries (although with mixed results).

Stations often combine their call letters and dial position in on-air identifiers—especially if they are rock stations. In Indianapolis, rocker WFBQ calls itself Q95, and rhythmic CHR WBBM in Chicago is B96. This practice generally involves rounding off a frequency to the nearest whole number (102.7 as 103, or 96.9 as 97). The increase in the numbers of stereo receivers with digital dial displays, however, has discouraged the use of rounding off. Most stations now give their actual dial location on the air, such as Rock 100.5 ("Rock One Hundred Point Five"), KATT in Oklahoma City.

The Attitude

Aside from the station personalities, the imaging is the only other element that really can set a station apart from its competition. These pieces of audio are used in various places throughout the broadcast hour and "position" the radio station, and will establish the attitude of the station. For example, rock stations will almost always use a deep male voice with phrases like "everything that rocks," and attitude statements like "turn it up, and rip the knob off." Adult Contemporary stations conversely will use a

11.14 Key Personalities of Dayparts

MORNING DRIVE: Most morning jocks are friendly, funny and entertaining, all keys to relating to the target audience. Morning jocks generally talk more than air talent in other dayparts because their shows are especially service oriented. Morning-drive air talent are more than mere jokesters—*they provide the day's survival information to the audience:* how cold (or hot) it will be, whether it will rain (or snow), what time it is, frequent updates on traffic problems that will keep them from dropping the kids at daycare and getting to work on time and so on. Reports of a pile-up on one expressway give listeners a chance to switch their commuter routes—and the station a chance to earn a brownie point.

Traditionally, morning drive lasted from 6 to 10 A.M., and it is still defined that way by Arbitron. For PDs and morning jocks, however, the reality could be different. People are spending more and more time in their cars as the suburbs surrounding many large urban areas continue to sprawl outward. Commutes take new forms (suburb to suburb rather than suburb to city), and people's work schedules have changed to incorporate flex time or earlier (or later) shifts. As a result, the real "drivetime" has extended. In many markets, traffic builds to significant volume by 5:30 or even 5 A.M. Therefore, most large-market stations and some midmarket stations begin their morning shows at those earlier times. Some also end earlier, getting to their midday programming by 9 A.M.

Morning jocks are often paired in teams of a lead DJ and a sidekick—someone to bounce jokes off of—or a co-anchor who can add to the act—commonly a male plus a female. On most stations, the morning jock is the only performer permitted to violate format to any appreciable extent (the "morning zoo" approach). Indeed, morning can be almost music-free on some music stations. Normally, morning drivetime personalities are also the most highly paid, but with that pay comes greater pressure. They have a greater responsibility than other jocks because the audience is bigger in the time period than at any other time of day, and stations earn a substantial part (if not a majority) of their revenue during that daypart. For most stations, "If you don't make it in the morning drive, you don't make it at all." But how far are you willing to go to make it?

In many major markets, shock jocks rule the morning airwaves, at least among the male audience aged 18 to 49. These hosts (almost all are men) target that group with a mix of crude sexual humor and innuendo, risqué audience phone calls and titillating interviews with pop culture icons from athletes to porn stars. Some of the best known, such as Howard Stern and Opie & Anthony, have left broadcast radio for less restrictive satellite or online services. And the shock format is not confined entirely to mornings. Although some stations downplay personality in favor of heavy doses of music after 9 A.M., some practitioners of crude humor have found success (at least for limited times) in afternoon drivetime or evenings. Most large or medium markets probably have at least one performer, local or via syndication, that might be described in this vein. Some of the more well-known names often associated with this style (or who have at least attracted regular attention from the FCC for on-air antics) besides those listed above include Doug "Greaseman" Tracht, Mancow Muller and Bubba the Love Sponge.

The question for programmers is always, "What is best for the station in my situation?" A number of factors affect the decision as to whether the station should go the shock route—including the target audience and the market's taste for the material, the talent's track record (in terms of ratings and FCC enforcement), and the station owner's content policies and expectations for revenue. These performers can be consistent moneymakers, but the price can be steep. Some advertisers will shy away, no matter how big the ratings get. There is no easy answer, nor one that is correct for all stations in all markets. Programmers need to carefully juggle competing needs when selecting morning talent. *If you were programming a low- or mid-rated rock*

more conversational, upbeat station voice with phrases like "more music while you work," or "today's hits and all your favorites."

The imaging will always incorporate the name of the station in some way, and can be used in the form of sweepers, liners and jingles. In the past, imaging could last as long as 30 seconds, but the recent trend is to keep them as short as possible—sometimes as short as 5 or 8 seconds. The PD will work closely with the imaging director, who is often *station with a so-so morning show, and Mancow was available in your market, what would you do?*

MIDDAY: The midday jock is frequently conversational in style, warm and friendly. Incidental services (requiring talk) during this daypart normally are curtailed—although not eliminated—in favor of longer music sweeps. Most of the audience is at work or school. Music rotations may be slowed and more recurrents, golds and oldies added so as not to seem too repetitious to the all-day, at-work audience. Although there is still out-of-home listening during the 10 A.M. to 3 P.M. period, Arbitron data show that the majority of listeners are at home or at work. Many midday jocks capitalize on the dominantly female audience by using liners (brief continuity between songs) that have special appeal to women and by talking about what the listener might be doing at home or after work. At-work listeners may also be targeted through daytime-specific promotions (giving away lunch to everybody in the office after entrants have mailed in business cards or faxed in requests, for example). Noontime may lend itself to special programming as people leave the office or take a break from work; for example, the all-request "dinner" hours popular on many country, AC, oldies and rock stations.

AFTERNOON DRIVE: The afternoon jock (3 to 7 P.M.) is more up-tempo, as is the music rotation during this period if the station is dayparting. Teens are out of school, and adults are driving home from work. In small markets, this necessitates a delicate balance between teen-oriented music and music suiting the moods and attitudes of the going-home audience. Again, weather and traffic are important in this period (especially traffic), although not quite as much as in the morning. Information is more likely to take the form of the afternoon jock alluding frequently to evening activities—about how good it is to finish work and to look forward to whatever events people in your audience will be a part of that evening—a concert, a ball game, a movie sneak preview and so on. By Thursday, and certainly on Friday, weekend plans become a focus.

EVENING: More teens and young adults are available to listen at night, making this daypart especially strong for CHR and urban stations, as well as younger-skewing rock or country stations. The ability to use listener phone calls on the air, juggling the phones along with music and everything else, is an essential ingredient of many CHR evening jocks' shows. They may open the request lines and play specific records for specific people, get listeners to introduce songs or play along with pranks, or engage in short funny bits (with the calls always edited before playback).

Because the majority of adults over 25 are doing something other than listening to the radio (most often watching television, dealing with children and household chores and so on), AC stations, older rock outlets and other adult formats may try slightly altering their programming in the evening to attract an audience. Syndicated programs such as *Delilah* or *Rockline* offer programming that is different yet similar enough to have broad appeal for the AC or rock audience.

OVERNIGHTS: Only large-market stations typically still have live air talent in overnights, from midnight to 6 A.M. But regardless of whether the shift is live or voice tracked, the jock's attitude is usually one of camaraderie. "We're all up late tonight, aren't we? We have to work nights and sleep days." This jock must commune with the audience: the taxi drivers, revelers, police officers, all-night restaurant and grocery store workers, insomniacs, parents up giving babies two o'clock feedings, shift workers at factories, bakers and the many others active between the hours of midnight and 6 A.M. The commercial load is almost nil during this period, so the jock can provide listeners with a lot of uninterrupted music. If they're not voice tracking it, many stations will run network or syndicated material here to save on costs or use some of this time period to offer public-affairs programming.

one of the on-air personalities or the production director, to establish the overall idea, and then the imaging director will complete the clips and place them into the automation system for use in rotation.

Most stations will use *sweepers* between songs during music sweeps (hence the name). These short, highly produced imaging elements include the call letters, an identifying slogan, or air talent identifier. They move the audience from one song to the next while reminding them of the station they're listening to (for diary purposes) and reinforcing the station's image, often by making aural connections between other elements of popular culture and the station. Companies like TM Studios (*www.tmstudios.com*) can provide produced imaging spots or just the production elements (music, sound effects, drop-ins from popular movies or TV shows) for local producers to use in creating these important pieces. Music skills as well as creative audio production abilities are valuable commodities in this regard. Some companies will differentiate between different types of sweepers by assigning them different names including **stabs** or **quickies**, or categorize them into **(a) sweeps**, **(b) sweeps**, and **(c) sweeps**.

Liners serve a similar imaging and transitional purpose but are simple scripted voice tracks or live reads without music or effects. They can be used to promote upcoming station events, music coming up after the break, or a general image for the station. To be effective, however, liners must be kept fresh, constantly rewritten and replaced.

Singing *jingles*, sometimes as long as 30 or 60 seconds, were frequently the centerpiece of station imaging in most formats other than AOR prior to the mid-1980s. Companies like JAM Creative Productions (*www.jingles.com*) still produce short, custom radio IDs and jingles that consist of a few bars of music with the station call letters and identifying slogan sung over them. Producers create several versions for use between songs of different tempos and in different dayparts. Stations that purchase a jingle package generally receive not only complete jingles but also the individual components (music tracks, vocal elements, and so on) that they can remix themselves. Although available for nearly any format, they are seldom used today except on oldies, AC and country stations (as well as some news and talk outlets). Historically-minded readers can find examples of older jingles at both the JAM website and at *www.pams.com* (PAMS Productions was one of the original jingle producers in the 1950s).

The Spots

Just as there is no one "right" way to program a radio station, there is *no single set of clock formulas that will drive a station to the top of the market*. Remember that a change in one area of the clock will also change other aspects of the clock. Increasing the number of commercials per hour to satisfy demands for higher revenues means less room in a given hour for music. Less music on a music intensive station means fewer listeners, which in turn leads to lower ratings, and then to lower revenues in the long run. Spot loads will vary considerably, depending on the format. For example, news-talk stations historically carry the heaviest spot loads—potentially as many as 18 or 20 minutes per hour. Music intensive stations, however, generally do best running between 8 to 12 minutes per hour. This number may increase slightly during morning drive when music is less of a focus (and the ads have greater value).

Finding this delicate balance is often the work of intense negotiation between the PD, the sales manager and the general manager. Once an agreement is made, there should be no deviation from the plan until the time comes for a re-negotiation of the current terms. Most companies will decide on one of two systems by which to set the number of avails in an hour, either by units or by time.

In a unit system, there is a definite *number* of avails in a given hour, regardless of the duration of a spot. Most radio commercials are either (:30) or (:60) in length, but in a unit system, length is of little concern. If the consensus of management is to run three stopsets an hour with three avails per stopset, there are only ever nine avails per hour, and stopsets can be filled with any combination of spots. For example, the stopset could only ever be as long as three minutes (three sixty's), or as short as a minute and a half (three thirties). The stopset could also be comprised of two sixties and a thirty, or two thirties and a sixty, but never more than three commercials running back-to-back. This strategy is employed more often by programming-driven companies, and often times both the listener and the advertiser win;

the listener knows that the commercial breaks are usually short, and the advertiser knows they won't be lost in the clutter. Also by limiting the number of avails, a station can charge a premium price for each of the avails because fewer exist.

In a time system, management agrees to allow for a certain number of minutes per stopset. Using the previous example of three stopsets an hour, now with three minutes of avails per stopset, the commercial load could significantly increase, and spot duration is of the utmost concern. In this scenario, the stopset will still only be a maximum of three minutes in length but could contain as many as six spots per break, or conceivably as many as eighteen in a given hour if all of the spots are (:30) in duration. According to a stopwatch, the same duration of time has passed (three minutes) but perceptually the listener has endured as many as six commercials in one break. The danger in this scenario is that listeners will perceive the station as having "too many commercials," and may be inclined to tune to another station as soon as they hear the first commercial. For the station's relationship with advertisers, there can be concerns about perceptions of clutter.

In these cases, stations may try to change listener perception by having long music sweeps. Remember a change to one area of the clock means changes to other areas of the clock. Stations running "10 songs in a row," or "50 minute music hours" leave room for only one or two very long breaks. A listener staying through a ten-song sweep will have been tuned in for 35 to 45 minutes, or three quarter hours. The tradeoff is the six- or eight-minute commercial break that follows and the second long stopset that will come up after just one or two more songs. The strategy may work, at least in the short run, if everybody in the market follows along. The risk is that a heavier-than-normal spot load opens a station up to attack by a "more music" competitor.

Perceptions that audiences consider commercials to be, at best, a necessary evil, have led stations to have kicked off new formats with no commercial load whatsoever. In 2004 Nine-FM (WRZA, 99.9) launched in Chicago with 9,999 songs in a row and a promise to restrict the commercial load to just nine

units per hour afterward. A risk-filled tension always exists between the number of commercials and the number of interruptions that can be tolerated. Setting the audience up to believe that commercials will be non-existent or severely restricted makes the likelihood of long-term station success very limited—the revenue has to come from somewhere, and advertising is usually the most efficient means of generating substantial revenue (if you have a substantial audience). *One key to understanding radio programming strategy is to compare stations with regard to commercial load and the number of interruptions per hour (stopsets).* Because advertising is necessary to keep the lights on, management must establish a policy that is reflected in clocks and stick to it (see 11.15).

The Clock in Practice

Once all of the elements are established—the music is assembled into categories, the station imaging is in place, the number and duration of stopsets are decided upon and the air talent is selected—then

11.15 Quality in Commercials

Spot quality and production is critical to the station and advertiser's success. Too often, radio spots (including promos and PSAs) are full of clichéd copy and fail to grab the audience's attention. Listeners don't so much hate commercials as they hate poorly executed, pointless commercials that don't address a recognizable need of the audience. Commercials should sell the audience on the product or service by explaining how that product or service fills some need or desire, and they must complement the format rather than clash with it. Stations that will take any spot so long as it's paid for, or rely on poorly or untrained salespeople as copywriters and producers risk alienating their audiences and failing in the long run. Stations best serve their audiences and their advertisers by making sure that the commercials they run fit the format, address the target audience directly, and are creative, effective selling tools aired in a relatively uncluttered environment.

the PD can finalize the clocks and prepare them for broadcast. The clock can be created in scheduling programs like *Selector*, and the computer "knows" that at six minutes after the hour it should play the next power song. Because the computer plans ahead, it will adhere to the usual restrictions, making sure, for example, that another song by the same artist has not played recently and is not scheduled too closely in the future.

Besides structuring information (news, weather, traffic), promos and commercials, the clock also structures the music for a given hour. The music portion of an hour depends on the number of commercials to be aired. A commercial-free hour, for example, requires many more songs than an hour with 14 spots. A clock for a basic morning-drive hour designed to handle one newscast and 16 minutes of commercials appears in 11.16. This leaves room for up to 10 or 11 songs, depending on how much the DJ talks (if the station has a star morning personality, there may actually be a clock with little or no music scheduled). The music for this morning hour with approximately 10 songs might consist of four powers, two currents, two recurrents, one power gold and one gold. The service elements—news, weather, traffic—are spaced more or less evenly throughout the hour. As is typical of a contemporary music station, news has been placed in the middle of a quarter-hour. Station imaging, promotion and identification elements, either recorded or voiced live by the air talent, occur between every song.

11.16 Morning Drive

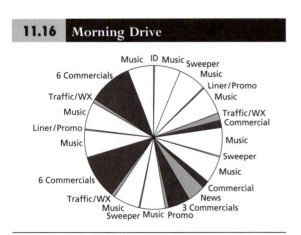

11.17 Evening Hot Clock

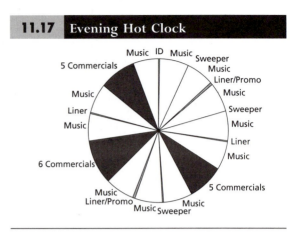

The clock in 11.17 is intended for an early-evening show. The music selection contains 12 songs made up of six powers, two currents, two recurrents, one power gold and one gold. Note the long music sweep from before the top of the hour until approximately 20 or 22 minutes past. This selection fits a CHR or urban contemporary station but would be different on a rock or mainstream country station (where the rotation of currents would be slower and more golds would be played). A midday clock might look similar to this one but with more golds and recurrents scheduled to slow down the current rotation a bit so at-work listeners aren't hearing the same song four or five times. The rotation pace of the currents would then pick up again during afternoon drivetime and evening.

Once the music log is completed using the clock as the template, it is merged with the traffic (commercial) log to create one seamless schedule known as a *broadcast log* that then is loaded in the on-air computer in the control room. In some cases, the log may even include scrollable live copy or other performance notes for the air talent. The automation software then will take over and play the log element by element until the jock in the control room stops it to talk on air. In voicetracked environments, the automation system will simply keep on running until interrupted. In some stations, the automation software is put in "auto" at 7 P.M. on a Friday, and is left running unattended until the morning team shows up on Monday.

Controlling "the Sound"

Many of the tricks used by program directors to control the sound of a radio station are not immediately noticeable to listeners but greatly affect the presentation of a station on-air. Perhaps you've heard a station that just sounds better than its competition, but you don't know why or can't quite put your finger on it. That sense is the cumulative result of all of the small factors that contribute to "the sound."

Part of controlling the sound is the processing that is placed on the station. Once the audio stream leaves the control room, it passes through a series of audio processors before making it to the transmitter and eventually over the air. Most of the processors that are used in broadcast facilities have endless settings, and a good program director will work with the engineer to get the processing just right. Oftentimes this processing will use significant *compression* on the audio signal, making it "sparkle" when it hits your receiver.

Another trick programmers will use is *speeding the music*—just slightly—before it is placed into the automation system. It was falsely believed for many years that top 40 stations sped up the playback speed on their turntables slightly to fit more music (or spots) into an hour, but that wasn't the reason. Instead, programmers speed music both to give their station more energy and thus take energy away from their competition. If you hear a song on a station that is speeding music, then tune in to the competition, that same song on the competition's station seems to drag on which makes the competing station seem slow and boring (the kiss of death).

Even on an iPod or CD, the music will never sound the same as it does on the radio station speeding the music. A famous example was a song released called "Baker Street" by Gerry Rafferty in 1977. Most stations playing that record sped the song up significantly, and in that context the song was a huge hit, making it to #2 on the Billboard hot 100. However the album, "city to city" was one of the most returned albums in music history, because the song never sounded the same at home as it did on the radio. If people returned records because the songs didn't sound the same, then it is likely that the same

perception would exist when comparing, for instance, two CHR stations. The listener will choose the one that makes them feel better and more energetic.

Another consideration for program directors is the overall *tightness* of the radio station—that is, how quickly the station moves from one element to the next. In the past, this was a trademark of a good DJ in the studio who was "jockeying" records, carts and tapes while also talking on air. In today's radio environment where almost everything is automated, the degree of tightness falls back on the program director. Tightness is achieved by placing *trip tones* or *aux marks* on the audio files before they are loaded into the automation system. These trip tones are inaudible cues that tell the computer it is time to begin playing the next element on the log. Without the use of trip tones, the song (or sweeper, commercial or voicetrack) would completely fade out to "dead air" before beginning the next element (Eeek!). The more dead air, the more *listener fatigue* sets in. Subconsciously, the listener feels exhausted just from listening to the station in part because of the constant, jerky starting and stopping of audio. With proper trip tones placed on all audio, a smooth fade happens between all elements; when one song fades out, another begins before reaching dead air. This also helps to aid in the pacing of a station, keeping it moving forward and not stopping or losing momentum.

Every program director has his or her own style that influences "the sound" of the radio station and helps to provide the station with its own unique personality. No two program directors will use the same list of tricks and procedures to make their stations unique. As discussed at the beginning of this section, ultimately the listener decides the PD's success or failure when a new ratings book is released.

Marketing and Promotion

The modern radio station pays almost as much attention to marketing as to programming. Marketing is essential for keeping a station from simply disappearing in the crowd. A carefully designed and executed social media strategy is critical for drawing listeners to the community the station wants to create, and stations continue to use television, newspapers, billboards, bumper stickers, bus cards, cab tops and other graphic media because they also help reach the target audience. Promotional stunts have long been the special province of pop radio and involve the cooperation of programming personnel. If this chapter's hypothetical station were trying to launch in a large market, the station might need as much as $2.5 million the first year for promotion.

Station promotion takes two forms: *on-air* and *off-air*. On-air promotion is suited for retaining current listeners through reinforcing their positive image of the station or extending the amount of time they listen through contesting or other incentives. Social media are also suited for image reinforcement and are the best means of building a stronger relationship with your existing audience. But social media platforms can also be used to attract new listeners—if your existing audience will serve in the messenger role. Creating evangelists out of your most dedicated listeners can be very effective—we all respond more favorably if we get a recommendation from somebody we know and trust. For a new station, attracting new listeners without that personal touch is increasingly difficult in a cluttered market space and requires a significant investment in off-air promotion, often in conjunction with on-air stunts and events, to have any chance of success. Going viral is the goal.

Off-air alternatives include billboards, television, online and direct mail. The first two are useful for broad market awareness; the latter two for more targeted campaigns. In a medium-sized market (500,000), television and billboard advertising might run $25,000 a month for good exposure. It may cost five times that in a Dallas- or Chicago-sized market. Not only are unit prices higher in large markets but more territory must usually be covered. Reaching the whole population in one market with a set of painted billboards may require 35 billboards, for example, although a similar showing in Dallas would require 125 billboards at an average cost of several thousand dollars each per month.

Some markets are now utilizing digital billboards which, though more expensive per month, give the station the ability to change what is on the billboard weekly or even daily. Television advertising, which is even more expensive but often necessary for launching a new format, can help generate the kind of top-of-mind awareness among the audience that drives ratings. Occasionally, a radio station will be able to *trade* advertising with a television station, offering mutual promotion of each other's programming.

Station promotion can have three possible goals: to *build audience share* (by extending the listening of the current audience), to *build cume* (by attracting new listeners), or to simply *enhance the audience's expectations* of the station without having to meet an immediate ratings goal (positioning). In any case, it is essential that the promotional effort be focused on the listener and the specific goal if it is to succeed. Too often, promotions happen because of advertisers' or a station's own economic concerns rather than through a focused attempt to achieve one or more of these three goals (see 11.11, which discusses the way the industry pays to get songs on the air).

Contests can build the station's share of audience if they are constructed to extend a listener's time spent with the station (see 11.18). Thus, their elements need to stretch over multiple quarter hours (but be careful not to overdo it). To build the cumulative audience, a sufficient budget is needed for reaching and enticing potential listeners with billboards, print or television or direct mail. In addition, stations should concentrate their efforts on one promotion at a time. Multiple concurrent promotions simply dilute the impact of each and may confuse and frustrate listeners. At the same time, plenty of FCC rules and regulations apply to contests and other station promotion (see 11.19).

Community involvement projects are as important as contests for programming and promoting a successful radio station. The station must be highly visible at local events to gain a strong, positive, local image. The event should be one that is of significant interest for the station's target audience and that fits their lifestyle and the station's image. The following

11.18 Contesting

The traditional promotional stunt is the contest, but the industry favors the term "word game." Many people think they cannot win contests, but they like to play games. For many stations, a contest approach emphasizes a superprize of $25,000 or more. Such amounts can be offered only a few times each year (during the Arbitron survey sweeps). And because a station cannot afford to risk losing the big prize on the first day of the game, winning has to be made difficult.

Traditional promotion theory holds that people are more likely to think they can win a small prize than succeed in a $25,000 treasure hunt or win a safe containing $50,000. With a superprize, one person is made happy, but thousands are disappointed. Thus, it would be better to break up the $25,000 prize into $250 prizes and scatter them through a more extended period. But the growth of huge national station groups has added an interesting twist. Those stations regularly pool resources and jointly run a contest with larger daily or weekly prizes than would be possible for a single station or single market cluster. Thus, instead of giving away $102 (or whatever number corresponds to a station's dial position) in the birthday game, a station may award several thousand dollars to the one hundredth caller. The catch is that the same prize is being offered simultaneously by the morning jocks on dozens or hundreds of stations across the country, making the odds of winning infinitesimal, although many in the local audience may not realize it unless they listen very carefully to the contest rules.

There are three steps to properly promoting a contest: (1) Tell 'em you're gonna do it: "It's coming—your chance to win a zillion dollars!" (2) Do it: "Listen every morning at 7:20 for the song of the day. When you hear it played later in the day, be the first caller at 555-0000 and win the money!" (3) Tell 'em you did it: "KPPP congratulates Mary Jones of your town, winner of a zillion dollars in the KPPP song-of-the-day game!" (and preferably include Mary's hyperexcited response to winning as part of the message). It is important to avoid giving exact addresses on the air. The station might be legally culpable if a robbery or other crime occurs. Also, in order to discourage possible unpleasantness for their listeners, many DJs do not use the last names of callers on the air.

Exercise caution when recording and airing telephone conversations. It is illegal to record and play back a phone call unless the person being recorded is informed of the recording and consents before recording starts or could reasonably assume from circumstances that the call might be recorded and aired. Thus, most stations avoid call-outs because the phone-call target does not respond spontaneously after going through the consent process. Listeners who call in to the studio phone line, however, are assumed to be aware that their voice may go out on the air. Management should seek legal counsel on call-out questions and should write specific instructions for programming personnel on how call-out calls are to be handled.

are community promotions that, depending on the format and market, might benefit both the station and the community:

- The station's van (often wrapped or decaled with the station's logos, armed with CDs, bumper stickers and T-shirts) sets up a tent and broadcasts live outside a venue before a big concert.
- Station jocks emceeing community events or the county fair.
- Two or three jocks take the van and sound equipment to the beach (or a public park) on the Fourth of July to provide music and "freebies" to listeners and friends.

- Stations near rivers or lakes may purchase (or more likely hire) a boat to cruise around passing out t-shirts, drink coozies or other recreation goodies to people who are listening to the radio station on weekends in the summer.
- The station runs announcements and then helps collect clothing and other items to benefit the victims of a recent tornado by letting people drop off goods at the station and has the station van parked at different collection points in the community.

Radio stations will also seek out various charity events in the community that also matter to the listeners. For example, in most communities, radio

11.19   Constraints on Programming and Promotion

Radio broadcasters have to be aware of myriad rules, regulations and guidelines. To keep up with them, radio programmers read trade journals, retain legal counsel specializing in communication law, and join the National Association of Broadcasters (NAB) as well as state broadcast organizations. Programmers have to be aware of legal constraints that may limit their ingenuity. Illegal or unethical practices such as fraud, lotteries, plugola and the like can cost a fine, a job or even a license.

Contests and Games The principal point to remember about on-air contests and games is to keep them open and honest, fully disclosing the rules of the game to listeners. Conniving to make a contest run longer or to produce a certain type of winner means trouble.

The perennial problem with many brilliant contest ideas is that, by the FCC's definition, they are lotteries—and advertising of lotteries is explicitly prohibited by federal law (although there are many exemptions for things like legal commercial casinos and Indian gaming, charity bingo nights, and state lotteries). If your contest includes a prize, requires some form of consideration and is a game of chance, it is a lottery and probably illegal. (*Consideration* here refers to payment of some kind—which could be money or extraordinary effort—that needs to be made in order for someone to be allowed to participate in a contest.) Consult the station's lawyers or the NAB legal staff if there is the slightest question.

Because of the way it conducts national contests across multiple stations in the group, at least one large group has also run afoul of the Federal Trade Commission (FTC) rules regarding deceptive advertising practices. The stations were accused of misleading listeners about the nature of the contest and their chances of winning by failing to make the multimarket, multistation nature of the contest sufficiently clear in the rules (which must be broadcast several times each day during the run of the promotion) and by broadcasting the winners' comments without identifying them as residents of other markets (thus implying they were local residents).

Sounds That Mislead Similarly, opening promos or commercials with sirens or other attention-getting gimmicks (such as "Bulletin!") cause listeners to believe unjustifiably that they are about to receive vital information. Listener attention can be gained in other more responsible ways that do not offend FCC rules or deceive listeners. Monitoring locally produced commercials or promos for misleading production techniques is especially important. Similarly, hoaxes perpetrated by air talent, even in the name of entertainment, can result in FCC penalties. For example, a station in St. Louis was cited for airing a phony emergency alert (on April Fool's Day) that claimed that the United States was under attack. Particularly offensive in the commission's view was the DJ's use of the actual emergency alert tone at the beginning of the bit to heighten the realism.

Plugola and Payola Fifty years ago, the radio industry was rocked by a series of *payola* scandals involving some of the industry's biggest names and stations, in which bribes were paid by record promoters to DJs in return for playing certain songs on the air. The bribes could be in the form of cash but just as often involved drugs, sex, trips or other inducements. Although a number of reforms were implemented in the 1960s, record promotion (the attempt to influence airplay) remains a high-stakes, high-pressure part of the music and radio businesses. Similarly, announcers who "plug" their favorite bar, restaurant or theater (in return for goods or services) are asking for trouble for themselves and the licensees (*plugola*). Certainly, any tainted jock is likely to be fired instantly. Most responsible licensees require air personnel to sign statements once every six months confirming that they have not been engaging in any form of payola or plugola; some require drug tests for their employees.

Program Logs Any announcement associated with a commercial venture should be logged as commercial matter (CM), even though the FCC has done away with requirements for program logs per se. Logs have many practical applications aside from the former legal requirement, including advertising billing, record keeping, format maintenance and format organization.

stations are heavily involved in events like Relay for Life, and will align themselves with large national charities like the American Cancer Society, American Red Cross or the National Diabetes Association.

Some stations will also leverage their audiences to put on radiothons once a year to benefit charities like St. Jude Children's Research Hospital or Children's Miracle Network. It is perfectly acceptable for a station to ask listeners to donate to a cause, and most listeners are happy to oblige for their favorite station, but care should be taken to not ask listeners to give too much or too often as it may have the opposite effect and alienate the listener.

Many station owners now expect promotional efforts (aside from those done for charity) to directly generate nontraditional revenue for the station. These events are similar to traditional promotion in the ways they try to connect the station to the audience's lifestyle. But nowadays, the station's sales staff (or a single, dedicated NTR account executive) works with the promotion director and PD to put together a package that will involve several large advertisers in an event. The projects can take many forms, but a typical one for many is the "Taste of …" The stations sell sponsorships to food and beverage distributors, which gain the sponsors plenty of visibility on all promotional literature and often exclusive rights in their product category to sell at the event (a single beer distributor, for example).

At the same time, the parent station group can use the event to promote several of its adult formats (AC, news/talk, country, some variants of rock and urban) on its other stations. Local restaurants can purchase booth space to offer their products. Live music or other entertainment can be involved, creating an additional potential revenue stream in the form of tickets for attendance (but be sure the station can at least cover the cost!).

Some stations will go so far as to build entire promotions in an NTR environment. For example, a sales rep may get a local car dealership to agree to trade a Jeep Wrangler in exchange for being given the promotion plus the cost of additional advertising, and a local marina or powersports dealer is brought on board to trade a JetSki with a similar arrangement. The station makes money on the advertising schedule and now has a Jeep and a JetSki to giveaway, simply for mentioning the dealers in airtime that would have already been dedicated to a promotion. Theoretically, everyone wins: the station has a great grand prize to give away just in time for summer (and makes money), and because of the listener's frenzy to try to win the grand prize, the advertisers build name recognition (and hopefully

sell additional vehicles) by being associated with the promotion.

The key to strong promotion of a station is visibility, and the station should be everywhere the target listener would be in the community. This is becoming an increasing struggle for those stations who continue to cut back both promotion and air staff. Radio stations need people to succeed, and those stations that find ways to retain their staff and keep the station visible will be those that succeed in the coming years.

News and Other Nonentertainment Programming

The FCC has no formal requirements for nonentertainment programming, although licensees are required to ascertain the problems, needs and interests of their communities (by whatever means they deem appropriate) and to provide programming that addresses those issues. Each station's public file must contain a quarterly list of programming that the licensee has broadcast to meet those needs.

Stations targeting younger listeners often do not want to carry news, believing that their listeners are bored by it. (However, adult-oriented stations must provide information to their audiences, especially during morning drivetime.) News, public affairs and "other" nonentertainment programming create a flow or continuity problem for the format. The complaint is, "We have to shut down the radio station to air that junk." Junk, of course, is any programming not directly related to the music format. However, that assumes that all nonentertainment content must be long form. The programmer's trick is weaving into the format an appropriate kind and amount of nonentertainment material, which can be effectively woven into any format. Much important information, from traffic and weather reports to upcoming events in the community, can be dished out in 60, 30 or 10 seconds, for example. *Public service announcements (PSAs)* are both nonentertainment and community-oriented programming, and a station can make significant contributions to the community welfare with an aggressive PSA policy. The key for programmers is to be as careful and deliberate about the choices they make with this material as they are with their music. These nonentertainment elements should be as timely and relevant to the lives of the target audience as the music. The morning jock shouldn't be wasting several minutes rehashing the weekend on Monday morning—he or she should be letting listeners know whether to grab their umbrellas or their sunglasses as they struggle to get out their doors and off to work. On Thursday and Friday, the afternoon-drive talent should be focused on events coming up that weekend as well as on helping the audience avoid the overturned semi at the airport freeway exit.

Radio will probably always be a service medium, and broadcasters will always differ on what constitutes community service. In a competitive major market served by a number of communications media such as newspaper, cable, television, radio, MMDS, LPTV and DTH satellite, the FM radio station that plays wall-to-wall rock music is doubtlessly providing a service, even though it is solely a music service. When the audience has so many options for music, from iPods to satellite radio, a programmer must ask just what it is that the station provides that will convince the audience to listen. In information-poor markets, owners may elect to mix talk shows with music, air editorial comments on community affairs, and in general provide useful information to the community. The services and information provided should be based on competitive market factors, the owners' and managers' personal choices, and a realistic understanding of the role a radio station can play in the particular market situation.

The Big News Question

Do listeners want news on music stations? Early studies by consultants concluded that a large percentage of rock listeners were "turned off" by news. These same listeners also hated commercials, PSAs and anything else not related to music and fun. Some studies found, however, that everybody

wanted lots of news on their music stations. More contemporary views hold that the task for programmers is to find news and information that is relevant to the target audience because it will provide an important component in the overall station identity. Listeners do value information—*but only if they understand how it is relevant to their lives right now.*

Some thinking on news scheduling hinges on the habits of listeners and Arbitron's method of calculating ratings by the quarter-hour: The idea is to hold a listener for at least five minutes in any quarter hour by playing some music so that the station will get credit in a listener diary even if the listener tunes away at news time. News is therefore often placed in the middle of one or two 15-minute periods each hour. This strategy assumes that a significant number of listeners are turned away by news. Music stations, especially those targeting younger listeners, have generally eliminated newscasts except in morning drivetime.

Journalistic Content

Having decided where to put news, the programmer must then decide how to handle it. For some stations, it is enough to have jocks (or sidekicks) **rip and read** newswire copy as it comes out of the machine. Some have been tempted to satisfy the need for local news by simply stealing from the local newspaper or *USA Today.* Programmers tempted to go this route should be aware, however, that stations have been successfully sued under copyright law for engaging in this practice. Although the facts of the news cannot be copyrighted, the specific expression of those facts can be.

On a slightly more elevated level, there are now local news services available that will provide local and regional news (including traffic and weather) for any station willing to pay for the service. The best known of these is Metro, a service that Westwood One sold to Clear Channel in 2011. The advantage to the station is the ability to deliver timely and valuable local information at less than what it would cost to hire its own news staff. The disadvantage is the loss of any exclusivity. The same reporter filing the story for your station on the downtown fire and resulting traffic jam at 8:05 A.M. is likely to be on your competition at 8:08 (or 8:03).

Another option is to enter into a joint agreement with one of the local television stations or the local newspaper. The local evening television news anchor or a sports reporter may be a valuable addition to the radio station's morning show, and the teaming has promotional advantages for each company. Some clustered stations have adopted a variation of this cross-promotional approach if the cluster includes a news or news/talk AM station—the FM music stations get their morning news from the AM station news staff. Opinions are divided about the advisability of identifying the anchor as from the FM or the AM station during an FM newscast; some stations believe that maintaining a single brand identity is crucial to the station's image and success, while others trade on the legitimacy associated with the news station by identifying the anchor as being from that station. The lack of exclusivity is still an issue.

Programmers who set the highest goals for themselves do well to hire at least two persons to staff the news operation who trade anchoring and reporting duties during the day. This news operation would be extremely luxurious for a music station, however. The typical full-time news staff in radio stations throughout the country—if they have one—is one person, perhaps supplemented by part-time stringers or a service. And even at stations that have a news staff, the news staff is most likely serving multiple stations in a market.

Network and Syndicated Programming

For economic reasons or other factors, stations may not wish to locally program 24 hours a day, 7 days a week. Thanks to digital technology, satellites and the internet, national or regional programming is easily available from either a radio network or a radio syndicator. Both offer similar types of programming, but they can be distinguished by the nature of the relationship between the program supplier and the local

station. Networks provide an integrated, full-service product (music, news, air talent, national spots, other features) that airs simultaneously on all affiliated stations, while syndicators provide one element (a single program, a music service and so on) to individual stations that may sometimes air the material at different times.

National and regional syndication can be divided into three categories: short form, long form and continuous music formats. A program of sufficiently broad appeal can run in more than one format (thus increasing the odds that the supplier will be able to sell the program in most markets). Stations use short-form programs as spice in the schedule, airing most longer syndicated fare on weekends or at night (some network material may air in other dayparts). Many syndicators and networks also provide material not only for broadcast but also for online platforms (podcasts, website content, etc.). Short-form offerings include individual network newscasts as well as syndicated programs and series. Many syndicators provide material not only for broadcast but also for online platforms (podcasts and other digital content). Familiar long-form programming includes shows that run several hours on a daily or weekly basis, for example, Cumulus' *American Country Countdown* with Kix Brooks or *American Top 40* with Ryan Seacrest from Premiere Radio Networks (a Clear Channel subsidary). In addition to Cumulus and Premiere, major national syndicators include Dial Global (*www.dial-global. com*), Westwood One and United Stations (*www. usrn.com*).

Continuous music formats are just what the name suggests—24-hour, 7-day-a-week music selections. Until the late 1970s, stations programmed their own music or purchased long-form all-music programming tapes from such syndicators as Drake-Chenault. Syndicated formats are available from a number of companies, including many of those mentioned above. The increased availability of satellite delivery in the 1980s brought a new type of national music programming service—the full-time, live network radio format. Modern satellite-delivered networks supply the combined services of a traditional network (news and advertising) and a formatted program service (music and entertainment programs). Satellite Music Network (SMN) was the first provider of real-time satellite radio in ten different music formats, including two versions of country, two rock formats, two formats targeted toward adult African-Americans, two adult contemporary formats, one version of nostalgia and one version of oldies. That service was eventually consolidated with ABC Radio (*www.abcradio.com*), and is now owned by Citadel. Dial Global, part of the TM Studios company, is another major provider of network music formats. There are others who offer a limited number of formats, including United Stations.

The decision to go with one of these services instead of locally generated programming can reduce operating costs by one-half. About half of all commercial stations use at least some national or regional radio programming, from overnight filler to 24-hour *turnkey* operations (in turnkey arrangements, management is turned over to another entity). Although local programming is desirable, nationally programmed song selections are based on the kinds of professional research that smaller local stations find difficult to afford. Using a network or syndicated format package, a small-market station can achieve a consistent "big-market" sound with a recognized appeal to audiences and advertisers.

Network formats offer a complete package that includes practically everything but local commercials. *Syndicated* formats at their most basic provide only music that is intended for use on fully automated stations. A station running a syndicated format may choose to run without air talent or may use local air talent, or for an additional fee the syndicator may also provide voice-tracking service. Unlike networks, format syndicators traditionally do not sell commercial time or produce newscasts.

Network formats are generally available on a barter basis (two minutes per hour is the norm), although stations in unrated markets or brand-new stations may be required to take the service on a cash-plus-barter contract. Full-time satellite programming eliminates the need for large staffs, large facilities and large equipment budgets. In the most extreme form, current digital automation systems allow stations to replace a complex of air studios, production

studios and a programming/production staff of several people with a small production studio (for local commercials, weather forecasts and so on), an on-air computer and a staff of one or two. In smaller markets, going with such a service may allow a reformatted station to break even in less than a year.

Like a locally produced format, the network or syndicated service operates from a clock, each hour following a set pattern of music sweeps, some combination of mandatory and optional stopsets and perhaps other material (jingles, sweepers and so on). The typical network clock shown in 11.20 might be used in the daytime for an oldies or AC format. There are 11 minutes of avails in three stopsets: 2 minutes for the network (the first minute in each mandatory break) and 9 for the local station. Also note the long music sweep (or two long sweeps if the local station doesn't take the optional break at about 35 minutes after the hour), and note the opportunities for *localization* (liners to be recorded by the network air talent as well as things that can be done within the station breaks).

Local stopsets and other content are triggered at the local station by a network command using subaudible tones (different tones can be used to trigger different local elements). After the three- or four-minute

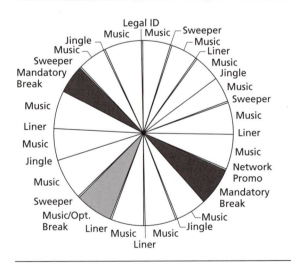

11.20   Network Clock

break, the station's automation system then seamlessly rejoins the network at the appropriate point. For liners, the network channel is kept open, so the liner plays over the music as a song fades or the intro begins.

In the late 1990s, many of the networks and syndicators settled on a single technological standard for satellite receivers provided by StarGuide Digital Networks (*www.starguidedigital.com*). At each mandatory break, the local station must fill the time with local content, such as commercials, promos, PSAs, weather and traffic. The network then uses this time to send important information (last-minute changes in the network's lineup of air talent or the network's spot log, for example) or other material (such as copies of the network commercials for use in hours where local stations are not using the full network feed) to the affiliated stations using their regular channel. In an optional break, the network will program a precisely timed song so stations that don't have local spots scheduled there can continue with music.

It's a system that can be a bit awkward at times for the network PD—after all, how many songs in a particular format remain popular and run exactly 3:30? The timed song is generally a secondary gold or oldies because the programmer wouldn't want to miss playing a top current hit in its regular rotation.

The key to successfully operating with a satellite-delivered format is effective localization—making the station sound like a part of the community even though the programming isn't locally produced. Networks offer major-market-quality personalities, thoroughly tested and carefully scheduled music and (sometimes) network news.

Another part of their service is aimed at helping stations localize the product, but it is always up to the local station to direct the effort. At the request of the local station, network talent will record local station IDs, liners and other voice tracks (intros to weather or news, contest wraps so that the tenth caller sounds like she's talking to the network DJ and so on). These are then sent to the local station for insertion in the programming. Most stations have their call letters or slogans voice tracked by the appropriate network talent. Placed at the start of every break, song intro or *backsell* (telling the audience what music is coming up or what just played), the slogan sounds to the listener like the network DJ is at the station. Most of this process is really common sense and involves little more than the kinds of things a programmer would do if the air talent were indeed at the station (for example, having the air talent repeat the call letters or slogan when coming out of music, so the station and music are associated in the listener's mind).

But it's surprising how many stations fail to follow through and wind up sounding like a satellite station because they create localizing material too infrequently or irregularly. Others make the mistake of completely eliminating local programming and production personnel, leaving account executives to write and produce commercials and the receptionist to voice track a weather forecast a couple of times a day—employees who are often without the training or talent to effectively execute those tasks.

Local information remains important: regardless of the market, people still want the weather forecast; they want survive-the-day information like traffic during the morning and afternoon drivetimes, and they expect the local radio station to provide it. Many network-affiliated stations adopt a middle-ground approach, running local information in morning drivetime and perhaps during one or two additional shifts during the day while using the satellite primarily at night and on weekends. Most networks require the affiliated stations to air the scheduled network spots, however, even during hours when the station is not airing the network programming.

One downside to running full-service satellite-delivered music programming is the lack of control at the local station. Sometimes the network personality talks too much or makes inappropriate comments. One station became upset when the network DJ (in Dallas) told Christmas listeners to "avoid the crowds and stay in today," which was then followed by local commercials asking people to do exactly the opposite! By choosing a format syndicator, a station may exert more control because the music and all other program elements (especially DJ tracks) can be located (and therefore altered or eliminated as needed) at the station. The price of such control, however, is paying someone to mind the format, to handle voice tracking and ads. For locally controlled stations, this is not a huge concern, and format syndication works well. For an automated station with a distant owner and a skeleton staff, however, the network format is a better option.

Concerts and Specials

Special music programs have long been popular with both stations and advertisers. Concerts command premium prices because they provide exclusive access to top-ranked music in a live setting. Some acts are particularly valuable because they cross over a variety of station formats (for example, from country to AC, like Shania Twain or Alternative to CHR, like Green Day), making it fairly easy for some music shows to air on at least one station in most markets. Since the mid-1990s, however, only a few musical megastars have been able to attract audiences on the scale necessary for both meeting the costs associated with national production and distribution and justifying local stations' preemption of regular programming. (Access to these rare concerts and major performers remains beyond the financial reach of most local stations on an individual basis.)

Syndicators capable of recording such shows generally offer them to stations on a barter or cash-plus-barter basis at prices ranging from $25 to $50 per hour in small markets to several hundred dollars per hour in large markets. Networks may include these music specials as part of the full-service network programming of music, news and sports. Networks can also go into the syndication business, offering music specials on a station-by-station basis.

As with any other type of network program, *the key to revenue for a music special or concert series is the size of its cleared audience.* Fitting a particular concert or series of concerts to a demographic category that matches a salable number of affiliates is very difficult. Most of these programs target either the youth demographic, aged roughly 18 to 34 (it may include teens), or the adult demographic, aged 25 to 54. Each group presents programming problems, and local stations can be understandably reluctant to preempt traditional programming that

they know will deliver a given audience and amount of revenue for an unknown. Stations will expect a careful fit between special programs and their regular formats. Contemporary radio listeners have many choices and are ready to push a button if the sound or voices are too staid, too serious or otherwise perceived as "not for them."

For a network that seeks musical concerts and specials, three alternative strategies exist:

- Produce many shows of varied appeal to capture fragments of the youth or adult audiences.
- Concentrate on the relatively small number of stars that appeal across the broadest format spectrum.
- Buy or produce programs that have unique, broad appeal.

The third strategy is often the most economically efficient, although many national programmers also follow the first strategy to at least some extent. For example, countdown shows target specific groups who will listen to a wide variety of music over the course of the show. Countdown shows succeed best as regularly scheduled weekend features, and audiences tend to seek them out. These unique music programs usually clear the broadest range of affiliates, which makes them potentially the most profitable syndicated programs and competitive with top-rated radio sports.

Feature Syndicators

Radio broadcasters may use features to attract a specific target audience during mornings, evenings or weekends. Most popular syndicated feature programs are brief inserts such as the *ET Radio Minute, Late Show with David Letterman Top-Ten List* and *CBS HealthWatch*. Stations producing their own programming include short features to add spice and variety to programming and use the longer programming to fill unsold or low-audience time periods.

Syndicated features are as varied as their producers, which include many of the companies previously mentioned in this chapter: Dial Global, Cumulus, Premiere Radio Networks (*www.premiereradio. com*), Westwood One and United Stations are among the biggest. A few major-market stations also syndicate their talent (for example, KLOS in Los Angeles offers morning duo Mark & Brian to stations in other markets).

One of the most important types of feature programming today is the syndicated morning show. Several successful major-market morning shows have made the transition to national syndication, including Kid Kraddick (Dallas), Rick Dees (Los Angeles), Mancow Muller (Chicago) and Bob & Tom (Indianapolis). As with the other programming discussed in this section, a syndicated morning show can offer small- and medium-market stations talent that would otherwise be far beyond their reach, albeit at a still significant cost in cash and avails.

A wide range of styles are available, from Bob & Tom's Midwestern, occasionally risqué, humor to the outrageous and frequently offensive style of Mancow. As with all choices, programmers should be aware of the tastes and interests of their audience and market when selecting a syndicated morning show. All of the shows can point to significant ratings successes; most have also failed in some markets where they were on the wrong station or the show was just not appropriate for the market.

Many companies that syndicate long-form format packages also supply short features that fit within their long formats and provide other prep services for local air talent (entertainment news, joke services, other short items that can be used on the air). The short features are also made available to other stations in the same market on a format-exclusive basis. If a feature is format-exclusive, that same short feature can be sold to more than one station in a market if their formats differ, but only one rock or one country or one talk station can license the program. This arrangement assumes non-duplicated listeners.

What's Coming for Radio?

It's clear that "radio" will no longer be delivered only via broadcast transmission but also via other wireless (and wired) services. While the greatest threat to radio as it existed is 4G wireless broadband

services because they will further fragment the audience and reduce the time spent with other media including radio. At the same time, terrestrial broadcasters retain significant competitive advantages over many of the competing technologies, because radio remains free to the listener, plus stations have the ability to make use of those same next-generation platforms to distribute their content to listeners who prefer those platforms.

Changing technology and listener lifestyles have left local stations with no exclusive property in music genres or key artists to be used as a competitive driver in a market. That's not to say that music will disappear as a programming staple. It remains attractive to a large audience and is a very cost-effective way to fill time. But personality and local service—the things offered besides the music on a station—has always been the soul of successful radio. These are things that Pandora, Spotify and similar newer entrants to the audio space do not (and probably will never) offer. Thus, many local stations will best be able to fend off the challenge from newer services by emphasizing their people and their local commitment, along with their free cost to the audience and their availability everywhere their audience wants them to be.

On the other hand, stations have to be present in the mobile space (smartphones, tablets) as audiences—especially younger audiences—move more (and, in some cases, all) of their media use to those platforms. Apple leads that market as we write this; but the lead is shrinking rapidly and the Android operating system will almost certainly be the dominant mobile platform by the time you're reading this chapter (and Blackberry may have disappeared). In any case, stations will probably need to have apps running on at least a couple of platforms so the only real question is which one is the most important—where to start when you launch something new? The answer to that question, as has been the case for radio, begins by understanding on what devices and where your audience is most likely listening.

Convenience (as defined by the listener) will be the primary driver for strategic decision making in almost every case. The mantra recited by leaders in most media companies is "the content you want, anytime, anywhere." While there are still occasional licensing hurdles to overcome before that ideal can be realized, those barriers are fewer for radio than for other media businesses. The radio companies that survive will do so by not only creating compelling broadcast fare but also through the development of mobile apps and by taking advantage of distribution platforms in addition to the broadcast signal—by making that content available in a wide range of forms and engaging listeners in whatever way that listeners prefer.

The industry consolidation that followed the 1996 Telecommunications Act has permanently and fundamentally altered the strategies and economics of radio programming and thus the day-to-day nature of the work the employees of those groups perform. Owners and programmers seek to counter the technological pressures fragmenting the audience by finding different ways of engaging their fans. This requires leveraging their best talent across not only multiple stations (probably in multiple markets) but also across multiple platforms. Your morning jock or team doesn't just do four or five hours on the air. She, he or they (or, more likely, their producer) will certainly also be expected to produce high-involvement content for all the other platforms including the station's website, perhaps a daily podcast (or series of podcasts) available for listeners to download or stream to their smartphone or tablet or desktop. Personas or characters they create could be extended into other media, from video to games that listeners can play on their mobile device—either within a station app or as a stand-alone ... anything that keeps the audience engaged.

The nature of ownership is also changing. Although there may be some exceptions (Cumulus), most radio owners are no longer looking to emulate the Clear Channel approach of the past decade. Indeed, even Clear Channel slimmed down after the company was taken private, shedding many smaller stations and some other lines of business. Rather than trying to dominate everywhere, groups such as Merlin (a large market example) and Townsquare Media (a small-market example) are focused on more narrowly defined geographic, demographic, product and market-size segments; or on providing services to companies in those markets (such as Triton Digital). Other entrepreneurs are individuals or groups focused primarily on new media audio opportunities presented by the spread of 4G networks and platforms. All of them are hoping to prosper in the changing marketplace; and, most importantly, none of them believe that "radio is dead."

Notes

1. Arbitron, "Radio Today 2010," p. 87. This study is available at *www.arbitron.com*.

2. See *http://ibiquity.com/automotive* for updated figures.

3. Arbitron and Edison Media Research, "The Infinite Dial 2011." This study is part of an annual series and is available at *www.arbitron.com and www.edisonmedia research.com*. See more recent versions of this study for updates on listening patterns.

4. In the United States, the AM band runs from 520 to 1710 kilohertz (kHz), with station allocations spaced at 10-kHz intervals. The FM band runs from 88 to 108 megahertz (MHz), with allocations spaced every .2 MHz beginning with 88.1 (then 88.3, 88.5 and so on through 107.9), although the lower 4 MHz (88.1 through 91.9) are reserved for noncommercial educational (NCE) stations only. Note that interference concerns will prevent assignments of stations on adjacent frequencies within a market.

Information Radio Programming

Matthew S. Pierce and Robert F. Potter

Just what is meant by *information radio?* It is traditionally viewed by broadcasters as a fairly expansive term encompassing various formats where the spoken word—rather than music—makes up the main content feature. These formats occur on satellite radio channels and the internet as well as on analog and digital terrestrial broadcasting, and are known individually by such names as talk, news, news/talk and sports talk. All fall under the larger umbrella of information radio but raise the following question for programmers: What is the overall goal of information radio—is it to educate or to entertain its audience?[1]

Information Versus Entertainment Radio

A quick first answer is that with a name like *information radio,* the format must be designed to educate (and that sounds boring). However, some industry analysts believe all radio formats—not just delivering the news or talk about issues—function to educate and are thus a form of information radio. If this sounds extreme, consider that about 14 percent of the broadcast stations in the United States are officially programmed as what the industry calls *information radio,* that is, full-time talk, news or sports (Ahh: not so boring to fans). Add to that another 12 percent of stations categorized as programming religious or Christian formats offering a focused type of information (in the form of sermons, religion-themed talk shows, call-in prayer shows and so on) to an audience with a specific psychographic profile. Of the remaining 74 percent of stations, most schedule some talk, some news or some sports, typically during drivetimes, in late night and on the weekends, even though their "official" formats are some sort of music programming. In addition, surprisingly, more than 90 channels on the SiriusXM satellite service focus on information rather than music. Even noncommercial radio stations—those that we usually associate with classical music, opera and jazz—devote substantial portions of their programming to delivering information in the form of large news blocks (*Morning Edition* and *All Things Considered*), interview shows (*Talk of the Nation, Fresh Air with Terry Gross* and *The Tavis Smiley Show*), comedy (*A Prairie Home Companion* and *Wait, Wait ... Don't Tell Me!*), and call-in talk shows such as the hilarious *Car Talk.*

Even the most highly targeted "all music" stations provide generous amounts of information to their audiences in the form of pop psychology, humorous stories and discussions of "what's hot," all presented in the latest lingo of the target audience. These stations know that, even though they tie their brand images closely to their music mix, to succeed in the ratings they still must offer substantial amounts of useful information to their listeners—such as traffic, weather and lifestyle news—especially during drivetime dayparts.

If you are still having trouble thinking of *all* radio as information radio, consider that more than one-fifth of the average commercial radio station's airtime is set aside for advertising and promotion—almost all forms of which contain spoken information about products, services or the station itself. Even commercial-free public radio uses enhanced underwriting announcements between programs.

Furthermore, the on-air signal is only part of a modern radio station's or satellite service's business strategy. Stations and their program hosts now take advantage of multiple distribution paths to reach an audience. Podcasts, online streaming and apps for smartphones and tablets make content available to listeners whenever and wherever they want to listen. A station's or satellite service's reach now goes beyond the radio waves that carry its signal.

The challenge for content providers, whether they are traditional broadcast stations or webcasters, is to "monetize" these various distribution paths (often referred to as *platforms*). *That means finding a way to make money from the content no matter how it is delivered.* For example, advertising may support a talk program delivered to listeners over an AM broadcast station, but that *same content* can be provided commercial-free to a listener's smartphone through an app that requires a subscription fee to access the content.

Consultant Kipper McGee observes that traditional broadcasting seeks to import listeners to a station by encouraging them to tune to the station's frequency ("Hear weather and traffic on the 10s!"), but now broadcasters also have the opportunity to export their stations' content to listeners in ways that allow them to consume the content on their own time schedule.[2]

Station websites have evolved from simply offering information about station events, biographies of station DJs and personalities, and details on movies, concerts and other happenings in the station's city of license. Now they export content through daily podcasts, free downloads and live streams of the station's broadcast signal. Websites encourage greater interaction with visitors and link to social media sites such as Facebook.

Chicago music station WXRT, for example, invites listeners to become an "XRT VIP" and "access exclusive experiences and XRT ticket giveaways." VIPs get access to the "XRT VIP lounge" where they can earn points by participating in station promotions, filling-out surveys, using advertisers' coupons and clicking through to advertiser websites. Earned points can then be used to enter contests, participate in online auctions or trade for prizes.

The VIP lounge has elements of popular social media games and gives listeners an incentive to participate in marketing campaigns they might otherwise avoid. WXRT "monetized" its website by creating a place where businesses can reach potential customers.

So, a lot of information is being disseminated by radio stations and their personalities, regardless of format, both on and off the air. However, many industry consultants believe it's more important for all stations—even those that are formally information formats—to focus on being a source of *entertainment* for listeners. These analysts suggest that a station can dominate in ratings and revenue only when it is programmed as a form of audio entertainment. *The most successful news/talk/sports programmers require their air talents to remain focused on the entertainment value of their presentations.* According to consultant Holland Cooke, both information stations and popular music stations "play the hits," but in information radio that

means discussing the hot topics and news that the audience really wants to hear.[3] This attitude puts off serious news junkies, but it makes money.

Just as Chapter 11 discussed how hot songs are tracked by music station programmers in trade magazines like *Billboard,* information station programmers refer to publications like *Talkers Magazine* (*www.talkers.com*), which offers a Week in Review feature listing the top-10 people, issues and topics being discussed on information stations across the country. *Only programmers and hosts who recognize the importance of presenting these issues in an entertaining way are likely to succeed big time.*

There are plenty of examples in radio history of talk-radio personalities who took themselves too seriously, abandoned their focus on the *entertainment* value of their presentations, and suffered revenue and ratings decline. One personality who suffered from this lack of focus on the entertainment value of her show is Dr. Laura Schlessinger. Her increasingly strident anti-homosexual rhetoric in the late 1990s resulted in censure by the Canadian Broadcast Standards Council, a loss of several key U.S. affiliates, and the loss of several national advertisers, including the biggie of Procter & Gamble, which withdrew support from her proposed television show.

Controversy again swirled around Schlessinger in 2010 when she used a racial epithet 11 times while responding to a caller on her radio show. She apologized the next day and then announced she would stop hosting a radio show at the end of her contract, saying she would be freer to speak her mind through books, a YouTube channel, blogs and her website. Nonetheless, in 2011 she copied the path of other program hosts too controversial for broadcast radio and moved her show to satellite radio.

At a radio industry conference, a panel of news/talk programmers clearly explained the entertainment value of their programs. One programmer summed it up this way: "All highly rated radio is, first, entertaining, and in radio there're only two ways to entertain an ear—with spoken words [as in] news/talk or with music. When we got our staff to realize their spoken words had to be as entertaining as the music down the street, or the movie on HBO, we started to have success."[4]

To a certain extent, then, *all radio formats have information as a key ingredient.* For some formats, the most engaging way to deliver information is to present it between musical segments the audience will find appealing. In information formats, of course, the majority of the broadcast day is filled not with music, but with the spoken word, and the formats are growing in popularity among programmers and listeners—in the form of all-news, all-talk or the combination of the two known as news/talk. Consider that in 1980, only 75 radio stations in the United States offered full-time information programming. By 1985, that number had grown to only 100 stations. Then, during the next 25 years, the number of stations officially programming the information format skyrocketed! The *Broadcasting Cable Yearbook 2010* listed 2,793 full-time news, talk and news/talk stations—moving ahead of the number of stations with country music formats.

This surge in the number of stations is not the only sign of the format's popularity. Arbitron's *Radio Today 2010* reported that information radio also had the second-highest 12+ share of all formats in 2009, with an average 12.9 percent of those listening to the radio at any time tuning to an information station. That was just behind country music's 13.4 percent share of 12+ listeners. During the historic 2008 presidential election year, information radio had the largest share of 12+ listeners.

Perhaps even more important, large portions of those listening to information programming are in the demographic segments desirable to many advertisers. Moreover, advertisers believe their commercials are more effective in information formats because listeners are more engaged with the content, making it more likely they will actually pay attention to the messages being delivered in advertisements. Do you agree?

Information radio has become popular with programmers because it is a format that really engages listeners. One reason for its persistent popularity is the presentation of timely "hit" topics. However, much of the driving force behind the

format undoubtedly comes from the on-air personalities who present the topics in compelling, interesting and often controversial ways.

Identifiable Personalities

Among dominant information formats, *talk is almost always live and delivered by identifiable personalities.* Having recognizable individuals is extremely important. Research has repeatedly shown that the most loyal radio listeners seek feelings of pseudo-friendship or imagined personal relationships with media personalities. These relationships are evidenced by unexpectedly intense love/hate reactions to national talk hosts such as Howard Stern, Rush Limbaugh, Tom Joyner, Jim Rome, G. Gordon Liddy, Dr. Joy Browne and Phil Hendrie. *An emotional connection, whether positive or negative, has been shown to be absolutely necessary for sustained listener involvement and long-term ratings and revenue success.* A list of selected nationally syndicated and satellite radio talk hosts from *Talkers Magazine's* "Heavy Hundred," along with their web addresses, appears in 12.1.

Often even local personalities can develop sizable loyal followings. These hosts tend to be long-time residents of the broadcast city. They know the history of the area, and long-time local listeners develop a sense of having "grown up" with them. Even those new to the area become attracted by how tuned in to the happenings of the city such local personalities are—they know about everything from family activities happening in the coming week to the hot-button local political issues.

Sometimes information stations that have a comparatively small share of the listening audience can still be successful because of the connections they make with their niche audiences and the loyalty that follows. For example, consider WVON-AM (Chicago). Rarely does the talk station register more than one percent of the available listening audience. However, the station has remained successful by developing close ties between its local personalities and its primarily African-American audience. According to communication scholar Catherine Squires, who spent time observing

12.1 Popular Nationally Syndicated or Satellite Radio Talk Hosts

Talk Personality	Description	Website
Glenn Beck	"High-profile star of the current conservative talk media genre. King of controversy.	www.glennbeck.com
Jim Bohannon	"Seasoned late-night broadcaster with journalistic qualities. Political moderate heard in syndication."	www.jimbotalk.net
Sean Hannity	"A multimedia mega star in conservative talk. Solid mainstay of the genre."	www.hannity.com
Clark Howard	"Respected consumer advocate and personal financial advice expert."	www.clarkhoward.com
Don Imus	"Legendary talk media personality still performing daily syndicated morning show simulcast on cable news/talk TV."	http://www.wabcradio.com/showdj.asp?DJID=40880
Laura Ingraham	"A major fixture in the world of conservative talk entertainment. Top female in talk radio."	www.lauraingraham.com
Rush Limbaugh	"Twenty-three years in syndication and still the most important talk show host in America."	www.rushlimbaugh.com
George Noory	"Ubiquitous purveyor of late-night paranormal and oddities chat."	www.coasttocoastam.com
Dave Ramsey	"A media superstar in the world of personal financial advice and multi-media industry icon."	www.daveramsey.com
Randi Rhodes	"Progressive talk radio pro earning success in national syndication"	www.therandirhodesshow.com
Jim Rome	"Still the 'champ' of nationally syndicated sports talk radio."	www.jimrome.com
Michael Savage	"Boisterous talk radio personality heard on more than 300 affiliates."	www.michaelsavage.com
Dr.Laura Schlessinger	"Still an important player with legendary status. Unique personal advice host. Heard exclusively on satellite radio."	www.drlaura.com
Bev Smith	"Important player in African American targeted talk radio."	www.aurnol.com
Howard Stern	"King of satellite radio and 'pop culture' talk. Still a multi-media superstar and one-of-a-kind radio legend."	www.howardstern.com

WVON talents and listeners, the station sustains a loyal audience that counts on the station to "talk their talk" when it comes to issues of concern and interest to the African-American audience in the third largest market in the United States. So loyal is the WVON audience, in fact, that Squires reported listeners were willing to make financial contributions to the station when its advertising revenues were lower than anticipated.[5] Although some of those listed in 12.2 have begun to branch out to national audiences via syndication, their reputations initially developed by establishing long-term relationships with listeners in their local markets.

Branding Stations and On-Air Personalities

Carrying a syndicated show with an identifiable national personality and developing local talents for the surrounding hours—who then become local household names—should be the goals of every

| 12.2 | Popular Local Hosts |

New York	WNYM	www.am970theapple.com
	Curtis Sliwa	
Los Angeles	KFI	www.kfi640.com
	Bill Handel	
	KABC	www.kabc.com
	Larry Elder	
Chicago	WVON	www.wvon.com
	Cliff Kelley	
	WGN	www.wgnradio.com
	Garry Meier	
	WLS	www.wlsam.com
	Roe Conn	
San Francisco	KGO	www.kgoam810.com
	Ronn Owens	
Dallas	WBAP	www.wbap.com
	Mark Davis	

information radio programmer. How does a programmer identify the right ones?

Arbitron's research revealed an *important fact about strong personalities: Listeners will find them on the dial even if they change stations in the market.* In other words, listeners are often more loyal to the personality than they are to any individual station. A successful program host creates his or her own unique style or "brand." Just as consumers often become loyal to a particular brand of laundry detergent and other products, they can also become loyal followers of a popular on-air personality.

Once a program host has created a unique brand with a loyal audience, he or she can deliver content on many platforms and monetize them to generate profits. In the early days of the internet and before the rise of social media sites, syndicated talk programs used periodic newsletters as a source of revenue for the host and/or syndicator. Rush Limbaugh, for example, offered yearly subscriptions to his monthly newsletter *The Limbaugh Letter* for purchase on his website (*www.rushlimbaugh.com*). Limbaugh still offers the traditional newsletter, but he has expanded his offerings to take advantage of new digital platforms.

Subscribers to "Rush 24/7" are given access to audio and video podcasts through the iTunes library, including downloads of his minute long "Morning Updates," archives of his complete programs for the past four weeks, live streaming video of him during his radio show, and commercial-free versions of his radio program. (That's a LOT of Rush.) In addition, subscribers can download documents discussed during the show, related articles and audio, plus other reference materials. A free app is available for subscribers who want to consume the content on their smartphones or tablet computers. The 24/7 package even claims to include a super-secret email address that allows subscribers to reach Limbaugh directly.

Some stations or personalities, on the other hand, send out newsletters free of charge in an attempt to make more personal connections with their listeners while also developing databases of contact information for future direct marketing campaigns. Kim Komando, host of a weekly syndicated tech-talk show, also sends out daily computer tips and weekly newsletters via email to millions of people who have signed up for the free service on her website (*www.komando.com*). Komando also offers alternate access to content through a subscription service called "Kim's Club." For a monthly fee, club members get access to podcasts, streaming audio and streaming video of her (radio) program. Club members are also automatically entered into show contests.

What was once a business of attracting listeners to a broadcast station to boost advertising sales has now become a multi-platform marketing operation. Content is now recycled and repackaged to generate profits long after the program host has said "Goodbye, until tomorrow" to his or her broadcast station listeners.

Scott Betram, program director for Rockford, Illinois, station WROK-AM, is an example of a broadcaster who recognizes the importance of maintaining these many digital platforms. "Website, streaming audio, Twitter, Facebook—they all help put WROK on the computer or cell-phone or iPad of listeners every day. It helps brand us as a news/information/opinion source that will continue to provide content even when the consumer is away from the radio."[6]

Many hosts have further capitalized on their popularity by writing books. For example, Howard Stern's *Private Parts,* Limbaugh's *The Way Things Ought to Be,* Michael Savage's *The Savage Nation,* and Dr. Laura Schlessinger's *The Proper Care and Feeding of Husbands* not only gave those hosts another stream of income, but the publicity the books received likely directed new listeners to their radio programs. Publicity surrounding a new book can be substantial. For example, talk-show host Mitch Albom's *Tuesdays with Morrie,* a memoir of his time spent with one of his former college professors, lasted over five years on *The New York Times* best-seller list! And every copy sold mentions his daily syndicated radio show originating on WJR-AM in Detroit.

Knowing about syndication agreements is crucial for programmers. National hosts who have developed brands that can generate the most revenues sell themselves for fixed periods of time—one year, two years, etc. Beginning the next round of negotiations with the syndicator at exactly the proper time gives an edge. To continue a station's association with the personality, locking the agreement up early (before a competitor moves in) is an important strategic move.

However, if a programmer, sales manager and general manager decide that a new agreement with the syndicator is not cost-effective because of increases in the contract costs or decreases in projected sales revenue (see Chapter 3 for a related discussion of television syndication), it is better to know sooner rather than later that the station may lose that personality from its programming lineup. It is also not a bad idea to estimate when competitors' national syndication contracts will be renegotiated. It could be that a favorite personality might unexpectedly become available as a result of failed negotiations with a competing station, and a clever information programmer would be ready to act quickly to sign that big-name personality, knowing that his or her loyal audience will follow.

The strong loyalty between listeners and personalities also impacts the information programmer's relationship with local hosts. Often, management insists on *noncompete clauses* in contracts with the most popular "franchise" personalities. These clauses prevent local personalities from leaving one station and going to another in the same market without a lot of time (sometimes a year or more) passing. The logic behind these clauses is that having noncompetes in place will prevent the personalities from bringing their stations' strategic secrets—along with their loyal listeners—to competitors.

This approach is not without its critics, many of whom argue that noncompete clauses have a negative effect on station morale that does far more harm than any "strategic secrets" that may get into the competition's hands. The American Federation of Radio and Television Artists (AFTRA) continues to lobby state legislatures and Congress to outlaw noncompete clauses in broadcasters' employment contracts. Arizona, California, Connecticut, Illinois, Massachusetts, Maine and New York are among the states that have made these noncompete clauses unenforceable. Still, the initial motivation for noncompete clauses should not be lost amid the controversy: Once a station has a successful local personality on its airwaves, the programmer needs to try to do everything possible to keep that person there!

The rise in the number of recognizable personalities and the greater loyalty they command are, indeed, important reasons behind the increase in the number of information stations and their ratings successes over recent years. However, other factors also led to the popularity of the format among programmers and the listening public.

The Rise of Information Radio

Aside from social and cultural influences contributing to an interest in information radio, several technological, economic and policy changes have also played a role, especially affecting terrestrial broadcast radio. The six key factors are summarized in 12.3.

Cost Decline in Distribution Technology

The shows of Rush Limbaugh, Dr. Laura Schlessinger, Ed Schultz or others wouldn't be available today without the dramatic drop in the cost of distributing broadcast-quality audio over long distances that

12.3 Factors in the Rise of Talk Radio

1. Decline in distribution costs due to satellite technology
2. Repeal of the Fairness Doctrine in 1987
3. Acceptance of formerly taboo topics
4. Migration of music-oriented audiences to FM
5. Proliferation of cellular phones
6. Attraction of format for advertisers

occurred in the early 1980s. Prior to that time, radio network operators were forced to pay premium fees to the telephone monopolies for land-based distribution. This created the "chicken and egg" question common to most new technologies: Which will come first, the nationally-distributed radio personalities or the expensive distribution system? By the mid-1980s, commercial satellites magically appeared in the sky, and thanks to the much lower cost of satellite distribution, national syndication of unproven programming became economically feasible for the first time. One of the earliest of these shows was Limbaugh's talk show, and in an interview, Limbaugh noted that his popular show airs during the midday daypart, as opposed to perhaps the more strategically advantageous slot of morning or afternoon drivetime. This occurred because satellite time was only available during the midday hours when his syndicated show was first developed.[7]

The Abandonment of the Fairness Doctrine

Fairness was another problem. Prior to 1987, the FCC's Fairness Doctrine required radio stations to cover all sides of controversial public issues *equally*. In application, this severely limited the topics aired on talk radio because station owners feared lawsuits or complaints at license renewal time by those who felt they were treated "unequally." Indeed, both sides of a controversial issue would often claim less than equal treatment. Because of this, few station owners were willing to take the risk of programming anything more than the blandest kinds of talk. Rather than risk complaints at renewal time, it was easier to avoid all controversy.

The Fairness Doctrine was merely an FCC policy that had not been made law, so the FCC could decide to drop it at any time, and that time arrived at the height of deregulation under the Reagan administration. Although many members of Congress and some lobbyists fought to write the Fairness Doctrine into law, each of three attempts ended in failure. After several years, it became clear that the Fairness Doctrine was not likely to return, and broadcasters subsequently felt increasingly free to engage in even the most outrageously slanted forms of talk programming.

By the early 1990s, radio talk hosts had more freedom than ever before to advocate one view of a controversial issue and ridicule opposing points of view. Show hosts could take—or even distort—one side of an issue and demean opposing perspectives, often with tremendous success in audience ratings. Such talk was apparently much more interesting than talk that tried to be fair or equal to both sides (see 12.4). Despite complaints of extremism, the FCC decided to rely on the marketplace to provide fairness. In theory, if one station took one side of an issue, other stations in the market would program opposing views to attract the disaffected audience. Overall fairness would be found across the dial, rather than forced on each individual station as had been the case before.

By 2000, journalists, media scholars and even politicians were commenting that talk radio—particularly at the national level—had become primarily a haven for such politically conservative hosts such as Rush Limbaugh, G. Gordon Liddy, Ken Hamblin and Sean Hannity. Although this was no problem for the conservatives in the audience, polls showed that almost three-quarters of liberals felt that the information radio format did not provide balanced programming. Many conservatives pointed to failed programs hosted by such liberal icons as Mario Cuomo and Alan Dershowitz as evidence of the marketplace at work.

However, in 2004, Air America Radio debuted on stations in New York, Los Angeles, Chicago and

12.4 Blogs 'n Talk Radio

For listeners eager to have their say on radio, the surest way is through the web. Recognizing that a daily smorgasbord of opinions and ideas flow freely online, talk radio programs like *Open Source* and *Air America* are turning to bloggers to provide content for their shows.

Open Source, distributed by Public Radio International, draws on comments and information posted by bloggers on its website, *www.radioopensource.org*. Bloggers suggest ideas for the program, recommend guest speakers and questions, and even appear as guest speakers. According to its site, *Open Source* sees itself not as "a public radio show with a web community" but "a web community that produces a daily hour of radio." To date, about 40 stations (out of nearly 10,000) carry the program, whose topics range from global warming to national service in America to Groundhog Day to what to do in outer space.

Bloggers are also playing bigger roles in balancing and policing the air waves. For an independent talk radio show like *Air America*, which was created during the 2004 presidential elections to counter conservative talk radio shows like *The Rush Limbaugh Show* and *The Sean Hannity Show*, bloggers' input is critical because the show doesn't employ its own reporters. In 2007, hundreds of blogs demanded that advertisers pull their ads from San Francisco-based radio station KSFO-AM after several of its talk show hosts allegedly made racist and violence-inciting remarks. Audio clips of the shows were posted on blogs—and some were sent to advertisers, causing companies like Bank of America and Mastercard to stop advertising with the station.

Debbie Goh, Ph.D.
Nanyang Technological University

San Francisco and was touted by some as the beginning of syndicated "liberal radio." Relying on easily identifiable personalities, Air America Radio signed on with dayparts hosted by comedians Al Franken, Janeane Garofalo and Public Enemy rapper Chuck D. With the Fairness Doctrine now a distant memory, such "one-sided" left-leaning programming content became just as fair as the conservative radio that had been around for decades.

Despite reaching 2.1 million listeners on 75 affiliates, in 2006 the company filed for bankruptcy claiming it had lost more than $40 million in the two years since signing on. On top of that, the network also lost Franken—by far its highest-profile host—who resigned to run for the U.S. Senate in Minnesota. Still, in early 2007 Air America was purchased by Stephen Green, a real-estate entrepreneur who guaranteed to bring what he called an "underperforming asset with unrealized potential" to profitability.[8] His effort also failed, and Air America—as live radio—folded in early 2010.

The failure of Air America reignited the debate about why conservative talk radio was dominating the format. Conservative talkers pointed to the demise of Air America as proof that Americans reject liberal ideals and have no interest in listening to progressive talk show hosts. However, former Air America employees blamed the network's failure on a series of owners and managers with little broadcasting business experience.[9]

Proponents of progressive talk radio note that many liberal or left-leaning personalities are doing well. Air America alumus Randi Rhodes left the network to be syndicated by Premiere Radio Networks that also syndicates conservative Rush Limbaugh's program. Rachel Maddow moved from Air America to a prime time show on the MSNBC cable network. Progressive hosts Ed Schultz and Stephanie Miller who chose to remain independent of Air America remain nationally syndicated.

Embracing Formerly Taboo Topics

Although the elimination of the Fairness Doctrine removed most government-imposed restrictions on the nature of talk programming, several social and cultural events in the 1990s appeared to give broadcasters the public's permission to stretch the limits of what is considered acceptable on radio in another direction. What had once been confined to the seamier sections of porn magazines, internet chat rooms and X-rated movies was by the late 1990s suddenly fair game. Media frenzies such as the O. J. Simpson trial, the Jon Benet Ramsey murder, and the Clinton impeachment hearings encouraged on-air listeners to vent their reactions to topics as intense as murder, child sexual abuse and oral sex. Many programmers heard from citizen action groups outraged by the sordid and often sexual details being broadcast during morning drivetime— not coincidentally the times when parents drive their kids to school with the radio on. Most of these programmers held their ground against such groups, claiming First Amendment protection of the "information" being broadcast. The truth for many, however, was that regardless of the programmers' opinions about the Bill of Rights, many of the personalities who caused such an outcry with their titillation were also generating huge ratings numbers and advertiser revenue.

In early 2004, however, things began to change. Some content aired on broadcast stations seemed to go too far. One was a radio stunt created by Opie &

Anthony (former talkers on WNEW in New York) in which listeners were encouraged to have sex in public places. At first, this seems no more shocking than other stunts hosted by syndicated personalities on hundreds of stations across the country. Still, when the Opie & Anthony bit resulted in a broadcast "play-by-play" of copulation—at New York City's St. Patrick's Cathedral during a mass—the ever-elusive line of public acceptability was crossed.

Then, Janet Jackson and Justin Timberlake had a "wardrobe malfunction" that led to Jackson's breast being exposed to 800 million people during CBS's 2003 Super Bowl halftime broadcast. Shortly thereafter, the FCC began to strengthen its public stance against indecency. Congress, too, began to give the FCC a bigger club to swing at station owners who allowed their personalities to be overly prurient: The legislators increased indecency fines from a measly $27,500 to as much as $500,000. This greatly increased the motivation of station owners to keep their personalities on a shorter leash. In the past, many had decided that the small fines were a price they were willing to pay for ratings success (see 12.5).

12.5 Indecency *Eventually* Costs Infinity

When does programming result in a broadcaster making a million-dollar "voluntary contribution" to the United States Treasury? When it's indecent. Since the late 1980s, the FCC had been frequently issuing notices of apparent liability (fines) against Infinity Broadcasting for Howard Stern's allegedly indecent broadcasts. Infinity's president, Mel Karmazin, first reacted by saying the company would refuse to pay the fines, claiming that Stern's program content was protected by the First Amendment. But in 1995, Infinity Broadcasting finally agreed to pay (and as a reward, got its record of indecent broadcasts expunged).

Two developments brought about the Infinity settlement. First, in 1995 the U.S. Court of Appeals in Washington, DC, upheld the FCC's ban on indecent broadcasts in the daytime and evening (between 6 A.M. and 10 P.M.). Second, and much more important, Infinity was trying to buy nine radio stations (in addition to the 22 it already owned). Unfortunately (or fortunately, depending on your point of view), the purchase would require the FCC's approval.

After Karmazin failed to persuade the commissioners to lighten Infinity's penalty, he then agreed to the $1.7 million "contribution" while claiming his intention was to "conserve the time, expenses and human resources of the parties" involved. Howard Stern called the settlement "extortion" and the "biggest shakedown in history."

The actual amount paid, negotiated down to $1,175,000, was the largest fine ever paid by a broadcaster. Of course, it pales when compared with the value of the stations Infinity acquired as a result of the settlement ($375 million) or Infinity's $3 billion value. If you won't laugh, I'll tell you that Infinity also agreed to establish a program to *educate* its on-air personnel about the FCC's indecency actions. Educate Howard Stern?

And Infinity has morphed into CBS Radio to clean up its name.

Lindsy E. Pack, Ph.D.
Frostburg State University

Increased reaction against vulgar conversation led radio ownership giant Clear Channel Communications to drop *The Howard Stern Show* from several markets and to fire long-time morning host Bubba the Love Sponge in early 2004. These moves have forced even the milder talkers who rely on innuendo rather than blatantly sexual topics to rein in their content. For example, Tom Griswold, one-half of the *Bob & Tom Show,* said that the show is "not going to take the chance of being anywhere near the line. We've pulled way, way back." The current goal, according to Griswold, is to produce a show "that a soccer mom can listen to with her kids in the car."[10]

The pendulum may have swung back to caution when it comes to bad taste on information stations. However, public taste is fickle, and daring programmers have made names for themselves and their stations by pushing the envelope. That may be the reason why Stern's show was immediately picked up by competitors in four of the markets where Clear Channel removed him from the airwaves. Eventually, however, the three big-mouths—Stern, Bubba the Love Sponge, and Opie & Anthony—moved to satellite radio, safe from all FCC restrictions.

Migration to FM

Another important factor in the rise of the information format was the drastic migration of listeners from the AM to FM bands. In the largest markets, audiences began abandoning AM stations for FM stations in the early 1970s. Those music formats that had proved successful on an AM station were rapidly duplicated by FM stations with higher quality sound and then got higher ratings. By the late 1980s, it was clear no all-music format could survive on the AM band. As Chapter 11 points out, program directors of AM music stations were quick to find that *when AM and FM stations offer similar music programming, the bulk of the audience will choose to listen to the FM stations,* leaving the AM stations struggling for advertisers and revenue.

At roughly the same time as the Fairness Doctrine was abandoned by the FCC, many AM stations faced financial pressures unseen since the advent of television, leading radio personalities to start supplying strong, one-sided political opinions or sexual innuendo rarely before heard. By the mid-1980s, with a nothing-left-to-lose philosophy, AM stations, even in large markets, were willing to gamble on unknown syndicated talk personalities. Visionary talk syndicators initially offered the programming for free (in exchange for clearance of the commercials), and local AM station owners were thus able to cut the expense of paying a local personality. Although almost no one in the industry believed daytime talk programming on AM could succeed, much less draw audiences back from FM, there really were no other viable programming options.

While information programming gave AM radio a new lease on life, new dynamics are shifting talk radio onto the FM band. Just as AM radio found it could not compete with music formats against FM stations, FM now must compete with digital platforms that allow consumers to listen to all of their favorite music on cells, MP3s and tablets. Internet music services like Pandora allow listeners to customize their music listening experience, and webcasters now offer a variety of streaming music on the internet that is easily accessible through wireless portable devices. Listeners, particularly younger people, have stopped letting radio stations decide which songs they should hear. FM then has to go after whoever will best please its advertisers.

While FM stations are facing the reality that they are no longer the preferred platform for music delivery, AM stations are coping with a listening audience that is aging and technical problems that can make hearing AM stations sometimes difficult. The population of older people who are accustomed to listening to AM radio is shrinking, yet they are not being replaced by younger people because most don't listen to AM radio. This is a particularly difficult problem for AM because advertisers most want to reach younger listeners.

AM signals are more susceptible to interference and static than FM from things like thunderstorms and various kinds of machinery. AM signals also have a harder time penetrating the steel structures of big-city skyscrapers where thousands of potential listeners work. Finally, many AM stations must reduce their power or sign-off at night when AM radio waves travel farther to avoid interfering with other stations on their frequencies that have been given a higher priority by the FCC. As you can imagine, this is a major problem when those stations carry sporting events that last into the evening hours! These AM reception problems, the need for news/talk formats to grow younger audiences, and the migration of FM's music formats to digital platforms are triggering the shift of news/talk formats to FM.

Mobile Phones

Most talk shows depend on call-in listeners. Until the 1990s, talk shows had low levels of participation, especially during the peak periods of the morning and afternoon drivetimes. To people who have *always* owned a cellular telephone, this may seem illogical, but keep in mind that mobile phone technology was not widely used until the 1990s. Luckily for the format, just as the content of talk on radio was becoming more interesting, cell technology emerged to allow easier participation by listeners...wherever they were. The ability of broadcasters to offer free cell-phone calls to the station's phone numbers (in return for running advertising for the cellular service) made it easy for listeners call in any time of day—but especially during their morning and afternoon commutes.

Moreover, it quickly became standard procedure for the hosts of many talk shows to move callers on cell phones to "the top of the list," thereby giving the impression that the opinions of cell-phone callers had a greater chance of being aired—and leading more and more commuters to chime in. The proliferation of cell phones has been a boon for information programmers because research shows listeners are more likely to tune in when they can call in, even if most are unlikely to actually call.

Synergistic Advertising Environment

Information radio provides an environment uniquely attractive to radio advertisers. For one thing, the audiences tend to be more loyal to the format than audiences of other formats. This, coupled with the fact that in many smaller markets only one information station exists, means that listeners are less likely to tune out during commercial breaks. Music stations, on the other hand, often have many competitors both within and between their formats. Even more detrimental to advertisers are those music stations that promote a "more music, less talk" format. This, in effect, equates talk (that is, the information that happens between music, such as commercials!) with negative emotions and invites listeners to tune out once a commercial set starts.

On information stations, however, commercials seem less of an interruption and are merely more information that the station wants to impart to its audience. Thus, *given equally-sized audiences on both a talk station and a music station, advertisers are willing to pay a higher price to place their commercials on the news/talk/sports station—because more of the listeners will stay tuned during the commercial breaks.*

Although the synergies between programming and commercial content have undoubtedly contributed to the talk format's rise in popularity, changes in the media environment mean that information programmers may need to reevaluate their strategies on commercial spot loads. First, *more minutes of commercials are broadcast per hour on information stations than on any other format.* While originally viewed as a benefit to station owners, commercial clutter has reached an all-time high: Marketing messages appear in more and more places all the time, and consumer fatigue may not be far behind. Information listeners may eventually become less forgiving of an overload of commerce.

Furthermore, the popularity of the format has brought competition from other sources hoping to capitalize on the public's desire for information. Listeners can now find information programming in the form of news, talk or sports talk from multiple radio stations in a single market, not to mention web-based talk networks, satellite-delivered radio, cable television networks and podcasts. *Loyalty to a particular source is likely to go down in this competitive environment.* The wise information programmer will try to convince upper management that ultimate station success may be as much a factor of keeping listener loyalty as maximizing the number of commercials played per hour.

Information Programming Formats

Before discussing individual formats specifically, a reminder of how syndication delivery works in the media industries may be helpful. (For a more in-depth discussion, see Chapter 3.) Although many programmers initially think of television when they hear the word *syndication*, a vast number of highly-rated syndicated radio shows exist as well. Any of the formats described in the following sections could either originate in the local station's studio hosted by local personalities or, instead, be delivered by a national personality via satellite by such companies as Premiere Radio Networks, Westwood One and Citadel Media.

Many syndicated shows that once relied on only terrestrial broadcast signals for distribution struck deals with satellite radio services. For example, Sean Hannity and Glenn Beck are syndicated to AM and FM broadcast stations via satellite by

Premiere Radio Networks, but also have their shows distributed directly to listeners on the Patriot channel of Sirius/XM satellite radio.

This satellite radio presence, along with web-based delivery, podcasting and the growth of syndicated radio, has all but obliterated a clear line of distinction between traditional network radio and syndicators. Premiere and Westwood One are syndication companies, while ESPN Radio is a traditional network. According to some, there is *no* difference between such entities, especially in radio. When a single personality such as sports talk host Jim Rome appears on hundreds of stations via syndication, the impact for advertisers on a show is the same as the impact of Colin Cowherd, whose program is available only to ESPN Radio affiliates. Few of the tens of thousands of people listening across the nation care whether a show is coming from a network or a syndicator or appears online (see 12.6). The distinction may continue to remain important to some programmers, however, because of the prestige and branding associated with being

---

12.6 | Wi-Fi Radio

Thousands and thousands of audio services are streamed over the internet—simulcasts of many AM/FM broadcast stations, internet-only webcasters, and radio stations from foreign countries. You can listen to these internet audio streams over a computer, tablet or smartphone that has access to the internet.

Wi-Fi radios look and act more like traditional AM/FM tabletop or clock radios but link to internet radio stations through a wireless access point using Wi-Fi technology. Unlike a wireless carrier's wide area network (WAN) that covers several miles around each of its tower sites, a Wi-Fi "hotspot" is a local area network (LAN) with a range of only a few hundred feet that is intended to be an extension of a nearby wired internet connection. So Wi-Fi radios will only work if they are within range of a Wi-Fi hotspot.

With a broadcast radio, listeners can quickly tune up and down the AM or FM band looking for programs that interest them. A Wi-Fi radio must know the specific web

address of any audio service you want and then connect itself to that service's own computer (called a "server"). You must then wait several seconds to establish the digital audio stream, so it's not practical to browse internet audio offerings on a Wi-Fi radio.

To help listeners search through the thousands of audio services available on the internet and quickly access their favorites, Wi-Fi radios usually interact with a portal or aggregator web site such as Reciva Internet Radio (*www.reciva.com*), or vTuner Internet Radio (*www.vtuner.com*). These sites catalogue and organize internet audio services by location, language and genre. Listeners visit the sites to browse through audio services and designate their favorites. Those favorites then appear as "presets" on their Wi-Fi radios much like favorite radio stations are assigned to buttons on car radios.

Internet connection ➡ Modem ➡ Wireless router ➡ Wi-Fi radio waves))))))) Wi-Fi radio an affiliate of a highly regarded and widely recognized network such as ESPN Radio.

As a result of the vastness of the national audience, radio remains a gold mine for talented syndicated entertainers. For example, in 2008, Premiere signed Limbaugh to an eight-year contract extension reported to pay him $38 million per year plus a $100 million signing bonus. That same year, Sean Hannity signed a five-year contract reported to be worth around $100 million. The reason for paying

such enormous fees to syndicated personalities is that they generate huge advertising revenue. Talk show hosts like Limbaugh have fiercely loyal audiences (see 12.7) who are very responsive to advertisers who support the programs.

One worry is that paying such big bucks for superstars in national syndication deals will leave talented newcomers no place to develop their skills on local radio. Michael Harrison, publisher of *Talkers Magazine*, said, "It's really sad that so much

---

12.7 **Rush Stumbles But Doesn't Fall**

Rush Limbaugh started his radio career at the young age of 16, working as an afternoon drivetime disc jockey in his hometown of Cape Girardeau, Missouri. After a relatively nondescript career in music radio and a short stint in the advertising office of the Kansas City Royals' baseball team, he found his voice as the host of a political talk show in Sacramento, where he tripled the ratings for his time slot. Eventually, *The Rush Limbaugh Show*, with its decidedly conservative political stance, found an audience at stations across the nation. Today more than 20 million listeners tune in each day to hear Limbaugh pontificate on his self-proclaimed E.I.B. (Excellence in Broadcasting) Network. Limbaugh's success in the 1990s spread to other media, too; he authored two books that were bestsellers and hosted a syndicated television program for a while.

Although his politically-focused TV show was eventually canceled, in 2003, he had another shot at TV stardom—this time as a commentator for ESPN's *Sunday NFL Countdown*. Limbaugh said he wanted his role to be providing the "fan's perspective" on what long-time ESPN sportscasters Chris Berman, Chris Mortensen and other announcers said during the show. It was understood among cable programming insiders, however, that ESPN had hired the talk host to do what he did best: generate controversy.

After only five appearances, Limbaugh did just that. During a preview of a Philadelphia Eagles game, Limbaugh commented that Eagles quarterback Donovan McNabb's abilities had been overrated by the media because he was an African-American. In hindsight, what may have been more shocking than the claim itself was that none of the other hosts (two of whom were African-Americans) challenged Limbaugh on it. Nor were they instructed to do so by the

ESPN producers, either during that segment or after the subsequent commercial break. Although Berman and other sportscasters on the show later made public statements denouncing Limbaugh's comment, ESPN executives did not. Less than one week later, however, Limbaugh resigned.

Personal troubles continued that year for the man who often says his "talent is on loan from God." In October the newspaper tabloid *The National Enquirer* published a story claiming Limbaugh's former housekeeper had provided his employer with thousands of prescription pills over the course of four years. A short time later, Limbaugh announced on his radio program that he was addicted to prescription painkillers and was checking himself into a rehabilitation program. According to Limbaugh, the drugs had first been prescribed to him by his doctor following spinal surgery six years earlier. This prompted a state investigation and attempts to unseal his medical records to determine whether he used his public personality to "shop" for physicians who would provide him with the drugs.

After 30 days in rehab, though, Limbaugh was back and as bombastic as ever. What is remarkable is the extent to which Limbaugh's audience remained loyal. Survey research found that more than 90 percent of his regular listeners said they listened to him as much now as they had before the scandal. According to the researcher who conducted the study, there was "no increase in defections or negative comments even at the height of the most negative publicity. The majority of his regular listeners are still rock-solid behind him."[11]

Robert F. Potter
Indiana University

money will go to the superstars and so little to the new talent."[12] However, some predict the next crop of talented talk personalities will come from digital platforms, not the traditional route of working their way to national syndication from smaller market broadcast stations. Personalities who can prove their talent by building a unique brand with a loyal audience through podcasting or web streaming will catch the attention of syndicators looking for the next big talk personality.

All-News Formats

Amid the earlier discussion of personalities and commentary, it is easy to forget that some radio programs do not comment on the news but simply deliver it. Radio did not become a primary source for news coverage until World War II, when radio technology, although still new to many, became the source of the memorable voices of Edward R. Murrow, William Shirer and the other great war correspondents who offered listeners the sounds of battle and bombing. Today, the use of radio to keep in touch with what is happening in the world and in local communities remains popular. In such major markets as Chicago (WBBM-AM), New York (WCBS-AM) and Philadelphia (KYW-AM), all-news stations are consistently among the most highly rated.

The all-news format consists of continuous newscasts, usually in 20- or 30-minute segments, for 24 hours each day. One example is WINS-AM (New York), whose slogan for a long time was, "At 10-10 WINS, give us 22 minutes and we'll give you the world." Because stations following this format repeat news cycles over and over, they tend to attract listeners for short periods of time—only long enough to hear one or two of the cycles. By the second time, most listeners recognize that the content is nearly identical to what they heard only minutes before. This means the all-news format is a *high-cume, low-TSL* format; in other words, it depends on high cumulative ratings to counteract low time-spent-listening numbers. Because cume ratings are based on the number of unduplicated listeners who tune in, locally produced all-news stations

are normally found just in larger markets with big enough population bases to generate the needed audience flow.

Given that listeners are constantly tuning in and out of all-news stations, commercials, program elements and promos must be scheduled much more frequently than in other formats in order to obtain an *effective frequency* among the constantly changing audience. While station managers and air talent will get "sick of hearing the same thing over and over and over," the program director must look out for the typical listener, who tunes in for perhaps 20 minutes a day and relies on the heavy frequency in order to be sufficiently exposed to the information.

Another important philosophical decision for an all-news programmer is to decide on an optimal ratio of different types of news: hard news, entertainment news, economic news, human-interest stories and so on. Some all-news programmers insist that as many stories as possible should contain a local angle. In other words, even if the story focuses on something taking place overseas, such as the 2011 Pacific earthquake and tsunami, in order to get on the air the story must be written in such a way as to have a simple, clear answer to the question, "How does this affect our local audience?" This is often accomplished by the presence of an "exemplar," a local resident or expert either affected by or offering their opinions on the story.

Other programmers make sure their content contains an ample supply of news about motion picture celebrities, television stars, famous athletes and sex scandals. To them, "news" is the type of information that can be talked about in the break room at work or with a friend you meet for lunch. For these reasons, stories about international relations, macroeconomic policy, scientific discovery—news that cannot easily be put directly into a human context—is seldom covered.

Network-Delivered Newscasts

Most large-market stations are now so tightly formatted that they want newscasts more tailored to their format than any network can provide. In response, the traditional radio networks have shifted from delivering newscasts to becoming sources of original sound bites. Stations then use the network sound bites to craft their own custom newscasts.

Increasingly, network news material is delivered not by a local anchor or as part of a traditional newscast but by a sidekick to the station's drivetime personality. One model for the newscaster as sidekick is Robin Quivers, who began as a newscaster but who now is, in effect, one of the team of co-hosts of *The Howard Stern Show* on satellite radio. Using members of the wacky "morning zoo" team as newscasters may make traditional journalists shudder, but the practice has increased program consistency, reduced audience turnover and resulted in increased ratings. As local stations increasingly model their formats after Stern/Quivers or Imus/McCord, entertainment environments become the primary sources of local and national news on radio.

Ironically, what were once the great radio network news departments have assisted in killing themselves off by passing along sound bites of everything from presidential addresses to Hollywood stars pushing their latest productions. In 2004, however, Fox News surfaced as a radio power on stations owned by Clear Channel Radio, reviving network-delivered newscasts in about 400 markets. Bringing its uniquely conservative slant, Fox builds radio interview shows around current and former cable news hosts such as Brian Kilmeade and Alan Colmes.

In smaller markets and on less successful stations in larger markets, network newscasts can still be heard in their entirety. Because these stations have much smaller audience sizes, the radio networks could not survive financially if these were the only audiences their national advertisers could reach. *Stations that choose not to carry the newscasts in full (mostly major-market affiliates) are required by network affiliation contracts to at least broadcast the commercials that were included within the newscast.* Stations receive private feeds of the commercials from the networks for local recording and insertion into local programs. They also receive schedule information from the network. They must then schedule the network's commercials in time periods equivalent to when they would have aired in the newscasts. After these replacement commercials air, station personnel produce affidavits for the networks affirming the times and dates the network spots ran (as proof so their advertisers pay the bills).

News Scheduling Priorities

Because the programming of all-news stations is based on repeating cycles, scheduling considerations tend to be tighter than for talk stations. On the average, news occupies about 75 percent of airtime on an all-news station. The basic elements of newcasting at an all-news station include the following:

- Hard news copy
- Recapitulations (recaps) of major stories
- Question-and-answer material from outside reporters
- Results of public opinion polls
- Telephone actualities from exemplars

Earthshaking news developments on a global or national scale are not necessarily uppermost in the audience's notion of what is news. During morning drivetime, weather and traffic reports should be emphasized as they will determine how listeners start their day. A typical urban schedule runs in this way: time announcements at least every 2 minutes; weather information (current and forecast) no more than 10 minutes apart; traffic information every 10 minutes; plus, interspersed, related information such as school closings, major area sports events and so on. In other words, *the top priority in any all-news format is* local, personal, service *programming*. Item repetition slows during midday as average listener TSL increases, and is stepped up again during afternoon drivetime (4 to 6 P.M.).

Predictability is important in news programming because the audience will get used to coming to the station at specific times for program elements such as weather, traffic and sports. During drivetimes, in fact, many all-news stations develop on-air slogans that emphasize when listeners can count on hearing what matters to them most during their commute to work. For example, WWJ-AM (Detroit) gives its listeners "traffic and weather together on the 8s," meaning listeners know that they can tune into the station at 8, 18, 28, 38, 48 and 58 minutes past each hour and be sure to get the information they need.

Talk Formats

Just as there is format fragmentation in music radio (discussed in Chapter 11), traditional talk has fragmented to include hot talk, advice talk, business talk, sports talk, success talk and other niche formats. Such variations of talk radio differ in approach, sound, and "attitude" and appeal to quite different audiences. Most consultants now identify at least ten major talk formats, shown in 12.8 and described in more detail in this section.

Heritage Talk

Heritage talk stations typically are 50,000-watt clear channel stations that have included at least some talk programming for 40 years or more (see 12.9). Twenty years ago, these were classified as full-service stations

with a mix of news, talk, sports and midday music. Increasingly, these stations have moved to all-information formats with emphasis on local news, weather, traffic, sports and local talk. They are also able to attract the highest rated of the nationally syndicated talk programming, primarily because of the wide signal coverage they have at night. These stations typically carry heavy commercial loads, often up to 20 minutes an hour.

Politics/Issues Talk

Political talk occupies a formidable spot on any list of information radio formats. Rush Limbaugh is certainly the king of the genre, but there are many other well-known syndicated personalities out there, such as Sean Hannity, Michael Savage, Glenn Beck and Ed Schultz. Politics/issues talk is sometimes described as programming hosted and listened to by "angry white men"—leaning to either the left or the right politically. However, that characterization is not altogether accurate. There are examples of successful hosts of color in this format, such as

---

12.8   Ten Top Talk-Radio Formats

1. **Heritage talk:** Traditional news/talk formats, mostly on the AM band. Broad appeal with mix of news, sports, talk, health and financial features.

2. **Politics/issues talk:** Discussion of the latest issues coming from Washington, DC, around the world, or from the local city and state.

3. **Sports talk:** Discussion of the issues surrounding major team sports of interest to men: football, baseball and basketball. Often also supplemented with play-by-play and "guy talk."

4. **Success talk:** Formerly, money talk or business radio. A mix of investment and personal advice for financial success. May include talk about upscale travel, recreation and relaxation.

5. **Hot talk:** Younger demographic appeal with sexually-oriented content. Found on FM stations, but mostly on satellite radio and digital platforms.

6. **Urban talk:** Similar to heritage talk but with African-American appeal. Tends to be in urban areas.

7. **Faith talk:** Also called "religious radio." Used to be exclusively Christian, but now characterized by a growing multitude of faiths.

8. **Spanish/foreign-language talk:** Similar to heritage talk but appealing to the needs of the demographic audience that speaks the programmed language. One of the fastest-growing formats.

9. **Health and help talk:** Advice given to callers about anything from health to finances to home improvement. Includes many syndicated weekend programs.

10. **Technology talk**: Initially limited to discussion of computer and networking issues, but expanding to include discussions of all types of electronic gadgets.

12.9 Heritage News and Talk

In the mid-1960s, the foundation for all-news radio was laid by two major broadcasting groups. The first was Group W, the Westinghouse Broadcasting Company, which converted three AM stations—WINS (New York) and KYW (Philadelphia) in 1965 and KFWB (Los Angeles) in 1968—to an all-news format. CBS followed suit with several of its owned-and-operated AM stations, first at WCBS (New York), KCBS (San Francisco) and KNX (Los Angeles), and later at WBBM (Chicago), WEEI (Boston) and finally WCAU (Philadelphia).

By the mid-1990s, hundreds of stations, mostly AM, were identifying themselves as all-news or news/talk stations, and the format was spreading beyond major cities into smaller markets. Although the all-news format is dependent on local programming, network affiliation provides coverage most local stations cannot supply. In addition, a growing number of syndicators supply both affiliated and nonaffiliated stations with news services and programs.

The term *talk station* was generally adopted when KABC in Los Angeles and a few other major-market stations discarded their music formats around 1960 and began airing information programming featuring the human voice. KABC started with a key four-hour news and conversation program, *News/Talk*, from 5 to 9 A.M. KGO in San Francisco later adopted the name of that program to describe its overall format. KGO used news blocks in both morning and evening drivetime and conversation programs throughout the balance of the day. KABC focused on live call-in programs, interviews and feature material combined with informal and formal news coverage. KABC first promoted itself as "The Conversation Station," but *news/talk* stuck as the generic industry term for stations that program conversation leavened with news during drivetimes.

Lincoln Ware on WDBZ in Cincinnati and Jo Madison, "The Black Eagle," on WOL-AM in Washington, DC, who can also be heard on SiriusXM satellite radio. At the local market level, Ray Taliaferro was the first black talk-show host in a major market. He started in talk radio in 1967 and joined KGO-AM (San Francisco) in 1977 where he has been talking politics in the Bay Area ever since.

Many programmers find success by scheduling female hosts who can intelligently communicate a political viewpoint to an audience. Progressive talker Randi Rhodes broadcasts live from Washington, DC, during afternoon drivetime and is syndicated nationally by Premiere Radio Networks. Diane Rehm of National Public Radio (NPR) and WAMU-FM (Washington, DC) has been effectively discussing political issues on the air for more than 30 years. *The Laura Ingraham Show* is syndicated by Talk Radio Network, and its host was described by *Talkers Magazine* as the "leading nationally-syndicated female political talker [with a] razor wit."[13]

Scholars have recognized that political talk radio is more effective than many other forms of mass media at generating a sense of solidarity and community among its audience members. Many believe the format provides "a venue for a public that feels ignored, isolated, alienated, and powerless to channel their anger concerning…actions by political elites… ."[14] Politics/issues talk stations can also take the lead in affecting political attitudes and social change. Some believe that the impeachment hearings of President Clinton would never have come about had it not been for hosts of political talk radio keeping listeners focused on the Clinton/Monica Lewinsky scandal. Others believe the historic recall election of California governor Gray Davis would not have occurred had it not been for the efforts of such political talk stations such as KSFO (San Francisco), KTZK (Sacramento) and KFI (Los Angeles). These stations not only consistently raised the topic of public dissatisfaction with Davis, but also actively collected listener signatures on petitions that led to the eventual recall.

Sports Talk

Sports talk radio is a rising star in information radio. Growing from only a handful of stations dedicated to sports programming, there are now more than one thousand commercial sports talk stations on the air, with some major markets supporting at least two sports talk stations. The vast majority of these stations are AM, but a few FM sports talk stations exist as well. Some of the leading stations in this genre include WFAN-AM (New York), WSCR-AM (Chicago) and WIP-AM (Philadelphia).

The growth of sports talk has been fueled not only by the overall success of information radio but also by the sports format's appeal to men in the 25 to 54 and 18 to 34 age groups, two elusive demographic groups much sought by advertisers. Another huge factor in sports talk's success was the development of a syndicated radio network as a brand extension of the cable television network ESPN. ESPN Radio is carried on hundreds of affiliates in the United States, with many of them airing the feed around the clock. Beyond getting the allure of the ESPN brand, affiliate programmers acquire some of the hot personalities that viewers are familiar with, such as Mike and Mike (Mike Greenberg and Mike Golic), Doug Gottlieb, and Brian Kenny. ESPN Radio is not the only full-time syndicated sports talk source: Sporting News Radio and Fox Sports Radio also reach millions of listeners each on hundreds of affiliates in North America.

Often, programmers who affiliate with these networks choose not to schedule all of the available programming, electing instead to schedule local hosts to discuss professional, minor league, collegiate and even high school sports of interest to the local market. Of course, play-by-play coverage of pro and college games is an important element, but other popular sports talk staples include scoreboard shows, interview shows and talk programs with a sports slant. Ultimately, decisions in this format, just like any other, must be made according to the desired target market of the programmer. For example, some ESPN Radio affiliates felt that the network's *The Tony Kornheiser Show* skewed too old for their programming strategies and opted instead to go after *The Jim Rome Show*, a stand-alone talk show syndicated by Premiere Radio Networks. Rome's in-your-face style as he "gives his take to the clones" (translation for those unfamiliar with

the show: "states his opinion to his listeners") is viewed as more attractive to the 18 to 34 male demographic. Similarly, *The Herd with Colin Cowherd* was picked up because it is a faster-paced show skewing to younger males.

Sports programmers agree that a successful sports talk station is more than just discussion of sports. In fact, some consultants prefer to call the format "guy talk" because what makes the format work is a combination of the games themselves and a celebration of the lifestyle that goes with them. The fun surrounding a football game is far more than just going to the game. The game becomes an excuse for a day-long or weekend-long party with tailgating, road trips and barbecuing. In sports radio, capturing on the air the lifestyle of the sports fans is what really makes this format work. Sports talk personalities commonly discuss movies, celebrities, politics, music and much more—as well as sports. In fact, ESPN Radio's morning drivetime show—*Mike & Mike in the Morning*—even has a daily stock report because the programmers at the network recognize that many of the males in their target market are interested not only in sports but also in business and investing.

Success Talk

This format, also known as money talk or business radio, offers listeners a mix of investment and personal advice for financial success. Segments include discussion of stock trading, retirement planning, insurance issues and taxes. Some programmers of success talk also include programs that focus on health and recreation, chic travel and vacations, and upscale entertainment. Just like the sports talk format, some stations choose to sign on to a 24-hour syndicated network such as Bloomberg Radio. Others, however, use a mixture of nationally syndicated personalities (Clark Howard and Dave Ramsey) and locally known financial gurus. Although stations in this format rarely deliver large ratings, those that succeed do so because they convince advertisers that the listeners are very loyal and upwardly mobile. One of the best known of these shows appears only on the weekends: *Bob Brinker's*

Moneytalk, which focuses on financial advice. Examples of stations that program the success format include WBIX-AM (Boston) and KBNP-AM (Portland, Oregon).

Hot Talk

This format focuses on discussions of sexual issues that are presented in a titillating way to appeal to the male audience. Hot Talk programmers are trying to develop a sound that expresses a "rock and roll" attitude without the music. However, the format has mostly retreated to satellite radio and digital platforms after the government's crackdown on indecent content on broadcast stations.

It will come as no surprise that Howard Stern is one of the most successful hosts of talk radio with a "rock and roll" attitude. His move to satellite radio in 2006 left opportunities for others to grow even larger in their broadcast popularity, although the window of opportunity seems to be closing. *The Adam Carolla Show With Teresa Strasser* replaced Stern on KLSX (Los Angeles) when he moved to satellite. However, Carolla lost his job in 2009 when CBS radio converted the station from Hot Talk to a Top 40 music format. Corolla is now showing success as a podcaster (*www.adamcarolla.com*). Tom Leykis, a legendary name in the hot talk format, was also a casualty at KLSX. Steve Dahl, who was a hot talker at WCKG-FM (Chicago), also now hosts a podcast (*www.dahlcast.org*).

Urban Talk

Stations programming this format tend to be in metro areas where the available listening audience includes a large number of middle to upper-middle-class African-Americans. The approach usually follows that of heritage or political talk, but the issues are those with a strong appeal to black listeners. A syndicated leader is *The Tom Joyner Morning Show,* which is delivered by Joyner's Reach Media to over 8 million listeners on more than 100 stations (see 12.10). Although music takes up a substantial portion of Joyner's show, the key programming element is the information he and his co-hosts provide to their audience. Local stations programmed to focus on the urban issues of their communities are also highly popular in major urban areas. In addition to WVON-AM (Chicago), others in this format include WOL-AM (Washington, DC) and satellite radio's "The Power."

12.10 **African-American Talk on Radio**

*T*he Tom Joyner Morning Show has made a big place for itself in the radio syndication history books. Begun in 1994, the show is one of the first nationally syndicated radio programs hosted and produced by an African-American and distributed by a nonblack network. It reaches about 8 million listeners on some 115 stations. Moreover, in 2003, Joyner (majority shareholder and chairman of Reach Media) assumed control and syndication of his own show, making this a rarity in syndication—a black-owned program.

Distributed as a four-hour morning-drive radio program, *The Tom Joyner Morning Show* appeals to an urban contemporary audience of affluent adults. It schedules a mix of oldies urban music, guests from politics and entertainment, and multiple local tags or promos to give the show a "hometown feel."

Tom Joyner, the self-proclaimed "hardest working man in radio," made his name a household word with African-Americans while raising money for black colleges and other political causes. A daily segment called "It's Your World" is one of the few present-day radio soap operas. Listeners say following the on-again, off-again relationships of various characters keeps them on the edge of their seats, and the rating books show that the segment certainly keeps them tuned in.

George L. Daniels, Ph.D.
University of Alabama

Faith Talk

This format has long consisted primarily of talk programming that focuses on Christian topics. Stations typically have a combination of syndicated program elements from such nationally known clergy as Max Lucado, T. D. Jakes and Joyce Meyer; they are accompanied by national and local political talk hosts offering their positions on topics from a Christian worldview. The faith talk format is expanding, however, with many more beliefs now represented. Some broadcast stations program exclusively Jewish talk and Catholic talk, supported by national Jewish and Catholic network programming. *Jewish Moments in the Morning* has been on New York/New Jersey's community radio WFMU since 1977 (*www.jmintheam.org*), and online sources include *www.jewishradio.com*. Those of the Muslim faith can also find a talk-radio outlet on the web at *www.radioislam.com*, and Bahais can listen to *www.bahairadio.org*. Moreover, podcasting provides for listeners a wealth of information across a wide range of religious and spiritual topics.

Spanish/Foreign-Language Talk

This format, similar to the urban talk format, is one where the information being provided focuses on the needs of those whose native language is not English. Although the largest markets may have low-powered AM stations programming information in almost any native tongue, by far the dominant and fastest-growing foreign-language talk format is Spanish. The popularity of this format has grown rapidly along with the number of Spanish-speaking people in the United States and has been recognized by national networks.

Univision Radio owns or operates 70 radio stations in top markets across the country. Its strategy is to acquire English-language stations in markets with the largest Hispanic populations and relaunch them with Spanish language formats. Univision also syndicates its popular KSCA-FM (Los Angeles) program *Piolin por la Manana* (*Piolin in the Morning*) hosted by Eddie "Piolin" Sotelo.

ESPN recognized the importance of this growing demographic when it launched ESPN Deportes Radio, an around-the-clock national Spanish-language sports radio network that serves Hispanic sports fans in the United States. The network has 44 affiliates throughout the country, reaching nearly 60 percent of the Hispanic population in the U.S. The network is also available via SiriusXM Satellite Radio. Of course, regardless of the language, many information stations now stream their signals over the web, giving non-English speakers easy access to foreign-language talk stations from around the globe with the click of a mouse.

Health and Help Talk

Although it is rare to find a station that programs this format exclusively, many programmers find that a regular offering of some type of advice to listeners is a good addition to their broadcast schedule. The type of advice varies widely and is usually limited only by the host's expertise. Advice programming contains information on nutrition, health, relationships, home improvement, sexuality, the law—the list is almost endless. Some syndicated weekday leaders in this area include *Duke and the Doctor* (for health-related concerns) and Dr. Joy Browne (for relationship issues). Also in this category falls the network devoted to serving the nation's truckers who are often on the road during the overnight hours. The Midnight Trucking Radio Network reaches all of the United States and over 75 percent of Canada and Mexico, thanks to overnight broadcasts on many 50,000-watt stations in the United States (see 12.11).

Often, shows falling in the health/help talk category air only once a week—usually on the weekend. Well-known nationally syndicated examples include *At Home With Gary Sullivan*, a show about home improvement, and *On the Garden Line*. Many such weekend shows also produce "daily minutes" offering tidbits of advice to listeners while also promoting their long-form weekend programming.

Technology Talk

Originally referred to as "internet talk," this format has now expanded to include discussions of anything to do with computers and technology. Although it is

12.11 | Midnight Trucking Radio Network

Calling itself the "national clearinghouse of information, thoughts, and opinions of the American Truck Driver," the Midnight Trucking Radio Network (MTRN) airs nightly from midnight until 5 A.M. on 60 affiliates. The number of MTRN affiliates may seem miniscule compared to the hundreds of stations carrying *The Rush Limbaugh Show*. However, the network can actually be heard in almost every market of the country because ten of its affiliates broadcast on 50,000-watt clear channel transmitters that have tremendous geographic reach during the overnight hours. This national reach is also expanded by MTRN's availability on mobile devices and the web.

MTRN hosts Eric Harley and Gary McNamara take calls from truckers and deliver information precisely targeted toward their specific audience, including hourly reports of weather along the nation's highways, announcements of road closings and construction delays, news about legislation affecting the trucking industry, and daily maintenance tips. They also take calls from truckers behind the wheel during segments focusing on everything from semi-truck insurance issues to the latest in truck technologies. So, as the network's website (*www.midnighttrucking.com*) says, "Whether you're behind the wheel or just can't sleep, you're never alone ... when you've got The Midnight Trucking Radio Network."

---

unlikely that a programmer will choose to focus on this topic 24 hours a day, weekly programs focusing on computers have been highly successful. *The Kim Komando Show* is a weekly syndicated show remarkable not only for explaining technical issues about computers in very simple terms to callers but also for being hosted by a very knowledgeable female personality in a stereotypically male-dominated genre.

The Content Infrastructure

Most information radio formats are constructed to showcase different types of content during different dayparts. Heritage talk stations, for example, schedule a heavy load of news during morning drivetime (from 5 to 9 A.M. or 6 to 10 A.M.) and again during afternoon drivetime (from about 4 to 6 P.M. depending on the market). The rest of their program days are devoted to various kinds of talk programs and often include some type of sports programming.

Although news and talk stations are often seen as similar because their spoken-word formats are so distinct from music stations, they are in fact very different from one another. The all-news programmer oversees the equivalent of a single program that recycles for 24 hours throughout each day, whereas talk programmers fill most of their days with diverse shows lasting from one to six hours. The talk

programmer must also consider the gratifications desired by various kinds of talk listeners. Some are attracted by the personality of such hosts as Schlessinger or Limbaugh. Others use talk radio primarily as a way to gather information. While some listen to hear viewpoints that differ from their own, many appreciate hearing their own opinions validated by the program host.

The programming infrastructures for both news and talk formats, however, are usually created on computers and form the skeletons on which hang the sections of hard news, features, talk programs, game coverage, sports commentaries, editorials and so on. At all-news stations, newscasts are repeated in 20-, 30-, 45- or 60-minute sequences, although most stations prefer the shorter 20-minute cycles. Cycle length affects spot and headline placement; time, traffic, weather and sports scheduling; major news story development; and feature scheduling. Advantages and disadvantages are inherent in all lengths; which cycle pattern a programmer chooses depends on local market conditions, staff capability, editorial supervision, program content and commercial load.

As mentioned earlier, *information formats usually program a larger commercial load than music stations because the spots seem less intrusive.* Typically, each hour on an information station contains 12 to 18 minutes of spot announcements. Talk stations tend to have fewer breaks per hour, and often the number and location are dictated by the programs' syndicators. All-news stations, especially those with frequent news and traffic updates, may run as few as one or two spots in breaks coming every five minutes or less.

Hosts

In the all-news format, many of the on-air talent are **experienced journalists**. Some have spent years in television or print news prior to joining a radio staff. Sometimes, radio hosts have many information careers going at once. Mitch Albom hosts a syndicated talk show and writes for the *Detroit Free Press*. Brian Kilmeade hosts a three-hour talk show on Fox News Radio just after completing duties as a co-host of *Fox and Friends* on the Fox News cable network. Talk hosts are sometimes experts in their particular field (for example, the doctors or scientists in the health/help talk format), but usually could best be described as generalists. They have developed the ability to grasp a subject's essence. The host of a general-interest issues talk program will discuss world and local affairs, politics, medicine, economics, science, history, literature, music, art, sports and entertainment trivia—often on a single show. It thus becomes a vital part of the host's daily preparation to keep abreast of current events and to have at least some familiarity with a wide range of topics. Hosts can subscribe to "show prep" services to receive background information and summaries of news events and political happenings.

Callers and Listeners

It is important for an information programmer (*any* radio programmer, really) to remember that people who are motivated enough to call the station and try to get on the air represent only a small fraction of the audience. According to surveys by the Times Mirror Center for the People and the Press, only 11 percent of Americans say they have attempted to call a talk-radio program; of these, only 6 percent report that they made it on the air. It is common for show producers and screeners to choose callers to put on the air according to their likelihood of offering an interesting perspective on the topic being discussed or saying

something that may hit a nerve with the host or other listeners. Programmers should keep in mind that, although the audience may like *listening* to this controversy, most people will not hold such extreme viewpoints. Callers do not provide an accurate profile of listeners, but station personnel frequently become so focused on calls that they forget about the larger audience—which should be their prime concern. Switching the emphasis to the listening audience usually makes ratings go up. What is known about the talk-radio *listener* appears in 12.12.

Commercial Interests

Of all radio formats, talk is the most vulnerable to the appearance of what is really unscheduled commercial matter. *Payola* and *plugola* have long been associated with the music industry, but the talk format offers greater opportunities for such abuses. An hour of friendly conversation presents frequent chances for the on-air host to mention a favorite resort or restaurant or to comment on a newly acquired automobile. Moreover, the program host is often in the position of booking favored business acquaintances as guests. The on-air personality receives many offers from potential guests and local businesses, ranging from free dinners to discounts on major purchases. Policies aimed at preventing regulatory violations must emphasize that

12.12 ## Demographic Profile of News/ Talk/Information Radio Listeners

1. Almost 60 percent of the audience is male.
2. More than three-fourths are age 45 or older.
3. Three-fourths have attended college, with 44 percent holding college degrees.
4. Almost two-thirds live in households earning more than $50,000.
5. More than two-thirds own their homes.

Radio Today 2010: How America Listens to Radio, Arbitron Marketing Communications, 2010, retrieved from *http://www.arbitron.com/home/radiotoday.htm*.

management will severely penalize culprits. Stations often require their on-air talent and producers to sign affidavits showing that they understand the law on these points, and some hire independent agencies to monitor their talk programs for abuses. More than one station has reinforced this message by billing on-air performers for the time when their casual conversations became "commercials."

However, guests representing commercial enterprises may certainly appear on the station. It is appropriate, for instance, for a local travel agent to discuss travel in mainland China or for the proprietor of a health food store to present opinions on nutrition. And, obviously, many personalities on the talk-show circuit have something to sell—a book, a movie, a sporting event, a philosophy and so on. Some mention of the individual's reason for appearing is appropriate because it establishes the guest's credentials. An apt reference might be, "Our subject today is the popularity of computer games, and our guest is Dr. Ted Castronova, author of a new book entitled *Synthetic Worlds.*" A gray area arises on those occasions when the host seems to be strongly encouraging listeners to buy the book. If the host has no financial interest in the publication, however, a claim of violating FCC regulations is unlikely.

On-Air Talk Techniques

Call-in programs are the backbone of talk radio. They can also be complicated to produce, especially if a program has a dozen phone lines to deal with. To help the on-air personality run a smooth show, the *call screener* or producer has become a vital part of the talk-radio staff. The screener is partly a "warm-up artist" for the host—building up the caller's enthusiasm and excitement so that it comes through in the caller's interaction with the host— and partly serves as a traffic cop.

Telephone Screeners

Screeners add substantially to station budgets, but a station can control its programming only through careful screening. Many hosts and programmers view airing "cold" or unscreened calls as a dangerous practice. Jim Bohannon of Westwood One, on the other hand, prefers the spontaneity of unscreened calls, saying to his listeners, "If you get in, you get on."

The screener for a talk program functions as a gatekeeper, exercising significant control over the information that reaches the air. Screeners constantly manipulate the lineup of incoming calls, giving priority to more appropriate callers and delaying or eliminating callers of presumably lesser interest. The screener asks each caller a series of questions to determine whether the call will be used: "What topic do you want to talk about? How do you feel about it? Why do you want to speak on the air?" At the same time, the screener determines whether callers are articulate, whether their comments are likely to promote the flow of the program, and whether they possess some unique quality that the host and audience will find appealing (see 12.13). In the case of *The Dr. Laura Show,* for example, the screener prompts callers to begin by thanking the host and tries to get each one focused on a specific question to ask.

The screener also asks for the caller's name. Most stations prohibit the use of full names to forestall imposters from identifying themselves as prominent people in a community and then airing false statements to embarrass the individuals they claim to be. Another job for the screener is to filter out the "regulars" who call the station too frequently as well as those unable or unlikely to make a coherent contribution. When screeners must dump a caller, they say something like, "Thank you for calling, but I don't think we'll be able to get you on the air today." Callers thus dismissed and those asked to hold for long periods often complain of unfair treatment, but the screener must prevail, insisting on the right to structure the best possible conversational sequence. The most effective screeners perform their jobs with tact and graciousness, but a few callers always go away mad.

When a program depends on callers, what happens in those nightmare moments when there are none? For just this emergency, most talk-show hosts maintain a clipping file containing newspaper

12.13 Host Displays

Various systems are used for the screener to signal to the on-air host which incoming call is to be aired next. Most talk stations now utilize computer software they have developed themselves or a commercial product. Using computers shifts greater program control to the on-air host. The computer display indicates the number and nature of the calls prepared for airing as well as the first name, gender and approximate age of each caller, and it may specify the point the caller wishes to discuss. The host can then alter the complexion of the program by orchestrating call order.

The display also frequently includes material of practical conversational value, such as the current weather forecast and news headlines. Hosts often use a timer to monitor call length, and many hosts cut a caller off, as politely as possible, after 90 seconds to two minutes to keep the pace of the program moving. *Listeners will tune out a poor phone call on a talk station just as they would a weak song on a music station*. Thus, hosts must control the on-air subject matter and the flow of program material rather than let callers dictate the programming. The point is to move the show along rather than get bogged down making sure each caller gets his or her "full" say.

Almost all talk stations use an electronic unit that delays the programming about seven seconds to allow the host or audio board operator to censor profanity, personal attacks and other questionable utterances. The on-air host generally controls a "cut button" that diverts offensive program material, although the engineer should have a backup switch. Because the program is delayed, the screener instructs all callers to turn off their radios before talking on the air. If they fail to do this, callers hear their voices coming back at them on a delayed basis and cannot carry on a conversation, causing the host to exclaim, "Turn your radio down!" Listening only on the telephone, callers hear the real-time program material and can talk normally with the host.

and magazine articles saved from their general reading to provide a background for monologues when no calls come in. Another strategy is the expert phone list, a list of 10 or 20 professionals with expertise in subjects of broad appeal. Resorting to the list should yield at least one or two able to speak by phone when the host needs to fill time in order to sustain a program.

Controversy, Balance, and Pressure

Although information radio programmers get many opportunities for creative expression, they also must devote considerable time to administration. Because the station deals almost constantly with public-affairs issues, its programmers spot-monitor the station's programs for compliance with FCC rules, and to avoid legal problems such as slander. A programmer, however, having many other duties as well, rarely knows as much about the minute-by-minute program as heavy listeners do. Therefore, digital backup systems must be established. Many stations keep archived recordings of previous broadcasts in order to respond to complaints made by the public.

Talk stations frequently find themselves the targets of pressure groups, activist organizations and political parties trying to gain free access to the station's airtime. Although most partisans deserve some airtime in the interest of fairness and balance, management must turn away those seeking inordinate amounts of airtime. Because of this, and the fact that an effective talk station frequently deals with controversial issues, management can expect threats of all kinds from irate audience members. A provoked listener will demand anything from a retraction to equal time, and on occasion, someone will threaten legal action.

Potential lawsuits usually vanish, however, when management explains the relevant broadcast law to the complainant. Review of the archived program proves very handy in these situations. When the station is even slightly in the wrong, it is good policy to provide rebuttal time for an overlooked point of view.

A primary ingredient in the recipe for success in any talk format is commitment at the top—at the station management level. A timely and innovative music format can catapult a station from obscurity to the number-one ranking during a single rating period. Talk stations and all-news stations, on the other hand, generally take years to reach their potential. Once success is achieved, however, the talk station enjoys a listener loyalty that endures long after the more fickle music audience shifts from station to station in search of the hits. *High figures for time-spent-listening and long-term stability in cumulative ratings demonstrate audience loyalty in the information format.*

Information Formats on Public Radio

Until now this chapter has focused on programming *commercial* information stations—a task that is ultimately guided by the specific goal of gathering either a large audience or one with an extremely desirable demographic and psychographic profile that can then be sold to advertisers. The discussion now turns toward another type of information radio, the public stations, usually guided more by delivering what the programmers believe is important information than by the struggle to gain high ratings.

Information programming is among the most popular formats on public radio stations—at least during large blocks of the day. Talk shows such as *Car Talk* and *A Prairie Home Companion* attract large, loyal audiences (see 12.14). Similarly, news programs such as *All Things Considered* and *Morning Edition* are popular and trusted sources for millions of Americans. Because of their popularity, the potential for earning commercial revenue from these shows is great. However, public stations are prohibited from airing advertisements and explicitly committed to serving as an alternative to commercial broadcasting by providing programs for specialized, small-audience needs. Instead of selling commercial spots, the major public radio networks sell their programs to affiliates (the member stations), who must in turn find funds from local

underwriting by businesses and from listener donations during periodic pledge drives. The three major networks, National Public Radio (NPR), Public Radio International (PRI) and American Public Media (APM), also look for underwriting from national companies and foundations in order to fund their production operations and keep the program acquisition fees charged to affiliates as low as possible.

Sometimes, donations to the national public networks can create a catch-22 situation. This was experienced in a grand way in 2003. In January of that year, NPR received a $14 million grant from the John D. and Catherine T. MacArthur Foundation. At the time it was the largest grant the public radio network had ever received. Only a few months later, it was announced that Joan B. Kroc—late millionaire widow of the founder of the McDonald's restaurant chain—had bequeathed more than *$200 million* to NPR; it was one of the largest individual gifts to any cultural organization in history and far overshadowed the extraordinary MacArthur gift. Referring to Kroc's gift, NPR's President Kevin Klose said, "This remarkable act of generosity will help secure the future of NPR as a trusted and independent source of news," but he also worried that news of the gift would keep listeners of local stations from making individual contributions, something that would severely hurt the local affiliates because none of the gift would go directly to the local level.[15]

Unlike affiliates of traditional commercial networks, public radio stations are free to choose programs from any source, including from the three major national competitors, PRI, NPR and APM. Individual public radio programmers often decide that their local audiences are best served by airing NPR's *Morning Edition* followed immediately by APM's business news program *Marketplace Morning Report*. More important than allegiance to one network are a station's philosophy toward its audience and its fundraising capability, degree of localism, and integrity.

As in public television, the nature of the licensee determines many of the station's goals. About 60 percent of public radio stations have colleges and universities as their licensees, while about one-third are licensed to independent community organizations, 6 percent to local school districts or local

12.14 A Companion to Prairie Home Companion

"It's been a quiet week in Lake Wobegon, Minnesota, my home town." For almost 30 years, those words have introduced listeners to the lives of the most famous nonexistent residents of Minnesota's most famous nonexistent town. Those are also the words associated with Garrison Keillor, one of the world's greatest living storytellers. But few could have seen his genius in the beginning.

The name *A Prairie Home Companion* was borrowed from the Prairie Home Cemetery in Moorhead, Minnesota, back in 1969 when Keillor was doing a morning show on Minnesota Public Radio. While researching the Grand Ole Opry for an article, Keillor had one of those incredibly brilliant moments that most others would have considered insane. His idea was to produce an old-fashioned radio variety show. Never mind that live radio plays had been declared dead for more than 20 years. NPR wasn't interested, but about five years later, with the help of the more adventurous Minnesota Public Radio, Garrison Keiller's first variety broadcast occurred on the campus of Macalester College in St. Paul. There were 12 people in the audience. As they say, the rest is history.

News of the seemingly innovative program quickly spread by word of mouth, audiences grew, and a decade later the show moved into a larger St. Paul theater (later renamed the Fitzgerald Theater) where it has been—with brief interruptions—ever since. Those interruptions included renovations in 1986, Keillor's retirement from radio in 1987 to marry and move to Europe, and the period from 1989 to 1993 when the show was broadcast from New York under the name *Garrison Keillor's American Radio Company*.

Today, alongside Garrison Keillor, a small group of people keep the show going. These include Pat Donohue,

Andy Stein, Richard Dworsky, Arnie Kinsella and Gary Raynor (making up Guy's All-Star Shoe Band), and Tom Keith and Fred Newman handling sound effects. Tim Russell, Sue Scott and Erica Rhodes contribute as actors. These people, along with a seemingly endless list of guest stars (the show is considered one of the most significant outlets for all genres of folk music) keep the only regularly scheduled live radio variety show in the United States fresh and innovative every week.

People everywhere now know about "The Catchup Advisory Board" (a compromise between the two spellings of catsup and ketchup) and "natural mellowing agents," The Professional Organization of English Majors, Be-Bop-A-Re-Bop Rhubarb Pie, the Café Beouf, and Ralph's Pretty Good Grocery (where "if you can't find it, you can probably get along without it"). Guy Noir and Dusty and Lefty have become household names; Dusty and Lefty even have their own sponsor (Prairie Dog Granola Bars—"healthier than chewing tobacco and you don't have to spit"). Perhaps the reason the program seems to speak to so many people, and has lasted so long, are its regular looks into the ordinary lives of the citizens of the fictional Lake Wobegon.

Carried by about 500 radio stations and listened to by nearly 4 million people in the United States, *A Prairie Home Companion* has become a worldwide broadcasting phenomenon, aired in different versions by New Zealand's National Radio, WRN in Europe, BBC 7 in England and RTE in Ireland, among other places. It has also become the flagship program for its distributor, American Public Media, which challenges NPR for the public broadcasting crown.

William J. Adams, Ph.D.
Kansas State University

governments, and 4 percent to state governments. Because most public stations rely on NPR, PRI and APM for much of their information programming, a brief look at each appears in 12.15, 12.16 and 12.17. Pacifica, one of the most influential of public station groups, is described in 12.18.

A myriad of other sources for programming— informational and otherwise—are available to

noncommercial radio programmers. WFMT's Beethoven Satellite Network, the Association of Independents in Radio (AIR) and a variety of station programming consortia that have emerged to provide program elements. The appetite is strong for more information programming than NPR, PRI, APM or any commercial outlet, for that matter, can supply.

12.15 National Public Radio

A private, nonprofit corporation, NPR contributes programming to more than 900 nonprofit radio stations that broadcast to communities in all 50 states, Puerto Rico, the District of Columbia and even the Virgin Islands. It programs two channels on SiriusXM Satellite Radio, produces multiple international services heard in more than 150 countries, provides programming for Armed Services Radio and operates NPR FM 104.1 in Berlin, Germany.

The considerable international reach of NPR's information programming through satellite delivery is now extended through digital media platforms. NPR.org presents constantly updated news, streaming audio, downloadable multimedia content (including video and photojournalism) and podcasts. NPR has launched several apps for smartphones and tablet computers.

In the United States, each NPR station is itself a production center, capable of producing and distributing programming to the entire system. Each station mixes locally produced programs with those transmitted from the national production center. A combined satellite and internet content distribution service allows better-quality transmission of existing programs. The high quality of national programs frequently entices stations to use NPR's offerings.

NPR schedules news, public affairs, arts, music and drama programs to fit into whatever formats member stations choose. The news programs *Morning Edition, All Things Considered* and *Weekend Edition* are its most distinguished trademarks and the core of its program service. NPR also successfully programs talk about politics and social issues with shows such as *Talk of the Nation* and *Fresh Air*. NPR also has provided leadership in music and arts programming for the public radio system with such shows as *From the Top, JazzSet, Radiolab* and live broadcasts of musical events from Europe and around the United States. It has provided stations with in-depth reporting on education, bilingual Spanish news features, and live coverage of Senate and House committee hearings.

However, not everyone applauds NPR programs. Conservative members of Congress complain that NPR's programs have a liberal bias (denied by NPR) and have proposed prohibiting any federal funds from being used to pay for NPR programs. While NPR does not receive funding directly from Congress for its operations, its member stations rely on grants from the taxpayer-funded Corporation for Public Broadcasting (CPB) to help pay NPR programming fees. Threats to NPR funding rise and fall depending upon which political party controls Congress. Efforts to cut-off funds and growing pressure to reduce government spending mean NPR and public radio stations across the country need to rally listeners periodically to contact Congress in support of public broadcasting.

12.16 Public Radio International

In 1983 a group of five stations formed a second public national radio network called American Public Radio (APR). Minnesota Public Radio, KUSC-FM in Los Angeles, KQED-FM in San Francisco, WNYC AM/FM in New York and WGUC in Cincinnati initially joined together to market and distribute programs they produced and to acquire other programming to distribute to affiliates. The name was changed to Public Radio International (PRI) in 1994 to help end confusion between APR and NPR and also to underline the network's interest in importing and exporting radio programs in the international marketplace.

Today, PRI programming is carried by over 880 affiliated stations. Its content is also available on pri.org through a smartphone app and podcasts. Its stated mission is "to serve audiences as a distinctive content source for information, insights and cultural experiences essential to living in our diverse, interconnected world."[16] Although well-known for its music programs, it is telling that the first goal PRI claims is to provide information. PRI distributes news programs such as *BBC World Service, The World* and *America Abroad*. It also has the urban-talk program *The Tavis Smiley Show*, the popular storytelling program *This American Life* and health information shows such as *Zorba Paster on Your Health*.

That was certainly part of the logic behind the 1999 FCC rules that introduced noncommercial low-power FM (LPFM) radio service. LPFM consists of stations with either maximum power levels of just 10 watts (reaching areas with a radius of 1 to 2 miles) or 100 watts (reaching areas with a radius of approximately 3.5 miles). Despite vigorous lobbying against the idea by National Association of Broadcasters (NAB)—who were concerned that the presence of even low-power transmission towers would interfere with existing commercial broadcast station signals—today hundreds of LPFM stations broadcast information programming to local communities. Most are programmed by educational facilities, local church groups or city governments.

Finally, the government is, itself, in the noncommercial information radio business. The National Oceanic and Atmospheric Administration (NOAA) broadcasts local weather information over 1,000 NOAA stations in the 160-megahertz band, and state governments operate numerous Highway Advisory Radio (HAR) stations within the AM broadcast band (see 12.19 and 12.20).

What Lies Ahead

When it comes to the future of information radio, perhaps the most obvious statement is that the format is not going to disappear any time soon. Our society has developed a high level of urgency about obtaining relevant news and information. However, programmers might wonder whether traditional terrestrial radio is going to disappear now that content can be delivered on multiple digital platforms.

In simpler times, programmers only worried about competition from the radio stations in their markets and had the straightforward task of attracting listeners to their stations' frequencies and keeping them listening for as long as possible. Now that cell phones and computers have evolved into wireless multimedia devices, consumers can access audio, video, text and more from around the world in the palm of their hands and listen, watch or read on their own terms. *Programmers must now export content to listeners rather than just importing listeners to the content on radio stations.*

12.19 NOAA Weather Radio

NOAA Weather Radio is a nationwide network of radio stations broadcasting continuous weather information direct from a nearby National Weather Service office. NOAA Weather Radio broadcasts National Weather Service warnings, watches, forecasts and other hazard information 24 hours a day. Under the FCC's new Emergency Alert System, NOAA Weather Radio has become an "all hazards" radio network, making it the single source for the most comprehensive weather and emergency information available to the public. NOAA Weather Radio broadcasts warning and post-event information for both natural (such as earthquakes and volcano activity)

and technological (such as chemical releases or oil spills) hazards.

Known as the "Voice of the National Weather Service," NOAA Weather Radio is provided as a public service by the Department of Commerce's National Oceanic and Atmospheric Administration. The NOAA Weather Radio network has more than 1,000 transmitters that cover the 50 states, adjacent coastal waters, Puerto Rico, the U.S. Virgin Islands and the U.S. Pacific Territories. NOAA Weather Radio requires a special radio receiver or scanner capable of picking up the signal. Broadcasts are found in the public service band at these seven frequencies (MHz): 162.400, 162.425, 162.450, 162.475, 162.500, 162.525 and 162.550.

12.20 Highway Advisory Radio

Along highways people see bright orange signs with flashing lights along the side of the road. Such signs read, "Motorist Advisory When Flashing: Tune Radio to 1610 AM" (or some similar frequency). This is an invitation to listen to Highway Advisory Radio (HAR) stations. HAR stations give motorists a wide variety of information, such as details about the latest highway construction and maintenance projects, details on local traffic and weather conditions that may impede travel, locations of upcoming rest stops and descriptions of local points of interest.

These broadcasts are possible as the result of an FCC authorization for "Travelers' Information Stations." According to FCC regulations, radio frequencies 530 through 1700 kHz may be used by governmental entities and parks districts to inform the public about traveler safety information. There are some limitations, however, such as the output power of HAR stations cannot exceed 10 watts, and transmissions may not interfere with any existing commercial stations (which is why HAR stations are usually at the very far ends of the AM band). In addition, identifying the commercial names of businesses is prohibited.

Broadcasters will hang onto the traditional radio advertising business model as long as possible while they struggle with learning how to best make money from digital platforms like podcasting, web streaming and smartphone apps. Some form of multiplatform strategy has become crucial, but at present, user payments for apps get divided among several parties, leaving only a trickle for stations. However, advertisers are likely to be less than pleased if listeners prefer commercial-free digital downloads over listening in real time to the advertiser-supported version on the radio. Broadcast programmers need to work closely with sales managers and general managers to develop business models that maximize both audiences and revenue.

Programmers will also be wondering where they will find the talent necessary to attract a loyal audience and build a brand that can be marketed on multiple platforms. No matter how content is delivered, it will always be essential to have compelling personalities who can attract listeners. And those new talk-radio personalities will likely be found with loyal followings on digital platforms rather than working their way up from small market broadcast stations. Some may see a brighter future building their own empires on digital platforms rather than sharing profits with station owners and syndicators.

Finally, talk radio programmers will continue seeking ways to attract younger audiences that advertisers say they prefer. As the baby boom ages and AM radio station audiences get older, look for more talk radio formats to migrate to the FM band. With more people preferring to listen to music on MP3 players and through web streaming services, FM broadcast stations will have to reinvent themselves just as AM radio did when music formats migrated to FM.

It would be easy to count radio out, but it has faced challenges before and adjusted to continue being a viable medium. "I believe there is a future for traditional radio, but we also have to remember we're in the communications business, not the radio business," says Jerry Bader, the news/talk program director for Midwest Communications. "The challenge for radio is to use print and video formats to grow the on-air product to the new platforms, not just move them over."[18]

Notes

1. Credit goes to former authors Robert F. Potter and Joseph G. Buchman for much of this discussion of information's multiple meanings and other portions of this chapter.

2. Kipper McGee, Kipper McGee, LLC, introduction to "Digital Media Workshop" at the 13th annual New Media Seminar, March 19, 2010. Retrieved 26 May 2011 from *http://www.podjockey.com/2010/04/08/2010-new-media-seminar-videos/*.

3. Smith, Andy, "A Whole New Wavelength," *Providence Journal-Bulletin*, 13 July 2003, p. E-1.

4. Personal communication from Rollye James, talk-show host and radio consultant, to Joseph G. Buchman, Philadelphia, PA, May 2000. Quoted from Buchman's chapter, "Information Radio Programming," in the sixth edition of this book.

5. Squires, C. R., "Black Talk Radio: Defining Community Needs and Identity," *Harvard International Journal of Press/Politics* 5(2), 2000, pp. 73–95.

6. As quoted in "The Big Questions: A special report on the state of news/talk radio," *Radio Ink*, 16 May 2011.

7. Marcucci,Carl, "Numero Uno: Rush!" Retrieved 25 July 2004 from *www.rbr.com/interviews/rushrlimbaugh.asp*.

8. "Green Brothers Close Deal to Buy Liberal Talk Radio Network Air America," Associated Press Worldstream, 6 March 2007. Retrieved from Lexis-Nexis.

9. Stelter, Brian, "Liberal Radio, Even Without Air America," *The New York Times*, 25 January 2010, p. C1.

10. As quoted in "'Bob & Tom Show' Pulls Back from Edgy Content," Associated Press wire story, 26 February 2004. Retrieved from Lexis-Nexis.

11. The quote is from Dr. Rob Balon, CEO of The Benchmark Company, in "Study: Rush Limbaugh's Audience Remains Solid," *Radio & Records Online*, 3 February 2004. *www.radioandrecordsonline.com*.

12. Personal communication from Michael Harrison to Joseph G. Buchman, 27 April 2000. Quoted from Buchman's chapter, "Information Radio Programming," in the sixth edition of this book.

13. "The 100 Most Important Radio Talk Show Hosts in America—Class of 2004." Retrieved 26 July 2004 from *www.talkers.com.heavy.html*.

14. Hoffstetter,C. Richard, "The Skills and Motivations of Interactive Media Participants: The Case of Political Talk Radio." In Erik P. Bucy and John E. -Newhagen (eds.), *Media Access: Social and Psychological Dimensions of New Technology Use*. Mahawah, NJ: Erlbaum, 2004, p. 211.

15. Kaltenbach,C., and McCauley,M. C., "Public Radio Gets Bequest of More Than $200 Million; Donation Is from Widow of McDonald's Founder," *The Baltimore Sun*, 7 November 2003, p. 1A.

16. Quoted from the Public Radio International (PRI) website. Retrieved 1 June 2011 from *http://www.pri.org/pri-facts.html*.

17. Quoted from the Pacifica Network website. Retrieved 1 June 2011 from *http://www.pacificanetwork.org/radio/content/section/4/40/*.

18. As quoted in "The Big Questions: A special report on the state of news/talk radio," *Radio Ink*, 16 May 2011.

Annotated Bibliography

This is a selective, annotated listing of recent books, articles, guides, reports and trade magazines on broadcast and cable programs and online programming published since 2006. Additional citations of books, articles and websites appear at each chapter's end under Notes. See also Internet Media Sites. For publications relevant to programming prior to 2006, consult the bibliographies to the previous editions of this book.

Abbott, Jon. *Stephen J. Cannell Television Productions: A History of All Series and Plots*. Jefferson, NC: McFarland, 2009. Compilation of Cannell's work in television with brief discussion of its impact.

Albarran, Alan B. *Management of Electronic Media*, 3rd ed. Belmont, CA: Wadsworth, 2006. Textbook for teaching management of new and mature media businesses.

Albarran, Alan B., Chan-Olmstead, Sylvia M., and Wirth, Michael O. (eds.). *Handbook of Media Management and Economics*. Mahwah, NJ: Erlbaum, 2006. A synthesis of current research and industry practice relating to media management.

Alten, Stanley. *Audio in Media*, 8th ed. Belmont, CA: Wadsworth, 2008. Techniques and principles of audio production from planning to post-production.

Arbitron Cable Television Study: Exploring the Consumer's Relationship with Cable TV. Columbia, MD: Arbitron, Inc., 2006. Report of a telephone survey taken in 2006 describing use and distribution of new media and cable in subscribers' homes.

Aylesworth, John. *The Corn Was Green: The Inside Story of Hee Haw*. Jefferson, NC: McFarland, 2010. History and impact of the television comedy *Hee Haw*.

Banet-Weiser, Sarah, Chris, Cynthia, and Freitas, Anthony (eds.). *Cable Visions: Television Beyond Broadcasting*. New York: New York University Press, 2007. Comprehensive survey of the limits and opportunities in the new video media.

Baym, Geoffrey. *From Cronkite to Colbert: The Evolution of Broadcast News*. Boulder, CO: Paradigm Publishers, 2010. Analysis of the changing news culture at CBS television and its effects.

Beaty, Bart, and Sullivan, Rebecca. *Canadian Television Today*. Alberta, Canada: University of Calgary Press, 2006. Discussion of challenges facing the Canadian television industry and government in the face of cable importation, high-speed internet access and mobile media.

Bennett, James. *Television Personalities: Stardom and the Small Screen*. New York: Routledge, 2011. Insightful view of television celebrities, their rise to stardom and their impacts.

Berman, Margo. *Street-Smart Advertising: How to Win the Battle of the Buzz*. New York: Rowman & Littlefield, 2006. Advice on the creative side of marketing strategy.

Billboard: The International Newsweekly of Music and Home Entertainment. New York, 1894 to date, weekly. Trade magazine of the radio industry. www.billboard.com.

Bissell, Tom. *Extra Lives: Why Video Games Matter*. New York: Pantheon, 2010. Academic essays on the meaning and experiences of video game playing.

Blakeman, Robyn. *Integrated Marketing Communication: Creative Strategy from Idea to Implementation*. New York: Rowman & Littlefield, 2007. Textbook on building brand equity.

Broadcaster Magazine. Toronto, Canada, 1942 to date. Canadian trade magazine covering the radio, television and cable industries, with special emphasis on current news.

Broadcasting & Cable Market Place (replaced *Broadcasting Yearbook* in 1992). Washington, DC: Broadcasting Publications, 1935 to date, annually. Basic trade directory of radio and television stations and support industries; added cable in 1980.

Broadcasting & Cable: The Business of Television. New York: Reed Business Information, 1931 to date, weekly. (Cable added in 1972; radio and Washington politics dropped in 1992.) Major trade magazine of the broadcasting industry; see especially Special Reports on cable, children's television, digitalization, high-definition TV, internet technology, journalism, media corporations, radio, reps, satellites, sports, syndication and television programming.

Broadcasting and the Law. Knoxville, TN: Perry Publications, 1972 to date, twice monthly. Newsletter and supplements explaining findings of the Federal Communications Commission, courts, and Congress affecting broadcast operations.

Burgess, Jean, and Green, Joshua. *YouTube: Online Video and Participatory Culture.* Polity Press, Cambridge, Mass., 2009. Scholarly assessment of the societal functions and politics of YouTube from a social science perspective.

Butler, Jeremy G. *Television: Critical Methods and Applications*, 3rd ed. Mahwah, NJ: Erlbaum, 2007. Introductory textbook about the production of television programs and commercials from a critical and cultural media perspective.

By the Numbers: Street & Smith's SportsBusiness Journal (weekly). Street & Smith since 1998. Ongoing updating of events and facts about sports, especially televised sports.

Cable Services Directory. Washington, DC: National Cable Television Association, 1978 to date, annually (title varies). Directory of information on individual cable systems, including amounts and types of local origination.

Cable Strategies. Monthly trade magazine concentrating on the operations and marketing of local cable services. Denver, CO, 1986 to date.

Cable Television Business (formerly *TVC*). Biweekly trade magazine covering cable system management. Englewood, CO, 1963 to date.

Cable World. Denver, CO: Cable World Associates, 1988 to date, weekly. Trade articles on national cable programming and other topics from a managerial perspective.

Chambers, Todd. " The State of Spanish-Language Radio." *Journal of Radio Studies 13* (Winter 2006), pp. 34–50.

Update on radio stations and programs targeting the Hispanic market.

Chan-Olmstead, Sylvia M. *Competitive Strategy for Media Firms: Strategic and Brand Management in Changing Media Markets.* Mahwah, NJ: Erlbaum, 2006. Review of the analytic frameworks behind current industry practices with application to the products of the electronic media.

Children's Educational Television, FCC Consumer Facts. Federal Communications Commission, 11 December 2006. www.fcc.gov/cgb/consumerfacts/childtv.html. Summary report of research findings about children's viewing of television and commercial advertising.

Cohen, Noam. " Bloggers Take on Talk Radio Hosts." *The New York Times.* 15 January 2007, p. C3. Analysis of reactions to the excesses of right-wing radio talk based on blogged messages.

Collins, Kathleen. *Watching What We Eat: The Evolution of Television Cooking Shows.* New York: Continuum, 2009. An exploration of cooking programs' shift from education to entertainment and their impact on social attitudes.

Comm/Ent: A Journal of Communications and Entertainment Law. San Francisco: Hastings College of the Law, 1978 to date, quarterly. Law journal containing articles summarizing the law on specific issues, including broadcasting and new technologies.

Communications & Convergence Review. Published by Korea Information Society Development Institute, Gwacheon, Korea, since 2009. A journal of multidisciplinary research about convergence of technologies, users, applications and regulations relating to mobile and online media and other forms of electronic communication.

Community Television Review. Washington, DC: National Federation of Local Cable Programmers, 1979 to date, bimonthly. Newsletter of the NFLCP for local cable programmers. Covers public, educational, and government access television on cable and local cable origination.

C-SPAN Update. Washington, DC: C-SPAN Network, 1982 to date, weekly. Newspaper of program content and issues affecting the broadcasting of public affairs on radio and television.

Current. Washington, DC: Public Broadcasting Service, 1981 to date, weekly. Washington newspaper focusing on public broadcasting. www.current.org.

Daily Variety. Hollywood/New York: Variety, 1905 to date, daily. Trade newspaper of the film and television industries. Daily version of *Variety* magazine that is oriented toward film and television production and programming.

Darnell, Simon C., and Wilson, Brian. " Macho Media: Unapologetic Hypermasculinity in Vancouver's 'Talk Radio for Guys.'" *Journal of Broadcasting & Electronic Media*, 50 (Fall 2006), pp. 444–466. Contextual analysis of on-air programming of MOJO Radio.

David, Nina. *TV Season*. Phoenix, AZ: Oryx, 1976 to date, annually. Annotated guide to the previous season's commercial and public network and major syndicated television programs.

DBS News. Washington, DC: Phillips Publishing, 1983 to date, monthly. Newsletter covering international regulatory, technical and programming developments in direct broadcasting.

De Vito, John, and Frank Tropea. *Epic Television Miniseries: A Critical History*. Jefferson, NC: McFarland, 2010. An analysis of the blockbuster miniseries and their impact on the industry and culture.

Dominick, Joseph R., Sherman, Barry L., and Messere, Fritz. *Broadcasting, Cable, the Internet, and Beyond: An Introduction to Modern Electronic Media*, 5th ed. New York: McGraw-Hill, 2007. Up-to-date edition of this basic text, with several chapters on programming and the internet.

Duncan, James H., (ed.). *American Radio Quarterly Ratings Reports*. Cincinnati, OH: Duncan's American Radio, Inc., 1976 to date, quarterly plus supplements. Industry sourcebook for radio ratings and programming information for all markets, with extensive tables and charts.

———. *Duncan's Radio Market Guide*. Cincinnati, OH: Duncan's American Radio, 1976 to date, annually. Companion reference volume on the revenue ratings histories and projections for 173 markets, including market descriptions and many charts and tables.

Eastman, Susan Tyler, Ferguson, Douglas A., and Klein, Robert A. (eds.). *Media Promotion and Marketing*, 5th ed. (formerly *Promotion of Marketing for Broadband, Cable, and the Web*). Boston, MA: Focal Press, 2006. Strategic planning for marketing networks, stations, cable systems and websites to audiences and advertisers,

Edgerton, Gary R., and Jeffrey P. Jones (eds.). *The Essential HBO Reader*. Lexington, KY: University Press of Kentucky, 2008. Essays interpreting major films carried by HBO and assessments of their importance and impacts.

Erickson, Hal. *Encyclopedia of Television Law Shows: Factual and Fictional Series About Judges, Lawyers and the Courtroom, 1948–2008*. Comprehensive listing of law-related television series, including actors, producers, ratings history and plot synopses.

Farhi, Paul. " Tomlinson Cited for Abuses at Broadcast BoardL CBS Ex-Chief Puts Friend on Payroll, State Dept. Says." *Washington Post*, 22 January 2007, p. C1.

Federal Communications Commission. *Tenth Annual Report: In the Matter of Annual Assessment of Competition in the Market for the Delivery of Video Programming* [MB Docket No. 03-172]. Washington, DC: 28 January 2004.

Fentuck, Mike, and Varney, Mike. *Media Regulation, Public Interest, and the Law*, 2nd ed. Edinburgh, UK: Edinburgh University Press, 2006. British perspective on law and the media.

Gomery, Douglas. *The Studio System*. Berkeley, CA: University of California Press, 2005. Overview of the history of the Hollywood Studios and the movies they made.

Grant, August E., and Meadows, Jennifer H. (eds.). *Communication Technology Update*, 10th ed. Boston, MA: Focal Press, 2006. Latest in a quickly updated series on the newest media technologies, written by academics and media experts in their specialties.

Green, Andrew. *From Prime Time to My Time: Audience Measurement in the Digital Age*. London, Warc, 2010. Scholarly assessment of the problems of television ratings.

Greene, Doyle. *Politics and American Television Comedy: A Critical Survey from* I Love Lucy *through* South Park. Jefferson, NC: McFarland, 2008. Analyses of the broad sweep of comedy television, stressing political implications.

Greven, David. *Gender and Sexuality in* Star Trek: *Allegories of Desire in the Television Series and Films*. Jefferson, NC: McFarland, 2009. Analysis of gendered images and language in this classic set of programs.

Groebel, Jo, Noam, Eli M., and Feldmann, Valerie. (eds.). *Mobile Media: Content and Services for Wireless Communications*. Mahwah, NJ: Erlbaum, 2006. Scholarly chapters discussing the likely content, policies, economics and business models of the new mobile media in international markets.

Ha, Louisa S., and Ganahl, III, Richard J. *Webcasting Worldwide: Business Models of an Emerging Global Medium*. Mahwah, NJ: Erlbaum, 2006. Examination of the business practices of webcasters around the world.

Halper, Donna H. *Icons of Talk: The Media Mouths That Changed America*. Westport, CT: Greenwood Press, 2009. Analyses of the major talk radio and television figures and their individual and collective impact.

Hausman, Carl, Benoit, Philip, Messere, Frank, and O'Donnell, Lewis B. *Modern Radio Production:*

Production, Programming, and Performance, 7th ed. Belmont, CA: Wadsworth, 2007. Handbook for introducing students to producing and performing on radio, including programming aspects.

Holmes, Su. *The Quiz Show*. Edinburgh: Edinburgh University Press/New York: Columbia University Press, 2009. Analysis of television quiz shows in Great Britain and America, from a British perspective.

Howard, Herbert H. *Ownership Trends in Cable Television*. Washington, DC: National Association of Broadcasters, 1987 to date, annually. Continuing comparative series on the 50 largest cable multiple-system operations; tables and charts.

International Journal on Media Management. Mahwah, NJ: Erlbaum and the University of St. Gallen, Switzerland (Institute for Media and Communications Management), 1999 to date. Scholarly articles on management and economics of media in many countries, especially focusing on the transition from old to new media.

Jermyn, Deborah. *Sex and the City*. Detroit, MI: Wayne State University Press, 2008. Analysis of the classic television series *Sex and the City*.

Journal of Broadcasting & Electronic Media. Washington, DC: Broadcast Education Association, 1955 to date. Scholarly journal covering research in all aspects of television and radio broadcasting, especially emphasizing those topics with industry impact.

Journal of Consumer Research. Chicago, IL: University of Chicago Press, 1974 to date. Interdisciplinary journal reporting empirical studies and humanistic analyses that describe and explain consumer behavior.

Journal of Mass Media Ethics: Exploring Questions of Media Morality. Mahwah, NJ: Erlbaum, 1986 to date, quarterly. Essays, reports, and literature reviews about ethical issues of interest to professionals and scholars.

Journal of Radio Studies. Washington, DC: Broadcast Education Association, 1991 to date. Scholarly articles on historical and contemporary radio, including programming.

Keith, Michael C. *The Radio Station: Broadcast, Satellite, and Internet*, 7th ed. Boston, MA: Focal Press, 2007. Newest edition of this classic guide to the business of running radio stations. Emphasizes station operations and marketing, satellite radio, web radio and podcasting.

Keith, Michael C. *Radio Cultures: The Sound Medium in American Life*. New York: Peter Lang Publications, 2008. Scholarly analysis of the influence of radio on American culture.

Lochte, Bob. *Christian Radio: The Growth of a Mainstream Broadcasting Force*. Jefferson, NC: McFarland & Co., 2006. Brief history and analysis of the surge in Christian-oriented radio talk.

Lotz, Amanda D. *The Television Will Be Revolutionized*. New York: New York University Press, 2007. Analyses and explications of the impact of the convergence of prime-time television and the computer on the media industry.

The LPTV Report. Butler, WI: Kompas/Biel & Associates, 1985 to date, monthly. Trade magazine that is the official information channel of the Community Broadcasters Association, an organization of low-power television broadcasters.

MediaPost's TV Board: "Big Thoughts on the Future of the Small Screen." *MediaPost Publications*, *www.tvboard@mediapost.com*. Near daily blogs from Jack Myers and others about advances and problems in media, advertising and technology.

Meizel, Katherine. *Idolized: Music, Media and Identity in American Idol*. Bloomington, IN: Indiana University Press, 2011. Analysis of the production techniques of this blockbuster television show and its impact on other programs and the television business.

Multichannel News: The Newspaper for the New Electronic Media. New York: Reed Business Information, 1980 to date, weekly. Trade newspaper of regulatory, programming, financial and technical events affecting electronic media.

NAB News. Washington, DC: National Association of Broadcasters, 1989 to date, monthly. Reports during the 1989 to 1990 period on developments in federal regulation, ratings research and other matters affecting broadcasters, later becoming a report on the NAB convention.

NATOA News. 1980 to date, bimonthly. Newsletter of the National Association of Telecommunications Officers and Advisors and the National League of Cities. Short reports on current events affecting local cable franchise regulation and technology, including legislative updates.

NATPE International Newsletter (formerly *NATPE Programmer*). Washington, DC: National Association of Television Program Executives, 1990 to date, monthly. Trade newsletter of the national programmers' association.

The New York Times. 1850 to date, daily. National newspaper covering business and entertainment aspects of broadcasting, cable television and the internet.

NRB Magazine. Manassas, VA: National Religious Broadcasters Association, 1968 to date, nine times per year. Magazine emphasizing evangelical broadcasting on radio and television, with informal style.

Palmer, Shelly. *Television Disrupted: The Transition from Network to Networked Television.* 2nd ed. Boston, MA: Focal Press, 2008. Examines the changing technologies, business rules and legal issues of television, directed toward professionals and business executives.

The Pay TV Newsletter. Carmel, CA: Paul Kagan Associates, 1983 to date, weekly. Trade summaries of analyses and events affecting premium cable television.

Pondillo, Robert. *America's First Network TV Censor: The Work of NBC's Stockton Helffrich.* Carbondale, IL: Southern Illinois University Press, 2010. Explication of Helffrich's influence on NBC's policies regarding explicit and implied sexuality, indecency and race in series, movie and comedy during the 1950s.

Producers Quarterly. Port Washington, NY: Producers Quarterly Publications, 1991 to date. Trade magazine for executives in the movie and television production business. Covers developments in production technology and animation, production problems and success stories, and interviews with producers.

Radio Ink. Biweekly magazine for radio managers, 1998 to date.

Radio and Internet Newsletter (RAIN). Free, daily web-based commentary on issues, published by Kurt Hanson, 1999 to date. www.kurthanson.com.

Radio & Records: The Industry's Newspaper. Los Angeles, 1974 to date, weekly. Trade magazine of the record industry, ranking songs and albums. Available online at *www.radioandrecords.com.*

R&R Ratings Report. Los Angeles: Radio & Records, Inc., semiannually. Special reports on the state of radio programming.

RadioWeek. Washington, DC: National Association of Broadcasters, 1960 to date, weekly. Newsletter on matters affecting radio broadcasters, including proposed changes in federal regulations and standards.

Raney, Arthur, and Bryant, Jennings (eds.). *Handbook of Sports and Media.* Mahwah, NJ: Erlbaum, 2006. Comprehensive scholarly analyses of mediated sports' history and development, economics and marketing, coverage and audiences, and critical issues by major scholars.

Robinson, Tom, and Anderson, Caitlin. " Older Characters in Children's Animated Television Programs: A Content Analysis of Their Portrayal." *Journal of Broadcasting & Electronic Media,* 50 (Spring 2006), pp. 287–304. Descriptive analysis of portrayals of older characters in cartoons, revealing negative mental

and physical characteristics that feed into harmful stereotyping by children.

RTNDA Communicator. 1946 to date, monthly. Newsletter of the Radio-Television News Directors Association.

SkyResearch. Monthly trade magazine concentrating on the satellite industry. Golden, CO, 1994 to date.

Sterling, Christopher H., Bernt, Phyllis W., and Weiss, Martin B. H. *Shaping American Telecommunications: A History of Technology, Policy, and Economics.* Mahwah, NJ: Erlbaum, 2006. An authoritative explanation of the stages of telecommunications development. Covers policy decisions, innovations and regulations.

Sterling, Christopher H., and Keith, Michael C. *Sounds of Change: A History of FM Broadcasting in America.* Chapel Hill, NC: University of North Carolina Press, 2008. Definite chronicle of FM radio, its influence on government regulation, politics and society, and its major figures.

Stolarz, Damien, and Felix, Lionel. *Hands-On Guide to Video Blogging and Podcasting.* Boston, MA: Focal Press, 2006. Covers technology, production techniques, licensing and launch instructions for podcasts and video blogs, including uses in business, education and entertainment.

Strangelove, Michael. *Watching YouTube: Extraordinary Videos by Ordinary People.* Toronto, Canada: University of Toronto Press, 2010. Examples of the range and types of unusual videos on YouTube. Also, www.watchingyoutube.com.

Stratyner, Leslie, and James R.Keller (eds.). *The Deep End of South Park: Critical Essays on TV's Shocking Cartoon Series.* Jefferson, NC: McFarland, 2009. Essays explicating the elements that create this program's impact and symbolism, as well as its implications for understanding American culture.

The Television Audience. Northbrook, IL: A. C. Nielsen Company, 1959 to date, annually. Trends in television programming and audience viewing patterns.

Television Digest. Washington, DC: Warren Publishing, Inc., 1945 to date, weekly. Trade summary of events affecting the television business.

Television Week (formerly Electronic Media). Chicago: Crain Communications, 1982 to date, weekly. Trade periodical covering topical news in broadcasting, cable, and new media technologies. Available online at *www.tvweek.com.*

TVI: Television International Magazine. Universal City, CA: TVI Publishing Company, 1956 to date. Daily media news on the internet derived from the major international news service. Print and online at *www.tviNews.net*.

TV Today. Washington, DC: National Association of Broadcasters, 1970 to date, weekly. Newsletter addressing matters of interest to broadcast station members, including developments in technology, regulation and member services.

Variety. New York and Hollywood, 1925 to date, weekly. Trade newspaper covering the stage and the film, television and recording industries.

Vorderer, Peter, and Bryant, Jennings. *Playing Video Games: Motives, Responses, and Consequences*. Mahwah, NJ: Erlbaum, 2006. Psychology of mediated game playing as entertainment; includes simulations, gambling and role-playing games.

Webster, James G. " Audience Flow Past and Present: Television Inheritance Effects Reconsidered." *Journal of Broadcasting & Electronic Media*, 50 (Spring 2006), pp. 323–337. Scholarly replication of an earlier study of audience flow between back-to-back programs; finds the same predictors and strength of influence 20 years later.

Webster, James G., Phalen, Patricia F., and Lichty, Lawrence W. *Ratings Analysis: The Theory and Practice of Audience Research*, 3rd ed. Mahwah, NJ: Erlbaum, 2006. Authoritative description and analysis of audience ratings data for industry and scholarly users of ratings. Covering applications, collection methods, and models for data analysis—especially for electronic media.

Wimmer, Roger D., and Dominick, Joseph R. *Mass Media Research: An Introduction*, 9th ed. Belmont, CA: Wadsworth, 2011. Updated version of this classic text on applied research methods in mass media, emphasizing broadcasting; includes survey methods and people meter ratings.

Yuan, Elaine J., and Webster, James G. " Channel Repertoires: Using Peoplemeter Data in Beijing." *Journal of Broadcasting & Electronic Media*, 50 (Summer 2006), pp. 524–536. Report of regression analysis of minute-by-minute viewing in China, showing that total time spent with television and cable subscriptions explained 65 percent of variance.

Zettl, Herbert. *Television Production Handbook*, 9th ed. Belmont, CA: Wadsworth, 2006. Update of the widely-used classic text that introduces students to the skills and techniques of producing television programs (including high-definition video) in the studio and field.

Internet Media Sites

This list was current for 2012 and is continually updated on the home page link for this textbook, searchable from *http://media-programming.com*. If you encounter difficulties with any of the addresses below, try entering the minimal URL address by preceding it with *http://* and then deleting any material after the *.com* portion.

General Interest Sites

www.zap2it.com/tv/
www.broadcastingcable.com
www.disney.com
www.fcc.gov
www.hollywoodreporter.com
www.mediaweek.com
www.nab.org (broadcast industry)
www.natpe.org (programming industry)
www.ncta.com (cable industry)
www.sbca.com (satellite industry)
www.sia.org (satellite industry)
www.tvb.org (TV broadcast industry)
www.newscorp.com
www.timewarner.com
www.viacom.com
www.warnerbros.com

For other media organizations and associations, see the list in 1.22 on page 36 of this textbook.

Updates and News Summaries

tv.yahoo.com
tv.zap2it.com
www.adweek.com
www.allcommunitymedia.org (Alliance for Community Media)
www.billboard.biz/bbbiz/industry
www.bitpipe.com
www.broadcastingcable.com
www.cable360.net/
www.ctam.com
www.dsl-forum.org
www.kagan.com
www.mediapost.com/publications/
www.multichannel.com
www.newschannels.org
www.soapcentral.com
www.sportsbusinessjournal.com
www.tvguide.com/
www.tvnewscheck.com
www.tvweek.com
www.variety.com
www.zap2it.com/tv

Schedules

tvlistings.zap2it.com
www.allmytv.com
www.allyourtv.com
www.clicktv.com
www.tvguide.com/Listings/
www.tviv.org/Category:ProgrammingGrids (best source of current and historical program grids)

Ratings Research

tvbythenumbers.zap2it.com/
www.adage.com (Ad Age online)
www.arbitron.com
www.billboard.biz/bbbiz/charts/currentsingles
www.katz-media.com
www.krgspec.com/ (Katz Media)
www.MediaMetrix.com (comScore)
www.ncta.com
www.nielsenmedia.com
www.nielsen.com/us/en/insights/top10s/television.html
www.nielsen.com/us/en/measurement/online-measurement.html
www.tvweek.com
www.zap2it.com/tv/ratings/

Broadcast Networks
www.abc.com
www.cbs.com
www.cwtv.com
www.fox.com
www.iontelevision.com
www.mntv.com
www.nbc.com
www.pbs.org
www.telefutura.com
www.telemundo.com
www.thecw.com
www.univision.com

Cable
abcfamily.go.com
dsc.discovery.com
espn.go.com
soapnet.go.com
www.aetv.com
www.amctv.com
www.bet.com
www.bravotv.com
www.cartoonnetwork.com
www.cbn.org
www.cinemax.com
www.cnbc.com
www.cnn.com
www.comedycentral.com
www.disneychannel.com
www.eonline.com
www.foodtv.com
www.foxnews.com
www.fxnetworks.com
www.galavision.com
www.hbo.com
www.hgtv.com
www.historychannel.com
www.lifetimetv.com
www.money.cnn.com
www.msnbc.com
www.mtv.com
www.nationalgeographic.com/tv/channel
www.oxygen.com
www.playboy.com/pbtv
www.ppv.com or *www.indemand.com*
www.scifi.com
www.showtimeonline.com
www.soapcentral.com
www.sportsbusinessjournal.com
www.spiketv.com
www.superstation.com

www.tbn.org
www.tnt.tv.com
www.turnerclassicmovies.com
www.travelchannel.com
www.trutv.com
www.usanetwork.com
www.vh1.com
www.vvtv.com
www.weather.com
www.wewomensentertainment.com

Public Broadcasting
www.aptonline.org
www.cpb.org
www.current.org
www.npr.org
www.pbskids.org
www.pbs.org
www.pri.org

Satellite
www.directv.com
www.dishnetwork.com
www.newschannels.org
www.sbca.com

Radio
www.allaccess.com
www.billboard.com
www.citadelmedianetworks.com
www.clearchannel.com
www.cumulus.com
www.npr.org
www.radio-info.com
www.siriusxm.com

Online
video.aol.com
www.amazon.com/gp/video/ontv/ontv
www.atom.com
www.blockbuster.com/download
www.chooseandwatch.com
www.crackle.com
www.funnyordie.com
www.hulu.com
www.itvt.com
www.movielink.com
www.netflix.com
www.streamingmedia.com
www.vodpod.com
www.vudu.com
www.youtube.com

About the Contributing Authors

William J. Adams, professor of Communication in the School of Journalism & Mass Communication at Kansas State University, has a B.A. from Brigham Young University, an M.A. from Ball State University, and a Ph.D. from Indiana University. He teaches, researches and writes about programming, and especially focuses on network television programming for prime time and on motion pictures. Professor Adams has published extensively as a journalist and scholar. His work includes chapters in the area of television and movie programming in eight editions of *Media Programming: Strategies and Practices* (Wadsworth, 1985 to 2013); on promotion in *Promotion & Marketing for Broadcasting & Cable* (Focal Press, 2006); and on movies in *Research in Media Promotion* (Erlbaum, 2000). He has also published articles in the *Journal of Broadcasting & Electronic Media*, the *Journal of Communication* and the *Journal of Media Economics*. Professor Adams brings considerable historical expertise in television programming to his analysis of present-day prime-time strategies at the major networks. He can be reached at *wadams@ksu.edu*.

Robert B. Affe, senior lecturer in Telecommunications and International Studies at Indiana University, also directs the Telecommunications Management Institute. His teaching and research center on advertising, management and international media issues. A former television executive and attorney, he was educated at Georgetown University (A.B.) and the New York University School of Law (J.D.). After admission to practice before the New York State Supreme Court and the District of Columbia Court of Appeals, he practiced communications law in Washington, DC. Drawn to the business of television, he subsequently helped to launch or rebrand stations in several major markets. While in Florida, Professor Affe taught courses in communications law and media management at the University of South Florida and recently lectured at several leading Chinese universities, including Peking University. He has published chapters in several telecommunications texts, including six editions of *Media Programming: Strategies and Practices* (1993 to 2013). He can be reached at *raffe@indiana.edu*.

Glenda R. Balas is associate professor and chair of the Department of Communication and Journalism at the University of New Mexico. She holds a B.A. in Mass Communication and an M.B.A. from Eastern New Mexico University and received her Ph.D. from the University of Iowa. Prior to a career in academics, Dr. Balas worked in the non-profit and public broadcasting sectors, spending more than a decade in public information, programming and development at public television stations KCTS-Seattle and KENW-Portales, NM. Her research interests include the history, theories and practices of mass communication, focusing particularly on U.S. public broadcasting. Work in this area includes journal articles in *Critical Studies in Media Communication*, *Journal of Communication Inquiry* and *Democratic Communique*, as well as a book entitled *Recovering a Public Vision for Public Television*. Professor Balas presented the Leah Vande Berg 2007 Lecture on Media at the University of Iowa. In Spring 2009, she was a Fulbright Scholar at Dalhousie University, Nova Scotia, Canada, where she focused on the study of public broadcasting in Canada. Dr. Balas can be reached at *gbalas@unm.edu*.

Robert V. Bellamy, professor in the Department of Journalism & Multimedia Arts at Duquesne University in Pittsburgh, has his B.A. from Morehead State University, his M.A. from the University of Kentucky, and his Ph.D. from the University of Iowa. His teaching and research interests include television programming and promotion, media globalization, media and sports, and the impact of technological change on media industries. He has professional experience as a NATPE Fellow and program consultant to KLRT in Little Rock, Arkansas, and as a newscast producer, air talent and engineer for stations in Lexington and Morehead, Kentucky. Professor Bellamy has published widely about sports and television, network branding, U.S. media economics and institutions and international media communication, including chapters in such books as *Sport, Public Broadcasting and Cultural Citizenship* (Routledge, 2012), *The Twenty-First Century Media Industry* (Lexington, 2010), the *Handbook of Media and Sports* (Erlbaum, 2005), *Artificial Ice* (Garamond, 2006), *Promotion & Marketing for Broadcasting & Cable* (Focal Press, 2006), *Research in Media Promotion* (Erlbaum, 2000), *Television and the American Family* (Erlbaum, 2000), *Media-Sport* (Routledge, 1998) and the last four editions of *Media Programming: Strategies and Practices* (Wadsworth, 2002 to 2013). His research appears in such publications as the *Journal of Broadcasting & Electronic Media*, the *Journal of Communication*, the *Journal of Sport & Social Issues* and *Journalism & Mass Communication Quarterly*. Professor Bellamy is coauthor of *Centerfield Shot: A History of Baseball and Television* (University of Nebraska Press, 2008) and *Television and the Remote Control: Grazing on a Vast Wasteland* (Guilford, 1996), and coeditor of *The Remote Control in the New Age of Television* (Praeger, 1993). He is a member of the Editorial Board of *NINE: A Journal of Baseball History and Culture*. He can be reached at *bellamy@duq.edu.*

Susan Tyler Eastman, professor emerita of Telecommunications at Indiana University in Bloomington, has her B.A. from the University of California at Berkeley, her M.A. from San Francisco State University, and her Ph.D. from Bowling Green State University. She is senior author/editor of nine editions of *Media Programming: Strategies and Practices* (Wadsworth, 1981 to 2013), five editions of *Promotion & Marketing for Broadcasting & Cable* (Focal Press, 1982 to 2006) and *Research in Media Promotion* (Erlbaum, 2000). Professor Eastman has published over a hundred book chapters and scholarly articles, most of which focus on the structural, content and industry factors affecting programming and promotion in television, radio

and cable. She has served on several editorial boards, and her articles have appeared in such journals as the *Journal of Broadcasting & Electronic Media, Critical Studies in Mass Communication*, the *Journal of Communication*, the *Journal of Applied Communication Research*, the *Howard Journal of Communication*, the *Sociology of Sport Journal*, the *Journal of Sport & Social Issues* and *Communication Yearbook*. She can be reached at *eastman@indiana.edu.*

Douglas A. Ferguson is a professor in the Department of Communication at the College of Charleston, South Carolina, where he served as the inaugural chair. His B.A. and M.A. are from the Ohio State University and his Ph.D. from Bowling Green State University. Early in his career, he was program director of NBC-affiliated WLIO (TV) and a station manager. In addition, he was program director for a local origination cable channel in Bay City, Michigan, that carried local game shows, children's shows, sporting events, movies and off-network syndication. He teaches, researches and writes about programming and promotion on the internet and other new media technologies and has authored several chapters on aspects of information technology, economics and media programming. He coauthored *The Broadcast Television Industry* (Allyn & Bacon, 1998) and coedited three editions of *Promotion & Marketing for Broadcasting & Cable* (Focal Press, 1999 to 2006) and five editions of *Media Programming: Strategies and Practices* (Wadsworth, 1997 to 2013). Professor Ferguson's scholarly work has been published in the *Journal of Broadcasting & Electronic Media, Communication Research, Journalism Quarterly* and *Communication Research Reports*. He can be reached at *fergusond@cofc.edu.*

Matthew T. Kaiser holds a B.A. from the University of North Carolina at Greensboro and an M.A. from Ohio University, where his research focused on interrelationships among radio programming, telecommunication law and regulations, and management. He is presently an on-air talent for market leader WQBE-FM, owned by Bristol Broadcasting Company, and an account executive for their five station cluster in Charleston, WV. Additionally, he serves weekends as on-air talent for Golden Isles Broadcasting in Brunswick, GA. He is both a Certified Radio Marketing Consultant (CRMC) and Certified Digital Marketing Consultant (CDMC) through the Radio Advertising Bureau. He combines an interest in digital and social media with a strong reverence for terrestrial broadcasting, accompanied by familiarity with marketing and consumer behavior. He can be reached at *matt@kaiseraudio.com.*

Timothy P. Meyer, professor, holds the John P. Blair Endowed Chair in Communication and is Chair of the Communication Program at the University of Wisconsin-Green Bay. He received his B.A. from the University of Wisconsin and his M.A. and Ph.D. from Ohio University. Before joining the University of Wisconsin-Green Bay, he taught at the University of Texas at Austin and the University of Massachusetts, Amherst. He actively consults in marketing and advertising research and works in organizational and management communications. Professor Meyer is coauthor of *Mediated Communications: A Social Action Perspective* (Sage, 1988). He has published numerous chapters and articles on programming and marketing in edited books and such major scholarly journals as the *Journal of Communication*, the *Journal of Broadcasting & Electronic Media*, the *Journal of Marketing* and the *Journal of Advertising*. He has contributed to seven editions of *Media Programming: Strategies and Practices* (Wadsworth, 1989 to 2013). He can be reached at *meyert@uwgb.edu.*

Gregory D. Newton is associate director of graduate studies in the School of Media Arts & Studies at Ohio University. In addition to conducting research in media programming and television law, he teaches courses in programming, management, and law and regulation in the Department of Telecommunications. He is the faculty advisor for Ohio University's online student radio station, cern.com, and has several years of radio station experience, serving as operations manager, program director and production director as well as air talent for several stations with AC, CHR, oldies, country, big band, jazz and news/talk formats. He holds a B.A. from Northern Illinois University, an M.A. from Northwestern University, and a Ph.D. from Indiana University. Professor Newton has published in the *Journal of Broadcasting & Electronic Media*, the *Journal of Communication*, the *Journal of Radio Studies*, the *Journal of Media Business Studies*, the *Journal of Promotion and Marketing* and the *Journal of Applied Communication Research*. He has contributed to four editions of *Media Programming: Strategies and Practices* (Wadsworth, 2002 to 2013). He can be reached at *newtong@ohio.edu.*

Matthew S. Pierce lectures in the Department of Telecommunications at Indiana University while also serving as a member of the Indiana House of Representatives. He has a B.A. and J.D. from Indiana University. He is licensed to practice law in Colorado, the District of Columbia, Indiana and Pennsylvania. After serving in a variety of staff positions for the Indiana House of Representatives, as

a member of the Bloomington, Indiana, City Council and then as chief of staff for Congressman Baron Hill (9th District-Indiana), he was first elected to the Indiana House of Representatives in 2002 and has been reelected every two years since then. Representative Pierce also serves on the board of directors of Bloomington's community radio station, WFHB. His teaching centers on media industries and management and the history of media development. He can be reached at *mspierce@indiana.edu.*

Robert F. Potter is an associate professor in the Department of Telecommunications at Indiana University, following several years on the Telecommunication & Film faculty at University of Alabama. He teaches in the area of telecommunication programming, advertising, marketing and management. His primary research interest lies in cognitive processing of audio in media messages. He was also a radio professional for a decade, primarily in the programming and promotion departments at a CHR station in the Pacific Northwest. His B.A. and M.S. degrees are from Eastern Washington University and his Ph.D. is from Indiana University. Professor Potter has contributed to the last three editions of *Media Programming: Strategies and Practices* (Wadsworth, 2006–2013). His research is published in *Journal of Broadcasting & Electronic Media, Communication Research, Media Psychology*, the *Journal of Advertising*, and the *Journal of Interactive Marketing*. He can be reached at *rfpotter@indiana.edu.*

John von Soosten is program director and air personality for SiriusXM Satellite Radio's "On Broadway" music channel, based in New York City. He was for many years the senior vice president and director of programming for Katz National Television, part of the nation's largest television representative firm, dealing with syndicated programming. Before joining Katz in 1984, Mr. von Soosten was vice president and program manager of Metromedia's WNEW-TV, New York (now WNYW-TV), and before that, he was production manager at the same station and production technician at WOR-TV, New York (now WWOR-TV). He also has consulted for program syndicators and software companies and authored numerous magazine articles about the business of television and radio. His B.S. is from Ithaca College and his M.S. from Brooklyn College, and he taught television production for many years at the college level. He brings a wide experience with syndicated television programming from the perspective of hundreds of U.S. stations and their foreign counterparts to his chapters in seven editions of *Media Programming: Strategies and Practices* (Wadsworth, 1989 to 2013). Mr. von Soosten has been president of the National Association of Television Program Executives (NATPE), a director of the International Radio Television Society (IRTS), a vice president of the International Radio Television Foundation (IRTF), and chairman of the NATPE Educational Foundation. He can be reached at *johnvons@msn.com*.

James R. Walker, professor in the Department of Communication at Saint Xavier University in Chicago, has his B.A. and M.A. from Penn State University and his Ph.D. from the University of Iowa. He has many years of experience as a producer and host of a daily consumer affairs program aired on public television. His teaching and research have focused on television programming practices, the effectiveness of television program promotion, televised sports, and the impact of remote control devices on television viewing behaviors and the television industry. His most recent book is *Centerfield Shot: A History of Baseball on Television* (University of Nebraska Press, 2008) with Robert V. Bellamy, Jr. Professor Walker coauthored *The Broadcast Television Industry* (Allyn & Bacon, 1998) and *Television and the Remote Control: Grazing on a Vast Wasteland* (Guilford, 1996), and coedited *The Remote Control in the New Age of Television* (Praeger, 1993). In addition, he has published more than 30 articles in national and regional journals, including the *Journal of Broadcasting & Electronic Media, Journalism Quarterly, Nine: A Journal of Baseball History and Culture* and the *Journal of Popular Culture*. He has contributed to the last four editions of *Media Programming: Strategies and Practices* (Wadsworth, 2002 to 2013). He can be reached at *walker@sxu.edu*.

Michael O. Wirth is dean of the College of Communication and Information at the University of Tennessee, after many years as director of the School of Communication and professor and chair of the Department of Mass Communications and Journalism Studies at the University of Denver. He was also a Senior Fellow of the Magness Institute for cable telecommunications. He has been a visiting professor at Renmin University in Beijing, Zhejiang University in Hangzhou, and Curtin University of Technology in Perth, Australia. Professor Wirth is an internationally known expert who teaches and does research in the areas of cable telecommunication and broadcast economics, management and regulation. He has provided consulting services for a number of multi-channel television distributors, television networks and station groups. For five years, he hosted a public affairs program on Denver television for KWGN-TV. His B.S. came from the University of Nebraska-Lincoln and his M.A. and Ph.D. from Michigan State University. He is coeditor of the *Handbook of Media Management and Economics* (Laurence Erlbaum, 2006), coauthor of *Costs, Benefits, and Long-Term Sustainability of Municipal Cable Television Overbuilds* (GSA Press, 1998), and he has published numerous research articles in such periodicals as the *Journal of Broadcasting & Electronic Media*, the *Journal of Media Economics, Journal of Regulatory Economics, Information Economics and Policy, Quarterly Review of Economics and Business* and the *Journal of Economics and Business*, as well as in scholarly books. He has contributed to three editions of *Media Programming: Strategies and Practices* (Wadsworth, 2006 to 2013). Dr. Wirth can be reached at *mwirth@utk.edu*.

Index to Program Titles

Note: This is a guide to specific television, radio, cable, and online **programs** and **movies** mentioned in the text. (Television, radio, and cable **networks** appear in the General Index.)

General Index